THE ESSENTIAL CUISINES OF MEXICO

CLARKSON POTTER/PUBLISHERS
NEW YORK

THE
ESSENTIAL
CUISINES
of
MEXICO

DIANA KENNEDY

Published by Clarkson Potter/Publishers, New York, New York.
Member of the Crown Publishing Group.
Random House, Inc. New York, Toronto, London, Sydney, Auckland
www.randomhouse.com
CLARKSON N. POTTER is a trademark and POTTER and colophon are registered
trademarks of Random House, Inc.

Printed in the United States of America

DESIGN BY JANE TREUHAFT

Library of Congress Cataloging-in-Publication Data
Kennedy, Diana.
    The essential cuisines of Mexico / by Diana Kennedy.—1st ed.
    Includes bibliographical references and index.
    1. Cookery, Mexican.   I. Title.
TX716.M4 K473   2000
641.5972—dc21

ISBN 0-609-60355-8

10   9   8   7   6   5   4   3   2   1

First Edition

TO MY BELOVED PAUL,

who was my reason for being in

Mexico in the first place

TO MY MOTHER,

Who just expected me to cook everything she did

TO ELIZABETH DAVID,

who inspired me to write about what I was cooking

AND TO CRAIG CLAIBORNE,

who launched me and so many others

In humble dishes,

the Most Holy Mary served

to her beloved son and husband

well-seasoned food.

En pobres trastos, servía

A su Hijo y Esposo amados,

Manjares bien sazonados

La Purísima María.

—WORDS WRITTEN BY THE CURATE ON THE WALL INSIDE AN
EIGHTEENTH-CENTURY COUNTRY CHURCH IN GUANAJUATO

CONTENTS

ACKNOWLEDGMENTS My sincere thanks to my editor at Clarkson Potter, Roy Finamore, who recognized the value of putting my first three books together in one volume. He has been a joy to work with. And for Lauren Shakely, who supported him so enthusiastically.

My deep appreciation and thanks to Frances McCullough, my editor and friend of now thirty years, who has guided me through the labyrinth of publishing, calmed my idiosyncrasies (or tried to), and given shape to my manuscripts.

It is impossible to thank adequately all those who have contributed one way or another to my traveling and writing life in Mexico for so many years. I have tried to attribute wherever possible the names of the persons who gave me each recipe and would like them to know how much pleasure their recipes have given to so many people all over the world.

Copyediting is always an unenviable task, but I would like to thank Carole Berglie for her painstaking and sympathetic approach to this hefty manuscript, and designer Jane Treuhaft for fitting it admirably into these pages.

And to Marike Janzen, who patiently and carefully typed the final manuscript.

INTRODUCTI�֍N

It would by no means be an exaggeration to say that this book—a compilation of my first three books, *The Cuisines of Mexico*, *The Tortilla Book*, and *Mexican Regional Cooking*—came about because of a chance meeting in 1957. After spending three years in Canada, I was traveling home to England via the Caribbean, and I met my future husband, Paul Kennedy, a foreign correspondent for the *New York Times*, during one of the many revolutions in Haiti. We fell in love and a few months later I found myself disembarking from a Dutch freighter in the port of Veracruz, Mexico. And so a new life and adventure began.

My first vivid impressions of Mexico City, engraved forever in my memory, were of wide, tree-lined avenues, brilliant blue skies, and magnificent snow-capped volcanoes that seemed to be standing guard over the lakes and city beyond. The streets were calm and orderly, especially during the hours of the afternoon siesta, but the neighborhood marketplaces dotted throughout the city were a hive of activity, full of exotic chiles, herbs, and fruits of vibrant colors and aromas. I was instantly captivated. I began exploring, talking about food to anyone who would answer my endless questions, and, of course, cooking and trying all those strange, exciting new tastes and textures.

A few years later Craig Claiborne, then Food Editor of the *New York Times*, and his colleague Pierre Franey came to Mexico to research an article about restaurants there. Over drinks I offered to give Craig a Mexican cookbook. "No," he said, "I'll wait until the day you write one." That came somewhat as a jolt—enough to leave a subconscious, nagging idea.

Several years later, after Paul's untimely death from cancer, it was Craig again who jolted me into giving my first classes in Mexican cooking in my New York apartment. It was the beginning of a golden era of learning about different cuisines, with their exotic ingredients, and how to prepare them. For that we were, and still are, indebted to Craig, for bringing a new sophistication to food journalism, and to the infectious enthusiasm of Julia Child, convincing us on television that every housewife could produce, without tears, a wonderful French meal.

Craig announced the impending classes in the *Times*. I was inundated with inquiries and soon had the six stools in my small, Upper West Side kitchen occupied for a series of four classes.

One of those callers was to become, and still is, my editor, Frances McCullough. Although at the time she was the poetry editor at Harper & Row, Fran was also an expatriate Californian desperate for some good Mexican food; she wanted to know if I would write a Mexican cookbook for Harpers.

I was very nervous. I warned Fran that I couldn't write. She persisted, so I sent in some drafts—later she told me she privately agreed about the writing but wisely didn't tell me at the time. I went off to Mexico again for my usual research trip, came back, read what I had written, tore it up, and started again. I had a call from Fran at midnight. She had just finished reading the new material and couldn't wait to talk to me. "What happened over the summer—you've taught yourself how to write." That was in 1969.

And so my first book, *The Cuisines of Mexico*, was born, a culmination of invisible forces propelling me along an uncharted course of food writing—and there was nothing I could do about it.

While *Cuisines* was in the making, very few people (apart from Fran) knew what I was talking about, perhaps only those who had traveled and eaten well in Mexico. It was the era of the combination plate, and we soon realized that just within Harpers itself there was an awful lot of convincing to do about the very existence of the authentic regional cuisines of Mexico. We then and there decided to feed all the people in charge of various stages of the book's production the real thing with, of course, lots of well-made margaritas.

We had to convince everyone: the art department to give us four-color photographs instead of the cute little drawings they had suggested, the sales force to make the right pitch, the designer to catch the spirit, the book clubs to get excited, not forgetting the booksellers all across America. I cooked and cooked; the Harper staff got into the swing of things and helped me haul thirty huge cazuelas of food to Washington, D.C., in a heatwave for the annual booksellers' convention; our guests were astounded, and happy. Finally everyone understood what we were talking about and gave us carte blanche. *The Cuisines of Mexico* came out in the fall of 1972 to much acclaim.

There was a lot more to be written about, and once again fate intervened. A jogging accident, which knocked me off my feet for several months, got me started again in a most unlikely fashion. In the sheer frustration of having my movements curtailed, I began to delve into my—now growing—collection of Mexican cookbooks in Spanish, especially those of Señora Josefina Velázquez de León, who was a pioneer in recording recipes of housewives from the states of Mexico. I then realized how little there was published in English on those delectable Mexican foods that were becoming so popular in the United States: tacos, enchiladas, and tostadas. I decided I had to devote a smallish book to the subject of the corn tortilla and what you can do with it, in combination with chiles, cheese, cream, and sauces, as well as meats and vegetables, to make delicious and usually inexpensive dishes. The idea took root and, despite the fact that a good tortilla was hard to come by in those days, *The Tortilla Book* was published in 1975.

My yearly visit to Mexico was extended to almost six months as I doggedly traveled—mostly cheaply and uncomfortably—to remote places where some, often unrecorded, culinary surprise awaited me. I did my apprenticeship in a Mexico City bakery learning the secrets of good *pan dulce*—and mine were actually sold alongside those of the professional bakers. (They were wonderful teachers and so proud of my efforts.) On these trips, I got to know, and work with, some extraordinary regional cooks whom I have written about in *The Regional Cooks of Mexico*, which was now, unbeknownst to me, being formed. It was published in 1978.

Throughout those years I was teaching classes in cooking schools across the United States, striving to give my students insight into the diversity of the regional foods of Mexico. Even these enthusiasts were as much surprised as the Harpers staff had been at that first lunch. Of course, authentic ingredients were few and far between at that time, but I persevered, carrying things across the continent so I could duplicate these different tastes as faithfully as possible until there was a wider distribution of the chiles and herbs so essential to that end. (I can claim the recognition and diffusion of epazote, which I found growing in Central Park in New York and various other places over the United States.)

Now, of course, things have changed, and are still changing; with mass immigration of Mexicans into the United States, and the effect of NAFTA, more and more ingredients are being imported as the demand for them grows: avocados from Michoacán, real *criollo* tomatoes (I suspect from Guerrero), *chilacas* from Michoacán and Guanajuato, dried shrimp from the Isthmus of Oaxaca, *guajes* from the hot country, and even fresh *hierbas de olor*—pot herbs including thyme, marjoram, and Mexican bay leaf—as well as the small, fragrant Mexican limes. One day soon, I hope, we shall see the large fragrant *hoja santa* leaf in the supermarkets (although it does actually grow wild in Texas and is being cultivated in California and Texas).

The task of putting these three early cookbooks together has not been an easy or happy one. I felt as though I were dismembering my offspring as I cut and shaped them into one, not too cumbersome, volume. Each one of these books represented a milestone in my life, and I have lived happily with them ever since their publication. Now I have simplified the recipes when possible, bringing them up to date without losing the spirit of their generation. I have tried to leave the introductory texts untouched because they are "word pictures" of what I saw and experienced during those years: a Mexico of the past.

There are thirty-three new recipes from different regions of Mexico: a pico de gallo with peaches from the state of Mexico, the very popular *arroz a la tumbada* (rice with seafood) from Veracruz, *pollo en cuiclacoche* (chicken in a corn fungus sauce) from Puebla, wonderful snacks from the cantinas of Mérida and Yucatán, and barbecued chicken from Chiapas, all of them intriguing and delicious.

I am sure that this reincarnation of old friends will reach a new audience as future generations of Mexican Americans become more aware of their culinary heritage and a new wave of young chefs delves into these exciting, authentic recipes. Among them, I am sure, will be my devoted fans, to whom I am so grateful for their continued enthusiasm for my books and classes, and for their letters of appreciation, which I have carefully saved over the years. They, too, have helped preserve the spirit of these fascinating cuisines. ❁

DIANA KENNEDY, 2000

F O R E W O R D It is a long time between an idle remark, a casual wish, and a much desired reality.

I first met Diana Southwood Kennedy over twenty years ago in her home on the Calle Puebla in Mexico City. I was the food news editor and restaurant critic for the *New York Times* and her husband Paul, a gentle, effusive soul with a lust for life, was the *Times* correspondent for Central America, Mexico, and the Caribbean. During his lifetime—he died in 1967—their home was an international gathering place, a crossroads where men and women from many of the world's more interesting milieus came to discuss art, politics, revolutions here and there, and the state of the world in general. And—foremost perhaps—to eat Diana's food.

But the thing that I most vividly recall about our first meeting was her offer to buy me a Mexican cookbook. "No," I demurred, "I'll wait for the genuine article. The day you publish one."

I have always had a passion for the Mexican table since, as an infant, I ate hot tamales sold by a street vendor in the small town where I lived in Mississippi. (There were dreadful rumors about what the meat filling consisted of but, poof, I couldn't have cared less.) Never have I eaten such glorious Mexican food as I have in Diana's home, and with good reason. I know of no one else with her dedication to the pursuit of great Mexican cooking. (If her enthusiasm were not beautiful, it would border on mania.)

Diana introduced me to and taught me to make what I consider one of the greatest drinks (Is it a cocktail? I've never been able to decide) in the world, the sangrita (not sangria). It is made with sour orange juice and the juice of crushed fresh pomegranates. Drunk, of course, with tequila. But beyond that, her food! Good lord, where is there anything to equal her *papa-dzules*, that Yucatecan specialty made with the pulp of pepitas, eggs, and tortillas; or her pork in chile sauce, or squash in cream, or tamales fixed in any of a dozen fashions. No wonder that Diana's kitchen smells better than most kitchens.

Long ago, she and I agreed on the merits of Mexican food. It is, we decided, earthy food, festive food, happy food, celebration food. It is, in short, peasant food raised to the level of high and sophisticated art. On the publication of the original edition of the book I wrote, "If this book is a measure of Diana's talent, it will probably rank as the definitive book in English on that most edible art." Time has proved this to be the case, and all lovers of true Mexican cooking will share in my enthusiasm for this revised edition.

CRAIG CLAIBORNE, 1986

PREFACE After many wanderings, in the summer I met Paul Kennedy in Haiti, where he was covering one of the many revolutions for the *New York Times*. We fell in love and I joined him in Mexico later that year.

And so life in Mexico began. Everything was new, exciting, and exotic. Luz, our first maid, loved to cook. One day she brought her corn grinder to the house and we made tamales, first cooking the dried corn in a solution of lime and water, washing the skin of each kernel, and then grinding it to just the right texture. It seemed to take forever, and our backs ached from the effort. But I shall never forget those tamales. She introduced us both to the markets and told us how to use the fruits and vegetables that were strange to us.

Finally Luz had to go, and Rufina came from Oaxaca; it was her first job. She was young and moody, but she was a really good cook and my apprenticeship continued as she taught me how to make her rather special *albóndigas*, rabbit in adobo, and how to draw and truss a hen.

But I suppose it is Godileva to whom I am most indebted. I always loved the evenings when she would stay to do the ironing; we would chat about her life when she was a young girl on her father's small ranch in a remote area of Guerrero. They had lived well, and she loved good food. She would pat out our tortillas, and before lunch would make us *gorditas* with the fat of marrow bones to enrich them, and as we came in the door would hand us, straight from the comal, sopes smothered with green sauce and sour cream. We would take turns grinding the chiles and spices on the metate, and it is her recipe for chiles rellenos that I have included in this book.

I had other influences as well.

My friend Chabela Marín, on several trips into the interior, taught me almost all I know about the handicrafts of Mexico; together we visited craftsmen in remote areas and on those journeys we would try all the local fruits and foods. It was she who spent many hours in my kitchen showing me, accompanied by meticulous instructions, the specialties of her mother's renowned kitchen in Jalisco.

At last our stay had to come to an end. Paul had been fighting cancer courageously for two years, and it was time to return to New York. By then we had traveled extensively together, and on my own I had driven practically all over the country, seeing, eating, and asking questions. I started to collect old cookbooks and delve into the gastronomic past to learn more for the cookbook that I hoped someday to write.

Paul died early in 1967, and later that same year Craig Claiborne suggested that I start a Mexican cooking school. I suppose I wasn't ready to start a new venture; I was too saddened and worn by the previous three years. But the idea had planted itself, and in January 1969, on Sunday afternoons, I did start a series of Mexican cooking classes—the first in New York. A wintry Sunday afternoon is a wonderful time to cook, and the idea caught on.

The classes expanded beyond those Sunday afternoons, and the work for the book went on as well. But while the classes continue to flourish and grow, the research and testing have come at least to a temporary halt—if only to allow the book to be published at last. For I find myself involved in a process of continual refinement, owing both to the frequent trips I make to Mexico to discover new dishes and to refine old ones, and to the constant dialogue between myself and my students and friends who try these recipes with me.

DIANA KENNEDY, APRIL 1972

APPETIZERS

Sikil P'ak ※ *Pumpkin Seed Dip*

Queso Relleno ※ *Yucatecan Stuffed Cheese*

Papas Escabechadas ※ *Yucatecan Pickled Potatoes*

Ibis Escabechados ※ *Yucatecan Pickled Lima Beans*

Calabaza Frita ※ *Fried Pumpkin*

Salpicón Yucateco ※ *Yucatecan Shredded Meat*

Guacamole ※ *Avocado Dip*

Cacahuates Enchilados ※ *Chilied Peanuts*

Mariscos a la Marinera ※ *Seafood Cocktail*

Caviar de Chapala ※ *Carp Roe Snack*

Ostiones Pimentados ※ *Peppered Oysters*

Salpicón de Jaiba ※ *Shredded Crabmeat and Vegetables*

Chicharrón en Escabeche ※ *Pickled Pork Rind*

Queso Flameado ※ *"Flamed" Cheese*

Chilorio ※ *Chile-Seasoned Pork*

Mochomos Sinaloenses ※ *Sinaloan Shredded Beef*

Salsa para Mochomos ※ *Tomato Sauce for Mochomos*

Carne Cocida en Limón ※ *Ground Meat Marinated in Lime Juice*

Botanas de Camarón Seco ※ *Dried Shrimp Fritters*

Salsa de Albañil ※ *Bricklayers' Sauce or Botana*

Carnitas ※ *Little Pieces of Browned Pork*

Frijoles Puercos Estilo Jalisco ※ *Rich Well-Fried Beans from Jalisco*

ANTOJITOS Without doubt the Mexicans are the most persistent noshers in the world. Who wouldn't be, with such an endless variety of things to nibble on along the streets and in the marketplaces? Even if you think you are not hungry you will be enticed by the smell, by the artistry with which the food is displayed, or just because it is something new to try, for Mexican cooks are among the most creative anywhere. Next time you wander the streets of any Mexican city or small town, pause at the *taquería* on the corner and see if your mouth doesn't start to water as the floppy, hot tortillas are crammed with shredded meat or carnitas and doused in a robust green tomato sauce from an enormous black molcajete, or as the quesadillas are patted out and stuffed with squash flowers and browned on a comal. Any hour of the day, and well into the night, there will be groups of people standing and eating with great concentration—for this is no time to talk. In Ensenada it is the pismo clam that is the favorite of the sidewalk carts; in the La Paz market the tacos are made of shredded fish, and in Morelia they are made of brains sprinkled with chopped cilantro. As you wander around the markets of central Mexico you will be offered completely pre-Hispanic food, small fish wrapped in corn husks and cooked over charcoal, or *tlacoyos*, oval pieces of rather thick dough filled with a paste of beans; at the back of the Oaxaca market you can snack on toasted grasshoppers and the perennial favorite everywhere, ears of corn hot from the steamer or roasted to a dark brown over charcoal. And with all the marvelous *antojitos* that exist in Yucatán, I can't help but raise my eyebrows every time I see a little cart, proudly displaying a "hot dogs" sign, being pushed around the cathedral plaza. If you are looking for something less substantial there are always peanuts and pumpkin seeds, still warm and their shells blackened slightly from the recent toasting, and in Chihuahua the tiniest acorns I have ever seen, slightly sweet and at the same time bitter.

At practically any street corner a woman may come along with her charcoal brazier and a large metal cooking sheet with a shallow circular well in the center for the fat and wide, sloping sides to hold the cooked filling or the newly fried enchiladas. I shall never forget the streets around the Puebla market at dusk on a Saturday evening. Everybody seemed to be scurrying around with braziers, charcoal, or baskets of food, and the smoke drifting out of every other doorway brought with it the pungent fragrance of *ocote*—the thin strips of resinous pine—used to fire the charcoal.

To combat the midday heat, stands covered with decorative green leaves sell skinned mangoes, cut like flowers and stuck onto thin sticks like lollipops, as well as another recent innovation: small paper cones, held in racks, and brimming over with mixed fruits—watermelon, melon, pineapple, and cucumber—and everything sprinkled with salt and powdered chile piquín as it is served. And later on in the year, sliced jicama, cucumbers opened up lengthwise like flowers, and hot yams appear.

Food vendors push their little barrows for miles to post themselves outside some big institution or government office, hospital, school, or prison to offer sustenance to the constant flow of people. Whenever a crowd gathers to watch the police or firemen at work, out of nowhere appears a little man pushing his cart of goodies to sustain the excited onlookers. Antonio Mayo Sánchez, in his book *Cocina Mexicana*, writes: "Any of the dozens of varieties make ideal snacks to appease the appetite while waiting for dinner or to bolster the stomach against the effect of cocktails when entertaining guests, or simply to justify their very name *antojito*—a little whim."

SIKIL P'AK Pumpkin Seed Dip
MAKES ABOUT 1½ CUPS (375 ML)

According to the late eminent Mayan ethnologist Dr. Alfredo Barrera Vásquez, the correct name for this dish is ha'-sikil-p'ak: ha' (water), sikil (pumpkin or squash seed), and p'ak (tomato). It is a truly Mayan concoction, except for the addition of the cilantro, which must have crept in later, and the substitution of chives, which very much resemble in taste and appearance the cebollina—a variety of the same plant—used so much in the cooking of Campeche and Yucatán.

Sikil P'ak is served in Yucatán today as a dip (horrible word!) with crisp-fried or toasted tortillas—and what a healthy dip it is, compared to those packaged soup and gummy cheese affairs. If you are feeling extravagant with your calories, you can eat it on top of pimes, small masa cakes piled with the delicious pork pieces called Lomitos (page 281).

Many cooks will tell you that the tomatoes should be boiled, but some prefer the flavor of them broiled; you may, therefore, do as you like. The chile is optional, although, as I have said many times before, the habanero chile has an enticing flavor of its own.

In Yucatán the tiniest, unshelled pumpkin seed, locally called chinchilla, is used; it is about ½ inch long and ¼ inch wide. However, I have made this dish with practically every squash seed I have come across, and the seeds taste fine providing you toast them very well indeed and grind them very fine, until they are almost pulverized, and add a small amount of hulled seeds.

1 CUP (250 ML) UNHULLED RAW PUMPKIN SEEDS
¼ CUP (65 ML) HULLED RAW PUMPKIN SEEDS
1 HABANERO CHILE OR ANY FRESH, HOT GREEN CHILE, WIPED CLEAN
1½ TEASPOONS SALT, OR TO TASTE
12 OUNCES (340 G) TOMATOES, BROILED (SEE PAGE 490)
⅔ CUP (165 ML) WATER, APPROXIMATELY
2 HEAPED TABLESPOONS ROUGHLY CHOPPED CILANTRO
2 HEAPED TABLESPOONS FINELY CHOPPED CHIVES

Heat a thick frying pan or comal and toast the unhulled seeds slowly, turning them constantly, until the hulls are well browned and crisp (some types of seeds will start to pop open). Add the hulled pumpkin seeds and toast for 1 minute more. Set them aside to cool. Meanwhile, toast the chile, turning it from time to time until it is blistered and black-brown in spots.

Using an electric coffee/spice grinder, grind the toasted seeds, together with the salt, to a coarse powder. Transfer to a small serving bowl.

Blend the unskinned tomatoes briefly with ⅓ cup (85 ml) of the water. Stir into the ground pumpkin seeds together with the cilantro, chives, and whole chile. (If you prefer a more picante dish, blend a small piece of the chile with the tomatoes before mixing them with the seeds.) The mixture should have the consistency of mayonnaise. If it is too thick, you may have to add a little more water to dilute it.

Serve it at room temperature, as a dip.

NOTE: Sikil P'ak can be made ahead of time and will keep for a few days, although the fresh cilantro taste does suffer a little. I do not recommend freezing.

QUESO RELLENO Yucatecan Stuffed Cheese
SERVES 8   YUCATÁN

This stuffed cheese dish served as an appetizer in Yucatán is a most elaborate affair, in terms of both preparation and flavors. It is a relative latecomer to the foods of the Yucatán Peninsula and an intriguing way of using the round Dutch cheeses that were found at a reasonable price (then) in the free port shops of Chetumal and Cozumel.

Any leftovers, although not likely, could be frozen and reheated gently (so as not to toughen the cheese) for tacos.

It is very difficult to give an exact cooking time, as it will vary tremendously depending upon the age of the cheese and such considerations as the conditions under which it has been stored. Always hollow out the cheese the day before using. If it is dry and rather hard, then leave it to soak overnight in cold water. If the cheese is new and soft, do not soak it, but leave it out of the refrigerator overnight and until you finally cook it. The cheese will sag when it is cooked through, but the trick is to have the inside and outside cheese melted evenly without letting it lose its shape and go completely flat. Both warming the stuffing before you put it into the cheese and cooking it over medium heat will help. The time can vary from 15 to 35 minutes. After the first 10 minutes, feel the cheese to see how soft it is.

One of the Campeche cooks likes to wrap the cheese in a banana leaf first. Not only does the leaf give it a subtle flavor, but the leaf also forms an attractive base for the cheese on the serving dish. Some cooks in Yucatán submerge the cheese in the meat broth to soften it, but I find it becomes rather messy to untie and serve.

A 4-POUND (1.8-KG) EDAM CHEESE

MEAT FOR THE STUFFING

8 OUNCES (225 G) PORK
8 OUNCES (225 G) BEEF
3 ½ CUPS (875 ML) WATER
SALT TO TASTE
3 GARLIC CLOVES, UNPEELED AND TOASTED (SEE PAGE 492)
¼ TEASPOON DRIED MEXICAN OREGANO (YUCATECAN IF POSSIBLE), TOASTED
    (SEE PAGE 487)

THE TOMATO BASE (FOR THE STUFFING AND THE TOMATO SAUCE)

2 TABLESPOONS LARD OR VEGETABLE OIL
½ MEDIUM GREEN PEPPER, FINELY CHOPPED
½ MEDIUM WHITE ONION, FINELY CHOPPED
1 HEAPED TABLESPOON DRAINED LARGE CAPERS
1 ¼ POUNDS (565 G) TOMATOES, FINELY CHOPPED (3 CUPS/750 ML)
15 SMALL PITTED GREEN OLIVES, ROUGHLY CHOPPED
1 HEAPED TABLESPOON RAISINS
½ TEASPOON SALT

THE STUFFING

10 PEPPERCORNS
2 WHOLE ALLSPICE
2 WHOLE CLOVES
¼-INCH (.75-CM) PIECE OF CINNAMON STICK
SALT TO TASTE
3 GARLIC CLOVES
½ TABLESPOON MILD WHITE VINEGAR
4 HARD-COOKED EGGS
A LITTLE VEGETABLE OIL

THE GRAVY

2 CUPS (500 ML) RESERVED MEAT BROTH
2 TABLESPOONS ALL-PURPOSE FLOUR
A PINCH OF SAFFRON
1 X-CAT-IK CHILE OR GÜERO, CHARRED (DO NOT SKIN; SEE PAGE 464)

THE TOMATO SAUCE

THE REMAINING TOMATO BASE

$^{1}\!/_{2}$ CUP (125 ML) TOMATO JUICE OR WATER

SALT TO TASTE

TO PREPARE THE CHEESE: Pare off the red skin. Cut a $^{1}\!/_{2}$-inch (1.5-cm) slice off the top of the cheese to make the "lid." Hollow out the inside of the cheese until the shell is about $^{1}\!/_{2}$ inch (1.5 cm) thick. If the cheese is very hard, leave it to soak overnight (see note above). Reserve the scooped-out cheese for another use.

TO PREPARE THE MEAT FOR THE STUFFING: Cut the meat into $^{1}\!/_{2}$-inch (1.5-cm) cubes, and add it with the rest of the ingredients to the pan. Bring to a boil, lower the heat, and cook until the meat is tender—30 to 35 minutes. Let the meat cool in the broth.

Strain the meat, reserving the broth. Chop the meat fine.

TO PREPARE THE TOMATO BASE FOR THE STUFFING AND THE TOMATO SAUCE: Heat the lard and fry the pepper, onion, and capers slowly, without browning, until they are soft.

Mash the tomatoes and add them, with the rest of the ingredients, to the pan. Cook over medium heat for about 8 minutes.

Divide the mixture in two, half for the stuffing and half for the sauce.

TO PREPARE THE STUFFING: Crush the spices together with the salt, garlic, and vinegar.

Put the meats, spice mixture, and tomato base into a large skillet and mix well.

Separate the egg whites from the yolks, being careful to keep the yolks whole. Set the yolks aside. Chop the whites fine and add them to the ingredients in the pan.

Cook the mixture over medium heat for about 8 minutes—it should be almost dry.

Put half the stuffing into the cheese; set the whole yolks into it and cover with the remaining stuffing. Replace the top slice of the cheese.

Smear the outside of the cheese well with oil and wrap it tightly in a cloth, tying it on top. Place the cheese on a small plate in the steamer. Cover the steamer with a tightly fitting lid and cook the cheese until it is soft (see note above).

TO PREPARE THE GRAVY: Meanwhile, prepare the gravy. Heat the broth. Add a little of it to the flour and stir to a smooth paste. Stir the rest of the broth into the paste until it is smooth. Return to the pan and cook over gentle heat until the gravy thickens slightly, stirring constantly. Add the saffron and chile, set aside, and keep warm.

TO PREPARE THE TOMATO SAUCE: Heat the tomato base and juice together and add salt as necessary.

To serve, unwrap the cheese, remove the "lid," and pour the hot tomato sauce and the gravy over it. Serve with plenty of hot tortillas and Salsa de Chile Habanero (page 248). Each person will make his own tacos.

PAPAS ESCABECHADAS Yucatecan Pickled Potatoes
MAKES ABOUT 2²/₃ CUPS (665 ML)   YUCATÁN

This and the two following recipes—Ibis Escabechados and Calabaza Frita—are three of the very tasty botanas served free of charge to accompany drinks in the cantinas of Mérida. Of course, these tidbits should also encourage you to drink more, so they should be slightly salty. They happen to be among my favorites and along with Sikil P'ak (page 4) make delicious vegetarian snacks. The juice of bitter orange gives this snack a very special flavor.

These potatoes are best when made about 1 hour before serving and are still good the following day.

1 CUP (250 ML) LOOSELY PACKED, THINLY SLICED WHITE ONION
BOILING WATER TO COVER
SALT TO TASTE
¼ CUP (65 ML) BITTER ORANGE JUICE OR FRESH LIME JUICE
½ HABANERO CHILE, FINELY CHOPPED
12 OUNCES (340 G) WAXY POTATOES, CUT INTO ¾-INCH (2-CM) CUBES
⅓ CUP (85 ML) FIRMLY PACKED, FINELY CHOPPED CILANTRO

Cover the onion with the boiling water and leave to soak for 1 minute. Drain, add salt to taste, and stir in the bitter orange juice and chile. Set aside in a nonreactive bowl at room temperature to macerate while you cook the potatoes.

Put enough water into a small saucepan to cover the potatoes. Bring the water to a boil, add the potatoes, and cook over medium heat until just tender—about 8 minutes. Drain, cool off a little, and peel—but while still slightly warm add to the onion. Stir in the cilantro and add more salt as necessary. Serve at room temperature.

IBIS ESCABECHADOS Yucatecan Pickled Lima Beans
MAKES ABOUT 3 CUPS (750 ML)   YUCATÁN

Ibis, both fresh and dried, are used in the food of the Yucatán Peninsula. They very closely resemble lima beans.

1 CUP (250 ML) LOOSELY PACKED, THINLY SLICED WHITE ONION
BOILING WATER TO COVER
SALT TO TASTE
¼ CUP (65 ML) BITTER ORANGE JUICE OR FRESH LIME JUICE
½ HABANERO CHILE, FINELY CHOPPED
12 OUNCES (340 G) LIMA BEANS (ABOUT 2½ CUPS/625 ML)
⅓ CUP (85 ML) FIRMLY PACKED, FINELY CHOPPED CILANTRO

Cover the onion with the boiling water and leave to soak for 1 minute. Drain, add salt to taste, and stir in the bitter orange juice and chile. Set aside in a nonreactive bowl at room temperature to macerate while you cook the beans.

Put enough water into a small saucepan to cover the beans. Bring the water to a boil, add the beans, and cook over medium heat until just tender—about 10 minutes. Drain, and while still warm add to the onion. Stir in the cilantro and add salt as necessary. Serve at room temperature.

CALABAZA FRITA Fried Pumpkin
MAKES ABOUT 5 CUPS (1.25 L)   YUCATÁN

Although this recipe has a prosaic name, it is a delicious way of preparing pumpkin either tender or mature—I prefer the latter, as does one of my gurus for Yucatecan cooking, Señora Berta López de Marrufo. I first ate this dish in a Mérida cantina where it was served with totopos as a botana with drinks. With the addition of cooked pork ribs it can be converted into a main dish.

When tender the pumpkin or squash resembles a large pattypan squash except for the fact that it has a dark green skin and pale orange flesh. It does not need to be pre-cooked for this recipe. Once it matures, like all pumpkins, it has a hard rind. I prefer to leave this on when pre-cooking.

The small chile dulce, or botanik, *is typically used in Yucatán and, although it does not have as delicate a flavor and texture, an ordinary green pepper may be substituted.*

Calabaza Frita is the sort of dish that can be prepared several hours, or even one day, ahead—in fact, it improves in flavor. But I do not suggest freezing as it will become too mushy.

2 POUNDS (900 G) UNPEELED PUMPKIN, CUT INTO SMALL PIECES
$\frac{1}{3}$ TO $\frac{1}{2}$ CUP (85 TO 125 ML) OLIVE OIL (NOT EXTRA VIRGIN)
I SMALL WHITE ONION, FINELY CHOPPED ($\frac{1}{2}$ CUP/125 ML)
I GREEN PEPPER, SEEDED AND FINELY CHOPPED (I SCANT CUP/235 ML)
12 OUNCES (340 G) TOMATOES, FINELY CHOPPED (ABOUT 2 CUPS/500 ML)
SALT TO TASTE

TO SERVE
$\frac{1}{3}$ CUP (85 ML) FINELY GRATED AÑEJO OR ROMANO CHEESE

Put the pumpkin pieces into a large pot, cover with water, bring to a boil, lower the heat, and cook, covered, until still a little firm, about 20 minutes depending on the type of pumpkin. Drain, peel, and cut into $\frac{1}{2}$-inch (1.5-cm) cubes. Set aside.

Heat the oil in a deep flameproof casserole; add the onion, pepper, and tomatoes with salt to taste and cook over medium heat, stirring from time to time to avoid sticking, until well seasoned and still a little juicy—about 8 minutes.

Add the cubed pumpkin and mix well. Continue cooking over low heat, stirring from time to time to avoid sticking, adding a little water if mixture is too dry, for about 15 minutes. Test for salt, then set aside to season for at least 30 minutes.

Serve sprinkled with the cheese and accompanied by tostadas.

SALPICÓN YUCATECO   Yucatecan Shredded Meat
SERVES 6

YUCATÁN

In Tampico, on the Gulf Coast, one is offered tacos of salpicón de jaiba, *shredded crabmeat cooked with onion, chiles, and cilantro. Farther down the coast, along the Lagoon of Tamiahua, the* salpicón *would be a more complicated one, of shredded fish with olives, raisins, and capers, called* saragalla. *But in Yucatán the most common* salpicón *is made of shredded venison that has first been cooked in a pit barbecue called a* pib. *It is then mixed with Seville orange juice and very finely chopped radishes and cilantro to make a fresh, crisp filling for tacos on a hot day.*

Once assembled, the salpicón should be eaten within the hour, if possible. After that time the ingredients will lose their freshness and the color will leach from the radishes.

Actually, any meat can be used. It would, in fact, make an interesting way of using up a leftover roast.

1 CUP (250 ML) COOKED AND SHREDDED MEAT
½ CUP (125 ML) SEVILLE ORANGE JUICE OR SUBSTITUTE (SEE PAGE 494)
⅔ CUP (165 ML) VERY FINELY CHOPPED RADISHES
3 TABLESPOONS VERY FINELY CHOPPED CILANTRO
SALT TO TASTE

Mix all the ingredients and let them season for about 30 minutes before serving.

This *salpicón* is, of course, served at room temperature with a pile of freshly made tortillas.

GUACAMOLE Avocado Dip

MAKES ABOUT 2⅓ CUPS (585 ML)   CENTRAL MEXICO

The word guacamole *comes from the Nahuatl words for "avocado"* (ahuacatl) *and "mixture," or "concoction"* (molli) — *and what a beautiful "concoction" guacamole is, pale green sparked with the cilantro's darker green and the red of the tomato. Its beauty is definitely enhanced if it is served in the molcajete in which it has been made and where it rightfully belongs. (Never, never use a blender for the avocado to turn it into one of those smooth, homogeneous messes!) If you don't possess a molcajete, then use a blender for the base ingredients and mash avocados into it.*

Guacamole is usually eaten in Mexico at the beginning of a meal with a pile of hot, freshly made tortillas or with other botanas (snacks), like crisp pork skins (chicharrón) or little pieces of crispy pork (carnitas). It will also often accompany a plate of tacos. It is so delicate that it is best eaten the moment it is prepared. There are many suggestions for keeping it—covering it airtight, leaving the pit in, and so forth—but they will help only for a brief time; almost immediately the delicate green will darken and the fresh, wonderful flavor will be lost.

2 TABLESPOONS FINELY CHOPPED WHITE ONION

4 SERRANO CHILES, OR TO TASTE, FINELY CHOPPED

3 HEAPED TABLESPOONS ROUGHLY CHOPPED CILANTRO

SALT TO TASTE

3 LARGE AVOCADOS (ABOUT I POUND, 6 OUNCES/630 G)

4 OUNCES (115 G) TOMATOES, FINELY CHOPPED (ABOUT ⅔ CUP/165 ML)

TO SERVE

I HEAPED TABLESPOON FINELY CHOPPED WHITE ONION

2 HEAPED TABLESPOONS ROUGHLY CHOPPED CILANTRO

Grind together the onion, chiles, cilantro, and salt to a paste.

Cut the avocados into halves, remove the pits, and squeeze the flesh out of the shells and mash into the chile base to a textured consistency—it should not be smooth. Stir in all but 1 tablespoon of the tomatoes, adjust seasoning, and top with the remaining chopped tomatoes, onion, and cilantro.

Serve immediately at room temperature (see note above). I do not recommend freezing.

CACAHUATES ENCHILADOS Chilied Peanuts
MAKES ABOUT 1 CUP (250 ML)

These fiery little snacks invariably turn up on the table in a Mexican bar, providing a great incentive to drink more tequila and then tone it all down by sucking on those half-moon wedges of lime. But if you eat too many of them or make them too picante, you may as well forget about eating carefully prepared, delicate foods; your palate can easily be burned out.

The ordinary commercial chile powder sold in the United States is not sharp enough for this or the following recipe. Use a powder of piquín chile, chile de árbol, or cayenne.

I TABLESPOON VEGETABLE OIL

I CUP (250 ML) UNSALTED SHELLED PEANUTS, WITH BROWN PAPERY SKINS REMOVED

10 SMALL GARLIC CLOVES

I TO I ½ TEASPOONS POWDERED CHILE, OR TO TASTE

I TEASPOON SALT, OR TO TASTE

In a frying pan just large enough to accommodate the peanuts in one layer, heat the oil. Add the peanuts and garlic cloves and fry for about 2 minutes, turning them over constantly. Lower the heat a little, add the powdered chile and salt, and cook for a minute or two longer, stirring from time to time to avoid sticking; take care that the chile powder does not burn.

Set aside to cool before serving with drinks.

MARISCOS A LA MARINERA Seafood Cocktail
SERVES 6
VERACRUZ

This cocktail can be prepared with any seafood: raw clams or scallops, abalone, conch, or cooked shrimps. And how much fresher and crunchier a cocktail it is than the usual version of rubbery shrimps drowned in a commercially made tomato sauce. It is perhaps best eaten immediately after it is prepared, but if you do want to prepare it ahead, don't let it stand for more than 2 hours or the ingredients will lose their fresh flavor and crispness. Naturally, it should not be so cold that the flavor is lost and the oil congealed.

I prefer to serve this with hot, freshly made tortillas, or with dried tortillas, toasted until crisp on a comal or in the oven.

3 DOZEN LARGE RAW CLAMS OR SCALLOPS OR MEDIUM-SIZE COOKED SHRIMPS
½ CUP (125 ML) FRESH LIME JUICE
ABOUT 12 OUNCES (340 G) TOMATOES, FINELY CHOPPED (ABOUT 2 CUPS/500 ML)
1 SMALL WHITE ONION, FINELY CHOPPED (ABOUT ¼ CUP/65 ML)
1 LARGE AVOCADO, CUBED
3 TO 4 SERRANO CHILES OR ANY FRESH, HOT GREEN CHILES, FINELY CHOPPED
2 HEAPED TABLESPOONS FINELY CHOPPED CILANTRO
3 TABLESPOONS OLIVE OIL
SALT AND FRESHLY GROUND PEPPER TO TASTE

If you are using clams, open them or have them opened for you, saving both the clams and their juice. If you are using scallops, let them marinate in the lime juice for an hour or so. Combine the clams (and their liquid) or other seafood with the rest of the ingredients, adjust the seasoning, and serve slightly chilled (see note above).

CAVIAR DE CHAPALA Carp Roe Snack
SERVES 6

The name speaks for itself. Sometimes it is called caviar autóctono *("indigenous" caviar), as it is made from the roe of fish from Lake Chapala. When I first ate it there in a lakeside restaurant, it was made from carp roe, but in fact you could substitute cod or any less expensive roe. It is served as an appetizer with hot tortillas and little dishes of finely chopped onion, serrano chile, cilantro, and green (unripe) tomatoes, so that each person can make a taco, seasoning it* al gusto.

1 TABLESPOON SALT
1 POUND (450 G) CARP OR COD ROE
¼ CUP (65 ML) VEGETABLE OR OLIVE OIL
ABOUT 6 OUNCES (180 G) TOMATOES, FINELY CHOPPED (ABOUT 1 CUP/250 ML)
2 TABLESPOONS FINELY CHOPPED WHITE ONION
1 GARLIC CLOVE, FINELY CHOPPED

THE TOPPINGS
½ CUP (125 ML) FINELY CHOPPED WHITE ONION
⅓ CUP (85 ML) FINELY CHOPPED GREEN, UNRIPE TOMATOES OR TOMATE VERDE
⅓ CUP (85 ML) FINELY CHOPPED CILANTRO
⅓ CUP (85 ML) FINELY CHOPPED SERRANO CHILES OR ANY OTHER FRESH,
   HOT GREEN CHILES

Put the salt and enough water to cover the roe in a shallow pan and bring to the simmering point. Add the roe and let it simmer for 8 to 10 minutes, depending on thickness, then remove and drain. When it is cool enough to handle, remove the skin and crumble the roe.

Heat the oil in a heavy pan. Add the tomatoes, onion, and garlic and fry over fairly high heat, stirring from time to time and scraping the bottom of the pan, until the onion is soft and the mixture is almost dry. Add the crumbled roe with salt to taste and continue frying the mixture over medium heat, turning it over constantly, until dry and crumbly, about 5 minutes.

Serve hot, accompanied by the onion and the other finely chopped toppings, in small separate bowls, and a pile of hot corn tortillas.

OSTIONES PIMENTADOS Peppered Oysters

INSPIRED BY SEÑOR ANGEL DELGADO,
RESTAURANTE LAS DILIGENCIAS, TAMPICO
SERVES 6 TO 8   TAMAULIPAS

*When trying out and writing a recipe like this, I can hear my own and other voices saying,
"What a crime . . . good oysters are best raw," etc. Yes, but this does make an interestingly
tasty snack with drinks or served, atypically, as a first course with wafer-thin black bread.
Come to think of it, not everyone likes raw oysters, while they will happily consume a can of
smoked ones. Enough of excuses. These oysters may be served hot or at room temperature,
preferably on the half shell. Champagne is a wonderful accompaniment.*

4 DOZEN OYSTERS, SHUCKED, SHELLS AND LIQUID RESERVED
2 TEASPOONS WHOLE PEPPERCORNS
$\frac{1}{2}$ TEASPOON SALT, OR TO TASTE
6 GARLIC CLOVES
I TABLESPOON FRESH LIME JUICE, MORE IF DESIRED
2 TABLESPOONS OLIVE OIL
2 MEXICAN BAY LEAVES

Heat the liquid from the oysters to the simmering point, then add the oysters and poach
until the edges start to curl, about 2 minutes. Drain the oysters, reserving the broth.

Crush the peppercorns with the salt and garlic in a molcajete or mortar. Pound in
the garlic and gradually add the lime juice. Last of all, add about 3 tablespoons of the
reserved oyster broth. Mix well.

Heat the olive oil in a skillet. Add the bay leaves and the peppercorn mixture and
cook over high heat for about 3 minutes. Remove the pan from the heat and add the
oysters. Adjust the seasoning, then add a squeeze of lime juice and a little more of the
oyster liquid if desired.

Serve warm or at room temperature in half shells.

NOTE: For best results for a large quantity, poach the oysters lightly and drain. Then
prepare the seasoning, and assemble at the last moment. Do not attempt to freeze.

SALPICÓN DE JAIBA Shredded Crabmeat and Vegetables
MAKES ENOUGH TO FILL 12 SMALL TORTILLAS   TAMAULIPAS

When I first visited Tampico at the beginning of the seventies, I found what was to become one of my favorite regional restaurants at that time in the Hotel Inglaterra. The owner, Fidel Loredo, the brother of José Inés Loredo, the famous restaurateur whose restaurants in Mexico City are still renowned today, gave me this simple but delicious recipe. It smacks of Chinese food and perhaps the influence came from the Chinese merchant ships frequenting the port of Tampico.

The crabmeat was from the small blue crabs from that area that are certainly time-consuming to clean—but most cooks can buy crabmeat already prepared.

This salpicón *makes a delicious filling for small tacos or can be served with plain white rice.*

1/4 CUP (65 ML) VEGETABLE OIL
1/3 CUP (85 ML) FINELY CHOPPED WHITE ONION
1/2 CUP (125 ML) FINELY CHOPPED CELERY
5 SERRANO CHILES, FINELY CHOPPED, WITH SEEDS
1 CUP (250 ML) COOKED, SHREDDED CRABMEAT
3 TABLESPOONS FINELY CHOPPED CILANTRO
SALT TO TASTE

Heat the oil in a skillet and cook the onion gently until translucent.

Add the celery, chiles, and crabmeat and fry until they just begin to brown slightly. The mixture should be rather dry. Lastly, add the cilantro and salt and cook for 1 minute more.

Serve with hot tortillas.

CHICHARRÓN EN ESCABECHE Pickled Pork Rind
SERVES 6   PUEBLA

When visiting Tehuacán, Puebla, many years ago to do a story on the Matanzas, or mass killing of goats (see My Mexico*), I was taken by friends who lived there to visit a grand old lady who had a great reputation as a cook. She lived in a large turn-of-the-century house in a sad state of disrepair, but the family portraits and faded furniture spoke of a bygone* *elegance. Most of the dishes she prepared reflected her upbringing in Alvarado, Veracruz, by Andalusian parents, so it surprised me that this recipe, Mexican through and through, was one of her favorites.*

1/4 CUP (65 ML) VEGETABLE OIL

2 MEDIUM PURPLE ONIONS, THICKLY SLICED

6 GARLIC CLOVES, LEFT WHOLE

1 1/2 CUPS (375 ML) VINEGAR, MILD OR DILUTED WITH 1/2 CUP (125 ML) WATER,
    APPROXIMATELY

1/2 TEASPOON DRIED MEXICAN OREGANO

3 SPRIGS FRESH THYME OR 1/8 TEASPOON DRIED

1/2 TEASPOON SALT, OR TO TASTE

FRESHLY GROUND PEPPER

8 OUNCES (225 G) CHICHARRÓN (SEE PAGE 496), THE THINNER THE BETTER, BROKEN
    INTO 2-INCH (5-CM) SQUARES

2 JALAPEÑO CHILES EN ESCABECHE, CUT INTO STRIPS

I AVOCADO, PEELED AND SLICED

Heat the oil and gently fry the onions and garlic without browning for about 2 minutes. Add the vinegar, oregano, thyme, salt, and pepper to the pan and bring to a boil. Add the chicharrón pieces and chiles and cook over fairly high heat, stirring from time to time to avoid sticking, until the chicharrón has softened and absorbed almost all the vinegar—about 5 minutes. Set aside to cool, then serve, topped with slices of avocado.

To my mind, Chicharrón en Escabeche is best served as soon as it has cooled off, but it will keep indefinitely in the refrigerator (although it congeals and must be brought up to room temperature before serving).

QUESO FLAMEADO "Flamed" Cheese
SERVES 6   NORTHERN MEXICO

This is the Mexican version of a cheese fondue — not as delicate, of course, but robust and very well complemented by a picante tomato sauce and a stack of flour tortillas.

In and around Guadalajara this is called queso fundido *(melted cheese), but in the northern states, where it is a favorite first course in restaurants specializing in broiled meats, it is called* queso flameado *or* queso asado *(roasted or broiled cheese); the cheese is melted*

*in a shallow metal dish over the hot embers of the constantly burning wood fire and brought
sizzling to the table.*

*Queso Flameado can be served either plain or with fried and crumbled chorizo sprinkled
all over it. A picante tomato or green tomato sauce is put on the table, along with a stack of
wheat-flour tortillas, so that each one can help himself,* al gusto. *The cheese can be served
either in individual dishes or one large one. Allow 3 flour tortillas per person; for the sauces,
see Salsa Ranchera (page 238), Salsa de Tomate Verde (page 236), or Salsa Mexicana
Cruda (page 235).*

12 OUNCES (340 G) CHIHUAHUA CHEESE OR MUENSTER, THINLY SLICED
6 OUNCES (180 G) MEXICAN CHORIZOS, SKINNED, CRUMBLED, AND FRIED (OPTIONAL)
1 ½ DOZEN FLOUR TORTILLAS (SEE PAGE 52)

Place the cheese in two layers in a shallow, flameproof dish. Melt the cheese either on
top of the stove or in the oven, sprinkling the chorizo over it. Heat the tortillas and serve
immediately, with the sauce on the side.

CHILORIO Chile-Seasoned Pork

MAKES ENOUGH TO FILL 12 TORTILLAS   SINALOA

*This recipe was given to me in 1971 by a Señora Castro (alas, her full name disappeared
with the notebook) who lived very modestly in Culiacán and had been recommended to me
as an expert in making Chilorio. In those days Culiacán was a sleepy little town where no
one seemed to be in a hurry—especially in the heat of summer—and we spent the best part
of the day cooking and talking about the local foods. Her excellent recipe has stood the test of
time—I have never come across a better one, or a better cook than Señora Castro.*

2 POUNDS (900 G) PORK SHOULDER, WITHOUT BONE BUT WITH SOME FAT
2 TEASPOONS SALT
8 ANCHO CHILES, SEEDS AND VEINS REMOVED
⅓ CUP (85 ML) MILD VINEGAR; MAKE UP TO ½ CUP (125 ML) OF LIQUID BY ADDING WATER
8 GARLIC CLOVES, ROUGHLY CHOPPED
⅛ TEASPOON CUMIN SEEDS, CRUSHED
¼ TEASPOON DRIED MEXICAN OREGANO
SALT TO TASTE
LARD AS NECESSARY

Cut the meat into 1-inch (2.5-cm) cubes and cook with salt as for Carnitas (page 23). When the water has evaporated and the fat has rendered out of the meat but the meat has not browned—about 45 minutes—remove the meat from the dish and pound it in the molcajete until it is in shreds, or shred it finely with two forks.

Meanwhile, prepare the sauce. Cover the chiles with hot water. Soak for 10 minutes and drain.

Put the diluted vinegar into the blender jar with the garlic and spices and blend as smooth as possible. Gradually add the chiles and blend after each addition. The sauce should be thick, more like a paste. You will have to keep stopping the blender to release the blades. Only add more liquid if necessary to release the blades of the blender.

There should be about ¼ cup (65 ml) of fat in the dish in which the meat was cooked; if not, make up to that amount with lard. Add the meat and mix the chile sauce well into it. Cook over low heat for 15 to 20 minutes, or until the meat is well seasoned and the mixture rather dry, scraping the bottom of the dish to avoid sticking.

Chilorio will keep for months in the refrigerator.

MOCHOMOS SINALOENSES Sinaloan Shredded Beef

RECIPE INSPIRED BY BONNY ROJO OF CULIACÁN
MAKES ABOUT 6 CUPS (1.5 L)   SINALOA

Mochomos *is a curious name. It is the Opata Indian word—in eastern Sonora—for night-working ants. This very popular dish from Sinaloa is made of* carne machaca, *or* machacada—*literally meaning pounded. It is usually served for* almuerzo *with corn tortillas,* frijoles refritos, *and a simple tomato sauce, or it is often added to scrambled eggs. In other parts of Mexico,* carne machacada *is made of thinly cut dried beef, while in Sinaloa steaks about 1 inch (2.5 cm) thick are well salted and dried in the sun for two or three days. In this dehydrated state they can be kept for a long time. Before using the meat, it is broiled on both sides over a wood fire, then pounded—sometimes with garlic—to a fluff with a heavy, flat stone kept especially for that purpose. If you live in the dry Southwest this should present no problem—except for the time involved—but if you live elsewhere with a damp climate and need to hurry it along, here are two solutions. You may cut the meat into large cubes, rub in 1½ tablespoons finely ground sea salt, and place on a rack set over a roasting pan in a slow oven—250°F (120°C) to 300°F (150°C)—until the meat has dried out. Since this method takes from 3½ to 4 hours, I suggest a second method in the following recipe as a compromise. It produced pretty good results, but lacks, of course, the smoky flavor of the original method. (I could never recommend the addition of that artificial smoke flavor.)*

This type of meat is always rather salty, but you can tone it down with barely salted sauce and, of course, a tortilla that has no salt in it. The food of this area is not picante and therefore only one poblano chile is added for this quantity of meat while often the milder Anaheim chile is used in Sinaloa. The onion should remain crunchy, so do not allow it to overcook. A wok would be the ideal pan for cooking this dish.

2 POUNDS (900 G) ROUND STEAK (WITH SOME FAT ON)
1 ½ TABLESPOONS COARSE SEA SALT
½ CUP (125 ML) LARD OR VEGETABLE OIL
8 OUNCES (225 G) WHITE ONIONS, ROUGHLY SLICED
1 POBLANO CHILE, CHARRED, PEELED, CLEANED, AND CUT INTO SMALL SQUARES
   (SEE PAGE 469)
SALSA PARA MOCHOMOS (RECIPE FOLLOWS)

Cut the meat into 1-inch (2.5-cm) cubes. Place the meat in one layer in a large pan. Add the salt and water to barely cover. Bring the water to a boil, lower the heat, and cook slowly, uncovered, until the water has evaporated and the meat is tender but not too soft—35 to 40 minutes. Continue drying the meat out over low heat so that it is dried and slightly crusty on the outside. Allow to cool.

Put 3 pieces of the meat into a blender and blend at medium speed until meat is finely shredded. Continue in the same way until all the meat has been shredded.

Heat half of the lard in a skillet, add the onions, and fry briefly for about 1 minute— they should be crisp and still opaque. Remove the onions with a slotted spoon and drain. Set aside.

Add the rest of the lard to the skillet, heat, add the shredded meat and chile, and stir until the meat is well heated through and just browning—5 to 8 minutes.

Stir in the onions, heat through, and serve immediately with a little of the Salsa para Mochomos on top.

SALSA PARA MOCHOMOS Tomato Sauce for Mochomos
MAKES 2 CUPS (500 ML)

1 POUND (450 G) TOMATOES, BROILED (SEE PAGE 490)
2 OR 3 SERRANO CHILES, CHARRED (SEE PAGE 470)
1 THICK SLICE WHITE ONION
SALT TO TASTE
2 WHOLE BLACK PEPPERCORNS, ROUGHLY GROUND
2 TABLESPOONS ROUGHLY CHOPPED FRESH CILANTRO (OPTIONAL)

Blend the unskinned tomatoes together with the chiles and onion until fairly smooth. Season to taste, and decorate with the cilantro.

CARNE COCIDA EN LIMÓN Ground Meat Marinated in Lime Juice
SERVES 4

The pulquerias of Mexico City and the cantinas in the smaller towns have always been famous for their—mostly—thirst-provoking snacks provided free of charge with drinks. When I first visited Tuxtla Gutierrez, Chiapas, in 1970 I was amazed at the endless variety and quality of these snacks—rivaled only by the cantinas of Mérida in Yucatán today. Apart from the Carne Cocida en Limón, and the Botanas de Camarón Seco given here, they included fried fish roe, chicharrón in a fresh sauce, crispy pork ribs, fried beans, fresh crumbly cheese, and small cups of a picante broth of dried shrimp or fresh water snail called shote, *to name only a few.*

½ CUP (125 ML) FRESH LIME JUICE
8 OUNCES (225 G) FRESHLY GROUND SIRLOIN, ABSOLUTELY FREE OF FAT
4 OUNCES (115 G) TOMATOES, FINELY CHOPPED (⅔ CUP/165 ML)
2 TABLESPOONS FINELY CHOPPED WHITE ONION
4 SERRANO CHILES, FINELY CHOPPED
SALT TO TASTE

Mix the lime juice well into the ground meat and set it aside to "cook" in the refrigerator for at least 4 hours in a nonreactive bowl.

Mix in the rest of the ingredients and set the meat aside to season for at least 2 hours more.

Serve with crisp tortillas, either toasted or fried.

BOTANAS DE CAMARÓN SECO Dried Shrimp Fritters
MAKES ABOUT 24 BOTANAS

4 OUNCES (115 G) FLOUR (ABOUT 1 SCANT CUP)
1 CUP (250 ML) COLD WATER
SALT TO TASTE
3/4 CUP (190 ML) SMALL DRIED SHRIMPS, CLEANED (SEE PAGE 498)
1 EGG WHITE
1/2 CUP (125 ML) FINELY CHOPPED WHITE ONION
5 SERRANO CHILES, FINELY CHOPPED
VEGETABLE OIL FOR FRYING

Blend the flour, water, and salt together for 2 minutes and leave the batter to stand for at least 1 hour.

Rinse the shrimps to remove excess salt. Cover with warm water and leave them to soak for about 5 minutes—no longer.

Beat the egg white until stiff and fold it into the batter.

Drain the shrimps (if large, cut into 2) and add them, with the chopped onion and chiles, to the batter.

Heat the oil in a skillet and drop tablespoons of the mixture into it, a few at a time. Fry the botanas until they are golden brown, turning them over once. Drain them on the paper toweling and serve immediately.

SALSA DE ALBAÑIL Bricklayers' Sauce or Botana
MAKES 12 TACOS

There are many sauces and egg dishes ascribed to bricklayers, albañiles. *This is more than just a sauce; it was a favorite botana served with drinks at the Lincoln Grill in Mexico City in the late fifties.*

It is very easy to prepare at the last moment, especially if you have some leftover salsa verde. It should be served with freshly made tortillas so that each diner can make his or her own tacos.

1 ¼ CUPS (315 ML) SALSA DE TOMATE VERDE (PAGE 236)
4 OUNCES (115 G) QUESO FRESCO OR MUENSTER CHEESE, CUT INTO 12 STRIPS ABOUT
     ¼ INCH (.75 CM) THICK
1 MEDIUM AVOCADO (ABOUT 6 OUNCES/180 G), PEELED AND CUT INTO 12 SLICES
OPTIONAL TOPPING: 2 TABLESPOONS ROUGHLY CHOPPED CILANTRO

Spread the sauce over a shallow dish about 8 inches (20 cm) in diameter and place the pieces of cheese in spiral fashion over it. Top the cheese with avocado slices and sprinkle with the optional cilantro.

CARNITAS Little Pieces of Browned Pork
SERVES 6

CENTRAL MEXICO

For aficionados of pork, carnitas are an all-time favorite in Mexico. Traditionally, large hunks of pork are fried until tender in large vats of lard. When sold, they are cut into smaller pieces or chopped fine and stuffed inside a taco. The meat is succulent and delicious.

For some reason the carnitas in Michoacán have always been considered the best, but they have many a rival in other parts of the country. There are some fancier ways of preparing them (see recipe in The Art of Mexican Cooking *from the State of Mexico), but traditionalists prefer the simple method.*

This recipe is for cooking them at home and they are surprisingly addictive.

Carnitas can be eaten as a main course or as a hearty botana accompanied by guacamole or preferably a fresh green sauce or Salsa Mexicana Cruda (page 235).

3 POUNDS (1.35 KG) PORK SHOULDER, SKIN AND BONE REMOVED
2 TEASPOONS SALT, OR TO TASTE

Cut the meat, with the fat, into strips about 2 by ¾ inches (5 by 2 cm). Barely cover the meat with water in a heavy, wide pan. Add the salt and bring to a boil, uncovered. Lower the heat and let the meat continue cooking briskly until all the liquid has evaporated—by this time it should be cooked through but not falling apart.

Lower the heat a little and continue cooking the meat until all the fat has rendered out of it. Keep turning the meat until it is lightly browned all over—total cooking time is about 1 hour and 10 minutes.

Serve immediately for best flavor and texture.

FRIJOLES PUERCOS ESTILO JALISCO
Rich Well-Fried Beans from Jalisco

SERVES 6

There are many variations of Frijoles Puercos in northwest Michoacán, Colima, and Jalisco and this is one of them. They are served as a botana with drinks. In Jalisco they are topped with a queso ranchero, a strong, dry, and salty cheese.

1 CHORIZO, ABOUT 3 OUNCES (85 G)
6 STRIPS BACON
LARD AS NECESSARY
8 OUNCES (225 G) PINTO OR PINK BEANS, COOKED AS FOR FRIJOLES DE OLLA (PAGE
    154)—3 1/2 TO 4 CUPS (875 ML TO 1 L) WITH BROTH
20 SMALL, PITTED GREEN OLIVES, CHOPPED
2 JALAPEÑO CHILES EN ESCABECHE
2 TABLESPOONS FINELY GRATED QUESO RANCHERO OR ROMANO
TOASTED TORTILLAS OR TOTOPOS (SEE PAGE 94)

Skin and crumble the chorizo, and chop the bacon. Cook in a skillet over low heat, covered, until most of the fat has rendered out. Be careful not to let them burn. Remove chorizo and bacon and reserve.

There should be about 1/3 cup (85 ml) fat in the pan. Take out or make up to that amount with lard. Add the beans and broth and cook them over high heat, mashing them as you would for Frijoles Refritos (page 155). If they start to dry out and stick to the pan, add a little more lard.

When the beans have been mashed to a coarse texture and are almost dry, ready to roll, add the bacon and about two thirds of the olives, chiles, and chorizo.

Roll the beans, then turn onto the serving dish and top with the remaining olives, chiles, and chorizo.

Sprinkle the roll with the cheese and serve with the toasted tortillas or totopos.

MASA FANTASIES

Garnachas Yucatecas ✳ *Filled Masa Tartlets*

Picadillo Sencillo para Garnachas

✳ *Ground Meat Filling for Garnachas*

Garnachas Veracruzanos de Masa Cocida ✳ *Garnachas of Cooked Masa*

Enchiladas del Santuario ✳ *Sanctuary Enchiladas*

Bocoles de Frijol ✳ *Masa and Black Bean Snacks*

Gorditas de Chiles Serranos ✳ *Cakes of Masa with Serrano Chiles*

Chalupas

Quesadillas

Sesos para Quesadillas ✳ *Brains Filling for Quesadillas*

Flor de Calabaza Guisada ✳ *Squash Flower Filling*

Chorizo con Papa ✳ *Chorizo and Potato Filling*

Green Chile Gordas

Potato and Masa Gordas

Sopes

Panuchos

Empanadas de Requesón

✳ *Empanadas Filled with Ricotta and Squash Flowers*

"Enchiladas" Tultecas

Gordas, *sopes*, *chalupas*, quesadillas—enchanting names, but these are just a few of the masa fantasies, for wherever you travel in Mexico there are the specialties of that region—the *garnachas* of Yucatán and Veracruz, the *panuchos* of Yucatán and Campeche; the *molotes* of Oaxaca; *bocoles* of Tamaulipas; and the *tlacoyos*, *memelas*, *picadas*, and *pelliscadas* of central Mexico. They are all variations on a theme—corn dough flattened into little cakes, thick or thin, fried or toasted, some reddened with dried chiles, enriched with creamy cheese or marrow fat, stuffed with beans, or seasoned with dried shrimps. Some are topped with shredded meats or crumbled cheese, doused with a fiery sauce, and decorated carefully with radish, tomato, or lettuce—or whatever is at hand. The corn dough is patted and coaxed into a hundred different little forms, enticing you to nibble from morning until night. These are just a few of the hundreds of variations on what the Mexicans call *antojitos*, "little whims."

GARNACHAS YUCATECAS Filled Masa Tartlets

SEÑORA TRÁNSITA, QUINTA MARI, MÉRIDA

MAKES 12 GARNACHAS

1 ¼ POUNDS (565 G) TORTILLA MASA (ABOUT 2 ¼ CUPS/563 ML)

1 TABLESPOON ALL-PURPOSE FLOUR

SALT TO TASTE

MELTED LARD OR VEGETABLE OIL

1 CUP (250 ML) FRIJOLES COLADOS YUCATECOS (PAGE 158), WARMED

1 CUP (250 ML) PICADILLO SENCILLO PARA GARNACHAS (PAGE 28), WARMED

½ CUP (125 ML) SALSA DE JITOMATE YUCATECA (PAGE 240), WARMED

3 TABLESPOONS FINELY GRATED QUESO SECO OR SUBSTITUTE ROMANO

Mix the masa together with the flour and salt.

Roll the masa into 12 balls, each roughly 1¾ inches (4.5 cm) in diameter.

Press each ball of dough onto a floured surface and make a well in it, using both thumbs together. Press out the sides of the well and mold the dough into a small basket shape about 3 inches (8 cm) across and ¾ inch (2 cm) deep. The dough should be about ¼ inch (.75 cm) thick.

Heat the fat in a large skillet and fry the *garnachas*, hollow side down first, until they are a pale gold and just a little crisp on the outside, 8 to 10 minutes. Drain the *garnachas* on the paper toweling and keep them warm.

Fill one half of each *garnacha* with a tablespoon of the bean paste and the other half with a scant tablespoon of the picadillo. Cover the filling with a large teaspoon of the tomato sauce and sprinkle it with the cheese.

Garnachas should be served as soon as possible after frying or they will become leathery. They can be prepared up to the point of frying some hours ahead, but they should be kept covered so that the masa does not dry out.

The picadillo, bean paste, and sauce will freeze perfectly well, so you could always keep some on hand and whip up some *garnachas* at the drop of a hat—a sort of Mexican pizza.

PICADILLO SENCILLO PARA GARNACHAS
Ground Meat Filling for Garnachas
MAKES APPROXIMATELY 2 CUPS (500 ML)

1 TABLESPOON MELTED LARD OR VEGETABLE OIL
1 GARLIC CLOVE, FINELY CHOPPED
1/3 CUP (85 ML) FINELY CHOPPED WHITE ONION
2 CUPS (500 ML) FINELY CHOPPED TOMATOES
1 POUND (450 G) GROUND BEEF
SALT TO TASTE

Heat the fat in a large skillet and fry the garlic and onion until translucent.

Add the tomatoes and fry over fairly high heat until reduced—about 3 minutes. Stir in the meat with salt to taste and cook over medium heat, stirring from time to time, until cooked—about 10 minutes. The mixture should be moist but not juicy.

GARNACHAS VERACRUZANOS DE MASA COCIDA
Garnachas of Cooked Masa
SEÑORA OCHOA DE ZAMUDIO
MAKES 16 2½-INCH (6.5-CM) GARNACHAS

These garnachas made of an unusual, cooked masa are sold along the waterfront of Alvarado, Veracruz, in the evenings. Señora Ochoa de Zamudio, who was born in Alvarado, prepared them for me, working the masa with her hands. When prepared and ready to serve, the bottom of the garnacha will be slightly browned and firm while the rest is still soft. Like all antojitos of this kind, they are addictive!

1 POUND (450 G) TORTILLA MASA
SALT TO TASTE
2 HEAPED TABLESPOONS LARD
LARD OR VEGETABLE OIL FOR FRYING

THE FILLING

²⁄₃ CUP (165 ML) FRIJOLES REFRITOS A LA VERACRUZANA (PAGE 155)

12 OUNCES (340 G) WAXY POTATOES, COOKED, PEELED, AND DICED
(ABOUT 2¼ CUPS/563 ML)

²⁄₃ CUP (165 ML) SALSA DE JITOMATE VERACRUZANA (PAGE 240)

½ CUP (125 ML) FINELY CHOPPED WHITE ONION

½ CUP (125 ML) FINELY GRATED COTIJA OR ROMANO CHEESE

Work the masa and salt together until very smooth, either by hand or in the food processor, adding a little water if the masa is rather dry. Divide the dough into three parts and form into round, flat cakes about ½ inch (1.5 cm) thick and cover with a damp cloth until ready to cook.

Choose a pot that is about 8 inches (20 cm) in diameter and fill with water to the depth of about 5 inches (13 cm). Bring to a boil over medium heat. Lower the heat slightly so that the water is not boiling so fiercely and add one piece of the masa. It will sink to the bottom but after a minute shake the pan gently to ensure that the masa is not sticking to the bottom. If it is, gently loosen it with a wide spatula. Continue cooking the masa cake until it floats to the surface of the water—about 4 minutes—then turn it over and cook on the second side for about 2 minutes more. Drain and set aside. Continue with the other two masa cakes. Transfer the cakes to the bowl of a food processor with the lard and process until you have a very smooth, cohesive dough. (This process was done by hand with movements like the *fraisage* for a pastry dough, working the cooked dough and lard together hard three times.)

Put a shallow layer of lard or oil in a large skillet and melt over medium heat. Divide the dough into 1¼-inch (3.25-cm) balls and cover them with a damp cloth. Press one of the balls out to about 2½ inches (6.5 cm) in diameter. Form a small ridge around the circumference and place in the hot fat. Continue with the rest. From time to time flip some of the hot fat into the *garnacha*. While it is still in the pan, spread a heaped teaspoonful of the bean paste inside the *garnacha*, add a few cubes of potato and 1½ teaspoons of the sauce, and continue frying until the dough is slightly browned on the bottom. Top with a little of the onion and cheese and serve immediately.

ENCHILADAS DEL SANTUARIO Sanctuary Enchiladas
MAKES 12 ENCHILADAS   SAN LUIS POTOSÍ

I remember so clearly those lovely balmy evenings in San Luis Potosí in the early seventies. It seemed that every family was out ambling along the long paseo lined with fragrant trees which led to the santuario. From way off you could see the blinking specks of light from candles set up in the little food stands at the foot of the steps leading to the church. Most were serving the specialty of San Luis, Enchiladas del Santuario. They were not enchiladas in the general sense, more like quesadillas made with a reddish masa and filled with cheese and onion: they were so simple but delicious. The cheese I remember was one of the most delicious quesos fresco I have ever tasted, made by a local factory called Carranco.

1 TABLESPOON LARD
1 ANCHO CHILE, WIPED CLEAN, SEEDS AND VEINS REMOVED
1/4 CUP (65 ML) WATER
2 PEPPERCORNS, CRUSHED
SALT TO TASTE
10 OUNCES (285 G) TORTILLA MASA (SCANT 1 1/4 CUPS/313 ML), FAIRLY DRY
4 OUNCES (115 G) QUESO FRESCO, CRUMBLED (ABOUT 3/4 CUP/188 ML)
MELTED LARD OR VEGETABLE OIL FOR FRYING
1/3 CUP (85 ML) FINELY GRATED QUESO SECO OR ROMANO
1/3 CUP (85 ML) FINELY CHOPPED ONION

Heat the lard and fry the chile lightly on both sides, then remove with a slotted spoon, and tear into pieces. Put the chile pieces in a blender, add the water, peppercorns, and salt, and blend until smooth.

Mix the ground chile into the masa and knead the dough well. Set it aside—do not refrigerate—to season for 1/2 hour.

Divide the dough into 12 portions and roll each into a ball about 1 1/4 inches (3.25 cm) in diameter. Press a ball of the dough out in a tortilla press to make a slightly thicker tortilla about 4 1/2 inches (11.5 cm) in diameter. Put 1 scant tablespoon of queso fresco on one half of the dough, then fold the second half over to cover the cheese, pressing the edges firmly together. Cook on a comal or griddle over medium heat for about 2 minutes, turn it over, and cook on the second side for another 2 minutes. Continue with the rest of the masa balls.

Heat the fat, about ¼ inch (.75 cm) deep, in a frying pan, and fry the enchiladas lightly on both sides—they should not be crisp—for about 1½ minutes on each side. Drain on paper toweling and serve immediately with the cheese and onion.

Like all masa *antojitos* they are best eaten the moment they are made, but if you have to make some ahead, cook them on the comal, wrap in a thick cloth, and do the frying at the last moment.

BOCOLES DE FRIJOL Masa and Black Bean Snacks

SEÑORA HORTENSIA DE FAGOAGA

MAKES 12 BOCOLES—2½ INCHES (6.5 CM) TO 3 INCHES (8 CM) IN

DIAMETER, AND JUST OVER ¼ INCH (.75 CM) THICK

PUEBLA

The mixture of masa and black beans for antojitos *is not unique to this area; there are the* gorditas de frijol *from Veracruz (see recipe in* My Mexico*), negritos from Campechein, and even some unusual totopos from the Isthmus among others, not to mention the many tamales incorporating beans and masa. It is a happy marriage!*

These bocoles resemble gorditas (see the following recipe) in size and shape, but they are briefly submerged in a hot tomato sauce and therefore slightly softer on the outside. They are served with a little of the sauce and topped with very finely grated queso añejo and finely chopped onion. They make for a delicious, albeit slightly caloric, snack.

1½ CUPS (375 ML) TORTILLA MASA, AS DRY AS POSSIBLE

1 CUP (250 ML) BLACK BEAN PASTE

4 TABLESPOONS LARD

½ TEASPOON BAKING POWDER

SALT TO TASTE

TO SERVE

2 CUPS (500 ML) SALSA RANCHERA (PAGE 238), OMITTING THE ONION, DILUTED WITH
   ABOUT ⅔ CUP (165 ML) MEAT OR CHICKEN BROTH

⅓ CUP (85 ML) FINELY GRATED QUESO AÑEJO

⅓ CUP (85 ML) FINELY CHOPPED WHITE ONION

Mix the masa with the bean paste, lard, baking powder, and salt. Divide into 12 equal balls about 1¾ inches (about 4.5 cm) in diameter. Press each ball into a disk about 3½ inches (9 cm) in diameter and just over ¼ inch (.75 cm) thick.

Heat the comal, then lower the heat and cook the *bocoles* for about 6 minutes on each side. Meanwhile, warm the tomato sauce. While the *bocoles* are still warm, immerse them in the warm tomato sauce, then serve with a little of the sauce and sprinkle with a little of the cheese and chopped onion.

These are best eaten immediately—even if you do burn your mouth. By adding more lard they can be reheated even a day later.

GORDITAS DE CHILES SERRANOS
Cakes of Masa with Serrano Chiles

SEÑORA HORTENSIA DE FAGOAGA

MAKES 12 GORDITAS—3 INCHES (8 CM) IN DIAMETER
AND JUST OVER ¼ INCH (.75 CM) THICK   PUEBLA

These little masa antojitos *are called either* gorditas *or* itacates. *The word* itacate *comes from the Náhuatl, denoting provisions or food taken on a journey or to the fields.*

This particular recipe is from the Sierra de Puebla and was given to me by my never-failing source of information for recipes of that area, Señora Hortensia de Fagoaga. Many recipes of hers appear in The Art of Mexican Cooking *for this type of delectable masa concoctions or* antojitos. *They are eaten like bread, either alone or to accompany an egg or rice dish.*

These simple foods rely on a very good quality masa and, of course, pork lard or, more delicious still, rendered beef fat—as do the very similar bocoles *of the Tampico area.*

When cooking these itacates *on either a metal or a clay comal, I like to spread a thin coating of cal (lime) over the surface to prevent the masa from sticking. They should be cooked slowly so that the heat penetrates the thick dough. The gorditas should be slightly crisp on the outside but soft inside.*

2 CUPS (500 ML) TORTILLA MASA (ABOUT 18 OUNCES/510 G)
3 TABLESPOONS PORK LARD, SOFTENED
SALT TO TASTE
4 SERRANO CHILES ASADOS, OR MORE TO TASTE

Mix the masa with the lard and salt. Roughly chop the chiles and crush to a textured paste. Mix the chiles into the masa well. Divide the dough into balls about 1¾ inches (about 4.5 cm) in diameter. Press each ball into a disk about 3 inches (8 cm) in diameter and just over ¼ inch (.75 cm) thick.

Heat the comal, then lower the heat and cook the *itacates* (see note above) for about 6 minutes on each side.

These are best eaten immediately—even if you do burn your mouth. By adding more lard they can be reheated even a day later.

CHALUPAS

MAKES 12 CHALUPAS MEXICO CITY

Because of its narrow elongated shape this little antojito *was named* chalupa *after the narrow canoes that navigated the waterways between the* chinampas, *or floating gardens, of Xochimilco—presumably since pre-Columbian times. But nobody can give me an explanation of why in Puebla and around Chilpancingo, Guerrero, the* chalupas *are round!*

A favorite topping for chalupas *is some shredded, poached chicken and a little green sauce, sprinkled with finely chopped onion and crumbled queso fresco.*

12 OUNCES (340 G) TORTILLA MASA (ABOUT 1 $\frac{1}{3}$ CUPS/233 ML)
MELTED LARD OR VEGETABLE OIL FOR FRYING (OPTIONAL)

TOPPING
1 CUP (250 ML) SHREDDED, POACHED CHICKEN (PAGE 499)
$\frac{3}{4}$ CUP (188 ML) SALSA DE TOMATE VERDE (PAGE 236)
$\frac{1}{2}$ CUP (125 ML) FINELY CHOPPED WHITE ONION
$\frac{1}{2}$ CUP (125 ML) CRUMBLED QUESO FRESCO

Work the masa with your hands until perfectly smooth—it should be soft and pliable—and divide into 12 separate balls. Form one piece of the dough into a sausage shape about 3½ inches (9 cm) long and ½ inch (1.5 cm) wide and press out lightly in a lined tortilla press (see page 49) to an oval shape slightly thicker than a tortilla.

Cook the *chalupa* on an ungreased comal until firm on the bottom, about 2 minutes. Turn the *chalupa* over and cook on the second side for about 1 minute, pressing up the sides of the dough to form a small ridge around the edge.

Spread the top with some of the shredded chicken, cover with the sauce, and sprinkle with the onion and cheese.

Optional—immerse the *chalupas* in hot, melted lard or vegetable oil for a few seconds and serve immediately: this is pan-to-mouth food.

QUESADILLAS
MAKES 12 QUESADILLAS

Quesadillas are one of the Mexicans' favorite simple snacks. These uncooked tortillas are stuffed with one of various fillings and folded over to make a turnover. They are then toasted on a hot griddle or fried until golden. Only too often they are just a cooked tortilla filled with strips of Chihuahua cheese, which melts and "strings" nicely—a Mexican requirement. In central Mexico the simplest ones are filled with some of the braided Oaxaca cheese, a few fresh leaves of epazote, and strips of peeled poblano chile. Potato and chorizo filling—the one used for tacos (see page 36)—is also a favorite version, while the most highly esteemed of all are those of sautéed squash blossoms (flor de calabaza) or the ambrosial fungus that grows on the corn (cuiclacoche), both of which are at their best during the rainy months of summer and early fall. I have tried quesadillas with a delicious filling of brains (see page 35) in Morelia and I remember one of our maids making them with cooked potato peelings and a few epazote leaves—they were delicious.

1 ⅓ ROUNDED CUPS (335 ML) TORTILLA MASA (ABOUT 12 OUNCES/340 G)
MELTED LARD OR VEGETABLE OIL FOR FRYING

Preheat a lightly greased griddle.

Divide the dough into 12 equal parts and roll into balls about 1½ inches (4 cm) in diameter. Using the tortilla press and plastic bags (see How to Make Corn Tortillas, page 49) press out a ball of dough to make a tortilla 3½ to 4 inches (9 to 10 cm) in diameter. Peel off the top bag. Lift up the bottom bag and place it flat on your hand with the dough on the palm. Put a little of the filling onto one half of the dough, not too near the edge. Bring the bag up and over so that the other half of the dough doubles over and covers the filling. Press the edges of the dough gently together and then gently peel the bag from the "turnover." Place it onto the griddle and cook for 3 to 4 minutes on each side, then stand it up so that the U-shaped fold is also cooked. (Take care that the griddle is not too hot or the dough will be burned on the outside without cooking through sufficiently; it should be thoroughly opaque and speckled with brown.)

Or cook them as follows: Heat the lard and fry the quesadillas for 2 to 3 minutes on each side, or until they are golden brown but not too dry and crisp. Drain and serve immediately.

NOTE: Quesadillas should be served immediately after they are cooked or they will soon become leathery. They could be formed ahead of time and kept wrapped in a slightly damp cloth or a piece of plastic wrap so they do not dry out.

SESOS PARA QUESADILLAS Brains Filling for Quesadillas
ENOUGH FOR 12 QUESADILLAS CENTRAL MEXICO

12 OUNCES (340 G) CALVES' BRAINS

SALT TO TASTE

2 TABLESPOONS MILD WHITE VINEGAR

3 TABLESPOONS VEGETABLE OIL

1 TABLESPOON FINELY CHOPPED WHITE ONION

1 GARLIC CLOVE, FINELY CHOPPED

8 OUNCES (225 G) TOMATOES, FINELY CHOPPED (ABOUT 1 1/3 CUPS/335 ML)

2 SERRANO CHILES, FINELY CHOPPED

SALT TO TASTE

1 HEAPED TABLESPOON CHOPPED EPAZOTE

Cover the brains with cold water and leave them to soak for at least 4 hours. Change the water frequently.

Rinse the brains carefully in warm water to remove all traces of blood.

Bring the water to a simmer in a small pan; add the salt, vinegar, and brains—the water should cover the brains completely—and poach for 15 minutes but *do not let the water boil on any account*. It should just shudder. Let the brains cool in the liquid.

Drain the brains and remove the outer membrane; chop roughly.

Heat the oil and cook the onion and garlic over medium heat until translucent, about 1 minute.

Add the tomatoes and let cook over medium heat for about 3 minutes.

Add the brains, chiles, and salt and continue cooking until the brains are well seasoned and the mixture almost dry—about 5 minutes, stirring in the epazote after about 3 minutes.

FLOR DE CALABAZA GUISADA Squash Flower Filling

ENOUGH FOR 12 QUESADILLAS, ABOUT 1 1/2 CUPS (375 ML)   CENTRAL MEXICO

2 TABLESPOONS VEGETABLE OIL

3 TABLESPOONS FINELY CHOPPED WHITE ONION

1 GARLIC CLOVE, FINELY CHOPPED

2 POBLANO CHILES, CHARRED, PEELED, SEEDS REMOVED, AND CUT INTO NARROW STRIPS
    (SEE PAGE 469)

1 1/4 POUNDS (565 G) SQUASH FLOWERS, CLEANED AND ROUGHLY CHOPPED (ABOUT
    9 CUPS/2.25 L; SEE PAGE 497)

SALT TO TASTE

1 TABLESPOON ROUGHLY CHOPPED EPAZOTE

Heat the oil in a large frying pan, add the onion and garlic, and cook over medium heat until translucent—about 1 minute. Add the chile strips and cook for about 2 minutes. Stir in the flowers and salt, cover the pan, and cook over medium heat, stirring from time to time until the bulbous base of the flower is tender—about 10 minutes. If the flowers are rather dry, add a little water, if they are very juicy, remove the lid to reduce a little. The mixture should be moist but not juicy. Stir in the epazote and cook for 3 minutes more.

VARIATION: Substitute 12 ounces (340 g), weighed when cut from the ears, *cuiclacoche* (about 3 cups/750 ml) for the squash flowers. Follow the method above, cooking the *cuiclacoche* until tender but not soft—about 15 minutes.

CHORIZO CON PAPA Chorizo and Potato Filling

MAKES 2 ROUNDED CUPS (500 ML) FILLING FOR 12 QUESADILLAS OR TOPPING FOR 12 TO 15 SOPES, DEPENDING ON SIZE

If you want, you can peel the potatoes for this filling. I never do.

3 CHORIZOS, ABOUT 6 OUNCES (180 G)

8 OUNCES (225 G) WAXY POTATOES, COOKED AND CUT INTO SMALL CUBES (ABOUT 1 1/2
    CUPS/375 ML)

2 CANNED CHIPOTLES EN ADOBO, OR MORE TO TASTE, ROUGHLY CHOPPED

SALT TO TASTE

Remove the skin from the chorizos and crumble into a small skillet. Cook over low heat until the fat renders, taking care not to let them burn—about 5 minutes. If they are very greasy, drain off all but 3 tablespoons of the fat. Add the potatoes, chiles, and salt. Cook over medium heat, stirring from time to time, until the potatoes just begin to brown—about 8 minutes.

GREEN CHILE GORDAS
BASED ON A RECIPE BY SEÑORA JOSEFINA VELÁZQUEZ DE LEÓN
MAKES 12 GORDAS   ZACATECAS

12 DRIED TORTILLAS
3 FRESH CHILE VERDE DEL NORTE (ANAHEIM), CHARRED AND PEELED (SEE PAGE 471)
²⁄₃ CUP (165 ML) HOT MILK
SALT TO TASTE
1 TABLESPOON MELTED LARD
APPROXIMATELY ¼ CUP (65 ML) MILK, IF NECESSARY
MELTED LARD OR VEGETABLE OIL FOR FRYING

TO SERVE
1 ½ CUPS (375 ML) PREPARED SOUR CREAM (SEE PAGE 489)
1 ¼ CUPS (315 ML) FINELY CHOPPED WHITE ONION

Break the tortillas into small pieces and blend until they are reduced to the texture of fine bread crumbs. Transfer to a mixing bowl.

Blend the chiles, including their seeds, and the milk until smooth. Add the chile mixture, salt, and lard to the ground tortillas and knead the mixture well. Set aside, covered, for at least 2 hours to soften. Knead well again, then divide the dough into 12 equal portions. If the dough is crumbly, then add about ¼ cup (65 ml) more milk.

Roll the dough into balls—they should be about 1½ inches (4 cm) in diameter. Flatten them to form small cakes about 2 inches (5 cm) in diameter and ¼ inch (1 cm) thick.

Heat the lard in a large skillet over high heat, then lower the heat and let it cool a little. Fry the cakes gently, a few at a time, for 3 to 5 minutes on each side. Drain well and serve immediately, topped with the sour cream and onion.

I do not recommend freezing this masa.

POTATO AND MASA GORDAS

BASED ON A RECIPE BY SEÑORA JOSEFINA VELÁZQUEZ DE LEÓN

MAKES 12 GORDAS　　　　　　　　　　　　　NORTHERN MEXICO

THE MASA

1 ⅓ ROUNDED CUPS (335 ML) TORTILLA MASA (ABOUT 12 OUNCES/340 G)

⅓ CUP (85 ML) FINELY GRATED QUESO AÑEJO

¾ TEASPOON BAKING POWDER

SALT TO TASTE

4 SMALL POTATOES (ABOUT 12 OUNCES/340 G), COOKED, PEELED, AND ROUGHLY MASHED

VEGETABLE OIL FOR FRYING

THE TOPPING

1 ¼ CUPS (315 ML) FINELY CHOPPED WHITE ONION

1 ½ CUPS (375 ML) FINELY SHREDDED LETTUCE

2 CHORIZOS, CRUMBLED AND FRIED

6 OUNCES (180 G) QUESO FRESCO, CRUMBLED (ABOUT 1 CUP/250 ML)

4 POBLANO CHILES, PEELED (SEE PAGE 469) AND CUT INTO STRIPS

¾ CUP (185 ML) PREPARED SOUR CREAM (PAGE 489)

Mix the masa, cheese, baking powder, and salt. Add the mashed potatoes and knead the dough well. It should be smooth, not too dry, and just hold its shape when formed into a patty.

Heat a lightly greased griddle or frying pan over medium heat. Divide the dough into 12 equal parts; roll into 1¾-inch (4.5-cm) balls and flatten them to make patties about 3½ inches (9 cm) in diameter and ⅜ inch (1 cm) thick. Cook the cakes for about 2 minutes on the first side, then turn them over, and while they cook on the second side—for about 2 minutes—carefully pinch up a small ridge around the edge of each one.

Heat the oil in a large skillet and fry the cakes lightly on either side. Drain, then sprinkle lavishly with the onion and lettuce and either the chorizos and queso fresco or the chile strips and sour cream. Serve immediately.

SOPES

MAKES 12 SOPES

Sopes are small round cakes of masa. The dough is slightly thicker than that for tortillas and the edge is pinched up to form a small ridge. They are spread with a bean paste and topped with any number of ingredients—see list below. They are enticingly delicious and addictive.

1 ¼ CUPS (315 ML) TORTILLA MASA (ABOUT 11 OUNCES/300 G)
ABOUT 2 TABLESPOONS MELTED LARD
FRIJOLES REFRITOS (PAGE 155)

Divide the masa into 12 parts and roll each into a ball of 1¼ inches (3.25 cm) in diameter. While you work with one, keep the rest of the balls covered with a damp towel.

Press each ball out—either with your hands or a tortilla press—to a thickish tortilla about 3½ inches (9 cm) in diameter. Cook on an ungreased comal or skillet over medium heat for about 1 minute or until the bottom masa is firm and slightly speckled with brown. Turn the *sope* over and cook on the second side for about 1 minute more. Turn it once again and try, without burning your fingers, to pinch up a small ridge—so that the sauce won't run off—around the circumference.

Put a little lard on top of the dough and when it sizzles remove the *sope* from the comal, spread with some of the Frijoles Refritos, and trim with one of the following, or whatever you have on hand. Serve immediately or they'll get soggy.

FILLINGS FOR SOPES

- A layer of *Frijoles Refritos* (page 155), some *Chorizo con Papa* (page 36) with chipotle en vinagre, chopped onion, and crumbled white cheese
- *Frijoles Refritos* (page 155), chorizo, *Salsa de Tomate Verde* (page 236), chopped onion, and crumbled white cheese
- *Salsa de Tomate Verde* (page 236), chopped onion, crumbled white cheese, and/or sour cream
- *Salsa de Chile Cascabel* (page 246), chopped onion, crumbled white cheese, and/or sour cream
- *Frijoles Refritos* (page 155), shredded meat, a little *Salsa Ranchera* (page 238), shredded lettuce, radish slices, and crumbled white cheese
- Shredded chicken or pork with *Salsa de Tomate Verde* (page 236), chopped onion, and crumbled queso fresco

PANUCHOS
MAKES 12 PANUCHOS

Before my husband, Paul, and I even went to Yucatán for the first time in the late fifties, the Yucatecan restaurant Círculo del Sureste was one of our favorite eating places in Mexico City. We would drop in just before the evening rush hour to eat panuchos. *So often we resolved to try something else, but the sight of those piles of carefully shredded succulent pork—Cochinita Pibil—and the Pollo en Escabeche Oriental on the counter in the tile-lined entrance was too much. It was* panuchos *again.*

The crunchiness of the acidy onion, the delicately spiced meat, and the bean-filled tortilla make it, I think, the supreme antojito.

I learned how to make panuchos *from Yucatecan cooks in private homes, but nowadays most families go out to eat them in places specializing in this type of evening food—they are not what they used to be, alas!*

1 ¼ CUPS (315 ML) TORTILLA MASA (ABOUT 11 OUNCES/300 G)

12 SLICES HARD-COOKED EGG

¾ CUP (185 ML) FRIJOLES COLADOS YUCATECOS (PAGE 158)

LARD OR VEGETABLE OIL FOR FRYING

1 ½ CUPS (375 ML) SHREDDED COCHINITA PIBIL (PAGE 277) OR POLLO EN ESCABECHE ORIENTAL (PAGE 345)

1 ½ CUPS (375 ML) CEBOLLAS ENCURTIDAS PARA PANUCHOS (PAGE 249)

Divide the masa into 12 parts and roll each into a ball about 1 ¼ inches (3.25 cm) in diameter. While you work with one, keep the rest of the balls covered with a damp towel or plastic wrap.

Follow the instructions for making tortillas (see page 49) about 4 inches (10 cm) in diameter, trying to make the top layer of dough puff up. Very often it will do it of its own accord, but much will depend on whether you let the dough dry out too much before turning it for the first time, and the heat of the pan. If it doesn't look very promising, then press the dough down gently with a towel and that should do it. It should then puff up enough at least to make a slit around at least a third of the circumference of the dough to form a pocket.

Hold a slice of egg inside the pocket while you put some of the bean paste under it. Press the top of the tortilla down to flatten the paste a little. The *panucho* is now ready to fry—and can be prepared up until this point several hours ahead and kept covered with a damp cloth.

Heat the lard in a skillet—it should be about ¼ inch (.75 cm) deep—and fry the *panuchos* on both sides until the edge is crisp but not too hard. Drain well and then top with the shredded meat and onion rings. Serve immediately.

I do not recommend freezing these.

EMPANADAS DE REQUESÓN
Empanadas Filled with Ricotta and Squash Flowers
MAKES 15 5-INCH (13-CM) EMPANADAS   O A X A C A

The empanadas of Oaxaca are larger—about 7 inches (18 cm)—and more delicious than any others I know in Mexico. Like real quesadillas, they are made with uncooked masa, and handling them requires the deftness of the Oaxacan cooks, so accustomed to handling delicate masa for their large, thin tortillas.

A late breakfast, almuerzo, *in the Mercado Libertades in the city of Oaxaca is a must for aficionados, if you are prepared to wait while the long line of customers is served. It is an agonizing wait if you are hungry, with the appetizing aromas of fresh masa and their delicious fillings wafting as you watch the empanadas being carefully prepared by one young woman, and then consumed with gusto by the people who got there before you.*

Perhaps the most delicious and surprising almuerzo *I have ever eaten was in Tlaxiaco in an improvised kitchen and eating area at the back of a modest house on the edge of town. Every Sunday from early morning an enormous array of breakfast foods is prepared, including pozole, soups, and* machucados—*a freshly made tortilla all scrimped up and served with a green sauce or beans and finely grated cheese. The cooks also made another local specialty called* tutuni: *half-cooked masa mixed with crumbled hoja santa and costeño chile.*

There were empanadas filled with chicken livers and gizzards or intestines and even the chicken's intestines and unlaid eggs, cooked with a corn masa—admittedly not to everybody's taste! But the most popular were those filled with ricotta and squash flowers, the recipe for which I give here.

The usual way to cook empanadas is to cook one face of the dough lightly, cover it copiously with filling, then double the masa over the filling and cook on both sides. This ensures that the inside masa is cooked properly. The finishing touch is to toast the empanada on a small wire rack right on top of the glowing wood or charcoal.

I suggest you make quesadillas in the normal way with this filling. I have tried cooking the masa on one side first, but it invariably breaks and the filling oozes out.

THE FILLING

9 OUNCES (250 G) DRAINED RICOTTA (ABOUT 1 ⅓ CUPS/315 ML)

¾ CUP (185 ML) SQUASH FLOWERS, CLEANED AND ROUGHLY CHOPPED (SEE PAGE 497)

2 HEAPED TABLESPOONS ROUGHLY CHOPPED EPAZOTE

3 COSTEÑO CHILES OR PUYA CHILES, TOASTED WHOLE AND CRUMBLED

SALT TO TASTE

12 OUNCES (340 G) TORTILLA MASA (ABOUT 1 ⅓ CUPS/315 ML)

Mix the filling ingredients well.

Divide the masa into 15 parts and roll each into a ball about 1¼ inches (3.25 cm) in diameter. Follow instructions for making quesadillas (see page 34) and see note above. Empanadas should be eaten immediately or they become leathery. Of course, you could also fry them and blot well before eating.

"ENCHILADAS" TULTECAS

BASED ON A RECIPE BY SEÑORA JOSEFINA VELÁZQUEZ DE LEÓN
MAKES 12 ENCHILADAS

TAMAULIPAS

Once again the name is misleading. These are not enchiladas in the accepted "cooking method" sense, so I have included them here, as antojitos.

This is such a colorful and abundant dish, but you may begin to wonder as you read the recipe whether it is all worth the trouble. I did at first, then one day I happened to have all the ingredients handy and somehow it just fell together. I shredded the chicken for the topping because I wanted to pick the enchilada up to eat it — knives and forks are somehow all wrong — and as I crunched my way through all those layers of different textures, some fresh and some cooked, I knew it had been worth it. Of course, the recipe lends itself to many variations, depending on what you have around.

These enchiladas are better served on individual plates rather than attempting to arrange them on a platter, only to have them collapse as you serve them.

2 ANCHO CHILES, WIPED CLEAN, VEINS AND SEEDS REMOVED, AND TOASTED (SEE PAGE 473)

1/3 CUP (85 ML) HOT WATER

2 CHORIZOS

1 CUP (250 ML) DICED, COOKED CHAYOTE

1 CUP (250 ML) DICED, COOKED POTATO (ABOUT 8 OUNCES/225 G)

1 1/3 CUPS (585 ML) TORTILLA MASA (ABOUT 12 OUNCES/340 G), AS DRY AS POSSIBLE

SALT TO TASTE

VEGETABLE OIL OR MELTED LARD FOR FRYING

TO SERVE

2 CUPS (500 ML) SHREDDED, DRESSED LETTUCE

JELLIED PIGS' FEET

1 CUP (250 ML) COOKED PEAS, WARMED

4 OUNCES (115 G) QUESO FRESCO, CRUMBLED (ABOUT 3/4 CUP/188 ML)

6 RADISHES, THINLY SLICED

2 CUPS (500 ML) SHREDDED POACHED CHICKEN (PAGE 499)

STRIPS OF JALAPEÑO CHILES EN ESCABECHE

Put the chiles into a blender jar, cover with the hot water, and leave to soak for 10 minutes. Drain off all but 1/4 cup (65 ml) of the water.

Meanwhile, skin and crumble the chorizos, and then cook them over low heat until the fat starts to render out, about 5 minutes. Add the cooked vegetables and let them brown lightly with the chorizos, turning them over from time to time, about 8 minutes. Remove from the heat and keep warm.

Blend the chiles until smooth with the 1/4 cup (65 ml) water. Mix the puree into the masa, add the salt, and knead the dough well. Divide the dough into 12 equal parts and roll each one into a ball about 1 1/2 inches (4 cm) in diameter. Press out with the tortilla press to make tortillas about 5 inches (13 cm) across and cook in the usual way (see page 49).

Heat the oil—about 1/4 inch (.75 cm) in depth—in a medium skillet and fry the tortillas lightly on both sides (do not let them become too crisp). Drain, then place 2 tortillas on each plate and top with chorizos and vegetables, lettuce, pigs' feet, peas, cheese, radishes, chicken, and chile strips and eat immediately.

NOTE: All the component parts to this recipe can be prepared ahead and the tortillas made but not fried until ready to serve.

TORTILLAS
AND TORTILLA DISHES

PREPARATION OF DRIED CORN FOR TORTILLA MASA

TAMALE MASA

Corn Tortillas

Tortillas de Quintonil ※ *Corn Tortillas with Wild Greens*

Tortillas de Harina de Trigo ※ *Flour Tortillas*

Burritos

ENCHILADAS

Enchiladas Placeras o Pollo de Plaza

Enchiladas de Jalisco

Enchiladas Sencillas ※ *Simple Enchiladas*

Enchiladas Rojas de Aguascalientes ※ *Red Enchiladas*

Enchiladas Verdes de Aguascalientes ※ *Green Enchiladas*

Enchiladas de Fresnillo

Enchiladas Verdes de San Luis Potosí ※ *Green Enchiladas*

Enchiladas Verdes con Carnitas ※ *Green Enchiladas with Carnitas*

Enchiladas Verdes Veracruzanas ※ *Green Enchiladas from Veracruz*

Enchiladas Verdes ※ *Green Enchiladas*

CHILAQUILES

Chilaquiles Verdes Tampiqueños ※ *Green Chilaquiles*

Chilaquiles de Aguascalientes

Chilaquiles Veracruzanos

Chilaquiles de Guanajuato

BUDÍNES OR SOPAS SECAS DE TORTILLAS

❈ *Layered Tortilla Casseroles*

Budín Azteca ❈ *Moctezuma Pie*

Caserola de Tortillas en Chiles Guajillo

❈ *A Casserole of Tortillas in Chile Sauce*

Caserola de Tortillas Sencilla ❈ *Simple Tortilla Casserole*

Caserola de Tortillas y Legumbres ❈ *Tortilla and Vegetable Casserole*

Budín de Hongos ❈ *Mushroom Pudding*

TACOS

Tacos de Papa ❈ *Potato Tacos*

Taquitos ❈ *Little Tacos*

Taquitos de Natas ❈ *"Sour Cream" Tacos*

Tacos de Rajas de Zacatecas ❈ *Tacos of Chile Strips*

Tacos de Res ❈ *Beef Tacos*

Tacos de Hongos ❈ *Mushroom Tacos*

Puerco en Salsa de Jitomate ❈ *Shredded Pork and Tomato Filling for Tacos*

TOSTADAS

Tostadas de Manitas de Puerco ❈ *Pigs' Feet Tostadas*

Tostadas de Guacamole y Crema ❈ *Guacamole and Sour Cream Tostadas*

Tortillas como Sandwich ❈ *Tortilla "Sandwich"*

Tortillas Piladas con Guacamole y Salsa de Jitomate

❈ *Tortillas Stacked with Guacamole and Tomato Sauce*

Indios Vestidos ❈ *"Dressed Indians"*

Totopos ❈ *Crisp-Fried Tortilla Pieces*

What is it that goes along the foothills of the mountains patting out tortillas with its hands? A butterfly.

—FROM *Náhuatl Proverbs, Conundrums, and Metaphors*
COLLECTED BY SAHAGÚN; TRANSLATED BY THELMA D. SULLIVAN

You always know when you are nearing a Mexican village anytime during the morning; there is that unmistakable smell of wood smoke intermingled with that of tortillas cooking on the comal, and the rhythmic patting of hands as the masa is fashioned into tortillas—I am told it takes thirty-three pats. Unwittingly your steps quicken to make sure you arrive in time to try one straight off the comal with a few grains of rough salt. It is one of those simple eating experiences that cannot be equaled. When I went to Mexico for the first time in the late fifties I wondered why people were so passionate about such humble, everyday food, but it did not take long for me to become an aficionado of the first degree. In those days the commercial tortillas in the cities were quite good. I remember well that each little *tortillería* had its group of women and young girls standing around a high drum of a stove with a large circular metal top heated by huge gas jets, chatting and joking as they patted out hundreds upon hundreds of tortillas daily. But now things have changed, and the machine has taken over from start to finish. The art of *tortear* is dying fast, and more and more people are buying them ready-made.

The ground masa is fed into a large hopper and pushed out at the bottom through a press, which stamps the tortillas out onto a narrow conveyor belt. The tortilla goes on its way as the belt jiggles over jets of hot flame; the belt goes just so far and then doubles back in such a way that the tortilla is flipped over, and as it cooks through it starts to puff and dance, and very soon it is thrown onto a fast-growing pile in a cloth-lined basket on the floor.

And how the tortilla can vary from one region to another! But for me the Oaxaca Valley still holds pride of place with its delicious, white *blandas*—large, thin, white tortillas. Nowhere else are they quite as fine. There are tortillas made of corn of different colors: blue, yellow, red, purple, and variegated, depending on what is grown or local tastes. The masa can be mixed with wheat, or wild greens, or roots of the banana plant, coconut, and other ingredients, not only for flavor but also to extend the masa as the corn supply dwindles at the end of the season.

I learned very quickly during my years in Mexico that a tortilla is never thrown away: fresh and pliable, it is used as an edible spoon; wrapped around food and seasoned with one of a hundred sauces, it becomes a taco. When a tortilla is slightly stale and dry, it can be cut into small pieces, fried, and cooked in a sauce as *chilaquiles*; or fried crisp in triangles, it becomes a little shovel for a dip; fried crisp in strips, it can be used like croutons to top a soup. When a tortilla is thoroughly dried out, it can be ground to a textured consistency, moistened, and reformed to make *gordas*, little fat cakes, or balls to drop into a soup. Tortillas can also be used like layers of pasta in a casserole, *budin*, or *sopa seca*.

Whole tortillas can be fried quite flat for tostadas and spread with bean paste and/or topped with shredded meat, crumbled cheese, vegetables; the variations are infinite. It is perhaps the most versatile piece of foodstuff in the world!

The recipes that follow provide a small sampling of what exists, but there are no hard-and-fast rules here and your imagination can do the rest.

PREPARATION OF DRIED CORN FOR TORTILLA MASA

No meal in Mexico is complete without the corn tortilla to accompany it. The tortilla is made of dried corn cooked with lime (calcium oxide) and ground to a masa, or dough.

The first lesson a young Mexican woman living in the country learns is how to prepare the *nixtamal* (the corn cooked in a solution of lime and water) for the next day's tortillas. Because it is such an intuitive thing among my neighbors, they find it impossible to give precise quantities of lime or the time for cooking the corn. I have often asked them, "How much lime do I need for one kilo of dried corn?" and the answer is *"Lo necesario,"* and to the question "How long do I cook the corn?" the answer is "When you shake the *olla* the corn should no longer sound like raw beans." So there you have it . . . but since I have often watched the process and done it myself under their watchful eyes, I feel a little more qualified to explain it here.

Pick over the dried corn to make sure there are no stones or other rarities. Rinse in cold water and put into a large, nonreactive pot. Cover with cold water—it should come about 2 inches (5 cm) above the surface of the corn. Bring the water up to a simmer, stir in the powdered lime (see page 462)—1 heaped tablespoon for 2 pounds (900 g) dried corn—and the outer skin of the kernels will almost immediately turn an intense yellow. Continue cooking uncovered, stirring from time to time, over low heat until you can scrape the membranous skin from the kernels—this should take about 20 minutes. Make sure that you do not let the corn go past this stage because it will be overcooked, the masa gummy, and your tortillas a disaster.

Remove from heat, cover, and set aside for the corn to soak overnight. The following day, rinse the corn in fresh water, rubbing it a little to remove some of the skin and lime, drain, and repeat the process. Drain well; now you have *nixtamal,* ready to take to the mill to be ground to a very smooth dough.

If you add too much lime, your tortillas will be a dull yellowish color and taste slightly bitter, *neja,* and if you add too little, the skin cannot be softened and removed. But the lime does act as a preservative and in hot, humid weather you could go overboard if you are not using your *masa* right away (see note on lime, page 462).

TAMALE MASA

If you are making tamales that call for this masa (see Tamales chapter) you will need to rub all the skin meticulously from the kernels, leaving them as white as possible, then have the mill grind them to a textured dough.

For tamale recipes that require a very dry, textured masa, it can be ground twice with the metal corn grinder available in all Mexican markets.

CORN TORTILLAS

MAKES 15 5-INCH (13-CM) TORTILLAS

A friend and great cook from Hidalgo, Señora Lara, once after a meal presented her guests with crisped tortilla halves sprinkled with salt. "Even if you think you have no room, eat it; it aids the digestion," she said.

1 ¼ POUNDS (565 G) TORTILLA MASA (ABOUT 2 ¼ CUPS/563 ML), APPROXIMATELY
WATER IF NEEDED
2 1-QUART (1-L) PLASTIC BAGS FOR PRESSING TORTILLAS

If the tortilla masa has been freshly made, it will probably be the right consistency for working immediately—a soft, smooth dough. If the masa has been sitting around and drying out a little, then add a very little water and knead until it's smooth and pliable, not the slightest bit crumbly.

Divide the dough into 15 equal parts—each one should weigh just over 1 ounce (30 g)—and roll into smooth balls about 1½ inches (4 cm) in diameter. Place all but one of the balls under plastic wrap so they do not dry out.

Heat an ungreased comal or griddle over medium heat. Open up the tortilla press and place a small plastic bag (Alligator Baggies are ideal but may be hard to find) on the bottom plate. Place a ball of the dough on the bottom plastic bag, a little off center toward the hinge rather than the pressing lever (it presses too thin on that side), and press it out with your fingers to flatten it a little. Cover with the second plastic bag and press down firmly but not too fiercely (or the dough will be too thin and you will never be able to pry it off the bag in one piece). Open the press, remove the top bag, lift the bottom bag up in one hand, place the dough onto the fingers of your other hand, and very carefully peel the bag off the flattened dough. Do not try to peel the dough off the bag.

Keeping your hand as horizontal as possible, lay the tortilla flat onto the comal. There should be a slight sizzle as the dough touches the surface of the comal. Leave for about 15 seconds; the underside will have opaque patches and be slightly speckled with brown. Flip the tortilla over onto the second side and cook for another 30 seconds; the underside should now be opaque and speckled. Flip back onto the first side again and cook for 15 seconds more.

If you have done all the correct things and the comal is the correct heat, the tortilla should puff up, showing that the extra moisture has dried out of the dough. If the tortilla doesn't puff up and it's necessary in order to make *panuchos*, for example, then press it gently on the last turn with your fingers or a towel.

As the tortillas are made, they should be placed one on top of the other in a basket or gourd lined with a cloth to preserve the heat and keep them moist and flabby.

Tortillas can be made ahead and reheated and can also be frozen.

VARIATION

TORTILLAS MADE WITH QUAKER MASA HARINA
MAKES ABOUT 15 5-INCH (13-CM) TORTILLAS

2 CUPS (500 ML) QUAKER MASA HARINA (10½ OUNCES/300 G) OR MASECA
1⅓ CUPS (325 ML) WATER, APPROXIMATELY
2 1-QUART (1-L) PLASTIC BAGS SUCH AS ALLIGATOR BAGGIES FOR PRESSING TORTILLAS

Mix the masa harina with the water and work well so that it is evenly distributed through the flour and forms a cohesive mass when pressed together. The dough should be of medium consistency, neither too firm nor wet and sticky. Set aside for about ½ hour.

Follow the instructions for making tortillas in the preceding recipe.

NOTE: Tortillas made of this powdered product are not suitable for chilaquile and layered casserole dishes, as they disintegrate easily.

TORTILLAS DE QUINTONIL Corn Tortillas with Wild Greens

MAESTRA GUDELIA LÓPEZ

MAKES 15 4½-INCH (11.5-CM) TORTILLAS OAXACA

On one of my trips to Tlaxiaco in the northern Mixtec region of Oaxaca, I met a retired schoolmistress who came from a small isolated village not too far from Tlaxiaco. During her working life she had lived and taught in many remote areas and was familiar with the foods prepared there. Of the many she talked about, this recipe caught my fancy.

There are many examples of extending the corn masa for the daily tortillas by adding other ingredients: wheat, the root of the banana plant (or so I'm told), mango pits, and so on, as well as this recipe for adding cooked wild greens. These tortillas would have been made if the corn crop was poor, or stores were dwindling at the end of the year, or simply because people liked the flavor; they are certainly nutritious.

Tortillas with wild greens of various types were generally served alone with some sauce and perhaps, if the budget allowed, a little cheese. They make a very tasty snack and you could make them bite-size to serve with drinks. Although quintoniles (Amaranthus spp.) are called for, spinach can be substituted: 1¼ pounds (570 g) raw greens will make about 1 cup (250 ml) cooked.

I CUP (250 ML) COOKED SPINACH

I ½ CUPS (375 ML) TORTILLA MASA

SALT TO TASTE

Squeeze as much of the liquid as possible out of the spinach and chop as finely as possible. Put into a bowl with the masa and salt and mix with your hands. Divide the mixture into about 15 portions and roll each into a ball about 1¼ inches (3.25 cm) in diameter.

Heat an ungreased comal or griddle over medium heat.

Using a tortilla press lined with a plastic bag (see page 49), flatten each of the balls out to about 4½ inches (11.5 cm) and cook for about 2 minutes on each side. Serve immediately.

TORTILLAS DE HARINA DE TRIGO Flour Tortillas
MAKES ABOUT 10 TORTILLAS

Mexico produces wheat as well as corn. The most important wheat-growing area is the flat, irrigated land in Sonora and the northern part of Sinaloa. Tortillas of wheat flour (tortillas de harina de trigo) are common all over the north of Mexico, but they really come into their own in Sonora. There are the sweet ones, thicker and shorter, more like pastry, usually called tortillas de manteca *(lard tortillas); and then the largest tortillas in Mexico (*tortillas de agua), *as thin as tissue paper and about 18 inches (46 cm) across. When served with a meal these come to the table folded into quarters and wrapped in a napkin. Folded just like that they are often used for burritos—rolled around a filling of meat or* machaca *(dried beef) or beans.*

Most people buy the large tortillas ready-made, since it takes skill to produce them without a great deal of practice, but in 1971 Señor Colores, a restaurant owner in Hermosillo, had them made for his restaurants daily, and I went there to see how they were prepared.

An older couple who had worked for him for years were making them. They rolled the dough into 2-inch (5-cm) balls and let them sit a while. To make the tortilla, they rolled and stretched the dough until it was translucent—this has to be done with lightly greased hands. Then they cooked it on a comal over a hot wood fire. After a few seconds it ballooned up and had to be flattened back onto the comal. They flipped it over, just a few seconds more, and then stacked it on top of the others, wrapped up in a cloth to keep them moist and warm.

The recipe they gave me was "a handful of lard to a kilo of flour, salt, and water. Hot water if the weather is cold; cold water if the weather is hot." Later on I had one toasted crisp with the biggest piece of meat, cooked over the wood fire, that I have ever seen on any plate.

You can make the dough either by hand or with an electric mixer.

I POUND (450 G) BREAD FLOUR (FROM HARD WINTER WHEAT)
4 OUNCES (115 G) SOFTENED VEGETABLE SHORTENING (ABOUT ½ CUP/125 ML)
I SCANT TEASPOON SALT
ABOUT I CUP (250 ML) WARM WATER

Put the flour onto a work surface or pastry board. Rub the fat into the flour with your fingertips. Dissolve the salt in the warm water and mix into the flour, a little at a time, so that you can see how much the flour will absorb. Using a plastic dough scraper, gather up all the flour around the periphery and work the dough into a cohesive mass—about 2 minutes with the mixer, 4 minutes by hand.

Divide the dough into 10 equal parts—about 3 ounces (85 g) each—and roll into very smooth balls about 2 inches (5 cm) in diameter. Cover with well-greased plastic wrap and set aside for at least 20 minutes or up to 2 hours.

Heat an ungreased comal or griddle over medium heat.

Flatten one of the balls on a lightly floured work surface and roll it out, with a dowel for a rolling pin, to form a 6-inch (15-cm) circle. Now it is a matter of choice about thinness and size. You can stretch the dough like a pizza to about 15 inches (38 cm) in diameter.

Carefully lay the tortilla on the griddle; it should sizzle if the heat is correct.

The dough will become opaque and the bottom slightly browned in patches. Turn the tortilla over and cook on the second side; the whole process should take less than ½ minute. Do not overcook or the tortilla will become hard instead of soft and pliable.

As soon as each tortilla is cooked, stack inside a cloth.

These tortillas keep well and, although I hesitate to say so, can be prepared well ahead and reheated on a warm comal.

BURRITOS

Flour tortillas filled and rolled up become burritos. They can be filled with the following:

CHILORIO (PAGE 18)

MOCHOMOS SINALOENSES (PAGE 19)

MACHACADO DE HUEVO (PAGE 179)

PINTO OR PINK BEANS FRIED TO A LOOSE PASTE WITH PIECES OF MUENSTER CHEESE ADDED
  AT THE LAST MOMENT SO THAT THEY JUST START TO MELT

Burritos can also be fried crisp, just like a fried taco, at which point they become chivichangas.

All of these should be served with Salsa de Jitomate Sonorense (page 239).

ENCHILADAS

Enchiladas, a greasy tortilla sandwich containing chilies and a number of uninviting looking compounds and other nasty messes, are sold everywhere, filling the air with a pungent, nauseous smell.

—"THROUGH THE LAND OF THE AZTECS" BY "A GRINGO," 1883

So many aficionados of the enchilada would heartily disagree, I among them, because enchiladas can be so delicious and satisfying. Again it all depends on the care with which they are put together and on making sure they're not too greasy.

There are two main types: the tortilla is either first fried and then dipped into a cooked chile sauce or the tortilla is first dipped into a sauce and then fried—a messy business with delicious results!

Here are just a few examples of an endless array of regional recipes.

ENCHILADAS PLACERAS O POLLO DE PLAZA
SERVES 6   MICHOACÁN

This is the most substantial supper dish of enchiladas and chicken that I know of. As dusk falls in Pátzcuaro the sidewalks become alive with activity as small stands are assembled: tables, benches, improvised stoves with large metal comales, and gas tanks, all sheltered by canvas or plastic awnings for when the rains start. It seems that every family in town comes out to eat this colorful and delicious evening fare. Granted it's a little bit greasy, but once in a while! . . . Actually I have given suggestions for cutting down on the amount of oil, but do leave the skin on the chicken!

There are only very slight variations of recipes from stand to stand: some cooks use only guajillo chiles, the quality of the cheese varies, and it's difficult to choose among the enchiladas of the many cooks who devote themselves to this evening ritual, either in Patzcuaro or in the Plaza San Agustín in Morelia.

Every element of this dish can be prepared ahead so there is just the final frying and no waiting around to eat; it is pan-to-mouth food!

THE TOPPING

8 OUNCES (225 G) RED BLISS OR WAXY NEW POTATOES (3 SMALL ONES), UNPEELED

8 OUNCES (225 G) CARROTS (3 MEDIUM)

1 TEASPOON SALT

1/3 CUP (85 ML) MILD VINEGAR

THE SAUCE

3 GUAJILLO CHILES, SEEDS AND VEINS REMOVED

3 ANCHO CHILES, SEEDS AND VEINS REMOVED

ABOUT 1 1/2 CUPS (375 ML) WATER

2 GARLIC CLOVES, ROUGHLY CHOPPED

1 SLICE WHITE ONION

1/4 TEASPOON DRIED MEXICAN OREGANO

SALT TO TASTE

THE ENCHILADAS

LARD OR VEGETABLE OIL FOR FRYING

12 FRESHLY MADE TORTILLAS (SEE PAGE 49)

8 OUNCES (225 G) QUESO FRESCO, CRUMBLED AND LIGHTLY SALTED
    (ABOUT 1 1/3 CUPS/333 ML)

1/2 CUP (125 ML) FINELY CHOPPED WHITE ONION

A 3-POUND (1.35-KG) CHICKEN, POACHED AND CUT INTO SERVING PIECES

TO SERVE

STRIPS OF CANNED JALAPEÑO CHILES EN ESCABECHE

2/3 CUP (165 ML) PREPARED SOUR CREAM (PAGE 489)

1 CUP (250 ML) FINELY SHREDDED LETTUCE OR RAW CABBAGE

Rinse the potatoes and cut them into small cubes; scrape the carrots and cut them into smaller cubes. Cover the carrots with boiling water, add the salt, and cook them for about 5 minutes over high heat. Add the potatoes and cook them for about 8 minutes—they should still be al dente—then drain.

Cover the vegetables with cold water and add the vinegar. Stir and set aside.

Heat a griddle and toast the chiles lightly, turning constantly so they don't burn.

Cover the chiles with hot water and leave them to soak for 10 minutes.

Put 1/2 cup (125 ml) of the water into a blender jar, add the guajillos, and blend until smooth. Strain. Add the remaining 1 cup (250 ml) water, the anchos, garlic, and onion and blend until smooth. Add the guajillo puree, the oregano, and salt to taste.

Melt a little of the lard, and when it is sizzling, dip each tortilla into the raw sauce—it should just lightly cover it (if the sauce is too thick dilute it with a little more water) and fry it quickly on both sides.

Remove from the frying pan and put about 1 scant tablespoon of the cheese and ½ tablespoon of the onion across each tortilla. Roll them up loosely and set them side by side on the serving dish. Keep warm.

In the same fat, fry the pieces of chicken until they are golden brown. Drain and arrange them around the enchiladas.

In the same fat, fry the vegetables until just beginning to brown, and drain well. In the same fat, cook the remaining sauce for a few moments and pour it over the enchiladas. Cover with the fried vegetables.

Top with the chile strips and on each serving add a spoonful of sour cream and a sprinkling of cheese, with lettuce on the side.

NOTE: *To reduce the amount of oil,* drain the fried vegetables in a strainer and shake gently. Coat the chicken pieces with the chile sauce and place under a hot broiler, turning them from time to time so that they are evenly cooked.

ENCHILADAS DE JALISCO
SEÑORA VICTORIA MARÍN DE TECHUELO
SERVES 6

JALISCO

In preparing this dish I have followed, word for word, the cooking methods of Señora Victoria Marín de Techuelo, a marvelous cook and daughter of one of the most distinguished cooks in Jalisco, because behind every step there is a reason: to enhance either the flavor or the texture of each ingredient.

In Mexico, queso añejo would be used, and the dish would be served with frutas en vinagre—*such vegetables as carrots, beans, zucchini, onion, and chiles preserved in a fruity vinegar.*

If you are making your own tortillas (see page 49), try to make them puff up on the comal so that while they are still warm you can remove the thin, loose layer of dough on top, which is then discarded. Or try and buy them freshly made, then reheat them and remove the top layer. The reason for this is so that the tortillas are as thin as possible.

I have prepared this dish of enchiladas at least 3 hours ahead, taking care that the filling was not too juicy or it would make the tortillas soggy, and that the extra chile sauce was poured down the sides and over the top of the enchiladas just before they were put into the oven.

THE FILLING (OR PICADILLO)

1 ZUCCHINI SQUASH (ABOUT 4 OUNCES/115 G)

2 SMALL CARROTS (ABOUT 4 OUNCES/115 G)

3 SMALL RED BLISS OR WAXY NEW POTATOES (ABOUT 8 OUNCES/225 G)

2 TEASPOONS SALT, OR TO TASTE

8 OUNCES (225 G) GROUND PORK

8 OUNCES (225 G) GROUND BEEF

SALT TO TASTE

1 POUND (450 G) TOMATOES

3 TABLESPOONS LARD

$\frac{1}{2}$ CUP (125 ML) FINELY CHOPPED WHITE ONION

1 TABLESPOON FINELY CHOPPED PARSLEY

$\frac{1}{3}$ CUP (85 ML) RESERVED MEAT BROTH

THE CHILE SAUCE

10 GUAJILLO CHILES (ABOUT 2 OUNCES/60 G), VEINS AND SEEDS REMOVED

1 CUP (250 ML) RESERVED MEAT BROTH

2 WHOLE CLOVES, CRUSHED

$\frac{1}{4}$-INCH (.75-CM) PIECE OF CINNAMON STICK, CRUSHED

SALT TO TASTE

2 TABLESPOONS LARD

THE ENCHILADAS

$\frac{1}{4}$ CUP (65 ML) LARD

24 4-INCH (10-CM) HOMEMADE TORTILLAS (SEE PAGE 49)

TO SERVE

SHREDDED LETTUCE

THINLY SLICED RADISHES

STRIPS OF JALAPEÑO CHILES EN ESCABECHE

$\frac{1}{4}$ CUP (65 ML) GRATED QUESO AÑEJO, OR SUBSTITUTE ROMANO OR SARDO

$\frac{1}{2}$ CUP (125 ML) FINELY CHOPPED WHITE ONION

Trim the squash and leave whole. Trim and scrape the carrots and cut into quarters lengthwise. Peel the potatoes and cut into halves. Cover the vegetables with boiling water in a large saucepan, add the salt, and let them cook for 5 minutes.

Mix the meat with salt to taste. Press tightly into two large balls and add them, with the whole tomatoes, to the vegetables in the pan. Cover and cook all together over low heat until the vegetables are just tender—do not overcook—and the meat balls are almost cooked through—about 10 minutes. Drain and reserve the broth.

When the vegetables are cool enough to handle, chop them into small cubes and set aside.

Blend the tomatoes for a few seconds. Set aside.

Melt the lard in a large skillet and cook the onion until translucent.

Crumble the cooked meat balls into the pan, add the parsley, and fry for about 5 minutes over medium heat. Add the blended tomato puree and cook over brisk heat until some of the juice has evaporated. Add the broth and vegetables and continue cooking the mixture until it is well seasoned—about 10 minutes. Add salt as necessary. Set aside.

Heat a comal and toast the chiles lightly, turning them constantly, since they burn very quickly. Cover the chiles with hot water in a bowl and leave to soak for about 10 minutes. Transfer with a slotted spoon to a blender jar. Add the broth, blend, and strain to remove any traces of the tough skin, return to the blender, add the spices and salt, and blend until smooth.

Melt the lard and cook the sauce until it is well seasoned and a rich, dark-red color—about 8 minutes.

Preheat the oven to 350°F (180°C).

Heat a little of the lard in a skillet, and fry the tortillas on both sides, adding more lard as necessary—they should just soften and heat through in the hot fat. Pile one on top of the other between sheets of toweling and keep warm.

Dip the tortillas into the sauce, which should lightly cover them (if it is too thick, then add a little more broth). Place some of the picadillo across each tortilla and roll up. Put one layer of the enchiladas in the bottom of an ovenproof dish about 4 inches (10 cm) deep. Pour a little of the remaining sauce over them. Then place another enchilada layer on top and pour over the rest of the sauce.

Cover the dish and heat the enchiladas through in the oven for about 15 minutes, then serve immediately, topped with the lettuce, radishes, and canned chiles, and sprinkled with the cheese and chopped onion.

NOTE: The chile sauce and tortillas can be done the day before, but the picadillo really has to be prepared the same day or the potato gets that warmed-over taste. To heat the enchiladas through, cover tightly with foil so that the top layer does not get dried up. They should just fit snugly into the dish used.

I do not recommend freezing.

ENCHILADAS SENCILLAS Simple Enchiladas

MAKES 12 ENCHILADAS

CENTRAL MEXICO

THE TOMATO SAUCE

1 POUND (450 G) TOMATOES, BROILED (SEE PAGE 490)

1 GARLIC CLOVE

2 FRESH SERRANO CHILES, TOASTED

2 TABLESPOONS VEGETABLE OIL

SALT TO TASTE

½ CUP (125 ML) THICK SOUR CREAM (PAGE 489), AT ROOM TEMPERATURE

THE ENCHILADAS

VEGETABLE OIL FOR FRYING

12 FRESHLY MADE TORTILLAS (SEE PAGE 49)

7 LARGE EGGS, SCRAMBLED WITH PLENTY OF SALT, OR 1 ½ CUPS (375 ML) COOKED AND
   SHREDDED CHICKEN, WELL SALTED

1 CUP (250 ML) FINELY CHOPPED WHITE ONION

TO SERVE

1 CUP (250 ML) GRATED CHIHUAHUA CHEESE OR CHEDDAR

In a blender, puree the tomatoes, garlic, and chiles until smooth—you'll have about 2 cups (500 ml).

Heat the oil in a large skillet and fry the sauce for about 5 minutes, or until it has reduced and thickened. Add the salt. Set aside to cool a little.

Stir the sour cream well into the sauce and just heat it through gently. *Do not let the sauce come to a boil after the cream has been added or it will curdle.*

Heat the oil in another skillet and fry the tortillas quickly, one by one, without letting them become crisp around the edges.

Preheat the oven to 350°F (180°C).

Dip the tortillas into the warm sauce—they should be just lightly covered—then put about 2 tablespoons of the scrambled egg or shredded chicken across each tortilla and sprinkle it with a little of the onion. Roll the filled tortillas up loosely and set them side by side in an ovenproof dish.

Cover the enchiladas with the remaining sauce and sprinkle with the cheese and remaining onion. Put the dish into the oven and just heat them through for a very short time, no more than 10 minutes. Serve immediately.

NOTE: A good alternative would be to use Salsa de Tomate Verde (page 236). Like all enchiladas, they go rather soggy if left to stand around after they are prepared.

I do not recommend freezing.

ENCHILADAS ROJAS DE AGUASCALIENTES Red Enchiladas
BASED ON A RECIPE BY SEÑORA JOSEFINA VELÁZQUEZ DE LEÓN
MAKES 12 ENCHILADAS   AGUASCALIENTES

THE SAUCE

4 ANCHO CHILES, WIPED CLEAN, SEEDS AND VEINS REMOVED, LIGHTLY TOASTED
    (SEE PAGE 473)
1 ½ CUPS (375 ML) HOT MILK
SALT TO TASTE
1 GARLIC CLOVE
1 HARD-COOKED EGG YOLK
2 TABLESPOONS VEGETABLE OIL

THE FILLING

VEGETABLE OIL FOR FRYING
12 TORTILLAS
8 OUNCES (225 G) QUESO FRESCO, CRUMBLED (ABOUT 1 ½ CUPS/375 ML)
1 CUP (250 ML) FINELY CHOPPED WHITE ONION

TO SERVE

1 HARD-COOKED EGG WHITE, FINELY CHOPPED
1 ½ CUPS (375 ML) FINELY SHREDDED LETTUCE
6 RADISHES, THINLY SLICED
STRIPS OF JALAPEÑO CHILES EN ESCABECHE

Tear the chiles into pieces and add to a blender jar with the milk and leave to soak for about 10 minutes. Add the salt, garlic, and egg yolk and blend until smooth. (You will have about 2 cups/500 ml of sauce; add water if necessary to make up that quantity.)

Heat the oil in a medium skillet, add the sauce, and cook for about 5 minutes over medium heat, stirring and scraping the sides and bottom of the pan from time to time. Remove from the heat and keep warm.

Heat the oil in another skillet and fry the tortillas, one by one, briefly on both sides. Drain well and keep warm.

Dip the tortillas, one by one, into the sauce. Fill each one with some of the cheese and onion, then roll and place side by side in a serving dish. Dilute the remaining sauce, if necessary, and pour it over the enchiladas. Top with the chopped egg white, the lettuce, sliced radishes, and chile strips and serve immediately.

ENCHILADAS VERDES DE AGUASCALIENTES Green Enchiladas

BASED ON A RECIPE BY SEÑORA JOSEFINA VELÁZQUEZ DE LEÓN

MAKES 12 ENCHILADAS   AGUASCALIENTES

THE SAUCE

3 POBLANO CHILES, CHARRED, PEELED, AND SEEDS REMOVED (NOT VEINS; SEE PAGE 469)

2 LARGE ROMAINE LETTUCE LEAVES

1 WHOLE CLOVE, CRUSHED

1 CUP (250 ML) CHICKEN BROTH

2 TABLESPOONS VEGETABLE OIL

SALT TO TASTE

1/2 CUP (125 ML) SOUR CREAM, COMMERCIAL OR HOMEMADE (SEE PAGE 489)

THE FILLING

VEGETABLE OIL FOR FRYING

12 TORTILLAS

1 1/2 TO 2 CUPS (375 TO 500 ML) COOKED, SHREDDED, AND WELL-SALTED CHICKEN (SEE PAGE 499)

TO SERVE

1 1/2 CUPS (375 ML) FINELY SHREDDED LETTUCE

6 LARGE RADISHES, THINLY SLICED

1/2 CUP (125 ML) PITTED, HALVED GREEN OLIVES

Blend the chiles together with the lettuce, clove, and ½ cup (125 ml) of the chicken broth until very smooth.

Heat the 2 tablespoons of oil in a large skillet, add the sauce, and cook over fairly high heat for about 5 minutes, stirring and scraping the bottom of the pan to avoid sticking. Add the salt, sour cream, and the remaining ½ cup chicken broth and just heat through, then remove from the heat and keep warm.

Heat the oil in another skillet and fry the tortillas, one at a time, briefly on both sides. Drain well and keep warm.

Dip the tortillas, one by one, into the sauce, then fill each one with some of the chicken. Roll up and place side by side on a warmed dish. Pour the remaining sauce over the enchiladas, top with the lettuce, sliced radishes, and olives, and serve immediately.

ENCHILADAS DE FRESNILLO

BASED ON A RECIPE BY SEÑORA JOSEFINA VELÁZQUEZ DE LEÓN
MAKES 12 ENCHILADAS

ZACATECAS

THE SAUCE

3 ANCHO CHILES, SEEDS AND VEINS REMOVED, LIGHTLY TOASTED (SEE PAGE 473)

¼-INCH (.75-CM) PIECE OF CINNAMON STICK, CRUSHED

I WHOLE CLOVE, CRUSHED

⅛ TEASPOON DRIED MEXICAN OREGANO

3 SPRIGS FRESH THYME OR ⅛ TEASPOON DRIED

3 SPRIGS FRESH MARJORAM OR ⅛ TEASPOON DRIED

3 PEPPERCORNS, CRUSHED

I TABLESPOON SESAME SEEDS, TOASTED AND CRUSHED

¼ CUP (65 ML) SHELLED PEANUTS, TOASTED AND CRUSHED

I ½ CUPS (375 ML) COLD WATER

SALT TO TASTE

2 TABLESPOONS VEGETABLE OIL

THE FILLING

VEGETABLE OIL FOR FRYING

12 TORTILLAS

8 OUNCES (225 G) QUESO FRESCO, CRUMBLED (ABOUT I ½ CUPS/375 ML)

I MEDIUM WHITE ONION, FINELY CHOPPED

TO SERVE

1 AVOCADO, THINLY SLICED

6 LARGE RADISHES, THINLY SLICED

¾ CUP (185 ML) PREPARED SOUR CREAM (SEE PAGE 489)

2 CHORIZOS, CRUMBLED AND FRIED

Cover the chiles with hot water and leave them to soak for about 5 minutes. Drain, then transfer the chiles to a blender jar, add the rest of the sauce ingredients, and blend until smooth.

Heat the oil in a skillet and cook the sauce over medium heat for about 8 minutes, stirring and scraping the bottom of the pan almost constantly. Remove from the heat and keep warm.

One by one, fry the tortillas lightly on both sides, drain well, and keep them warm while you do the rest.

Dip the tortillas into the sauce, then fill each one with some of the cheese and onion. Roll up loosely and place side by side in the serving dish. Add a little water to the remaining sauce, then bring to a boil and pour over the enchiladas. Top with the avocado slices, sliced radishes, sour cream, and chorizos and serve immediately.

ENCHILADAS VERDES DE SAN LUIS POTOSÍ Green Enchiladas

BASED ON A RECIPE BY SEÑORA JOSEFINA VELÁZQUEZ DE LEÓN

MAKES 12 ENCHILADAS   SAN LUIS POTOSÍ

THE SAUCE

2 CUPS (500 ML) COOKED TOMATE VERDE (SEE PAGE 492), DRAINED

4 SERRANO CHILES

3 SPRIGS CILANTRO

⅓ CUP (85 ML) MILK

1 GARLIC CLOVE

SALT TO TASTE

2 TABLESPOONS VEGETABLE OIL

2 TABLESPOONS SOUR CREAM, COMMERCIAL OR HOMEMADE (SEE PAGE 489)

THE TORTILLAS

VEGETABLE OIL FOR FRYING

12 TORTILLAS

THE FILLING

1 ½ TO 2 CUPS (375 TO 500 ML) SHREDDED COOKED CHICKEN

TO SERVE

¾ CUP (190 ML) FINELY CHOPPED WHITE ONION

3 OUNCES (85 G) QUESO FRESCO, CRUMBLED (ABOUT ½ CUP/125 ML)

½ CUP (125 ML) PREPARED SOUR CREAM (SEE PAGE 489)

Blend the tomate verde with the chiles, cilantro, milk, garlic, and salt until smooth.

Heat the oil in a large skillet and cook the sauce over fairly high heat until reduced and seasoned—about 5 minutes. Remove from the heat, add the sour cream, and set aside. Keep warm.

Heat the oil in a second skillet and fry the tortillas, one by one, briefly on each side. Drain well and keep warm.

One by one, dip the tortillas into the sauce. Fill each one with some of the chicken, then roll and place side by side in the warmed dish. Dilute the rest of the sauce, if necessary, and pour it over the enchiladas. Top lavishly with the onion, cheese, and sour cream and serve immediately.

ENCHILADAS VERDES CON CARNITAS

Green Enchiladas with Carnitas

BASED ON A RECIPE BY SEÑORA JOSEFINA VELÁZQUEZ DE LEÓN

SERVES 6

COAHUILA

These were originally called taquitos but were prepared like enchiladas. This recipe makes a rich, but very satisfying, main course.

3 POUNDS (1.35 KG) COUNTRY-STYLE SPARERIBS

2 GARLIC CLOVES, CRUSHED

SALT TO TASTE

THE SAUCE

2 TABLESPOONS VEGETABLE OIL

⅓ CUP (85 ML) FINELY CHOPPED WHITE ONION

1 CUP (250 ML) COOKED TOMATE VERDE (SEE PAGE 492), DRAINED

2 LARGE ROMAINE LETTUCE LEAVES

2 SPRIGS EPAZOTE

2 GARLIC CLOVES

SALT TO TASTE

¼ CUP (65 ML) BROTH OR WATER

2 POBLANO CHILES, CHARRED, PEELED, SEEDS AND VEINS REMOVED (SEE PAGE 469)

6 SPRIGS CILANTRO

THE FILLING

3 TABLESPOONS VEGETABLE OIL

5 LARGE EGGS

SALT TO TASTE

¼ MEDIUM WHITE ONION, FINELY CHOPPED

6 OUNCES (180 G) TOMATOES, FINELY CHOPPED (ABOUT 1 CUP/250 ML)

4 SERRANO CHILES, FINELY CHOPPED

THE TORTILLAS

VEGETABLE OIL FOR FRYING

12 TORTILLAS

TO SERVE

2 CUPS (500 ML) FINELY SHREDDED LETTUCE

6 LARGE RADISH FLOWERS

Put the meat into a wide pan just large enough to accommodate it in no more than two layers. Barely cover the meat with water (see note below), add the garlic and salt, and bring to a boil. Lower the heat to medium and let the meat cook until it is tender, the water evaporates, and the fat is rendered out. Let the meat fry in its fat, turning it from time to time until well browned—about 1 hour. Set aside and keep warm.

Heat the oil in a skillet and fry the onion until translucent.

Blend the remaining ingredients for the sauce until smooth. Add to the onion in the pan and fry over fairly high heat, stirring and scraping the bottom of the pan until it has reduced a little and is well seasoned—about 5 minutes. Remove from the heat and keep warm.

Heat the oil in a second skillet.

Meanwhile, beat the eggs together well, then stir in the salt, onion, tomatoes, and chiles. Pour into the hot oil and scramble them over very low heat; they should be just set and tender. Remove from the heat and keep warm.

Heat the oil in a skillet and fry the tortillas, one by one, lightly on both sides. Drain and keep warm.

Dip the tortillas into the green sauce, fill each one with some of the egg mixture, then roll up and place them on the serving dish. Dilute the remaining sauce, if necessary, and pour over the enchiladas. Place the pork, lettuce, and radish flowers around the dish, and serve immediately.

NOTE: The sauce can, of course, be done ahead of time. The pork could be done about 1 hour ahead, but would have to be kept tightly covered and heated through gently.

It is better to put less water with the meat than too much; you can always add some if the water has evaporated and the meat is still not tender enough. If you put in too much, then the meat will fall apart by the time the frying stage is reached.

ENCHILADAS VERDES VERACRUZANAS
Green Enchiladas from Veracruz
BASED ON A RECIPE BY SEÑORA JOSEFINA VELÁZQUEZ DE LEÓN
MAKES 12 ENCHILADAS

VERACRUZ

THE SAUCE

1 CUP (250 ML) COOKED TOMATE VERDE (SEE PAGE 492), DRAINED

½ CUP (125 ML) COOKING LIQUID FROM THE TOMATOES

4 POBLANO CHILES, CHARRED, PEELED, AND CLEANED (SEE PAGE 469)

½ CUP (125 ML) ROUGHLY CHOPPED WHITE ONION

SALT TO TASTE

2 TABLESPOONS VEGETABLE OIL

½ CUP (125 ML) SOUR CREAM, COMMERCIAL OR HOMEMADE (SEE PAGE 489)

THE TORTILLAS

12 FRESHLY MADE TORTILLAS

THE FILLING

2 CUPS (500 ML) GUACAMOLE (PAGE 11)

TO SERVE

¼ CUP (65 ML) ROUGHLY CHOPPED FLAT-LEAF PARSLEY

3 OUNCES (85 G) QUESO FRESCO, CRUMBLED (ABOUT ½ CUP/125 ML)

Blend the tomate verde with the cooking liquid, chilies, onion, and salt until smooth.

Heat the oil in a skillet and cook the sauce over fairly high heat for about 5 minutes, stirring and scraping the bottom of the pan from time to time to avoid sticking. Remove from the heat and add the sour cream, then set the sauce over a very low heat just to heat it through. Set aside and keep warm.

If the tortillas are not freshly made and still warm, heat them briefly in a steamer. Dip them, one by one, into the sauce, put about 1½ tablespoons of the guacamole across the face of each, roll up loosely, and place side by side in the serving dish. Dilute the remaining sauce with a little water or milk and pour over the enchiladas. Sprinkle with the parsley and cheese and serve immediately.

NOTE: Because of the guacamole, this is obviously a dish that will not hold, so it must be served as soon as it is assembled. The sauce can be made well ahead, but for best results the guacamole, as always, should be made at the last moment.

ENCHILADAS VERDES Green Enchiladas
MAKES 12 ENCHILADAS

CENTRAL MEXICO

THE SAUCE

1 CUP (250 ML) COOKED TOMATE VERDE (SEE PAGE 492), DRAINED

3 POBLANO CHILES, CHARRED, PEELED, AND CLEANED (SEE PAGE 469)

2 SPRIGS CILANTRO, THICK STEMS REMOVED

½ CUP (125 ML) TOASTED (SHELLED), UNSALTED PEANUTS, CRUSHED

SALT TO TASTE

2 TABLESPOONS VEGETABLE OIL

⅓ CUP (85 ML) PLUS ½ CUP (125 ML) CHICKEN BROTH

THE TORTILLAS

12 FRESHLY MADE TORTILLAS

THE FILLING

1½ TO 2 CUPS (375 TO 500 ML) SHREDDED, COOKED CHICKEN

TO SERVE

⅓ CUP (85 ML) CRUMBLED QUESO FRESCO (ABOUT 2 OUNCES/60 G)

⅔ CUP (165 ML) FINELY CHOPPED WHITE ONION

½ CUP (125 ML) PREPARED SOUR CREAM (SEE PAGE 489)

Blend the tomate verde with the rest of the sauce ingredients, except the oil and ½ cup (125 ml) chicken broth, until smooth.

Heat the oil in a large skillet and fry the sauce over fairly high heat for 5 minutes, stirring and scraping the bottom of the pan from time to time to avoid sticking. Add the remaining ½ cup (125 ml) broth and bring to a boil, then remove from the heat and keep warm.

If the tortillas are not freshly made and still warm, heat them briefly in a steamer. Dip them, one by one, into the sauce, fill each one with a little of the chicken, roll loosely, and set side by side in the serving dish. Reheat the remaining sauce, diluting it if necessary with a little broth or water. Pour it over the enchiladas and top with the cheese, onion, and sour cream and serve.

CHILAQUILES

The name *chilaquiles*, according to the *Diccionario de Mejicanismos*, derives from the Náhuatl words *chilli* and *quilitl*, the latter meaning an edible wild green. We now know it as a dish of stale tortillas fried and then immersed in a chile sauce topped with shredded chicken or cheese and cream, and so on. I know this sounds very dull, but—when well made—they are a most delicious Mexican breakfast food that can fast become addictive. Here is just a sampling of recipes.

CHILAQUILES VERDES TAMPIQUEÑOS Green Chilaquiles

INSPIRED BY A RECIPE BY SEÑORA JOSEFINA VELÁZQUEZ DE LEÓN

SERVES 6   TAMAULIPAS

THE SAUCE

8 OUNCES (225 G) TOMATE VERDE, COOKED AND DRAINED (ABOUT 1 CUP/250 ML; SEE PAGE 492)

3 POBLANO CHILES, CHARRED, PEELED, SEEDS AND VEINS REMOVED (SEE PAGE 469)

2 SPRIGS EPAZOTE

3 SPRIGS CILANTRO

⅓ MEDIUM WHITE ONION, ROUGHLY CHOPPED

SALT TO TASTE

1 TABLESPOON VEGETABLE OIL

1 CUP (250 ML) CHICKEN BROTH

THE TORTILLAS

VEGETABLE OIL FOR FRYING

12 TORTILLAS, EACH CUT INTO 6 TRIANGULAR PIECES AND LEFT TO DRY

TO SERVE

4 OUNCES (115 G) QUESO FRESCO, CRUMBLED (ABOUT ⅔ CUP/165 ML)

½ CUP (125 ML) ROUGHLY CHOPPED WHITE ONION

2 HARD-COOKED EGGS, SLICED

6 LARGE RADISHES, THINLY SLICED

2 TABLESPOONS ROUGHLY CHOPPED CILANTRO

Blend the tomate verde with the chiles, epazote, cilantro, onion, and salt until smooth.

Heat the oil in a large skillet and fry the sauce over medium heat, stirring from time to time to avoid sticking, for 5 minutes. Add the broth and continue cooking for 1 minute more, then remove from the heat and set aside.

Heat the oil and fry the tortilla pieces, about one third at a time so they will be evenly cooked, until they just begin to stiffen but do not brown. Drain well.

Return the sauce to the heat and bring to a boil; stir in the tortilla pieces and cook them over medium heat, scraping the bottom of the pan almost constantly, until most of the liquid has been absorbed and the tortillas are *just* softening—5 to 8 minutes. Sprinkle the cheese, onion, eggs, radishes, and cilantro over the top and serve immediately.

CHILAQUILES DE AGUASCALIENTES

INSPIRED BY A RECIPE BY SEÑORA JOSEFINA VELÁZQUEZ DE LEÓN

SERVES 4   AQUASCALIENTES

The chipotles lend a pungent and smoky flavor to the sauce here. Like many other chilaquile *dishes, this would be good served with eggs for brunch, or leaving out the chorizo, with plain roasted chicken and a green salad.*

THE SAUCE

4 CANNED CHIPOTLE CHILES EN ADOBO

2 SPRIGS CILANTRO

$^1/_4$ CUP (65 ML) ROUGHLY CHOPPED WHITE ONION

1 $^1/_2$ TABLESPOONS SESAME SEEDS, TOASTED AND CRUSHED

$^1/_8$ TEASPOON DRIED MEXICAN OREGANO

$^2/_3$ CUP (165 ML) COOKED AND DRAINED TOMATE VERDE (SEE PAGE 492)

2 GARLIC CLOVES, CRUSHED

SALT TO TASTE

2 PLUM TOMATOES (ABOUT 6 OUNCES/180 G), BROILED (SEE PAGE 490)

2 TABLESPOONS VEGETABLE OIL

THE TORTILLAS

VEGETABLE OIL FOR FRYING

12 STALE TORTILLAS, EACH CUT INTO 6 TRIANGULAR PIECES

TO SERVE

3 CHORIZOS (ABOUT 8 OUNCES/225 G), SKINNED, CRUMBLED, AND FRIED

8 OUNCES (225 G) QUESO FRESCO, CRUMBLED (ABOUT 1 $^1/_3$ CUPS/335 ML)

$^3/_4$ CUP (190 ML) THINLY SLICED WHITE ONION

1 TABLESPOON ROUGHLY CHOPPED CILANTRO (OPTIONAL)

In a blender, blend all the sauce ingredients except the oil until smooth.

Heat the oil in a skillet and cook the sauce over a fairly high heat, stirring and scraping the bottom of the pan for about 5 minutes. Remove from the heat and set aside. Preheat the oven to 350°F (180°C).

Heat the oil in another skillet and fry the tortilla pieces, about one third at a time so they are evenly cooked, until they just begin to stiffen but do not brown. Drain well.

Put one third of the tortillas at the bottom of the dish, then add half the chorizos and cheese and $^1/_3$ cup (85 ml) of the sauce. Repeat the layers and top off with the rest of the tortillas and sauce. Cover the dish with foil and bake for 15 to 20 minutes, or until it is well heated through and the tortillas are *just* soft. Sprinkle with the onion and cilantro and serve immediately.

CHILAQUILES VERACRUZANOS

BASED ON A RECIPE BY SEÑORA JOSEFINA VELÁZQUEZ DE LEÓN

SERVES 4

VERACRUZ

This is one of the most delicious versions of chilaquiles. *Everything can, of course, be prepared ahead of time and the sauce reheated and cooked with tortilla pieces at the last moment. With a plain green salad it makes a most satisfying meal.*

THE CHICKEN

1 WHOLE CHICKEN BREAST, OR 2 LARGE LEGS, IF PREFERRED

SALT TO TASTE

1 LARGE GARLIC CLOVE

$^1/_4$ CUP (65 ML) ROUGHLY SLICED WHITE ONION

2 SPRIGS CILANTRO

2 SPRIGS FRESH MINT, OR 1 SCANT TABLESPOON DRIED

2 CUPS (500 ML) WATER

THE SAUCE

2 TABLESPOONS VEGETABLE OIL

1 ANCHO CHILE, SEEDS AND VEINS REMOVED

8 OUNCES (225 G) ROUGHLY CHOPPED TOMATOES (ABOUT 1 $^1/_2$ CUPS/375 ML)

1 LARGE GARLIC CLOVE

SALT TO TASTE

$^1/_4$ CUP (65 ML) WATER

1 CUP (250 ML) CHICKEN BROTH

THE TORTILLAS

VEGETABLE OIL FOR FRYING

12 STALE TORTILLAS, EACH CUT INTO 6 PIECES

TO SERVE

1 CUP (250 ML) PREPARED SOUR CREAM (SEE PAGE 489)

1 SMALL AVOCADO, PEELED, CUT INTO SMALL SQUARES, AND DRESSED WITH A SIMPLE VINAIGRETTE

1 CUP (250 ML) THINLY SLICED WHITE ONION

3 OUNCES (85 G) QUESO FRESCO, CRUMBLED (ABOUT $^1/_3$ CUP/85 ML)

Put the chicken, salt, garlic, onion, cilantro, and mint with the water into a large saucepan. Bring to a simmer, then lower the heat and simmer until the chicken is just tender—about 20 minutes for breast, 25 or more for legs. Allow the chicken to cool off in the broth. When the meat is cool enough to handle, remove from bones and shred. Strain and reserve the broth.

Heat the oil in a skillet. Fry the chile for about 1 minute on each side, flattening it down in the pan with a spatula. Remove the chile, cover with hot water, and leave to soak for 5 to 10 minutes. Leave the oil in the pan.

Transfer the drained chile to a blender jar, add the rest of the sauce ingredients except the broth, and blend until smooth.

Reheat the oil and fry the sauce over fairly high heat for about 3 minutes, scraping the bottom of the pan to avoid sticking. Add the broth and cook for 1 minute more. Adjust the seasoning, remove from the heat, and set aside.

Heat the oil and fry the tortilla pieces, about one third at a time so they cook evenly, until they just begin to stiffen but do not brown. Drain well.

Return the sauce to the heat. As it begins to boil, stir in the tortillas and cook over medium heat for 5 to 8 minutes, or until most of the sauce has been absorbed and the tortilla pieces are just beginning to soften. Stir almost constantly or the sauce and tortillas will stick and burn.

Put the *chilaquiles* into the dish, then top with the sour cream, chicken, avocado, onion, and cheese. Serve immediately.

CHILAQUILES DE GUANAJUATO

BASED ON A RECIPE BY SEÑORA JOSEFINA VELÁZQUEZ DE LEÓN
SERVES 4

GUANAJUATO

This is a strong, picante dish with a great flavor. Try serving this dish with fried eggs on top for brunch; it is an almost surefire way to kill a hangover. It is also very good served with sour cream on top, with scrambled eggs, or with plain roasted chicken.

THE SAUCE

6 GUAJILLO CHILES WIPED CLEAN, SEEDS AND VEINS REMOVED, AND LIGHTLY TOASTED
  (SEE PAGE 476)
12 OUNCES (340 G) TOMATE VERDE, COOKED AND PARTIALLY DRAINED
  (ABOUT 1 ½ CUPS/375 ML; SEE PAGE 492)
SALT TO TASTE
¼ CUP (65 ML) ROUGHLY CHOPPED WHITE ONION
2 GARLIC CLOVES, CRUSHED
2 TABLESPOONS VEGETABLE OIL

THE TORTILLAS

VEGETABLE OIL FOR FRYING
12 STALE TORTILLAS, EACH CUT INTO 6 TRIANGULAR PIECES

TO SERVE

6 OUNCES (180 G) GRATED CHIHUAHUA CHEESE OR MUENSTER (ABOUT 1 ¼ CUPS/315 ML)
½ CUP (125 ML) FINELY CHOPPED WHITE ONION

Put the chiles into a blender jar. Add the rest of the sauce ingredients except the oil and blend until quite smooth.

Heat the oil in a skillet, add the sauce through a strainer, and fry over medium heat for about 5 minutes, scraping the bottom of the pan from time to time. Remove from the heat and set aside.

Heat the oil in another skillet and fry the tortillas, about one third at a time so they are cooked evenly, until they just begin to stiffen but do not brown. Drain well.

Preheat the broiler or oven.

Heat the sauce, stir in the tortilla pieces, and cook over medium heat, stirring from time to time to avoid sticking, for about 5 minutes, or until they are just beginning to soften and some of the sauce has been absorbed. (Take care, as the sauce sticks and burns easily.) Transfer the *chilaquiles* to the serving dish. Cover with the cheese, then run the dish under a hot broiler or into the oven until the cheese just begins to melt. Top with the onion and serve immediately.

BUDÍNES OR SOPAS SECAS DE TORTILLAS ❄
LAYERED TORTILLA CASSEROLES

Layered tortilla casseroles are sometimes served as a *sopa seca*, literally dry soup, as the pasta course would be in Italy. They make an excellent lunch dish with a salad. Although they tend to be rather heavy, and slightly fattening, they are delicious when made with good quality tortillas that do not disintegrate—as do those made of *maseca* or masa harina. Here are just a few examples, but from here you can elaborate and invent.

BUDÍN AZTECA Moctezuma Pie
SERVES 6

MEXICO CITY

This is a delicious calorie-laden dish and a great favorite when I first came to Mexico. There are many variations depending on what you have on hand.

THE GREEN TOMATO SAUCE

3 CUPS (750 ML) COOKED TOMATE VERDE (ABOUT 1 ½ POUNDS/680 G), DRAINED, RESERV-
ING ½ CUP (125 ML) OF THE LIQUID (SEE PAGE 492)

3 SERRANO CHILES, COOKED WITH THE TOMATE VERDE

2 SMALL GARLIC CLOVES, ROUGHLY CHOPPED

2 TABLESPOONS FINELY CHOPPED WHITE ONION

2 TABLESPOONS VEGETABLE OIL

THE RAJAS

7 POBLANO CHILES, CHARRED, PEELED, AND CLEANED (SEE PAGE 469)

3 TABLESPOONS VEGETABLE OIL

⅓ CUP (85 ML) THINLY SLICED WHITE ONION

SALT TO TASTE

THE BUDÍN

⅓ CUP (85 ML) VEGETABLE OIL

18 FRESHLY MADE TORTILLAS (SEE PAGE 49), CUT INTO HALVES ABOUT 5 INCHES (13 CM)
ACROSS

2 CUPS (500 ML) SHREDDED, POACHED CHICKEN (PAGE 499), WELL SALTED

TO SERVE

1 ½ CUPS (375 ML) THICK SOUR CREAM (SEE PAGE 489)

1 ¾ CUPS (440 ML) GRATED CHIHUAHUA CHEESE OR CHEDDAR (ABOUT 8 OUNCES/225 G)

Have ready an ovenproof dish about 10 inches (25 cm) in diameter and 4 inches (10 cm) deep.

Preheat the oven to 350°F (180°C).

In a blender, blend the tomate verde with the ½ cup (125 ml) reserved liquid and the chiles, garlic, and onion to a smooth sauce.

Heat the oil in a skillet, add the sauce, and cook over high heat for about 5 minutes, stirring from time to time to avoid sticking, by which time it will have thickened a little and will be well seasoned. Set aside.

Cut the chiles into narrow strips and set aside.

Heat the 3 tablespoons of oil in another skillet, then add the onion and fry until translucent— about 1 minute. Add the chile strips and salt, cover the pan, and cook over gentle heat until the chiles are tender but not too soft—about 5 minutes.

Heat the oil in another skillet and fry each tortilla for a few seconds—they should not get crisp or hard. Blot off excess oil on the next unfried tortilla.

Spread one third of the tortillas over the bottom of the dish. Then spread, in layers on top of them, half the chicken, half the *rajas*, and a third each of the sauce, sour cream, and cheese. Repeat the layers and finish off with a layer of tortillas, sprinkled with the rest of the sauce, sour cream, and cheese.

Bake the *budín* for about 25 minutes, or until it is well heated through and the cheese has melted.

NOTE: The dish could be assembled about 2 hours ahead of time, but it would be best not to add all the sauce. Just use half of it between the layers, and then, at the last moment before putting the dish into the oven, pour in the sauce around the edges. Be careful not to cook it for too long or the tortillas will disintegrate—they should be soft but keep their shape.

This pie does not freeze successfully.

CASEROLA DE TORTILLAS EN CHILES GUAJILLO
A Casserole of Tortillas in Chile Sauce

SEÑORA GODILEVA

SERVES 6

GUERRERO

THE SAUCE

12 GUAJILLO CHILES, SEEDS AND VEINS REMOVED

1/2 CUP (125 ML) ROUGHLY CHOPPED WHITE ONION

2 GARLIC CLOVES, ROUGHLY CHOPPED

1/4 TEASPOON CUMIN SEEDS, CRUSHED

1 CUP (250 ML) CHICKEN BROTH OR WATER

2 TABLESPOONS VEGETABLE OIL

SALT TO TASTE

THE CHILAQUILES

VEGETABLE OIL FOR FRYING

18 TORTILLAS, CUT INTO STRIPS OR TRIANGLES AND DRIED

8 OUNCES (225 G) QUESO FRESCO, CRUMBLED, OR SUBSTITUTE MILD CHEDDAR, GRATED
    (ABOUT 1 1/3 CUPS/335 ML), OR MUENSTER (1 1/4 CUPS/315 ML)

2 CUPS (500 ML) CHICKEN BROTH, APPROXIMATELY

2 LARGE SPRIGS EPAZOTE

TO SERVE

1 CUP (250 ML) PREPARED THIN SOUR CREAM (SEE PAGE 489)

2 CHORIZOS (ABOUT 5 OUNCES/140 G), CRUMBLED AND FRIED

3/4 CUP (185 ML) THINLY SLICED WHITE ONION RINGS

2 LIMES, CUT INTO WEDGES

Have ready a flameproof dish about 10 inches (25 cm) in diameter and 4 inches (10 cm) deep.

Heat the griddle and toast the chiles lightly on both sides. Be careful—they burn very quickly.

Cover the chiles with hot water and leave them to soak for about 10 minutes, then transfer with a slotted spoon to a blender jar. Add the onion, garlic, and cumin seeds and blend to a smooth sauce with 1/2 cup (125 ml) of the broth.

Heat the oil and add the sauce through a fine strainer, pressing down to extract as much of the substance and juice as possible.

Add the other ½ cup broth and let the sauce cook over high heat for a few minutes longer. Add salt to taste. Set aside.

Heat the oil and fry the tortilla strips until they are a pale gold, but not too crisp. Remove and drain on paper toweling.

Cover the bottom of the dish with one third of the tortilla pieces, then one third of the cheese and one third of the sauce. Repeat the layers twice more.

Add the 2 cups broth and bring to a boil. Lower the heat and continue cooking the *chilaquiles* at a brisk simmer, until most of the broth has been absorbed—about 15 minutes. Add the epazote a minute or so before the *chilaquiles* have finished cooking.

Pour the sour cream around the edge of the dish, then top with the chorizos and the onion rings. Serve in small deep bowls with lime wedges on the side.

CASEROLA DE TORTILLAS SENCILLA Simple Tortilla Casserole
BASED ON A RECIPE BY SEÑORA JOSEFINA VELÁZQUEZ DE LEÓN
SERVES 4   NUEVO LEÓN

This casserole of tortillas in tomato sauce is often served as a "dry soup," which can be served as you would a pasta course, alone or with simply cooked meats, fish, or chicken.

THE SAUCE
1 POUND (450 G) TOMATOES, ROUGHLY CHOPPED (ABOUT 3 CUPS/750 ML)
¼ CUP (65 ML) ROUGHLY CHOPPED WHITE ONION
1 LARGE GARLIC CLOVE, ROUGHLY CHOPPED
SALT TO TASTE
2 TABLESPOONS VEGETABLE OIL

THE FILLING
VEGETABLE OIL FOR FRYING
12 TORTILLAS CUT INTO STRIPS AND DRIED
4 OUNCES (115 G) CHIHUAHUA CHEESE (ABOUT ¾ CUP/185 ML), OR QUESO FRESCO
    (ABOUT ⅔ CUP/165 ML)
⅓ CUP (85 ML) BROTH OR HOT WATER

TO SERVE
2 TABLESPOONS FINELY CHOPPED PARSLEY (OPTIONAL)
1 CUP (250 ML) PREPARED SOUR CREAM (SEE PAGE 489)

Have ready a lightly greased ovenproof dish about 9 by 6 by 3 inches (23 by 15 by 8 cm).

Blend the tomatoes with the rest of the sauce ingredients except the oil until smooth.

Heat the oil in a medium skillet and fry the sauce over a fairly high heat to reduce and season—about 4 minutes. Remove from the heat and set in a warm place.

Heat the oil in a second skillet and fry the tortilla pieces, about one third at a time so they will cook evenly, until they are just stiffening but not brown. Drain well.

Preheat the oven to 375° F (190°C).

Put one third of the tortilla pieces at the bottom of the dish; sprinkle with ⅓ cup (85 ml) of the sauce and one third of the cheese. Repeat with half of the remaining tortillas, sauce, and cheese, then top off with the remaining ingredients. Moisten the top layer with the broth. Cover the dish with foil and set in the top level of the oven for 15 to 20 minutes, or until heated through and bubbling. (The liquid should have been absorbed and the tortilla pieces just soft, not falling apart, at the bottom and still a little chewy on top. Slight adjustments may be needed to suit the tortillas that are available to you.)

Serve, sprinkled with parsley, if you like it. Pass the sour cream separately.

CASEROLA DE TORTILLAS Y LEGUMBRES

Tortilla and Vegetable Casserole

BASED ON A RECIPE BY SEÑORA JOSEFINA VELÁZQUEZ DE LEÓN

SERVES 4   CENTRAL MEXICO

The original recipe included chorizo, but it rather overpowers the taste of the vegetables and I prefer it without. This casserole can be served as a separate course, alone or with plainly broiled meats, fish, or roast chicken.

Be sure not to overcook the vegetables—they should be just tender, almost crisp, so that they do not become mushy during baking.

THE SAUCE

1 ½ TABLESPOONS VEGETABLE OIL

⅓ CUP (85 ML) THINLY SLICED WHITE ONION

12 OUNCES (340 G) TOMATOES, BROILED (SEE PAGE 490)

SALT TO TASTE

⅔ CUP (165 ML) CHICKEN BROTH OR VEGETABLE BROTH FOR VEGETARIANS

THE FILLING

VEGETABLE OIL FOR FRYING

12 TORTILLAS, CUT INTO STRIPS AND DRIED

1 CUP (250 ML) COOKED PEAS, OR DEFROSTED UNCOOKED

1 CUP (250 ML) COOKED, DICED CARROT

1 CUP (250 ML) COOKED GREEN BEANS, CUT INTO SMALL PIECES

TO SERVE

4 OUNCES (115 G) MILD CHIHUAHUA CHEESE OR SUBSTITUTE GRATED
   (ABOUT 1 HEAPED CUP/265 ML)

Have ready a lightly greased ovenproof dish about 9 by 6 by 3 inches (23 by 15 by 8 cm).

Heat the oil in a large skillet and cook the onion gently until soft, about 3 minutes; do not brown.

Blend the unskinned tomatoes briefly, then add, with the salt, to the onion in the pan. Cook over fairly high heat, stirring from time to time, until it reduces—about 3 minutes. Add the broth or vegetable water and cook for a minute or so longer, then set aside.

Heat the oil in another skillet and fry the tortilla pieces, about one third at a time so they fry evenly, until just beginning to stiffen, not brown. Drain well.

Preheat the oven to 375°F (190°C).

Spread half of the tortilla pieces over the bottom of the dish. Sprinkle with about one third of the sauce, then cover with the vegetables, the rest of the tortillas, and finally the rest of the sauce. Cover the dish with foil and bake for about 20 minutes, or until the bottom tortillas are soft but not falling apart and the top ones are still slightly chewy. Remove the foil.

Sprinkle the cheese over the top of the casserole and return the dish to the oven just until the cheese melts. Once this casserole is assembled it should be cooked and served, or it will become rather soggy.

BUDÍN DE HONGOS Mushroom Pudding

INSPIRED BY A RECIPE BY SEÑORA JOSEFINA VELÁZQUEZ DE LEÓN

SERVES 4   CENTRAL MEXICO

The original recipe calls for cuiclacoche, *the delicious fungus that grows on corn (see page 497). But mushrooms are cheap and plentiful, and this recipe provides a delicious variation on the usual ways of preparing them. Any type of mushrooms may be used.*

You may use more or fewer chiles, depending on your taste.

THE FILLING

2 TABLESPOONS VEGETABLE OIL

½ CUP (125 ML) THINLY SLICED WHITE ONION

2 GARLIC CLOVES, PEELED AND FINELY CHOPPED

1 POUND (450 G) MUSHROOMS, RINSED AND THINLY SLICED, OR ROUGHLY CHOPPED CUICLACOCHE

3 SERRANO CHILES, FINELY CHOPPED

SALT TO TASTE

1 LARGE SPRIG EPAZOTE OR PARSLEY, LEAVES ONLY, ROUGHLY CHOPPED

THE SAUCE

1 POUND (450 G) TOMATOES, ROUGHLY CHOPPED (ABOUT 3 CUPS/750 ML)

¼ CUP (65 ML) ROUGHLY CHOPPED WHITE ONION

1 GARLIC CLOVE, ROUGHLY CHOPPED

1 TABLESPOON VEGETABLE OIL

SALT TO TASTE

THE TORTILLAS

VEGETABLE OIL FOR FRYING

12 TORTILLAS, CUT INTO FOUR AND DRIED

4 OUNCES (115 G) MILD CHIHUAHUA CHEESE OR MUENSTER, GRATED (ABOUT 1 HEAPED CUP/265 ML)

Have ready a lightly greased ovenproof dish about 9 by 6 by 3 inches (23 by 15 by 8 cm).

Heat the oil in a large skillet and fry the onion and garlic for 2 minutes, stirring from time to time to avoid sticking—they should not brown. Add the mushrooms, chiles, and salt, then cover the pan and cook over medium heat until the mushrooms are tender—about 20 minutes; they should be juicy. Add the epazote and cook for 1 minute more. Set aside in a bowl.

Blend the tomatoes, onion, and garlic together until smooth.

Heat the oil in a skillet and cook the sauce over fairly high heat, stirring it from time to time, for about 4 minutes to reduce. Add salt.

Heat the oil in a second skillet and fry the tortillas, about one third at a time so they fry evenly, until they are just becoming stiff but do not harden and brown. Drain on paper toweling.

Preheat the oven to 375°F (190°C).

Put one third of the tortilla pieces at the bottom of the dish, then add half of the mushroom mixture, one third of the cheese, and ⅓ cup (85 ml) sauce. Repeat the layers and top off with the rest of the cheese, sauce, and any mushroom juice left in the pan. Bake until well heated through and bubbling—20 to 25 minutes.

TACOS

To many people outside Mexico, a taco is a tortilla bent in half to form a deep U shape, fried crisp, and stuffed with ground beef, iceberg lettuce, sliced tomato, and grated cheese. Throughout Mexico, however, the simple taco consumed by millions daily is a fresh, hot corn tortilla rolled around one of a hundred or so fillings and liberally doused with one of a hundred or so sauces. The variety is endless.

There are, of course, tacos that are fried fairly crisp: *no deben de tronar*—they shouldn't crackle as you bite them—is one admonition, no doubt from a dyed-in-the-wool aficionado of great experience. Of course, there are always exceptions to the rule because their counterparts in Jalisco, *la flauta*, and in Yucatán, *el cotzito*, are tightly rolled and crisp to a crackling point.

Apart from the ordinary soft taco and the fried, there is the *sudado*, which means literally (and unattractively) "sweated," or steamed, and the *taco de canasta*, basket taco, which is almost the same because as the filled soft tacos are placed one on top of the other in layers in a cloth-lined basket, it is virtually the same as steaming.

Although you can use whatever you have on hand, here are a few ideas for different fillings.

TACOS DE PAPA Potato Tacos

BASED ON A RECIPE BY SEÑORA JOSEFINA VELÁZQUEZ DE LEÓN

MAKES 12 TACOS

The original recipe calls for a plain mashed-potato filling. I happen to like potato skins and the texture they give to the filling, and have improvised this, keeping within the Mexican tradition. Surprisingly, the potato and masa go very well together, and make a simple and tasty budget dish.

You could even use some chopped epazote leaves in the filling.

THE FILLING

12 OUNCES (340 G) COOKED RED BLISS OR OTHER WAXY POTATOES, UNPEELED AND DICED
(ABOUT 2¼ CUPS/563 ML)
½ MEDIUM WHITE ONION
4 OUNCES (115 G) QUESO FRESCO, CRUMBLED (ABOUT ¾ CUP/190 ML)
SALT TO TASTE

TO SERVE

12 TORTILLAS
VEGETABLE OIL FOR FRYING
⅔ CUP (165 ML) PREPARED SOUR CREAM (SEE PAGE 489)
1 CUP (250 ML) SALSA RANCHERA (PAGE 238), OMITTING THE ONION, WARMED
1½ CUPS (375 ML) SHREDDED LETTUCE
JALAPEÑO CHILES EN ESCABECHE

Mix the potatoes with the rest of the filling ingredients.

Fill each tortilla with about 2 tablespoons of the mixture and secure with toothpicks.

Heat the oil and fry until the tortilla is just crisp on the outside. Drain well.

Serve immediately, topped with the sour cream, warm sauce, and lettuce. Serve the chiles separately.

TAQUITOS Little Tacos
MAKES 12 TACOS

I came upon this simple suggestion for tacos when I had a refrigerator full of Mexican bits and pieces. There was half a big avocado, a little package of frozen refried beans that kept falling out with the ice trays, and a half-finished can of chipotle chiles. You don't have to have these ingredients, but it does make you stop and realize that practically all leftovers can be made up into savory and simple tacos.

TO PREPARE THE TACOS

12 TORTILLAS
1 SMALL AVOCADO, CUT INTO 12 SLICES
4 OUNCES (115 G) CHIHUAHUA CHEESE OR MUENSTER (ABOUT 1 CUP/250 ML)
4 TO 6 CANNED CHIPOTLE CHILES, EACH CUT INTO 3 PIECES
3/4 CUP (185 ML) FRIJOLES REFRITOS (PAGE 155)
12 THIN SLICES WHITE ONION
SALT TO TASTE

TO SERVE

VEGETABLE OIL FOR FRYING
6 ROMAINE LETTUCE LEAVES, SHREDDED
6 LARGE RADISHES, THINLY SLICED
APPROXIMATELY 3 TABLESPOONS ROUGHLY CHOPPED CILANTRO SPRIGS

On each tortilla put a slice of avocado, some strips of cheese, a piece or two of chile, a tablespoon of beans, and a thin slice of onion. Sprinkle well with salt, roll the tortillas up, and secure with a toothpick.

Fry until golden but not too crisp. Drain on paper toweling and serve topped with the lettuce, radishes, and chopped cilantro.

TAQUITOS DE NATAS "Sour Cream" Tacos
BASED ON A RECIPE BY SEÑORA JOSEFINA VELÁZQUEZ DE LEÓN
MAKES 12 TACOS   SAN LUIS POTOSÍ

Taquitos de natas *is the original name for this dish—referring to when the sauce was thickened with* natas, *which are the skimmings from good rich, unhomogenized milk as it is scalded.*

The original recipe did not call for the chile or the onion topping, but they are authentic touches that I think improve this very simple and delicious dish.

The tacos are not completely smothered by the sauce, so the ends are slightly crisp.

THE FILLING

12 OUNCES (340 G) TOMATOES, BROILED (SEE PAGE 490)

2 TABLESPOONS FINELY CHOPPED WHITE ONION

1 GARLIC CLOVE

SALT TO TASTE

2 TABLESPOONS VEGETABLE OIL

1 ½ TO 2 CUPS (375 TO 500 ML) COOKED, SHREDDED, AND WELL-SALTED CHICKEN

1 FRESH JALAPEÑO CHILE, CUT INTO THIN STRIPS

1 TABLESPOON VEGETABLE OIL

½ CUP (125 ML) SOUR CREAM, COMMERCIAL OR HOMEMADE (SEE PAGE 489), AT ROOM
    TEMPERATURE

TO SERVE

VEGETABLE OIL FOR FRYING

12 TORTILLAS

⅔ CUP (165 ML) FINELY CHOPPED WHITE ONION

Blend the tomatoes with the onion, garlic, and salt and divide into two parts. Heat the oil in a skillet and fry the shredded chicken and chile strips for a minute or so over fairly hot heat, stirring from time to time to avoid sticking, until they just begin to brown. Add half of the tomato puree and continue cooking and stirring until almost dry. Set aside and keep warm.

Heat the oil in another skillet and fry the remainder of the puree over fairly high heat for about 3 minutes, stirring from time to time. Remove from the heat and stir in the sour cream. Set aside and keep warm.

Heat the oil in a skillet and lightly fry the tortillas, a few at a time, on both sides. Preheat the oven to 375°F (190°C).

Put a little of the filling on each of the tortillas, roll up, and place side by side on the serving dish. Pour the sauce down the center of the tacos and bake for 10 minutes. Sprinkle with the onion and serve immediately.

NOTE: The tacos should not be left for a longer period in the oven or they will become tough and the sauce will dry out. You could get the filling and sauce made ahead and then assemble and bake at the last moment.

TACOS DE RAJAS DE ZACATECAS Tacos of Chile Strips

BASED ON A RECIPE BY SEÑORA JOSEFINA VELÁZQUEZ DE LEÓN

MAKES 12 TACOS   ZACATECAS

THE FILLING

2 TABLESPOONS VEGETABLE OIL

3 POBLANO CHILES, CHARRED, PEELED, CLEANED, AND CUT INTO NARROW STRIPS
(SEE PAGE 469)

8 OUNCES (225 G) TOMATOES, BROILED (SEE PAGE 490)

3 TABLESPOONS ROUGHLY CHOPPED WHITE ONION

SALT TO TASTE

3 LARGE EGGS

TO SERVE

VEGETABLE OIL FOR FRYING

12 TORTILLAS

1 1/3 CUPS (335 ML) PREPARED SOUR CREAM (SEE PAGE 489)

Heat the oil in a large skillet. Add the chile strips and cook over low heat for about 3 minutes.

Blend the tomatoes with the onion until smooth, then add the puree to the chiles in the pan. Season with salt and cook over medium heat for about 5 minutes, stirring and scraping the bottom of the pan from time to time.

Beat the eggs lightly and stir them into the mixture. Continue stirring until they are just set, then remove from the heat and keep warm.

Heat the oil in a skillet and fry the tortillas on both sides. Fry a little more than you would for enchiladas, but not allowing them to get so crisp that you cannot easily fold them over. Drain well, then fill each one with a little of the chile-egg filling. Double the tortillas over and set on the serving dish.

Pour the sour cream over the tacos and serve immediately.

TACOS DE RES Beef Tacos
BASED ON A RECIPE BY SEÑORA JOSEFINA VELÁZQUEZ DE LEÓN
MAKES 12 TACOS

GUANAJUATO

This is a good way of using up leftover roast beef. Atypically, I like to add a strip or two of fresh jalapeño chiles to the meat in the tacos.

THE FILLING
1 ½ TABLESPOONS VEGETABLE OIL
½ CUP (125 ML) THINLY SLICED WHITE ONION
1 POUND (450 G) COOKED AND SHREDDED BEEF (ABOUT 2 CUPS/500 ML; SEE PAGE 500)

TO SERVE
12 TORTILLAS
VEGETABLE OIL FOR FRYING
1 CUP (250 ML) SALSA RANCHERA (SEE PAGE 238)
¾ CUP (185 ML) PREPARED SOUR CREAM (SEE PAGE 489)
3 OUNCES (85 G) QUESO FRESCO, CRUMBLED (ABOUT ½ CUP/125 ML)

Heat the oil in a large skillet and fry the onion gently until translucent. Add the meat and cook over medium heat, stirring from time to time, until it is lightly browned. Set aside to cool a little.

Fill the tortillas and fry until slightly crisp on the outside. Drain, then serve immediately topped with the sauce, sour cream, and cheese.

TACOS DE HONGOS Mushroom Tacos
MAKES 12 TACOS   CENTRAL MEXICO

The original recipe called for cuiclacoche *but any wild or cultivated mushroom could be used.*

THE FILLING
3 TABLESPOONS VEGETABLE OIL
¼ CUP (65 ML) FINELY CHOPPED WHITE ONION
2 GARLIC CLOVES, PEELED AND CHOPPED
12 OUNCES (340 G) TOMATOES, FINELY CHOPPED (ABOUT 2 CUPS/500 ML)
3 SERRANO CHILES, CUT INTO STRIPS, WITH SEEDS AND VEINS
1 POUND (450 G) MUSHROOMS OR CUICLACOCHE (SEE PAGE 497), ROUGHLY CHOPPED
    (ABOUT 4 CUPS/1 L)
SALT TO TASTE
2 SPRIGS EPAZOTE OR PARSLEY, FINELY CHOPPED

TO SERVE
12 TORTILLAS
VEGETABLE OIL OR MELTED LARD FOR FRYING
PREPARED SOUR CREAM (SEE PAGE 489; OPTIONAL)

Heat the oil in a large skillet and fry the onion and garlic gently for a few seconds; do not let them brown.

Add the tomatoes, chiles, mushrooms, and salt. Cook over medium heat, uncovered, stirring the mixture from time to time until the mushrooms are soft and the juices reduced—about 15 minutes.

Add the epazote and cook for 1 minute more. Set aside to cool a little.

Put a little of the mixture onto each of the tortillas, roll them up, and secure with a toothpick. Heat the fat and fry the tacos until they are just crisping but not hard. Drain them well and serve them immediately, either plain or with a little prepared sour cream.

PUERCO EN SALSA DE JITOMATE
Shredded Pork and Tomato Filling for Tacos
MAKES ENOUGH FILLING FOR 12 TO 15 SMALL TACOS, 1½ CUPS (375 ML)

12 OUNCES (340 G) TOMATOES, BROILED (SEE PAGE 490)

1 GARLIC CLOVE, ROUGHLY CHOPPED

2 TABLESPOONS LARD OR VEGETABLE OIL

⅓ CUP (85 ML) FINELY CHOPPED WHITE ONION

2 FRESH JALAPEÑO CHILES, WITH SEEDS, FINELY SLICED

SALT TO TASTE

1 ⅓ CUPS (335 ML) COOKED AND SHREDDED PORK (PAGE 500; ABOUT 12 OUNCES/340 G)

Blend the tomatoes with the garlic until almost smooth. Set aside.

Heat the lard in a large skillet and cook the onion and chiles, without browning, until translucent. Add the tomato mixture and cook over medium heat for about 5 minutes; add salt.

Add the meat and continue cooking the mixture for 8 minutes, or until it is all well seasoned and the sauce moist but not juicy.

TOSTADAS

A tortilla fried flat until crisp is a tostada, which acts as an edible plate for a variety of toppings to make a luscious, if hazardous, snack that tends to break and scatter at a bite (see recipes pages 89–90).

In Mérida and Queretero I have eaten a tostada that had a small amount of fat mixed in the masa and had been toasted and not fried.

Of course you can always let the tortillas dry out, then brush them with oil and bake them until crisp.

TOSTADAS DE MANITAS DE PUERCO Pigs' Feet Tostadas

INSPIRED BY SEÑORA JOSEFINA VELÁZQUEZ DE LEÓN

MAKES 12 TOSTADAS   SAN LUIS POTOSÍ

Any jellied pigs' feet left over can be used as it is for an appetizer, served with lime quarters and plenty of chopped parsley.

The tendency generally is to overcook pigs' feet, so that the flesh becomes too soft and insipid. They vary considerably in size, so cooking time may have to be adjusted. Try to choose ones that are between 12 ounces (340 g) and 1 pound (450 g) each. I often err on the time and undercook them in an effort to get the right consistency—forgetting that, soft as they may be when hot, they stiffen up considerably as they cool down.

TO PREPARE THE PIGS' FEET

2 FRESH PIGS' FEET, SPLIT IN HALF

1 SMALL MEXICAN BAY LEAF

3 SPRIGS FRESH THYME OR $^1/_8$ TEASPOON DRIED

$^1/_4$ TEASPOON DRIED MEXICAN OREGANO

2 GARLIC CLOVES

$^1/_3$ CUP (85 ML) THICKLY SLICED WHITE ONION

6 PEPPERCORNS

SALT TO TASTE

FRESHLY GROUND PEPPER

TO SERVE

VEGETABLE OIL FOR FRYING

12 TORTILLAS

THE PIGS' FEET JELLY

1 $^1/_2$ CUPS (375 ML) FINELY SHREDDED AND DRESSED LETTUCE

1 SMALL AVOCADO, SLICED

1 $^1/_2$ CUPS (375 ML) SALSA RANCHERA (PAGE 238), OMITTING THE ONION

3 TABLESPOONS FINELY GRATED QUESO AÑEJO (SEE PAGE 481)

1 CUP (250 ML) THINLY SLICED PURPLE ONION

Put all the ingredients for the pigs' feet into a large saucepan and cover with cold water by $^1/_2$ inch (1.5 cm). Bring slowly to a boil, then lower the heat and simmer for about 2$^1/_2$ hours. (The meat should be tender but not too soft.) Set aside to cool in the broth.

When the pigs' feet are cool enough to handle, remove all the bones carefully and chop the meat, gelatinous gristle, and rind together into small pieces and place in a shallow dish and season with salt and pepper (bearing in mind that cooked foods served cold need to be more highly seasoned). Strain the broth and pour 1⅓ cups (335 ml) of it over the meat. Set the dish in the refrigerator until firmly set—about 1 hour.

Heat the oil in a skillet and fry the tortillas until crisp. Drain well.

Cut the pigs' feet jelly into small squares and put 2 to 3 heaped tablespoons onto each tostada. Cover with lettuce, some slices of avocado, sauce, cheese, and last of all the onion rings.

NOTE: The pigs' feet can be prepared a day or two ahead.

TOSTADAS DE GUACAMOLE Y CREMA
Guacamole and Sour Cream Tostadas
BASED ON A RECIPE BY SEÑORA JOSEFINA VELÁZQUEZ DE LEÓN
MAKES 12 TOSTADAS   SONORA

VEGETABLE OIL FOR FRYING
12 CORN TORTILLAS
8 OUNCES (225 G) CHIHUAHUA CHEESE, CUT INTO THIN SLICES
2 CUPS (500 ML) GUACAMOLE (PAGE 11)
1 CUP (250 ML) PREPARED SOUR CREAM (SEE PAGE 489)
1½ CUPS (375 ML) FINELY SHREDDED LETTUCE
4 TO 6 JALAPEÑO CHILES EN ESCABECHE, CUT INTO STRIPS

Heat the oil in a skillet and fry the tortillas until crisp. Drain well.

Cover the tortillas with the sliced cheese and melt under a broiler or in the oven. Top each tostada with a large spoonful of the guacamole, a little sour cream, some shredded lettuce, and some chile strips. Serve immediately.

TORTILLAS COMO SANDWICH Tortilla "Sandwich"

MAKES 6 TORTILLA SANDWICHES   CENTRAL MEXICO

The Mexicans' delicious answer to the American ham and cheese sandwich that lends itself to many interpretations.

12 TORTILLAS

6 OUNCES (180 G) COOKED HAM, THINLY SLICED

6 OUNCES (180 G) CHIHUAHUA CHEESE OR CHEDDAR, FINELY SLICED

VEGETABLE OIL FOR FRYING

¾ CUP (185 ML) PREPARED SOUR CREAM (SEE PAGE 489)

¾ CUP (185 ML) SALSA DE TOMATE VERDE (PAGE 236), GUACAMOLE (PAGE 11),
    OR SALSA RANCHERA (PAGE 238)

½ CUP (125 ML) FINELY CHOPPED WHITE ONION

1 ½ CUPS (375 ML) FINELY SHREDDED LETTUCE

6 RADISHES, CUT INTO FLOWERS OR SLICED

Lay 6 of the tortillas out flat; spread each one with some of the ham and cheese. Cover each with another tortilla to form a sandwich, then secure each pair of tortillas together with 2 toothpicks, one on each side.

Heat the oil and fry each sandwich on either side until just beginning to get crisp, not hard. Drain well, then top with the sour cream, sauce, and chopped onion. Decorate each plate with the lettuce and radishes, which will serve as a foil for the richness of the tortillas. Serve immediately.

TORTILLAS PILADAS CON GUACAMOLE Y SALSA DE JITOMATE Tortillas Stacked with Guacamole and Tomato Sauce
SERVES 4 TO 6   CENTRAL MEXICO

This was called simply "tortilla soup" in the book where I found this recipe—what an under-statement! It is in fact a delicious fanciful and colorful concoction of fried tortillas stacked with guacamole, sour cream, and cheese and smothered in tomato sauce.

THE SAUCE
2 TABLESPOONS VEGETABLE OIL
5 SCALLIONS, FINELY CHOPPED
1 POUND (450 G) TOMATOES, ROUGHLY CHOPPED (ABOUT 3 CUPS/750 ML)
2 GARLIC CLOVES
SALT TO TASTE

TO SERVE
VEGETABLE OIL FOR FRYING
12 TORTILLAS, FRESHLY MADE, IF POSSIBLE, AND NOT TOO THIN
1 ½ CUPS (375 ML) GUACAMOLE (PAGE 11)
4 OUNCES (115 G) CHIHUAHUA CHEESE OR MILD CHEDDAR CHEESE, GRATED
¾ CUP (185 ML) PREPARED SOUR CREAM (SEE PAGE 489)

Heat the oil in a large skillet and cook the scallions gently until they are soft but not browned.

Blend the tomatoes with the garlic. Add to the pan with the salt and fry the sauce over fairly high heat, stirring and scraping the bottom of the pan almost constantly, until it has reduced and seasoned—about 5 minutes. Set aside and keep warm.

Heat the oil in another skillet and fry the tortillas briefly on both sides. Drain well.

You need to make 3 piles. Dip 3 of the tortillas into the sauce and lay them flat onto the serving dish. Spread them with about 2 tablespoons each of the guacamole, a little cheese, and some sour cream.

Dip 3 more tortillas into the sauce and cover the filling. Repeat with another layer of tortillas on top of the first "sandwich," then repeat a layer of guacamole, cheese, and sour cream, ending with a layer of the remaining tortillas.

Pour the rest of the sauce over the stacks of tortillas and sprinkle the remaining cheese over the top. Cut into wedges and serve immediately.

N O T E : This is quite obviously a dish that has to be prepared at the very last moment. Only the sauce can be done ahead of time. The minute the guacamole is made, preparations for the rest should start.

INDIOS VESTIDOS "Dressed Indians"

BASED ON A RECIPE BY SEÑORA JOSEFINA VELÁZQUEZ DE LEÓN

SERVES 6

GUANAJUATO

"Dressed Indians" is the whimsical name of this dish, and sometimes it is known as "little Indians." It's rather like a simple version of chiles rellenos, only instead of chiles, tortillas are used. They can be stuffed with either shredded meat or cheese.

THE SAUCE

2 TABLESPOONS VEGETABLE OIL

$\frac{1}{3}$ CUP (85 ML) FINELY CHOPPED WHITE ONION

1 $\frac{1}{4}$ POUNDS (565 G) TOMATOES, BROILED (SEE PAGE 490)

2 CANNED CHIPOTLE CHILES EN ADOBO

SALT TO TASTE

THE FILLING AND FRYING

1 POUND (450 G) SHREDDED, COOKED PORK (PAGE 500; ABOUT 1 $\frac{1}{3}$ CUPS/313 ML), OR
    8 OUNCES (225 G) QUESO FRESCO, CRUMBLED (ABOUT 1 $\frac{1}{3}$ CUPS/335 ML)

12 TORTILLAS, CUT INTO HALVES

ABOUT $\frac{1}{2}$ CUP (125 ML) ALL-PURPOSE FLOUR

VEGETABLE OIL FOR FRYING

5 LARGE EGGS, SEPARATED

SALT TO TASTE

TO SERVE

1 LARGE AVOCADO, THINLY SLICED

4 TABLESPOONS FINELY GRATED QUESO AÑEJO (SEE PAGE 481)

Heat the oil in a large skillet and fry the onion gently until translucent. Blend the unskinned tomatoes with the chiles, then add to the pan, along with the salt. Cook the sauce over fairly high heat for about 3 minutes so that it reduces a little. Season. Remove from the heat and keep warm.

Put a little of the filling onto each piece of tortilla. Fold in half and fasten with a toothpick, then dust lightly with flour.

Heat the oil, about ½ inch (1.5 cm) deep, in a skillet.

Meanwhile, beat the egg whites and salt until stiff but not dry, then add the yolks, one by one, and continue beating until they are well incorporated. Dip the tortilla "packages" into the beaten egg—they should be lightly but well coated—and fry until golden brown. Drain well, then put onto the serving platter, pour the heated sauce over, top with the avocado and cheese, and serve immediately.

NOTE: When the *indios* have been fried in the batter, they could be held on a baking sheet, with plenty of paper toweling underneath, in a 350°F (180°C) oven for about 2 minutes. The batter will become a little sodden, but then it does under the sauce anyway.

Do not freeze.

TOTOPOS Crisp-Fried Tortilla Pieces

Totopos, squares or strips of crisped corn tortillas, are used as a topping for soups, and even for chilaquiles in Michoacán, or added to scrambled eggs. Cut into larger triangles, they are used as scoops with guacamole or refried beans.

It is preferable to prepare your own totopos, since the commercially packaged ones, known as "fritos" in the United States, are too thin and highly seasoned. First, cut your corn tortillas into the required shapes and spread them onto a rack to dry out overnight—so they will absorb less oil in the frying process. Heat vegetable oil to the depth of about ½ inch (1.25 cm) in a smallish skillet and fry a small quantity of the totopos until crisp and a deep golden-brown in color. Drain well on paper toweling. They are best used immediately, but if you have leftovers, freeze them and reheat in a hot oven.

TAMALES

You may not be able to tell at first that tamales are being cooked except perhaps by the steamy windows—but later on a rich, subtle smell of corn husks, masa, and good lard, all intermingled, fills the house and gets stronger as the cooking nears completion. After their allotted time, you open one up to see if it is done. You heave a sigh of relief as a soft, spongy, white tamal rolls quite easily away from the husk. It could so easily have been heavy and damp. ✳ Tamales are made for an occasion, and an occasion is made of making them. Men, women, children, and servants all join in with good humor, shredding, chopping, stirring, and cleaning the husks until all is prepared. Then everyone converges to form a real assembly line, some daubing the husks with masa while others add the filling, fold, and stack into the steamer. And there is nothing quite as delicious as that first tamal, straight from the steamer. ✳ Tamales are fiesta food, Sunday supper food in popular restaurants, and early morning market food. They are prepared for graveside suppers on All Saints' Day. Many varieties of tamales were prepared in pre-Columbian times. And what an enormous variety there is today, from the smallest *norteño* to the yard-long *sacahuil* made in the Sierra Huasteca.

I had often read of this giant tamal yet I could find no one who had eaten it or seen it prepared until I went to Tampico. There I was told that it was the favorite breakfast fare in Pánuco, less than an hour away by road. "But you have to get there early," I was warned. I got up at the crack of dawn and braved hurricane winds and torrential rains to get to the bus station on time. After countless delays the bus was finally cruising along the highway at a maddeningly slow pace. When we arrived in Pánuco, no one was in sight and the air was hot and sultry as I made my way without success from one little *puesto* to another. I was just about to give up when a passerby enlightened me: "But *sacahuiles* are only made on Sunday. Anyway go and see Señorita Chanita, she makes the best ones," and she pointed the way to the house.

Señorita was a striking woman, tall, dark skinned, with gleaming white hair. After the usual polite greetings I came to the point: could she make a two-foot *sacahuil* for me early tomorrow, as I had a plane to catch. "But no one slaughters pigs on Friday," she demurred. She must have seen that I was on the verge of tears because she finally agreed to do it.

Back in Tampico I immediately started to negotiate for a car with a steady driver and good brakes. We did indeed leave early, but when we were halfway there the engine began to falter. The driver was optimistic, contrite, and silent in turn—I was furious. He coaxed the car to the edge of town, where it stopped dead. As I neared Chanita's house a savory smell wafted on the damp air and there she was, opening up her huge adobe oven in which the *sacahuil* had been cooking all night. She eased it out cautiously. The giant tamal thickly wrapped in layers of banana leaves was held taut within a framework of tough palm leaves. We opened it reverently and broke into the moist, textured dough of *maiz martajado* (roughly crushed) that encased a whole loin of pork seasoned with a paste of ancho chiles and spices. What a breakfast we made of it, accompanied by earthenware mugs of local coffee boiled with raw sugar and cinnamon.

Probably the most surprising members of the tamal family are the shrimp ones from Escuinapa in Sinaloa. Small shrimps in their shells are used, and their little spines and feelers stick out through the dough. Of course you have to know where to eat them or you will find yourself with a mouthful of spines and debris. In Sinaloa, too, they make large tamales like elongated bonbons. They are filled with the usual pork and tomato sauce, but added to it are all sorts of vegetables cut into little strips—zucchini, potatoes, green beans, plantains, and serrano chiles.

Chiapas seems to have more than its share of varieties. On the coast there are those of iguana meat and eggs, and inland around Tuxtla Gutiérrez there are countless varieties. I was told of at least ten kinds, of different herbs, beans, chicharrón (the crisp-fried pork), and those called *cuchunuc,* to which small pink flower buds are added. But probably the best known of all are the *tamales de bola,* with the corn husk tied on top making them round, as their name implies, and inside a rib of pork, a prune, and a small dried local chile called *simojovel.*

You will have to persevere to find the *tamales colados* in Campeche and Mérida. They are cooked in banana leaves, with a wonderfully savory filling seasoned with achiote and epazote. The tamal itself is made of tortilla dough that has been diluted in water, strained, and thickened over the fire; as one Campeche cookbook says, "the dough must be almost transparent and so delicate that it trembles at a touch." There are small tamales whose dough is studded with little beans called *espelón,* the skin of which turns black when cooked, and the completely pre-Columbian *dzotobichay,* which is a large tamal of masa flecked with cooked *chaya* (tastes rather like Swiss chard) and formed like a jelly roll, with a filling of well-toasted pumpkin seeds. It is then steamed in a banana leaf and served with a tomato sauce.

Michoacán, too, is famed for its tamales: the fresh corn *uchepos* and the *corundas*— *tamales* leavened with wood ash and wrapped in the long leaf of the corn stalk to form a fat, triangular shape. There are tamales of wild cherries *(capulines)* and those made of fermented dough of black corn. There are *uchepos de leche* or *cuchara*: fresh corn is finely ground with milk, the liquid strained and then cooked with sugar and cinnamon until thickened. Briefly blanched fresh corn husks are filled with the mixture and set aside to set firmly before eating.

Elsewhere there are tamales filled with fish, pumpkin, or pineapple and peanuts. Doughs vary too: there are those made of black and purple corn, ground rice, and pulque bread dough to name only a few.

When I first went to Uruapan, I would go very early in the mornings to the *portales* around the central plaza to eat tamales of wild blackberries and drink atole of fresh corn. And just when I decided that there could surely be no more types of tamales, a friend's cook produced some *del campo*—tortilla dough beaten with lard and sandwiched between avocado leaves. The steamer was lined with the leaves as well, giving off a delicious anisey aroma. We ate them with a dish of pork and zucchini cooked in green sauce.

There are a great variety of tamales, too, in Oaxaca, which has so many geographical and cultural areas. The best known of these perhaps are those with paper-thin masa filled with mole negro; simple but delicious ones filled with beans and hoja santa; masa flecked with wild green, called *chepil*; those from the Isthmus, made of masa flavored with epazote and filled with dried fish or shrimp; and those of the Pacific coast filled with a type of mussel, shell and all—to name but a few.

NORTHERN TAMALES

The two recipes for small, slim tamales that follow were given to me by the García Quintanilla family from Monterrey when they were talking to me nostalgically about the dishes their late mother used to prepare.

The *tamales de frijol* were always prepared for family gatherings and festive occasions; they were topped with finely shredded lettuce or cabbage and chopped tomatoes seasoned with lime juice and salt. Curiously they were made with imported pinto beans, which were much more commonly used in the north than those from central Mexico.

Señora Hortensia always beat the masa—not very long—by hand, but nowadays most cooks prefer to use a heavy-duty mixer. She put two crossed forks in the top of the steamer to support the tamales at a slight angle.

Traditionally these tamales, and many other types, were reheated in the husk on a comal over medium heat. The husk will become slightly charred.

TAMALES DE FRIJOL NORTEÑOS Northern Bean Tamales

SEÑORA HORTENSIA QUINTANILLA DE GARCÍA

MAKES ABOUT 33 4-INCH (10-CM) TAMALES   NUEVO LEÓN

THE BEAN FILLING AND CHILE SAUCE

8 OUNCES (225 G) FLOR DE MAYO OR PINTO BEANS

2 LARGE ANCHO CHILES, SEEDS AND VEINS REMOVED

2 GARLIC CLOVES

2 CUPS (500 ML) MEAT BROTH OR WATER

3/4 TEASPOON CUMIN SEEDS, CRUSHED

4 PEPPERCORNS, CRUSHED

3 TABLESPOONS PORK LARD

SALT TO TASTE

THE MASA

1 POUND (450 G) TAMALE DOUGH (ABOUT 2 CUPS/500 ML)

4 1/2 OUNCES (130 G) PORK LARD (1/2 CUP/125 ML, PLUS 2 TABLESPOONS)

3 TABLESPOONS RESERVED CHILE SAUCE

ABOUT 1/3 CUP (85 ML) MEAT BROTH OR WATER

SALT TO TASTE

ABOUT 36 HALVED CORN HUSKS—ABOUT 3 INCHES (8 CM) WIDE AT THE TOP, SOFTENED IN
  WATER, DRAINED, PATTED DRY

Have ready a tamale steamer (see page 460).

Pick through the beans to make sure there are no small stones. Rinse in cold water and skim the surface of any flotsam. Put the beans into a large saucepan or slow cooker, cover with fresh water, and bring to a boil. Cook until the beans are quite soft and most of the water has been absorbed—you should have about 4 cups (1 l).

Meanwhile, prepare the chile sauce. Put the chiles and garlic into a small saucepan, cover with water, bring to a simmer, and cook for about 5 minutes. Drain and set aside. Put 1/2 cup (125 ml) of the broth or water into the blender jar, add the cumin and peppercorns, and blend well. Tear the chile into pieces and add, with the garlic and another 1/2 cup (125 ml) of the broth or water, to the blender jar and blend to a fairly smooth sauce.

Heat the 3 tablespoons of lard in a deep skillet, add the beans, and mash over medium heat to a rough-textured consistency. Stir in all but 3 tablespoons of the chile sauce and salt to taste and continue cooking over medium heat, stirring from time to time to avoid sticking until reduced—the bean paste should just plop off the spoon—and well seasoned, about 15 minutes. Set aside to cool. You should have about 3½ cups (875 ml).

In a large bowl, mix the masa with the lard, the reserved 3 tablespoons chile sauce, and about ⅓ cup (85 ml) of the broth or water—with either your hand or an electric mixer—until all the ingredients are well incorporated. Add salt as necessary.

Line the top of the steamer with some of the corn husks and place an inverted soup plate in the middle. Set over medium heat.

Spread 1 rounded tablespoon of the dough very thinly over the entire width of the top of the corn husk and for about 4 inches (10 cm) down the husk. Place some of the bean paste down the center of the dough and fold one edge of the husk over the other to form a slender tamale—the overlapping masa will stick and help to close the husk more securely. Double the point of the husk up to cover the seam.

Stack the tamales in circular layers, the first layer supported at a gentle angle by the top of the plate. Cover the steamer and cook over high heat for about 50 minutes. The tamale is cooked when the dough separates cleanly from the husk.

TAMALES DE PUERCO NORTEÑOS Northern Pork-Filled Tamales

SEÑORA HORTENSIA QUINTANILLA DE GARCÍA

MAKES ABOUT 33 4-INCH (10-CM) TAMALES   NUEVO LEÓN

Traditionally, a whole pig's head was cooked, and the rind, ears, and tongue were all chopped and used, as well as some lean meat from the leg.

THE MEAT FILLING

1 POUND (450 G) STEWING PORK WITH SOME FAT, SEE NOTE ABOVE, CUT INTO ½-INCH (1.5-CM) CUBES

SALT TO TASTE

2 LARGE ANCHO CHILES, SEEDS AND VEINS REMOVED

2 GARLIC CLOVES

¾ TEASPOON CUMIN SEEDS, CRUSHED

4 PEPPERCORNS, CRUSHED

THE MASA

1 POUND (450 G) TAMALE DOUGH (ABOUT 2 CUPS/500 ML)
4 1/2 OUNCES (130 G) PORK LARD (1/2 CUP/125 ML, PLUS 2 TABLESPOONS)
3 TABLESPOONS OF RESERVED CHILE SAUCE
SALT TO TASTE

ABOUT 36 HALVED CORN HUSKS—ABOUT 3 INCHES (8 CM) WIDE AT THE TOP,
    SOFTENED IN WATER, DRAINED, PATTED DRY

Have ready a tamale steamer (see page 460). Put the meat into a large saucepan, cover with water, add salt, and bring to a simmer. Continue cooking until the meat is tender —35 to 40 minutes. Drain the meat and set aside. You will need at least 2 1/2 cups (625 ml) of broth; add water if necessary to make up to that amount.

Put the chiles and garlic into a small saucepan, cover with water, bring to a simmer, and cook for about 5 minutes. Strain and set aside.

Put 1/2 cup (125 ml) of the broth into the blender jar, add the cumin and peppercorns, and blend well. Tear the chiles into pieces and add to the blender jar along with the garlic and another 1/2 cup (125 ml) broth. Blend to a fairly smooth sauce.

Put the meat into a skillet, add all but 3 tablespoons of the sauce and 1 cup (250 ml) of the broth, and cook over medium heat, stirring from time to time, until well seasoned and the sauce is slightly reduced—to a medium consistency—about 15 minutes. Adjust salt and set aside to cool.

In a large bowl, mix the masa with the lard, the reserved 3 tablespoons of chile sauce, and about 1/3 cup (85 ml) of the remaining broth with your hand, or an electric mixer, until all the ingredients are well incorporated—about 5 minutes. Add salt as necessary.

Line the top of the steamer with some of the corn husks and place an inverted soup plate in the middle. Set over medium heat.

Spread 1 rounded tablespoon of the dough very thinly over the entire width of the top and for about 4 inches (10 cm) down the corn husk. Place a few pieces of the meat and some of the sauce down the center of the dough and fold one edge of the husk over the other to form a slender tamale—the overlapping masa will stick and help to close the leaf securely. Double the point of the husk up to cover the seam.

Stack the tamales in circular layers, the first layer supported at a gentle angle by the top of the plate. Cover the steamer and cook over high heat for about 50 minutes. The tamale is cooked when the dough separates cleanly from the husk.

MUK-BIL POLLO Yucatecan Chicken and Pork Tamale Pie
SERVES 6

This is a Yucatecan tamal pie, filled with a highly seasoned mixture of chicken and pork and cooked in a banana leaf. It is offered to the dead on All-Saints' Day, traditionally accompanied by a cup of hot chocolate. Muk-bil *literally means "to put in the ground," or to cook in a* pib.

John L. Stevens, in Incidents of Travel in Yucatán, *describes the feast of* todos los santos *in the middle of the nineteenth century in Yucatán:*

. . . and besides the usual ceremonies of the Catholic Church throughout the world, there is one peculiar to Yucatán, derived from the customs of the Indians and called Mukpipoyo. On this day every Indian, according to his means, purchases and burns a certain number of consecrated candles, in honor of his deceased relatives, and in memory of each member of his family who has died within the year. Besides this, they bake in the earth a pie consisting of a paste of Indian corn, stuffed with pork and fowls, and seasoned with chili, and during the day every good Yucateco eats nothing but this. In the interior, where the Indians are less civilised, they religiously place a portion of this composition out of doors, under a tree, or in some retired place, for their deceased friends to eat, and they say that the portion thus set apart is always eaten, which induces the belief that the dead may be enticed back by appealing to the same appetites which govern them when living; but this sometimes accounts for malicious and skeptical persons, who say that in every neighbourhood there are other Indians, poorer than those who can afford to regale their deceased relatives, and these consider it no sin, on a matter of this kind, to step between the living and the dead.

We have reason to remember this fete from one untoward circumstance. A friendly neighbour, who, besides visiting us frequently with his wife and daughter, was in the habit of sending us fruit and dulces more than we could eat, this day, on top of a large undisposed-of present, sent us a huge piece of mukbipoyo. It was as hard as an oak plank, and as thick as six of them; and having already over-tasked ourselves to reduce the pile on the tables, when this came, in a fit of desperation we took it out into the courtyard and buried it. There it would have remained until this day but for a malicious dog which accompanied them on their next visit; he passed into the courtyard, rooted it up, and, while we were pointing to the empty platters as our acknowledgment of their kindness, this villainous dog sneaked through the sala and out at the front door with the pie in his mouth, apparently grown bigger since it was buried.

The dish is still cooked in the villages in pibs *and comes out with a golden, crisp top and a faintly smoky flavor. Very often the chicken will just be jointed, but it makes it a great deal easier to serve if the bones are removed.*

As you can imagine, it is a very solid dish, and needs perhaps just a green salad with it.

THE FAT FOR THE DOUGH

8 OUNCES (225 G) PORK FAT, CUT INTO SMALL CUBES

THE FILLING

A 3-POUND (1.35-KG) CHICKEN

8 OUNCES (225 G) PORK SHOULDER

4 GARLIC CLOVES, TOASTED (SEE PAGE 492)

$^1/_4$ TEASPOON DRIED MEXICAN OREGANO, YUCATECAN IF POSSIBLE

1 $^1/_2$ TEASPOONS SALT

1 $^1/_2$ CUPS (375 ML) RESERVED MEAT BROTH

2 TABLESPOONS TORTILLA MASA

$^1/_4$ TEASPOON PEPPERCORNS

1 TABLESPOON ACHIOTE SEEDS

SALT TO TASTE

2 GARLIC CLOVES, CRUSHED

1 TABLESPOON MILD WHITE VINEGAR

3 TABLESPOONS OF THE RENDERED PORK FAT

$^1/_3$ CUP (85 ML) FINELY CHOPPED WHITE ONION

1 HABANERO CHILE, WHOLE

$^1/_2$ MEDIUM GREEN PEPPER, SEEDED AND DICED

1 LARGE SPRIG EPAZOTE

8 OUNCES (225 G) TOMATOES, FINELY CHOPPED (ABOUT 1 $^1/_3$ CUPS/333 ML)

THE DOUGH

2 POUNDS (900 G) TORTILLA DOUGH (ABOUT 4 CUPS/1 L)

2 TEASPOONS SALT

$^1/_4$ TEASPOON YUCATECAN CHILE SECO OR HOT PAPRIKA (SEE PAGE 480)

BANANA LEAVES TO LINE THE PAN (SEE PAGE 462)

Lay two pieces of string—each 30 inches (76 cm) long—parallel across the length of a metal baking pan about 8 by 8 by 2½ inches (20 by 20 by 6.5 cm) and two other pieces of string of the same length across the width—there will be a large overlap for tying.

Quickly pass the banana leaves over a flame to make them more pliable, and line the dish with them, smooth, shiny side up, so that they overlap the pan by about 5 inches (13 cm) all the way around. Cut one leaf slightly bigger than the size of the pan.

Heat the fat in a skillet over medium heat, or in the oven, until the lard renders out of it. Turn the pieces from time to time so that they do not burn but become evenly crisp and brown. Spoon out 3 tablespoons fat for frying the filling and reserve the rest for the dough.

Cut the chicken into serving pieces and the pork into 1-inch (2.5-cm) cubes. Put them into a pan with the garlic, oregano, and salt and barely cover with water. Bring up to a simmer and cook over low heat until the meat is just tender—the chicken should take about 30 minutes; the pork a little longer.

Strain the meat, reserving the broth. Remove the bones from the chicken. Set the meat aside. Return the broth to a clean pan.

Stir the masa gradually into the broth. Bring to a boil, lower the heat, and stir the mixture until it thickens a little. Set the thickened broth aside.

Grind the peppercorns, achiote, and salt and mix with the crushed garlic and vinegar.

Heat the 3 tablespoons of rendered fat in a large pan and fry the onion, chile, green pepper, epazote, and tomatoes until soft and still slightly juicy—about 8 minutes.

Add the ground seasoning and continue cooking the mixture for about 3 minutes.

Add the cooked meats and continue cooking the mixture for 5 minutes over medium heat. Set aside.

Preheat the oven to 350°F (180°C).

To the dough add the salt, *chile seco* or paprika, and remaining rendered fat and browned pieces and mix thoroughly.

Press about two thirds of the dough into the prepared baking pan to form a crust about ¼ inch (1 cm) thick on the bottom and sides of the pan. Add the filling and pour the thickened broth over it.

Press the remaining dough onto the smooth, shiny side of the reserved banana leaf. This will be the cover for the pie. Carefully turn the leaf upside down so that the dough completely covers the pan, with enough of an overlap to seal the pie together with the dough around the sides of the pan.

Fold the leaves over the top of the pie and tie them down firmly with the string.

Bake the *Muk-Bil Pollo* for 1½ hours and serve it immediately.

NOTE: If you can time it so that you serve it hot, straight out of the oven, it is well worthwhile. However, if you have to reheat it, then put it into the oven in a water bath to keep the dough soft. Any leftovers can be frozen well. To reheat, put it frozen into a water bath in a 350°F (180°C) oven.

UCHEPOS Michoacán Fresh Corn Tamales

SEÑORA ESQUIVEL

MAKES 20 UCHEPOS

MICHOACÁN

The uchepo *is a small tamal of fresh corn, a specialty of central Michoacán. Many people just grind the corn, add sugar, salt, and sometimes baking powder or soda, and fill the fresh corn husks, ready to steam like any other tamales. However, the most delicate and delicious uchepos I have ever tasted are made by Señora Esquivel for her restaurant Los Comensales, in Morelia. She grinds the corn twice through the corn grinder — she insists that a blender makes the puree too frothy — and then beats in milk,* natas *(clotted cream, from milk that has been scalded), sugar, and salt. She serves them as a first course or supper dish with some tomato sauce, thick cream, and slices of queso fresco.*

For this recipe, and any fresh corn tamales, you will need to look for juicy but mature field corn. Sweet corn does not have the necessary starch and you can use it only with the addition of a "filler" like corn starch, although it will not have such a good texture or flavor.

A food processor is ideal for this recipe, but you can also use a blender: grind the corn in several small batches and let the froth subside a little before stirring in the rest of the ingredients. Select six ears with the husks still wrapped around them. Using a very sharp knife, carefully cut around the base of the husks just above the spot where they are attached to the stalk. Carefully unfurl the husks, rinse them well in cold water, and shake them dry (or spin in a salad spinner) and set aside.

Line the top part of the steamer with the toughest outside husks and set the rest aside for covering the uchepos.

Shave the kernels off the cobs; this should yield about 5 cups (1.25 l).

Serve the uchepos *as suggested above with Salsa Ranchera (see page 238), omitting the onion, cream, and queso fresco, or with the pork dish (see page 276).*

5 CUPS (1.25 L) WHITE STARCHY FIELD CORN KERNELS

¼ CUP (65 ML) MILK

2 TABLESPOONS SUGAR

2 TABLESPOONS UNSALTED BUTTER

2 TABLESPOONS NATAS, OR CRÈME FRAÎCHE OR THICK CREAM

I ROUNDED TEASPOON SALT

ABOUT 20 FRESH CORN HUSKS

Put half of the corn into the bowl of a food processor, add the milk, and process until the corn has been reduced to a textured consistency—about 1½ minutes. Add the remaining corn and continue grinding until you have a finely textured puree—about 2½ minutes more. Add the rest of the ingredients except the husks and mix well.

Shake the husks once again to get rid of any surplus water. Place 1 heaped tablespoon of the mixture down the center of the husk, starting just below the cupped top and extending about 2 inches (5 cm) down the husk. Taking care not to flatten the mixture, or let it ooze out, roll, rather than fold, the husk over so that it overlaps the other side completely.

Fold the point end up to the back of the *uchepo* and immediately place it horizontally in the top of the steamer. (Because of the loose consistency of the mixture they have to be cooked immediately and cannot sit around while you finish making them.)

To ensure that the bottom layer will not be squashed flat, steam for about 10 minutes before you add the rest. Remember to stir the mixture well before you continue with the subsequent layers. Steam for about 1¼ hours and then test. The *uchepos* should barely separate from the husk. Set the *uchepos* aside to firm up for about 2 hours before using.

NOTE: Uchepos freeze very successfully and can be kept for about 2 months. When reheating, put them, still frozen, into a hot steamer until soft—about 15 minutes.

TAMALES DULCES DE ELOTE Sweet Fresh Corn Tamales

SEÑORA ISABEL MARÍN DE PAALEN

MAKES ABOUT 24 TAMALES

JALISCO

I had my first lesson on fresh corn tamales from my friend Chabela Marín from Jalisco. One morning we set out promptly at five and drove down to the big wholesale market in Jamaica (a part of Mexico City). For one square block there was nothing but mounds and mounds of fresh corn, and it was still coming in from the countryside around. It took at least an hour to choose twenty-five ears of just-right cacahuazintle corn, going from one pile to another and choosing one here and one there to meet Chabela's very high standards.

Once home again, she told me how to cut the cob at exactly the right spot to unravel the leaves without tearing them, to shave the kernels off as near to the core as possible, and to grind them to just the right texture on the metate. We then ground piloncillo (cones of raw

*sugar) with anise seeds and cinnamon, and gently melted the butter and lard so that it did
not overheat. The most difficult part was filling the fresh husks and folding them in just the
right way to hold the loose, pasty dough firmly in place. It seemed like an endless process, but
finally the tamales were cooking and that wonderful smell of fresh corn mixed with spices was
filling the apartment.*

*I am afraid we'll have to start a movement to have more starchy, not-so-sweet corn avail-
able, but if you can get white field corn, do make these delicious tamales.*

30 (TO BE SAFE) FRESH CORN HUSKS, RINSED AND SHAKEN DRY

4 CUPS (1 L) FIELD OR WHITE STARCHY CORN KERNELS

ABOUT ½ CUP (125 ML) WATER

1 SCANT TABLESPOON ANISEED

8-INCH (20-CM) PIECE OF CINNAMON STICK

1 CUP (250 ML) GRATED PILONCILLO OR DARK BROWN SUGAR

¼ TEASPOON SALT

4 OUNCES (115 G) UNSALTED BUTTER (½ CUP/125 ML), MELTED AND COOLED

4 OUNCES (115 G) PORK LARD (½ CUP/125 ML), MELTED AND COOLED

½ TEASPOON BAKING POWDER

Prepare a tamale steamer or an improvised one (see page 460) and line the top part
with fresh corn husks.

Using a food processor or blender, blend the corn with the water, in two batches,
to a rough-textured consistency—you will have to keep stopping the machine and loos-
ening the mixture with a spatula, but do not add more liquid.

Grind the spices to a powder and add with the sugar and salt to the corn, mixing
thoroughly. Gradually stir in the fats and lastly the baking powder. Again mix thoroughly. The consistency should be that of a loose, textured paste.

Put about 1½ tablespoons of the corn mixture down the center of each husk to
extend about 3 inches (8 cm) long. Curl one side of the leaf over the mixture, making
sure there is a good overlap and the mixture cannot ooze out. Press the leaf firmly where
the mixture ends and fold the empty part, and pointed end, to the back of the tamale.

Make sure that the water is boiling in the steamer, then lay the tamales in horizontal layers in the top of the steamer. It is best to put one layer in first and let it firm up a
little—about 10 minutes—before stacking the other layers on top. Steam for about 1½
hours until, when tested, the dough separates cleanly from the husk.

Eat accompanied by a cup of atole or hot chocolate. Reheat this type of tamale, with the husk removed, on a comal or griddle over medium heat.

N O T E : Freeze any leftovers. To reheat, steam for about 15 minutes, or heat through in their husks on an ungreased comal.

TAMALES DE POLLO Chicken Tamales

ADRIANA JEFFRIES

MAKES ABOUT 30 3-INCH (8-CM) TAMALES

MEXICO CITY

I was shown how to make these tamales many years ago by a Mexican acquaintance and excellent cook, Adriana Jeffries.

THE FILLING

ONE 3 ½-POUND (1.575-KG) CHICKEN CUT INTO SERVING PIECES

THE CHICKEN GIBLETS

ABOUT 6 CUPS (1.5 L) WELL-SEASONED CHICKEN BROTH TO COVER

THE SAUCE

1 ½ POUNDS (680 G) TOMATOES, BROILED (SEE PAGE 490)

1 LARGE GARLIC CLOVE, ROUGHLY CHOPPED

¼ TEASPOON CUMIN SEEDS, CRUSHED

4 WHOLE CLOVES, CRUSHED

6 PEPPERCORNS, CRUSHED

3 TABLESPOONS VEGETABLE OIL OR MELTED CHICKEN FAT

1 CUP (250 ML) THINLY SLICED WHITE ONION

SALT TO TASTE

THE MASA

8 OUNCES (225 G) PORK LARD

1 ½ POUNDS (675 G) TAMALE DOUGH

ABOUT ½ CUP (125 ML) OF THE RESERVED CHICKEN BROTH, WARM

SALT TO TASTE

TO ASSEMBLE THE TAMALES

30 CORN HUSKS, SOAKED TO SOFTEN AND SHAKEN DRY

30 STRIPS OF FRESH JALAPEÑOS

30 PITTED GREEN OLIVES

MAKE THE FILLING: Put the chicken, giblets, and broth into a large saucepan, bring to a simmer, and continue cooking over low heat until almost tender—about 30 minutes. Remove the chicken and set aside to cool. Strain the broth. There should be at least 3 cups (750 ml). Shred the chicken roughly.

MAKE THE SAUCE: Put a few of the tomatoes into a blender jar with the garlic and spices and blend thoroughly. Add the rest of the tomatoes and blend to a textured sauce.

Heat the oil in a large skillet, add the onion, and fry over medium heat until translucent—about 3 minutes. Add the blended ingredients and cook over fairly high heat until reduced and seasoned—about 5 minutes. Stir in the chicken pieces, adjust salt, and set aside to season.

Using an electric mixer, beat the lard about 5 minutes until well aerated—it will become very white and opaque. Gradually beat in the masa alternately with the warm broth, add salt, and beat again for about 5 minutes or until a small ball of the mixture floats on the surface of a glass of water.

ASSEMBLING THE TAMALES: Spread a large tablespoon of the dough thinly over the inside of a corn husk. Put some of the sauced chicken down the middle with a strip of the chile and an olive. Fold the husk so that the masa is completely covered and turn the pointed end up to the back of the tamale—this will tighten up the seam.

Stack the tamales vertically in the top of a tamale steamer (see page 460) and steam for about 1 hour, then test. If the dough separates easily from the husk the tamale is cooked sufficiently.

NOTE: These tamales freeze very successfully and can be kept for about three months in the freezer. To reheat, place still frozen into the hot steamer and steam until well heated through, 15 to 20 minutes.

TAMALES DE DULCE Sweet Tamales

ADRIANA JEFFRIES

MAKES ABOUT 24 3-INCH (8-CM) TAMALES   MEXICO CITY

This recipe is another from the family of Adriana Jeffries.

Sweet tamales are very popular in Mexico for breakfast or supper with a cup of hot chocolate or atole. They are usually reheated from the day before, in their husks, on an ungreased comal or griddle.

7 OUNCES (200 G) PORK LARD

1 ¼ POUNDS (570 G) TAMALE DOUGH (ABOUT 2 ½ CUPS/625 ML)

⅓ CUP (85 ML) CHICKEN BROTH OR WATER

½ TEASPOON SALT

1 TABLESPOON CINNAMON

½ CUP (125 ML) SUGAR

⅔ CUP (165 ML) ROUGHLY CHOPPED PECANS

ABOUT 24 CORN HUSKS (ALWAYS DO A FEW EXTRA) SOAKED TO SOFTEN AND SHAKEN DRY

¾ CUP (185 ML) RAISINS

Put a prepared tamale steamer (see page 460) over low heat.

Put the lard into a bowl and beat with an electric beater until the lard is very white and opaque—about 5 minutes. Gradually beat in the masa, broth, and salt, beating well after each addition. Continue beating for another 5 minutes, gradually adding the cinnamon and sugar. Stir in the chopped pecans.

Spread a thin layer of the dough over the inside of the husk and put a teaspoon of raisins down the middle of the dough. Fold the husk over so that it covers the dough and turn the pointed end up to the back of the tamale.

When the water is boiling stack the tamales vertically in the top part, cover, and steam about 1 hour or until the pale pink dough comes cleanly away from the husk.

NOTE: For a variation use ¼ cup (65 ml) sugar, 2 tablespoons grenadine syrup, ⅔ cup (165 ml) raisins, ½ cup (125 ml) diced acitron (candied biznaga cactus) or other candied fruit, and ½ cup (125 ml) pine nuts or blanched and slivered almonds.

TAMALES CERNIDOS DE RAJAS Y QUESO

Spongy Tamales Filled with Chile Strips and Cheese

MAKES ABOUT 30 3-INCH (8-CM) TAMALES   CENTRAL MEXICO

The curious name of these tamales, literally "sifted tamales," comes from the sifting of the specially prepared, textured flour made from the broad, white corn kernels that are also used for pozole, cacahuazintle, or maiz pozolero.

The masa is generally whiter and more spongy than that of tamales made of corn masa. In fact these were the first tamales I ever knew in Mexico City and I have certainly never found any like them in southern Mexico. This harina para tamales is not easy to find outside of Mexico City, and perhaps the Bajío, the center-north, but you could make your own (see

The Art of Mexican Cooking, page 59) or substitute a tamale dough that is fairly dry—you will need about 1½ pounds (675 g). The lard should be reduced to 6 ounces (180 g) and the broth to about ½ cup (125 ml).

Another popular filling is mole poblano with shredded, poached chicken, or pork in a tomato sauce. These tamales can also be ciegos, *or blind, just masa without a filling, to be served with a mole.*

THE MASA

8 OUNCES (225 G) PORK LARD (ABOUT 1 CUP/250 ML)
1 POUND (450 G) TAMALE FLOUR
ABOUT 1 CUP (250 ML) WARM CHICKEN BROTH
SALT TO TASTE

36 (TO BE SAFE) CORN HUSKS, SOAKED TO SOFTEN AND SHAKEN DRY

THE FILLING

2 CUPS (500 ML) RAJAS OF POBLANO CHILES (SEE PAGE 469), ABOUT 8 CHILES
12 OUNCES (340 G) CHIHUAHUA, MEXICAN MANCHEGO, OR MUENSTER CHEESE, CUT INTO
    STRIPS ABOUT ½ INCH (1.5 CM) WIDE
2 CUPS (500 ML) SALSA DE TOMATE VERDE (PAGE 236)

Using an electric mixer, beat the lard until light and fluffy—about 5 minutes. Gradually beat in the flour alternately with the broth, beating thoroughly after each addition. Add salt. If beaten sufficiently, a small piece of dough should float on the surface of a glass of water.

Put a prepared tamale steamer (see page 460) over low heat.

Spread 1 heaped tablespoon of the masa thinly over the upper part, and about 3 inches (8 cm) down the leaf. Place 2 strips of the chile, a strip of the cheese, and a tablespoon of the sauce over them. Fold the husk so that the filling is mostly covered by the masa and turn the spare part of the husk up the back of the tamale.

Set the tamales vertically in the top part of the steamer, cover well, and steam for about 1¼ hours. To test, open up a tamale; the masa should separate cleanly from the husk. Leave the tamales in the steamer until they have cooled; they will become a little firmer and less likely to break as you serve them.

Any leftovers can be frozen successfully. See note on storing and reheating on page 109.

TAMALES TIPO RANCHEROS VERACRUZANOS

Veracruz Ranch Tamales

SEÑORA ROSITA DE GONZÁLEZ

MAKES ABOUT 20 TAMALES

VERACRUZ

These tamales are also known as rancheros. *Some cooks insist that the meat be put raw into the tamales, some say the masa should be cooked first and be much thicker. And so the discussion goes on. I have perhaps unwittingly made these tamales more delicate than they should be, given their rustic origin, but they are delicious.*

THE MEAT FOR THE FILLING

1 POUND (450 G) PORK SHOULDER WITH SOME FAT, CUT INTO ¼-INCH (.75-CM) CUBES

¼ WHITE ONION, ROUGHLY CHOPPED

1 GARLIC CLOVE

SALT TO TASTE

THE SAUCE FOR THE FILLING

4 ANCHO CHILES, SEEDS AND VEINS REMOVED

1 CHIPOTLE CHILE, DRIED OR CANNED

1 CUP (250 ML) RESERVED PORK BROTH

1 TABLESPOON ROUGHLY CHOPPED WHITE ONION

1 GARLIC CLOVE, ROUGHLY CHOPPED

6 OUNCES (180 G) TOMATOES, BROILED (SEE PAGE 490)

1 ½ TABLESPOONS PORK LARD OR VEGETABLE OIL

SALT TO TASTE

THE MASA

5 OUNCES (140 G) PORK LARD (ABOUT 1 HEAPED CUP/265 ML)

ABOUT ½ CUP (125 ML) OF THE RESERVED BROTH, WARM

1 ¼ POUNDS (565 G) TAMALE DOUGH (ABOUT 2 ½ CUPS/625 ML)

SALT TO TASTE

ASSEMBLING THE TAMALES

5 LARGE HOJA SANTA LEAVES, CUT INTO QUARTERS

20 PIECES OF BANANA LEAVES, ABOUT 9 BY 7 INCHES (23 BY 18 CM) (SEE PAGE 462)

Put the pork, onion, garlic, and salt into a large saucepan. Barely cover with water and bring to a boil. Lower the heat and simmer the pork for about 35 minutes. Allow the pork to cool off in the broth, then strain the meat, reserving the broth, and set both aside. There should be about 2 cups (500 ml) of broth; if not, make up to that amount with water.

Heat the comal and toast the chiles lightly, turning them from time to time so they do not burn.

Cover the chiles with hot water and let them soak for about 10 minutes, then remove with a slotted spoon and put into a blender jar. Add $^{1}/_{2}$ cup of broth, the onion, garlic, and tomatoes and blend to a smooth sauce.

Heat the lard in a large skillet, add the chile sauce, and cook for about 5 minutes, stirring from time to time to avoid sticking. Add salt to taste.

Add the pork and $^{1}/_{2}$ cup of broth to the sauce and let the mixture cook for about 5 minutes over medium heat until it is all well seasoned and the liquid has reduced a little. Add salt to taste. Set aside.

To prepare the dough, beat the lard until white and well aerated—about 5 minutes.

Beat the remaining broth and dough alternately into the lard, adding the salt. Continue beating for about 5 minutes more. (Don't try to float a piece of the dough; it will be a much softer and damper consistency than that for ordinary tamales.)

Pass the leaves over a bare flame to make them a little more flexible. Spread 1 large tablespoon of the dough over an area about 4 by 3 inches (10 by 8 cm) and $^{1}/_{4}$ inch (.75 cm) thick. Put two cubes of the meat and a little of the sauce into the center of the dough and cover with a piece of the hoja santa. Fold the edges of the banana leaf over until they completely cover the dough and filling. Stack the tamales horizontally in overlapping layers in the top of the steamer. Cover them with more leaves and then cover the top of the steamer with a thick cloth or piece of toweling and the steamer lid. Steam in the normal way for 1 hour.

NOTE: These tamales freeze extremely well. To reheat, put them still frozen into a very hot shallow steamer for about 15 minutes.

SOUPS

Sopa de Tortilla ✳ *Tortilla Soup*

Sopa de Bolitas de Tortillas ✳ *Tortilla Ball Soup*

Caldo de Habas ✳ *Dried Fava Bean Soup*

Sopa de Pan ✳ *Bread Soup*

Sopa de Fideo Aguada ✳ *Angel Hair Pasta in Tomato Broth*

Sopa de Lentejas Estilo Querétaro ✳ *Lentil Soup*

Sopa de Puerros ✳ *Leek Soup*

Sopa Verde de Elote ✳ *Green Corn Soup*

Sopa de Elote ✳ *Fresh Corn Soup*

Sopa de Elote y Rajas ✳ *Fresh Corn and Poblano Soup*

Crema de Flor de Calabaza ✳ *Cream of Squash Flower Soup*

Sopa de Aguacate ✳ *Avocado Soup*

Sopa de Ajo y Migas ✳ *Garlic and Bread Soup*

Caldo Tlalpeño ✳ *Chicken and Vegetable Broth*

Sopa Tarasca Tipo Conde ✳ *Tarascan Bean and Tortilla Soup*

Sopa de Lima ✳ *Sour "Lima" Soup*

Caldo de Queso Sonorense ✳ *Cheese Broth*

Consomé de Camarón Seco ✳ *Dried Shrimp Consommé*

Caldo Michi ✳ *Fish Soup*

Caldo de Piedra ✳ *Broth of "Stones"*

Summing up all my "soup experiences" through many years of travel, I firmly believe that no country's cooks can rival those of Mexico when it comes to soup making. Whether it is a traditional soup made in a specific way with specific ingredients or one thrown together with whatever is around, they win hands down.

The following recipes, and those in my other books, provide just a small sample of the hundreds of regional soups that play so important a part in the Mexican meal.

SOPA DE TORTILLA Tortilla Soup
SERVES 6   CENTRAL MEXICO

When I first came to Mexico City in 1957, Sopa de Tortilla was by far the most popular. It was quite simple but delicious, with the distinctive tastes of epazote and good corn tortillas (before commercial tortillas took a downhill tumble). Dried chiles were cheaper then and a whole pasilla, inflated with frying, was placed across the surface of the soup bowl. Through the years this soup has acquired many embellishments, depending on each cook's fancy.

VEGETABLE OIL FOR FRYING

12 SMALL TORTILLAS, CUT INTO STRIPS AND DRIED

12 OUNCES (340 G) TOMATOES, BROILED (SEE PAGE 490)

¼ CUP (65 ML) ROUGHLY CHOPPED WHITE ONION

1 GARLIC CLOVE

6 CUPS (1.5 L) CALDO DE POLLO (SEE PAGE 499)

2 LARGE SPRIGS EPAZOTE

3 PASILLA CHILES, FRIED CRISP AND CRUMBLED

6 HEAPED TABLESPOONS GRATED CHIHUAHUA CHEESE OR MUENSTER

Heat the oil in a large skillet and fry the tortilla strips until they are lightly browned but not too crisp. Drain them on paper toweling. Pour off all but 1 tablespoon of the oil.

Blend the tomatoes, onion, and garlic to a smooth sauce, then add to the oil and fry for about 5 minutes, until the sauce is well seasoned and has reduced somewhat.

Add the sauce to the Caldo de Pollo and bring to a boil. Adjust seasoning. Add the tortilla strips and cook them for about 3 minutes.

Just before serving, add the epazote. Cook for 1 minute more.

Serve each portion topped with pieces of crumbled chile and grated cheese.

NOTE: The base could be prepared (and even stored frozen) hours ahead but the final steps, adding tortillas and epazote, should be done a few minutes before serving.

SOPA DE BOLITAS DE TORTILLAS Tortilla Ball Soup
SERVES 6

The temptation, I think, might be to compare these with matzo balls, which can be deliciously light and delicate. These are much more solid, but they have a nice grainy texture and a gentle corn flavor. It is a popular "family" soup in Central and Northern Mexico.

THE SOUP

12 STALE TORTILLAS, DRIED
½ CUP (125 ML) HOT WHOLE MILK
½ CUP (125 ML) FINELY GRATED QUESO AÑEJO (ABOUT 1 ½ OUNCES/45 G)
1 LARGE EGG, WELL BEATEN
SEA SALT TO TASTE
APPROXIMATELY ¼ CUP (65 ML) WHOLE MILK, COLD
MELTED LARD OR VEGETABLE OIL FOR FRYING
6 CUPS (1.5 L) TOMATO-CHICKEN BROTH (SEE RECIPE FOR SOPA DE TORTILLA, PAGE 116)

TO SERVE

⅓ CUP (85 ML) PREPARED SOUR CREAM (SEE PAGE 489)
FINELY CHOPPED FRESH CILANTRO OR PARSLEY

Break the tortillas into small pieces and blend until they are like fine bread crumbs; this amount will make about 1 cup (250 ml). Add the hot milk, cheese, egg, and salt and knead the dough well, then set it aside for several hours or refrigerate it overnight, to allow the tortilla particles to soften.

Again knead the dough well, adding the cold milk. Roll the dough evenly into one long piece; divide this into 12 pieces, and each piece in half again. Roll the 24 pieces into small balls about 1 inch (2.5 cm) in diameter.

Heat the lard in a skillet and fry the balls *very gently*, turning them from time to time until they are a golden brown—about 5 minutes. Drain well. Put the balls into the heated broth, bring to a boil, then reduce the heat and simmer for about 2 minutes.

Serve in individual bowls—four balls per serving—and top each with a spoonful of the cream and some chopped cilantro.

CALDO DE HABAS Dried Fava Bean Soup

SEÑORA MARÍA ELENA LARA

SERVES 6   HIDALGO

This is quite the most delicious version of dried fava bean soup that I have ever eaten. Even those who say they can't stand cilantro will eat it in this soup—providing you don't let on. Actually, this is a Lenten dish in Mexico, and a friend of mine there was almost shocked when I served it to her on a cool, rainy summer day.

Cooking time varies enormously, depending, of course, on the age of the beans and their density, which varies between those grown in the United States and those grown in Mexico. Be sure to buy the peeled pale yellow beans. There are some brown unpeeled ones on the market that take forever to cook—and then you have the messy business of removing the skins.

8 OUNCES (225 G) DRIED, PEELED YELLOW FAVA BEANS (ABOUT 1 ½ CUPS/375 ML)
2 TABLESPOONS VEGETABLE OIL
⅔ CUP (165 ML) ROUGHLY CHOPPED WHITE ONION
2 GARLIC CLOVES, ROUGHLY CHOPPED
ABOUT 8 OUNCES (225 G) TOMATOES, FINELY CHOPPED (1 ⅓ CUPS/333 ML)
ABOUT 10 CUPS (2.5 L) HOT WATER
10 SPRIGS FRESH CILANTRO, ROUGHLY CHOPPED
2 TEASPOONS SALT, OR TO TASTE

TO SERVE
6 TABLESPOONS FRUITY OLIVE OIL
2 PASILLA CHILES, FRIED AND CRUMBLED (SEE PAGE 475)

Rinse the beans well, picking out any loose pieces of skin or fiber.

Heat the oil in a heavy-bottomed pot and fry the beans, together with the onion and garlic, until they are lightly browned and the onion and garlic are translucent. Add the tomatoes and fry over high heat, stirring constantly, until the mixture is almost dry— about 3 minutes. Add the water, cilantro, and salt and let the soup cook over low heat until the beans are mushy and almost disintegrated—about 3½ hours (see note above).

Serve each bowl with a tablespoon of the olive oil and some crumbled pasilla chile on top.

NOTE: This soup can be prepared several hours or even a day ahead, but since it will thicken up considerably, it will have to be diluted with water or chicken broth. The soup freezes successfully.

SOPA DE PAN Bread Soup
SEÑORA MARÍA, CASA BLOM, SAN CRISTOBAL DE LAS CASAS
SERVES 6   CHIAPAS

There are many versions of this recipe among the old families of Spanish origin in different regions of Mexico. In Chiapas it is always prepared for fiestas, and was probably a Lenten dish until the chicken broth crept in.

I like to use a sourdough bread, which has a tougher crumb than most white breads so that it will not absorb too much fat when frying.

4 CUPS (1 L) STALE BREAD CUBES, PREFERABLY SOURDOUGH

½ CUP (125 ML) VEGETABLE OIL, MORE IF NECESSARY

4 OUNCES (115 G) UNSALTED BUTTER (ABOUT 1 CUP/250 ML)

6 CUPS (1.5 L) CHICKEN BROTH

4 OUNCES (115 G) GREEN BEANS, TRIMMED AND CUT INTO THIRDS

4 OUNCES (115 G) CARROTS, SCRAPED AND THINLY SLICED (ABOUT 1 CUP/250 ML)

6 SPRIGS FRESH THYME OR ¼ TEASPOON DRIED

SALT TO TASTE

2-INCH (5-CM) PIECE OF CINNAMON STICK

2 WHOLE CLOVES

10 PEPPERCORNS

2 WHOLE ALLSPICE

LARGE PINCH OF SAFFRON

8 OUNCES (225 G) POTATOES, PEELED AND CUT INTO ½-INCH (1.5-CM) SLICES (ABOUT
   1 ¼ CUPS/315 G)
2 MEDIUM PLANTAINS (ABOUT 1 POUND/450 G), PEELED, QUARTERED, AND CUT INTO
   3-INCH (8-CM) LENGTHS
1 POUND (450 G) TOMATOES, THICKLY SLICED
1 CUP (250 ML) THINLY SLICED WHITE ONION
2 GARLIC CLOVES, THINLY SLICED
4 HARD-COOKED EGGS, SLICED

Preheat the oven to 300°F (150°C).

Place the bread cubes on a baking sheet in one layer and bake until they are crisp on the outside but not dried all the way through—20 to 30 minutes.

Heat some of the oil in a large skillet and melt a portion of the butter in it. Fry the bread cubes lightly until golden brown, adding more oil and butter as necessary (if you add it all at once, the bread cubes will absorb it and become soggy). Drain and set aside, reserving the oil in the pan.

Heat the chicken broth, and when it comes to a boil, add the beans and carrots and simmer until just tender—10 to 15 minutes. Drain the vegetables and set aside. Add the thyme, salt, and spices to the broth and simmer for about 10 minutes. Strain and reserve the broth—there should be about 5 cups (1.25 l).

Reheat the oil in which the bread was fried, adding about ½ cup (125 ml) more as necessary, and fry the sliced potatoes on both sides until well browned; remove and drain. In the same oil, fry the plantain slices until golden brown; remove and drain. Fry the sliced tomatoes, onion, and garlic together until soft, then remove and set aside.

Preheat the oven to 350°F (180°C). Grease an ovenproof dish, ideally 8½ by 13½ by 2 inches (21.5 by 34 by 5 cm). Spread alternate layers of the vegetables and the tomato mixture in the dish. Cover with the bread cubes and top with the slices of egg. Pour the broth over and bake for about 15 minutes.

Serve immediately in deep bowls.

NOTE: The components of this dish can be prepared ahead and assembled just before putting in the oven. The soup does not freeze.

SOPA DE FIDEO AGUADA Angel Hair Pasta in Tomato Broth
SERVES 6   CENTRAL MEXICO

This soup is Mexican soul food and turns up predictably several days a week on the Mexican dinner table; it is both economical and easy to prepare. Because it is so popular and I am asked constantly for a recipe, I have included it. But it's not one of my own favorites.

The soup thickens considerably as it stands, so it may have to be thinned down with more stock if you make it ahead.

3 TO 4 TABLESPOONS CHICKEN FAT OR VEGETABLE OIL
4 OUNCES (115 G) ANGEL HAIR PASTA
12 OUNCES (340 G) VERY RIPE TOMATOES, ROUGHLY CHOPPED (2⅓ CUPS/585 ML)
1 GARLIC CLOVE, ROUGHLY CHOPPED
¼ CUP (65 ML) ROUGHLY CHOPPED WHITE ONION
7 CUPS (1.75 L) LIGHT CHICKEN BROTH
2 SPRIGS FLAT-LEAF PARSLEY

Heat the fat in a large skillet and add the whole bundles of pasta without breaking them up. Fry until the pasta is a deep golden brown, stirring all the time and taking care not to burn. Drain off all but about 2 tablespoons of fat in the pan.

Blend the tomatoes with the garlic and onion until smooth. Add to the fried pasta and continue cooking over very high heat about 4 minutes, stirring and scraping the bottom of the pan, until the mixture is almost dry. Add the broth and the parsley and bring to a boil. Lower the heat and simmer until the pasta is soft. Adjust the seasoning. (It should take about 20 minutes to cook and season well.)

NOTE: This soup may be prepared several hours ahead, but does not freeze.

SOPA DE LENTEJAS ESTILO QUERÉTARO Lentil Soup
OBDULIA AND ANA MARÍA VEGA, QUERÉTARO
SERVES 6   QUERÉTARO

When I rented a house one summer, I was delighted to find that the maids who came with it were from a small rural community in Querétaro. They loved to cook their simple peasant dishes for me, and this is one of them.

If fresh nopales are not available, then leave them out. Cooking time varies depending, of course, on how dry the lentils are or whether they were grown in the United States or Mexico. The Mexican lentils seem to have a denser consistency and thus thicken the soup more. When using American lentils, increase the amount to 6 ounces (180 g). Dilute the soup with water or chicken broth if it thickens too much.

4 TO 6 OUNCES (115 TO 180 G OR ½ ROUNDED CUP/125 ML) SMALL BROWN LENTILS

6 CUPS (1.5 L) WATER, APPROXIMATELY

8 OUNCES (225 G) NOPALES (ABOUT 3 MEDIUM-SIZE CACTUS PADDLES), CLEANED OF
   PRICKLES (SEE PAGES 208, 498) AND CUT INTO SMALL SQUARES (ABOUT 1¾ CUPS/
   440 ML)

SALT TO TASTE

1 LARGE SCALLION, GREEN PART INCLUDED, QUARTERED

8 OUNCES (225 G) TOMATOES, ROUGHLY CHOPPED (1½ CUPS/375 ML)

1 GARLIC CLOVE, ROUGHLY CHOPPED

2 TABLESPOONS VEGETABLE OIL

¼ CUP (65 ML) FINELY CHOPPED WHITE ONION

1 JALAPEÑO CHILE, OR 2 SERRANO CHILES, OR ANY FRESH, HOT GREEN CHILE, THINLY
   SLICED

1 CUP (250 ML) CHICKEN BROTH

3 LARGE SPRIGS CILANTRO

Rinse the lentils well and drain. Put them into a pan with 6 cups (1.5 l) of cold water. Bring to a boil, then lower the heat and cook over a low heat until mushy—about 3 hours for Mexican lentils, 2 hours for American.

Cover the cactus pieces with cold water, add ½ teaspoon of the salt and the scallion, and simmer until *just* tender—about 20 minutes. Rinse in cold water and drain, discarding the onion.

Blend the tomatoes with the garlic until smooth. Set aside.

Heat the oil in a skillet and fry the onion and chile gently, without browning, until they are soft. Add the tomato puree and fry for another 3 minutes or so over a high heat, stirring constantly, until the mixture is almost dry. Add to the lentils with the chicken broth and nopales. Cover the pan and cook over low heat for about 20 minutes, then add the cilantro and cook for 1 minute longer. Salt to taste.

N O T E : This dish could be prepared several hours ahead. It could be frozen for about a week.

SOPA DE PUERROS Leek Soup

SEÑORA DOMATILA SANTIAGO DE MORALES

SERVES 6   OAXACA

This is a very interesting and delicious recipe—Señora Domatila has never failed me. I have changed it in only one respect: I fry the leeks first, whereas she just boils them; I think the frying improves the flavor. Señora Domatila could never tell me where this recipe originated.

2 TABLESPOONS UNSALTED BUTTER

2 TABLESPOONS VEGETABLE OIL

4 CUPS (1 L) FINELY CHOPPED LEEKS, WHITE AND TENDER GREEN PART ONLY

¼ CUP (65 ML) FINELY CHOPPED FLAT-LEAF PARSLEY

6 CUPS (1.5 L) LIGHT CHICKEN BROTH

5 HARD-COOKED EGGS

SALT AND FRESHLY GROUND PEPPER TO TASTE

THE TOPPING

FRIED BREAD CROUTONS OR CRISP-FRIED TORTILLA PIECES (SEE PAGE 94)

Heat the butter with the oil in a large, heavy saucepan and fry the leeks and parsley until just soft, without browning—about 8 minutes. Add 5 cups (1.25 l) of the chicken broth and cook over medium heat until the leeks are tender—about 8 minutes.

Shell the eggs and separate the whites from the yolks. Chop the whites fine and set aside. Blend the yolks, together with the rest of the broth, until smooth and add with the chopped whites to the soup. Season and continue cooking for another 10 minutes, or until the leeks are completely soft and well seasoned.

Serve the soup with croutons or crisp-fried tortilla pieces.

NOTE: This recipe could be prepared up to about 4 hours ahead. I do not recommend freezing.

SOPA VERDE DE ELOTE Green Corn Soup
SERVES 6   SAN LUIS POTOSÍ

This unusual and delicious soup, with all its wonderfully different flavors, is from Mi Libro de Cocina, *a book published in San Luis Potosí in 1965. Unless you can get corn that is not too sweet, use frozen corn, measured before it defrosts.*

¼ CUP (65 ML OR ABOUT 2 OUNCES/60 G) UNSALTED BUTTER
½ CUP (125 ML) FINELY CHOPPED WHITE ONION
2 SMALL GARLIC CLOVES, FINELY CHOPPED
⅔ CUP (165 ML) TOMATE VERDE, COOKED (SEE PAGE 492) AND DRAINED
4½ CUPS (1.125 L) CORN KERNELS
5 CUPS (1.25 L) LIGHT CHICKEN BROTH
⅔ CUP (165 ML) GREEN PEAS, FRESH OR FROZEN
6 LARGE SPRIGS CILANTRO
2 SMALL POBLANO CHILES, CHARRED AND PEELED (SEE PAGE 469)
3 LARGE ROMAINE LETTUCE LEAVES, ROUGHLY CHOPPED
1 TEASPOON SALT, OR TO TASTE

TO SERVE
6 TABLESPOONS SOUR CREAM, COMMERCIAL OR HOMEMADE (SEE PAGE 489)
CRISP-FRIED TORTILLA PIECES (SEE PAGE 94)

Melt the butter in a large saucepan and fry the onion and garlic until translucent.

Blend the tomate verde until smooth. Add to the onion in the pan and fry over high heat for about 3 minutes, stirring constantly.

Put the corn kernels into a blender jar (one third at a time) with 2 cups (500 ml) of the chicken broth and the peas, cilantro, chiles, and lettuce leaves and blend until quite smooth. Pass this puree through the medium disk of a food mill or strainer, then add to the pan and cook over fairly high heat for about 3 minutes, stirring and scraping the bottom of the pan constantly, since the mixture tends to stick.

Add the remaining broth and the salt and cook the soup over low heat until it thickens and is well seasoned—about 20 minutes.

Serve in soup bowls with a large spoonful of the sour cream and a sprinkling of tortilla pieces for each serving.

NOTE: This soup can be made ahead and it can be frozen. On defrosting, blend it for a few seconds before heating and serving.

SOPA DE ELOTE Fresh Corn Soup
SERVES 6   CENTRAL MEXICO

This is a delicious and comforting soup, but much will depend on the corn, which should not be sugary sweet. Unless you can get very fresh corn it is best to use frozen. Measure it frozen and then let it defrost. Do not on any account use canned corn, which has been precooked.

4 CUPS (1 L) CORN KERNELS (ABOUT 1 ½ POUNDS/675 G FROZEN CORN)
1 CUP (250 ML) WATER
¼ CUP (65 ML) BUTTER
3 ½ CUPS (875 ML) MILK OR LIGHT CHICKEN BROTH
½ TEASPOON SALT, OR TO TASTE
2 POBLANO CHILES, CHARRED, PEELED, AND CLEANED, THEN DICED AND BRIEFLY FRIED
    (SEE PAGE 469)
6 TABLESPOONS CRUMBLED QUESO FRESCO
6 SMALL TORTILLAS, CUT INTO SMALL SQUARES, DRIED, AND FRIED CRISP AS FOR TOTOPOS
    (SEE PAGE 94)

Blend the corn with the water at high speed until you have a smooth puree. Put the puree through the medium disk of a food mill or a coarse strainer.

Melt the butter in a large saucepan but do not let it get too hot. Add the corn puree and let it cook over medium heat for about 5 minutes, stirring all the time.

Add the milk and the salt to the mixture and bring it to a boil. Lower the heat and let the soup simmer for about 15 minutes, stirring it from time to time to avoid sticking. By this time it will have thickened slightly.

Put about ½ tablespoon diced chile and 1 tablespoon of crumbled cheese into each bowl. Pour the hot soup over them and top with the crisp tortilla squares.

NOTE: The soup freezes quite well.

SOPA DE ELOTE Y RAJAS Fresh Corn and Poblano Soup
SEÑORA CANTÚ
SERVES 6   CENTRAL MEXICO

8 OUNCES (225 G) TOMATOES, BROILED (SEE PAGE 490)
2 TABLESPOONS ROUGHLY CHOPPED WHITE ONION
3 SMALL POBLANO CHILES, CHARRED, PEELED, CLEANED OF VEINS AND SEEDS
3 TABLESPOONS BUTTER
ABOUT 3 CUPS (750 ML) CORN KERNELS, OR 1 ½ 10-OUNCE (285-G) PACKAGES FROZEN
    CORN
3 CUPS (750 ML) MILK
¾ CUP (185 ML) WHOLE CORN KERNELS, FOR ADDING LATER
SALT TO TASTE
6 HEAPED TABLESPOONS QUESO FRESCO OR SUBSTITUTE, CRUMBLED

Blend the tomatoes and onion and set aside.

Cut the cleaned chiles into narrow strips. Melt the butter in a large saucepan and fry the chiles gently for about 2 minutes—they should not brown. Add the blended tomatoes to the chile strips and cook the mixture for about 5 minutes over medium heat until the sauce has reduced a little.

Blend the 3 cups of corn, together with the milk, at high speed to a very smooth consistency. This will probably have to be done in two stages. Put the corn mixture through the medium disk of a food mill or strainer and stir it in very gradually into the tomato sauce, stirring all the time.

Add the whole kernels and salt and cook the soup over very low heat—it should just simmer—for about 15 minutes.

Add a little cheese to each bowl before pouring the hot soup into it.

CREMA DE FLOR DE CALABAZA Cream of Squash Flower Soup
SERVES 6   CENTRAL MEXICO

When the squash plants are in full spate during the summer rains, huge baskets of the flowers come into the markets early every morning. It is best to rush home and cook them while the flowers are still wide open and delicately perfumed. (See page 497 for preparation of flowers for cooking.) In Mexico the flowers used most commonly are those of the calabacita criolla, *which have large yellow petals, about 50 to the pound (450 g) after cleaning. The zucchini squash blossoms you find in American farmers' markets are much smaller and therefore 90 should be right for 1 pound (450 g). If using the latter the soup will have a slightly greenish yellow hue, as the proportion of petal is smaller.*

3 TABLESPOONS UNSALTED BUTTER

⅓ CUP (85 ML) FINELY CHOPPED ONION

I LARGE GARLIC CLOVE, ROUGHLY CHOPPED

I POUND (450 G) SQUASH FLOWERS, CLEANED AND FINELY CHOPPED (ABOUT 8 CUPS/2 L, FIRMLY PACKED)

SALT TO TASTE

3½ CUPS (875 ML) LIGHT CHICKEN BROTH

⅔ CUP (165 ML) CRÈME FRAÎCHE OR HEAVY CREAM

SALT TO TASTE

THE RESERVED FLOWERS

2 POBLANO CHILES, CHARRED, PEELED, CLEANED, CUT INTO SMALL SQUARES, AND LIGHTLY FRIED (SEE PAGE 469)

Melt the butter, add the onion and garlic in a deep saucepan, and cook gently until translucent—do not brown. Add the chopped flowers and salt, cover the pan, and cook over low heat until the flowers are quite tender—10 to 15 minutes. Set aside a scant ½ cup (125 ml) of the flowers.

Blend the remaining flowers with 1½ cups (375 ml) of the broth and return to the pan. Add the remaining broth and cook over low heat for about 8 minutes.

Stir the cream into the soup and heat gently until it reaches the simmering point. Adjust seasoning and serve topped with the unblended flowers and the chile pieces.

SOPA DE AGUACATE Avocado Soup
SERVES 6   CENTRAL MEXICO

This is a lovely, pale green soup that can be served hot or cold. However, much will depend on the quality of the avocados; they must be very fresh and creamy. While I prefer the simple topping of chipotle chiles and tortilla squares, there are endless ways of dressing up this soup.

2 LARGE AVOCADOS, OR ENOUGH TO YIELD 2 CUPS (500 ML) PULP

6 CUPS (1.5 L) WELL-SEASONED CALDO DE POLLO (PAGE 499)

SMALL TORTILLA SQUARES, FRIED CRISP AS FOR TOTOPOS (SEE PAGE 94)

CHIPOTLE CHILES ADOBADOS, TORN INTO SMALL PIECES

Cut the avocados into halves. Remove the pits and scoop out the flesh.

Place 2 cups (500 ml) of broth in a blender jar, add the avocado pulp, and blend to a smooth puree. Add to the rest of the broth in the pan and just heat it through gently. *Do not let it boil.*

Serve the soup immediately, topped with the tortilla squares and pieces of chipotle chile.

SOPA DE AJO Y MIGAS Garlic and Bread Soup

SEÑORA MARÍA ELENA LARA

SERVES 6   HIDALGO

Prepared as described below, the eggs will form rough strands like egg drop soup. On one of my early cooking tours in San Diego, Jerrie Strom taught me a Chinese trick to keep the strands of eggs smoother and more silky: when beating the eggs, add about 1 teaspoon oil.

6 THICK SLICES FRENCH-TYPE BREAD, PREFERABLY SOURDOUGH

1/3 CUP (85 ML) VEGETABLE OIL, APPROXIMATELY

4 GARLIC CLOVES, SLICED

6 CUPS (1.5 L) STRONG CHICKEN BROTH

2 LARGE EGGS

2 LARGE SPRIGS EPAZOTE

SALT TO TASTE, IF NECESSARY

VEINS FROM 3 PASILLA CHILES, LIGHTLY TOASTED

Preheat the oven to 300°F (150°C).

Place the bread slices on a baking sheet in one layer and bake until they are crisp on the outside but not dried all the way through—about 30 minutes.

Heat a little of the oil in a heavy pan and fry the bread on both sides until very crisp and golden brown, adding more oil as necessary. Drain on paper toweling and set aside to keep warm.

Add or make up to 1 tablespoon of oil in the pan, and cook, rather than fry, the garlic over a low heat so that it flavors the oil. Remove the garlic and discard. Pour a little of the broth into the pan, swirl it around, and add to the rest of the broth.

Heat the broth to a simmer in a saucepan. Beat the eggs lightly with a teaspoon of oil (see note above) and, stirring constantly in a circular motion, add to the broth. Add the epazote and simmer until the eggs are set. Adjust the seasoning, then add the fried bread and simmer for half a minute, no longer.

Serve in deep soup bowls, with a crouton in each bowl, and top with chile veins to taste.

CALDO TLALPEÑO Chicken and Vegetable Broth
SERVES 6

MEXICO CITY

Nobody can tell me how this broth came to be named for Tlalpan, a community that used to be on the outskirts of Mexico City but is now swallowed up by rapid urbanization. It used to be a favorite place for a Sunday outing to eat barbacoa or carnitas. Caldo Tlalpeño was quite possibly served in the pulquerias *there—I have a theory that many a new soup or* antojito *were created in* pulquerias *and* cantinas.

There are, of course, many variations of the recipe, some adding rice instead of chickpeas, for example. It is customary to serve a whole piece of chicken in each bowl but for the uninitiated it is more difficult to eat. I have therefore substituted shredded chicken.

8 OUNCES (225 G) GREEN BEANS

4 OUNCES (115 G) CARROTS (ABOUT 2 MEDIUM)

4 OUNCES (115 G) TOMATOES, ROUGHLY CHOPPED (ABOUT 1 CUP/250 ML)

2 TABLESPOONS ROUGHLY CHOPPED WHITE ONION

1 GARLIC CLOVE, ROUGHLY CHOPPED

1 TABLESPOON LARD OR VEGETABLE OIL

6 CUPS (1.5 L) CALDO DE POLLO (SEE PAGE 499)

1/2 CUP (125 ML) COOKED AND SKINNED CHICKPEAS

2 LARGE SPRIGS EPAZOTE

2 CHIPOTLE CHILES, DRIED OR CANNED, TORN INTO STRIPS

1 CUP (250 ML) COOKED AND SHREDDED CHICKEN (SEE PAGE 499)

1 AVOCADO, CUBED

6 LIME WEDGES

Trim the beans and cut them in two. Trim and scrape the carrots and cut into rounds. Blend together the tomatoes, onion, and garlic. Heat the lard in a medium skillet, add the blended ingredients, and fry over medium heat for about 3 minutes.

Heat the Caldo de Pollo in a large saucepan, add the vegetables, chickpeas, and tomato mixture, and cook over medium heat until tender—about 15 minutes.

Add the epazote and chiles and cook for about 5 minutes more.

Serve the soup in deep bowls, adding some of the shredded chicken and topping with the avocado. Lime wedges are passed separately.

NOTE: This soup can be prepared several hours ahead up to the point of adding the epazote and chiles. It does not freeze.

SOPA TARASCA TIPO CONDE Tarascan Bean and Tortilla Soup
SEÑORA BEATRIZ DE DÁVALOS
SERVES 6   MICHOACÁN

When I was researching recipes for The Cuisines of Mexico *many years ago, I was fortunate to meet and learn from one of the outstanding cooks at that time, Señora Beatriz de Dávalos. She introduced me to this soup and many other regional recipes from the Morelia area. Nowadays it is more likely that you will be served a Sopa Tarasca that resembles a tortilla soup, but this is* tipo conde, *meaning that it is thickened with pureed beans. It is a delicious and filling cold-weather soup.*

8 OUNCES (225 G) COOKED PINK OR PINTO BEANS (ABOUT 3 1/2 TO 4 CUPS; 875 ML TO
    1 L) WITH BROTH
1 POUND (450 G) TOMATOES, BROILED (SEE PAGE 490)
1 GARLIC CLOVE
2 TABLESPOONS ROUGHLY CHOPPED WHITE ONION
3 TABLESPOONS LARD OR VEGETABLE OIL
2 1/2 CUPS (625 ML) CHICKEN OR PORK BROTH
SALT AS NECESSARY
1/4 TEASPOON DRIED MEXICAN OREGANO
1 CUP (250 ML) QUESO FRESCO
3 ANCHO CHILES, CLEANED OF SEEDS AND THEN CUT INTO NARROW STRIPS AND FRIED
3 SMALL TORTILLAS CUT INTO STRIPS, FRIED CRISP AS FOR TOTOPOS (SEE PAGE 94)
THICK SOUR CREAM (SEE PAGE 489)

Blend the beans, together with their broth, to a smooth consistency and transfer to a large, heavy saucepan.

Blend the tomatoes, garlic, and onion together to a smooth sauce. Melt the fat in a skillet and cook the tomato mixture over high heat for about 5 minutes, then stir into the bean puree and let it cook over medium heat for about 8 minutes, stirring it all the time.

Add the broth and let the soup cook for another 5 minutes over low heat. Add salt to taste and add the oregano just before serving.

Put a few pieces of the cheese into each bowl. Pour the hot soup over them and top with the chiles, some tortilla strips, and a dollop of sour cream.

NOTE: This soup will thicken considerably as it stands and will have to be diluted with broth or water. It freezes well.

SOPA DE LIMA Sour "Lima" Soup

SEÑORA BERTA LÓPEZ DE MARRUFO

SERVES 6   YUCATÁN

Sopa de Lima is the *soup of Yucatán. It is named for the sour* lima agria *(see page 493), as opposed to lime, the juice and rind of which give the soup a subtle flavor and astringency. Even in the hottest weather you will be served a sizzling bowl — sizzling as the hot, crisp-fried tortillas are added at the last moment.*

This recipe produces a slightly more sophisticated soup than the usual restaurant offering.

8 CUPS (2 L) WATER

10 GARLIC CLOVES, TOASTED (SEE PAGE 492)

¼ TEASPOON DRIED MEXICAN OREGANO, YUCATECAN IF POSSIBLE, TOASTED

6 PEPPERCORNS

SALT TO TASTE

4 CHICKEN GIZZARDS

2 CHICKEN BREASTS WITH SKIN AND BONES

6 CHICKEN LIVERS (ABOUT 8 OUNCES/225 G)

1 ½ TABLESPOONS LARD OR CHICKEN FAT

⅓ CUP (85 ML) FINELY CHOPPED WHITE ONION

¼ CUP (65 ML) FINELY CHOPPED CHILE DULCE OR GREEN PEPPER

8 OUNCES (225 G) TOMATOES, FINELY CHOPPED (1 ⅓ CUPS/335 ML)

½ LIMA AGRIA OR SUBSTITUTE FRESH LIME

VEGETABLE OIL FOR FRYING

12 TORTILLAS, CUT INTO STRIPS AND DRIED

TO SERVE

¾ CUP (185 ML) FINELY CHOPPED WHITE ONION

⅓ CUP (85 ML) HABANERO CHILES, CHARRED AND FINELY CHOPPED
   (SEE PAGE 466)

6 THIN SLICES LIMA AGRIA

Put the water into a soup pot. Add the garlic, oregano, peppercorns, and salt. Bring to a simmer and cook for about 10 minutes. Add the gizzards and cook for 15 more minutes.

Add the chicken breasts and continue cooking for another 15 minutes. Add the livers and cook for 10 more minutes, or until the meats are tender.

Strain the broth and set it aside. Remove the meat from the breasts and shred. Chop the livers, remove the gristle from the gizzards, and chop them. Set the meats aside.

Heat the lard in a saucepan and gently fry the onion and pepper until they are soft, but not browned. Add the tomatoes to the mixture in the pan, and cook for about 5 minutes over medium heat. Add to the broth and let it simmer uncovered for about 5 minutes. Add salt as necessary, then add the chopped and shredded meats and heat them through.

Squeeze the juice of the ½ *lima agria* into the broth. Drop the squeezed *lima* shell into the broth for a few seconds only, then remove. Keep the broth warm.

Heat the oil in a skillet and fry the tortilla strips until they are crisp. Drain them on the toweling, and while they are still very hot, drop some of them into the broth in each soup bowl.

Pass the chopped onion, the chiles, and slices of *lima* separately.

CALDO DE QUESO SONORENSE Cheese Broth

SEÑORA CONSUELO M. MARTÍNEZ

SERVES 6 SONORA

When I first tried this simple, peasant soup in Hermosillo, Sonora, the potatoes were cut into quite large pieces and the cheese was cut from a huge wheel. It was homemade cheese from a nearby ranch—crumbly, slightly acidy, and tasting of pure cream. It melted immediately in the hot broth.

12 OUNCES (340 G) RED BLISS OR WAXY NEW POTATOES

5 CUPS (1.25 L) BEEF BROTH

1 POUND (450 G) LARGE TOMATOES

2 TABLESPOONS VEGETABLE OIL

1/3 CUP (85 ML) SLICED WHITE ONION

1 SMALL GARLIC CLOVE, FINELY CHOPPED

1 ANAHEIM CHILE, CHARRED AND PEELED (SEE PAGE 471)

SALT TO TASTE

12 THIN STRIPS QUESO FRESCO OR MUENSTER CHEESE

Peel the potatoes and cut them into 1-inch (2.5-cm) squares. Bring the broth to a boil, add the potatoes, and let them cook over medium heat for 10 minutes. They should be *just* cooked.

Cut a thin slice off the top of each tomato and grate the flesh on the coarse side of a grater. In a very short time you will have the skin of the tomato left flat in your hand. Don't forget to grate the flesh from the top slices.

Heat the oil in a large skillet and gently fry the onion and garlic, without browning, until translucent. Add the tomato pulp and cook the sauce over brisk heat for 10 minutes, by which time it will have thickened somewhat and be well seasoned. Add the tomato sauce to the broth and potatoes.

Remove the seeds from the chile and cut it into strips. Add the chile strips to the broth and let it cook over medium heat for 5 minutes. Add salt as necessary. Just before serving, add the cheese. Serve the soup as the cheese melts.

CONSOMÉ DE CAMARÓN SECO Dried Shrimp Consommé

SEÑORA CLARA ZABALZA DE GARCÍA
SERVES 6

This is a wonderfully strong-flavored, slightly picante soup. Señora García says that she often serves small cups of it just before a meal of Caldo Michi (see page 135). It is great for cold days, to end a long night, or to pep up a dull low-calorie diet.

8 OUNCES (250 G) MEXICAN DRIED SHRIMPS (SEE PAGE 498)
4 TO 5 CUPS (1 TO 1.25 L) WATER
6 CASCABEL OR 4 GUAJILLO CHILES
1 MULATO OR 2 PASILLA CHILES
1 GARLIC CLOVE, LEFT WHOLE

TO SERVE
ROUGHLY CHOPPED CILANTRO SPRIGS
FINELY CHOPPED WHITE ONION
LIME QUARTERS

Rinse the uncleaned shrimps in cold water and drain, cover the shrimps with 2 cups (500 ml) of the water, and bring them to a simmer. Cook for 1 minute, then remove from the heat and set them aside to soak for 5 minutes longer—no more, as the shrimps soon lose their flavor. Drain the shrimps and reserve the cooking water.

Remove the stems from the chiles and veins and seeds from half of them. Put the chiles into a saucepan, cover with water, and simmer for about 5 minutes, or until soft (time varies, depending on how dry the chiles are). Remove from the heat and set aside to soak for about 5 minutes longer. Drain, discard the water in which they were cooked, and transfer to a blender jar with 1 cup (250 ml) of fresh water and the garlic. Blend until smooth.

Clean the shrimps: remove the legs, tails, and heads. Divide the cleaned shrimps into two parts. Roughly break up or chop one half and reserve. Transfer the other half with the shrimp debris to the blender jar. Add the water in which they were cooked and blend as smooth as possible.

Put the chile sauce and the blended shrimps into a large, heavy saucepan, bring to a simmer, and cook, stirring all the time and scraping the bottom of the pan, for about 3 minutes. Add 1 more cup (250 ml) of the water, bring back to the simmering point, and continue cooking over low heat for about 5 minutes. Pass the mixture through a fine sieve. Add the shrimp pieces and continue cooking for 5 minutes, no longer. The soup should be rather thick, but dilute with water if preferred.

Serve in small cups and pass the toppings separately.

NOTE: This soup can be prepared several hours ahead and it can also be frozen.

CALDO MICHI Fish Soup

SEÑORA CLARA ZABALZA DE GARCÍA
SERVES 6   JALISCO

Two of the largest lakes in Mexico are Pátzcuaro, in the state of Michoacán, and Chapala, in the neighboring state of Jalisco. Both have their own versions of a fish and vegetable soup called Caldo Michi (caldo means "broth" and michi, "fish," in the language of the Tarascan Indians) and made with fish from the lakes—catfish, carp, or the unique little pescado blanco (white fish), with its sharply pointed head and transparent flesh with wide silver stripes along each side.

Usually the whole fish is used because the gelatinous quality of the head adds substance to the broth (leave it out if you can't bear the thought, but do not skin or bone the fish slices). For Caldo Michi, do not first make a broth using the heads, as you would for most fish stews. I have tried it and it doesn't seem to work—perhaps because, with notable exceptions, freshwater fish of this type do not have a particularly fine flavor. Chicken broth is used locally.

Out of many recipes given to me for Caldo Michi, I have chosen that of Señora García. I like the flavor of her soup much better, and in talking to her about the regional food I've found she has a great respect both for traditional cooking methods and for fresh ingredients. Every year she pickles all her own chiles and frutas *in homemade pineapple vinegar, for this and other recipes.*

As a substitute for frutas en vinagre, *I suggest you put in a couple of slices of lime and a few sour pickles.*

2 ½ POUNDS (1.125 KG) WHOLE CATFISH OR CARP

SALT AND FRESHLY GROUND PEPPER TO TASTE

¼ CUP (65 ML) VEGETABLE OIL

10 OUNCES (285 G) SLICED TOMATOES, ABOUT 1 ½ CUPS (375 ML)

½ CUP (125 ML) THINLY SLICED WHITE ONION

3 GARLIC CLOVES, LEFT WHOLE

8 CUPS (2 L) CHICKEN BROTH

3 MEDIUM CARROTS (ABOUT 4 OUNCES/115 G), SCRAPED AND SLICED

2 ZUCCHINI (ABOUT 6 OUNCES/180 G), TRIMMED AND CUT INTO ROUNDS

¼ TEASPOON DRIED MEXICAN OREGANO

3 JALAPEÑO CHILES EN ESCABECHE, ROUGHLY CHOPPED

⅔ CUP (165 ML) LOOSELY PACKED FRUTAS EN VINAGRE OR AN EQUIVALENT AMOUNT OF
    SOUR PICKLES PLUS 2 SLICES LIME

8 LARGE SPRIGS CILANTRO, ROUGHLY CHOPPED

Rinse and dry the fish well. Cut the body into 1-inch (2.5-cm) slices and the head, if used, into four pieces. Season with salt and freshly ground pepper.

Heat the oil in a large, heavy pan and fry the fish pieces very lightly; the flesh should just turn opaque. Remove and set aside.

In the same oil, fry the tomatoes, onion, and garlic together until the onion is soft and the mixture has a saucelike consistency. Add the broth, carrots, zucchini, oregano, chiles, and *frutas en vinagre* (or substitutes) to the pan and cook until the vegetables are just tender, about 20 minutes. Add the fish pieces and simmer until the flesh flakes easily from the bone—about 10 minutes.

Remove the pan from the heat and add the chopped cilantro. Serve the soup accompanied by freshly made tortillas.

NOTE: This soup may be prepared a few hours ahead of time, but add the fish pieces about 10 minutes before serving. It will not freeze.

CALDO DE PIEDRA ❋ BROTH OF "STONES"

Many years ago now on one of my early trips to Oaxaca, friends there told me about a cooking method that would provide a pre-hispanic culinary surprise; I had to see it for myself. It wasn't until last summer, when I was driving through Tuxtepec on my way to Veracruz, that I had time to make a detour to Usila, famous for its unique way of cooking fish in *caldo de piedra*. This small, isolated village is situated near a river of the same name that winds through a valley cut off by a high mountain.

There was not enough time to go by bus, because the journey takes several hours over a rocky, difficult track that becomes almost impassable in the rainy season, but with the help of Relámpago Negro (Black Lightning), a taxi driver in Tuxtepec, I finally found a driver to take me in his pickup truck—which usually transports ten people out of Tuxtepec—for quite a tidy sum of money because, he said, his tires wear out in three months.

It was a spectacular trip, with lush vegetation that seemed to close in on us as the truck slowly made its way along the deeply rutted, rocky track. At one point we passed under a natural arch of immense, overhanging rocks thickly festooned with tropical creepers. But as we began our descent, there was an abrupt curve in the road and suddenly there was a magnificent panorama of the valley below, with the river Usila winding through it in dramatic loops.

By then it was almost midday and I doubted there would be time to arrange for the preparation of the *caldo de piedra*. But in Mexico you never give up hope—somehow there is always a way. And there was.

It was disappointing not to go fishing and have the fish cooked right there by the river, but instead, the owner of a small restaurant there offered to prepare it for us. There was a glowing wood fire on the raised adobe cooking surface and small river pebbles were put into the hot ashes. Señor Gachupín, our host, set a hollowed-out gourd for each of us and put into each a small amount of sliced tomato, white onion, a jalapeño chile, and some sprigs of cilantro, and on top five small crayfish from the river—he apologized for not having fish to add to it. He added water almost to the surface of each gourd and then, retrieving the stones, now red hot, one by one from the fire with a pair of sticks for tongs, dropped them into the gourd. There was a fierce hissing as the water boiled up like a geyser and subsided into a foam on the surface. In perhaps 3 minutes, all the ingredients were cooked into a fragrant broth. He continued with the rest of the gourds and then reheated freshly made corn tortillas by hanging them over sticks, over the fire.

It was one of those memorable meals and we talked about it as we drove slowly back—this time with a family of four behind to give us ballast up the steep track. They made themselves useful, too. I had despaired of getting a wild plant (*xonequi*; see recipe in *My Mexico*) for a class I was giving in Veracruz the next day but there it was, creeping over the bushes by the side of the road. Everybody got down to help and within a short time there was a large enough pile of leaves for the class.

SOUP STEWS

The following recipes from different regions of Mexico represent just a few of the popular soup stews, as I call them, that constitute a meal in themselves. In Jalisco, pozole is eaten for supper, while in Guerrero it is a morning or midday meal. Mole de Olla and Gallina Pinta are main dishes for comida (the main meal of the day, generally eaten early or mid-afternoon), while Menudo is eaten in the morning—a must for New Year's Day, or any morning for that matter, to cure a hangover.

PREPARATION OF CORN FOR POZOLE, MENUDO, AND GALLINA PINTA

The dried corn with broad, white kernels known as cacahuazintle *or* maiz pozolero *is generally used for pozole, some types of menudo, and Gallina Pinta (page 147). In Mexican and Latin American groceries it is often found already prepared—cooked briefly with lime and with the pedicel (the portion that connects the kernel to the cob) removed so that it will open up like a flower—in bags in the freezer section. It then needs to be cooked in water until it does "flower."*

But for those who have time and patience, and want to prepare the corn from scratch— and are rewarded with more flavor and texture—here is how you do it.

If you think of it, put 1 pound (450 g) of corn to soak in cold water overnight. This step is not essential, but it helps reduce the final cooking time. Remove any bits that float to the top of the water, then strain.

Put the corn into a deep pot, cover well with water, add 1 tablespoon lime juice, and bring to a simmer—it will turn yellow. Continue cooking uncovered over low heat for about 15 minutes. Remove from heat and set aside to cool and soak for about

20 minutes. When cool enough to handle, rinse in fresh water and rub the kernels through your hands until the rather slimy skin has been removed—you may need several changes of water until it is clean and white. With a paring knife—or strong fingernails—remove the pedicels at the top of the kernels.

Return the cleaned kernels to the pot and cover with water to come about 3 inches (8 cm) above the level of the corn—a little difficult because the kernels tend to float. Cook over medium heat, covered, until the kernels open up like a flower—about 3 hours depending on how old and dry the corn is. Add salt to taste. (Some cooks add salt at the beginning, others say it impedes the flowering—I tend to dither from one to the other with no visible difference.)

In some stores in Mexico and the United States you may be offered a reddish-hued corn for pozole, but I warn you it may take many more hours to cook. The canned corn for pozole should be used only as a last, desperate resort. It is too soft and tasteless, with obvious preservatives.

MENUDO COLORADO NORTEÑO Tripe Soup with Chile

SEÑORA BERTHA GONZÁLEZ DE MORALES

SERVES ABOUT 16   NUEVO LEÓN

In Nuevo León, menudo, or tripe soup, is prepared either red, colored with ancho and guajillo chiles, or plain, blanco. It is a hearty soup/stew at best, but here it is fortified with corn that has been cooked until it "opens like a flower"—as the expression goes in Mexico. (The preparation of the corn is detailed above.)

Menudo is the sine qua non for an early-morning pickup for New Year's revellers or for almuerzo, a hearty breakfast, on a Sunday morning. It is a fact that the enzymes in tripe greatly help a hangover—and, I am told, a stomach ulcer.

It is worthwhile making a large quantity while you are at it, not only because it freezes so well but also because it seems that the flavors of both menudo and pozole are better when cooked in large quantities.

Traditional cooks still prefer to cook menudo slowly overnight in large earthenware ollas.

This recipe was given to me by one of my constant oracles when it comes to the food of Nuevo León, Señora Bertha González de Morales. She says the number of chiles used is a matter of taste, and she includes the pigs' feet to add flavor and enhance the gelatinous quality of the broth.

The dried oregano used in this area is from a wild plant with small, elongated leaves that grows in the mountains surrounding Monterrey, but many cooks now have some growing in pots.

5 ½ POUNDS (2.5 KG) TRIPE OF DIFFERENT TEXTURES
1 ½ POUNDS (675 G) CALF'S FOOT, CUT INTO 4 PIECES
OPTIONAL: 3 PIGS' FEET, ABOUT 1 POUND (450 G)
1 HEAD OF GARLIC, UNPEELED, CUT IN HALF HORIZONTALLY
SALT TO TASTE

THE CORN

1 POUND 2 OUNCES (500 G) POZOLE CORN, COOKED AND "FLOWERED" (SEE PAGE 139)

THE CHILE

3 GUAJILLO CHILES, SEEDS REMOVED (LEAVE THE VEINS)
2 ANCHO CHILES, SEEDS REMOVED (LEAVE THE VEINS)
ABOUT 1 ¼ CUPS (315 ML) WATER
1 TEASPOON CUMIN SEEDS, CRUSHED
1 HEAPED TABLESPOON DRIED MEXICAN OREGANO, LONG-LEAFED FROM NUEVO LEÓN
    IF POSSIBLE
3 GARLIC CLOVES (OPTIONAL)

TO SERVE

SLICES OF LIME
CRUMBLED, DRIED MEXICAN OREGANO
FINELY CHOPPED WHITE ONION
FINELY CHOPPED SERRANO CHILE

Rinse the tripe twice in cold water, drain, and cut into 2-inch (5-cm) squares. Rinse the calf's and pigs' feet and drain. Put into a large stockpot or Mexican earthenware *olla*. Fill the pot with water almost to the top—the level should be several inches above the meats. Add the garlic and salt and set over low heat, uncovered, until it comes to a simmer. Continue cooking for 1 hour, then cover and continue cooking until the tripe and feet are tender—anywhere from 4 to 6 hours, depending on the quality of the tripe.

Meantime, the corn should be cooking (with salt; see page 140). When it is tender and has opened up, or "flowered," drain, reserving about 3 cups (750 ml) of the broth.

Put the chiles into a bowl, cover with cold water, and leave to soak for 35 minutes. Drain and tear into pieces.

Put ¼ cup (65 ml) of the water into the blender jar, add the cumin, oregano, and optional garlic, and blend until smooth. Add the remaining 1 cup (250 ml) of water and blend the chiles, a few at a time, until smooth. If some pieces of guajillo skin remain, pass the sauce through a strainer, pressing down hard to extract as much of the chile as possible.

When the meats are tender, add the chile sauce and corn with the reserved broth. Adjust the salt, and continue cooking uncovered until the meats are soft—about 1 hour more.

Remove the pieces of calf's foot from the broth and cut the gelatinous parts into small cubes. Return them to the pot.

Serve the menudo—about 2 cups (500 ml) per person is a healthy portion—in deep bowls and pass the toppings separately. Bread rolls or corn tortillas are served alongside in Nuevo León.

N O T E : Menudo can be prepared a day ahead and freezes excellently for up to a year.

MENUDO BLANCO NORTEÑO Northern Tripe Soup
SERVES ABOUT 16   S O N O R A

5 ½ POUNDS (2.5 KG) TRIPE OF DIFFERENT TEXTURES
1 ½ POUNDS (675 G) CALF'S FEET, CUT INTO 4 PIECES
OPTIONAL: 3 PIGS' FEET, ABOUT 1 POUND (450 G)
1 HEAD OF GARLIC, UNPEELED, CUT IN HALF HORIZONTALLY
SALT TO TASTE

THE CORN
1 POUND 2 OUNCES (500 G) POZOLE CORN, COOKED AND "FLOWERED" (SEE PAGE 139)

THE SEASONING
⅓ CUP (85 ML) WATER
1 TEASPOON CUMIN SEEDS, CRUSHED
1 HEAPED TABLESPOON DRIED MEXICAN OREGANO, LONG-LEAFED FROM NUEVO LEÓN
    IF POSSIBLE
3 GARLIC CLOVES (OPTIONAL)

TO SERVE

SLICES OF LIME

CRUMBLED, DRIED MEXICAN OREGANO

FINELY CHOPPED WHITE ONION

½ CUP (125 ML) TOASTED AND POWDERED ANCHO CHILE (SEE PAGE 473)

Rinse the tripe twice in cold water, drain, and cut into 2-inch (5-cm) squares. Rinse the calf's and pigs' feet and drain. Put into a large stockpot or Mexican earthenware *olla*. Fill the pot with water almost to the top—the level should be several inches above the meats. Add the garlic and salt and put over low heat, uncovered, until it comes to a simmer. Continue cooking for 1 hour, then cover and continue cooking until the tripe and feet are tender—anywhere from 4 to 6 hours depending on the quality of the tripe.

Meantime, the corn should be cooking (with salt; see page 140). When it is tender and has opened up, or "flowered," drain, reserving about 3 cups (750 ml) of the broth.

Put the ⅓ cup (85 ml) of water into the blender jar, add the cumin, oregano, and optional garlic, and blend until smooth.

When the meats are tender, add the seasoning mixture and corn with the reserved broth. Adjust the salt, and continue cooking uncovered until the meats are soft—about 1 hour more.

Remove the pieces of calf's foot from the broth and cut the gelatinous parts into small cubes. Return them to the pot.

Serve the menudo—about 2 cups (500 ml) per person is a healthy portion—in deep bowls and pass the toppings separately. Bread rolls or corn tortillas are served with it in Nuevo León.

NOTE: Menudo can be prepared a day ahead and freezes well for up to a year.

MONDONGO EN KABIK   Tripe in a Spicy, Picante Broth

SEÑORA BERTA LÓPEZ DE MARRUFO

SERVES 6   YUCATÁN

Besides being just what its Mayan title says it is, tripe in a picante broth, Mondongo en Kabik is a cheap, nutritious dish. I first tried this many years ago in a humble little eating place opposite the Mérida railroad station. For ten pesos—after devaluation in the 1970s—I had a large bowl of broth and a plate of tripe and cow's foot, served with French bread—rather soggy, generally, in Yucatán—a slice of sour lima, chopped chives, and chopped verde chile (the verde chile of Yucatán—a long, thin, pale green chile with a smooth surface—has a distinctive flavor, quite unlike those in other parts of the country). It was quite a meal in itself, and very good, even in the heat of the day.

I find myself going back to Doña Berta constantly with any new recipe I may acquire, as there is something very special about her food compared to that of other cooks I have come across. This is her slightly more refined version.

The type of tripe that should be used, according to Yucatecan cooks, is called toalla *(towel), since it has the surface texture of a towel. Tripe in the United States is always well scrubbed and deodorized, so the orange juice step could be omitted—but apart from that it does tenderize the tripe, and gives it a pleasant, acidy flavor. If you cannot find the Seville oranges, then use the substitute, and for the verde chiles use any fresh, hot green chile.*

Start the preparation the day before you plan to serve the dish. This dish can be prepared up to one day ahead of serving. It can also be frozen for about 1 month.

THE MEATS

1 POUND (450 G) TRIPE, CUT INTO 1-INCH (2.5-CM) SQUARES

2 CUPS (500 ML) SEVILLE ORANGE JUICE OR SUBSTITUTE (SEE PAGE 494)

1 SMALL CALF'S FOOT, CUT INTO 8 PIECES

½ HEAD GARLIC, UNPEELED AND TOASTED (SEE PAGE 492)

1 TEASPOON DRIED MEXICAN OREGANO, TOASTED, YUCATECAN IF POSSIBLE

1 TABLESPOON SALT

THE TOMATO SEASONING

2 TABLESPOONS VEGETABLE OIL

8 OUNCES (225 G) TOMATOES, FINELY CHOPPED (ABOUT ⅓ CUP/85 ML)

⅓ CUP (85 ML) FINELY CHOPPED WHITE ONION

1 SMALL GREEN PEPPER, CLEANED AND CHOPPED INTO SMALL SQUARES

4 SPRIGS EPAZOTE, LEAVES AND TOPS OF STEMS ONLY, ROUGHLY CHOPPED

3 YUCATECAN GREEN CHILES, GÜERO CHILES, OR ANY FRESH, HOT GREEN CHILES, TOASTED
   (SEE PAGES 480, 464)

1 TEASPOON SIMPLE RECADO ROJO (PAGE 485)

SALT TO TASTE

TO SERVE

6 YUCATECAN GREEN CHILES OR ANY FRESH, HOT GREEN CHILES, CUT INTO ROUNDS

$\frac{1}{2}$ CUP (125 ML) FINELY CHOPPED WHITE ONION

$\frac{1}{3}$ CUP (85 ML) FINELY CHOPPED CHIVES

SLICES OF LIMA-AGRIA OR LIME

Wash the tripe well, cover with the orange juice, and leave to soak for at least 4 hours, turning the pieces occasionally. Scrub the pieces of calf's foot. Put into a large saucepan with the garlic, oregano, and salt, and cover well with water. Bring to a boil, then lower the heat and let cook gently for about 4 hours, or until the meat is just beginning to get tender. Set aside, in the cooking liquid, in the refrigerator overnight.

The next day, drain the tripe, rinse, and add to the calf's foot, in its broth. Bring to a boil and cook slowly until both meats are tender—2½ to 3 hours.

Meanwhile, heat the oil in a heavy pan and add the tomatoes, onion, green pepper, and chopped epazote. Fry over medium heat until the mixture is reduced and seasoned, about 8 minutes. Add the chiles and recado rojo, along with 2 tablespoons of the meat broth, and cook for a few minutes more. Season and set aside.

When the meats are tender, drain, reserving the broth. Remove the bones from the calf's foot and chop the meat, gristle, and skin (all edible) into large pieces. Put the pieces, along with the tripe, onto a warmed serving dish and set aside in a warm place.

If necessary, add water to the reserved broth to make up to 8 cups (2 l). Add the tomato seasoning and simmer for about 5 minutes, or until well flavored. (If there is too much fat on top of the broth, skim as necessary.) Serve the broth in large soup bowls; serve the meat separately. Let everyone help themselves to the chiles, onion, chives, and slices of lime al gusto. Serve with French bread.

MOLE DE OLLA Mole Cooked in a Pot
SERVES 6

MICHOACÁN

*This is a substantial brothy soup of meat and vegetables seasoned with a few dried chiles.
Generally a sour tuna,* xoconostle, *is added to give a pleasant touch of acidity. It is a meal
in itself, served with corn tortillas.*

THE MEAT
3 POUNDS (1.35 KG) PORK NECK BONES OR 3 POUNDS (1.35 KG) BOILING BEEF
   (BRISKET OR A SHOULDER CUT), WITH BONE
2 QUARTS (2 L) WATER
2 TEASPOONS SALT, OR TO TASTE

THE SEASONING SAUCE
4 ANCHO CHILES, WIPED CLEAN, SEEDS AND VEINS REMOVED
4 PASILLA CHILES, WIPED CLEAN, SEEDS AND VEINS REMOVED
1 CUP (250 ML) TOMATE VERDE, COOKED AND DRAINED (SEE PAGE 492)
1/2 MEDIUM WHITE ONION, ROUGHLY CHOPPED
2 GARLIC CLOVES, ROUGHLY CHOPPED
1/8 TEASPOON CUMIN SEEDS
3 TABLESPOONS VEGETABLE OIL

THE VEGETABLES
8 OUNCES (225 G) ZUCCHINI
4 OUNCES (115 G) GREEN BEANS
1 LARGE EAR OF CORN
1 SMALL CHAYOTE (ABOUT 8 OUNCES/225 G)
8 OUNCES (225 G) POTATOES
3 SPRIGS EPAZOTE

THE GARNISH
WEDGES OF LIME AND FINELY CHOPPED WHITE ONION

Have the butcher cut the meat and bones into serving pieces. Cover them with the water,
add the salt, and bring to a boil. Lower the heat and simmer the meat, uncovered, until
it is tender—about 50 minutes for the pork and 1 hour and 10 minutes for the beef.

Meanwhile prepare the chiles. Heat the comal and toast the chiles on both sides,
taking care not to burn. When cool they should be easy to crumble into the blender.

Blend the chiles with the rest of the seasoning ingredients except the oil until smooth.

Heat the oil in a skillet and fry the sauce for about 5 minutes. Add it to the meat.

Clean and trim the squash and cut them into halves, then into four lengthwise. Trim the beans and cut them into halves. Cut the corn into six pieces. Cut the chayote open and remove the core, then cut into ¼-inch (.75-cm) wedges. Skin the potatoes and cut them into cubes.

When the meat is tender, add the vegetables and cook the mole slowly, uncovered, for about 30 minutes, or until the vegetables are cooked. Add the epazote about 5 minutes before the mole is ready, and add salt as necessary.

Serve in large, deep soup bowls, with hot tortillas, wedges of lime, and finely chopped onion on the side.

GALLINA PINTA Oxtail, Pork, and Bean Soup

SEÑORA CONSUELO M. MARTÍNEZ
SERVES 6 TO 8   SONORA

This curious name for a soup, Gallina Pinta, or speckled hen, refers to the various colors of the ingredients: the white corn (for pozole), brown beans, red chiles, and more. It is a regional specialty of Sonora and a very substantial one at that.

Traditionally it is much more likely to be served as the main dish of a comida, sometimes accompanied by a tomato sauce but always with some crushed, dried chiltepin (a small, round chile that grows wild in northern Mexico).

I OXTAIL (I ½ TO 2 POUNDS/675 TO 900 G), CUT INTO SMALL PIECES WITH MOST OF THE
   FAT REMOVED
½ WHITE ONION, ROUGHLY SLICED
2 GARLIC CLOVES
SALT TO TASTE
½ CUP (125 ML) PINTO BEANS
6 PEPPERCORNS
2 QUARTS (2 L) WATER
I POUND (450 G) COUNTRY-STYLE PORK SPARERIBS, CUBED
I ½ CUPS (375 ML) PREPARED AND COOKED WHITE CORN FOR POZOLE (SEE PAGE 139)
SALT TO TASTE
2 ANCHO CHILES, SEEDS AND VEINS REMOVED AND LIGHTLY TOASTED (SEE PAGE 473)

Put the oxtail into a large saucepan with the onion, garlic, salt, pinto beans, and peppercorns. Cover with the water and bring to a boil. Lower the heat and simmer for 1 hour.

Add the spareribs and white corn and continue cooking over low heat, uncovered, for another 1 to 1½ hours, until the meat is very tender and the beans soft. Add salt to taste.

About 20 minutes before the soup is done, blend one of the chiles with a little of the broth and add the mixture to the soup. Tear the other chile into thin strips and add to the soup.

Serve in deep bowls. I do not recommend freezing.

POZOLE DE JALISCO Pork and White Corn Soup

SEÑORA ISABEL MARÍN DE PAALEN
SERVES 12 TO 14

JALISCO

Through my job with the British Council for Cultural Relations I had the good fortune to meet many distinguished Mexicans, among them Isabel Marín, from a distinguished Jalisco family and widow of the painter Wolfgang Paalen. I can't remember how it came about, but I occasionally traveled with her on her trips into the country collecting folk crafts for a Mexico City museum. I still remember those trips, which contributed so much to my appreciation of rural Mexico.

Isabel had inherited a love of good food and was an excellent cook; it was she who generously took the time to give me my first lessons in making pozole and fresh corn tamales with her family's recipes. For all these years I have followed her instructions to the letter.

1 POUND (450 G) WHITE CORN KERNELS FOR POZOLE
1½ POUNDS (675 G) BONELESS STEWING PORK
½ PIG'S HEAD, ABOUT 3 POUNDS (1.35 KG)
1 POUND (450 G) PORK NECK BONES
APPROXIMATELY 14 CUPS (3.5 L) WATER
1½ TABLESPOONS SALT

TO SERVE

CHILE DE ÁRBOL SAUCE (RECIPE FOLLOWS)
I CUP (250 ML) FINELY CHOPPED WHITE ONION
I CUP (250 ML) SLICED RADISHES
2 CUPS (500 ML) FINELY SHREDDED LETTUCE OR CABBAGE
WEDGES OF LIME

Two days before serving, put the corn to soak, as indicated on page 139.

One day before serving, clean and prepare the white corn for cooking (see pages 139–40).

Cut the pork into large serving pieces and put it, with the head and bones, in cold water to soak overnight. Change the water as often as is practical.

On serving day, cover the white corn with the cold, unsalted water. Bring to a boil and cook, uncovered, over brisk heat until it opens up like a flower—about 1 hour. *Do not stir the corn* during this time, but, if necessary, skim the surface of the water from time to time.

Drain and cover the head with cold, unsalted water. Bring to a boil, then lower the heat and let it simmer, uncovered, until the flesh can be removed from the bone—but do not overcook—about 1 hour. Set it aside to cool.

When the head is cool enough to handle, remove all the meat and skin and cut it into serving pieces. Cut the ear up (there should be a piece for everyone) and set the eyes aside for the honored guest. Add the pieces of head, and the broth in which it was cooked, to the corn in its pot.

Add the salt. Place the meat on top of the corn and let the pozole cook, uncovered, over gentle heat for about 4 hours. Throughout the cooking time skim the fat from the surface. Keep some water boiling in a kettle at the side to add to the liquid in the pan. On no account should cold water be added. The liquid should be maintained at almost the same level from start to finish.

Place the meat onto a serving dish so it can be divided up more easily and everyone can have the part that he likes best. Serve the pozole with the corn in large, deep bowls, with the following small side dishes to which everyone can help himself: the Chile de Árbol Sauce, finely chopped onion, sliced radishes, finely shredded lettuce, and wedges of lime.

CHILE DE ÁRBOL SAUCE

3 OUNCES (85 G) ÁRBOL CHILES (ABOUT 2 CUPS/500 ML)
WATER TO COVER

Rinse the chiles briefly in cold water, drain, and cover with fresh water. Set aside to soak overnight.

Blend the whole chiles with the water in which they were soaking. Run the sauce through a strainer, discarding the debris. Do not add salt (traditionally no salt is added).

BEANS, RICE, AND PASTA

BEANS

Frijoles de Olla ※ *"Pot" Beans*

Frijoles Refritos ※ *Well-Fried Beans*

Frijoles Refritos a la Veracruzana ※ *Veracruz Refried Beans*

Frijoles a la Huacha ※ *"Dirty" Beans*

Frijoles Maneados Sonorenses ※ *Sonora Bean Puree*

Frijoles Colados Yucatecos ※ *Yucatecan Sieved Beans*

Frijoles a la Charra (Frijoles Borrachos) ※ *Drunken Beans*

RICE

Arroz a la Mexicana ※ *Mexican Rice*

Arroz Blanco ※ *White Rice*

Arroz Blanco con Chiles Rellenos de Elote

   ※ *White Rice with Corn-Stuffed Chiles*

Arroz Verde ※ *Green Rice*

Pastel de Lujo ※ *"Luxury Rice Cake"*

Sopa Seca de Fideo ※ *Dry Angel Hair Pasta "Soup"*

Lentejas con Piña y Plátano ※ *Lentils with Pineapple and Plantain*

Lentejas Guisadas ※ *Stewed Lentils*

The gentlemen Creoles or natives of Chiapa are as presumptuous and arrogant as if the noblest blood in the Court of Madrid ran through their veins. It is a common thing amongst them to make a dinner only with a dish of frijoles in black broth, boiled with pepper and garlic, saying it is the most nourishing meat in all the Indies; and after this so stately a dinner they will be sure to come out to the street-door of their houses to see and to be seen, and there for half an hour will they stand shaking off the crumbs of bread from their clothes, bands (but especially from their ruffs when they used them) and from their mustachios. And with their tooth-pickers they will stand picking their teeth, as if some small partridge bone stuck in them—and they will be sure to vent out some non-truth, as to say "O Sir, what a dainty partridge I have eaten today," whereas they pick out nothing from their teeth but a black husk of a dry frijol or Turkey bean.

—FROM THOMAS GAGE, *Travels in the New World*

BEANS

Frijoles (dried beans as opposed to fresh) are an indispensable part of the Mexican meal, and there is an astonishing variety to choose from: the black *veracruzanos,* the purple-mottled *flor de mayo,* the deep yellow *canarios,* the brownish *bayos* or *sabinos,* the white *aluvias,* and yellow *peruanos*—to name a few—overflowing in big woven sacks or poured into piles like small slag heaps. The stands where they are sold are usually grouped together at one side of the market, and there the peasant women will come and choose with great care and discussion, running the beans through their fingers to make sure their few dwindling pesos are well spent. Or on market days in the small towns and villages, canvas awnings like huge square umbrellas are set up along the streets by those with produce to sell: small bunches of fresh herbs, a basket of squash, or a new crop of fresh beans—frijoles nuevos—still in their pods, with just a few shucked ones at the side so that you can be assured they are full and fresh.

Each type of bean has its special flavor and quality. To savor them, they should be cooked (Mexicans never soak them) in the simplest of ways—*de olla*—very slowly in an earthenware pot, in water with a little onion, lard, and salt—and, if they are black, with a good sprig of epazote, the pungent flavor of which complements them. They are served in their broth in a small bowl, like soup, but usually after the main course of the meal. You can add a little cheese to melt and string into them, or a pungent, pickled chile, and scoop it all up with a tortilla—if you can manage it. Occasionally a few nopales—tender cactus pieces—are cooked in with them, or some chicharrón—pork cracklings. In the north, in Nuevo León for instance, they can become more complicated. Take, for instance, Frijoles a la Charra, with pieces of pork rind and some fried tomato, onion, and coriander; add some beer and they become *borrachos*, and slightly different still, with a strong flavor of cumin, the *rancheros*, to accompany the plainly roasted *agujas* or *cabrito* (ribs of beef or kid).

For a change they can be fried—but in their broth, so that all the flavor is absorbed. They can be lightly fried to a loose paste—no onion, nothing, just beans—and accompanied, as they were once served to me in a modest restaurant in Tacámbaro in Michoacán, with some thick, soured cream. In Veracruz the black beans are fried with chopped onions and a small, dried red chile, and farther east in the Yucatán, the beans are sieved to a smooth paste, *colados*, and then fried with onion and the whole, fiery habanero chile; while in Oaxaca the black beans are seasoned with varied wild herbs.

Beans are not only the food of the poor; they are everybody's food. Beans are served with *almuerzo*, the hearty midmorning breakfast; always after the main course of the *comida*, the heavy midday meal, and again at supper—this time perhaps just a few fried beans with cheese. No wonder an Englishman traveling across Mexico in 1864 wrote: "but for the frijoles which allowed, and which come in at the conclusion—like God Save the Queen at the end of a concert—we should have gone to bed famishing." Colloquially, to eat is *frijolear*.

FRIJOLES DE OLLA "Pot" Beans
SERVES 10   CENTRAL AND SOUTHERN MEXICO

Frijoles de Olla are usually served, both beans and broth, after the comida's *main course. It is traditional to serve them in small earthenware bowls, and they can be scooped up with a tortilla or eaten (less messily) with a spoon. You can dress them up with small pieces of creamy cheese, which will melt most appetizingly, or add a little zest to the taste with a small amount of chile, fresh or en escabeche.*

In Mexico use frijoles negros (black beans) or bayos, canarios, flor de mayo, etc. (you have a wide choice).

1 POUND (450 G) DRIED BEANS—BLACK (ABOUT 2¼ CUPS/565 ML) OR PINTO (ABOUT 2½ CUPS/625 ML)

10 TO 12 CUPS (2.5 TO 3 L) HOT WATER, APPROXIMATELY

⅓ CUP (85 ML) ROUGHLY SLICED WHITE ONION

2 TABLESPOONS PORK LARD

SALT TO TASTE

2 LARGE SPRIGS EPAZOTE, ONLY IF BLACK BEANS ARE USED

Rinse the beans in cold water and let them run through your hands to make sure there are no small stones or pieces of earth among them. Put them into a pot and cover with the hot water. Add the onion and lard and bring to a boil, then lower the heat and let the beans simmer, covered, until they are just soft and the skins are breaking open— about 4 hours for black beans and 2½ for other varieties, although it is very difficult to be precise. (Much will depend on the age of the beans, how long they have been stored, and if they have dried out too much, and on the efficiency of the pot or pan in which you are cooking them.) Add the salt and continue cooking over low heat for another ½ hour or more, until the beans are completely soft.

For black beans, add the epazote just before the end of the cooking time, as it tends to lose flavor if cooked too long.

These beans will keep in the refrigerator for about 2 days. They can also be frozen up to about 3 months.

FRIJOLES REFRITOS Well-Fried Beans

SERVES 6   CENTRAL MEXICO

Well-fried beans are used for tortas (see page 190) and other recipes in this book, but more commonly they accompany breakfast eggs and suppertime snacks. Pork lard is, of course, best for this recipe, but if you flinch at the quantity cut it down or use vegetable oil. Bacon drippings provide too strong a flavor if you want to cook beans authentically.

6 TABLESPOONS PORK LARD ($^1/_3$ CUP/85 ML)
2 TABLESPOONS FINELY CHOPPED WHITE ONION
8 OUNCES (225 G) BEANS COOKED AS FOR FRIJOLES DE OLLA (PAGE 154),
    3 $^1/_2$ TO 4 CUPS/875 ML TO 1 L, WITH BROTH

In a very heavy skillet—about 10 inches (25 cm) in diameter—heat the lard and fry the onion, without browning, until soft. Add 1 cup (250 ml) of the beans and their broth and mash well as you cook them over high heat. Gradually add the rest of the beans, little by little, mashing them all the time until you have a coarse puree.

As the puree begins to dry out and sizzle at the edges, it is ready to be used for the recipes calling for frijoles refritos.

NOTE: Frijoles Refritos freeze well and can always be ready to use; just reheat them.

FRIJOLES REFRITOS A LA VERACRUZANA
Veracruz Refried Beans
MAKES ABOUT 3 CUPS (750 ML)   VERACRUZ

This recipe from the area around the port of Veracruz differs from those prepared around Jalapa, which are flavored with avocado leaves. These beans are used for Garnachas Veracruzanos de Masa Cocida (page 28) and the gorditas de frijol of that area.

3 TABLESPOONS LARD OR VEGETABLE OIL
2 TABLESPOONS FINELY CHOPPED WHITE ONION
2 JALAPEÑO CHILES, FINELY CHOPPED
8 OUNCES (225 G) COOKED BLACK BEANS (SEE PAGE 154), WITH BROTH

Heat the lard in a large skillet, add the onion and chile, and fry over medium heat for 1 minute. Add the beans and their cooking liquid and fry over fairly high heat, mashing to a textured paste—about 15 minutes.

FRIJOLES A LA HUACHA "Dirty" Beans

SEÑORA BERTA LÓPEZ DE MARRUFO

SERVES ABOUT 10

The very idea of beans fried with mint is enough to make anyone stop in his tracks, especially the hardened aficionados of Mexican food. But it's done in Yucatán. Señora Berta, whose recipe this is, tells me that the Mayan word huacha *is used to describe someone from the interior of Mexico, and is usually derogatory, hence the "dirty" in the recipe title.*

¼ CUP (65 ML) PORK LARD

2 TABLESPOONS FINELY CHOPPED WHITE ONION

¼ HABANERO CHILE OR ANY FRESH, HOT GREEN CHILE, FINELY CHOPPED

I POUND (450 G) BLACK TURTLE BEANS COOKED AS FOR FRIJOLES DE OLLA (PAGE 154),
    3½ TO 4 CUPS/875 ML TO I L, WITH BROTH

7 LARGE MINT LEAVES, ROUGHLY CHOPPED

Melt the lard and fry the onion and chile, without browning, until soft.

Blend the beans with 1½ cups (375 ml) of the broth they were cooked in until smooth, and add them to the pan. Fry the beans until they reduce to a thick paste, about 10 minutes (see page 155), adding the chopped mint leaves toward the end of the cooking time. Fry for a few minutes longer and serve.

NOTE: These beans can be prepared several hours ahead and leftovers can be frozen for about 2 months.

FRIJOLES MANEADOS SONORENSES Sonora Bean Puree

SEÑORA MARÍA DOLORES TORRES YZÁBAL

SERVES 10

Some years ago, an old friend and culinary expert, María Dolores, served these beans to me during a late, sumptuous lunch — and I can only say that they are wickedly rich. I had heard that the original recipe was cooked with butter and cream, which is so good in the northwest of Mexico, but María Dolores assures me that this is how her family, los Izabál, always prepared them when she was growing up in Sonora. The name maneados *is derived from the continual stirring of the beans to incorporate the rest of the ingredients — before the days of the blender, of course.*

1 POUND (450 G) PINTO OR CALIFORNIA PINK BEANS (ABOUT 2½ CUPS/625 ML)

12 TO 14 CUPS (3 TO 3.5 L) HOT WATER, APPROXIMATELY

½ SMALL WHITE ONION, ROUGHLY SLICED

1 CUP (250 ML) PLUS 3 TABLESPOONS VEGETABLE OIL

1 TABLESPOON SALT, OR TO TASTE

⅔ CUP (165 ML) WHOLE MILK

3 ANCHO CHILES, WIPED CLEAN

8 OUNCES (225 G) ASADERO OR CHIHUAHUA CHEESE, OR MILD CHEDDAR, JACK, OR
DOMESTIC MUENSTER, CUT INTO ½-INCH (1.5-CM) CUBES

Run the beans through your hands slowly, picking out any small stones or pieces of dirt that might be among them. Rinse in cold water and put into a large flameproof bean pot.

Add 12 cups (3 l) of the hot water, the onion, and the 3 tablespoons oil and bring to a simmer. Cover the beans and continue simmering until they are just beginning to soften and the skins are splitting open—about 1 hour (depending on how dry the beans are). Add the salt and continue cooking until the beans are soft and mushy, about 30 minutes; there should be some broth in the pot. If the broth reduces too much during the cooking time, then add more water. Put the rest of the oil—1 cup (250 ml)—into a casserole. Put the casserole into the oven and set the temperature at 350°F (180°C).

Meanwhile, put one third each of the beans and milk into a blender jar with a little of the broth and blend until smooth. Repeat twice to use up the beans and milk.

By the time the beans have been blended, the oil should be very hot; if not, leave in the oven for a few minutes longer. When the oil is ready, stir the bean puree into the casserole and return to the oven to cook, uncovered, until the edges are just drying out and the mixture is reduced—about 1 hour 15 minutes.

After you put the bean puree into the oven, slit the chiles open, remove the veins and seeds, and toast lightly on both sides on a warm griddle or comal. Tear the chiles into thin strips and add to the bean puree.

At the end of the cooking time, add the cheese and return the casserole to the oven until the cheese has melted—about 10 minutes. Serve immediately.

FRIJOLES COLADOS YUCATECOS Yucatecan Sieved Beans
SERVES ABOUT 6   YUCATÁN

Only in southeastern Mexico—Yucatán, Campeche, and Quintana Roo—are beans sieved before they are fried to a smooth paste. Since this is time-consuming, they could be blended (not in a food processor) to a smooth consistency.

3 TABLESPOONS PORK LARD
¼ CUP (65 ML) ROUGHLY SLICED WHITE ONION
8 OUNCES (225 G) BLACK TURTLE BEANS, COOKED AS FOR FRIJOLES DE OLLA (PAGE 154)
1 HABANERO CHILE OR ANY FRESH, HOT GREEN CHILE, LEFT WHOLE AND WIPED CLEAN
2 LARGE STEMS EPAZOTE

Melt the lard in a large, heavy skillet and cook the onion, without browning, until translucent.

Add the blended beans, whole chile, and epazote, and cook over fairly high heat until the beans form a loose paste that plops off the spoon—about 15 minutes (depending, of course, how much liquid there is with the beans in the first place). Be sure to stir and scrape the bottom of the pan from time to time so the beans do not stick.

FRIJOLES A LA CHARRA (FRIJOLES BORRACHOS)
Drunken Beans
SERVES 6   NUEVO LEÓN

This is the Nuevo León version of frijoles de olla. *Literally it means "beans cooked in the way the lady* charro *would prepare them" (the* charros *are the elegant horsemen of Mexico).*

The green chiles and coriander give the beans a great flavor, making them a perfect complement to the simple broiled meats so popular in Monterrey, the capital of Nuevo León: the agujas *(ribs of beef) and* cabrito *(kid) cooked over wood or charcoal. There are many variations of this recipe and the very similar* frijoles rancheros *and* frijoles fronterizos. *Monterrey is an important center for the beer industry—add ⅓ small bottle of beer to the recipe and they become* frijoles borrachos *("drunken beans"), a very lusty plateful.*

These beans are served in individual bowls to accompany broiled meats.

THE PICADILLO FILLING

4 OUNCES (115 G) PORK RIND

8 OUNCES (225 G) PINK OR PINTO BEANS (ABOUT 1 ¼ CUPS/315 ML)

¼ MEDIUM WHITE ONION, SLICED

2 SMALL GARLIC CLOVES, SLICED

6 CUPS (1.5 L) WATER

SALT TO TASTE

3 THICK STRIPS BACON (ABOUT 4 OUNCES/115 G)

2 TABLESPOONS MELTED LARD OR PORK DRIPPINGS

12 OUNCES (340 G) TOMATOES, FINELY CHOPPED (ABOUT 2 ROUNDED CUPS/525 ML)

3 SERRANO CHILES, FINELY CHOPPED

4 LARGE SPRIGS CILANTRO

Cut the pork rind into small squares and put together with the beans, onion, and garlic into a bean pot.

Add the water and bring to a boil. Lower the heat, cover the pot, and let the beans cook gently until they are tender—about 1½ hours.

Add the salt and cook, uncovered, for another 15 minutes.

Cut the bacon into small pieces and cook it gently in the lard until it is slightly browned. Remove with a slotted spoon and set aside.

Add the tomatoes, chiles, and cilantro to the pan and cook the mixture over fairly high heat for about 5 minutes, until reduced and seasoned.

Add the tomato mixture and bacon pieces to the beans and let them cook together, uncovered, over low heat for about 15 minutes.

NOTE: These beans may be cooked a day ahead, adding the cilantro a short while before serving, but they must be refrigerated as they quickly sour. I do not recommend freezing.

RICE

In a typical Mexican *comida,* which is eaten about two o'clock in the afternoon, there will always be a *sopa seca*—a "dry soup" course—either of pasta cooked in a Mexican way or rice; it follows the "wet soup" course and precedes the main course. There is also a place for beans in the *comida,* after the main course.

ARROZ A LA MEXICANA Mexican Rice
SERVES 6

You can cook rice ahead, then heat it through gently, tightly covered, in a 300°F (150°C) oven for about 30 minutes. Leftover rice can be heated through in the same way the next day. (I do not recommend steaming, since the flavor of the rice will be diluted.) Arroz a la Mexicana also freezes successfully. To reheat, make a foil package of it and place, still frozen, in a 350°F (180°C) oven. Heat through for about 45 minutes.

1 ½ CUPS (375 ML) LONG-GRAIN UNCONVERTED WHITE RICE

⅓ CUP (85 ML) VEGETABLE OIL

8 OUNCES (225 G) TOMATOES, ROUGHLY CHOPPED (ABOUT 1 ½ CUPS/375 ML)

¼ SMALL WHITE ONION, ROUGHLY CHOPPED

1 GARLIC CLOVE, ROUGHLY CHOPPED

ABOUT 3 ½ CUPS (875 ML) WELL-SALTED CHICKEN BROTH

1 SMALL CARROT, SCRAPED AND THINLY SLICED (OPTIONAL)

2 TABLESPOONS PEAS (OPTIONAL)

1 WHOLE SPRIG PARSLEY (OPTIONAL)

SALT TO TASTE

For this quantity you will need a heavy-bottomed, flameproof pan about 4 inches (10 cm) deep and 9 inches (23 cm) across.

Pour hot water to cover over the rice and let it stand for about 5 minutes. Drain the rice and rinse well in cold water, then shake the colander well and leave the rice to drain for a few minutes.

Heat the oil. Give the rice a final shake and stir it into the oil until the grains are well covered, then fry until just turning color, stirring and turning the rice over so it will cook evenly and will not stick to the pan. This process should take about 10 minutes—depending, of course, on the size of the pan—but it should be done over high heat or the rice will become mushy in its final stage. Tip the pan to one side and drain off any excess oil or drain rice in a fine strainer.

Blend the tomatoes, onion, and garlic until smooth—there should be about 1 cup (250 ml). Add the puree to the fried rice, then, continuing to cook over high heat, stir and scrape the bottom of the pan until the mixture is dry.

Add the broth, carrot, peas, and parsley. Add salt as necessary, then stir well (do not stir again during the cooking time). Cook over medium heat, covered, until the liquid has been absorbed and small air holes appear in the rice. This will take about 10 minutes. Remove the pan from the heat and cover the rice with a piece of terry cloth. Cover with a tightly fitting lid so that no steam can escape, and set aside in a warm place for about 20 minutes, so the rice can continue cooking in its own steam and the grains will expand.

Before serving, loosen the rice with a fork from the bottom.

ARROZ BLANCO White Rice
SERVES 6

1 ½ CUPS (375 ML) LONG-GRAIN UNCONVERTED WHITE RICE
⅓ CUP (85 ML) VEGETABLE OIL
3 TABLESPOONS FINELY CHOPPED WHITE ONION
1 GARLIC CLOVE, FINELY CHOPPED
3 ½ CUPS (875 ML) WELL-SALTED LIGHT CHICKEN BROTH
⅓ CARROT, SCRAPED, TRIMMED, AND THINLY SLICED (OPTIONAL)
2 TABLESPOONS PEAS (OPTIONAL)
SALT TO TASTE

You will need a heavy-bottomed, flameproof pan about 4 inches (10 cm) deep and 9 inches (23 cm) across.

Pour hot water to cover over the rice and let it stand for about 5 minutes. Drain the rice and rinse well in cold water. Shake the colander well and leave the rice to drain for a few minutes.

Heat the oil. Give the rice a final shake, add it to the pan, and stir until all the grains are well covered with the oil. Fry until just turning color, then add the onion and garlic and fry a few moments longer until these two ingredients are translucent, stirring and turning almost constantly so that they cook evenly and do not stick to the pan. The entire process should take about 10 minutes—depending, of course, on the size of the pan—and it should be done over high heat or it will take too long and the rice will become mushy in the final stage.

Tip the pan to one side and drain off any excess oil (strain and refrigerate to use again). Add the broth, carrot, peas, and salt to taste and cook uncovered over medium heat—do not stir again—until the liquid has been absorbed and small air holes appear in the rice—about 10 minutes. Cover the rice with a piece of terry cloth and then cover with a tightly fitting lid so that none of the steam can escape. Set aside in a warm place for about 20 minutes, so it can continue to cook and the grains will expand.

Before serving, loosen the rice with a fork from the bottom. Serve, if desired, topped with Rajas de Chile Estilo Oaxaqueño (page 219) or Rajas de Chiles Jalapeños Frescos (page 238), or with fried plantain.

ARROZ BLANCO CON CHILES RELLENOS DE ELOTE
White Rice with Corn-Stuffed Chiles
SERVES 6   CENTRAL MEXICO

This is a particularly delicious combination of chiles, rice, and corn, and it can be made with either poblano or ancho chiles. A very substantial dish, this makes an excellent vegetarian main course.

ARROZ BLANCO (PAGE 161), USING 2 CUPS (500 ML) LONG-GRAIN UNCONVERTED RICE,
    MEASURED RAW, AND 4 CUPS (1 L) BROTH
CHILES RELLENOS DE ELOTE CON CREMA (PAGE 213)
1 ½ CUPS (375 ML) THICK SOUR CREAM (SEE PAGE 489) OR CRÈME FRAÎCHE
4 OUNCES (115 G) CHIHUAHUA CHEESE OR MILD CHEDDAR, GRATED (ABOUT 1 SCANT
    CUP/225 ML)

Preheat the oven to 350°F (180°C). Have ready a buttered ovenproof dish about 4 inches (10 cm) deep and 10 inches (25 cm) across or in diameter.

Spread half of the prepared rice over the bottom of the dish. Place the stuffed chiles in one layer over the rice and top with the remaining rice.

Cover the dish and bake for about 30 minutes or until the rice is bubbling at the bottom and well heated through. Remove the foil, pour the cream over the top, sprinkle with cheese, and return to the oven until the cheese has melted—but not browned.

ARROZ VERDE Green Rice

SEÑORA MARÍA LUISA CAMARENA DE RODRÍGUEZ
SERVES 6

PUEBLA

1 ½ CUPS (375 ML) LONG-GRAIN UNCONVERTED WHITE RICE
⅓ CUP (85 ML) VEGETABLE OIL
½ CUP (125 ML) COLD WATER, MORE IF NECESSARY
1 SMALL BUNCH FLAT-LEAF PARSLEY
3 SPRIGS CILANTRO
3 LARGE ROMAINE LETTUCE LEAVES
2 POBLANO CHILES, SEEDS AND VEINS REMOVED, ROUGHLY CHOPPED (NOT CHARRED)
2 TABLESPOONS ROUGHLY CHOPPED WHITE ONION
1 GARLIC CLOVE, ROUGHLY CHOPPED
2 ½ TO 3 CUPS (625 TO 750 ML) LIGHT CHICKEN BROTH
SALT TO TASTE

Have ready a heavy-bottomed pan about 4 inches (10 cm) deep and 9 inches (23 cm) across.

Cover the rice with hot water and let soak for about 5 minutes. Drain in a strainer, then rinse well in cold water and leave to drain for a few minutes.

Heat the oil in the pan. Give a final shake to the rice in the strainer and stir it into the oil. Fry over a very high heat, turning the rice thoroughly from time to time, until it is a pale golden color. Tip the pan to one side, holding back the rice with a wide metal spatula, and drain off about 3 tablespoons of the oil.

Pour the ½ cup (125 ml) of water into a blender jar. Add the greens, chiles, onion, and garlic and blend until smooth, adding more water only if absolutely necessary to release the blades of the blender.

Add the blended ingredients to the rice and fry over high heat, stirring constantly and scraping the bottom of the pan, until the rice is almost dry. Add the broth and salt to taste and cook over medium heat until all the liquid has been absorbed and small air holes appear in the surface of the rice—about 15 minutes.

Cover the pan with a lid or foil and cook for 5 minutes longer. Remove from the heat. Cover the rice with a piece of terry cloth and set aside to continue cooking in its own steam for 20 to 30 minutes.

PASTEL DE LUJO "Luxury Rice Cake"

SEÑORA ALICIA FERRER DE GONZÁLEZ

SERVES 6

THE MEAT FILLING

6 OUNCES (180 G) BONELESS STEWING PORK WITH SOME FAT, FINELY CHOPPED (NOT GROUND)

12 OUNCES (340 G) BONELESS CHICKEN, FINELY CHOPPED (NOT GROUND)

1/3 CUP (85 ML) FINELY CHOPPED WHITE ONION

1/4 GREEN BELL PEPPER, SEEDED AND FINELY CHOPPED

8 OUNCES (225 G) TOMATOES, FINELY CHOPPED (ABOUT 1 1/3 CUPS/335 ML)

12 SMALL PITTED GREEN OLIVES, ROUGHLY CHOPPED

1 TABLESPOON LARGE CAPERS, RINSED AND DRAINED

1 TABLESPOON RAISINS

3/4 CUP (185 ML) WATER

A PINCH OF GRANULATED SUGAR

SALT TO TASTE

THE SEASONING FOR THE MEAT

2 WHOLE ALLSPICE

1 WHOLE CLOVE

1/2-INCH (1.5-CM) PIECE OF CINNAMON STICK

16 PEPPERCORNS

2 GARLIC CLOVES, TOASTED AND PEELED (SEE PAGE 492)

1 TABLESPOON VINEGAR

1/2 CUP (125 ML) MEDIUM DRY SHERRY

THE RICE MIXTURE

3 CUPS (750 ML) CORN KERNELS

1/2 CUP (125 ML) MILK

1 CUP (250 ML) LONG-GRAIN UNCONVERTED WHITE RICE COOKED AS FOR ARROZ BLANCO (SEE PAGE 161), WHICH SHOULD MAKE ABOUT 4 CUPS (1 L)

2 LARGE EGGS, WELL BEATEN

2 TABLESPOONS UNSALTED BUTTER, SOFTENED

1 TABLESPOON SUGAR

SALT TO TASTE

1 TABLESPOON FINELY GROUND TOASTED BREAD CRUMBS

Preheat the oven to 350°F (180°C).

Mix all the ingredients for the meat in a bowl. Put into an ungreased large skillet over low heat.

Grind the spices together in a spice grinder to a powder.

In a small bowl, crush the garlic with the vinegar and add the ground spices. Stir this well into the meat in the skillet and continue cooking, uncovered, over medium heat until the meat is tender and the juices have evaporated—about 20 minutes.

Remove the skillet from the heat, stir in the sherry, and set aside to cool a little.

Put about one third of the corn into the blender with the milk and blend until smooth. Gradually add the rest of the corn by degrees, blending well after each addition. Stir the corn into the rice together with the eggs, butter, sugar, and salt.

In an ovenproof dish about 4 inches (10 cm) deep, spread half of the rice and corn mixture. Cover the rice evenly with the meat mixture and then spread with the remaining rice and corn mixture. Sprinkle the bread crumbs over the top of the rice and bake until well heated through—about 30 minutes. Serve as soon as possible.

NOTE: The meat mixture and rice can be cooked a few hours ahead, but the corn should be blended at the last moment since it tends to sour easily when blended.

I have frozen leftovers quite successfully for about 1 month.

SOPA SECA DE FIDEO Dry Angel Hair Pasta "Soup"
SERVES 6   CENTRAL MEXICO

As are all dry soups, this is traditionally served alone as a pasta course. In its final stage, this recipe may also be cooked in a water bath on top of the stove and will take 45 minutes to 1 hour. It is equally delicious but has a softer texture.

¼ CUP (65 ML) VEGETABLE OIL
8 OUNCES (225 G) ANGEL HAIR PASTA
1 POUND (450 G) TOMATOES, ROUGHLY CHOPPED (ABOUT 3 CUPS/750 ML)
2 TABLESPOONS ROUGHLY CHOPPED WHITE ONION
1 GARLIC CLOVE, ROUGHLY CHOPPED
½ CUP (125 ML) CHICKEN BROTH
SALT TO TASTE
4 CHIPOTLE CHILES EN ADOBO, ROUGHLY CHOPPED
2 TO 3 OUNCES (60 TO 85 G) GRATED CHIHUAHUA CHEESE OR MILD CHEDDAR

TO SERVE
¾ CUP (185 ML) CRÈME FRAÎCHE OR THICK SOUR CREAM (SEE PAGE 489)

Preheat the oven to 350°F (180°C). Grease a 1-quart (1-l) casserole or 8 by 8-inch (20 by 20-cm) ovenproof dish at least 2 inches (5 cm) deep.

Heat the oil in a large, deep skillet and fry the angel hair pasta until a deep golden color, about 3 minutes. (They brown quickly, so turn them over carefully from time to time so that they do not break up.) Drain off all but about 2 tablespoons of the oil.

Blend the tomatoes with the onion and garlic and add to the pan. Fry over high heat to reduce, stirring well and scraping the bottom of the pan to avoid sticking, about 5 minutes or until the mixture is almost dry. Add the broth and salt, cover the pan, and cook over low heat until the liquid has been absorbed—8 to 10 minutes. Press the pieces of chile into the mixture at 1½-inch (4-cm) intervals.

Turn the pasta into the prepared dish, cover loosely, and bake until the pasta is just beginning to shrink away from the sides of the pan and is bubbling.

Sprinkle the cheese on top and return to the oven until the cheese has melted but not browned. Serve, topping each portion with a little of the crème fraîche.

LENTEJAS CON PIÑA Y PLÁTANO

Lentils with Pineapple and Plantain

SEÑORA GODILEVA CASTRO

SERVES 6

MEXICO CITY

When I rented a house for part of the summer in Mexico City, it was a great joy to know that Godileva, my old maid (whom I wrote about in The Cuisines of Mexico)*, was living just three blocks away. She often popped in to help me and give her opinion on the recipes I was testing. This popular recipe was a favorite of hers. It can be served as a vegetable to accompany broiled or roasted meats.*

4 OUNCES (115 G OR ½ ROUNDED CUP/125 ML) DRIED LENTILS

6 CUPS (1.5 L) COLD WATER

8 OUNCES (225 G) TOMATOES, FINELY CHOPPED (ABOUT 3 CUPS/750 ML)

1 GARLIC CLOVE, ROUGHLY CHOPPED

2 TABLESPOONS ROUGHLY CHOPPED WHITE ONION

1 ½ TABLESPOONS VEGETABLE OIL

1 THICK SLICE PINEAPPLE, PEELED, CORED, AND CUT INTO SMALL CUBES

½ MEDIUM-SIZE, VERY RIPE PLANTAIN (ABOUT ½ POUND/225 G), PEELED AND CUT INTO
    THICK ROUNDS

SALT TO TASTE

Rinse the lentils in cold water and drain. Cover with the cold water and bring to a boil, then lower the heat and simmer until soft—2½ to 3 hours, depending on how dry they are. Drain and reserve the broth—there should be about 1½ cups (375 ml); add water if necessary to make up to this amount.

Blend the tomatoes with the garlic and onion until smooth. Heat the oil and fry the tomato puree over a high heat for about 3 minutes, stirring constantly and scraping the bottom of the pan. Lower the heat, add the pineapple and plantain, and continue cooking for 5 minutes more.

Add the lentils and 1½ cups (375 ml) of the reserved broth to the pan, then add the salt and cook until the fruit is tender—about 20 minutes (the lentil mixture should be neither too thick nor too runny).

This can be prepared several hours ahead. I do not recommend freezing.

LENTEJAS GUISADAS Stewed Lentils

SERVES 6   CENTRAL AND NORTHERN MEXICO

Lentils cooked in this way may be served as a soup or as an accompaniment to the main dish, served in a separate bowl. If you are serving it as a soup, you may have to dilute it with water. It can then be served with fried croutons or, better still, crisp-fried tortilla pieces (see page 94).

FOR COOKING LENTILS

8 OUNCES (225 G) OR 1 HEAPED CUP/265 ML DRIED BROWN LENTILS

1 MEDIUM CARROT, TRIMMED, SCRAPED, AND SLICED

2 SLICES WHITE ONION

8 CUPS (2 L) COLD WATER

3 TABLESPOONS VEGETABLE OIL

2 GARLIC CLOVES

1 MEDIUM WHITE ONION, FINELY CHOPPED

8 OUNCES FINELY CHOPPED TOMATOES (ABOUT 1 1/3 CUPS/335 ML)

SALT TO TASTE

2 GÜERO CHILES, LARGOS, OR JALAPEÑOS, OR ANY FRESH, HOT GREEN CHILES

2 TABLESPOONS ROUGHLY CHOPPED CILANTRO

FOR SERVING

2 TABLESPOONS FINELY CHOPPED WHITE ONION

Rinse the lentils in cold water, then drain and put into a large saucepan with the carrot, onion, and water. Bring to a boil, lower the heat, and simmer until soft, 2½ to 3 hours, depending on the quality of the lentils. They should be very brothy.

Heat the oil in a skillet and lightly brown the garlic. Discard the garlic, then, in the same oil, fry the chopped onion gently, without browning, until soft, about 1 minute. Add the chopped tomatoes and cook over high heat, stirring constantly and scraping the bottom of the pan, until the mixture has reduced to a sauce—about 3 minutes.

Add the tomato sauce to the lentils, with salt to taste, and cook over medium heat for 15 minutes longer. Cut a cross in the bottom of the chiles and add them to the lentils. Cook for another 15 minutes, then add the cilantro and cook for 5 minutes longer. Scatter the onion over the bowls of stewed lentils.

This dish can be prepared several hours ahead and can be frozen for a limited period—1 month maximum.

EGG DISHES

Huevos Rancheros ✳ *Country Eggs*

Huevos Revueltos a la Mexicana ✳ *Mexican Scrambled Eggs*

Huevos Revueltos con Chorizo ✳ *Eggs Scrambled with Chorizo*

Huevos Revueltos con Totopos y Jitomate

✳ *Mexican Scrambled Eggs with Totopos*

Huevos Revueltos con Totopos y Salsa de Chile Pasilla

✳ *Eggs Scrambled with Tortilla Crisps and Pasilla Sauce*

Huevos Revueltos del Rancho ✳ *Farmhouse Scrambled Eggs*

Salsa de Huevo ✳ *Oaxacan Scrambled Eggs*

Huevo a la Sorpresa ✳ *Egg Surprise*

Nopales con Huevo ✳ *Nopal Cactus with Egg*

Huevos en Rabo de Mestiza ✳ *Eggs Poached in a Chile-Tomato Broth*

Huevos Motuleños ✳ *Eggs as They Are Prepared in Motúl*

Machacado de Huevo ✳ *Eggs with Dried Beef*

Huevos con Epazote y Chile ✳ *Eggs with Epazote and Chiles*

The hearty mid-morning *almuerzo*, the Mexican equivalent to brunch, is still very much in vogue—and many a successful business deal has been completed over it—for those who have the luxury of escaping from their offices to enjoy it. *Almuerzo* serves as a comforting cushion until the late afternoon *comida*. I, who had been brought up with typically English breakfasts, had long believed that they could not be equaled. However it did not take many years of living in Mexico to find that bacon and eggs accompanied by fried mushrooms and tomatoes, or grilled kippers—delicious as they can be—began to pale beside luscious fresh tropical fruits, eggs cooked in one of the many recipes that follow, fried beans, café con leche, and a freshly made *pan dulce*.

🌾 The following recipes are just a sampling of the many creative ways in which the Mexican cook varies the breakfast meal using whatever is left over and can be deliciously combined with eggs. (Many others can be found in *The Art of Mexican Cooking*.)

HUEVOS RANCHEROS Country Eggs
SERVES 1

This popular way of preparing eggs is also the one that is best known outside Mexico, and rightly so. It combines refreshing tastes and textures to make a very satisfying breakfast dish.

To serve the eggs a little more elegantly—as I have eaten them in a Mexican home—cut the tortilla to fit a cocotte, a small, round, shallow ovenproof dish, and mask the eggs with half red and half green sauce. They can be sprinkled with a grated melting cheese and lightly browned under a broiler.

2 TABLESPOONS VEGETABLE OIL
2 SMALL TORTILLAS
2 LARGE EGGS
½ CUP (125 ML) SALSA RANCHERA (PAGE 238), WARM

Heat the oil in a skillet and fry the tortillas lightly on both sides, as you would for enchiladas—they should not become crisp. Drain them on paper toweling and place them on a warmed dish.

In the same oil, fry the eggs, then place them on the tortillas.

Cover the eggs with the warmed sauce and serve immediately.

HUEVOS REVUELTOS A LA MEXICANA Mexican Scrambled Eggs
SERVES 1

Next in popularity to huevos rancheros *is Huevos Revueltos a la Mexicana, eggs scrambled with a mixture of lightly fried—some cooks leave the ingredients raw—onion, chile, and tomato. There are many variations on this theme (see the recipes that follow).*

2½ TABLESPOONS VEGETABLE OIL
4 OUNCES (115 G) TOMATOES, FINELY CHOPPED (ABOUT ⅔ CUP/165 ML)
2 SERRANO CHILES OR TO TASTE, FINELY CHOPPED
2 TABLESPOONS FINELY CHOPPED WHITE ONION
SALT TO TASTE
2 LARGE EGGS

Heat the oil in a skillet and stir in the chopped ingredients with salt to taste. Cook for 1 minute.

Lightly beat the eggs with a little salt and stir into the tomato-chile mixture. Stir over medium heat until set.

Serve immediately with hot tortillas.

HUEVOS REVUELTOS CON CHORIZO
Eggs Scrambled with Chorizo
SERVES 1

1 CHORIZO, ABOUT 2 OUNCES (60 G)

2 LARGE EGGS

SALT IF NECESSARY

Heat the pan. Skin the chorizo and crumble it into the pan. Let it cook gently—if the heat is too high it will burn quickly—until the fat has rendered out of the meat. Drain off all but 2 tablespoons of the fat.

Break the eggs into the pan and stir until set. Add salt if necessary.

Serve immediately.

HUEVOS REVUELTOS CON TOTOPOS Y JITOMATE
Mexican Scrambled Eggs with Totopos
SERVES 4

This makes a very good brunch dish.

VEGETABLE OIL FOR FRYING

6 TORTILLAS, EACH CUT INTO 6 TRIANGULAR PIECES AND DRIED (SEE PAGE 94)

¼ CUP (65 ML) VEGETABLE OIL

3 TABLESPOONS FINELY CHOPPED WHITE ONION

8 OUNCES (225 G) TOMATOES, FINELY CHOPPED (ABOUT 1 ⅓ CUPS/335 ML)

4 TO 6 SERRANO CHILES, FINELY CHOPPED

6 LARGE EGGS

SALT TO TASTE

Heat the oil in a large skillet and fry the tortilla pieces, one half at a time, so they cook evenly. They should be just a little crisp but not too brown. Drain on paper toweling and keep warm.

Heat $\frac{1}{4}$ cup oil, then add the chopped ingredients to the pan and cook over medium heat for 5 minutes, stirring the mixture from time to time.

Beat the eggs together with the salt and add them, with the dried tortilla pieces, to the pan. Cook, stirring, until the eggs are set but not too dry.

The dish should be eaten immediately.

HUEVOS REVUELTOS CON TOTOPOS Y SALSA DE CHILE PASILLA Eggs Scrambled with Tortilla Crisps and Pasilla Sauce

SEÑORA MARÍA LUISA DE MARTÍNEZ

SERVES 1   MEXICO CITY

$\frac{1}{4}$ CUP (65 ML) VEGETABLE OIL

1 $\frac{1}{2}$ SMALL TORTILLAS, CUT INTO STRIPS AND DRIED (SEE PAGE 94)

2 LARGE EGGS

SALT TO TASTE

3 TABLESPOONS SALSA DE CHILE PASILLA (PAGE 246), AT ROOM TEMPERATURE

1 TABLESPOON FINELY CHOPPED WHITE ONION

1 TABLESPOON CRUMBLED QUESO FRESCO

Heat the oil in a large skillet and fry the tortillas until they are just crisp and a light golden brown.

Leaving the crisps in the pan, drain off all but about 1 tablespoon of the oil.

Beat the eggs together with the salt and add them to the crisps in the pan. Stir the eggs over medium heat until they are set.

Serve the eggs topped with the sauce and sprinkled with the onion and cheese.

HUEVOS REVUELTOS DEL RANCHO Farmhouse Scrambled Eggs

SEÑORA MARÍA LUISA DE MARTÍNEZ

SERVES 1   MEXICO CITY

2 TABLESPOONS VEGETABLE OIL

2 SMALL TORTILLAS

3 TABLESPOONS SALSA DE CHILE PASILLA (PAGE 246)

2 LARGE EGGS

SALT TO TASTE

A SLICE OF CREAM CHEESE

1 TABLESPOON FINELY CHOPPED WHITE ONION

1 TABLESPOON CRÈME FRAÎCHE OR THICK SOUR CREAM (SEE PAGE 489)

Heat the oil in a large skillet and fry the tortillas lightly on both sides. They should not get crisp. Drain them on the paper toweling and put them onto a warmed plate.

In the same oil, cook the sauce for a few seconds over high heat.

Beat the eggs lightly with the salt and add them to the sauce in the pan. Stir the eggs until they are set.

Serve the eggs on top of the tortillas and top with the cream cheese, onion, and crème fraîche or sour cream.

SALSA DE HUEVO Oaxacan Scrambled Eggs

SEÑORA DOMATILA SANTIAGO DE MORALES

SERVES 2   OAXACA

I had been served huevos en chilpachole at La Flecha restaurant in Tlacotalpan, but checking up again on the recipe I couldn't find a Veracruzano who knew anything about them. Then, in Oaxaca, when I was cooking with Señora Domatila, she prepared them for a late breakfast. They were the same, with the addition of the nopales typical of that area.

It has always fascinated me to see just how recipes travel, and perhaps this one had gone by my most favorite route in all Mexico, across the Sierra Madre Oriental. The road begins in the basin of the Papaloapan River and winds steeply and seemingly endlessly up through a dense and wonderfully lush rain forest that gives way at about nine thousand feet to silent pine forests, brilliant and fragrant in the crystal-clear air. As you look back toward the east you can see endless ranges of mountains and three snowy-capped volcanoes emerging through the light clouds that speck a brilliant blue sky.

10 OUNCES (285 G) TOMATOES, BROILED (SEE PAGE 490)

1 OR 2 FRESH SERRANO CHILES OR ANY FRESH, HOT GREEN CHILE, CHARRED
   (SEE PAGE 470)

2 TABLESPOONS ROUGHLY CHOPPED WHITE ONION

1 GARLIC CLOVE, ROUGHLY CHOPPED

1/4 TEASPOON SALT, OR TO TASTE

3 TABLESPOONS VEGETABLE OIL

1/2 CUP (125 ML) WATER

1 LARGE SPRIG EPAZOTE

1/3 CUP (85 ML) CHOPPED NOPALES, FRESHLY COOKED (SEE PAGE 208; OPTIONAL)

3 LARGE EGGS

Blend the unskinned tomatoes with the chile, onion, garlic, and salt. Heat 1 tablespoon of the oil and fry the mixture for 5 minutes, stirring from time to time. Dilute with the water, add the epazote and nopales, and cook over medium heat for 2 minutes more. Set aside.

Heat the remaining oil in a heavy pan. Beat the eggs briefly with a little salt and cook very lightly in the oil, turning them constantly, until they are just set. Add to the sauce, stirring constantly for a few minutes, and cook for about 3 minutes more.

NOTE: You could prepare the sauce ahead, but cook and add the eggs just before serving.

HUEVO A LA SORPRESA Egg Surprise

SEÑORA MAURA RODRÍGUEZ

SERVES 1   JALISCO

A student in an early cooking class at Rancho Santa Fe brought along this recipe from her maid, who came from Jalisco. Somewhere, sometime I had eaten this before and forgotten just how delicious it was. Topped with some shredded lettuce, Salsa Mexicana Cruda (page 235) or Salsa de Tomate Verde (page 236), and slices of avocado, this makes a delicious brunch dish.

Make a tortilla so that it puffs up (see pages 49–50). Make a small slit in the puffed side to form a pocket, then crack open an egg and slide it into the pocket. Press the cut edges of the dough to seal in the egg and fry in hot oil until it is golden brown and crisp. Drain well and serve with Frijoles Refritos (page 155).

Serve immediately.

NOPALES CON HUEVO Nopal Cactus with Egg
SEÑORA HORTENSIA DE FAGOAGA
SERVES 4　　　　　　　　　　　　　　　　　　CENTRAL MEXICO

This recipe for nopales combined with eggs, given to me by Señora Hortensia de Fagoaga, is unusual in that the nopales are not cooked before they are added. They are thus crisper in texture and add more flavor to the eggs.

Señora Fagoaga served this dish as a first course in a comida, *but it could be served for breakfast or as a filling for tacos.*

2 TABLESPOONS LARD OR VEGETABLE OIL
1 POUND (450 G) NOPALES (ABOUT 3 ½ CUPS/875 ML) CLEANED AND DICED (SEE PAGES 208, 498)
8 OUNCES (225 G) TOMATOES, FINELY CHOPPED (ABOUT 1 ⅓ CUPS/335 ML)
2 GARLIC CLOVES, FINELY CHOPPED
⅓ CUP (85 ML) FINELY CHOPPED WHITE ONION
4 SERRANO CHILES, FINELY CHOPPED
SALT TO TASTE
3 LARGE EGGS

Heat the lard in a skillet and add the rest of the ingredients (except the eggs). Add salt to taste. Cover the pan and cook over medium heat, shaking the pan from time to time, for about 25 minutes—until the mixture is dry and well seasoned.

Break the eggs into the nopales and stir rapidly until set.

HUEVOS EN RABO DE MESTIZA
Eggs Poached in a Chile-Tomato Broth

SERVES 6   SAN LUIS POTOSÍ

Although I recommend this as a substantial and delicious brunch dish, Huevos en Rabo de Mestiza were first served to me many years ago at the then renowned restaurant in San Luis Potosí, La Lonja, at a comida *preceding a Fiambre Potosino (page 303).*

Some cooks add hard-cooked eggs to the sauce, but this is frowned upon by traditional cooks in San Luis.

The sauce with the rajas can be made well ahead of time and the dish assembled at the last moment. I do not recommend freezing the sauce.

^{1}/$_{3}$ CUP (85 ML) VEGETABLE OIL

1 ^{1}/$_{2}$ CUPS (375 ML) THINLY SLICED WHITE ONION

7 POBLANO CHILES, CHARRED AND PEELED (SEE PAGE 469), CLEANED, AND CUT INTO NARROW STRIPS

2 POUNDS (900 G) TOMATOES, BROILED (SEE PAGE 490)

3 CUPS (750 ML) WATER

SALT TO TASTE

12 LARGE EGGS

6 SLICES QUESO FRESCO

Heat the oil in a large skillet and cook the onion until translucent—about 2 minutes. Add the chile strips to the pan and let them cook for about 3 minutes, stirring frequently to avoid sticking.

Blend the broiled tomatoes for a few seconds—do not overblend—and add them to the onion-chile mixture. The sauce should have some texture. Let them cook over fairly high heat for about 10 minutes, or until the sauce is well seasoned and has reduced somewhat. Add the water and salt and continue cooking for a minute or so more.

Crack the eggs, one by one, onto a saucer and carefully slide them into the hot broth. Arrange the slices of cheese on top. Cover the dish with a lid and let the eggs poach very gently until set—6 to 8 minutes.

NOTE: The sauce can, of course, be made well ahead of time and even frozen.

HUEVOS MOTULEÑOS Eggs as They Are Prepared in Motúl
SERVES 1

This way of preparing eggs was presumably invented in the small Yucatecan town of Motúl; I always think of it (them) as huevos rancheros *with a Yucatecan flourish. When I first went to research recipes in Mérida thirty years ago, I was struck by the number of restaurants that were doing a roaring trade at breakfast time with businessmen, all in their white* guayaberas, *consuming to a man* huevos motuleños *accompanied by tall glasses of café con leche while they heatedly discussed politics and the financial events of the day.*

All the component parts of this recipe can be prepared well ahead, but the final assembling should be done at the last moment.

I could never figure out why peas. They are always as hard as bullets, and tasteless, or mushy if they have come out of a can.

2 TABLESPOONS VEGETABLE OIL

2 SMALL TORTILLAS

2 TABLESPOONS FRIJOLES COLADOS YUCATECOS (PAGE 158)

1 OR 2 LARGE EGGS

½ CUP (125 ML) SALSA DE JITOMATE YUCATECA (PAGE 240), HEATED

1 TABLESPOON CHOPPED HAM

1 TABLESPOON COOKED PEAS

½ TABLESPOON GRATED ROMANO CHEESE

Heat the vegetable oil in a skillet and fry the tortillas lightly on both sides. They should not be crisp. Drain them and set aside on the warm plate.

Cover one of the tortillas with a thick layer of the bean paste.

In the same fat, fry the egg and put it on top of the bean paste. Cover the egg with the second tortilla. Mask with the sauce, sprinkle the ham and peas over the tortilla, sprinkle it with cheese, and serve.

MACHACADO DE HUEVO Eggs with Dried Beef

SEÑORA HORTENSIA QUINTANILLA DE GARCÍA
SERVES 6   NUEVO LEÓN

Many years ago I was given a completely different recipe for machacado *that was published in* The Cuisines of Mexico. *Some years later I received a letter from Abel Quezada — the distinguished artist whose cartoons had kept the newspaper-reading public amused for decades. It was delightfully illustrated, telling me that his mother never put tomato in her* machacado. *Of course, he was right, as I found out later from more traditional cooks in Nuevo León.*

This more traditional recipe comes from a friend's mother. It reflects perfectly the simplicity of the ingredients and cooking of the north that are nevertheless totally delicious.

The small round piquín chile that grows wild in the mountains of Nuevo León is used most of the year in its ripened and dried state and green and fresh in the rainy season. Indeed it is known as chile de monte (mountain chile) or pajarito (little bird).

The Machacado is served with a tomato sauce and mashed and lightly fried beans — usually pintos brought from the United States — accompanied, of course, by flour tortillas.

4 OUNCES (115 G) MACHACA (DRIED AND SHREDDED SALTED BEEF; SEE PAGE 19)
3 TABLESPOONS MELTED LARD
8 LARGE EGGS

Put the dried beef into a bowl, cover with cold water, and soak 1 minute to soften slightly. Drain, then squeeze to extract as much water as possible. Shred the beef coarsely.

Heat the lard in a skillet, stir in the beef, and fry lightly until the moisture has evaporated—do not brown—about 3 minutes.

Break the eggs into the mixture—do not beat beforehand—stir, and mix until they are set and curdy, about 2 minutes. Serve the eggs immediately with the tomato sauce.

The beef is usually salty enough that no extra salt should be required, but that is a matter of taste.

THE TOMATO SAUCE
1 ¼ POUNDS (570 G) TOMATOES
1 ½ TABLESPOONS LARD
½ CUP (125 ML) FINELY CHOPPED WHITE ONION
7 DRIED PIQUÍN CHILES
SALT TO TASTE

Cut the tomatoes into quarters lengthwise and, using the coarse side of the grater, grate the flesh and seeds of each section until you have only the skin left in your hand—take care not to grate your knuckles or nails in the process. Save all the juice that exudes. You should have about 2 cups (500 ml) of juicy flesh with seeds.

Heat the lard in a large skillet, add the onion, the chiles, and salt, and fry over medium heat until translucent—about 2 minutes. Add the grated tomatoes and continue cooking over high heat until seasoned—about 15 minutes, or until you have a juicy, textured sauce. Keep warm.

HUEVOS CON EPAZOTE Y CHILE Eggs with Epazote and Chiles

SEÑORA HORTENSIA DE FAGOAGA
SERVES 2   PUEBLA

As usual, Señora Tencha came back from a visit to her tierra *in the Sierra Norte de Puebla with a new plant, a new idea, and this time a new recipe for eggs that her sister had served her with a corn tortilla fresh off the comal.*

For regular egg eaters — and there are still some around — or Sunday brunchers who like a good chile pickup on a Sunday morning, this will do it. I have now adapted this recipe and serve it with an unchilied tomato sauce.

I was told to just break the eggs into the pan and stir a little just to mix, but you could mix in a bowl first if you wish — just more washing up.

²/₃ CUP (165 ML) WATER
6 SERRANO CHILES, BROILED UNTIL SOFT AND ROUGHLY CHOPPED (SEE PAGE 470)
¹/₃ CUP (85 ML) FIRMLY PACKED, ROUGHLY CHOPPED EPAZOTE
SALT TO TASTE
3 TABLESPOONS VEGETABLE OIL
4 LARGE EGGS

Put the water into the blender jar, add the chiles, epazote, and salt, and blend to a rough-textured consistency.

Heat the oil in a large skillet, break the eggs into it, add a little salt, and stir just to mix. Cook the eggs over medium heat, folding them over so that they cook evenly until well set. Pour the sauce over the eggs and continue cooking, without stirring, still over medium heat, until the sauce has reduced and seasoned a little—about 2 minutes.

LIGHT MEALS

HIDALGO PICNIC

Lolitas ※ *Savory Masa Cakes*

Tortillas Dobladas

Chiles Capones ※ *Cheese-Stuffed Chiles*

Plátanos Rellenos con Queso ※ *Plantains Stuffed with Cheese*

Molletes ※ *Bean-Filled Rolls*

Guajolotes ※ *"Turkeys"*

Semitas ※ *Bread Rolls from Puebla*

Torta Mexicana ※ *Mexican Sandwich Roll*

Empanadas de San Cristóbal de las Casas

　　※ *Savory Pastries Filled with Chicken*

HIDALGO PICNIC

Since the first day I was taken to María Elena Lara's restaurant, Los Migueles (which, alas, no longer exists), way up on Avenida Santa Lucía in one of the more remote sections of Mexico City, I had been impressed by the honest, well-cooked, hearty food, which had such great *sazón*. And since that day María Elena has generously shared her recipes and knowledge with me.

Early one September, María Elena's whole family was going on a picnic at their ranch in the state of Hidalgo, and they invited me to go along. María Elena said she would prepare the typical picnic meal of that region, *pollo en itacate* (or "chicken in a coarse string bag"; the word *itacate* has come to mean "provender"). It is all prepared the day before to improve the flavor, and then it is heated in the fields over a wood fire the following day.

When I arrived to watch the preparations, it seemed that the kitchen was filled with baskets, all of them lined with white or red-and-white checked cloths. Ready to be packed were bottles of tequila and a dozen limes, *"Para abrir el apetito"* (to "open" the appetite), as María Elena explained; manchego cheese to nibble on while sipping; red and green sweet *tunas* (prickly pears); hard-boiled eggs; and little pottery mugs—because someone was sure to bring fresh pulque from a neighboring ranch.

First María Elena simmered the chicken for the *pollo en frío*, a large fat one, with a whole head of garlic and salt—nothing else. While it was cooking she cut four fresh jalapeño peppers and four scallions, shredding the bottom of them in such a way that after a short time in iced water they opened like flowers. When the chicken was tender, it was very lightly browned in hot lard. Then María Elena tucked a chile and onion into each of the four joints and tied the chicken up tightly in a large cloth while it was still hot.

With the chicken broth she made rice, frying it with the blended tomato, onion, and garlic as is customary, but adding some corn kernels. When it was cooked she scattered the top with sprigs of flat-leafed parsley and decorated it with slices of hard-boiled eggs and whole, canned chipotle chiles en vinagre. The casserole was then covered tightly with yet another cloth, ready for the next morning.

María Elena then made red and green sauces into which she dipped hot tortillas, folding them into neat packages (see the recipe for Tortillas Dobladas, page 184) with large napkins, after which she started to make fillings, four of them, for the Lolitas (see the recipe below), which are little stuffed cakes of tortilla dough. She seemed to go on endlessly mashing and frying chickpeas, dried fava beans, beans, and chiles; best of all was the ancho chile sauce with lots of grated cheese. She beat tortilla dough with lard and salt and then, with wondrously dexterous hands, shaped a hundred little Lolitas— diamonds, triangles, and ovals—each stuffed with one of the many different fillings. They puffed up invitingly on the comal, and a little cheese oozed out, sizzled, and quickly dried up with a tantalizing smell. It seemed too long to wait until tomorrow, so we sampled them one at a time.

LOLITAS Savory Masa Cakes

SEÑORA MARÍA ELENA LARA

MAKES 2 DOZEN LOLITAS   HIDALGO

Lolitas can be prepared ready for cooking several hours ahead. But they should be covered with a damp cloth to prevent the dough from drying out. Ideally they should be eaten the moment they are cooked — providing of course you don't burn your mouth.

THE FILLING

2 LARGE ANCHO CHILES, SEEDS AND VEINS REMOVED

I GARLIC CLOVE

⅔ CUP (165 ML) WATER

SALT TO TASTE

½ TABLESPOON VEGETABLE OIL

4 OUNCES (115 G) CHIHUAHUA CHEESE OR MILD CHEDDAR, GRATED (ABOUT I SCANT CUP/235 ML)

THE DOUGH

3 OUNCES (85 G) PORK LARD (ABOUT ⅓ CUP/85 ML)

SALT TO TASTE

I ¼ POUNDS (565 G) TORTILLA DOUGH (ABOUT 2 ½ CUPS/625 ML)

Prepare the filling first. Lightly toast the ancho chiles on a hot griddle or comal. Cover the chiles with hot water and let them soak for about 5 minutes, or until they are soft. Drain and transfer to a blender jar. Add the garlic, water, and salt to the blender jar and blend until smooth.

Heat the oil in a small frying pan, add the chile puree, and cook over fairly high heat, stirring constantly to prevent sticking, for 5 minutes, or until it reduces and thickens. Set aside to cool and then stir in the grated cheese, adjust the seasoning, and set aside while you prepare the dough.

Work the lard and salt thoroughly into the masa. Roll the dough into balls about 1¼ inches (3.25 cm) in diameter. Press each ball out on the palm and lower fingers of your right (or left) hand, into a circle about 3 inches (8 cm) in diameter. If you have difficulty handling the dough, grease your hands lightly and start again.

Put 1 good teaspoon of the filling into the center of the dough. Fold up the edges so they meet, then fold them over to seal and pinch them well together into a crescent-shaped turnover. Put the turnover on its side, flatten it until it is about ½ inch (1.5 cm) thick, and shape it into a square, rectangle, triangle, or circle, however the fancy takes you, taking care that the filling does not break out through the dough. Repeat with the remaining balls of dough.

Heat a comal or griddle, grease very lightly, and cook the Lolitas over low heat until they are lightly browned and puffy and the dough is cooked well but not dried out—about 8 minutes on each side.

TORTILLAS DOBLADAS
SEÑORA MARÍA ELENA LARA
SERVES 6   HIDALGO

This is how María Elena made the red sauce and prepared the Tortillas Dobladas ("doubled over" tortillas, also called paseadas, *or "passed through the sauce"). Some would have red sauce, some green (see the recipe for Salsa de Tomate Verde on page 236). A lot of pork lard went into the sauces and for good reason—to make the tortillas soft and spongy when they were reheated at the picnic the following day.*

She then spread out a large napkin, and in the center of it placed some plain tortillas, cut or broken up to form about an 8-inch (20-cm) square—the idea was to protect the napkin from the rather messy dobladas stacked on top and to absorb some of the lard that would seep from them.

2 LARGE ANCHO CHILES, VEINS AND SEEDS REMOVED
2 GARLIC CLOVES, ROUGHLY CHOPPED
$\frac{1}{2}$ TEASPOON SALT, OR TO TASTE
ABOUT 1 $\frac{1}{4}$ CUPS (315 ML) CHICKEN BROTH OR WATER
ABOUT $\frac{1}{2}$ CUP (125 ML) PORK LARD, SOFTENED
12 FRESHLY MADE TORTILLAS (SEE PAGE 49), STILL WARM

Open up the chiles and toast them lightly on either side on a hot griddle or comal (see page 473). Cover them with boiling water and leave them to soak until soft—about 5 minutes. Drain and transfer to a blender jar. Add the garlic, salt, and 1 cup (250 ml) of the broth and blend until smooth.

Heat the lard in a heavy pan, add the blended chiles, and cook over fairly high heat, stirring constantly, to reduce a little for about 4 minutes. Add $\frac{1}{4}$ cup (65 ml) more of the broth and bring to the simmering point. Remove from the heat and set aside. The sauce should be of a medium consistency.

Put one of the tortillas, face down, in the sauce and coat the surface well. Double over the tortilla with the sauce inside and press the edges together, then dip the rounded edges into the sauce so there is a border of sauce about $\frac{1}{4}$ inch (.75 cm) wide. Place the Doblada, with the folded (unchilied) side parallel to the edge of the napkin, along one side of the prepared square of tortillas already on the napkin. Repeat the process with the second tortilla, placing it opposite the first one, with the curved edges touching.

Make two more Dobladas and place them on top of the first layer, with curved edges touching, in such a way that the other sides of the square are completed. Repeat until all the tortillas have been used up. Fold the edges of the napkin over the top of the tortillas and store until the following day.

Reheat on an ungreased griddle or comal.

CHILES CAPONES Cheese-Stuffed Chiles
MAKES 12 CHILES   PUEBLA

These cheese-stuffed chiles can also be prepared with poblano chiles—for a less fiery version. The chiles should be eaten literally from pan to mouth. No waiting!

THE CHILES
12 LARGE, FRESH JALAPEÑO CHILES, CHARRED AND PEELED AS FOR POBLANO CHILES
    (SEE PAGE 469)
SALT TO TASTE
4 TO 6 OUNCES (115 TO 180 G) QUESO FRESCO, CRUMBLED (¾ TO 1 CUP/188 TO 250 ML)
1 HEAPED TABLESPOON CHOPPED EPAZOTE LEAVES

TO SERVE
VEGETABLE OIL FOR FRYING
12 TORTILLAS, FRESHLY MADE AND STILL WARM
1 CUP (250 ML) PREPARED SOUR CREAM (SEE PAGE 489)

Make an incision down one side of each chile, leaving the top and stem intact, and carefully scrape away the veins and seeds. Put the chiles into a saucepan and cover well with cold water. Add the salt, bring to a boil, and let simmer for 5 minutes. Drain and dry on paper toweling.

Mix the queso fresco and epazote with salt to taste and stuff the chiles well.

Heat the oil and place the chiles, open side up, into a frying pan in one layer. Fry them gently for about 7 minutes, turning them at intervals slightly to one side and then the other (do not let them cook with the open side down or the filling will melt and run out).

Put each chile into a warm tortilla, cover with a little of the sour cream, fold over, and serve immediately.

PLÁTANOS RELLENOS CON QUESO Plantains Stuffed with Cheese

MARIA ELENA ROMERO

MAKES ABOUT 8 5-INCH (13-CM) "BANANAS"   VERACRUZ

These "bananas," made of cooked plantain dough reformed into the shape of bananas, make a typical Veracruz evening snack, particularly in Alvarado and Tlacotalpan. Along with empanadas made of the same dough, they are prepared in the little food stands that are set up along the banks of the immense river Papaloapan. The filling is a finely crumbled, strong cheese like that made in Chiapas, or a meat picadillo.

The soft dough does pick up a lot of oil in the frying process, so it is necessary to have ready plenty of paper towels (or recycled paper bags from the supermarket, which will absorb much more efficiently). Another very effective method is to reheat them on paper toweling in the oven — as you would for chiles rellenos — and the excess oil exudes readily.

I often serve them in an unauthentic way, with some white rice and a tomato sauce, as a main course.

You need to find plantains that are ripe and yellow but very firm to the touch.

1 ½ POUNDS (675 G) PLANTAINS

3 TABLESPOONS FLOUR

½ TEASPOON SALT

VEGETABLE OIL FOR FRYING

¾ CUP (185 ML) FINELY GRATED CHIAPAS CHEESE (SEE NOTE ABOVE) OR SUBSTITUTE
  ROMANO

Trim the ends of the plantains, but do not peel. Cut into pieces about 5 inches (13 cm) long. Put into a saucepan, cover with water, cover, and bring to a simmer. Continue cooking over medium heat until the flesh is soft—the skin will probably split open— about 1 hour. Drain and set aside to cool.

Peel the plantains, and break into the container of a food processor. Add the flour and salt and process to a fairly smooth consistency.

Heat the oil in a skillet—it should be about ¾ inch (2 cm) deep—over low heat.

Wet your palms a little and divide the mixture into eight equal parts. Roll one into a ball about 2 inches (5 cm) in diameter. Press it out either with your hands or with a tortilla press lined with plastic bags (see tortilla making on page 49) to a circle about 4 inches (10 cm) across and ¼ inch (.75 cm) thick. Put about 1 scant tablespoon of the cheese across the center of the dough, but not right to the edge.

Again wet or lightly oil your palms, and form the dough into a banana shape about 5 inches (13 cm) long and 1¼ inches (3.25 cm) wide. The oil should now be hot but not exceed 250°F (120°C) or the outside will brown too much while the inside is still raw.

Fry two or more of the bananas, depending on the size of the pan—remember that you need plenty of room to turn them over as they tend to stick to the bottom of the pan. Fry for a few seconds, then start to roll them over from time to time until they are an even, golden brown color—10 to 12 minutes. Remove and drain. See note above.

Serve hot for a snack.

NOTE: The dough can be prepared several hours ahead. I do not recommend freezing.

MOLLETES Bean-Filled Rolls
SERVES 6   MEXICO CITY

A popular brunch dish known as Molletes is made with the small, elongated, bobbin-shaped rolls called bolillos. Since good bolillos are hard to come by, even in the Mexican bakeries in the southwestern United States, these could be made with sourdough rolls or 4-inch (10-cm) lengths of good, crusty French bread.

6 BOLILLOS, HARD SOURDOUGH ROLLS, OR 4-INCH (10-CM) LENGTHS OF FRENCH BREAD
ABOUT ⅓ CUP (85 ML) UNSALTED BUTTER, MELTED
2 CUPS (500 ML) FRIJOLES REFRITOS (PAGE 155), HEATED
8 OUNCES (225 G) CHIHUAHUA CHEESE, MILD CHEDDAR, OR JACK, GRATED—ABOUT
   1¾ CUPS/440 ML)
2 CUPS (500 ML) SALSA MEXICANA CRUDA (PAGE 235)

Preheat the oven to 400°F (205°C). Cut the rolls into halves horizontally and pull out the doughy crumb, leaving a shell just less than ½ inch (1.5 cm) thick around the outside. Place the rolls on a well-buttered baking sheet—they should preferably be about ¼ inch (.75 cm) apart. Lightly brush the inside of the rolls with butter and bake until just beginning to crisp up around the outside—about 10 minutes.

Remove the rolls from the oven. Fill with the fried beans and return to the oven for about 5 minutes, or until the beans heat through. Remove from the oven briefly, sprinkle the top of the beans with the cheese, and just melt in the oven—do not brown the cheese. Serve immediately with the sauce liberally doused over the top.

GUAJOLOTES "Turkeys"

SEÑORA MARÍA LUISA DE MARTÍNEZ
SERVES 6   MEXICO CITY

María Luisa de Martínez, who was constantly giving me new ideas and recipes, prepared the round, bun-shaped rolls called pambazos *for lunch one day in Cuautla. She made them into a great sandwich she called* guajolotes *("turkeys"). They were very tasty, crunchy, and filling —but they do require a good digestive system. In Tulancingo, Hidalgo, bread rolls stuffed with tamales are also called* guajolotes.

2 ANCHO CHILES, SEEDS AND VEINS REMOVED

1 TEASPOON SALT, OR TO TASTE

1 TABLESPOON ROUGHLY CHOPPED WHITE ONION

1 GARLIC CLOVE, ROUGHLY CHOPPED

1 ¼ CUPS (315 ML) COLD WATER

4 CHORIZOS (ABOUT 3 ½ OUNCES/100 G EACH), SKINNED AND CRUMBLED

8 OUNCES (225 G) POTATOES, RED BLISS OR OTHER WAXY VARIETY, COOKED AND CUT INTO
   ½-INCH (1.5-CM) CUBES

2 CANNED CHIPOTLE CHILES EN ADOBO, BLENDED WITH ¼ CUP (65 ML) WATER

6 LARGE PAMBAZOS OR HARD ROLLS

4 TO 6 TABLESPOONS VEGETABLE OIL, APPROXIMATELY

4 OUNCES (115 G) CHIHUAHUA CHEESE, MANCHEGO, MILD CHEDDAR, OR JACK, GRATED,
   ABOUT 1 SCANT CUP (225 ML)

2 CUPS (500 ML) SHREDDED LETTUCE

Preheat the oven to 400°F (205°C). Place a baking sheet on the top shelf.

Toast the cleaned chiles lightly on a griddle or comal. Cover with boiling water and let soak until soft, about 5 minutes, then drain and transfer to a blender jar. Add the salt, onion, garlic, and cold water and blend until smooth. Pour into a shallow bowl and set aside.

Put the skinned, crumbled chorizos into a small frying pan. Cook over a gentle heat until the fat has rendered out and the meat is cooked, but take care not to keep frying until it is crisp and dried out. Drain off half of the fat and reserve for future use.

Add the cooked potato cubes and the blended chipotle chiles and fry for a few minutes longer, turning everything over constantly.

Cut the rolls in half horizontally and remove and discard some of the crumb. Heat

2 tablespoons of the oil in a small frying pan. Dip one half of a roll very quickly into the sauce—it should just have a light coating and not become too damp inside—and fry quickly on both sides, immediately afterward placing it on the hot baking sheet in the oven. Repeat the process until all the rolls are dipped and fried, adding a little oil at a time as necessary. (If you put too much oil in the pan at one time, the bread will absorb it and become very greasy.) Bake until the rolls become slightly crisp—about 10 minutes.

Fill the bottom halves of the rolls with some of the chorizo-potato mixture. Sprinkle them liberally with the grated cheese and top with a thick layer of shredded lettuce. Cover with the tops and serve immediately.

SEMITAS Bread Rolls from Puebla

The name semita *is confusing to anyone outside Puebla since it usually refers to one of the many semi-sweet yeast rolls. However in Puebla a* semita *is a roundish, flattish, crusty bread roll that is sprinkled with sesame seeds and has a small top-knot made by giving a little twist to the raw dough on top. The most delicious* semitas *are traditionally baked in wood ovens and there is no trace of sugar used to hurry the rising of the dough—the downfall of many Mexican bread rolls nowadays.*

Classic semitas *are stuffed with cubed potatoes, jellied calf's foot, and avocado, all seasoned with chipotle chiles and a pungent, round-leafed herb called papaloquelite.*

TORTA MEXICANA Mexican Sandwich Roll

A Mexican torta has no equal in the world of sandwiches. A telera, or round, flat roll with a ridge across the middle, is cut horizontally and stuffed to overspilling. It requires both hands to eat and a lot of paper napkins even then; if properly and generously stuffed the filling will exude at the first bite. While the ingredients listed below are more generally used, there is a lot of leeway for innovation.

First remove a little of the crumb. Then slather one open face thickly with a paste of refried beans (see page 155) and add several strips of chiles jalapeños en escabeche. The other face can be thickly spread with mashed avocado while the middle layer holds sliced queso fresco or Oaxaca cheese, tomato, sour cream, head cheese, or Puerco en Adobo (page 275), shredded chicken, or ham.

EMPANADAS DE SAN CRISTÓBAL DE LAS CASAS

Savory Pastries Filled with Chicken

SEÑORA RODE, SAN CRISTÓBAL DE LAS CASAS

MAKES 2 DOZEN PASTRIES

CHIAPAS

In Mexican Regional Cooking I wrote about the delicious, flaky empanadas filled with chicken and sprinkled with sugar that I had eaten on a previous visit to San Cristóbal. On a later visit there I was introduced, by a gourmand taxi driver called El Tigre, to Señora Rode, one of the few women remaining who make these empanadas commercially, preserving the same quality and tradition for which her aunt was renowned for many years before her.

There was no mistaking her house; walking along the street there was a sudden welcoming, savory smell of baking on the cool evening mountain air. Señora Rode, still quite young, plump, with rosy cheeks, was patiently finishing off a last batch of five hundred empanadas for a wedding the next day.

She had been working in her kitchen since five o'clock that morning. The kitchen was warm and the dough very soft, yet she still managed with wonderful dexterity to turn the edges of the dough around the empanada into neat, even little pleats. For local tastes she was filling some with potato, others with tuna, a solid custard, or just a sprinkling of grated, dry cheese. But the really luxurious ones were filled with chicken, and this is the recipe she gave me for them.

Following the recipe just as Señora Rode gave it to me with U.S. ingredients, the result was a very tough pastry, so I have had to adjust the recipe for ingredients in this country. It makes for a very short crust, which is most delicate to handle. The unusual technique intrigued me so I followed it slavishly.

THE DOUGH

14 OUNCES (400 G) UNBLEACHED ALL-PURPOSE FLOUR (ABOUT 3 ½ CUPS/875 ML)

2 OUNCES (60 G) FINE CAKE FLOUR OR CORNSTARCH (ABOUT ½ CUP/125 ML)

¾ TEASPOON SALT

6 OUNCES (180 G) PORK LARD, AT ROOM TEMPERATURE (⅔ CUP/165 ML)

2 OUNCES (60 G) SOLID VEGETABLE SHORTENING (¼ CUP/65 ML)

1 OUNCE (30 G) UNSALTED BUTTER (2 TABLESPOONS)

1 TO 2 TABLESPOONS WATER

3 WHOLE EGGS PLUS 3 EGG YOLKS

3 TABLESPOONS OR MORE MELTED LARD FOR BRUSHING

THE FILLING

1 TABLESPOON VEGETABLE OIL

¼ CUP (65 ML) FINELY CHOPPED WHITE ONION

3 SERRANO CHILES OR ANY FRESH, HOT GREEN CHILES, FINELY CHOPPED

8 OUNCES (225 G) TOMATOES, FINELY CHOPPED (ABOUT 1 ⅓ CUPS/335 ML)

½ CUP (125 ML) CUBED ZUCCHINI, IN ¼-INCH (.75-CM) CUBES

½ CUP (125 ML) CUBED COOKED CARROTS, IN ¼-INCH (.75-CM) CUBES

2 ½ CUPS (625 ML) FINELY CHOPPED POACHED CHICKEN

½ TEASPOON SALT, OR TO TASTE

FRESHLY GROUND BLACK PEPPER

THE TOPPING

2 OUNCES (60 G) GRANULATED SUGAR (⅓ CUP/85 ML)

Sift the flour, cake flour or cornstarch, and salt together, then put on a clean, smooth working surface and make a well in the center. Put the soft lard, shortening, and butter, together with the water, eggs, and egg yolks, into the well and work them together with your fingers until you have a smooth emulsion. Gradually work in the flour and knead the dough well until it is soft and smooth.

Divide the dough into three equal balls about 10 ounces (285 g) each. Brush them liberally with melted lard, cover with a towel, and set them aside (not in the refrigerator) for 2 to 3 hours.

One by one, flatten each of the balls and roll into 9 by 9-inch (23 by 23-cm) squares about ¼ inch (.75 cm) thick. Brush the surfaces liberally with melted lard, sprinkle with flour, and put one on top of the other. Roll them out to make one slightly bigger square, about 11 by 11 inches (28 by 28 cm). (Señora Rode rolls out one ball, brushes it with lard and flour, and then rolls the second one out on top of the first and the third on top of that. The way I suggest is much easier.)

Carefully roll the three layers together—not too tightly but not too loosely—into a sausage shape about 1½ inches (4 cm) in diameter. Brush the roll with plenty of the melted lard and set aside for another 2 hours in the refrigerator.

Meanwhile, prepare the filling. Heat the oil in a skillet and fry the onion, chiles, and tomatoes together over medium heat until reduced and seasoned—about 3 minutes. Stir in the vegetables and chicken, season, and let the mixture cool off thoroughly before filling the empanadas.

Preheat the oven to 425°F (220°C).

Cut the roll into rounds about ½ inch (1.5 cm) thick and roll each one out into a circle about 4 inches (10 cm) across. Put about a heaped tablespoon of the filling onto one side of the dough, then fold the other side over to cover the filling. Pinch the semi-circular edges together firmly, twisting with your fingers to form little scallops around the edge. Place the empanadas well apart on an ungreased baking sheet and bake for about 25 minutes, until well browned.

Sprinkle with the sugar and serve immediately, as a light supper dish or first course.

SALADS

Original Ensalada Alex-César Cardini

  The Original Alex-Caesar Cardini Salad

Chiles en Escabeche Colimenses *Pickled Chiles Stuffed with Beans*

Chiles de la Sierra *"Mountain" Chiles*

Ensalada de Chiles Rellenos *Stuffed Chile Salad*

Ensalada de Nopalitos *Salad of Nopal Cactus Pieces*

Ensalada de Ejote y Calabacita *Green Bean and Zucchini Salad*

Ensalada de Calabacita *Zucchini Salad*

Ensalada de Jícama Yucateca *Yucatecan Jicama Salad*

Those weekly Saturday morning visits to San Juan market in Mexico City in the late fifties were both mouthwatering and time-consuming. There were slim bunches of the most delicate scallions—*cebollitas de cambrai*; delicate little radishes, crisp and nutty; avocados of all shapes and sizes; watercress, cucumbers, and every type of greens imaginable. But often the freshest and most delicate were to be found not on the stands in the market but spread out in front of the peasant woman sitting on the floor in the entranceway. She would touch your skirt or make a little hissing sound of the word *marchanta* ("shopper") to gently attract your attention. She would have neat little bunches of freshly picked herbs, or squash blossoms, or some small, freshly shelled peas or fava beans, and very soon I would be carried away, completely forgetting what I had really come for, and return home laden with two huge baskets overflowing with lovely, delicate, perishable things that two people could never have disposed of before they wilted and lost their bloom. ⚜ But it was on Sunday mornings that there was a brisk run on the salads already prepared and displayed on large shallow wheels of trays, of nopalitos or green or fava beans mainly, elaborately topped with tomato and onion rings and sprinkled with chopped cilantro.

A salad is not as indispensable a part of a Mexican meal as, for instance, beans are. But that is not to say that raw vegetables are not eaten much in Mexico. On the contrary, to have *antojitos* served without a wealth of shredded lettuce, sliced tomatoes, and little radishes either sliced or cut into rose shapes is inconceivable. And then there are the table sauces or relishes, guacamole, salsa Mexicana cruda, and its Yucatecan counterpart *xni-pec*, eaten in great quantities with tacos or just tortillas. During the summer months the wandering street vendors offer cucumbers, peeled and slashed so that they spread out like a flower, and as they hand you one it is liberally sprinkled with powdered piquín chile, salt, and a squeeze of lime juice. In wintertime their place is taken by the jicama, which is thinly sliced and seasoned in the same way.

In the past *ensalada* was the name given to practically any accompaniment to the main meat course, and it fascinates me to read in nineteenth-century Mexican cookbooks of salads of raw pineapple and cooking apple liberally doused with sherry; of boiled, acidy prickly pears *(xoconostles)* cooked with cinnamon and sugar; and a salad for ladies—*ensalada de damas*—which was considered much more appropriate fare for them instead of the meats offered to men, because "they are not as strong and lead a more sedentary life." The ladies were to eat an incredible mixture of cooked vegetables—beets, green beans, peas, zucchini squash, cauliflower—chopped up with plantain, pineapple, sweet potato, apples, avocados, olives, and pickled chiles.

It was also suggested that for more elegant occasions salads of plain greens should be presented more colorfully adorned with edible flowers: borage, nasturtiums, mallow, wild chicory, or orange flowers.

Naturally influences from the United States have crept in and even salad bars have begun to appear in some of the popular restaurant chains and hotel restaurants, while more sophisticated salads are now offered in the more fancy restaurants. But in private homes you are much more likely to get a traditional salad of cooked vegetables—zucchini, cauliflower, and green beans—dressed with oil and vinegar and sprinkled with dried oregano and onion rings.

I could never quite take the eye-catching Christmas Eve salad seriously—lettuce, beets, sugarcane, oranges, bananas, sweet limes, jicamas, peanuts, and small hard sugar candies all mixed up. But two that always spring to mind as being just right, different, and very Mexican are the nopal and stuffed chile salads, for which the recipes are given, along with recipes for some cooked vegetable salads and a crisp, refreshing one of jicama.

ORIGINAL ENSALADA ALEX-CÉSAR CARDINI
The Original Alex-Caesar Cardini Salad

ALEX CARDINI, SR.

SERVES 2   MEXICO CITY

In the early 1970s one of the best-loved restaurateurs in Mexico, Alex Cardini Sr., died. He had started in the restaurant business in Italy at the age of ten, and by his late teens he had worked in some of the most distinguished restaurants in Europe. As an ace pilot in the Italian air force, he was decorated for his courage and daring during World War I.

In 1926 Alex Sr. joined his brother Caesar in Tijuana, where Caesar had a thriving restaurant business and where he had invented a famous salad dressing. Using this dressing and a unique combination of other ingredients, Alex invented his salad in honor of the pilots of Rockwell Field Air Base in San Diego. First known as Aviator's Salad, it then became popularly known and copied as Caesar, but I shall call it as it should be called: Alex-Caesar Cardini Salad.

A few months before he died, I had one of those long and wonderful lunches with the Cardini sons and their friends. We talked for hours about the rare and fascinating things in Mexican food, and Alex Sr. prepared his salad for us.

10 ROMAINE LETTUCE LEAVES, APPROXIMATELY

6 HALF-INCH (1.5-CM) ROUNDS OF STALE FRENCH BREAD

¼ CUP (65 ML) OLIVE OIL

3 GARLIC CLOVES

6 ANCHOVY FILLETS

1 LARGE EGG, RAW

1 TABLESPOON FRESH LIME JUICE

1 TEASPOON WORCESTERSHIRE SAUCE

¼ CUP (65 ML) FRESHLY GRATED PARMESAN CHEESE

SALT AND FRESHLY GROUND PEPPER TO TASTE

Wash the lettuce, spin dry, wrap in a dry towel, and set aside in the refrigerator to crisp.

Preheat the oven to 400°F (205°C). Put the bread slices onto an ungreased baking sheet and bake until crisp—20 minutes. Brush with 1½ tablespoons of the oil and return to the oven to brown—about 10 minutes.

Crush together the garlic and the anchovies and gradually add 1 tablespoon of the oil. Spread this mixture onto the bread slices and set aside.

Cover the egg with boiling water and cook for 1 minute; the white should be opaque and just setting.

Put the lettuce leaves into the salad bowl, add the remaining ingredients, and toss with the egg and bread until well incorporated.

CHILES EN ESCABECHE COLIMENSES
Pickled Chiles Stuffed with Beans

SEÑORA ESPERANZA OROZCO DE OLEA

SERVES 6   COLIMA

This is a deliciously different version of stuffed chiles given to me by a distinguished cook from Colima. You should start three days ahead for best results. One chile per serving should be plenty, as it is a very filling salad or first course.

THE CHILES

3 TABLESPOONS VEGETABLE OIL

6 MEDIUM-SIZE POBLANO CHILES

THE PICKLING MIXTURE

5 GARLIC CLOVES, HALVED

1 CUP (250 ML) THINLY SLICED PURPLE ONION

1 MEDIUM CARROT, SCRAPED AND THINLY SLICED

½ CUP (125 ML) WINE VINEGAR

2 TABLESPOONS WATER

1 TEASPOON SALT, OR TO TASTE

THE FILLING

8 OUNCES (225 G) PINTO OR CALIFORNIA PINK BEANS (CANARIOS OR FLOR DE MAYO IN MEXICO), COOKED (SEE PAGE 154), WITH THEIR BROTH

12 OUNCES (340 G) CHORIZOS

2 TABLESPOONS PORK LARD

3 TABLESPOONS FINELY CHOPPED WHITE ONION

ABOUT 6 OUNCES (180 G) TOMATOES, FINELY CHOPPED (ABOUT 1 ROUNDED CUP/265 ML)

3 TABLESPOONS GRATED QUESO RANCHERO SECO OR AÑEJO, OR SARDO OR ROMANO CHEESE

TO SERVE

ROMAINE LETTUCE LEAVES TO LINE THE DISH

6 SLICES QUESO PANELA OR DOMESTIC MUENSTER

Three days ahead, heat the oil in a skillet and fry the chiles over medium heat, turning them from time to time, until they are blistered and well browned, about 10 minutes. Remove the pan from the heat, cover, and let the chiles "sweat" for about 5 minutes in the pan. Remove the chiles from the pan, drain, and set them aside to cool while you prepare the pickling mixture.

In the same oil, fry the garlic gently until lightly browned. Add the other pickling ingredients and bring to a boil. Reduce the heat and let the mixture simmer, stirring from time to time, for about 2 minutes. Transfer the contents of the pan to a glass or china bowl.

Remove the skins from the chiles (if you have fried them sufficiently, they should slip off easily). Carefully slit the chiles open and remove the seeds and veins, taking care to keep the top and stem intact. Add the chiles to the ingredients in the bowl and store at the bottom of the refrigerator for 2 or 3 days, turning them over at intervals so they become evenly impregnated with the seasoning.

On the day you plan to serve the chiles, prepare the filling. Blend the beans and their broth (do not overblend, as they must have some texture). Set aside.

Skin and crumble the chorizo, then heat the lard in a skillet and cook the chorizo pieces gently—they will burn easily—until the fat has rendered out, about 5 minutes. Remove the chorizo pieces and set aside.

In the same fat, fry the onion gently, without browning, until translucent. Add the tomatoes and fry for 3 minutes longer. Add the blended beans and chorizo and fry the mixture, stirring and scraping the bottom of the pan, until it is reduced to a thick paste. Remove from the heat and set aside to cool, then stir in the grated cheese.

Stuff the chiles with the bean mixture and arrange them on a round platter lined with romaine lettuce leaves. Cover each chile with a strip of the cheese and the onion and carrot pieces from the pickling mixture, and serve at room temperature.

CHILES DE LA SIERRA *"Mountain" Chiles*
SERVES 6

PUEBLA

This very simple way of preparing whole ancho chiles to serve with roasted or broiled meats, or as a relish with cold cuts, comes from the Sierra de Puebla.

Some years ago I attended an exhibition of traditional Mexican foods in Morelia, where almost the same recipe was served as an appetizer: the anchos were stuffed with ricotta—a very nice idea! The chiles can be eaten the day they are made, or perhaps better still, when they have been left for a day or two to season at the bottom of the refrigerator.

ONE DAY AHEAD

6 MEDIUM ANCHO CHILES, WIPED CLEAN

3 TABLESPOONS VEGETABLE OIL

I SMALL WHITE ONION, THINLY SLICED

½ CUP (125 ML) VINEGAR

½ TEASPOON SALT, OR TO TASTE

½ CUP (125 ML) WATER

2 OUNCES (60 G) QUESO AÑEJO, ROMANO, OR SARDO CHEESE, FINELY GRATED
   (ABOUT ⅔ CUP/165 ML)

¼ TEASPOON DRIED MEXICAN OREGANO

TO SERVE

I SMALL WHITE ONION, THINLY SLICED

6 ROMAINE LETTUCE LEAVES

I MEDIUM TOMATO, SLICED

A day ahead, heat an ungreased skillet or comal over medium heat and let the chiles heat through, turning them over from time to time, until they have softened and become flexible. Flatten each chile out as much as possible, then make a slit down one side and halfway around the top, to which the stem is attached. Remove the seeds and veins.

Heat the oil in a skillet. Pressing the inside of one chile at a time into the oil, let it fry for a minute or so—its color will turn to an opaque tobacco brown. (Take care that the heat is not too high or the chile will readily burn.) When all the chiles have been fried, drain off the excess oil.

Add the sliced onion to the skillet and cook gently until it is translucent; do not let it brown. Add the vinegar, salt, water, and chiles and simmer for about 10 minutes, or until the chiles are completely soft. Remove the chiles from the skillet, drain, and set them aside to cool.

Sprinkle the inside of each chile with a little cheese. Reform them by folding the edges back in place, then set them in one layer in a serving dish and pour the liquid from the pan over them. Sprinkle them with oregano. Top with onion rings, both cooked and raw. At this point, the chiles can be left to marinate in the refrigerator for a day or two. Just before serving, decorate the sides of the dish with the lettuce and tomato.

ENSALADA DE CHILES RELLENOS Stuffed Chile Salad

ELIZABETH BORTON DE TREVIÑO

SERVES 6   NUEVO LEÓN

THE MARINADE

$^1/_3$ CUP (85 ML) WATER

2 TABLESPOONS VINEGAR

I GARLIC CLOVE, SLICED

3 SPRIGS FRESH MARJORAM OR $^1/_8$ TEASPOON DRIED

I MEXICAN BAY LEAF

SALT TO TASTE

3 TABLESPOONS OLIVE OIL

THE CHILES

6 SMALL POBLANO CHILES, CHARRED AND PEELED (SEE PAGE 469)

THE GUACAMOLE STUFFING

3 TABLESPOONS FINELY CHOPPED WHITE ONION

2 MEDIUM AVOCADOS

$^1/_2$ TEASPOON FRESH LIME JUICE

SALT TO TASTE

TO SERVE

LETTUCE LEAVES

POMEGRANATE SEEDS OR CHOPPED FRESH CILANTRO

Mix all the marinade ingredients well and set them aside.

Leaving the top of the chiles intact, slit down the side and carefully remove seeds and veins. Put the chiles into the marinade and refrigerate them at least 2 days, turning them from time to time.

When you are ready to serve the chiles, crush the onion. Cut open the avocados and scoop out the flesh. Mash with the onion, lime juice, and salt.

Drain the chiles and stuff them well with the guacamole. Arrange on a bed of lettuce leaves on a serving dish and decorate them with the pomegranate seeds or chopped cilantro.

ENSALADA DE NOPALITOS Salad of Nopal Cactus Pieces
SERVES 6   CENTRAL MEXICO

THE SALAD

2 CUPS (500 ML) NOPAL CACTUS PIECES, COOKED (SEE PAGE 208)

2 TABLESPOONS OLIVE OIL (OPTIONAL)

4 TEASPOONS MILD VINEGAR OR FRESH LIME JUICE

1/2 TEASPOON DRIED MEXICAN OREGANO

3 TABLESPOONS FINELY CHOPPED WHITE ONION

SALT TO TASTE

1/4 CUP (65 ML) ROUGHLY CHOPPED CILANTRO

TO SERVE

LETTUCE LEAVES

STRIPS OF JALAPEÑO CHILES EN ESCABECHE

4 OUNCES (115 G) QUESO FRESCO, CRUMBLED (ABOUT 2/3 CUP/165 ML)

1 SMALL PURPLE ONION, SLICED

2 MEDIUM TOMATOES, SLICED

Mix all the salad ingredients well and set aside to season for about 1 hour.

Line the dish with the lettuce leaves, put the salad on top, and top with the rest of the ingredients.

ENSALADA DE EJOTE Y CALABACITA

Green Bean and Zucchini Salad

SERVES 6   CENTRAL MEXICO

12 OUNCES (340 G) COOKED ZUCCHINI

12 OUNCES (340 G) COOKED GREEN BEANS

I SMALL WHITE ONION, THINLY SLICED

A WELL-SEASONED OIL AND VINEGAR DRESSING

2 PEACHES, PEELED AND SLICED

I SMALL AVOCADO, PEELED AND CUT INTO STRIPS

SEEDS OF HALF A POMEGRANATE, IF AVAILABLE

> Cut the zucchini lengthwise into halves and then into quarters. Cut the beans into thirds. Mix the onion with the squash and beans in a nonreactive bowl.
>
> Toss the vegetables in the dressing and spread onto a serving platter.
>
> To serve, decorate the salad with the peeled and sliced peaches, the avocado strips, and the pomegranate seeds.

ENSALADA DE CALABACITA Zucchini Salad

SERVES 6   CENTRAL MEXICO

I ½ POUNDS (675 G) COOKED ZUCCHINI (OR CAULIFLOWER, OR CHAYOTE),

   STILL SLIGHTLY CRISP

½ TEASPOON MEXICAN DRIED OREGANO

A WELL-SEASONED OIL AND VINEGAR DRESSING

SLICED WHITE ONIONS WILTED IN LIME JUICE

I SMALL AVOCADO, SLICED

GREEN OLIVES

4 OUNCES (115 G) STRIPS OF QUESO FRESCO (ABOUT ⅔ CUP/165 ML)

> Cut the squash lengthwise into halves and then into quarters. Divide the cauliflower into flowerets, or slice the chayote.
>
> Mix the vegetable with the oregano and salad dressing in a nonreactive bowl. Spread on a serving platter and decorate with the pickled onion rings, avocado slices, olives, and strips of the cheese.

ENSALADA DE JÍCAMA YUCATECA Yucatecan Jicama Salad
SERVES 6   YUCATÁN

2 SMALL JICAMAS OR 1 LARGE ONE (ABOUT 1 ½ POUNDS/675 G)
1 HEAPED TABLESPOON FINELY CHOPPED CILANTRO
SALT TO TASTE
½ CUP (125 ML) SEVILLE ORANGE JUICE OR SUBSTITUTE (SEE PAGE 494)
1 LARGE SWEET ORANGE

Peel the jicamas with a potato peeler, cut them into about ¼-inch (.75-cm) cubes, and put into a nonreactive bowl. Add the cilantro, salt, and Seville orange juice and set aside to season for at least 1 hour.

Peel and thinly slice the orange. Serve the salad topped with the orange slices.

VEGETABLES

Nopales al Vapor Estilo Otumba ※ *Steamed Cactus Paddles Otumba*

Legumbres en Pipián Oaxaqueño

※ *Vegetables in Oaxacan Pumpkin Seed Sauce*

Coliflor en Aguacate ※ *Cauliflower in Avocado Sauce*

Chayotes Rellenos ※ *Stuffed Chayotes*

Chiles Rellenos de Elote con Crema ※ *Chiles Stuffed with Corn and Cream*

Chiles Rellenos con Calabacitas ※ *Chiles Stuffed with Zucchini*

Chiles Rellenos de Picadillo ※ *Poblano Chiles Stuffed with Meat*

Chiles Rellenos de Queso ※ *Chiles Stuffed with Cheese*

Rajas de Chile Estilo Oaxaqueño ※ *Oaxacan Chile Strips*

Rajas de Chile Poblano ※ *Chile Poblano Strips*

Chile con Queso ※ *Chiles with Cheese*

Chiles en Nogada ※ *Stuffed (Poblano) Chiles in Walnut Sauce*

Esquites ※ *Corn Cooked with Epazote*

Elote con Crema ※ *Corn with Cream, Chiles, and Cheese*

Torta de Elote ※ *Fresh Corn Torte*

Cuiclacoche con Calabacitas Estilo Querétaro ※ *Corn Fungus with Zucchini*

Calabacitas con Crema ※ *Zucchini with Cream*

Torta de Calabacitas ※ *Zucchini Torte*

Calabacitas Rellenas de Elote ※ *Zucchini Stuffed with Fresh Corn*

Calabacitas Guisadas Estilo Michoacán

※ *Zucchini Cooked in Michoacán Style*

Budín de Chícharo ※ *Pea Pudding*

Budín de Zanahoria ※ *Carrot Pudding*

Budín de Elote ※ *Corn Pudding*

The Bounty of the Toltecs

They enjoyed great bounty;

there was an abundance of food, of the sustenances of life.

They say that the squash was so huge

that some measured six feet around

and that the ears of corn were as long as grinding-stone mullers;

they could only be clasped in both arms.

—FROM "CODEX MATRITENSE DE LA BIBLIOTECA REAL PALACIO,"
THELMA D. SULLIVAN, TRANS.

One of the most interesting sights to an inquisitive stranger in Mexico is a ramble early in the morning to the canal which leads to the Lake of Chalco. There hundreds of Indian canoes, of different forms and sizes, freighted with the greatest variety of animal and vegetable productions of the neighborhood, are constantly arriving; they are frequently navigated by native women accompanied by their families. The finest cultivated vegetables which are produced in European gardens, with the numberless fruits of the torrid zone, of many of which even the names are not known to us, are piled up in pyramids and decorated with the most gaudy flower.

—FROM W. H. BULLOCK, *Six Months Residence and Travel in Mexico*, NINETEENTH CENTURY

I remember so well an old man sitting on a sack of chiles in Mercado Juárez in Mexico City in the late 1950s. As I exclaimed over the variety and beauty of the chiles, herbs, and edible flowers that his wife was selling, he said, "*Sí, señora, aquí comemos a pie de la vaca* (Yes, señora, here we eat at the foot of the cow)!"

If you give a Mexican peasant a few square meters of land, in no time at all he will have built himself a little shack and hung the outside walls with a hundred little tin cans full of trailing plants and colorful flowers. In summer the little plot of ground will be bursting with growth: tall, strong cornstalks twined with wandering vines of pumpkins, squash, and beans. The peas will be in flower and the wild greens will be crowding themselves in wherever they can, exuberantly celebrating the arrival of the welcome rains.

Although Mexico City has grown so immense and unwieldy, even the supermarkets in the more sophisticated residential areas offer bunches of pumpkin flowers and *cuiclacoche*—the fungus that makes gray-black deformities of corn kernels—cheek by jowl with the more commonplace cauliflowers, spinach, and potatoes. And the large entranceways attract peasant women with their little piles of avocados, peanuts, or sweetmeats, for anywhere in the city, whether in the poor barrios or outside the homes of the rich, somebody has something to sell and another little curbside market is born.

But no longer do the canoes come into the city with their fresh produce; instead, for blocks around Merced market—the central wholesale market of Mexico City—there is a thick mass of slowly moving trucks from all over the republic, jostling for a place to stop and unload. The younger men have invested in small trolleys to haul the produce to the stands inside, but there are still many wrinkled old men bent under the weight of the enormous, overflowing hampers, attached by thick leather bands around their heads. They weave through the crowd, gently nudging people out of their way and saying in a low monotonous tone that can be heard, miraculously, above the din, their warning, "*Golpe . . . golpe . . . bulto.*"

Despite their stark, concrete edifices, the modern markets still retain a character uniquely Mexican. Take a walk through some of the smaller local markets: Santa Julia, Juárez, Medellín, or San Angel. Some stands will be piled high with produce that overflows onto the floor while others have just a few little piles—*montoncitos*—of dried, richly hued chiles; small *tunas*, red and orange, some of them carefully peeled ready to eat; a few *colorín* flowers for tortas; or some tiny, pale green limes. You wonder how the person sitting there manages to spin out the day, and at the end of it, how many pesos she will have made to buy food for her family.

San Juan and Santa Julia in particular have an amazing variety of mushrooms. From about the middle of July on through October, there are russet-colored cepes; the rich-brown, hooded morels; small white puffballs for salad; the spindly little clavitos for soups and quesadillas; and the rich-orange yemas; and once in a very great while, a few of the blue mushrooms from the sierras around Valle del Bravo.

There are tall bundles of *guauzoncles*, spindly *romeritos* to cook with dried shrimp cakes in a mole for Easter and Christmas, wild purslane to cook with pork, Swiss chard, cabbages, leeks, turnips—indeed, all the vegetables you can think of are there. If anything is new to you and you don't know how to cook it, within five minutes you will be given as many recipes as there are people to hear your question. And as you buy there will be that constant chorus of young voices . . . *"Le ayudo? Le ayudo?"* for everyone wants to earn a peso or two carrying your load.

Generally speaking in Mexico, vegetables are served as a separate dish, before the main course. They are made into *tortitas*—little fritters of light batter served in a tomato sauce; or cooked into rather solid *budínes*—puddings of eggs, cheese, and flour; or cooked in a stew of meat and fish or in substantial soups like the *mole de olla* or the favorite from Sonora, *pozole de milpa*.

NOPALES AL VAPOR ESTILO OTUMBA
Steamed Cactus Paddles Otumba
MAKES 2½ CUPS (625 ML), ENOUGH TO FILL 12 TACOS   ESTADO DE MÉXICO

The longer I live in Mexico, the more varied my recipe sources become. This one was given to me by a bus driver from the village of Otumba (near the pyramids of Teotihuacán), who loved to cook. His brother-in-law, also a bus driver, was driving the bus that was to take a group of us to the Merced market to buy our varied and exotic provisions for the week's cooking class I was holding many years ago. Curiosity got the better of the cook and he wanted to meet me, so he came with us for part of the journey. He told me that he had set up his "kitchen"—a small charcoal stove, two cazuelas, and a comal—in the bus garage, and with these he turned out, when time permitted, a full midday meal for his fellow drivers. Judging by their stomachs, it must be good—and also judging by this recipe, which is, to my mind, the best way of preparing nopales.

2 TABLESPOONS VEGETABLE OIL
2 GARLIC CLOVES, FINELY CHOPPED
1 POUND (450 G) PREPARED NOPALES (SEE PAGE 498), CUT INTO SMALL CUBES (ABOUT
   3½ CUPS RAW/875 ML)
1 LARGE SCALLION (1 LARGE CEBOLLA DE RABO IN MEXICO), FINELY CHOPPED

2 JALAPEÑO CHILES OR ANY HOT, FRESH GREEN CHILES (SEEDS AND VEINS LEFT IN),
  THINLY SLICED
1 TEASPOON SALT, OR TO TASTE
2 LARGE SPRIGS EPAZOTE, ROUGHLY CHOPPED

Heat the oil in a large, heavy saucepan and fry the garlic, without browning, for a few seconds. Add the rest of the ingredients, except the epazote. Cover the pan and cook over low heat, stirring the mixture from time to time, until the nopales are almost tender; their viscous juice will exude.

Remove the lid from the pan and continue cooking over slightly higher heat until all sticky liquid from the nopales has dried up—about 20 minutes, depending on how tender the nopales are. Stir in the epazote 3 minutes before the end of the cooking time.

To serve, fill a freshly made hot tortilla with some of the nopales and add a little crumbled queso fresco, if desired.

N O T E : This dish can be prepared ahead. I do not suggest freezing.

LEGUMBRES EN PIPIÁN OAXAQUEÑO
Vegetables in Oaxacan Pumpkin Seed Sauce
SEÑORA DOMATILA SANTIAGO DE MORALES
SERVES 6

OAXACA

Many years ago when I was cooking with my friend Señora Domatila, she suggested that we prepare a vegetable pipián *of nopales and peas. It makes an excellent vegetarian main course, deliciously satisfying in color, texture, and flavor.*

I call Domatila la regañadora, *"the scolder," because she was forever complaining and chiding as she cooked. As she was toasting the seeds for this dish, I asked her to what point they should be browned. "Ni muy, muy, ni tan, tan" (neither too much nor too little), she said with a click of her tongue, which indicated that I should know better than to ask. And later, as she was grinding the seeds on the metate—enough to make anyone complain, as I know from experience—she said that the preparation of Mexican food was "dura pero segura" (hard but sure). (The ground seeds, by the way, were strained through a small decorated gourd with small holes perforated in the bottom.)*

Of course, this pipián *can be made with poached chicken, stewed pork, or rabbit, and during the Lenten period with dried shrimps. I made it with cubed zucchini and quartered mushrooms precooked for a few minutes and it was very good.*

8 OUNCES (225 G) RAW, UNHULLED PUMPKIN SEEDS (ABOUT 2¾ CUPS/685 ML)
1 ANCHO CHILE
2 CHILCOSTLE OR GUAJILLO CHILES
1 GARLIC CLOVE
4 CUPS (1 L) COLD WATER, APPROXIMATELY
¼ TEASPOON CUMIN SEEDS
3 TABLESPOONS VEGETABLE OIL
2 TEASPOONS SALT, OR TO TASTE
1 POUND (450 G) NOPALES, DICED (ABOUT 2⅔ CUPS/665 ML), AND CRISP-COOKED
    (SEE PAGE 208; ABOUT 3½ CUPS/825 ML)
8 OUNCES (225 G) SHELLED, BARELY COOKED PEAS (ABOUT 2 CUPS/500 ML)
2 LARGE SPRIGS EPAZOTE OR 1 TOASTED AVOCADO LEAF

Put the seeds into a heavy frying pan over medium heat. Turn them constantly until they are evenly browned, keeping a lid handy, as they are likely to pop about fiercely. Set them aside to cool.

Remove the seeds and veins from the ancho chile; leave the chilcostles of guajillos whole. Cover the chiles with water and simmer them for 5 minutes, then leave them to soak for 5 minutes longer. Drain and transfer to a blender jar. Add the garlic and 1 cup (250 ml) of the water to the chiles and blend until smooth.

When the toasted seeds are cool, grind them, along with the cumin—preferably in a coffee/spice grinder—until they are rather fine but still have some texture. Transfer to a bowl and stir in the remaining 3 cups (750 ml) of water until smooth. Pass through the medium disk of a food mill or strainer and set aside. (Note: there will be quite a lot of debris of the husks left in the food mill.)

Heat the oil in a large, heavy pan. Add the chile sauce through a strainer, pressing down to extract as much of the juice as possible. Lower the heat and fry the chile sauce, scraping the bottom of the pan constantly, until it has reduced and seasoned—about 2 minutes.

Gradually stir in the pumpkin seed sauce and cook over low heat for about 20 minutes, stirring and scraping the bottom of the pan from time to time as it continues to thicken. Add the salt and vegetables and heat them through for 15 minutes longer, adding the epazote or avocado leaf just before the end of the cooking time. (When the sauce is properly cooked, pools of oil form on the surface.)

Serve hot, with freshly made tortillas.

NOTE: You can make the sauce ahead, since it both refrigerates and freezes well. After you defrost it, put it back into the blender and blend for a few seconds before reheating. The sauce should be of a medium consistency and lightly cover the back of a wooden spoon.

COLIFLOR EN AGUACATE Cauliflower in Avocado Sauce
SERVES 6   CENTRAL MEXICO

This recipe comes from Recetas de Cocina, *a 1911 Mexican cookbook. The idea of cooking cauliflower with aniseeds was rather intriguing; it does give an interesting flavor, but probably there was no more subtle reason than to diminish the gassy effect. This could be served as a vegetable dish or salad, but since it doesn't look too attractive by itself I prefer to serve it in the form of a dip—al dente cauliflower with guacamole—or masked with guacamole as a salad or side dish.*

This dish should all be prepared at the last moment. If not, the guacamole will lose its color and become rather watery and the cauliflower will become somewhat bitter and the subtle anise flavor will be lost. This is one case where a smooth guacamole is appropriate.

THE CAULIFLOWER
1 POUND (450 G) CAULIFLOWER, TRIMMED OF THE OUTER LEAVES
A LARGE PINCH OF ANISEEDS, TIED IN A SMALL PIECE OF CHEESECLOTH
1 TEASPOON SALT

THE GUACAMOLE
2 FRESH SERRANO CHILES OR ANY HOT, FRESH GREEN CHILES
3 SPRIGS CILANTRO
2 TABLESPOONS FINELY CHOPPED WHITE ONION
1/2 TEASPOON SALT OR TO TASTE
8 OUNCES (225 G) TOMATOES, BROILED (SEE PAGE 490)
2 AVOCADOS

THE TOPPING
2 OUNCES (60 G) QUESO FRESCO, CRUMBLED (ABOUT 1/3 CUP/85 ML)

Rinse the cauliflower well and divide it into florets. Bring a large pan of water to a rolling boil. Add the cauliflower, aniseeds, and salt and cook until just tender—about 5 minutes after returning to the boil. Drain and let cool.

While the cauliflower is cooking, make the guacamole. Crush the chiles, cilantro, onion, and salt to a paste in a blender. Add the tomatoes and blend a second or so longer. Skin the avocados and mash until smooth. Add the blended ingredients and mix well.

To serve as a vegetable dip, place the guacamole in a small bowl and top with the crumbled cheese. Put the bowl onto a large platter, on which you have arranged the cauliflower.

To serve as a vegetable dish or salad, place the cauliflower in one layer on a shallow serving dish. Mask with the guacamole and top with the crumbled cheese.

N O T E: This is best served as soon as the cauliflower is cooked and the guacamole prepared. I do not recommend freezing.

CHAYOTES RELLENOS Stuffed Chayotes
SERVES 6

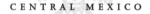

CENTRAL MEXICO

This is perhaps the best method of preparing chayotes, which tend to be rather insipid when cooked without a flourish. Choose a shallow ovenproof dish into which the chayote halves will just fit.

Chayotes Rellenos can be served as a first course with Salsa Ranchera (see page 238), omitting the onion, or as a vegetarian main course.

3 CHAYOTES, ABOUT 1 POUND (450 G) EACH

2 TEASPOONS SALT

2 HEAPED TABLESPOONS UNSALTED BUTTER

²/₃ CUP (165 ML) FINELY CHOPPED WHITE ONION

2 GARLIC CLOVES, FINELY CHOPPED

4 LARGE EGGS, WELL BEATEN WITH SALT AND PEPPER

6 OUNCES (180 G) QUESO FRESCO, CRUMBLED (ABOUT 1 CUP/250 ML)

12 SMALL STRIPS OF QUESO FRESCO OR CHIHUAHUA CHEESE

²/₃ CUP (165 ML) THICK SOUR CREAM (SEE PAGE 489), OR MORE TO TASTE

Cover the whole chayotes with boiling salted water, bring them to a boil, and then let them cook covered over medium heat until they are just tender—about ½ hour.

Drain the chayotes and let them cool. When they are cool enough to handle, cut into halves and remove the pithy core and almond-like seeds. (Eat the seed before anybody else does.) Scoop out the flesh carefully, leaving the outside skin intact. Mash the flesh well and leave it to drain in a colander for a few minutes, since the chayotes here are very watery. Put the chayote shells upside down to drain.

Preheat the oven to 400°F (205°C). Melt the butter in a skillet and cook the onion and garlic over medium heat until translucent. Add the eggs and stir them as you would scrambled eggs until they are just set.

Then add the mashed chayote flesh and let the mixture dry out a little for a minute or so over low heat.

Stir the crumbled cheese into the mixture, and stuff the reserved chayote shells. Place in the ovenproof dish.

Put the strips of cheese and sour cream on top of the filled shells and heat them through in the oven for about 15 minutes before serving. (Do not attempt to eat the shell.) I do not recommend freezing.

CHILES RELLENOS DE ELOTE CON CREMA
Chiles Stuffed with Corn and Cream
SERVES 6   CENTRAL MEXICO

Of all the combinations of chiles, corn, and cream, this is by far the most luscious. Either poblano or ancho chiles can be used; they are equally delicious. This dish makes a wonderfully rich and exotic first course. Use frozen kernels if you cannot get very fresh, tender corn. Crème fraîche or homemade sour cream should be used, as the commercial sour cream curdles when cooked.

These chiles baked in a dish of white rice make a delicious vegetarian dish (see page 162).

¼ CUP (65 ML) UNSALTED BUTTER

1 ¼ CUPS (315 ML) FINELY CHOPPED WHITE ONION

2 GARLIC CLOVES, FINELY CHOPPED

4 CUPS (1 L) CORN KERNELS (IF FROZEN, MEASURE BEFORE DEFROSTING)

SALT TO TASTE

⅓ CUP (85 ML) WATER, IF NECESSARY

3 TABLESPOONS FINELY CHOPPED EPAZOTE

12 SMALL POBLANO CHILES, CHARRED, PEELED, AND CLEANED (SEE PAGE 469), OR
    12 ANCHO CHILES, SEEDS AND VEINS REMOVED, SOAKED IN HOT WATER FOR
    15 MINUTES (SEE PAGE 473)

8 OUNCES (225 G) QUESO FRESCO, CUT INTO THICK SLICES

2 CUPS (500 ML) THICK SOUR CREAM (SEE PAGE 489) OR CRÈME FRAÎCHE

ABOUT 3 OUNCES (85 G) CHIHUAHUA CHEESE OR MILD CHEDDAR, GRATED
    (ABOUT 1 HEAPED CUP/275 ML)

Melt the butter in a large skillet and fry the onion and garlic gently, without browning, until soft—about 2 minutes. Add the corn kernels and salt, then cover the pan and cook over gentle heat until the kernels are tender. If the corn is very dry, add about ⅓ cup (85 ml) water. Cooking time is 10 to 15 minutes, depending on whether fresh or frozen corn is used. Add the epazote and adjust the seasoning. Set aside to cool a little.

Preheat the oven to 350°F (180°C).

Clean the chiles carefully, leaving the top and stem intact. Stuff the chiles well with the corn mixture. Put a slice of cheese in the center of the filling (the chiles should be fat but open).

Place the chiles in one layer in a shallow ovenproof dish into which they will just fit comfortably. Pour over the sour cream and bake until well heated through, then sprinkle with the grated cheese and continue to bake until the cheese is melted.

NOTE: You can make the corn stuffing ahead and refrigerate it. If you do, just heat it through a little before filling the chiles. Cover the dish with foil and put in a 350°F (180°C) oven for 20 to 30 minutes.

CHILES RELLENOS CON CALABACITAS

Chiles Stuffed with Zucchini

SERVES 6   CENTRAL MEXICO

This recipe caught my eye when I was leafing through a little book called Recetas de Cocina, *published in Mexico City in 1911. Like many cookbooks of its time, it was a compilation of recipes contributed by groups of women for some charitable cause. This one was for raising funds to build a temple to the Archangel San Rafael. I have included several of the most interesting recipes, such as Coliflor en Aguacate. They are always vague; the one for this dish directs the cook as follows: "Having roasted and cleaned [chiles], fill with cooked zucchini, onion, oregano, etc."*

This dish makes an unusual and delicious warm salad.

2 ½ TABLESPOONS VEGETABLE OIL

⅔ CUP (165 ML) FINELY CHOPPED WHITE ONION

2 GARLIC CLOVES, FINELY CHOPPED

1 ½ POUNDS (675 G) ZUCCHINI, TRIMMED AND CUT INTO ¼-INCH (.75-CM) CUBES
(ABOUT 5 ¼ CUPS/1.313 L)

SALT TO TASTE

¼ TEASPOON DRIED MEXICAN OREGANO

2 TABLESPOONS WINE VINEGAR

½ TABLESPOON FRESH LIME JUICE

2 TABLESPOONS FRUITY OLIVE OIL

6 OUNCES (180 G) QUESO FRESCO, CRUMBLED (ABOUT 1 CUP/250 ML)

6 MEDIUM POBLANO CHILES, PEELED AND CLEANED, READY FOR STUFFING (SEE PAGE 218)

2 TABLESPOONS UNSALTED BUTTER

THE TOPPING

ROMAINE LETTUCE LEAVES

6 RADISH FLOWERS

Heat 1½ tablespoons of the oil in a heavy skillet. Add 2 tablespoons of the onion and half the garlic and fry gently without browning for 2 minutes. Add the zucchini and salt, cover the pan, and cook over medium heat, shaking the pan from time to time so the mixture does not stick, until the zucchini is *just* done—about 8 minutes. (Squash vary in moisture content. In this recipe they should steam in their own juices, but if they seem too dry, add a little water; if too juicy, remove the lid and reduce the liquid.)

While the mixture is still warm, add the remaining chopped onion, the remaining garlic, and the oregano, vinegar, lime juice, olive oil, and cheese. Adjust the seasoning.

Stuff the chiles until they are full but will still meet at the opening. There should be about ⅓ to ½ cup (85 to 125 ml) of the stuffing left over, depending, of course, on the size of the chiles. Fasten each opening with a toothpick.

Melt the butter and remaining 1 tablespoon oil together in a skillet. Add the stuffed chiles and fry them over medium heat, turning them over gently so the stuffing does not fall out, until lightly browned.

Arrange the chiles on a serving dish and top with lettuce and the radish flowers. Sprinkle with the remaining stuffing. They can be served either hot or cold as a first course.

CHILES RELLENOS DE PICADILLO
Poblano Chiles Stuffed with Meat
SERVES 6   CENTRAL MEXICO

This recipe was the very first that I learned from my part-time maid Godileva. I still use it today.

There are, of course, many variations of chiles rellenos, but the best known, and most popular, are poblano chiles, charred, peeled, and cleaned of their seeds. With the top — the base for the stem — intact, the chiles are stuffed with either a meat or cheese filling, fried in a batter coating, and served in a tomato broth.

Many cooks take a shortcut and use ground meat, but the flavor and texture of the stuffing, or picadillo, is far better if the meat is first cooked and then shredded. The touch of sweet from the raisins and acitrón (see page 497), the crunch of the acitrón and almonds, and the acidity of the broth with the not-too-hot chiles combine to make an intriguing dish.

Poblano chiles ripened and dried become anchos. I particularly like them stuffed with cheese. The whole chiles should be soaked briefly to soften, slit open carefully, seeds and veins removed, and then stuffed.

THE PICADILLO

2 POUNDS (900 G) BONELESS PORK WITH SOME FAT, CUT INTO 1-INCH (2.5-CM) CUBES

$^1/_2$ WHITE ONION, SLICED

2 GARLIC CLOVES

SALT TO TASTE

$^1/_4$ CUP (65 ML) LARD OR VEGETABLE OIL

$^2/_3$ CUP (165 ML) FINELY CHOPPED WHITE ONION

3 GARLIC CLOVES, FINELY CHOPPED

8 PEPPERCORNS

5 WHOLE CLOVES

$^1/_2$-INCH (1.5-CM) PIECE OF CINNAMON STICK, BROKEN INTO SMALL PIECES

3 HEAPED TABLESPOONS RAISINS

2 TABLESPOONS BLANCHED AND SLIVERED ALMONDS

2 HEAPED TABLESPOONS ACITRÓN (SEE PAGE 497) OR CHOPPED CANDIED FRUIT

1 $^1/_4$ POUNDS (565 G) TOMATOES, ROUGHLY CHOPPED (ABOUT 2$^3/_4$ CUPS/685 ML)

THE TOMATO BROTH

1 $^1/_4$ POUNDS (565 G) TOMATOES, ROUGHLY CHOPPED (ABOUT 2$^3/_4$ CUPS/685 ML)

3 TABLESPOONS ROUGHLY CHOPPED WHITE ONION

2 GARLIC CLOVES, ROUGHLY CHOPPED

2 TABLESPOONS LARD OR VEGETABLE OIL

4 WHOLE CLOVES

6 PEPPERCORNS

2 MEXICAN BAY LEAVES

3 SPRIGS FRESH THYME, OR $^1/_4$ TEASPOON DRIED

1-INCH (2.5-CM) PIECE OF CINNAMON STICK, BROKEN IN 2

3 CUPS (750 ML) RESERVED PORK BROTH

SALT TO TASTE

THE CHILES

6 POBLANO CHILES, CHARRED AND PEELED (SEE PAGE 469)

THE BATTER

VEGETABLE OIL FOR FRYING

4 LARGE EGGS, SEPARATED

$^1/_4$ TEASPOON SALT

ABOUT $^1/_3$ CUP (85 ML) ALL-PURPOSE FLOUR

Put the meat into a large saucepan with the sliced onion, garlic, and salt and barely cover with water. Bring the meat to a simmer and continue cooking over low heat until the meat is tender—about 40 minutes. Leave the meat to cool in the broth. When cool, strain the meat, reserving the broth. First shred and then chop the meat to a medium texture—there should be about 3 cups (750 ml).

Skim the broth.

Melt the lard in a large skillet and cook the chopped onion and garlic until translucent—about 2 minutes.

Add the meat and let it cook until it begins to brown, about 8 minutes.

Crush the spices roughly and add them, with the rest of the picadillo ingredients, except the tomatoes, to the meat mixture. Cook the mixture a few moments longer.

Blend the tomatoes briefly and add them to the mixture in the pan. Continue cooking the mixture over high heat for about 10 minutes, stirring it from time to time to avoid sticking. It should be moist but not juicy.

TO PREPARE THE TOMATO BROTH: Blend the tomatoes with the onion and garlic until smooth.

Melt the lard in a wide pan and fry the blended tomatoes over high heat for about 3 minutes, stirring to prevent sticking. Add the rest of the ingredients, except the broth and salt, and cook them over high heat for about 5 minutes, stirring.

Add the pork broth and continue cooking the broth over medium heat for about 10 minutes. By that time it will be well seasoned and reduced somewhat—but still a broth rather than a thick sauce. Add salt as necessary.

TO PREPARE THE CHILES: Make a slit in the side of each chile and carefully remove the seeds and veins. Be careful to leave the top of the chile, the part around the base of the stem, intact.

Stuff each chile with about ½ cup (125 ml) of the picadillo until they are well filled out but the cut edges still come together.

TO PREPARE THE BATTER: Heat the oil in a deep skillet.

Meanwhile, beat the egg whites until they are firm, but not too dry. Add the salt and egg yolks one by one, beating well after each addition.

Prepare one chile at a time: pat the chile completely dry (or the batter will not adhere) and sprinkle them lightly with flour. Coat with the batter.

Fry in the hot oil, turning it from time to time, until the batter turns a deep golden color—about 2 minutes.

Drain the chiles on paper toweling and place them in the tomato broth—it should come about halfway up the chiles—to heat through over low heat. Serve immediately.

NOTE: You can prepare the stuffing and the sauce the day before, and clean the chiles. But do not put the stuffing into the chiles until about 2 hours before cooking.

If you do prepare the chiles 2 hours ahead, do not put them into the broth. Place them on a rimmed cookie sheet lined with several layers of paper toweling, and reheat in a 350°F (180°C) oven for about 20 minutes (5 minutes if filled with cheese, below). This method has the added advantage that the paper absorbs quite a lot of the grease. Then place the chiles in the broth or pour broth over and serve with hot tortillas.

I do not recommend freezing.

CHILES RELLENOS DE QUESO Chiles Stuffed with Cheese

CENTRAL MEXICO

Poblano chiles and anchos can be used for this recipe.

Follow the instructions on page 218 for preparing the chiles, and stuff them with strips of cheese instead of picadillo. In Mexico, queso Oaxaca or Chihuahua cheese is most commonly used, but you can substitute a good melting cheese like domestic muenster or Jack. Then follow the instructions for the tomato broth, the coating of batter, and frying on the preceding page.

RAJAS DE CHILE ESTILO OAXAQUEÑO Oaxacan Chile Strips

SEÑORA DOMATILA SANTIAGO DE MORALES

SERVES 6

OAXACA

In all my years in Mexico, I had never come across this recipe until I was cooking with my friend Señora Domatila in Oaxaca one August many years ago. The chile strips are traditionally eaten over white rice, which makes for a most unusual combination of flavors and textures. Like all rice dishes in Mexico, this rice is eaten as a "dry soup" or pasta course.

The long, light-green, very picante chiles de agua are used in Oaxaca, but you can substitute fresh poblano chiles or Anaheim chiles.

3 TABLESPOONS VEGETABLE OIL

½ CUP (125 ML) THINLY SLICED WHITE ONION

½ CUP (125 ML) WHOLE EPAZOTE LEAVES

9 CHILES DE AGUA, POBLANO CHILES, OR ANAHEIM CHILES, CHARRED, PEELED, CLEANED
    (SEE PAGE 469), AND CUT INTO STRIPS

SALT TO TASTE (DEPENDING ON THE CHEESE)

1 ½ CUPS (375 ML) WHOLE MILK

12 OUNCES (340 G) QUESO FRESCO, MUENSTER CHEESE, TELEME, OR JACK, CUT INTO THICK
    SLICES

In a heavy skillet about 10 inches (25 cm) in diameter, heat the oil, add the onion and
unchopped epazote leaves, and fry until they wilt, stirring from time to time—about
2 minutes. Add the chile strips and salt and fry for about 3 minutes, stirring from time
to time. Over low heat, gradually stir in the milk, then add the pieces of cheese and cook
until they melt. Serve hot, over Arroz Blanco (see page 161).

NOTE: These chile strips may be prepared ahead of time, adding the cheese just
before serving. I don't recommend freezing.

RAJAS DE CHILE POBLANO Chile Poblano Strips
SERVES 6

*Narrow strips of poblano chiles that have been charred and peeled, known as rajas, make a
delicious accompaniment to broiled meats. They can also be served on top of white rice, fried
with potatoes, added to a tomato sauce, or incorporated into dishes like Budín Azteca and
many others.*

12 POBLANO CHILES, CHARRED AND PEELED (SEE PAGE 469)

¼ CUP (65 ML) VEGETABLE OIL

1 CUP (250 ML) THINLY SLICED WHITE ONION

SALT TO TASTE

Remove stems, seeds, and veins from the chiles and cut the flesh into strips about
3 inches (8 cm) long and just less than ½ inch (1.5 cm) wide.

Heat the oil in a large skillet, add the onion, and cook until translucent—about
2 minutes. Add the chile strips and salt, cover the pan, and cook, shaking the pan from
time to time, for about 8 minutes. Serve hot.

N O T E : These chile strips can be prepared several hours ahead. They tend to become mushy when frozen.

CHILE CON QUESO Chiles with Cheese
SERVES 6   C H I H U A H U A

I had always thought of Chile con Queso as a Texas dish until the first time I went to Chihuahua. It is eaten there as a vegetable with broiled meats, and it is also served as an appetizer with hot tortillas. The chile here is the light green Anaheim chile grown extensively in the north of Mexico and in the southwestern United States. It is used a great deal in the cooking of Chihuahua and Sonora.

Two of the best Mexican cheeses come from Chihuahua: the queso Chihuahua made by the Mennonites who live there in settlements, and the queso asadero, a very creamy, slightly acidy cheese that is skeined like a mozzarella. It is always used cooked, and it gives the lovely creamy stringiness that the Mexicans hold in high esteem. It is curious that in some parts of the state they use the small berries—green when fresh and deep yellow when dried—of a wild plant to coagulate the milk instead of the more usual rennet.

5 TABLESPOONS VEGETABLE OIL

1 ½ CUPS (375 ML) THINLY SLICED WHITE ONIONS

1 CUP (250 ML) THINLY SLICED TOMATOES

15 GREEN ANAHEIM CHILES, CHARRED, PEELED, AND CUT INTO STRIPS (DO NOT REMOVE
   SEEDS; SEE PAGE 469)

SALT TO TASTE

¾ CUP (185 ML) MILK

3 TABLESPOONS WATER

8 OUNCES (225 G) CHIHUAHUA, ASADERO, OR MUENSTER CHEESE, THINLY SLICED

Heat the oil in a deep skillet and cook the onion over low heat until translucent—about 2 minutes.

Add the tomatoes with the chile strips to the pan with salt. Cover and cook over medium heat for about 5 minutes. Add the milk and water and let the mixture cook for a few minutes more.

Just before serving, add the cheese to the chile mixture. Serve as soon as the cheese melts.

NOTE: This should be eaten as soon as it is prepared. However, you can always prepare the chile-tomato mixture well ahead and add the cheese at the last moment.

CHILES EN NOGADA Stuffed (Poblano) Chiles in Walnut Sauce
SERVES 8   PUEBLA

Much has been written about this flamboyant dish of stuffed chiles covered with a sauce of fresh peeled walnuts and decorated with pomegranate seeds and parsley.

Every writer I have read on the subject concurs with the story that the recipe was concocted by the grateful people of Puebla who were giving a banquet in honor of Don Agustin de Iturbide's Saint's day on August 28, 1821. He and his followers had led the final revolt against the Spanish. As self-proclaimed emperor he had just signed the treaty of Cordoba. All the dishes at the banquet, or so the story goes, were concocted of ingredients the color of the Mexican flag: the green of the chiles, the white sauce, and red pomegranate seeds.

However, a noted cook and restaurateur begs to differ. She is Señora Lucila de Merlos, who was born in Teziutlán, Puebla, and whose very successful restaurant of the same name in Mexico City is devoted to dishes from that state. Señora Lucila says that in her youth it was customary, as it had been for generations, for the villagers in her area to compete with each other to produce the largest poblano chile on their land. Starting as early as July—weather patterns have since changed—whole families went into the fields to pick them along with the new crops of fruit in the orchards: large, white-fleshed peaches, red-cheeked pears and apples—varieties which no longer exist—for the stuffing of the chiles. They collected walnuts—from trees originally brought to Mexico by the Spaniards—for the sauce, or nogada, *and every member of the family took part in the laborious job of shelling them and then peeling off their soft, papery skin.*

Like so many other dishes that have been handed down through the years from one generation to another, the stuffing and the nogada *have undergone modifications and embellishments. One very well-known Puebla cook, Teresa Irigoyen, uses ground meat and adds a little cognac to the* nogada. *The mother of a great friend of mine there uses cooked and shredded pork and adds just a small amount of white bread crumbs to make the sauce a little smoother. The recipe for* nogada *in* La Cocinera Poblana *(published in 1877) calls for queso fresco, sugar, and a little oil; and so it goes, while most seem to agree that for each chile you need ten walnuts.*

The stuffing for these chiles is surprisingly sweet and has very little meat, contrary to the proportions published in most recipes, including my own.

It is always worth a visit to Mexico during the late summer months to eat this glamorous dish and especially to Casa Merlos, where you can be sure to find the real thing.

Chiles en Nogada are served as a main course with corn tortillas—some rice or soup or a ceviche could be served beforehand—but nothing else goes on the plate.

If it is easier, cook the pork first before shredding and chopping it.

12 OUNCES (340 G) PORK TENDERLOIN, FINELY CHOPPED, ABOUT 1 CUP (250 ML)
²/₃ CUP (165 ML) WATER
SALT TO TASTE
3 TABLESPOONS PORK LARD
6 OUNCES (180 G) TOMATOES, BROILED (SEE PAGE 490)
1 SLICE WHITE ONION
1 GARLIC CLOVE
1 POUND (450 G) PEACHES, PEELED, PIT REMOVED, AND CUBED (ABOUT 1 ¹/₂ CUPS/375 ML)
1 POUND (450 G) APPLES, PEELED, CORED, AND CUBED (ABOUT 1 ³/₄ CUPS/435 ML)
1 POUND (450 G) PEARS, PEELED, CORED, AND CUBED (ABOUT 1 ³/₄ CUPS/435 ML)
1 RIPE PLANTAIN (ABOUT 8 OUNCES/225 G), PEELED AND CUBED (ABOUT 1 CUP/250 ML)
¹/₃ CUP (85 ML) RAISINS
¹/₃ CUP (85 ML) SKINNED AND SLIVERED ALMONDS
3 TABLESPOONS SUGAR
8 LARGE POBLANO CHILES, CHARRED, PEELED, SEEDS AND VEINS REMOVED (SEE PAGE 469)

THE BATTER
VEGETABLE OIL FOR FRYING
4 LARGE EGGS, SEPARATED
¹/₄ TEASPOON SALT
FLOUR FOR DUSTING THE CHILES

TO DECORATE
1 CUP (250 ML) POMEGRANATE SEEDS
¹/₂ CUP (125 ML) FLAT-LEAF PARSLEY LEAVES

Put the pork into a large, heavy skillet, add the water and salt, cover, and cook over low heat until tender—about 25 minutes. You may need to add a little more water, depending on how tender the pork is. The meat should be moist but not juicy. Add the lard and fry over medium heat for about 3 minutes.

Blend the tomatoes with the onion and garlic and add to the pan. Cook over fairly high heat until almost dry—about 5 minutes.

Stir in the rest of the ingredients except the chiles and cook over low heat—covered for the first 10 minutes—stirring from time to time to avoid sticking—about 20 minutes. The fruit should be tender but not mushy. Set aside to cool.

Stuff the chiles well—each should take about ½ cup (125 ml). Then follow instructions (see page 218) for coating and frying them. Drain well on paper toweling. Cover each chile with the sauce and decorate with the pomegranate seeds and parsley.

THE WALNUT SAUCE

ABOUT 72 FRESH WALNUTS, SHELLED, PEELED, AND ROUGHLY CHOPPED
ABOUT ½ CUP (125 ML) WHOLE MILK (RAW IF POSSIBLE)
⅔ CUP (165 ML) MEDIUM DRY SHERRY
¼ TEASPOON SALT

Just before frying the chiles, blend the walnuts with the milk and mix in the sherry and salt. The sauce will be slightly textured.

NOTE: While these chiles are best cooked and served immediately, they could be prepared ahead up to the point of stuffing and frying. They can then be reheated in a 350°F (180°C) oven on a cookie sheet lined with paper toweling to absorb some of the excess oil. They do not freeze successfully.

ESQUITES   Corn Cooked with Epazote
SERVES 6   CENTRAL MEXICO

The name esquites *comes from the Náhuatl word* izquitl, *meaning "toasted corn." It probably referred to the corn that popped open when toasted, but it is now used very loosely to describe corn that is prepared very simply and sold from street vendors outside market places and on many street corners in Mexico City and Toluca. Sometimes the kernels are shaved off the cob and sometimes the whole ear is cut into thick rounds. But it is that epazote again that counts. The corn itself should be very fresh and tender.*

6 SMALL EARS OF CORN

2 TABLESPOONS UNSALTED BUTTER

3 TABLESPOONS LARD OR VEGETABLE OIL

1 ½ TEASPOONS SALT, OR TO TASTE

2 SERRANO CHILES OR ANY FRESH, HOT GREEN CHILES, FINELY CHOPPED

3 HEAPED TABLESPOONS CHOPPED EPAZOTE LEAVES

Cut through each ear of corn at the stalk end and remove all the leaves and silks. Cut the ears into slices about 1½ inches (4 cm) thick.

Heat a heavy pan into which the corn will just fit in one layer. Melt the butter and lard together in the pan, then add the corn, salt, and chiles. Cover the pan and cook the corn over medium heat, shaking the pan from time to time and turning the corn over once, until it is tender and slightly browned—about 15 minutes. Stir in the epazote for the last 3 minutes of the cooking time.

NOTE: This may be prepared ahead but the epazote should be added about 3 minutes before serving. I don't recommend freezing.

ELOTE CON CREMA Corn with Cream, Chiles, and Cheese
SERVES 6   CENTRAL MEXICO

However you put these ingredients together, the result is always delicious. I like to serve this as a first course with corn tortillas before a main course of fish.

¼ CUP (65 ML) BUTTER

⅔ CUP (165 ML) FINELY CHOPPED WHITE ONION

1 GARLIC CLOVE, FINELY CHOPPED

5 POBLANO CHILES, CHARRED, PEELED, AND SEEDS REMOVED (SEE PAGE 469)

ABOUT 4 CUPS (1 L) CORN KERNELS (FROZEN IS FINE)

1 TEASPOON SALT, OR TO TASTE

4 OUNCES (115 G) CHIHUAHUA CHEESE, IN SMALL CUBES, ABOUT 1 CUP (250 ML)

THICK SOUR CREAM (SEE PAGE 489)

Preheat the oven to 350°F (180°C).

Melt the butter in an ovenproof skillet and cook the onion and garlic over low heat until translucent.

Cut the chiles into narrow strips, add them to the pan, and cook them, covered, about 5 minutes.

Add the corn and salt to the chile mixture. Cover tightly with a lid and put in the oven to bake for 20 minutes. Add the cheese just before the end of baking time.

Serve hot, with the sour cream. This dish is best eaten right after it's cooked, as the cheese gets tough when reheated.

TORTA DE ELOTE Fresh Corn Torte
SERVES 6

This fresh corn torte makes a delicious first course, especially when served with rajas in a tomato sauce. (See page 177, with salt but no water.)

For best results you will need to find a starchy field corn that is not too sweet. If it is sweet, then reduce or omit the sugar.

5 CUPS (1.25 L) FIELD CORN KERNELS (SEE NOTE ON TAMALES, PAGE 106)
A LITTLE MILK
4 OUNCES (115 G) UNSALTED BUTTER, SOFTENED (¼ CUP/65 ML)
½ CUP (125 ML) GRANULATED SUGAR
4 LARGE EGGS, SEPARATED
SALT TO TASTE
1 TEASPOON BAKING POWDER
THICK SOUR CREAM (SEE PAGE 489)

Preheat the oven to 350°F (180°C).

Grease an ovenproof dish approximately 9 by 9 by 2 inches (23 by 23 by 5 cm) and sprinkle with toasted, finely ground bread crumbs.

Put about one third of the corn into a blender or food processor, adding only enough milk to loosen the cutting blades of the blender and blend the corn to a rough consistency. Add the rest of the corn by degrees and keep stopping the machine frequently to release the blades. Set the mixture aside.

Beat the butter and sugar together until they are fluffy.

Add the egg yolks one at a time to the creamed mixture and keep beating until they are well mixed in. Add the salt and the corn mixture and beat again.

Beat the egg whites until they are stiff and fold them into the mixture with the baking powder. Pour into the prepared dish. Place the dish on a hot baking sheet in the oven and bake for about 1 hour or until springy to the touch.

Serve immediately with Thick Sour Cream, crème fraîche, or Rajas de Chile Poblano con Salsa de Jitomate (see pages 220, 240).

CUICLACOCHE CON CALABACITAS ESTILO QUERÉTARO
Corn Fungus with Zucchini

OBDULIA AND ANAMARÍA VEGA

SERVES 6   QUERÉTARO

Cuiclacoche, *the delicious, exotic-looking grayish fungus that grows on corn, is now very much in vogue and therefore more expensive. AnaMaría and Obdulia Vega tell me that it was one of the cheapest meals at the small ranch in Querétaro where they were born and raised. Cooked in this way, it makes a wonderful filling for tacos; it can also be served as a vegetable.*

¼ CUP (65 ML) VEGETABLE OIL

2 LARGE SCALLIONS, FINELY CHOPPED

1 GARLIC CLOVE, CHOPPED

1 POUND (450 G) ZUCCHINI, TRIMMED AND DICED SMALL (ABOUT 3½ CUPS/875 ML)

1 CUP (250 ML) CORN KERNELS

1 POUND (450 G) CUICLACOCHE, SHAVED FROM THE CORN COB AND ROUGHLY CHOPPED
  (ABOUT 4 CUPS/1 L)

2 JALAPEÑO CHILES, SERRANO CHILES, OR ANY FRESH, HOT GREEN CHILES, CUT INTO
  THIN STRIPS

½ TEASPOON SALT, OR TO TASTE

1 HEAPED TABLESPOON ROUGHLY CHOPPED EPAZOTE LEAVES

Heat the oil in a large skillet and fry the scallions and garlic gently, without browning, until soft. Add one quarter of the diced zucchini and cook for a few seconds over a fairly high heat, turning constantly, then add another quarter, and so on. When all the zucchini is in the pan, fry for a few minutes more.

Add the corn kernels by degrees, the same way you did the zucchini. Add the *cuiclacoche* in the same manner. Add the chile strips and salt, then cover the pan and cook over a low heat, stirring from time to time, until the vegetables are tender—about

15 minutes. (The vegetables should remain moist and cook in their own juices, but if they do get rather dry, sprinkle liberally with water.)

When almost cooked, add the epazote leaves and simmer a few seconds longer.

NOTE: This can be prepared about ½ hour before serving, and reheated gently. I do not recommend freezing.

CALABACITAS CON CREMA Zucchini with Cream
SERVES 6

There are hundreds of ways of cooking zucchini in Mexico, and every cook has her own method and seasoning. This was our maid Godileva's way of preparing them, and the dish frequently appeared on our dinner table. It has an exotic flavor, and is quite unlike any other squash dish I have come across.

1 ½ POUNDS (675 G) ZUCCHINI, TRIMMED AND DICED (ABOUT 5 ¼ CUPS/1.313 L)

12 OUNCES (340 G) TOMATOES, FINELY CHOPPED (2 SCANT CUPS/500 ML)

6 PEPPERCORNS

4 SPRIGS CILANTRO

2 SPRIGS FRESH MINT

1/2-INCH (1.5-CM) PIECE OF CINNAMON STICK

4 WHOLE CLOVES

2 WHOLE SERRANO CHILES

½ CUP (125 ML) CRÈME FRAÎCHE OR THICK SOUR CREAM (PAGE 489)

½ TEASPOON SALT, OR TO TASTE

Put the squash into a heavy pan with the other ingredients. Cover the pan with a tightly fitting lid and cook the mixture over low heat, scraping the bottom of the pan and stirring the mixture well from time to time so that it does not stick. If the vegetables are drying up too much, add a little water. It will take about 30 minutes to cook.

NOTE: The dish can be prepared well ahead of time and it is perhaps even better heated up the next day.

TORTA DE CALABACITAS Zucchini Torte
SERVES 6

This recipe could be made with any tender squash—zucchini or yellow summer squash. The dark green zucchini are not grown in Mexico; theirs are pale green and smaller, or round—with the exception of the dark green squash of the Yucatán Peninsula, which resemble small flying saucers. There is also a criollo, or native squash, that is more delicate in flavor still. It has small vertical ridges and is pale green and is cultivated the year round in the valley of Oaxaca and in the rainy season in Michoacán.

I regret to say I do not know who gave me this recipe, which makes an excellent and colorful vegetarian dish.

1 ½ POUNDS (675 G) ZUCCHINI
SALT TO TASTE
2 TABLESPOONS FINELY GROUND, TOASTED BREAD CRUMBS
⅓ RECIPE RAJAS DE CHILE POBLANO CON SALSA RANCHERA (PAGES 220, 238), USING 4
    CHILES, 10 OUNCES (285 G) TOMATOES, AND ½ MEDIUM WHITE ONION
6 OUNCES (180 G) CHIHUAHUA CHEESE OR MUENSTER
3 LARGE EGGS, SEPARATED
3 TABLESPOONS SOFTENED BUTTER

Clean and trim the squash and cut them into rounds about ⅛ inch (.5 cm) thick. Put them in a large saucepan, cover with boiling water, add salt, and cook until they are just tender—about 3 minutes, depending on the squash. They should not be allowed to become too soft. Drain the squash and set it aside to cool.

In the meantime, preheat the oven to 350°F (180°C). Butter a 2-quart (2-l) souf-flé dish or casserole, and sprinkle it with bread crumbs.

Make the rajas, cool them, then slice the cheese thin and cut it into small pieces.

Beat the egg whites until stiff, then add salt to taste and the egg yolks, one by one, beating well after each addition.

Put a layer of the squash over the bottom of the dish, pour one half of the rajas over it, put one third of the cheese onto the sauce, and cover with one third of the beaten eggs. Dot with butter. Repeat in the same order and finish off the torte with a layer of squash, the rest of the beaten eggs, butter, and cheese.

Cook the torte in the top of the oven until the eggs are firmly set—25 to 30 minutes. Serve immediately.

NOTE: The separate elements of this dish can be prepared ahead of time and then the eggs beaten and the torte assembled at the last moment.

CALABACITAS RELLENAS DE ELOTE
Zucchini Stuffed with Fresh Corn
SERVES 6   CENTRAL MEXICO

1 ½ POUNDS (675 G) ZUCCHINI—CHOOSE 6 FAT ONES
2 HEAPED CUPS (525 ML) CORN KERNELS
2 LARGE EGGS
2 TABLESPOONS MILK
SALT TO TASTE
6 OUNCES (180 G) QUESO FRESCO, CRUMBLED (ABOUT 1 CUP/250 ML)
3 TABLESPOONS UNSALTED BUTTER, SOFTENED
1 ½ CUPS (375 ML) SALSA RANCHERA (PAGE 238), OMITTING THE ONION

Preheat the oven to 350°F (180°C). Have ready two shallow ovenproof dishes, lightly greased.

Clean and trim the zucchini. Cut them into halves lengthwise and scoop out the inner flesh, leaving a shell about ½ inch (1.5 cm) thick. Discard the pulp or reserve for another use. Place the zucchini in the dish and set aside while you prepare the filling.

Blend the corn, eggs, milk, and salt to a coarse mixture. Do not add more liquid unless absolutely necessary to release the blades. Mix about three quarters of the cheese into the corn mixture, saving the rest for the topping.

Fill the zucchini shells with the corn stuffing, which will be quite runny. Sprinkle with the remaining cheese and dot with the butter. Cover the dish and bake until the squash is tender—about 30 minutes. Serve covered with the tomato sauce.

NOTE: This is a dish that is far better eaten fresh than left to stand around. However, the filling, the zucchini, and the sauce can be prepared ahead of time, ready to assemble for the oven. I do not recommend freezing.

CALABACITAS GUISADAS ESTILO MICHOACÁN
Zucchini Cooked in Michoacán Style

SEÑORITA EFIGENIA HERNÁNDEZ

SERVES 6   MICHOACÁN

Of the many versions of zucchini cooked with tomatoes, this is my favorite. It was one, out of the two, dishes that a one-time maid from a neighboring family showed me how to cook—she didn't like to cook.

The recipe really does need the fresh epazote. It can be served as a vegetable with meat or fish. Topped with cheese it makes a very good vegetarian dish.

¼ CUP (65 ML) VEGETABLE OIL

2 POUNDS (900 G) ZUCCHINI, TRIMMED AND DICED (ABOUT 7 CUPS/1.75 L)

⅓ CUP (85 ML) FINELY CHOPPED WHITE ONION

⅓ CUP (85 ML) ROUGHLY CHOPPED EPAZOTE LEAVES

SALT TO TASTE

12 OUNCES (340 G) TOMATOES, BROILED (SEE PAGE 490)

2 SERRANO CHILES, CHARRED (SEE PAGE 470)

2 GARLIC CLOVES

Heat the oil in a large, deep skillet and add the zucchini, onion, epazote, and salt. Stir well, cover the pan, and cook over medium heat, stirring occasionally, until just tender—about 10 minutes.

Blend together the tomatoes, chiles, and garlic and stir into the zucchini mixture. Cook over medium heat, uncovered, until the zucchini is soft and the tomato sauce has been absorbed, about 15 minutes. The vegetables should be moist but not too juicy. Adjust the seasoning and serve immediately.

NOTE: This is best eaten as soon as it is cooked as it tends to go watery.

It does not freeze well.

BUDÍN DE CHÍCHARO Pea Pudding
SERVES 6

I was introduced to vegetable budínes—*I prefer the Spanish word, having had my fill of puddings, delicious though many of them were, in my youth in England—in Jalisco. They were served either as a first course, after the soup, or to accompany a meat dish.*

This recipe and the following one were given to me by a family from Ciudad Guzman.

2 POUNDS (900 G) FROZEN OR FRESH COOKED PEAS
6 OUNCES (180 G) UNSALTED BUTTER (2/3 CUP/165 ML)
3 LARGE EGGS, SEPARATED
1/2 CUP (125 ML) GRANULATED SUGAR
6 OUNCES (180 G) RICE FLOUR, SIFTED (ABOUT 1 1/2 CUPS/375 ML)
1 TEASPOON SALT
4 OUNCES (115 G) CHIHUAHUA OR MUENSTER CHEESE, GRATED (ABOUT 1 SCANT CUP/
   235 ML)
1 1/2 TEASPOONS BAKING POWDER
A SAUCE MADE BY COMBINING 2 CUPS (500 ML) FRESH ORANGE JUICE WITH 3/4 CUP
   (185 ML) FINELY CHOPPED WALNUTS

Preheat the oven to 500°F (260°C). Butter an 8-inch square baking dish.

Pass the peas through the medium disk of a food mill or process in a food processor. Melt the butter and set it aside to cool.

Setting the egg whites aside, beat the egg yolks until they are thick. Add the sugar and continue beating until it is well incorporated. Beat in the rice flour alternately with the butter.

Stir in the pea pulp, salt, and cheese, mix well, and add the baking powder.

Beat the egg whites until they are stiff and fold them into the mixture. Pour the mixture into the prepared dish. Place the dish on a baking sheet and bake for 10 minutes. Then lower the oven temperature to 350°F (180°C) and continue cooking for about 45 minutes. The *budín* should be soft and spongy to the touch—the top and sides nicely browned, but the inside moist.

Serve immediately, with the orange and walnut sauce to accompany it.

NOTE: I do not recommend freezing this *budín*.

BUDÍN DE ZANAHORIA Carrot Pudding
SERVES 6

2 POUNDS (900 G) COOKED CARROTS

Follow the recipe for Budín de Chícharo (see page 232), omitting the cheese and adding
½ cup (125 ml) raisins.

This can either be eaten hot as a coffee cake or served as a dessert with a thin syrup
and the addition of ¼ cup (65 ml) rum poured over it just before serving.

NOTE: I do not recommend freezing.

BUDÍN DE ELOTE Corn Pudding
SERVES 6

This *budín* is made with uncooked frozen corn.

Defrost 2 pounds (900 g) of corn kernels and blend them with as little milk as necessary to release the cutting blades of the blender. Follow the recipe for Budín de
Chícharo (page 232) and serve with coarsely ground salt and Thick Sour Cream (see
page 489).

This *budín* can be frozen for about 2 months.

SAUCES AND RELISHES

Salsa Mexicana Cruda ※ *Fresh Mexican Sauce*

Salsa de Tomate Verde ※ *Mexican Green Tomato Sauce*

Chiles Serranos o Jalapeños en Escabeche

    ※ *Pickled Serrano or Jalapeño Chiles*

Rajas de Chiles Jalapeños Frescos ※ *Fresh Jalapeño Chile Relish*

Salsa Ranchera ※ *Tomato Sauce*

Salsa de Jitomate Sonorense ※ *Sonoran Tomato Sauce*

Salsa de Jitomate Veracruzana ※ *Veracruz Tomato Sauce*

Salsa de Jitomate Yucateca ※ *Yucatecan Tomato Sauce*

Salsa de Muchos Chiles ※ *Sauce of Many Chiles*

Salsa de Chile de Árbol I ※ *Chile de Árbol Sauce I*

Salsa de Chile de Árbol II ※ *Chile de Árbol Sauce II*

Salsa de Chile Guajillo ※ *Guajillo Chile Sauce*

Salsa Arriera ※ *"Mule Driver's" Sauce*

Salsa de Chile Serrano Rojo ※ *Red Serrano Chile Sauce*

Salsa de Chile Cascabel ※ *Cascabel Chile Sauce*

Salsa de Chile Pasilla ※ *Pasilla Chile Sauce*

Salsa de Tía Georgina ※ *Aunt Georgina's Sauce*

Salsa de Chile Habanero ※ *Habanero Chile Sauce*

Cebollas Encurtidas Yucatecas ※ *Yucatecan Pickled Onions*

Cebollas Encurtidas para Panuchos ※ *Pickled Onions for Panuchos*

Salsa de Cebolla ※ *Onion "Sauce"*

Pico de Gallo con Duraznos ※ *Peach Pico de Gallo*

Salsa de Chile Pasilla de Oaxaca ※ *Sauce of Oaxacan Pasilla Chile*

It would be unthinkable to sit down to an authentic Mexican meal and not find a dish of sauce or some pickled jalapeños on the table; they are as common as salt and pepper. I suppose it is not surprising given the great variety of chiles that are cultivated—and some grow wild—throughout Mexico. There is a great difference, too, in heat level, color, and taste in chiles both fresh and dried. The ways in which the chiles are prepared, and the ingredients with which they are combined, are highly regional, as many of the following recipes will show. 🌾 I doubt that any other cuisine has such a variety of "condiments."

SALSA MEXICANA CRUDA   Fresh Mexican Sauce
MAKES ABOUT 1½ CUPS (375 ML)

This sauce is best eaten immediately. Although it could be made up to 2 hours ahead, it tends to lose its crispness and fresh flavor. It goes with just about everything.

6 OUNCES (180 G) TOMATOES, FINELY CHOPPED (ABOUT 1 ROUNDED CUP/265 ML)
½ CUP (125 ML) FINELY CHOPPED WHITE ONION
⅓ CUP (85 ML) FINELY CHOPPED CILANTRO
3 SERRANO CHILES OR ANY FRESH, HOT GREEN CHILES, FINELY CHOPPED
SALT TO TASTE
⅓ CUP (85 ML) WATER (OPTIONAL)

Mix all the ingredients well and serve at room temperature.

SALSA DE TOMATE VERDE Mexican Green Tomato Sauce
MAKES ABOUT 1 1/4 CUPS (315 ML)   CENTRAL AND NORTHERN MEXICO

This is the most popular of the Mexican table sauces; all the ingredients are raw except for the tomate verde, which is usually, but not always, cooked before using.

Diehard traditionalists with strong wrists can, of course, make this sauce in the molcajete—it is always better for texture and flavor—but if using a blender try to retain a little texture in the sauce; it is all too easy to overblend.

There are no rigid quantities for the ingredients; the chiles and cilantro especially are very much a matter of taste. But don't overdo the onion and the garlic.

2 OR MORE SERRANO CHILES, FINELY CHOPPED
1 HEAPED TABLESPOON FINELY CHOPPED WHITE ONION
1 SMALL GARLIC CLOVE, FINELY CHOPPED
1/3 CUP (85 ML) FIRMLY PACKED, ROUGHLY CHOPPED CILANTRO
8 OUNCES (225 G) TOMATE VERDE, COOKED (SEE PAGE 492) AND PARTIALLY DRAINED
    (ABOUT 1 CUP/250 ML)
SALT TO TASTE
1 ADDITIONAL TEASPOON FINELY CHOPPED CILANTRO (OPTIONAL)

Put the chiles, onion, garlic, and cilantro into a molcajete or blender and crush or blend—if the latter you may need a little water—to a paste. Gradually add the tomate verde and blend to a textured consistency. Add salt and sprinkle the remaining cilantro over the top.

NOTE: This sauce can be made up to 3 hours ahead but tends to lose color and flavor after that time. I do not recommend freezing.

VARIATIONS: Here are two variations that produce more rustic sauces:

1 Using the same quantity of ingredients: Chop all the ingredients together and blend briefly to a textured consistency.

2 Using the same quantity of ingredients: Toast the chiles and tomate verde on a comal over medium heat until soft and slightly browned, then blend with the rest of the ingredients to a textured consistency.

CHILES SERRANOS O JALAPEÑOS EN ESCABECHE

Pickled Serrano or Jalapeño Chiles

MAKES 6 HALF PINTS (1.5 L)

Important note: Partially cooked chiles allow the growth of bacteria, so it is important to make sure that the chiles have been cooked thoroughly if they are to be kept for any length of time.

1 ½ POUNDS (675 G) SERRANO OR JALAPEÑO CHILES

¾ CUP (185 ML) VEGETABLE OIL

2 MEDIUM WHITE ONIONS, THICKLY SLICED

3 MEDIUM CARROTS, SCRAPED AND THICKLY SLICED

1 HEAD GARLIC, CLOVES SEPARATED BUT NOT PEELED

3 CUPS (750 ML) MILD VINEGAR

2 TABLESPOONS SALT

2 MEXICAN BAY LEAVES

½ TEASPOON DRIED MEXICAN OREGANO

6 SPRIGS FRESH MARJORAM OR ¼ TEASPOON DRIED

6 SPRIGS FRESH THYME OR ¼ TEASPOON DRIED

1 TABLESPOON SUGAR

Wash the chiles, leaving the stems intact. Cut a cross in the tip end of each chile so the vinegar can penetrate.

Heat the oil in a large, deep skillet, then add the chiles, onions, carrots, and garlic, and fry over medium heat for about 10 minutes, turning them over from time to time. Add the vinegar, salt, herbs, and sugar, and bring to a boil. Lower the heat and simmer for 5 minutes for serranos or 10 minutes for jalapeños. Pack 6 sterilized half-pint jars with the chiles, vegetables, and herbs, top with the vinegar, and seal.

These should keep for about 1 month in the refrigerator.

RAJAS DE CHILES JALAPEÑOS FRESCOS

Fresh Jalapeño Chile Relish

SEÑORA ARCELIA VÁZQUEZ DE VALLES

MAKES ABOUT 2 CUPS (500 ML)

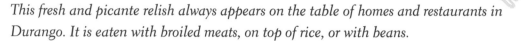

DURANGO

This fresh and picante relish always appears on the table of homes and restaurants in Durango. It is eaten with broiled meats, on top of rice, or with beans.

8 OUNCES (225 G) JALAPEÑO CHILES (ABOUT 13)

1 MEDIUM WHITE ONION, THINLY SLICED (ABOUT 1 ½ CUPS/375 ML)

4 GARLIC CLOVES, LEFT WHOLE

1 ½ TEASPOONS SALT, OR TO TASTE

½ TEASPOON DRIED MEXICAN OREGANO

¾ CUP (185 ML) MILD VINEGAR

¼ CUP (65 ML) VEGETABLE OIL

Wash and dry the chiles well. Remove the stems and cut in half lengthwise. Remove as many of the seeds as possible and cut each chile into four strips. Mix with the rest of the ingredients and set aside to marinate for at least 2 hours.

N O T E : The rajas can be used after about 2 hours but are better the next day. They will keep well for up to about a week in the refrigerator.

SALSA RANCHERA Tomato Sauce

MAKES ABOUT 1 CUP (250 ML)   CENTRAL AND NORTHERN MEXICO

Although Salsa Ranchera is most commonly associated with Huevos Rancheros (page 171), it is really an all-purpose sauce (see also Queso Flameado, page 17, and Molletes, page 188).

The number of chiles, of course, is a matter of taste.

There will always be arguments among cooks about whether the tomatoes should be used fresh or broiled. I prefer them broiled for flavor and texture, although it is a little more trouble to make.

1 POUND (450 G) TOMATOES, BROILED (SEE PAGE 490)

4 SERRANO CHILES OR ANY FRESH, HOT GREEN CHILES, CHARRED (SEE PAGE 470)

1 GARLIC CLOVE, ROUGHLY CHOPPED

2 TABLESPOONS VEGETABLE OIL

2 TABLESPOONS FINELY CHOPPED WHITE ONION

½ TEASPOON SALT, OR TO TASTE

Blend the tomatoes, chiles, and garlic together until fairly smooth.

Heat the oil, and fry the onion gently, without browning, until it is translucent. Add the blended ingredients and the salt and cook over fairly brisk heat for about 5 minutes, stirring and scraping the bottom of the pan until the sauce has reduced a little and is well seasoned.

Serve as described above.

NOTE: This sauce can, of course, be made several hours ahead; it will keep from one day to another. It also freezes well, but as it tends to separate it is best to defrost and blend briefly before using.

SALSA DE JITOMATE SONORENSE Sonoran Tomato Sauce
MAKES ABOUT 2 CUPS (500 ML)   SONORA

The people of Sonora are very proud of their local dishes. They say that they are very healthy and do not have the spices and hot chiles used in the rest of Mexico that irritate the stomach. This is certainly a rather soothing but delicious sauce to be found daily on the table, and a very good accompaniment to the typical carne asada sonorense—*a huge piece of steak cooked over a wood fire in one of the large open-air restaurants of Hermosillo. I have also had it served there with fresh clams and oysters from the nearby Gulf of California.*

1 POUND (450 G) TOMATOES, BROILED (SEE PAGE 490)

1 TABLESPOON ROUGHLY CHOPPED CILANTRO

⅓ CUP (85 ML) FINELY CHOPPED WHITE ONION

SALT TO TASTE

2 ANAHEIM CHILES, CHARRED AND CUT INTO STRIPS WITH SEEDS (SEE PAGE 471)

1 ½ TEASPOONS MILD WHITE VINEGAR

Blend the tomatoes until you have a textured consistency. Do not overblend.

Transfer the tomato sauce to a nonreactive serving dish and add the cilantro and onion with the salt. Add the chiles with their seeds. Last of all, add the vinegar and set aside to season for about 30 minutes.

NOTE: This sauce is best eaten the day it is made. It is not suitable for freezing.

SALSA DE JITOMATE VERACRUZANA Veracruz Tomato Sauce
MAKES ABOUT 1 1/2 CUPS (375 ML)   VERACRUZ

This is the typical sauce to accompany the Garnachas Veracruzanos or other antojitos *from the coastal area around the port of Veracruz, Alvarado, Tlacotalpan, and so on.*

This sauce will keep in the refrigerator for about 3 days. You can freeze it, but blend once again after defrosting as it tends to separate a little.

Most cooks now will use the blender, although traditionally this salsa would have been made in the molcajete.

12 OUNCES (340 G) TOMATOES, BROILED (SEE PAGE 490)
2 JALAPEÑO CHILES, BROILED
1 GARLIC CLOVE, ROUGHLY CHOPPED
SALT TO TASTE

Put all the ingredients (do not skin tomatoes or remove seeds from chiles) into the blender jar and blend to a smooth sauce, add salt, and blend to mix.

Serve at room temperature.

SALSA DE JITOMATE YUCATECA Yucatecan Tomato Sauce
MAKES ABOUT 2 CUPS (500 ML)   YUCATÁN

This is a simple tomato sauce, or chiltomate, *used for many Yucatecan recipes. It is used with Papadzules and Pan de Cazón (in* The Art of Mexican Cooking) *and Frijol con Puerco (page 279).*

The same argument goes on about the best way to cook it. It seems that after cooking the tomatoes traditionally on the hot stones of the pib, *or pit barbecue, they were just mashed and never fried—but times have changed.*

Despite the fact that the habanero chile has the reputation of being one of the hottest chiles—if one really can compare—it has a delightful flavor, and this, not its heat, is supposed to be imparted to the sauce. But, then again, some cooks blend a little piece of the chile with the tomato.

1 ½ POUNDS (680 G) TOMATOES, BROILED OR BOILED (SEE PAGE 490)
3 TABLESPOONS VEGETABLE OIL
¼ CUP (65 ML) ROUGHLY SLICED WHITE ONION
1 WHOLE HABANERO CHILE OR ANY FRESH, HOT GREEN CHILE
½ TEASPOON SALT, OR TO TASTE

If the tomatoes are broiled, remove any very blackened pieces of the skin and leave the rest on; if they are boiled, remove the skins, as boiled skins tend to be tougher. Mash or blend the tomatoes briefly—there should be some texture to the sauce.

Heat the oil in a deep skillet and fry the onion over low heat, without browning, until it is translucent. Add the tomatoes, whole chile, and salt and cook the sauce over medium heat, stirring from time to time until it has reduced and seasoned—about 5 minutes.

Serve as described above.

N O T E : This sauce can be kept refrigerated for about 2 days. I do not recommend freezing.

SALSA DE MUCHOS CHILES Sauce of Many Chiles
SEÑORA MARÍA ELENA LARA
MAKES ABOUT 1 ½ CUPS (375 ML)   MEXICO CITY

This is another of those picante, uncooked table sauces that are used as a condiment, as opposed to a cooked sauce, which becomes an integral part of a dish. There are so many excitingly different chile flavors here that, along with my chile cascabel sauce (see page 246), it has become a firmly established favorite in my kitchen.

María Elena Lara, of whom I have written elsewhere, always served this sauce (which she calls simply salsa) at her restaurant, Los Migueles, in Mexico City (now closed), with rich gorditas that she stuffed with crumbled chicharrón. A wonderful start, with a shot of tequila, to one of those wickedly enticing and fattening Sunday comidas. It can very comfortably accompany broiled meats or sopes or other antojitos.

If you don't have all the chiles called for in this recipe, then substitute from your stockpile, remembering always, of course, that ancho and mulato chiles are rarely, if ever, used for this type of sauce.

2 CASCABEL CHILES, WIPED CLEAN

2 MORITA CHILES, WIPED CLEAN

2 CHILES DE ÁRBOL, WIPED CLEAN

1 CHIPOTLE CHILE, WIPED CLEAN

1 GUAJILLO CHILE, WIPED CLEAN

10 OUNCES (285 G) TOMATOES, BROILED (SEE PAGE 490)

SALT TO TASTE

½ CUP (125 ML) COLD WATER

1 LARGE GARLIC CLOVE, ROUGHLY CHOPPED

1 TABLESPOON ROUGHLY CHOPPED CILANTRO

Heat an ungreased frying pan or comal and toast the chiles, turning them constantly so they do not burn. Let them cool, then crumble (which they should do easily), seeds and veins and all.

Put the unskinned tomatoes, salt, and water in the bottom of a blender jar, then add the garlic and the crumbled chiles, and blend until you have a rough sauce (pieces of the chile skins will and should be visible). Stir in the cilantro and serve the sauce at room temperature.

NOTE: This sauce can be prepared several hours ahead but don't add the cilantro until just before serving. It can also be frozen, without the cilantro, but should be defrosted and blended briefly before serving.

SALSA DE CHILE DE ÁRBOL I Chile de Árbol Sauce I

SEÑORA CLARA ZABALZA DE GARCÍA

MAKES ABOUT 1¼ CUPS (315 ML)

JALISCO

This is probably the best way of using the very fierce chile de árbol in a sauce — and even then you may wish to reduce the number of chiles to the proportion of tomatoes. The sauce, used with discretion, can be served with tacos, flautas, or other antojitos or on rice and pasta dishes.

5 CHILES DE ÁRBOL, WIPED CLEAN

1 TABLESPOON VEGETABLE OIL

10 OUNCES (285 G) TOMATOES, BROILED (SEE PAGE 490)

5 MEDIUM TOMATE VERDE, FRESHLY COOKED (SEE PAGE 492; ABOUT ½ CUP/125 ML)

2 GARLIC CLOVES, ROUGHLY CHOPPED

SALT TO TASTE

Slit the chiles open and remove the seeds and veins. Reserve the seeds and discard the veins. Heat the oil in a skillet and fry the chiles and seeds until they are well browned, but do not let them burn or the sauce will have a bitter taste.

Put the tomatoes, tomate verde, garlic, and salt into a blender jar. Add the fried chiles and seeds and blend briefly. (Do not overblend; the sauce should have some texture.)

NOTE: This sauce can be prepared well ahead and if refrigerated will last up to 3 days. It can also be frozen, but after defrosting it should be blended briefly before serving.

SALSA DE CHILE DE ÁRBOL II Chile de Árbol Sauce II
MAKES ABOUT 1½ CUPS (375 ML)   JALISCO

This is one of many uncooked table sauces from Jalisco used as a condiment with broiled meats and eggs, in soups, or as a topping for antojitos. It could also be diluted with water and fried with shredded meat to make a taco filling. It is fearsomely hot, so reduce the number of chiles to suit your own taste.

9 CHILES DE ÁRBOL, WIPED CLEAN
1½ CUPS (375 ML) TOMATE VERDE, COOKED AND PARTIALLY DRAINED (SEE PAGE 492)
½ CUP (125 ML) WATER
SALT TO TASTE
1 GARLIC CLOVE, ROUGHLY CHOPPED

Toast the chiles well on a hot griddle or comal, turning them constantly so they do not burn (see page 476).

Put the tomate verde into a blender jar with the water, salt, and garlic. Remove the stems from the chiles and crumble the chiles, with seeds and veins, into the blender jar. Blend the mixture until almost smooth. (Do not overblend; the sauce should have some texture and there should be some evidence of the chile skins.)

NOTE: For instructions on keeping, see previous recipe.

SALSA DE CHILE GUAJILLO Guajillo Chile Sauce
MAKES ABOUT 1 1/2 CUPS (375 ML)   MICHOACÁN

This sauce from central Mexico makes a wonderful accompaniment to plainly broiled meats and any tacos.

6 GUAJILLO CHILES, WIPED CLEAN, VEINS AND SEEDS REMOVED
1 CUP (250 ML) WATER, APPROXIMATELY
6 OUNCES (180 G) TOMATOES, BROILED (SEE PAGE 490)
1 SLICE WHITE ONION, ROUGHLY CHOPPED
1 GARLIC CLOVE, ROUGHLY CHOPPED
SALT TO TASTE

Heat a griddle or comal and toast the chiles well on both sides (see page 476)—when they cool they should be almost crisp—but be careful not to burn them or the sauce will have a bitter taste.

Put the water into the blender jar, add the rest of the ingredients, and blend until almost smooth (small pieces of chile skin should be evident in the sauce).

NOTE: Directions for keeping and freezing are on page 243.

SALSA ARRIERA "Mule Driver's" Sauce
MAKES ABOUT 1/2 CUP (125 ML)   CENTRAL MEXICO

The very simplest of tacos, reputedly eaten by mule drivers, consists of a hot tortilla, some rather strong white cheese (añejo), and a small amount of mouth-searing sauce.

20 FRESH SERRANO CHILES
2 TABLESPOONS ROUGHLY CHOPPED WHITE ONION
1 GARLIC CLOVE, ROUGHLY CHOPPED
3 TO 4 TABLESPOONS COLD WATER
SALT TO TASTE

Toast the chiles on a medium hot griddle or comal (see page 470), turning them from time to time until they are blistered and charred. While they are still hot, grind them with the rest of the ingredients to a rough paste in a molcajete (preferably) or in a blender.

NOTE: This sauce can be prepared several hours ahead. I do not recommend freezing.

SALSA DE CHILE SERRANO ROJO Red Serrano Chile Sauce

SEÑOR JOSÉ MEZA, RESTAURANTE EL PASTOR, MONTERREY

MAKES ABOUT 1¼ CUPS (315 ML) NUEVO LEÓN

When I was in Monterrey one year at the end of October, the markets were filled with shining piles of red (ripe) serrano chiles—their preferred condition, I was told, for sauces in this part of Mexico. (Farther south, on the other hand, the most popular sauces are made of green serrano chiles, which have a sharp, pungent flavor.) One could almost call this particular sauce a violent one, but very colorful. It goes very well with the cabrito al pastor *(goat) I ate while I was there. Cabrito cooked over a wood fire is a specialty of northern Mexico. I ordered a steamed head, too—just to prove that my memory of how delicious it was on a previous visit had not become exaggerated with time—and then some* machitos *(the small intestines wound into a skein and broiled over the fire). Everything went so well with a* tarro, *or mug, of draught beer and then a bowl of frijoles rancheros to finish up with (the best frijoles rancheros, incidentally, I have ever eaten).*

2 OUNCES (60 G) RED (RIPE) SERRANO CHILES (ABOUT 18)

6 OUNCES (180 G) TOMATOES

¼ CUP (65 ML) WATER

½ TEASPOON SALT, OR TO TASTE

Put the chiles into a small saucepan with the tomatoes. Cover with water, bring to a simmer, and cook uncovered for about 15 minutes, or until soft.

Drain the chiles and tomatoes and transfer to a blender jar. Add the ¼ cup of water and the salt and blend briefly. (Do not overblend; the sauce should have some texture.)

Serve with broiled or roasted meats.

NOTE: This sauce can be prepared several hours ahead but I do not recommend freezing it.

SALSA DE CHILE CASCABEL Cascabel Chile Sauce
MAKES ABOUT 1½ CUPS (375 ML)   CENTRAL AND NORTHERN MEXICO

This is another of those very satisfying rustic sauces. The toasted cascabel chile has a rich, nutty flavor, and even though the seeds are ground up in it, the sauce is not too picante. I first encountered it when we were visiting the archaeological zone and planning a trip into the selva to see the more remote ruins of Bonampak and Yaxchilán. It was served to us in a small restaurant on the outskirts of Palenque, run by a family from Chihuahua. When I got home it was adopted by our household, and it has been a great favorite ever since.

10 CASCABEL CHILES, WIPED CLEAN, SEEDS AND VEINS REMOVED, SEEDS RESERVED
12 OUNCES (340 G) TOMATOES, BROILED (SEE PAGE 490)
3 GARLIC CLOVES, ROUGHLY CHOPPED
½ TEASPOON SALT
ABOUT ⅔ CUP (165 ML) WATER

Toast the chiles over medium heat on a comal or skillet, turning them constantly so that they do not burn.

Toast the seeds to a deep golden brown, turning them constantly or they will burn.

Blend all the ingredients together for a minute or two, but be careful not to overblend—the sauce must have some texture. Add a little more water if necessary; the sauce should have quite a loose consistency, but will thicken as it stands.

NOTE: This sauce can be prepared well in advance and will keep in the refrigerator for about 3 days. I do not recommend freezing.

SALSA DE CHILE PASILLA Pasilla Chile Sauce
MAKES ABOUT 1 CUP (250 ML)   CENTRAL MEXICO

4 PASILLA CHILES, WIPED CLEAN, LEFT WHOLE
1 GARLIC CLOVE, ROUGHLY CHOPPED
SALT TO TASTE
¾ CUP (185 ML) COLD WATER
1 HEAPED TABLESPOON FINELY CHOPPED WHITE ONION

Toast the chiles well on a comal or skillet over medium heat (see page 475). Do not soak them.

Blend the toasted chiles with the garlic, salt, and water. Do not overblend—the sauce should have some texture. Put the sauce into the dish and top with the onion.

NOTE: This sauce can be kept refrigerated for about 3 days. It can be kept frozen for about 2 months. After defrosting it should be blended briefly before serving.

SALSA DE TÍA GEORGINA Aunt Georgina's Sauce

SEÑORA ROSAMARÍA CASAS

MAKES ABOUT 1½ CUPS (375 ML)   CENTRAL MEXICO

This is sometimes called salsa de tijera *(scissors sauce) since the chiles are cut into narrow strips with a pair of scissors. Strictly speaking it is more of a relish than a sauce. It will keep indefinitely, and it gets better as it matures. It has an interesting texture and provides a very earthy and crunchy accompaniment to broiled meats, Carnitas (page 23), and rice.*

This is a family recipe, a variation of several of its type; when pasilla chiles are used in the same way it is called salsa de moscas. Salsa de los reyes *has the three chiles—mulato, ancho, and pasilla—mixed together. All of these sauces are used principally with barbecued meats.*

It is advisable to rinse the chiles briefly and wipe them with a cloth carefully, to remove any dust or earth adhering to them.

8 ANCHO CHILES, WIPED CLEAN, SEEDS AND VEINS REMOVED
⅓ CUP (85 ML) FINELY CHOPPED WHITE ONION
4 GARLIC CLOVES, FINELY CHOPPED
½ CUP (125 ML) VEGETABLE OR LIGHT OLIVE OIL
½ CUP (125 ML) MILD VINEGAR
SALT TO TASTE
¼ CUP (65 ML) CRUMBLED QUESO FRESCO

Cut the chiles into small pieces or narrow strips. Mix all the ingredients except the cheese. Set the sauce aside to season for at least 2 hours, or overnight.

To serve, sprinkle with the crumbled cheese.

NOTE: This sauce will keep, refrigerated, for at least 9 months in the refrigerator.

SALSA DE CHILE HABANERO Habanero Chile Sauce
MAKES ALMOST 1 CUP (250 ML)   YUCATÁN

This is a very concentrated sauce that is used with restraint, more as a condiment than a sauce in the general sense of the word.

Traditionally the chiles are ground, or tamulado, with the lime juice and salt to a loose, pastelike consistency in a wooden mortar called a kokoic.

12 HABANERO CHILES
⅔ CUP (165 ML) FRESH LIME JUICE OR MILD WHITE VINEGAR
SALT TO TASTE

Toast the chiles lightly on a comal or skillet over medium heat, turning them constantly until they are quite soft. Blend the chiles with the rest of the ingredients for a few seconds.

NOTE: This amount of sauce will go a very long way; it also freezes well indefinitely.

CEBOLLAS ENCURTIDAS YUCATECAS Yucatecan Pickled Onions
MAKES ABOUT 2 CUPS (500 ML)   YUCATÁN

In traditional Yucatecan kitchens you can always see a large glass jar with these pickled onions, some flavored with allspice or chiles (see following recipe). They are always ready to add to a dish like Sierra en Escabeche (page 360) or Pollo en Escabeche Oriental (page 345) or to liven up a sandwich or soup.

1 LARGE PURPLE ONION, THINLY SLICED (ABOUT 1¾ CUPS/435 ML)
10 PEPPERCORNS
4 WHOLE ALLSPICE
1 SCANT TABLESPOON MEXICAN DRIED OREGANO, YUCATECAN IF POSSIBLE, TOASTED AND
   CRUMBLED
2 GARLIC CLOVES, SLICED
¾ CUP (185 ML) MILD VINEGAR
SALT TO TASTE

In a nonreactive bowl, mix the ingredients well and set aside in the refrigerator for at least 24 hours before using.

CEBOLLAS ENCURTIDAS PARA PANUCHOS
Pickled Onions for Panuchos

SEÑORA BERTA LÓPEZ DE MARRUFO

MAKES ABOUT 2 CUPS (500 ML)

YUCATÁN

These delicious, lightly pickled onions are used by traditional cooks as a topping for Panu-chos (page 40). Of course, they are even more delicious if you can use the juice of bitter (a variety of Seville) orange. They should be prepared at least 2 hours ahead and will keep for several days in the refrigerator. You may wonder at the yield, but the onions wilt considerably.

2 MEDIUM WHITE ONIONS, FINELY SLICED INTO RINGS (ABOUT 3 CUPS/750 ML)

4 CUPS (1 L) BOILING WATER

½ CUP (125 ML) SEVILLE ORANGE JUICE OR SUBSTITUTE (SEE PAGE 494)

½ CUP (125 ML) WATER

1 SCANT TABLESPOON DRIED MEXICAN OREGANO, YUCATECAN IF POSSIBLE,
TOASTED AND CRUMBLED

1 HABANERO CHILE, FINELY SLICED

SALT TO TASTE

Immerse the onion rings in a saucepan of boiling water for a few seconds until slightly blanched. Drain well and put into a nonreactive bowl.

Mix in the rest of the ingredients and set aside to season for at least 2 hours before using.

SALSA DE CEBOLLA Onion "Sauce"

MAKES ABOUT 1 CUP (250 ML)

CHIAPAS

This resembles a watery relish rather than a sauce as such, but it nonetheless provides a picante and acidy crunch to certain foods—rice, for example, or tamales. Señora Esperanza Murillo of Tapachula, Chiapas, served this with crisp-fried slivers of malanga—it would be great with potato chips, too.

⅔ CUP (165 ML) FINELY CHOPPED WHITE ONION

¼ CUP (65 ML) FRESH LIME JUICE

½ CUP (125 ML) WATER

2 SERRANO CHILES, FINELY CHOPPED

SALT TO TASTE

Mix all the ingredients and set aside for at least 1 hour before serving.

NOTE: Obviously this is a fresh sauce and not suitable for freezing, but it will keep for 2 or 3 days in the refrigerator.

PICO DE GALLO CON DURAZNOS Peach Pico de Gallo

DR. ALFREDO GARDUÑO

MAKES 2 SCANT CUPS (475 ML)   ESTADO DE MÉXICO

Pico de gallo, or rooster's beak, is the colorful name given to a fresh relish of finely chopped ingredients seasoned with chile. The first pico I tried was in Jalisco, and it was made with dried jicama and orange and served with drinks before the meal. A fresh salsa Mexicana of chopped tomatoes, chiles, onions, and cilantro is referred to as pico de gallo in parts of northern Mexico, and here is yet another version, this time with peaches.

In the sheltered valleys in the eastern part of Michoacán and neighboring Mexico State peaches can be grown for several months of the year. They are small and firm and the flesh is often very pale orange; they are ideal for peeling and dicing for this relish given to me by Dr. Alfredo Garduño from Coatepec de Harinas in the State of Mexico—a simpler version is made in San Pancho, my village in Michoacán.

1 ½ CUPS (375 ML) FINELY DICED PEELED FIRM BUT JUST RIPE PEACHES

3 TABLESPOONS FINELY CHOPPED WHITE ONION

2 TABLESPOONS FINELY CHOPPED EPAZOTE LEAVES

1 PERÓN (ROCOTO) CHILE, SEEDS REMOVED AND FINELY CHOPPED, OR 3 SERRANO CHILES FINELY CHOPPED WITH SEEDS

3 TABLESPOONS FRESH LIME JUICE

SALT TO TASTE

Mix all the ingredients and set aside to season for about ½ hour before using.

NOTE: This pico de gallo is served as a relish with rice dishes, in soups, or as a topping for *tlacoyos* and many *antojitos*.

SALSA DE CHILE PASILLA DE OAXACA
Sauce of Oaxacan Pasilla Chile

ABIGAIL MENDOZA

MAKES A LITTLE OVER 1⅓ CUPS (335 ML)

OAXACA

Señorita Abigail Mendoza, the star of the Zapotec kitchen — as I call her — generously allowed me to use her recipe for this table sauce. It closely resembles the dark paste chintesle, which traditionally is taken on long journeys or peregrinations and used to smear on tortillas. It is both nutritious and satisfying.

Abigail insists that the whole chiles be very lightly toasted in warm ashes, which gives a slightly different balance of flavors to the sauce, but if you don't have warm ashes, just heat the chiles through on a warm comal.

Though not comparable in flavor, the dried chile de agua is sometimes used in this sauce; however they are hard to come by except in the Oaxaca Valley.

When making this sauce in the traditional way the Mendoza sisters grind it either on the metate or in the clay chilmolera, *an earthenware mortar that is ridged inside. It is a fairly thick, slightly textured sauce.*

1 ⅓ CUPS (335 ML) WATER, APPROXIMATELY

6 MEDIUM-SIZE PASILLA DE OAXACA CHILES

4 LARGE HOJA SANTA LEAVES

¼ CUP (65 ML) DRIED SHRIMP HEADS (SEE PAGE 498), RINSED AND DRIED (THE BODIES
    CAN BE USED FOR RICE OR SOUP)

3 SMALL GARLIC CLOVES, ROUGHLY CHOPPED

SALT TO TASTE

Put the water into the blender jar.

On a warm comal or hot plate, heat the chiles through, turning them from time to time for about 2 minutes, taking care not to let them burn. Tear them up and add to the blender jar. Toast the hoja santa leaves on the warm comal until dry and crisp—about 3 minutes. Crumble into the blender jar.

Toast the dried shrimp heads, turning them over to avoid scorching, for about 2 minutes. Crumble into the blender jar. Add the garlic and blend to a textured sauce, adding salt if necessary.

A plentiful repast was served up in the Spanish style, in a house built of sticks. Of the greater portion of the dishes I could not learn the component parts; but one striking feature was a pig three months old roasted whole, and stuffed with walnuts, which I thought an excellent dish and well cooked.

—A NINETEENTH-CENTURY DESCRIPTION OF A RURAL DINNER OUTSIDE JALAPA, FROM W. H. BULLOCK, *Six Months Residence and Travel in Mexico*

In my early days in Mexico, Saturday mornings for me meant markets. I would start off early and go first to San Juan and then stop off at Juárez on my way home. By that time Señor Raúl, the butcher, was preparing his *almuerzo*; you could smell it the moment you entered the market almost a block away, and he used to make everyone very hungry and very envious. He loved to cook, and this *almuerzo* of his was no ordinary "brunch." A little girl would come by, always at the same hour, with a large, thick tumbler full of milky coffee and a bag of the *pan dulce* that has a rounded top latticed with cinnamon sugar; an old crone would push some steaming, flabby tortillas across the counter and we would all peer curiously toward the little stove to see what he was cooking that day. Quite often it would be a piece of *carne enchilada*—meat seasoned with a paste of guajillo chile—or a pork chop in adobo (see page 273) that he was preparing for his clients.

Once he was beating eggs and adding cooked and shredded flank steak. He dropped the mixture by spoonfuls into the hot fat and very soon the little *tortitas* were all puffed up and golden and ready for the tomato broth in which they were to be served.

He taught me how delicious veal kidneys could be; but his were not as large as those we are accustomed to. The whole kidney in its fatty sheath would be no more than about 2½ inches (6.5 cm) across, and each ripple about ¼ inch (1 cm). He would slice them, fat and all, and fry them lightly. At his suggestion, I would buy these little kidneys and bake them, complete with their fatty casing, until the outside was crisp and brown while the inside was still juicy and very tender.

Señor Raúl also taught me how to cut the filet for *carne asada* and how to prepare the adobo for pork chops. Since he didn't sell veal I would go to a nearby stand, where a group of cheerful and energetic young men would cut scaloppine to perfection and slice a whole calf's liver—pale reddish brown and weighing no more than two pounds—into paper-thin slices. I can never eat liver anywhere else. So even if you couldn't get the best roast beef or lamb chops, there were so many other things.

The Mexicans are great pork eaters, especially the country people, who will often fatten up a couple of pigs in their back yard as an investment. Our maid Godileva always did, and no household scraps, potato peelings, or outside lettuce leaves escaped her eye; they were carried home along with the neighbors' stale bread and dried tortillas for the pigs.

The butchers' stands in the markets in small villages and country towns are hung with yards and yards of thin meat—moist, drying, and dried *tasajo* or *cecina*. I wanted to learn how to cut it, so one Sunday morning on a trip to the Sierra de Puebla I went to the almost deserted market in Huauchinango, right on the border between Veracruz and Puebla. The two friendly butchers would take a rump of beef or pork, or a huge lump of ox lung, and with a long, thin knife cut a first fine layer, then turn the meat and cut the other way, backwards and forwards, turning it over and over until, in no time at all, the piece would be flattened out into one long continuous strip. With a flick of the wrist, they would throw on a fine layer of salt, squeeze plenty of lime juice on it, and fold the meat up into a basket pile of laundry, where it was left to season overnight. The next day they would hang it up in an airy place to dry. Broiled over char-coal and eaten with a green tomato or cascabel chile sauce, it is very tasty.

The beef country is in the north of Mexico, and Chihuahua City has some of the most opulent steak houses in the whole of Mexico. They say the beef has an extra-good flavor there because the animals feed on wild oregano. To the west, in Hermosillo, you were served the biggest steaks of all in the large open-air restaurants, where they are cooked to order over wood fires. Then they go to the other extreme and have the flim-siest beef jerky—*carne machacada*—pounded to a fluff.

I have eaten cabrito—kid—in many places, but nowhere is it as good as in Mon-terrey. The kid must not be older than thirty days, for after that time it ceases to be milk fed, and as it starts to browse the flavor of the flesh becomes strong and goaty. Prefer-ably it should be cooked, and eaten, out of doors, over a fire of *huisache* branches— but I would settle any day for the cabrito so carefully cooked in the Restaurante Princi-pal or El Tio in Monterrey. The tender animal is opened out flat and impaled on a stake set at a 70-degree angle at the edge of the fire. It takes two hours to cook, and every half hour its position is changed. The cooking follows a strict pattern, and when there are at least ten cabritos being cooked at once you wonder how the cook remembers exactly which way each one should go next—but he does. The *riñonada*, the choicest part, is the lower part of the back, where the drippings from the fatty kidney sheath continu-ally baste it. It is brown and crisp on the outside, but the flesh inside is as delicate and tender as the finest veal.

But there are other things that went along with the cabrito: a bowl of frijoles rancheros quite strongly seasoned with cumin; a sausage of intestine stuffed with liver and kidney called *machitos*. And, most delicate of all, the steamed head of the little goat, the tongue of which is the delicacy of all time. Or you would have a stew of cabrito thickened with the blood—*fritada*, which is more of an acquired taste.

The meat stands in the Culiacán market are piled with brick-colored *chilorio*, a ready-made filling for tacos of shredded, crisp pork seasoned with ground chiles and spices, and cuts of beef called *gusano* for the local Asado Placero Sinaloense (page 289). Curiously this is not roasted meat as the name implies, but boiled and then fried in cubes with potatoes, smothered in a tomato sauce, and topped with zucchini, carrots, onion rings, and lettuce. It is a very popular supper dish, especially in Mazatlán when the day has cooled off a little and you have eaten a light seafood lunch.

In Guadalajara the most touted meat dish is Birria (page 301), and throughout the central plateau of Mexico the Sunday marketplaces are full of lamb and *pancita* or *montalayo* barbecued in pits lined with maguey leaves. The *pancita* is lamb's stomach stuffed with chile-seasoned lamb's liver and kidney as well as the intestines of the lamb. In Hidalgo and Tlaxcala you can nearly always be sure of getting *mixiote*, which is lamb seasoned with dried chiles and cooked in little packages covered with the membrane stripped from the outside of the maguey leaves. In Oaxaca, the barbacoa is of sheep or goat cooked on a bed of crushed maize, which absorbs the juices and is wonderfully savory.

You used to go to the upper floor of the Mérida market to find every imaginable cut of cooked venison; they say it had been cooked in a *pib* in the ground. The flesh of the small deer that abounded in the Yucatán is light in color and delicate in flavor, much more like veal than the gamy dark-red venison we are more accustomed to. It is often served in a *pipián* made of very tiny pumpkin seeds that are toasted and ground, hull and seed together. Or it is shredded finely and mixed with minutely chopped radishes, onion, and cilantro and moistened with Seville orange juice to make a *salpicón* for tacos (see page 10).

Saturday still seems to be the day for slaughtering cattle in Campeche, for *chocolomo* is the Saturday night special. It is made only with freshly killed beef and offal. It is one of those hearty soup-stews that are found all over Mexico, but with a difference: along with the meat, the brains, kidney, liver, and heart are cooked with toasted garlic and onion and flavored at the last moment with the bitter *lima* that gives its name to the typical lime soup of the Yucatán.

One could go on forever. The variations are enormous, as can be seen by the following recipes.

PORK

Caldillo de Puerco Duranguense ※ *Durango Pork Stew*

Carne de Puerco en Chile Colorado ※ *Pork in Red Chile*

Ayocotes con Carne de Puerco Estilo Querétaro

※ *Ayocote Beans with Pork*

Cochito al Horno ※ *Chiapas Roast Pork*

Puerco en Naranja ※ *Pork Cooked in Orange Juice*

Asado de Puerco a la Veracruzana ※ *Veracruz Roast Pork*

Puerco en Mole Verde Veracruzano ※ *Pork in Veracruz Green Mole*

Puerco en Mole Verde de Cacahuate ※ *Pork in Green Peanut Sauce*

Calabaza Guisada con Puerco ※ *Pumpkin Cooked with Pork*

Guiso de Puerco ※ *Pork Stew*

Puerco con Verdolagas ※ *Pork with Purslane*

Tinga Poblana con Carne de Puerco ※ *Shredded Savory Pork*

Chuletas de Puerco Adobados

※ *Pork Chops Seasoned with Adobo Paste*

Puerco en Adobo ※ *Pork in Adobo Sauce*

Carne de Puerco con Uchepos ※ *Pork with Fresh Corn Tamales*

Cochinita Pibil ※ *Yucatecan Pit-Barbecued Pig*

Frijol con Puerco ※ *Beans with Pork*

Lomitos ※ *Yucatecan Pork Pieces*

Calzones del Diablo ※ *The Devil's Pants*

Puerco en Mole Chatino ※ *Pork in Chatino Mole*

CALDILLO DE PUERCO DURANGUENSE Durango Pork Stew

SEÑORA ARCELIA VÁZQUEZ DE VALLES

SERVES 6   DURANGO

The popular dish in the northern state is caldillo—*really a stew—made with filet of beef, or dried and shredded beef or pork. It resembles very much the Chihuahua dish Carne de Puerco en Chile Colorado.*

This recipe was given to me by Señora Arcelia Vázquez de Valles, a cook of great reputation, particularly renowned for her exquisite marzipan fruits.

8 ANCHO CHILES

5 $\frac{1}{2}$ CUPS (1.375 L) WATER, APPROXIMATELY

1 CUP (250 ML) TOMATE VERDE, COOKED (SEE PAGE 492) AND PARTIALLY DRAINED

3 TABLESPOONS VEGETABLE OIL OR PORK LARD

2 $\frac{1}{4}$ POUNDS (1 KG) BONELESS PORK, WITH SOME FAT, CUT INTO $\frac{1}{2}$-INCH (1.5-CM) CUBES

2 GARLIC CLOVES, FINELY CHOPPED

$\frac{2}{3}$ CUP (165 ML) FINELY CHOPPED WHITE ONION

SALT TO TASTE

2 TEASPOONS ALL-PURPOSE FLOUR

$\frac{1}{4}$ TEASPOON DRIED MEXICAN OREGANO

Cover the whole chiles with water and simmer until soft—about 10 minutes, depending on how dry the chiles are—then drain and transfer to a blender jar. Add 2 cups (500 ml) of the water and the tomate verde and blend until smooth. Set aside.

Heat the oil or lard in a wide pan and fry the meat, together with the garlic, onion, and salt, until golden, stirring constantly, about 5 minutes. Sprinkle the flour into the pan and fry, stirring until it is lightly browned. Add the blended chiles to the pan and cook, over fairly high heat, for about 10 minutes, scraping the bottom of the pan to avoid sticking.

Add the oregano and approximately 3 cups (750 ml) of the water—the meat should be covered with the sauce—then cover the pan and simmer until the meat is tender—about 30 minutes. (When cooked, the sauce should be quite soupy like a thin gravy; add more water if necessary.)

Serve in bowls, with lots of sauce and flour tortillas.

NOTE: This can be prepared several hours ahead and can be frozen for about 1 month.

CARNE DE PUERCO EN CHILE COLORADO Pork in Red Chile

SEÑORA ROSA MARGARITA J. DE MEJÍA

SERVES 6 CHIHUAHUA

When The Cuisines of Mexico was published, my northern Mexican friends gently chided me for not taking more notice of their favorite dishes. So for Mexican Regional Cooking, after another extended tour through the northern states, I gathered together a number of recipes from that region, including this one. Admittedly my taste lies south—with the fascinating herbs, chiles, and vegetables of central Mexico—but I do find these simple dishes extremely good, and very comforting after a lot of more complicated food.

Señora Rosa Margarita J. de Mejía, a talented cook from Chihuahua who has introduced me to many of her regional dishes, gave me this particular recipe. It is made with the chile de la tierra, but Californian or New Mexican chile pods can be substituted.

2¼ POUNDS (1 KG) BONELESS PORK, WITH SOME FAT, CUT INTO ½-INCH (1.5-CM)
  CUBES
2 TEASPOONS SALT, OR TO TASTE
3½ CUPS (875 ML) WATER, APPROXIMATELY
2 GARLIC CLOVES
⅛ TEASPOON CUMIN SEEDS
¼ TEASPOON DRIED MEXICAN OREGANO
8 CHILES DE LA TIERRA (SEE PAGE 477), OR NEW MEXICAN OR CALIFORNIAN CHILES,
  INCLUDING THEIR SEEDS
2 TABLESPOONS VEGETABLE OIL, APPROXIMATELY
2 TEASPOONS ALL-PURPOSE FLOUR

Put the meat, salt, and ¼ cup (65 ml) of the water into a large, heavy pan in which the meat will just fit in two layers. Cover the pan and cook over low heat, shaking the pan from time to time to prevent sticking, until the meat is *just* tender, all the liquid absorbed, and the fat rendering out—about 45 minutes, depending on the cut of meat and how tender it is. If it becomes too dry during the cooking time, then add a little more water.

Crush the garlic, cumin, and oregano in a molcajete or mortar. Cover the chiles with water in a small saucepan, and simmer uncovered for about 10 minutes, or until the skin is soft. Drain and transfer to a blender jar, along with 1 cup (250 ml) of the water and the crushed ingredients, and blend until smooth. Set aside.

Add oil as necessary to the fat in the pan to make up to 3 tablespoons, approximately. Heat the oil and fry the meat lightly, turning it over from time to time. Sprinkle the flour over the meat and keep turning and frying until it browns slightly. Pass the chile sauce through a strainer into the pan and fry for a few minutes longer, stirring and scraping the bottom of the pan. Add the remaining 2 cups (500 ml) of water—the sauce should be rather thin—and cook for 15 to 20 minutes more.

Serve in bowls, with lots of sauce and flour tortillas.

NOTE: This dish can be prepared several hours ahead and can be kept frozen for about 2 weeks.

AYOCOTES CON CARNE DE PUERCO ESTILO QUERÉTARO
Ayocote Beans with Pork

OBDULIA AND ANAMARÍA VEGA

SERVES 6   QUERÉTARO

Ayocotes *are large dried beans all shades of brown and purple that can be found in markets throughout central Mexico. They can be cooked when they are freshly picked, but more often they are dried and stored for the months ahead. The large pods are harvested and dried in the hot October sun, then they are beaten with sticks so they break open and release the beans. In Puebla they are often served to accompany a mole.*

I never really acquired a taste for them until AnaMaría and Obdulia Vega—who had brought a huge bag of them back from their last visit home—showed me how to cook them as their mother used to at their small Querétaro ranch. The chiles seem to bring out the delicious, earthy flavor of the ayocotes—*one would think quite the opposite, that they would mask the flavor. You could quite successfully substitute any large dried beans.*

THE BEANS

3 CUPS (750 ML) DRIED AYOCOTES, LARGE NAVY BEANS, OR HARICOT BEANS
    (ABOUT 18 OUNCES, 510 G)

8 CUPS (2 L) COLD WATER

2 TEASPOONS SALT, OR TO TASTE

THE MEAT

1 ½ POUNDS (675 G) COUNTRY-STYLE SPARERIBS, CUT INTO 1 ½-INCH (4-CM) CUBES
(HALF CARNE MACIZA AND HALF COSTILLITAS IN MEXICO)

SALT TO TASTE

PORK LARD, IF NECESSARY

THE SAUCE

9 PASILLA CHILES, SEEDS AND VEINS REMOVED

9 GUAJILLO CHILES, SEEDS AND VEINS REMOVED

5 PEPPERCORNS, ROUGHLY CRUSHED

¾ TEASPOON CUMIN SEEDS, CRUSHED

3 WHOLE CLOVES, CRUSHED

2 GARLIC CLOVES, CRUSHED

2 ½ CUPS (625 ML) HOT WATER

2 MEXICAN BAY LEAVES

Rinse the beans well, then place in a bean pot or slow cooker. Cover with the water and leave to soak for 30 minutes. In the same water, bring the beans to a boil, lower the heat, and simmer until tender—2 to 3 hours, depending on how dry they are. Add salt.

In the meantime, cook the pork. Put the cubes into a wide, heavy pan, barely cover with water, add salt, and cook, uncovered, over medium heat until all the water is consumed and the meat tender. Continue cooking, turning from time to time, so that the fat renders out and the meat browns well. If the pork is very lean you may have to add some lard, say ¼ cup (65 ml). Remove the meat and all but ¼ cup (65 ml) of the fat.

Heat a griddle or comal and toast the chiles thoroughly (see page 475), taking care not to burn them or the sauce will have a bitter taste. Cover the chiles with hot water separately and let them soak for about 5 minutes; drain.

Add the crushed spices and garlic with ½ cup (125 ml) water to the blender jar and blend thoroughly. Add another cup of water (250 ml) and the drained pasillas and blend until almost smooth. Reheat the lard in the pan, then add the blended ingredients and fry over medium heat. In 1 cup (250 ml) of water, blend the guajillo chiles thoroughly and add to the pan, pressing the mixture through a fine strainer to eliminate any tough pieces of skin. Continue cooking the sauce over medium heat, stirring occasionally.

Add the beans with their broth and the bay leaves, adjust the seasoning, and cook over low heat for another 20 minutes.

N O T E : This dish can be made a day ahead and frozen for a week.

COCHITO AL HORNO Chiapas Roast Pork
SERVES 6 TO 8

Cochito is the shortened form of cochinito *("little pig"), used in Chiapas and Tabasco. Traditionally the rind is left on and the pig cut into large pieces before being seasoned and roasted. The number and amount of spices used, with the predominant flavor of allspice, are characteristic of the food of that area around Tuxtla Gutiérrez, Chiapa de Corzo, and San Cristóbal de las Casas.*

I have mentioned before the famous botanas—hot and cold appetizers that are served in bars and small regional restaurants—and they often include cochito *cooked in this way. You won't find it on ordinary menus, but I have seen it served with a pile of hot tortillas as a substantial* almuerzo, *or late breakfast, in the small Tuxtla Gutiérrez airport, many years ago.*

Start one day ahead, preferably, to enhance the flavor.

4 ANCHO CHILES, SEEDS AND VEINS REMOVED

6 SPRIGS FRESH THYME OR 1/4 TEASPOON DRIED

4 MEXICAN BAY LEAVES

10 PEPPERCORNS, CRUSHED

6 WHOLE CLOVES, CRUSHED

20 WHOLE ALLSPICE, CRUSHED

2-INCH (5-CM) PIECE OF CINNAMON STICK, CRUSHED

4 GARLIC CLOVES, CRUSHED

1 1/2 TABLESPOONS SALT

2/3 CUP (165 ML) MILD VINEGAR, APPROXIMATELY

5 POUNDS (2.5 KG) PORK ROAST, WITH RIND, IF POSSIBLE

1 CUP (250 ML) WARM WATER

TO SERVE

2 CUPS (500 ML) THINLY SLICED WHITE ONION

2 CUPS (500 ML) SHREDDED ROMAINE LETTUCE

Cover the chiles with boiling water in a bowl and leave to soak for about 15 minutes, or until soft. Put the herbs, spices, garlic, salt, and vinegar into a blender jar and blend thoroughly. Gradually add the soaked and drained chiles and blend until smooth, stopping occasionally to release the blades of the blender—you may need to add a little water, but the mixture should have the consistency of a loose paste.

Pierce the meat all over with the point of a sharp knife. Smear the meat liberally with the seasoning paste and set aside for a minimum of 4 hours, but preferably overnight.

Preheat the oven to 350°F (180°C).

Put the meat into a casserole, cover, and cook for 1 hour. Turn the meat and cook for 1 hour more, still covered. At this point, scrape up the paste that is sticking to the bottom of the pan and dilute it with the warm water. Turn the meat again and cook for another 2 hours, or until the meat is very tender, basting from time to time with the pan juices. When the meat is cooked, there should be plenty of sauce in the casserole.

Serve the meat sliced, with some of the sauce from the pan and topped with plenty of onion rings and shredded lettuce. Eat with freshly made tortillas.

NOTE: The meat may be seasoned up to 2 days ahead—but once cooked it is best eaten the same day. I do not recommend freezing.

PUERCO EN NARANJA Pork Cooked in Orange Juice
SERVES 6 TO 8   CENTRAL MEXICO

When I first tasted this recipe the Mexican cook used a boneless loin. Since this cut tends to be fatless and dry, I use a rib end of loin which is much more succulent.

This is one of the many versions of Puerco en Naranja—every cook has her own secret touches—with my method for cooking it. It is often served with rajas—strips of poblano chiles fried together with onions—which complement the meat very well.

5 POUNDS (2.5 KG) RIB-END PORK LOIN (IN TWO PIECES, IF NECESSARY, TO MAKE UP THIS WEIGHT)
5 GARLIC CLOVES
SALT TO TASTE
2 TEASPOONS DRIED MEXICAN OREGANO
12 PEPPERCORNS
3 ORANGES

Pierce the meat all over with the point of a sharp knife. Crush the garlic, together with the salt, oregano, and peppercorns, and moisten with the juice of 1 orange. Rub this mixture into the pork and set aside to season for 1 hour.

Preheat the oven to 350°F (180°C).

Place the pork in a heavy casserole into which it will just fit comfortably and moisten it with the juice of a second orange. Add the skin of the orange to the casserole, then cover and bake for 2 hours.

Drain off all but about 3 tablespoons of the pan juices and reserve. Turn the meat over and bake for another hour, uncovered, basting the meat from time to time.

Drain off the pan juices again and reserve. Turn the oven up to 400°F (205°C) and brown the top of the meat, then turn it over and brown the other side.

Meanwhile, skim the reserved pan juices of most of their fat. Add the pan juices and the juice of the third orange and reduce quickly over a high heat. Slice the meat and either pass the sauce separately or spoon it over the sliced meat at the moment of serving.

N O T E : This pork roast is best served the same day. The next day, rather than reheating, I prefer to serve the meat at room temperature, sliced.

ASADO DE PUERCO A LA VERACRUZANA Veracruz Pork Roast
SERVES 6 TO 8   V E R A C R U Z

This recipe was given to me in Huatusco, Veracruz. Preparations should start the day before to improve the flavor. It was originally given for a leg of pork, which I find rather dry, so I have suggested a pork butt or shoulder for this recipe. You can use any small, hot dried chile if the moritas are not available.

This is also good the next day, sliced thin and eaten cold, excellent for sandwiches or tortas.

5 POUNDS (2.5 KG) PORK ROAST ON THE BONE, PREFERABLY BUTT
6 GARLIC CLOVES
1 TABLESPOON SALT
3 TABLESPOONS FRESH LIME JUICE
6 ANCHO CHILES, SEEDS AND VEINS REMOVED
4 MORITA CHILES, OR 1 CHIPOTLE OR 1 MORA
½ CUP (250 ML) WATER, APPROXIMATELY
4 WHOLE ALLSPICE, CRUSHED
BANANA LEAVES SUFFICIENT TO WRAP THE ROAST IN A DOUBLE LAYER (OPTIONAL;
    SEE PAGE 462)

Pierce the meat all over with the point of a sharp knife. Mash the garlic with the salt and moisten with the lime juice. Rub this mixture thoroughly into the roast and set aside to season while you prepare the chile mixture.

Lightly toast the ancho chiles (see page 473) on a hot griddle or comal. Cover them with hot water, add the whole, untoasted morita chiles, and simmer for 5 minutes. Turn off the heat and leave the chiles to soak for 5 minutes longer.

Transfer the chiles to a blender jar with the water. Add the allspice and blend until smooth. Add a little more water only if necessary to release the blades of the blender.

Coat the meat liberally with the chile paste. Hold the banana leaf over a hot heat until it softens and wrap it around the meat. Let the meat season overnight in the refrigerator. (If you are not using the banana leaf, simply leave the meat unwrapped.)

Preheat the oven to 325°F (165°C).

Place the meat in a Dutch oven or casserole with a tightly fitting lid and bake for 2 hours, by the end of which time there should be plenty of juices at the bottom of the casserole. Remove the lid and continue cooking the meat, basting it from time to time, for about 2 hours longer, or until soft.

Serve hot, with fresh corn tortillas.

NOTE: Rather than reheating this pork the next day, I prefer to eat it cold. I don't recommend freezing.

PUERCO EN MOLE VERDE VERACRUZANO
Pork in Veracruz Green Mole

SEÑORA ÁNGELA DE GALINDO

SERVES 6   VERACRUZ

The wife of Sergio Galindo, the well-known writer from Veracruz, gave me this family recipe from Jalapa. The predominant flavor comes from the hoja santa leaves, which are now more readily available in the United States. The original recipe called for some of the tender shoots of the chayote vine—if they are available, strip off the stringy layer around the lower part of the stem and cut into small lengths. There is no suitable substitute.

THE MEAT

4 POUNDS (1.8 KG) PORK, PREFERABLY COUNTRY-STYLE SPARERIBS

THE VEGETABLES

$\frac{1}{2}$ WHITE ONION, ROUGHLY SLICED

2 GARLIC CLOVES

8 PEPPERCORNS

I TABLESPOON SALT

I POUND (450 G) ZUCCHINI (ABOUT 3 MEDIUM)

I POUND (450 G) CHAYOTE

8 OUNCES (225 G) GREEN BEANS

10 TENDER SHOOTS OF CHAYOTE VINE, CUT INTO SMALL LENGTHS

8 OUNCES (225 G) LIMA BEANS

THE SAUCE

3 CUPS (750 ML) ROUGHLY CHOPPED RAW TOMATE VERDE

2 GARLIC CLOVES, ROUGHLY CHOPPED

6 SERRANO CHILES, ROUGHLY CHOPPED

$\frac{1}{4}$ CUP (65 ML) LARD OR VEGETABLE OIL

2 CUPS (500 ML) RESERVED BROTH

I LARGE SPRIG PARSLEY

4 SPRIGS FRESH CILANTRO

3 LARGE ROMAINE LETTUCE LEAVES

3 HOJA SANTA LEAVES

SALT TO TASTE

Have the meat cut up into serving pieces. Put them into a large saucepan with the onion, garlic, peppercorns, and salt, cover with water, and bring to a boil. Lower the heat and simmer for 25 minutes.

Clean and trim the zucchini and cut them into quarters. Peel the chayote and remove the core, then cut into wedges about $\frac{1}{2}$ inch (1.5 cm) thick. Trim the green beans and cut into halves. Add the vegetables (except the limas) to the meat in the pan and cook for 15 more minutes, or until both meat and vegetables are just tender. *Do not overcook.* Drain the meat and vegetables and set them aside. Cool and skim the broth and set aside.

Cook the lima beans separately and set them aside.

Blend the tomate verde, garlic, and chiles to a smooth sauce. Heat the lard in a deep pan and cook the sauce over high heat until it has reduced and thickened a little—about 10 minutes. Add the broth and continue cooking the sauce a few minutes more.

Add the meat and vegetables to the sauce and heat them through over low heat. Blend the parsley, cilantro, lettuce, and hoja santa until smooth and strain them into the mole at the last minute. Bring the mole just to a boil, add salt as necessary, and serve immediately.

This mole is traditionally served with tortillas only.

N O T E : Like any stew, this can be cooked ahead of time and heated through very slowly about 30 minutes before serving, but add the green puree at the very last moment. This type of stew does not freeze successfully.

PUERCO EN MOLE VERDE DE CACAHUATE
Pork in Green Peanut Sauce
SEÑORA VIRGINIA VILLALÓN
SERVES 6

VERACRUZ

In 1977, I returned to Pánuco, the small river town in northern Veracruz, in high hopes of visiting Señorita Chanita, who six years earlier had made a very special, huge tamal, called sacahuil, for me, only to find that she had died two years before. When I asked around for someone who really knew the local food and was a good cook, I was sent to Virginia Villalón's modest little restaurant in one of the main streets. She was quite young, and had learned from her aunt the simple dishes of the area. She patiently dictated her recipes, stopping now and then to give me tastes from one and then another of the several large cazuelas bubbling away on the stove. This mole was one of them.

THE MEAT
2 ¼ POUNDS (1 KG) PORK, WITH SOME FAT, CUT INTO 1-INCH (2.5-CM) CUBES, OR
    3 ½ POUNDS (1.58 KG) COUNTRY-STYLE SPARERIBS, IN SMALL PIECES
⅓ CUP (85 ML) ROUGHLY CHOPPED WHITE ONION
2 GARLIC CLOVES, ROUGHLY CHOPPED
2 TEASPOONS SALT, OR TO TASTE

THE SAUCE

4 TABLESPOONS VEGETABLE OIL OR PORK LARD

1 CUP (250 ML) RAW PEANUTS (ABOUT 5 OUNCES/140 G SHELLED WEIGHT)

9 OUNCES (250 G) TOMATE VERDE, ROUGHLY CHOPPED (ABOUT 2 CUPS/500 ML)

1 SMALL BUNCH CILANTRO

6 PEPPERCORNS, CRUSHED

3 TO 4 SERRANO CHILES, OR ANY FRESH, HOT GREEN CHILE

2 GARLIC CLOVES

1/2 CUP (125 ML) THINLY SLICED WHITE ONION

Put the pork, chopped onion, garlic, and salt into a saucepan, cover with water, bring to a simmer, and cook—about 30 minutes (much depending on quality and cut of meat). Drain the meat, reserving the broth.

Meantime, heat 1 tablespoon of the oil and fry the peanuts (or toast in a toaster oven), turning them constantly, until they are a golden brown. Crush and transfer to a blender jar. Add the tomate verde, cilantro, peppercorns, chiles, garlic, and ¾ cup (185 ml) of the meat broth and blend until smooth (you may need a little more broth, but be careful not to make the sauce too watery).

Heat the remaining 3 tablespoons of oil in a heavy pan and fry the pork and sliced onion together until golden, turning the pieces constantly. Add the blended sauce and cook for a few minutes longer, stirring and scraping the bottom of the pan all the time. Add approximately 2½ cups (625 ml) of the broth, then adjust the seasoning and simmer the stew for about 20 minutes, or until well seasoned. (You may need to dilute the sauce further—it should be of a medium consistency, like thin cream—and it will thicken considerably as it cooks.)

Serve with plenty of the sauce and fresh, hot tortillas.

NOTE: This dish can be prepared several hours ahead. I do not recommend freezing.

CALABAZA GUISADA CON PUERCO Pumpkin Cooked with Pork

SEÑORA DOMATILA SANTIAGO DE MORALES

SERVES 6 OAXACA

This is a very simple Oaxacan stew that is neither picante nor heavily spiced. In Oaxaca in the late summer and fall the markets are full of small green pumpkins that are incredibly sweet when picked fresh. We used them for this dish, but you could easily substitute summer or acorn squash.

THE MEAT

2 1/2 POUNDS (1 KG) COUNTRY-STYLE SPARERIBS, CUT INTO 1 1/2-INCH (4-CM) CUBES

2 TEASPOONS SALT

1/4 SMALL WHITE ONION, ROUGHLY CHOPPED

2 GARLIC CLOVES, ROUGHLY CHOPPED

THE SAUCE

1 1/2 TABLESPOONS VEGETABLE OIL

6 OUNCES (180 G) TOMATOES, FINELY CHOPPED (ABOUT 1 CUP/250 ML)

2 TABLESPOONS FINELY CHOPPED WHITE ONION

2 SMALL GARLIC CLOVES, FINELY CHOPPED

1 POUND (450 G) SMALL GREEN PUMPKIN OR ZUCCHINI, TRIMMED AND CUT INTO
     1/2-INCH (1.5-CM) CUBES

1 1/2 CUPS (375 ML) FRESH CORN KERNELS

1 THICK SLICE FRESH PINEAPPLE, PEELED AND CUT INTO SMALL PIECES

1 ANCHO CHILE

1/8 TEASPOON CUMIN SEEDS, CRUSHED

1 MEDIUM-SIZE, VERY RIPE PLANTAIN (ABOUT 8 OUNCES/225 G), SKINNED AND CUT INTO
     1/2-INCH (1.5-CM) ROUNDS

SALT TO TASTE

Put the pork into a large saucepan, together with the salt, onion, and garlic, and barely cover with water. Bring to a boil, then lower the heat and simmer uncovered until *just* tender—about 45 minutes. Drain the meat, reserving the broth.

Heat the oil in a large, heavy saucepan, then add the tomatoes, onion, and garlic and fry over high heat, stirring constantly, until the mixture is slightly reduced, about 4 minutes. Add the pumpkin, corn kernels, pineapple, and 2 cups (500 ml) of the pork broth.

Cover the pan and cook over medium heat, stirring from time to time, for about 10 minutes—the zucchini, if you're using it, and corn should be *just* tender.

Slit open the ancho chile, remove the seeds and veins, cover with hot water, and cook for 5 minutes. Transfer the chile to a blender jar, along with ⅓ cup (85 ml) of water and the cumin. Blend until smooth.

Add the plantain, the blended chile, and the meat to the sauce, adjust the salt, and simmer for about 15 minutes longer.

Serve with fresh hot tortillas.

GUISO DE PUERCO Pork Stew
SERVES 6   OAXACA

Rufina, the maid whose recipe this is and who was with us for some years, came from a very poor village in Oaxaca. She was young and impatient and didn't really like cooking—but she did like to eat and everything she made for us was delicious. This dish, pork cooked in a sauce of tomatoes and pineapple—spiced and slightly sweetened—is very simple and refreshing and perfect for those who don't like picante food, since the chile is cooked whole, and while it lends a flavor to the sauce, it does not make it picante. The long, thin yellow-green güero chile, which has such a delicious flavor, was used in Mexico.

THE MEAT
4 POUNDS (1.8 KG) COUNTRY-STYLE SPARERIBS, CUT INTO 12 PORTIONS
1 TABLESPOON SALT
6 PEPPERCORNS
2 GARLIC CLOVES
1½ CUPS (375 ML) THINLY SLICED WHITE ONION

THE SAUCE
¼ CUP (65 ML) LARD
1 MEDIUM WHITE ONION, THINLY SLICED
3 GARLIC CLOVES, SLICED
2½ POUNDS (1.125 KG) TOMATOES, ROUGHLY CHOPPED (ABOUT 7 CUPS/1.75 L)
1½ THICK SLICES FRESH PINEAPPLE, PEELED
1 LARGE RIPE PLANTAIN, PEELED
2 SPRIGS PARSLEY

SCANT $^1/_4$ TEASPOON DRIED MEXICAN OREGANO
1 HEAPED TABLESPOON SLIVERED ALMONDS
2 TABLESPOONS RAISINS
2 TEASPOONS GRANULATED SUGAR (OPTIONAL)
1 TEASPOON SALT
$^1/_2$-INCH (1.5-CM) PIECE OF CINNAMON STICK
4 WHOLE CLOVES
4 WHOLE SERRANO OR GÜERO CHILES
10 PITTED GREEN OLIVES
2 TO 3 CUPS (500 TO 750 ML) RESERVED MEAT BROTH, APPROXIMATELY
SALT AS NECESSARY

Put the meat, together with the salt, peppercorns, garlic, and onion, into a large pan, cover with cold water, and bring to a boil. Lower the heat and simmer the meat covered until it is just tender—about 35 minutes. Set aside to cool in the broth.

Melt the lard in a *cazuela* or flameproof casserole and cook the onion and garlic until translucent.

Blend the tomatoes for a few seconds only and add them to the onion and garlic in the pan. Cook over high heat until it has reduced and thickened—about 10 minutes.

Cut the pineapple into small wedges. Cut the plantain into thick rounds. Add them with the rest of the ingredients to the sauce and cook over fairly high heat for 15 minutes. By that time the sauce will have thickened considerably and be very well seasoned.

Strain the meat and add it with the broth to the sauce and cook for another 15 minutes over low heat. Add salt as necessary. The sauce should be neither too watery nor too dry—you may need to add a little extra broth.

NOTE: It is best prepared the same day you are going to eat it, but it could be made several hours ahead, just adding the meat and broth at the last moment. This sauce does not freeze well.

PUERCO CON VERDOLAGAS Pork with Purslane

SEÑORA MARÍA ELENA LARA
SERVES 6

You will always find verdolagas *(purslane) the year round in the markets of central Mexico and some farmers' markets in the United States. A ground creeper, with small, oval, fleshy leaves that are mid-green in color and fleshy, pinkish-green stems, it grows wild both here and in the United States. I have seen it growing in both California and Maryland, so it must turn up between the two extremes as well. It has a curiously acid flavor, rather like cactus paddles, and is very much an acquired taste. One of the preferred ways of cooking purslane in Mexico is with pork and tomate verde—a great peasant stew.*

I always like to cook country-style spareribs for this type of dish, but typically it is made with espinazo*—bones of the spine stripped of most of their meat—and the tail.*

4½ POUNDS (2 KG) COUNTRY-STYLE SPARERIBS, CUT INTO 1½-INCH (4-CM) PIECES

1 MEDIUM WHITE ONION, ROUGHLY SLICED

8 GARLIC CLOVES

SALT TO TASTE

2 POUNDS (900 G) PURSLANE (ABOUT 16 CUPS/4 L)

2 CUPS (500 ML) BOILING WATER, APPROXIMATELY

4 CUPS (1 L) TOMATE VERDE, COOKED (SEE PAGE 492) AND DRAINED, RESERVING 1 CUP (250 ML) OF THE COOKING WATER

4 TO 6 JALAPEÑO CHILES OR ANY FRESH, HOT GREEN CHILES, BOILED WITH THE TOMATE VERDE

2 OUNCES (60 G) PORK LARD

2 CUPS (500 ML) THINLY SLICED WHITE ONION

½ TEASPOON CUMIN SEEDS

¼ TEASPOON DRIED MEXICAN OREGANO

Put the meat into a large saucepan and barely cover with water. Add the roughly sliced onion, 2 garlic cloves, and salt and bring to a boil. Lower the heat and simmer until the meat is *just* tender—about 40 minutes; do not overcook. Drain the meat, straining and reserving the broth. There should be at least 3 cups (750 ml). Add water if necessary or reduce to make up that amount.

Wash the purslane. Remove the roots and very thick stems and chop the leaves and more tender stems roughly. Put approximately 2 cups (500 ml) of boiling water into a pan and add the purslane and 1 teaspoon salt. Cover the pan, bring to a boil over high heat, and cook the purslane for about 3 minutes, turning it over from time to time. Drain, discarding the cooking water, and set aside.

Blend the tomate verde and chiles with 1 cup (250 ml) of water in which they were cooked. Set aside.

In a large flameproof pan, melt the lard and fry the meat and thinly sliced white onion together until the meat is lightly browned and the onion is soft, turning the pieces constantly.

Crush the remaining garlic, cumin, and oregano together in a molcajete or mortar and add to the meat frying in the pan. Take a little of the tomate verde puree to "wipe out" the seasoning in the mortar. Add this and the remaining tomate verde puree to the pan and fry a few minutes more, stirring from time to time to avoid sticking.

Add the purslane to the pan with 3 cups (750 ml) of the reserved pork broth and simmer for 10 minutes longer. Adjust the seasoning before serving with freshly made tortillas.

NOTE: This dish can be prepared several hours ahead. I do not recommend freezing.

TINGA POBLANA CON CARNE DE PUERCO
Shredded Savory Pork
MAKES ENOUGH FOR ABOUT 12 TOSTADAS   PUEBLA

On every restaurant menu in Puebla you will find tostadas de tinga—*tortillas fried crisp and topped with this savory pork. It can, of course, be served as a main dish and goes very well, although untypically, with white Mexican rice (see Arroz Blanco, page 161).*

The Diccionario de Mejicanísmos *translates* tinga *as "vulgar" or "disorder." A very tasty disorder, I must say!*

1 POUND (450 G) BONELESS STEWING PORK, CUT INTO 1-INCH (2.5-CM) CUBES
1/2 TEASPOON SALT, OR TO TASTE
8 OUNCES (225 G) CHORIZOS
1 POUND (450 G) TOMATOES, FINELY CHOPPED (ABOUT 2 2/3 CUPS/665 ML)
1/3 CUP (85 ML) ROUGHLY SLICED WHITE ONION
3 SPRIGS FRESH THYME OR 1/8 TEASPOON DRIED
1/8 TEASPOON DRIED MEXICAN OREGANO
2 MEXICAN BAY LEAVES

3 CANNED CHIPOTLE CHILES EN VINAGRE, OR EN ADOBO, CUT INTO STRIPS

2 TABLESPOONS LIQUID OR SAUCE FROM THE CANNED CHILES

TO SERVE

1 AVOCADO, THINLY SLICED

1 CUP (250 ML) SHREDDED LETTUCE

Cover the pork cubes with water, add salt, and bring to a boil, then lower the heat and simmer until tender—about 40 minutes. Let the pork cool in the broth for a short period, then drain, reserving the broth, and shred the meat fine.

Skin the chorizos, crumble the meat into a skillet, and cook over low heat until the fat has rendered out. Remove the chorizo pieces from the pan and set aside.

Take out all but 2 tablespoons of the fat in the pan. Add the tomatoes and onion to the pan and fry over fairly high heat for about 5 minutes, stirring the mixture well and scraping the bottom of the pan from time to time. Add the shredded pork, fried chorizo, thyme, oregano, bay leaves, chiles, liquid or sauce from the chile can, and ½ cup (125 ml) of the reserved broth to the tomato sauce. Adjust the seasoning and let the mixture cook and season for about 10 minutes, stirring it well from time to time. It should be moist, not juicy.

Use as a topping for tostadas, topping with the avocado and shredded lettuce.

NOTE: This can be prepared up to a day ahead and can be frozen up to 1 month.

CHULETAS DE PUERCO ADOBADOS
Pork Chops Seasoned with Adobo Paste
SERVES 6   PUEBLA

Adobo is very popular for seasoning meats in Mexico and I became an aficionada of this way of preparing pork chops when eating in a small hostelry, Mi Ranchito, in Xicótepec de Juárez many years ago. The pork, from a criollo *pig (not a fine breed), was soft and delicious and the chops were served with a green sauce and of all things thick soured cream.*

Adobo is a seasoning made of dried chiles, spices, herbs, and salt ground together with vinegar to a pastelike consistency. In this recipe I recommend seasoning the meat one day ahead—it is worth it in terms of taste.

The pork chops should have some fat on them—you needn't eat it—but the flavor and texture will be better.

SEASONING

4 LARGE ANCHO CHILES, SEEDS AND VEINS REMOVED

$^{1}/_{8}$ TEASPOON CUMIN SEEDS, CRUSHED

$^{1}/_{8}$ TEASPOON DRIED MEXICAN OREGANO

3 SPRIGS FRESH THYME OR $^{1}/_{8}$ TEASPOON DRIED

1 TABLESPOON SALT

2 GARLIC CLOVES

$^{1}/_{2}$ CUP (125 ML) MILD WHITE VINEGAR OR SEVILLE ORANGE JUICE (SEE PAGE 494)

6 THICK SHOULDER PORK CHOPS

MELTED LARD OR PORK FAT FOR FRYING (JUST ENOUGH TO COVER THE BOTTOM OF
THE PAN)

TO SERVE

1 $^{1}/_{2}$ CUPS (375 ML) THINLY SLICED WHITE ONIONS

SLICED RADISHES

SHREDDED LETTUCE

One day before serving, toast the chiles lightly, turning them from time to time so that they do not burn.

Put the chiles into a bowl and cover them with hot water. Let them soak for about 10 minutes, then remove with a slotted spoon and transfer to a blender jar. Add the rest of the seasoning ingredients and blend into a fairly smooth paste.

Have the butcher pound the chops to the thickness required. Spread them with the paste on both sides and set aside to season, refrigerated, overnight.

The next day, heat the fat and fry the chops *very slowly* on both sides until they are well cooked—about 20 minutes depending on the thickness of the meat. When they have cooked through, raise the heat and brown them quickly.

Serve the chops immediately, topped with the sliced onion, and decorate the plate with the radishes and lettuces.

NOTE: You can actually season the pork and keep it for several days in the refrigerator. The meat tends to dry out, but the flavor improves daily.

PUERCO EN ADOBO Pork in Adobo Sauce

SEÑORA GODILEVA CASTRO

SERVES 6 TO 8   GUERRERO

One of our cleaning ladies in those early days in Mexico City was Godileva Castro. Her name appears several times in this book because she was a talented and enthusiastic cook who taught me so much about her local food. On many days, when I was not at work, the housecleaning was postponed.

Of course Godileva used an extravagant amount of lard for frying so the dish would shine and look more appetizing.

3 ½ TO 4 POUNDS (1.5 TO 1.8 KG) STEWING PORK WITH SOME FAT, CUT INTO 1 ½-INCH (4-CM) CUBES

1 POUND (450 G) PORK NECK BONES

½ WHITE ONION, SLICED

2 GARLIC CLOVES

8 PEPPERCORNS

1 TABLESPOON SALT

THE ADOBO

6 ANCHO CHILES, SEEDS AND VEINS REMOVED

10 PASILLA CHILES, SEEDS AND VEINS REMOVED

1-INCH (2.5-CM) PIECE OF CINNAMON STICK, CRUSHED

5 WHOLE CLOVES, CRUSHED

6 PEPPERCORNS, CRUSHED

6 SPRIGS FRESH THYME OR ¼ TEASPOON DRIED

6 SPRIGS FRESH MARJORAM OR ¼ TEASPOON DRIED

¼ TEASPOON CUMIN SEEDS, CRUSHED

6 GARLIC CLOVES, ROUGHLY CHOPPED

2 TABLESPOONS MILD WHITE VINEGAR

THE FINAL STAGE

¼ CUP (65 ML) LARD

2 MEXICAN BAY LEAVES

2 TABLESPOONS GRANULATED SUGAR

3 CUPS (750 ML) RESERVED MEAT BROTH

SALT TO TASTE

2 CUPS (500 ML) THINLY SLICED WHITE ONION

Put the meat, bones, onion, garlic, peppercorns, and salt into a large saucepan and barely cover with water. Bring the meat to a boil, then lower the heat and simmer it until it is *just* tender—about 35 minutes. Let the meat cool in the broth.

Drain the meat, reserving the broth. Set them aside.

Toast the chiles lightly, turning them from time to time so that they do not burn. Cover them with hot water and leave them to soak about 10 minutes. Transfer the chiles to the blender with 1 cup (250 ml) of water. Add the rest of the adobo ingredients and blend to a fairly smooth texture.

Melt the lard in a large casserole. Add the adobo sauce, bay leaves, and sugar to the dish and cook for about 15 minutes, stirring most of the time to avoid sticking. Keep a splatterproof lid handy. When the sauce becomes a very dark red and thickens so that it will barely slide off a wooden spoon, it is cooked. Add the cooked meat.

Gradually stir in the broth and add salt as necessary. Add the meat and continue cooking the adobo over low heat for another 10 minutes.

Serve topped with the onion rings.

NOTE: The sauce itself can be made 2 or 3 days ahead—in fact it improves in flavor —up to the point of adding the broth. The pork can then be cooked the day you are going to use it. If there is any left over, the sauce freezes very well and makes a very good filling, mixed with shredded meat, for tacos.

CARNE DE PUERCO CON UCHEPOS Pork with Fresh Corn Tamales
SERVES 6   MICHOACÁN

For years I had heard about Uchepos, *but I had never tried them until I went to Morelia for the first time in 1969. One of the great regional cooks, the late Beatriz Dávalos, had them prepared especially for me at the Casino Charro and gave me this recipe. It has such a wonderful contrast of flavors and textures: the slightly crunchy fresh corn of the tamales, the soft pork in its broiled tomato sauce, and the biting, inky flavor of the chilaca strips against the sour cream and cheese; not to mention the colors—yellow, red, and white with a lattice of black-green.*

THE MEAT
4½ POUNDS (2 KG) COUNTRY-STYLE SPARERIBS
2 TEASPOONS SALT

THE SAUCE

3 POUNDS (1.35 KG) TOMATOES, BROILED (SEE PAGE 490)

4 SERRANO CHILES, CHARRED (SEE PAGE 470)

2 LARGE GARLIC CLOVES

SALT TO TASTE

TO SERVE

18 SMALL UCHEPOS (PAGE 106) OR CORUNDAS (PAGE 70 IN *The Art of Mexican Cooking*)

1 CUP (250 ML) THICK SOUR CREAM (SEE PAGE 489)

8 OUNCES (225 G) QUESO FRESCO

3 LARGE CHILACAS OR POBLANO CHILES, CHARRED, PEELED, AND CUT INTO STRIPS
  (SEE PAGES 464, 469)

In a flameproof casserole, barely cover the meat with water, add the salt, and bring to a boil. Continue cooking the meat uncovered over medium heat for about 30 minutes. Remove about 2 cups (500 ml) of the broth and set aside. Then continue cooking the meat until it is just tender—about 15 minutes more. Let the fat render out of the meat and fry it until it is slightly browned (as for Carnitas; see page 23). Remove the meat and all but about 4 tablespoons of the fat.

Meanwhile, prepare the tomato sauce. Blend the tomatoes with the chiles, garlic, and salt, to a smooth consistency. Add the tomato sauce to the fat in the casserole and cook it over high heat for about 8 minutes, until it has reduced and thickened a little. Lower the heat, add the meat, and heat through gently.

Serve each portion of meat with two or three *Uchepos*, or *Corundas*, and plenty of sauce, some sour cream, strips of cheese, and finely shredded peeled chile.

NOTE: The sauce and the meat can be cooked several hours ahead. You may need to dilute the sauce a little with some broth when you reheat it.

COCHINITA PIBIL Yucatecan Pit-Barbecued Pig

SERVES 6   YUCATÁN AND CAMPECHE

The first time I tried Cochinita Pibil, it was shredded on top of Panuchos (page 40)—this was in the late fifties, in our then favorite Yucatecan restaurant, El Circulo del Sureste. I was hooked.

Pib is the Mayan word for the traditional oven, or pit barbecue, of the Yucatán Peninsula

and it is still used in the villages today. It is prepared by digging a rectangular pit about 2 feet deep. The bottom is lined with large stones that are heated with a wood fire. When the embers have died down and the stones are considered hot enough (only the experts know this by instinct) the meats to be cooked—pig, turkey, or meat pies like Muk-bil Pollo (page 103) —are wrapped in several layers of banana leaves, set in a metal container, and covered with sacking and earth. The cooking takes several hours. Meats cooked in this way have a very special flavor and succulence. This is how you can cook it at home.

ONE DAY AHEAD

$3^1/2$ TO $4^1/2$ POUNDS (1.5 TO 2 KG) PORK, PREFERABLY RIB END OF LOIN, WITH FAT

3 TEASPOONS SALT

2 TABLESPOONS SEVILLE ORANGE JUICE OR SUBSTITUTE (SEE PAGE 494)

1 HEAPED TABLESPOON ACHIOTE SEEDS

$^1/4$ TEASPOON CUMIN SEEDS

$^1/4$ TEASPOON DRIED MEXICAN OREGANO, YUCATECAN IF POSSIBLE

12 PEPPERCORNS

3 WHOLE ALLSPICE

4 GARLIC CLOVES

$^1/8$ TEASPOON POWDERED CHILE SECO YUCATECO (OPTIONAL; SEE PAGE 480) OR HOT
   PAPRIKA

3 TABLESPOONS SEVILLE ORANGE JUICE OR SUBSTITUTE, OR MILD WHITE VINEGAR

2 LARGE PIECES OF BANANA LEAF (SEE PAGE 462)

$^1/2$ CUP (125 ML) COLD WATER

The day before serving, pierce the pork all over and rub in 2 teaspoons of the salt and the juice. Set aside while you prepare the seasoning paste.

In an electric spice grinder, grind the achiote seeds, cumin, oregano, peppercorns, and allspice together to a fine powder. Pass through a fine strainer and grind the debris once more.

Crush the garlic together with the chile seco, remaining 1 teaspoon salt, and Seville orange juice and mix in the other powdered spices. The mixture should resemble a thick paste. Smear the paste all over the pork.

Lightly sear the banana leaves over a bare flame to make them more flexible. Wrap the meat up in them and leave to season in the refrigerator for at least 6 hours or overnight.

Preheat the oven to 325°F (165°C).

Place a rack at the bottom of the Dutch oven and set the wrapped meat on it. Add the water and cover the dish with a tightly fitting lid. Cook for 2½ hours. Turn the meat and baste it well with the juices at the bottom of the dish. Cook for another 2½ hours, or until the meat is soft and falling off the bone.

THE SAUCE

½ CUP (125 ML) VERY FINELY CHOPPED PURPLE ONION

3 HABANERO CHILES, VERY FINELY CHOPPED

½ TEASPOON SALT

⅔ CUP (165 ML) SEVILLE ORANGE JUICE OR SUBSTITUTE (SEE PAGE 494)

Meanwhile, prepare the sauce. Mix all the ingredients together. Set aside to season for about 2 hours.

To serve, shred the meat roughly. Pour the fat and juices from the pan over it. Serve hot, with tortillas and the sauce in a separate dish so that each person can make his own tacos.

FRIJOL CON PUERCO Beans with Pork

SEÑORA BERTA LÓPEZ DE MARRUFO

SERVES 6   YUCATÁN

This is one of those large, composite dishes reminiscent of its popular counterparts around the Caribbean and Brazil. Beans, meat, and rice are black, gaudily and lavishly strewn with finely chopped radishes, cilantro leaves, and tomato sauce, and served with lime quarters and slices of avocado—a hearty, crunchy, and filling dish.

I advise you to cook the beans the day before, just up to the point in the recipe where the meat is added. The tomato sauce could be prepared ahead, too, but even then cooking time is about 2½ hours, for not until the meat is cooked can you begin the rice.

THE BEANS

1 POUND (450 G) BLACK BEANS (ABOUT 2¼ CUPS/565 ML)

1 TABLESPOON PORK LARD

⅓ CUP (85 ML) ROUGHLY SLICED WHITE ONION

14 CUPS (3.5 L) COLD WATER, APPROXIMATELY

SALT TO TASTE

1 SPRIG EPAZOTE

Run the beans through your fingers and pick out any small stones or little pieces of earth that may be among them. Rinse the beans and put into a very large, flameproof bean pot with the lard, onion, and water. Bring to a simmer and continue cooking slowly until the skins start breaking, about 1 ½ hours. Add the salt and epazote and continue cooking until the beans are just tender but not soft, about ½ hour.

THE PORK

8 OUNCES (225 G) BONELESS STEWING PORK (CARNE MACIZA IN MEXICO), CUT INTO LARGE CUBES

1 POUND (450 G) PORK HOCKS (CHAMBERETE DE PUERCO IN MEXICO), CUT INTO ½-INCH (1.5-CM) SLICES

1 POUND (450 G) COUNTRY-STYLE SPARERIBS (COSTILLITAS IN MEXICO), CUT INTO 2-INCH (5-CM) CUBES

1 PIG'S EAR, CUT INTO SMALL PIECES (OPTIONAL)

1 GREEN BELL PEPPER, SEEDS AND VEINS REMOVED AND CUT INTO SMALL SQUARES

2 LARGE SPRIGS EPAZOTE

2 TABLESPOONS ROUGHLY CHOPPED WHITE ONION

1 TABLESPOON SALT, OR TO TASTE

Add the pork and remaining ingredients to the beans, then cover and continue cooking over low heat, stirring well from time to time. (There should be plenty of broth, bearing in mind that 3 cups/750 ml of it have to go into the rice. If it seems to have reduced too much, add a cup or so of water.) Cook until the beans are quite soft and the meat tender—1 hour 15 minutes, depending on the meat.

During the cooking time, start preparations for the rice.

THE RICE

1 ½ CUPS (375 ML) LONG-GRAIN UNCONVERTED WHITE RICE

⅓ CUP (85 ML) VEGETABLE OIL

¼ SMALL WHITE ONION, ROUGHLY CHOPPED (ABOUT 1 TABLESPOON)

1 GARLIC CLOVE, ROUGHLY CHOPPED

3 CUPS (750 ML) BEAN BROTH

SALT TO TASTE

Cover the rice with hot water and let it stand for about 5 minutes, then rinse in cold water twice and drain well. Heat the oil in a very heavy pan (the bean broth tends to stick rather badly) and stir the rice into it until the grains are evenly coated. Add the onion and garlic and fry the rice, turning it over from time to time so that it becomes an even, pale gold color. Tip the pan and drain off the excess oil.

Add the broth from the beans and salt, then cover the pot and cook the rice gently until all the liquid has been absorbed, about 15 minutes. Remove from the heat. Cover the rice with a piece of terry cloth and set aside for about 25 minutes, to allow the rice to continue cooking and expanding in the steam it generates.

ASSEMBLING THE DISH

2 CUPS (500 ML) SALSA DE JITOMATE YUCATECA (PAGE 240)
1 CUP (250 ML) VERY FINELY CHOPPED RADISHES
1/2 CUP (125 ML) VERY FINELY CHOPPED CILANTRO
4 SMALL LIMES, QUARTERED
2 AVOCADOS, SLICED

Remove the meat from the beans and serve on a warmed platter. Serve the rice in the casserole in which it was cooked. Serve the beans and their broth in individual small bowls and pass the rest of the ingredients separately so each person can serve himself, al gusto.

NOTE: See above for advance preparation. But when finally ready, this dish should be served without delay. It does not freeze well.

LOMITOS Yucatecan Pork Pieces
SEÑORA BERTA LÓPEZ DE MARRUFO
SERVES 6   YUCATÁN

This dish rarely appears on the menus of Yucatecan restaurants, but like many of the local specialties, it can be found at its best in the early morning in the marketplaces. I ate a local version of this recipe for the first time in the Valladolid market, where it was being served either in tacos or piled onto a pim *(a round cake made of tortilla dough beaten with lard and salt and cooked on a griddle or comal; a* pim *is usually 3 inches [8 cm] in diameter and "one finger" thick). This, Señora Marrufo's recipe, is a rather refined but equally delicious version.*

Lomitos (lit. "little loins") are also often served on a bed of cooked, sieved ibis—*small, round white beans grown in the Yucatán Peninsula—or white rice.*

1 TABLESPOON SIMPLE RECADO ROJO (PAGE 485)

2 TABLESPOONS SEVILLE ORANGE JUICE OR SUBSTITUTE (SEE PAGE 494)

2 POUNDS (900 G) BONELESS PORK, CUT INTO ½-INCH (1.5-CM) CUBES

2 TABLESPOONS VEGETABLE OIL OR PORK LARD

12 OUNCES (340 G) TOMATOES, FINELY CHOPPED (ABOUT 1¾ CUPS/435 ML)

½ GREEN BELL PEPPER, FINELY CHOPPED

⅔ CUP (165 ML) FINELY CHOPPED WHITE ONION

2 TEASPOONS SALT

1 SMALL HEAD OF GARLIC, UNPEELED

1 WHOLE HABANERO CHILE OR ANY FRESH, HOT GREEN CHILE

2 TO 2½ CUPS (500 TO 625 ML) COLD WATER, APPROXIMATELY

Dilute the Recado Rojo with the orange juice and rub it into the pieces of meat. Set aside for about 30 minutes to season.

Heat the oil in a skillet and fry the tomatoes, pepper, and onion together over fairly high heat, stirring well and scraping the bottom of the pan from time to time, for about 10 minutes. Add the salt and set aside.

Toast the whole head of garlic on a griddle or comal, turning it from time to time, until it is browned on the outside and the cloves inside are fairly soft. Toast the habanero chile.

Put the meat into a large, heavy saucepan with the water, which should barely cover the meat. Add the tomato mixture and the toasted, unpeeled garlic and chile and bring to a boil. Lower the heat and simmer the meat, uncovered, until it is tender—about 1 hour. (The sauce should be of a medium consistency; if it appears to be too watery, turn the heat higher and reduce quickly.) Serve hot.

N O T E : Lomitos may be prepared several hours ahead: in fact, the flavor is heightened with the standing. Lomitos could be stored frozen for a week or two.

CALZONES DEL DIABLO The Devil's Pants

SEÑORITA ELVIA CARRILLO

SERVES 4 TO 6

MICHOACÁN

Señorita Elvia Carrillo learned this recipe from her mother, who in turn learned it from an old lady living in the same village. Her mother, however, thought the name rather indecent and renamed the dish mole en blanco, *white mole.*

I had strict instructions about its preparation: the meat must be cooked in either an earthenware or enamel pot and on no account in the pressure cooker. Chiles serranos en escabeche must be used, not jalapeños, and the dish should have plenty of oil on top when served.

2 ¼ POUNDS (1 KG) COUNTRY-STYLE RIBS, CUT INTO 2-INCH (5-CM) CUBES

SALT TO TASTE

2 OUNCES (60 G) SESAME SEEDS (ABOUT ⅔ CUP/165 ML)

3 TABLESPOONS PORK LARD OR VEGETABLE OIL

1 ANCHO CHILE, VEINS AND SEEDS REMOVED

1 LARGE SCALLION WITH SOME OF THE GREEN TOP, OR 1 SMALL WHITE ONION CUT INTO
    THICK SLICES

1 GARLIC CLOVE

4 CHILES SERRANOS EN ESCABECHE (SHOULD NOT BE TOO HOT)

4 PLUM TOMATOES

2 SLICES FRENCH BREAD ABOUT 1 INCH (2.5 CM) THICK

1 WHOLE CLOVE

2 PEPPERCORNS

1 ALLSPICE

1 BAY LEAF, MEXICAN IF POSSIBLE

2 SPRIGS FRESH MARJORAM OR ⅛ TEASPOON DRIED

2 SPRIGS FRESH THYME OR ⅛ TEASPOON DRIED

In a deep pan, cover the pork with water, add salt, and cook covered over medium heat until tender but not soft—about 40 minutes. Drain, reserving the broth. Cool and skim, reserving the fat.

In an ungreased skillet, toast the sesame seeds until a deep gold color, taking care not to burn them. Cool and then grind to a textured powder in an electric coffee/spice grinder.

Melt 2 tablespoons of the lard in a skillet, flatten out the ancho chile, and fry for a few seconds until the inside turns a light brown. Drain, tear into pieces, and put into the blender jar. In the same fat fry the scallion, garlic, chiles, and whole tomatoes for about 1 minute or until the scallion is translucent. Transfer to the blender jar. Add the remaining lard to the pan and fry the bread until crisp on the outside; crumble into the blender jar. Add 1 cup (250 ml) of the reserved broth and blend until fairly smooth.

Put 2 tablespoons of the fat from the broth into a flameproof casserole, add the blended ingredients and the ground seeds, and fry over medium heat, stirring and scraping the bottom of the pan to avoid sticking, for about 5 minutes. Add the meat and the rest of the ingredients (whole), along with the remaining broth and cook over low heat for 10 more minutes. Adjust seasoning. The sauce should be of medium consistency and thinly cover the back of a wooden spoon.

PUERCO EN MOLE CHATINO Pork in Chatino Mole
SEÑORITA FRANCISCA PÉREZ
SERVES ABOUT 10

OAXACA

This is a very unusual, and very picante, mole from the area of Oaxaca around Sola de Vega. It was given to me by a young and talented cook from that area. It is unusual because it does not use chiles from the area but the more common and cheaper guajillos and de árbol, and it has a very rich base of nuts and seeds.

As you can see, nearly all the ingredients are toasted for this recipe. It is better to toast the chiles on a comal or griddle over medium heat so that they can be turned at the right time and not burned—they have to be well toasted so that they become crisp as they cool off. The nuts and seeds can be done in an oven, or better still a toaster oven, so that they can toast slowly and evenly and not burn.

Most moles made with dried chiles have a better flavor if the ingredients are toasted, or fried and then ground dry—traditionally this was done on the metate, and it still is in some rural areas. There are mills specifically for this only in areas of the United States where there is high concentration of Mexican immigration. But it is well worth the trouble to grind the ingredients in a large coffee/spice grinder or strong blender, in small quantities at a time, or break down the ingredients first in the food processor—which will never manage the whole process successfully.

The ground ingredients will need quite a bit of fat at the frying stage to avoid sticking and scorching, but the fat will float to the surface later on and can be removed.

I like to use pork with some bone and fat but that is a matter of taste. Chicken can also be used or a mixture of both.

If it seems too picante, increase the amount of tomatoes.

THE MEAT

3 ½ POUNDS (1.575 KG) COUNTRY-STYLE PORK RIBS, CUT INTO 2-INCH (5-CM) PIECES
1 LARGE TOMATO, ROUGHLY SLICED
½ MEDIUM WHITE ONION, ROUGHLY SLICED
6 UNPEELED GARLIC CLOVES
SALT TO TASTE

THE SAUCE

5 OUNCES (140 G) GUAJILLO CHILES, ABOUT 28, VEINS AND SEEDS REMOVED AND TOASTED
1 OUNCE (30 G) CHILES DE ÁRBOL, ABOUT 40, TOASTED WHOLE
4 ½ OUNCES (125 G) HULLED, RAW PUMPKIN SEEDS (ABOUT 1 CUP/250 ML), TOASTED
4 ½ OUNCES (125 G) RAW, SKINNED PEANUTS (ABOUT 1 SCANT CUP/225 ML), TOASTED
2 OUNCES (60 G) SESAME SEEDS (ABOUT ½ CUP/125 ML), TOASTED
2 OUNCES (60 G) WHOLE PEELED ALMONDS (ABOUT 40), TOASTED
2 OUNCES (60 G) PECAN PIECES (ABOUT ⅔ CUP/165 ML), TOASTED
2 TABLESPOONS DRIED OAXACAN OREGANO, OR 2 TEASPOONS DRIED MEXICAN
3 SPRIGS FRESH THYME OR ¼ TEASPOON DRIED
4 PEPPERCORNS
2 CLOVES
1 SMALL WHITE ONION, CUT INTO 6 PIECES AND TOASTED
8 UNPEELED GARLIC CLOVES, TOASTED
½ CUP (125 ML) MELTED LARD OR VEGETABLE OIL
9 OUNCES (250 G) PLUM TOMATOES, BROILED (SEE PAGE 490)

Put the meat into a large saucepan, then add the tomato, onion, garlic, and salt. Cover well with water and set over moderate heat to come to a simmer. Continue simmering covered until the meat is just tender, then set aside to cool in the broth. Drain the meat and set aside. You will need about 10 cups (2.5 l) of broth; make up to that amount with water if necessary.

Grind all the sauce ingredients, except the lard and tomatoes, to a crumbly paste consistency.

Heat the lard in a heavy, flameproof casserole, add the ground ingredients, and fry over medium heat, stirring all the time to avoid sticking, for about 10 minutes. Blend the tomatoes, stir into the fried mixture in the pan, and cook for another 5 minutes. Gradually stir in the reserved broth and cook over medium heat until it is well incorporated and the mole begins to thicken—it will splatter alarmingly at this stage. Test for salt, then add the meat and cook again for about 10 minutes. The mole will be quite thick and form a thin layer on the back of a wooden spoon.

NOTE: This mole can be cooked even a day ahead, using a pork or chicken broth that you may have on hand, but it is best to cook the meat the day you are serving the mole.

The sauce freezes very well but will need to be diluted when defrosted.

BEEF

Carne con Chile Verde ※ *Beef with Green Chile*

Asado Placero Sinaloense

※ *Meat and Vegetables with Tomato Sauce Sinaloa*

Bisteces Rancheros Sonorenses ※ *Sonoran Country Steaks*

Carne de Res con Col ※ *Ground Beef with Cabbage*

Estofado de Lengua ※ *Tongue in Oaxacan Sauce*

Carne Claveteada ※ *Pot Roast Studded with Almonds and Bacon*

Aguayón Estilo Leonor ※ *Pot Roast Leonor*

CARNE CON CHILE VERDE Beef with Green Chile

SEÑORA ROSA MARGARITA J. DE MEJÍA

SERVES 6   CHIHUAHUA

2 ¼ POUNDS (1 KG) STEWING BEEF, WITH SOME FAT, CUT INTO ½-INCH (1.5-CM) CUBES

SALT TO TASTE

3 GARLIC CLOVES, FINELY CHOPPED

2 CUPS (500 ML) WATER, APPROXIMATELY

2 TO 3 TABLESPOONS VEGETABLE OIL, APPROXIMATELY

1 ¼ CUPS (315 ML) FINELY CHOPPED WHITE ONION

1 ½ TABLESPOONS ALL-PURPOSE FLOUR

12 ANAHEIM CHILES, CHARRED, PEELED, SEEDS REMOVED (SEE PAGES 469, 471), AND CUT
    INTO SQUARES

8 OUNCES (225 G) TOMATOES, BROILED (SEE PAGE 490) AND MASHED

Put the meat—in two layers, no more—into a large, heavy pan. Add the salt, garlic, and ½ cup (125 ml) of the water, then cover the pan and cook over very low heat until the meat is almost tender, the liquid evaporated, and the fat rendering out—about 45 minutes, depending on the cut and quality of the meat. (It may be necessary to add a little more water to prevent the meat from sticking. On the other hand, if there is too much liquid as the meat approaches the correct point of tenderness, remove the cover, raise the heat, and reduce rapidly.) Shake the pan and turn the meat over from time to time.

Add enough oil to the fat in the pan to make about 3 tablespoons. Turn the heat to medium, then add the onion, and brown the meat lightly. Sprinkle the flour into the pan and let it brown lightly, stirring constantly. Add the chiles, tomatoes, and remaining 1½ cups (375 ml) water, then cover the pan and cook over low heat for another 20 minutes. (At the end of the cooking time there should be some liquid in the pan, but it should not be soupy; it may be necessary to add a little more water during the cooking time.)

Adjust the seasoning and serve hot, with flour tortillas.

NOTE: This dish can be prepared several hours ahead and reheated. I don't recommend freezing.

ASADO PLACERO SINALOENSE
Meat and Vegetables with Tomato Sauce Sinaloa

SEÑORA MARÍA LUISA CÁRDENAS, RESTAURANTE LA NEGRA, MAZATLÁN

SERVES 6   SINALOA

I must say at the outset that this dish did not "send" me. But it is a popular dish in Sinaloa and has a place in any collection of typical Mexican recipes. Nobody, of course, can agree just what vegetables should go into it, and some cooks include carrots, chayotes, and green beans.

In Mazatlán it is customary to eat seafood in the middle of the day and at night asado or, as in other parts of Mexico, tacos and antojitos. Some years ago if you had asked around about the best place to eat asado, the unhesitating answer would have been La Negra. I went there, and of course it was closed that week for painting. I found Señora Cárdenas sitting in her kitchen behind the restaurant, and when I explained that I had made a special trip to see her, she generously gave me her recipe.

I suggest that you use chuck or any good stewing beef, or leftover roast beef—in which case you should leave out the first part of the recipe.

THE MEAT AND VEGETABLES

2 ¼ POUNDS (1 KG) BEEF BRISKET, CUT INTO ½-INCH (1.5-CM) CUBES

½ MEDIUM WHITE ONION, ROUGHLY SLICED

3 GARLIC CLOVES

SALT

1 POUND (450 G) RED BLISS OR OTHER WAXY POTATOES, CUT INTO ½-INCH (1.5-CM) CUBES

2 CUPS (500 ML) THINLY SLICED WHITE ONION

½ CUP (125 ML) MILD VINEGAR

½ CUP (125 ML) CUBED, COOKED BEETS (OPTIONAL)

¼ CUP (65 ML) VEGETABLE OIL

1 CUP (250 ML) FINELY SHREDDED CABBAGE, BLANCHED IN BOILING WATER

2 CUPS (500 ML) SHREDDED LETTUCE

Put the meat, roughly sliced onion, garlic, and about 1 tablespoon salt into a large saucepan and cover with water. Bring to a simmer and cook the beef until tender, about 45 minutes—time will vary tremendously, depending on the thickness of the piece of meat. Let the meat cool off in the broth.

Cover the potatoes in a saucepan with water, add salt to taste, and boil until still slightly crisp. Drain and cool slightly, then peel.

Put the thinly sliced onion into the vinegar in a nonreactive bowl with the beets, if used, add salt to taste, and leave to macerate.

Heat the oil and fry the meat and potatoes together until lightly browned, then adjust the seasoning and serve topped with the onion, cabbage, and lettuce. Pass the sauce separately.

NOTE: This dish can be prepared several hours ahead. It is not suitable for freezing.

THE SAUCE

1 ¼ POUNDS (500 G) TOMATOES

1 GARLIC CLOVE

1 SERRANO CHILE OR ANY FRESH, HOT GREEN CHILE

SALT TO TASTE

½ TEASPOON DRIED MEXICAN OREGANO

PREPARE THE SAUCE: Cover the tomatoes with boiling water and simmer until soft—about 15 minutes. Drain, then blend with the garlic, chile, and salt until smooth. Add the oregano and set aside, but keep warm.

BISTECES RANCHEROS SONORENSES Sonoran Country Steaks

SEÑORA CONSUELO M. DE MARTÍNEZ

SERVES 6   SONORA

This dish is a typical example of the simple but robust country cooking of Sonora. None of the flavors predominate, and the touches of cilantro and rather mild chiles are just right. Although this recipe is usually cooked on top of the stove, I prefer the flavor when cooked in the oven.

6 SHOULDER OR CHUCK STEAKS, ABOUT ¼ INCH/.75 CM THICK (ABOUT 2 POUNDS/
    900 G)

1 LARGE GARLIC CLOVE, CRUSHED

SALT AND PEPPER TO TASTE

¼ CUP (65 ML) VEGETABLE OIL

2 CUPS (500 ML) THINLY SLICED WHITE ONION

2 POUNDS (900 G) TOMATOES

8 WHOLE SPRIGS CILANTRO

SALT TO TASTE

1 POUND (450 G) RED BLISS OR WAXY NEW POTATOES

3 ANAHEIM CHILES, CHARRED, PEELED, SEEDS AND VEINS REMOVED (SEE PAGES 469, 471)

Preheat the oven to 350°F (180°C).

Season the steaks on both sides with garlic, salt, and pepper and set aside for about 1 hour.

Heat 2 tablespoons of the oil in a skillet. Quickly brown the steaks on both sides, adding more oil as necessary. Place them in one layer on a shallow ovenproof dish, set aside, and keep warm.

Let the oil cool a little, then add the onion and cook it gently, without browning, until it is translucent.

Cut a slice off the top of each tomato. Grate the flesh on a coarse grater until only the flattened skin is left in your hand. Don't forget to grate the flesh from the top slices.

Add the tomato pulp, cilantro, and salt to the onion in the pan and let the sauce cook fast over fairly high heat for 5 minutes. Stir from time to time to prevent sticking.

Peel and slice the potatoes about ¼ inch (.75 cm) thick. Place the slices on top of the steaks. Pour the sauce over the meat and potatoes.

Cut the chiles into narrow strips, place the strips on top of the sauce, cover the dish, and bake for 35 minutes. Bake, uncovered, for another 35 minutes, by which time the sauce should be reduced and the potatoes just beginning to brown.

NOTE: This dish can be prepared a couple of hours ahead; in fact, it improves in flavor. I do not recommend freezing.

CARNE DE RES CON COL Ground Beef with Cabbage

SEÑORA PATRICIA MARTÍNEZ

MAKES ABOUT 4¼ CUPS (1.63 L) FOR TOSTADAS

SERVES 4 AS A MAIN COURSE

When I am in Tapachula, Chiapas, I always like to have breakfast in the market. One morning it was a rather unusual breakfast, tostadas topped with Carne de Res con Col. Señora Patricia said this mixture could also be used for stuffing chiles or serving as a main course with white rice.

I like to prepare this dish a little ahead so that the flavors intensify.

3 GARLIC CLOVES, ROUGHLY CHOPPED

6 PEPPERCORNS

SALT TO TASTE

1 POUND (450 G) GROUND SIRLOIN WITH A LITTLE FAT

3 TABLESPOONS VEGETABLE OIL

¼ CUP (65 ML) FINELY CHOPPED WHITE ONION

1 CHILE VERDE CRIOLLO OR JALAPEÑO, FINELY CHOPPED

6 OUNCES (180 G) TOMATOES, FINELY CHOPPED (ABOUT 1 ROUNDED CUP/265 ML)

4 CUPS (1 L) FINELY SHREDDED CABBAGE

⅔ CUP (165 ML) WATER

½ CUP (125 ML) FIRMLY PACKED, ROUGHLY CHOPPED CILANTRO

Crush the garlic, peppercorns, and salt together and mix well into the beef (hands are best). Set aside for a few minutes to season.

Heat the oil in a large, heavy skillet, add the onion, chile, and a sprinkle of salt, and cook over medium heat until the onion is translucent—about 1 minute. Add the tomatoes and continue cooking until most of the juice has been absorbed—about 3 minutes.

Stir the meat into the pan and cook over fairly high heat, stirring from time to time—about 7 minutes. Add the cabbage, water, and cilantro and continue cooking over medium heat, stirring from time to time until the mixture is well seasoned and moist but not juicy—about 15 minutes. Serve as suggested above.

ESTOFADO DE LENGUA Tongue in Oaxacan Sauce

SEÑORA DOMATILA SANTIAGO DE MORALES

SERVES 6 TO 8

OAXACA

A 5-POUND (2.25-KG) FRESH BEEF TONGUE

1 SMALL WHITE ONION, ROUGHLY CHOPPED

3 GARLIC CLOVES, ROUGHLY CHOPPED

8 PEPPERCORNS

SALT TO TASTE

THE SAUCE

2 TABLESPOONS SESAME SEEDS

6 TABLESPOONS LARD OR VEGETABLE OIL

2 ANCHO CHILES, WIPED CLEAN, SEEDS AND VEINS REMOVED

2 OUNCES (60 G) UNSKINNED ALMONDS—A GOOD $\frac{1}{3}$ CUP (85 ML)

1 SMALL DRY TORTILLA, BROKEN INTO PIECES

$\frac{1}{2}$ CUP (125 ML) TONGUE BROTH OR WATER

$\frac{1}{8}$ TEASPOON DRIED MEXICAN OREGANO, PREFERABLY OAXACAN

6 SPRIGS FRESH THYME OR $\frac{1}{4}$ TEASPOON DRIED

6 SPRIGS FRESH MARJORAM OR $\frac{1}{4}$ TEASPOON DRIED

$\frac{1}{2}$-INCH (1.5-CM) PIECE OF CINNAMON STICK, CRUSHED

2 POUNDS (900 G) TOMATOES, FINELY CHOPPED (ABOUT $5\frac{1}{3}$ CUPS/1.3 L)

SALT TO TASTE

$\frac{1}{2}$ CUP (125 ML) PITTED GREEN OLIVES

Put the tongue into a saucepan with the onion, garlic, peppercorns, and salt. Cover with water and bring to a boil. Lower the heat and simmer until the tongue is tender—about 3 hours. Let the tongue cool in the broth, and as soon as it is cool enough to handle, remove and discard the skin. Strain the broth and return the tongue to the broth. Keep warm.

Toast the sesame seeds in a skillet over low heat, stirring them and shaking the pan from time to time until they are a deep golden color—take care not to let them burn—about 5 minutes.

Heat 3 tablespoons of the lard in a small skillet and fry the chiles over medium heat for about $\frac{1}{2}$ minute on each side—the inside flesh should turn the color of tobacco. Drain and set aside.

In the same lard, fry the almonds over medium heat, turning them and shaking the pan until they turn a darker color. Drain and crush them well (so as not to strain the blender).

In the same lard, fry the tortilla pieces for a few minutes until crisp. Drain and set aside.

Put the ½ cup (125 ml) tongue broth or water into the blender jar, add the dried herbs and spices, and blend as smooth as possible. Gradually add the chiles, tomatoes, sesame seeds, almonds, and tortillas, blending thoroughly after each addition.

Heat the remaining 3 tablespoons lard in a heavy pan, add the sauce, and cook over medium heat for about 10 minutes, stirring and scraping the bottom of the pan from time to time to avoid sticking. Stir in salt to taste. The sauce should be of medium consistency and lightly cover the back of a wooden spoon. Add broth to dilute if necessary.

Drain the tongue and cut into thick slices. Arrange on a large platter in one slightly overlapping layer and cover with most of the sauce. Sprinkle the top with the olives and serve immediately. Pass the rest of the sauce separately.

N O T E : This dish can be prepared several hours, even a day, ahead and reheated. Leftovers can also be frozen successfully.

CARNE CLAVETEADA Pot Roast Studded with Almonds and Bacon
SEÑORA DOMATILA SANTIAGO DE MORALES
SERVES 6   OAXACA

This recipe was given to me by one of the most interesting cooks I met in Oaxaca: Señora Domatila Santiago de Morales, whom I have mentioned many times before because she was my first mentor for Oaxacan food way back in 1970.

The meat may be cooked on top of the stove but I prefer to put it in the oven.

A simple green salad would be a very good accompaniment to this dish.

3 POUNDS (1.35 KG) BRISKET IN ONE PIECE, TRIMMED OF SOME OF THE FAT
1 ½ TABLESPOONS SLIVERED ALMONDS
8 OUNCES (225 G) BACON OR HAM, CUT INTO SMALL PIECES
3 LARGE ANCHO CHILES, SEEDS AND VEINS REMOVED
1 ½ TABLESPOONS MILD VINEGAR
¾ CUP (185 ML) WATER
3 WHOLE CLOVES, CRUSHED
½-INCH (1.5-CM) PIECE OF CINNAMON STICK, CRUSHED

4 PEPPERCORNS, CRUSHED

6 SPRIGS FRESH THYME OR $\frac{1}{4}$ TEASPOON DRIED

6 SPRIGS FRESH MARJORAM OR $\frac{1}{4}$ TEASPOON DRIED

$\frac{1}{4}$ TEASPOON DRIED MEXICAN OREGANO

3 GARLIC CLOVES, ROUGHLY CHOPPED

3 TABLESPOONS LARD OR VEGETABLE OIL

SALT TO TASTE

1 $\frac{1}{2}$ POUNDS (675 G) RED BLISS OR NEW POTATOES

Preheat the oven to 325°F (165°C).

Pierce the meat all over with a knife point and insert the almonds and bacon. Set it aside while the sauce is prepared.

Toast the chiles lightly, turning them often so they won't burn. Put the chiles into a bowl, cover with hot water, and leave them to soak for about 10 minutes.

Put the vinegar and water into the blender jar, add the spices, herbs, and garlic, and blend as smoothly as possible. Add the chiles and blend to a fairly smooth consistency.

Heat the lard in a Dutch oven and when it is very hot sear the meat well all over. Remove the meat and set it aside. Drain off the fat, leaving only 2 tablespoons in the pan. Add the sauce to the pan and let it cook fast for about 5 minutes, stirring it all the time. Add salt to taste.

Return the meat to the pan and baste it with the sauce. Cover the casserole with a tightly fitting lid and cook the meat in the oven for about 2 hours.

Put the potatoes, unskinned, into a saucepan, cover them with boiling water, and let boil fast for 5 minutes. Drain them and set them aside to cool. When the potatoes are cool enough to handle, skin.

Remove the casserole from the oven, turn the meat over, and baste it well with the sauce. Scrape the sauce from the sides and bottom of the pan and add a little water if it has thickened too much.

Put the potatoes into the sauce around the meat, replace the lid, and let the meat cook until it is very tender but not falling apart—test after 1 hour and 10 minutes.

Slice the meat fairly thick and place it on a serving dish with the potatoes around it. Pour the sauce over it.

NOTE: The pot roast *could* be prepared a day ahead if necessary, but in that case the potato would have to be cooked separately and just warmed through in the sauce. I would not recommend freezing.

AGUAYÓN ESTILO LEONOR Pot Roast Leonor

SEÑORITA LEONOR

SERVES 6   OAXACA

This recipe was given to me by a friend's Oaxacan maid. Although it is not an outstanding dish, as such, it nevertheless has a delicious flavor, and guinea-pig friends of mine loved it when I was test-cooking. I always serve it with fried pasilla chiles on top to give it a little extra bite.

2 ½ TO 3 POUNDS (1.125 TO 1.35 KG) BEEF POT ROAST, IN ONE PIECE

2 TEASPOONS SALT, OR TO TASTE

FRESHLY GROUND PEPPER

3 TABLESPOONS VEGETABLE OIL

3 PASILLA CHILES, WIPED CLEAN, SEEDS AND VEINS REMOVED

2 ½ CUPS (625 ML) WATER, APPROXIMATELY

12 OUNCES (340 G) TOMATOES, ROUGHLY CHOPPED (ABOUT 2 CUPS/500 ML)

¾ CUP (185 ML) SESAME SEEDS, TOASTED

3 THICK, CRISPLY TOASTED ROUNDS OF FRENCH BREAD, CRUSHED

2 GARLIC CLOVES, ROUGHLY CHOPPED

TO SERVE

4 PASILLA CHILES, WIPED CLEAN AND FRIED CRISP (SEE PAGE 475)

SMALL, UNSKINNED WAXY POTATOES, BOILED

Season the meat with salt and pepper. Heat the oil in a heavy Dutch oven and brown the meat lightly all over. Remove from the oil and set aside.

Toast the chiles on a medium-hot griddle or comal; when they are cool they should be rather crisp, but take care not to burn them or the sauce will have a bitter taste. Put 1 cup (250 ml) of the water into the blender and add the tomatoes, the toasted chiles, sesame seeds, bread, and the garlic and blend until smooth. (You may need a little extra water but use only enough to loosen the blades of the blender.)

Fry the sauce over fairly high heat, stirring and scraping the bottom of the pot, for about 5 minutes. Add the meat and 1½ cups (375 ml) of water. Adjust the seasoning, then cover and cook over slow heat about 4 hours or until tender.

To serve, slice the meat rather thick, pour the sauce over, top with the fried pasilla chiles, and surround with the boiled potatoes.

NOTE: This dish can be prepared several hours ahead, even the day before, and reheated. Leftovers can be frozen up to 1 month.

ASSORTED MEATS

Conejo en Chile ※ *Rabbit in Chile Sauce*

Mixiotes ※ *Meat Steamed in Maguey Parchment*

Birria ※ *Seasoned and Baked Meat*

Fiambre Potosino ※ *Cold Meats in a Vinaigrette Sauce*

Albóndigas en Chipotle Quemado

   ※ *Meatballs in "Burnt" Chipotle Sauce*

Albóndigas de Jalisco ※ *Meatballs*

Albóndigas en Salsa de Jitomate y Chipotle

   ※ *Meatballs in Tomato and Chipotle Sauce*

BARBACOA

Barbacoa de Carnero Oaxaqueña ※ *Oaxaca Barbecued Mutton*

CONEJO EN CHILE *Rabbit in Chile Sauce*

SEÑORA MARÍA ELENA LARA

SERVES 6   HIDALGO

This is the recipe exactly as it was given to me by Señora Lara and it is particularly suitable for an older, compactly fleshed rabbit with rather a strong flavor. However, I have found by buying rabbits at random across the country they can vary enormously in the cooking time required. If you have a good source for tender rabbits or are using 2 smaller ones, then I suggest you omit the first boiling step and, after preparing the sauce, fry the rabbit pieces raw.

THE RABBIT

1 RABBIT (ABOUT 3 POUNDS/1.35 KG), CUT INTO 6 SERVING PIECES

2 TEASPOONS SALT

1/2 CUP (125 ML) MILD VINEGAR

2 MEXICAN BAY LEAVES

6 SPRIGS FRESH THYME OR 1/4 TEASPOON DRIED

6 SPRIGS FRESH MARJORAM OR 1/4 TEASPOON DRIED

THE CHILE SAUCE

15 GUAJILLO CHILES (ABOUT 2 1/2 OUNCES/75 G), WIPED CLEAN

10 PASILLA CHILES (ABOUT 2 1/2 OUNCES/75 G), WIPED CLEAN

2 CUPS (500 ML) WATER

1 1/4 POUNDS (565 G) TOMATOES, BROILED (SEE PAGE 490)

SALT TO TASTE

THE GARLIC SEASONING

2 LARGE GARLIC CLOVES

1/4 TEASPOON CUMIN SEEDS

1/2 TEASPOON DRIED MEXICAN OREGANO

6 SPRIGS FRESH MARJORAM OR 1/4 TEASPOON DRIED

6 SPRIGS FRESH THYME OR 1/4 TEASPOON DRIED

2 MEXICAN BAY LEAVES

1/2 TEASPOON SALT, OR TO TASTE

2 TABLESPOONS WATER

TO FINISH

3 TO 4 TABLESPOONS PORK LARD OR VEGETABLE OIL

1 ½ CUPS (375 ML) THINLY SLICED WHITE ONION

2 CUPS (500 ML) CHICKEN BROTH OR WATER, APPROXIMATELY

Put the rabbit into a large saucepan together with the salt, vinegar, bay leaves, and herbs. Cover with water and bring to a simmer. Simmer until just tender—about 40 minutes, depending on how tender the rabbit is to begin with. Drain and discard the cooking water.

While the rabbit is cooking, prepare the sauce. Remove the stems, seeds, and veins from the chiles. Open them up flat and toast them on a hot griddle or comal on either side (see page 475), taking care that they do not burn. (When they have cooled off they should be crisp.)

Put the 2 cups (500 ml) of water, unskinned tomatoes, and salt into a blender jar and crumble in half of the chiles. Blend until almost smooth. Crumble the remaining chiles into the jar and blend briefly; the sauce should be of a rough consistency. (You may have to add a little more water to the jar, but be sure it's only enough to release the blades of the blender.) Set aside while you prepare the garlic seasoning.

Crush the garlic in a molcajete or mortar, then grind together with the cumin, oregano, marjoram, thyme, bay leaves, and salt. Dilute with the water and set aside.

Melt the lard in a heavy pan and fry the rabbit pieces lightly together with the sliced onion. Add the garlic seasoning and fry for a minute more, stirring the mixture constantly. Wash the molcajete or mortar out with a little more water if necessary and add to the pan. Add the chile sauce and fry, constantly stirring and scraping the bottom of the pan, for about 2 minutes. Add the 2 cups (500 ml) broth or water and cook over low heat for about 20 minutes, stirring the sauce from time to time. (The sauce should be of a medium consistency. Add more broth or water if it reduces too much.)

Serve hot, with freshly made tortillas.

NOTE: This dish can be prepared several hours ahead, but I don't recommend freezing.

MIXIOTES Meat Steamed in Maguey Parchment

SEÑORA MARÍA ELENA LARA
SERVES 6   HIDALGO

Huge century plants, or magueyes, *are a predominating feature of the central Mexican landscape. The maguey has many uses apart from the making of pulque. The large, pointed, fleshy "leaf," or* penca, *is used to line barbecue pits, and it gives a very special flavor to the meat. The leaf is covered with a tough, transparent skin, which is stripped off and used for wrapping meat that is to be cooked in the barbecue pits. Apart from making a waterproof package, this also lends a special flavor to the meat. These little packages of chile-seasoned meat are called* mixiotes.

Since chances are good that you don't have a barbecue pit lined with maguey leaves, or the mixiote *skins, use an ordinary steamer and wrap the meat in cooking parchment (not foil, which in my opinion should not be used for cooking food). Señora Lara steams hers over a mixture of pulque and water, and some other cooks suggest using beer and water; I myself find that the latter gives rather too strong a flavor, but it is better than nothing. Although in central Mexico mutton and rabbit are used most commonly, any meat, even chicken, is, in fact, very good cooked in this way. I prefer meat on the bone as a general rule, as it is not dry and cooks better, and I find that ribs of beef are particularly tender and juicy for this dish.*

3 POUNDS (1.35 KG) MEAT, APPROXIMATELY, PREFERABLY WITH BONE, CUT INTO
    2¼-INCH (6-CM) SQUARES
4 TEASPOONS SALT, OR TO TASTE
8 GUAJILLO CHILES, WIPED CLEAN
7 PASILLA CHILES, WIPED CLEAN
1½ CUPS (375 ML) PULQUE OR BEER, OR ½ CUP (125 ML) MILD VINEGAR PLUS 1 CUP
    (250 ML) WATER
¼ TEASPOON CUMIN SEEDS
½ TEASPOON DRIED MEXICAN OREGANO
6 SPRIGS FRESH THYME OR ¼ TEASPOON DRIED
6 SPRIGS MARJORAM OR ¼ TEASPOON DRIED
5 WHOLE CLOVES
2 MEXICAN BAY LEAVES
3 GARLIC CLOVES
1 TABLESPOON MILD VINEGAR

12 SQUARES, APPROXIMATELY 7 BY 7 INCHES (18 BY 18 CM), MIXIOTES (SEE NOTE ABOVE)
  OR PARCHMENT PAPER
LIQUID FOR STEAMING (EQUAL PARTS PULQUE OR BEER AND WATER)

The day before, season the meat with 2 teaspoons of the salt and set aside while you prepare the chiles.

Remove the seeds and veins from the chiles. Flatten them out and toast them well (see page 475) on a hot griddle or comal. (They should be toasted enough so they crumble easily when cool, but care should be taken not to burn them, or the sauce will have a bitter taste.) Put the chiles, crumbled, into a blender jar, add the pulque, and leave to soak for about 15 minutes.

Meanwhile, crush the cumin, oregano, thyme, marjoram, cloves, bay leaves, and garlic together with the remaining 2 teaspoons salt. Add the vinegar and grind to a paste or add to the blender jar and blend briefly; the sauce should be textured.

Spread the meat thickly with the sauce and leave overnight in the refrigerator to season.

The next day, if you are using the *mixiotes*, cover them with hot water and leave to soak for about 5 minutes, or until fairly soft but pliable.

Divide the meat and sauce into 12 portions. Put one portion into the center of each *mixiote* square and gather up the sides to form a small bundle. Tie securely and put into the steamer. Put a coin into the bottom of the steamer (when it stops "dancing," you'll know you need to add more liquid), add the pulque (if available) and water, bring to a boil, and let the *mixiotes* cook until the meat is soft—about 2½ hours, depending on type and cut of meat. There should be plenty of juice in the packages.

Serve with hot, freshly made tortillas.

NOTE: This recipe can be prepared ahead, but it doesn't freeze successfully.

BIRRIA Seasoned and Baked Meat
SERVES 8 TO 10
JALISCO

The word birria *actually means something deformed or grotesque, and it is used colloquially in the northwest to mean a mess or failure. This certainly looks a mess when cooked, but it is a very savory one!*

This is a very rustic dish; usually a whole goat or lamb, although in some places just the offal, is seasoned with a paste of dried chiles and spices and cooked in a pit barbecue.

As you wander around Guadalajara at night, you can see that tacos de birria *head the list of* antojitos *sold on the street-side stands or in small* cenadurias *(modest supper places) and always appear prominently on the Sunday menus of small, family regional restaurants.*

Here is an unusual family version of Birria, but I have taken liberties with the recipe and used a variety of chiles that are more commonly used in the neighboring state of Zacatecas. The mixture of different meats gives the dish an interesting quality and texture. You will need about 7 pounds (3.25 kg).

2 LAMB SHANKS

A VEAL BREAST

A LAMB BREAST

3 POUNDS (1.35 KG) LOIN OF PORK, RIB, OR SHOULDER END

2 TABLESPOONS SALT

6 ANCHO CHILES, SEEDS AND VEINS REMOVED

3 GUAJILLO CHILES, SEEDS AND VEINS REMOVED

10 CASCABEL CHILES, SEEDS AND VEINS REMOVED

APPROXIMATELY 1 CUP (250 ML) HOT WATER

1/2 CUP (125 ML) MILD VINEGAR

18 PEPPERCORNS

4 WHOLE CLOVES

1/4 TEASPOON DRIED MEXICAN OREGANO

SCANT 1/4 TEASPOON CUMIN SEEDS

1/4 CUP (65 ML) ROUGHLY CHOPPED WHITE ONION

6 GARLIC CLOVES, ROUGHLY CHOPPED

1 1/2 CUPS (375 ML) WATER

2 TEASPOONS SALT

2 POUNDS (900 G) TOMATOES, BROILED (SEE PAGE 490)

1 CUP (250 ML) FINELY CHOPPED WHITE ONION

1/2 TEASPOON DRIED MEXICAN OREGANO

There will be approximately 6 to 7 pounds (2.75 to 3.25 kg) of meat. Slash the meats in several places down to the bone and rub the salt well into it. Meanwhile, prepare the chile paste.

Heat the comal and toast the chiles lightly, turning them from time to time so that they will not burn. Put the chiles to soak in the hot water for about 15 minutes and strain.

Put the vinegar, spices, onion, and garlic into a blender jar and blend thoroughly. Add the 1½ cups of water and the chiles a few at a time, blending thoroughly with each addition. Add the salt. The mixture should resemble a thick paste.

Cover the meat thickly with the paste and set it aside for 12 hours if time permits. Preheat the oven to 350°F (180°C).

Put the water into the bottom of a heavy casserole and place the meat on a rack so that it is just above the water. Seal the lid with a paste of flour and water and cook for 3½ to 4 hours, by which time the meat should be almost falling off the bones.

Strain off the juices from the bottom of the pan, cool, and skim off the fat. There should be about 2 cups (500 ml) of juices left—if not, make it up to 2 cups (500 ml) with water.

Blend the tomatoes to a smooth sauce. Add with the skimmed juices from the meat into a saucepan and bring to a boil.

Serve each portion of mixed meats in a deep bowl. Pour ½ cup (125 ml) sauce over the meat and sprinkle with the chopped onion and oregano. Eat with tortillas.

FIAMBRE POTOSINO Cold Meats in a Vinaigrette Sauce
RESTAURANT LA LONJA
SERVES 6   SAN LUIS POTOSÍ

Whenever my late husband, Paul, and I were making the drive north to Monterrey or Laredo, we would be sure to stop in San Luis Potosí for lunch at La Lonja, one of the really distinguished regional restaurants in those days. We would unfailingly order fiambre, *which was refreshing and light after a long, hot drive.*

Some years later, when I returned to San Luis to learn more about Potosino cooking, I met the owner/ manager Don Miguel Armijo — a most distinguished and charming old man who with his maître d' Arturo took a great delight in introducing me to the local food. One unforgettable meal — and I know that this is irrelevant here, but the meal was so incredible I can't resist putting it in — was designed to show me the delicacies the desert can produce. It started with what I called desert hors d'oeuvre, for the dish had on it yucca flower buds cooked with egg; the delicate heart of a local palm with an excellent vinaigrette; pickled maguey flower buds called chochas; *and the round buds of the large cushion-shaped biznaga cactus, called* cabuches. *After that came a strip of flattened filet of beef, charcoal-broiled* a la huasteca *and served with a small dish of* garambullos—*the round, grapelike fruit of the organ cactus, juicy and sweet, with small, crunchy seeds inside. And for dessert there was a special* queso de tuna *made by an old man in a nearby village who makes it better than anyone else; nobody knows his secret. It is a thick brown paste of red prickly pears cooked with raw sugar and dried in the sun.*

The meats should be cooked separately.

THE PIGS' FEET

3 PIGS' FEET, HALVED
1 MEXICAN BAY LEAF
10 PEPPERCORNS
$\frac{1}{2}$ MEDIUM WHITE ONION, ROUGHLY CHOPPED
2 GARLIC CLOVES
6 SPRIGS FRESH THYME OR $\frac{1}{4}$ TEASPOON DRIED
6 SPRIGS FRESH MARJORAM OR $\frac{1}{4}$ TEASPOON DRIED
SALT TO TASTE

THE CALF'S TONGUE

1 FRESH CALF'S TONGUE (ABOUT 1$\frac{1}{2}$ TO 1$\frac{3}{4}$ POUNDS/675 TO 800 G)
SALT TO TASTE
6 PEPPERCORNS
1 GARLIC CLOVE
$\frac{1}{4}$ WHITE ONION
$\frac{1}{2}$ MEXICAN BAY LEAF
3 SPRIGS FRESH THYME OR $\frac{1}{8}$ TEASPOON DRIED
3 SPRIGS FRESH MARJORAM OR $\frac{1}{8}$ TEASPOON DRIED
SALT TO TASTE

THE CHICKEN BREASTS

3 WHOLE CHICKEN BREASTS
$\frac{1}{4}$ SMALL WHITE ONION
1 GARLIC CLOVE

THE VEGETABLES

4 LARGE CARROTS
5 SMALL RED BLISS OR WAXY POTATOES (ABOUT 8 OUNCES/225 G)
SALT TO TASTE

THE VINAIGRETTE

½ CUP (125 ML) OLIVE OIL

¼ CUP (65 ML) VEGETABLE OIL

1 CUP (250 ML) BEST WINE VINEGAR

2 TEASPOONS PREPARED HOT MUSTARD

SALT AND FRESHLY GROUND PEPPER TO TASTE

2 TEASPOONS JUICE FROM CANNED JALAPEÑOS EN ESCABECHE

1 GARLIC CLOVE, CRUSHED

1 TABLESPOON VERY FINELY CHOPPED PARSLEY

3 HARD-COOKED EGG YOLKS, FINELY CHOPPED

Put the pigs' feet into the saucepan with the rest of the ingredients and cold water to cover. Bring the water to a boil, lower the heat, and simmer the feet until they are tender—2 to 2½ hours—then leave them to cool in the broth.

Meanwhile, trim the tongue of all excess fat. Put it into the saucepan with the other ingredients, cover with cold water, and bring to a boil. Lower the heat and simmer until the tongue is tender—1 hour and 20 minutes. Leave the tongue in the broth to cool a little. When it is cool enough to handle, skin it and put it back into the broth to get completely cold. Cut it into thick slices.

Put the chicken breasts into the pan with the rest of the ingredients, cover them with the broth, and bring to a simmer. Simmer for about 20 minutes. Let them cool in the broth, then remove the skin and slice them thinly.

Scrape the carrots and cut them into ¼-inch (1-cm) rounds. Peel the potatoes and cut them into quarters. Cover the vegetables with boiling water, add the salt, and let cook for about 10 minutes. They should not be soft but al dente. Drain and set aside.

Mix the ingredients for the vinaigrette.

Put the meats and vegetables into a large bowl and pour the vinaigrette over them. Mix all well and let the *fiambre* stand for at least 2 hours to season. Stir it well from time to time.

Arrange the meats and vegetables on the serving dish and pour the vinaigrette from the bowl over them.

ALBÓNDIGAS EN CHIPOTLE QUEMADO
Meatballs in "Burnt" Chipotle Sauce

SEÑORA MARÍA ELENA LARA

SERVES 6

This is, I believe, a brilliant innovation, a variation on the theme of albóndigas en chipotle.

THE MEATBALLS

6 SPRIGS FRESH THYME OR $\frac{1}{4}$ TEASPOON FRESH

6 SPRIGS FRESH MARJORAM OR $\frac{1}{4}$ TEASPOON DRIED

1 MEXICAN BAY LEAF

$\frac{1}{4}$ TEASPOON CUMIN SEEDS, CRUSHED

8 PEPPERCORNS, CRUSHED

2 TEASPOONS SALT

$\frac{1}{3}$ CUP (85 ML) WHOLE MILK

1 LARGE EGG

2 GARLIC CLOVES

1 SLICE STALE BREAD

12 OUNCES (340 G) GROUND BEEF

12 OUNCES (340 G) GROUND PORK, WITH SOME FAT

$\frac{1}{3}$ CUP (85 ML) HALF-COOKED LONG-GRAIN UNCONVERTED WHITE RICE

1 LARGE EGG, HARD-COOKED AND FINELY CHOPPED

THE SAUCE

6 CHIPOTLE CHILES (DRIED, NOT CANNED) OR MORAS

2 TABLESPOONS PORK LARD OR VEGETABLE OIL

1 $\frac{1}{2}$ POUNDS (675 G) RIPE TOMATOES, BROILED (SEE PAGE 490)

$\frac{1}{2}$ CUP THINLY SLICED WHITE ONION

2 GARLIC CLOVES

$\frac{1}{4}$ TEASPOON CUMIN SEEDS

1 TEASPOON SALT, OR TO TASTE

2 $\frac{1}{2}$ CUPS (625 ML) MEAT BROTH OR WATER, APPROXIMATELY

Put the herbs, spices, salt, milk, raw egg, and garlic into a blender jar and blend until smooth. Soak the bread in this mixture until it is mushy, then add it all to the ground meats, along with the rice and chopped egg, and work well with your hands. This quantity will make approximately 24 meatballs about 1¼ inches (3 cm) in diameter; form the meatballs and set them aside while you prepare the sauce.

Heat a griddle or comal and heat the chiles, turning them from time to time until they become soft and flexible. Slit the chiles open.

Heat the lard in a heavy pan and fry the chiles, flattening them in the fat with a spatula, until they are very dark brown, almost black. Remove from the pan, leaving the lard, and put into a blender jar with the broiled tomatoes, unskinned. Blend until smooth.

Reheat the lard in the pan and fry the onion gently, without browning, until soft. Crush the garlic, cumin, and salt together in a molcajete or mortar. Add 2 tablespoons of water—to clean the mortar out—and add the mixture to the onion in the pan. Fry, stirring and scraping, over a high heat until almost dry, then add the blended ingredients and fry over a fairly high heat, stirring and scraping the bottom of the pan constantly, until the sauce has reduced and thickened.

Add the broth and meatballs—the sauce should just cover them—cover the pan, and cook over gentle heat, turning the meatballs occasionally, until they are cooked through and spongy—30 to 45 minutes.

NOTE: This recipe can be prepared up to a day ahead and can be frozen for about 1 month.

ALBÓNDIGAS DE JALISCO Meatballs
SERVES 6   JALISCO

Every region has its albóndiga recipe, but I think this dish really comes into its own in the northwest of Mexico—Sonora, Sinaloa, and farther south in Jalisco. Señora Rubio, a delightful old lady in Guadalajara with a great reputation as a cook, gave me her family recipes and here they are—the recipe below and the one that follows. I think they are the best I have ever eaten. They are very soft because of both the finely ground meat and the long, gentle cooking; then there is the texture given by the zucchini and the fresh flavor of the mint.

Always leave a little fat on the meat for the meatballs as it adds flavor and makes for a more spongy texture. My good friend and great cook María Luisa Martínez grinds up some chicharrón and adds that to the mixture for the same reasons.

THE MEATBALLS

1 ½ TABLESPOONS LONG-GRAIN UNCONVERTED WHITE RICE

12 OUNCES (340 G) GROUND PORK

12 OUNCES (340 G) GROUND BEEF

6 OUNCES (180 G) ZUCCHINI

2 LARGE EGGS

¼ SCANT TEASPOON DRIED MEXICAN OREGANO

3 SPRIGS FRESH MINT

8 PEPPERCORNS

¾ TEASPOON SALT

¼ SCANT TEASPOON CUMIN SEEDS

⅓ CUP (85 ML) FINELY CHOPPED WHITE ONION

THE SAUCE

12 OUNCES (340 G) TOMATOES

2 TABLESPOONS VEGETABLE OIL

1 CUP (250 ML) THINLY SLICED WHITE ONION

4 CUPS (1 L) LIGHT MEAT OR CHICKEN BROTH

Cover the rice well with boiling water and leave it to soak for about 45 minutes.

Grind the meat using the finest screen of the meat grinder. Trim the zucchini and chop them very finely. Add to the meat. Blend the eggs with the rest of the meatball ingredients until smooth and mix well into the meat.

Drain the rice and add it to the mixture. Make 24 meatballs, each about 1 ½ inches (4 cm) in diameter.

Pour boiling water over the tomatoes to cover and cook for about 5 minutes. Drain and blend until almost smooth.

Heat the oil in a wide pan and cook the onion gently, until translucent. Add the tomatoes, bring it to a boil, and let it cook fast for about 3 minutes. Add the broth to the tomato sauce and bring it to a simmer. Add the meatballs, cover the pan, and let them simmer for 1 ¼ to 1 ½ hours. Serve in deep bowls with plenty of sauce.

N O T E: You can cook these albondigas ahead of time, the day before, or you can even freeze them.

ALBÓNDIGAS EN SALSA DE JITOMATE Y CHIPOTLE

Meatballs in Tomato and Chipotle Sauce

SERVES 6   JALISCO

THE MEATBALLS

12 OUNCES (340 G) GROUND PORK

12 OUNCES (340 G) GROUND BEEF

6 OUNCES (180 G) ZUCCHINI

2 LARGE EGGS

$\frac{1}{4}$ SCANT TEASPOON DRIED MEXICAN OREGANO

8 PEPPERCORNS

$\frac{1}{4}$ SCANT TEASPOON CUMIN SEEDS

$\frac{1}{3}$ ONION, FINELY CHOPPED

SALT TO TASTE

THE SAUCE

2 POUNDS (900 G) TOMATOES

3 TO 4 CHIPOTLE CHILES EN ADOBO, OR TO TASTE

3 TABLESPOONS VEGETABLE OIL

$\frac{3}{4}$ CUP (185 ML) LIGHT MEAT OR CHICKEN BROTH

SALT TO TASTE

Have the meat put through the finest screen of the grinder.

Trim the zucchini and chop very finely. Add to the meat.

Blend the eggs together with the rest of the meatball ingredients and mix well into the meat. Make 24 meatballs, about $1\frac{1}{2}$ inches (4 cm) in diameter.

Cover the tomatoes with boiling water and let them cook for about 5 minutes. Drain and blend with the chiles to a fairly smooth sauce.

Heat the oil in a wide pan, add the sauce, and when it comes to a boil, cook it over high heat for about 5 minutes. Add the broth and bring to a simmer. Add the meatballs and bring to a simmer once more.

Cover the pan and continue cooking the meatballs over low heat until they are done—about 50 minutes. Adjust the seasoning just before the end of the cooking time.

NOTE: You can prepare this dish ahead of time, even the day before. You can also freeze it.

A WEEKEND AND BARBECUE IN OAXACA I could never resist an invitation to a barbecue and especially this one, which was to be held late in September to celebrate the ripening of the corn in a remote village in the state of Oaxaca. My mouth began to water at the very thought.

My hosts, Teofilo and his wife, Blanca, were the caretakers of the small but fairly elegant house in Mexico City where I stayed with friends year after year. Teofilo was always neatly dressed, a stocky figure with a shock of graying black hair and large, owlish eyes behind thick horn-rimmed spectacles. He was for the most part monosyllabic but certainly pleasant, and whatever you said to him was always replied to with a smile. He also looked extremely well fed.

Doña Blanca, as the maids called his wife, had a great reputation as a cook. When I first heard this, I couldn't pass up the opportunity, and I hurried down to meet her formally. Doña Blanca is a monumental woman—*una mujer doble,* as the saying goes in Mexico—with heavy Indian features, soft, long wavy hair, and large, lustrous brown eyes, a constantly smiling woman with a soothingly soft voice.

From that first moment we were friends. I would proudly bring her some of the special breads I had personally baked in the nearby bakery, and she would send up to the kitchen door, much to the astonishment of my friends, a bowl of steaming stew or pungent mole from the family meal. We often cooked together, and we talked for hours about Teofilo's and her families and childhood in Tepzuitlán.

At first the invitations to visit their village had been tentative, but this summer the visit and barbecue were finally to take place—and I offered to pay for the goat.

It was a long drive, so we planned to be away for a three-day weekend. All Friday morning Teofilo had been packing things into the station wagon, a recycled job that, five years before, had literally been picked off the junk heap and that—unbent, reassembled, and with some minor additions—had been going strong ever since. It had been polished until it shone and was crammed full of linen and furniture for their new little house, still under construction in Tepzuitlán, and hideously colored plastic buckets and bowls for their rural relatives. The three of us sat in the front seat, while their adopted daughter, Francisca, who helped Doña Blanca with the housework and the cooking, sat huddled up in the back. And so we set off, punctually at midday, out through Mexico City and onto the Cuernavaca road. After about an hour we were halfway down the long descent into the valley of Morelos—a leisurely ride that gives one time to admire the breathtakingly beautiful panorama of fertile plains and distant mountains—at which point we turned off toward Cuautla. We drove past the dramatic overhanging rocks of Tepoztlán, past the tidy new resort developments of Cocoyoc and Oaxtepec, and for many miles through flat, fertile agricultural land, where vast tomato crops were being harvested and loaded into trucks at the side of the road.

Teofilo was always punctual about his meals, and at two-thirty it was time to stop, which we did at a pleasant, shady spot by a fast-flowing stream. Bordering the stream was a field in flower. I had heard that the seed of the amaranth has been used since pre-Columbian times to make different types of confections, and what a sight those flowers were.

Teofilo unloaded a large basket covered with an immaculately laundered cloth. Everything inside it was wrapped with care in white napkins—tortas made from the flat, crusty yeast rolls called *teleras*, which had been cut open and stuffed to overflowing with well-fried beans, chiles, ham, cheese, lettuce, and tomato. These were followed by a sweet, juicy cantaloupe whose delicate flavor had been incredibly enhanced by the heat of the sun. It was such a simple lunch, but so good.

We were soon on the road again and passed near Izúcar de Matamoros in the state of Puebla, then through the fields of sugarcane, and very soon we began winding through rocky limestone hills that were sparsely dotted with mesquite, small palms, and towering organ cacti. There were no signs of life until the road approached a river, where we found clusters of primitive houses with palm-thatched roofs, surrounded by straggly plantings of corn and occasional brilliant patches of alfalfa. Here for the first time I saw the curious, small cone-shaped granaries, *cuescomates*, with pointed thatched roofs I had only heard about; they were propped off the ground on stilts to protect the dried corn from predators.

We made a short stop in Huajuapan—a small town halfway between Mexico City and Oaxaca—and then turned off westward onto a dirt road. By now it was dark. The air was cool and fragrant after the noisy, smoggy city, and it was wonderfully quiet. The night was so clear I felt I could reach out and touch the stars, while all I could see around were the blurred outlines of rocky hills and brilliant patches of light from distant villages, which changed position constantly as the road twisted and turned. We drove on in complete silence.

It was late in the evening when we finally arrived at Tepzuitlán and the house of Blanca's sister, Petra. She and her husband, Pedro, a farmer, had nine children, and they were all there; two of the older sons who lived and studied in the city had made a special trip for the occasion with their wives. The family lived in a large, old rustic house set around a rectangular courtyard dotted with shrubs and flowers. The house was badly in need of repair, and the part of it that gave onto the main street and had once been the village store was now roofless and abandoned. There, set on a smoldering log fire, was a large pan containing parched corn kernels simmering in water, with a touch of lime to soften them, to be used for the tamal dough for tomorrow's barbecue. Nearby was another pan of corn, which had been put to soak until the following morning for a soup called *lligue*. And so my lesson began, and my many enthusiastic teachers were astonished that anyone from outside should take so much interest in the life and food that they took for granted.

We were called to supper, which was prepared and served, almost exactly as they might have done centuries before, by Petra, Francisca, and another young woman who had been adopted by the family at an early age. The "stove" was typical of those in Colonial haciendas, a broad, counterlike construction of adobe brick whose cementlike finish was the color of terra-cotta. Set into the counter, in a row, were small clay wells to hold the smoldering charcoal, and off to each side were counters on other levels, one just the right height for grinding on the metate, the rectangular grinding stone of volcanic rock; another for the cazuelas and ollas, the glazed earthenware cooking dishes and pots; and others for storing baskets of fruit and vegetables. There was a large pot of black beans simmering away next to a pan of milk with its thick, yellow crust of cream, and another earthenware pot contained coffee boiling with cinnamon and brown sugar.

Petra was at the metate, mashing and rolling curds of cheese that had been clabbered. When she was satisfied that the curds were smooth enough, she packed them firmly into a wooden ring about 6 inches (15 cm) in diameter and 1 inch (2.5 cm) deep; then, picking up the ring with both hands, she began pressing the cheese between her palms, first on one side and then the other, as though she were making a tortilla. When it was ready, she gently tapped the ring all around on the table and the cheese was loosened, a compact, creamy queso fresco (that fresh cheese sometimes called queso de metate), ready to be eaten for supper.

Most of the visitors chose to eat *cecina* (beef jerky), which had been salted and dried only two days before by the butcher, who lived a few doors away. It was simply flung onto the glowing charcoal and allowed to sizzle for about a minute on each side. There was a powerful but fragrant sauce of fresh chiles in the molcajete to complement the meat. Of course there were tortillas, and sweet yeast rolls fresh that evening from the bakery, and hot chocolate.

Petra had made the chocolate herself of toasted cacao beans, unskinned almonds, cinnamon, and sugar, crushing and grinding them on the metate, which had some hot charcoal beneath it to give the chocolate just the right consistency. Once ground, it was pressed into small round molds and left out in the sun to dry. The chocolate, now stored in a huge glass candy jar, was ready to be boiled with water and beaten with a hand-carved wooden beater, the four loose rings of which, carved from the same block of wood, would give the chocolate an appetizing, frothy top.

Teofilo and Blanca had not been home for some months, so there was a lot of gossip to catch up on, and we were not allowed to go on our way until quite late. But there was one more stop, this time at Teofilo's sisters' house, where we were to leave the car. Jealous that we had had our supper elsewhere, they insisted that we at least have a nightcap before we turned in, and as exhausted as I was, with a throbbing headache besides, I found it to be a surprisingly good homemade brandy, an infusion of *flor de jamaica (Hibiscus sabdariffa)* in alcohol.

At last we were able to be on our way, to unpack the car and haul the things up the street, a steep incline of massive rocks, that led to Teofilo's and Blanca's house. It seemed that the whole village was asleep, and only the incessant barking of dogs broke the silence. We had to shout for some time before we could rouse the old lady looking after the house, but she finally came to unlock the gate and let us in.

Teofilo and Blanca proudly showed me their home, still unfinished, of concrete with an asbestos-tiled roof. It was immaculately clean. It seemed an age before the things we had brought had been stowed away, the gas cylinder connected, and the water turned on. Fresh linen was found and beds made, and then, in my room, Blanca discreetly set a chamber pot on a small wooden stool and placed a carefully folded clean white mat in front of it so my feet wouldn't get cold on the cement floor.

It was a very short night. At five o'clock I was awakened with a start as *las mañanitas*, a special birthday song, boomed into my ears. Outside soft footsteps and low voices sounded as devout villagers climbed up the hill to the chapel, not more than two hundred yards away, while four loudspeakers set up on the church tower blared forth sentimental songs and Strauss waltzes. This was just one day in the month-long celebration in honor of the Virgin of the Rosary.

By now sleep had gone; there was obviously nothing else to do but get up. By the time we had dressed and walked down to Petra's house, foaming buckets of milk were being carried in. Some of it was put aside for breakfast, while the rest was immediately clabbered for cheese (this is not done with rennet tablets, but with a natural coagulant—an infusion made with a piece of dried cow's stomach). Almost immediately I was hustled off to the *molino*, the mill where the corn is ground for tortillas and tamales, with the two batches of corn for the barbecue. Meticulous instructions were given to the young man who was operating the grinder. The corn that had been cooked the night before was to be ground, but not too fine, for the tamal dough, while the soaked corn had merely to be broken up for the *lligue*. The young man kept stopping the machine and handing us a little piece of the dough so we could feel it and tell him when just the right point had been reached.

Then to breakfast. Petra offered us more of the same food we'd had the night before, along with some eggs that had been gathered that morning and *bolillos*, the crusty oval rolls. But time was getting on, and there was still a lot to be done.

A lot of rattling and shouting in the street announced the arrival of the truck that was to transport us, along with the food, to the fields where the barbecue was to take place. The loading began: a large sackful of fresh ears of corn, huge earthenware ollas, cases of beer and soft drinks, great branches of wood for the fire, chiles, salt, spices, and handfuls of fresh herbs—it seemed endless. At last all was packed in and we drove off through the streets, slowing down every few yards to greet yet another relative. Everybody stared at me curiously but was too polite to ask who I was and why I was there.

About fifteen minutes' drive from the village, the dirt road stopped abruptly at an unfinished bridge over a narrow, fast-flowing river. There we began to unload, and in relays we carried everything through a field where the corn towered above our heads until we came to a clearing farther up the river. There, very near a huge, shady tree, a pit had been dug, about a yard square and a yard deep. Teofilo, Pedro, and I were left there by the others, who went home to finish the rest of the day's chores, but we were shortly joined by three other people, two men who helped the family work their land and Señorita—as everyone called her.

Señorita was a woman in her fifties. Her gray hair, tightly plaited, hung down from under her wide-brimmed, man's straw hat. Her face was lined and weatherbeaten, her bright blue eyes sparkled, and she was lithe and muscular. She was the village specialist in preparing goats for barbecue.

Very few words were spoken between us; none were needed, for everybody knew what to do and I just tagged along and helped them collect small rocks from the river bed to cover the bottom of the barbecue pit. We gathered kindling and cut up the wood we had brought along and threw it all into the pit until it was piled high up over the edges. Someone found some matches and we lit the fire.

Pedro told me that the man who was selling us the goat had gone to fetch it. I somehow expected him to return with large hunks of meat ready to be cooked, but no—I soon saw him returning through the haze of smoke carrying a long, thin machete in one hand and leading a pretty little cinnamon and white goat by the other. It let out some ladylike bleats when it saw us, and when it caught a whiff of the smoke it rolled its eyes nervously. "Now you can learn how to kill a goat," said Petra's husband with a chuckle as the man sharpened his machete on a stone.

I berated them all for not choosing an ugly, cross-eyed animal, and then, covering my ears tightly, I turned my back and walked away along the riverbank, trying hard to concentrate on a large black butterfly with superb red markings that was hovering around a clump of purple cosmos. When I finally turned around and came back, they began laughing at me and telling me that I had missed an important part of my lesson.

By this time Señorita was supporting the goat's head, now quite limp, with one hand, while in the other she held a bucket under its pulsating neck as the brilliant, paint-red blood gushed out. When she was satisfied that she had got enough, she quickly beat some rough crystals of salt into it, to prevent it from clotting.

In minutes the men had skinned the animal and were deftly removing the organs. With accurate aim they threw the intestines and stomach onto a rock in the river, a few steps from where Señorita was standing, knee deep in the water, her long skirts tucked up into her waistband. I shall always remember her standing there, skillfully turning yards and yards of the intestines inside out as they floated downstream, all the time being pounded and washed by the swift current against the stones. She then picked up the stomach, tossed out the undigested fodder, and began to scrub it, rubbing it all over with cut limes to remove the strong odor. Very soon everything was washed, scraped, and cut, and the meat and entrails neatly hung along a bare branch in the shadiest part of the tree.

By this time the wood had burned down to ash, and more was piled on. With the renewed blaze, Teofilo decided that we had earned our first snack. He threw some of the ears of corn, still completely covered with their sheath of green leaves, onto the fire. Within minutes he was fishing them out again with a forked stick, and as soon as he could handle them he unfurled the leaves at the tip and blew hard into the husk. "It helps the final cooking of the corn," he explained. It was crisp and sweet, far more delicious than the overstewed corn we were offered later that afternoon.

Up until this point everything seemed surprisingly well organized, but then came the unforeseen delays so typical of life in Mexico. Someone had forgotten the lard, the avocado branches had not been cut from the neighbor's tree, and the molcajete was missing. Two of the men were sent off to get them, while we gossiped and watched Señorita prepare the filling for the stomach. The blood was thoroughly beaten once again, with more salt and water to smooth out the lumps. The small intestines of the goat were cut into short lengths; fresh mint and marjoram were chopped and cumin seed was ground with the garlic and onion. All these were stirred into the blood, and as I held the stomach open Señorita poured the mixture into it. She then gathered the uneven edges of the stomach together tightly and tied them with a strip of fiber torn from an agave "leaf," securing it firmly around a specially cut peg of wood about 4 inches (10 cm) long.

Teofilo's sisters had now arrived and were lending a hand. One of them beat the tamal dough with lard and salt until it was light and puffy. She then spread it "two fingers deep" onto a shallow baking pan that had been lined in overlapping layers with the heart-shaped leaves called hoja santa (*Piper auritum*, whose fragrant, aniselike flavor is touched with something else beyond description). The leaves extended well up over the sides of the pan, and were folded back over the edges of the dough. Another layer of leaves covered the top of the dough and it was ready.

One of the guests had contributed chickens, another rabbits, and again there was a slight delay while the seasoning was made for them—fiery dried costeño chiles ground with vinegar and herbs. This was thickly smeared over the little bodies, and they were set aside until the fire was hot enough.

By now Señorita had started the *lligue*. The roughly broken corn had been soaking in water brought up from the river, and she began to rub it hard between her palms, so that the tough, transparent outer skins of the kernels were loosened and floated up to the surface. These were carefully skimmed off and saved to be fed to the cattle. There were three more washings and much discussion before the corn was pronounced ready for the pot. By now the two large earthenware pots had been filled about two-thirds of the way up with water. Most of the water in which the corn had been soaking was saved to feed to the pigs that evening, but some of it went into the *lligue*. (Almost 8 pounds of corn were used to feed forty-five guests with some left over for the family.)

Blanca's mother now joined the helpers. She rinsed some dried chiles, guajillos and costeños (a thin, orange-red chile grown in the coastal area, as the name implies, and much esteemed by the Oaxaqueños), and ground them for a few minutes in the molcajete before straining the fiery sauce that resulted into each of the two pots. Someone else picked up some small sprays of avocado leaves and held them for a moment over the hot ashes so that the leaves sizzled and crinkled, letting off a burst of wonderful anise-avocado scent before they were plunged into the soup. Finally some rough salt, a little of the goat fat, a vigorous stirring, and that was it.

The wood had once again burned down to ashes, and the stones were now hot enough to begin the cooking. Two of the strongest men lifted the pots and, staggering a little under the weight, almost ran toward the pit, where they gently lowered their burden onto the hot stones below. Some of the men cut branches from the cazahuate trees across the river—a wood traditionally used since it chars but does not burn—which they trimmed into thin stakes; these they laid in crisscross fashion over the top of the pots to form grids. The thick, pointed leaves of the mescal agave were laid on top of the grids, and on these were placed the haunches, shoulders, and the doubled-over sides of the goat, along with the filled stomach and its whole liver. Then the chickens and rabbits went on, and lastly the two flat pans of tamal. Someone had forgotten the goat's head, and on it went as well. It had been trimmed of its horns, skinned, and scrubbed, and a small peg—the end of a corn cob—had been stuck, rather picturesquely, in the top of the skull to prevent the brains from falling out. Another large avocado branch had been placed over the top of the meat, and then two of the men dragged a couple of smoke-blackened *petates*, or locally woven straw mats, that had been soaking in the river over the top of it all. Several of the younger men set to enthusiastically and shoveled on the loose earth that had been excavated from the pit, covering the *petates* completely. A wisp of smoke was seen to escape, but this was quickly smothered with a final shovelful.

By now the party was growing. A big cattle truck had just driven up to the bridge, and we could hear the distant laughter of a group of young people just arriving, together with innumerable aunts, in-laws, and godparents; even Grandmother, who never stirred from her room in the family house, came, carried across the cornfield by two of the strongest young men.

Now the agonizing wait for food began in earnest. We had been up since five, it was now past one, and we had had no more than the corn and a tangerine to snack on since that early breakfast. Still with a throbbing headache, I decided to nap, but when I curled up under a tree the flies attracted by the killing, as well as some local bloodthirsty insects whose name I can't spell or pronounce, attacked me mercilessly. I gave up.

It was a brilliant day, but the water was too cold for me to even wade in, let alone bathe like the rest of the women. After brief greetings and introductions, I watched them troop upstream to find their favorite bathing place in the deeper pools. A hum of their chatter, and occasional shrieks as they dived into the icy water, reached us, punctuating the quiet conversation of the men, who were drinking Mexican brandy, neat and steadily, in the hot sunlight.

By the time the women had dressed themselves and wandered back in small groups to keep vigil over the barbecue, an hour or so had passed. It was now the men's turn for bathing. Sluggishly they walked off, some decidedly under the weather by now. The bracing water took its toll, and after a time we saw Teofilo, supported by the arms of his companions, stumbling along until he finally collapsed on the river bank a hundred yards or so from us—and he didn't stir again until we were ready to leave.

By now it was about four-thirty. We were all ravenous, and the children were complaining loudly that they couldn't wait any longer to eat. After some argument it was decided to open up the pit, and as the loose earth was pushed aside and the *petates* were drawn off, an incredibly fragrant smell emerged, the herbs, meat, chiles, and avocado leaves all contributing their share. A few of the older children snatched morsels as the meat was taken out, but most of them sat patiently around a huge rectangular cloth that had been spread out on the ground.

Two other fires had been set. On one a pot of corn was boiling (to its ultimate death), and on the other a comal, a huge, thin disk of unglazed clay, had been heating, ready for the tortillas.

Petra by this time was hurriedly making a sauce of charred chiles and tomatoes. Blanca's mother was stirring up the *lligue*, which had gained even more from the meat drippings, and began to serve powerful bowls of the broth with some of the tender, broken white corn from the bottom of the pot. I cut the tamale into squares, while Señorita sliced the stuffed stomach with her sharp knife and Blanca presided over the meat. There was no lack of enthusiastic help, and for a while a contented silence fell over the group.

The meat was succulent and wonderfully flavored, with a smoky avocado flavor. The broth, I must confess, was a little too pungent for my taste, but the tamal—rich and spongy and marvelously fragrant with hoja santa—was, to me, along with the stomach and its rich, savory stuffing, the height of gastronomic excellence. I helped myself time and time again, just a little bit more each time to make sure I wasn't imagining anything.

"The barbecue could have done with another hour at least," said Petra's husband, who was a brooding, sober pessimist. "And what's more, Señorita didn't beat the blood enough. It's lumpy"—this said as he ate sparingly, considering every mouthful. But he was alone with his comments. Everyone else came back for second and third helpings, until they could hold no more.

Some of the tastiest pieces of the meat were tucked away for Blanca to take back to the city. I suddenly remembered the head. Where was it? That was the part I really wanted to try, remembering as I did the delicate little heads that I had eaten in Monterrey, where *cabrito al pastor* (kid roasted over wood) is prepared par excellence, and as nowhere else in the Republic. But the head, too, had been discreetly tucked away, for, since the picnic was being held on her land, Blanca's mother had laid claim to it.

When we were stuffed and could hold no more, we sat around joking and singing, gossiping, and belching, until the shadows lengthened and the fires died down to gray ash. Just before the sun disappeared behind the mountains, we began to stow things away into huge baskets, which were hoisted up into the truck until there was hardly an inch of standing room left. Off went the truck, rocking precariously home along the dusty, uneven track, while the few of us who had decided to walk enjoyed the cool evening air and the extravagant blue brilliance of the evening sky.

By the time we had reached the house I wanted only to sleep, but no sooner had I laid my head on the pillow than the wretched loudspeakers blared forth their evening greetings to the Virgin of the Rosary. I felt desperate—but then, since I was the guest of honor for the weekend, Blanca's young nieces were sent hurrying up to the church with an unprecedented request, that the volume of the music be lowered. And to our surprise it was.

The weekend was far from finished, and to enjoy it to the full, Blanca had decided that we would have to join in the spirit of things: get up with the *mañanitas* in the morning and go up to the *peñas*, the rocks, to bathe.

It was barely light when we set off the following morning, carrying towels, shampoo, soap, and containers for water. Blanca had mentioned this trip several times, but I wasn't quite sure what she meant. As we walked up the hill past the church we could hear the congregation praying. The streets were deserted, and only the huge zebu cows tethered in a neighbor's yard turned to look at us curiously. Most of the houses we passed were constructed in the same rustic style and of the same materials—adobe brick with roofs of large, curved terra-cotta tiles that overhung to form broad eaves, and these supported by strong timbers to form galleries around the houses. There was a scent of burning in the air from fires started early to cook the first tortillas of the day.

We were now on the outskirts of the village. Climbing up between tall, overhanging rocks for a few hundred yards, we suddenly found ourselves in a landscape of huge, smooth boulders that sloped down for perhaps half a mile to flat grassland beyond. A few people had been there before us and were driving their donkeys, laden on both sides with tin cans filled to the brim with fresh water. Ahead of us were two small boys, who were balancing buckets of water suspended from the homemade yokes of rough timber across their shoulders.

We went first to the main spring of water, which seemed to be hardly more than a trickle as it came out of the crevice between two huge boulders but soon collected in a small catch basin below, to form a small but very clear pool. We bent down to drink from a hollowed gourd and found the water icy cold and delicious. Little wonder people came from miles around to collect it daily, and would drink nothing else.

Blanca and I left our water containers with Teofilo while the two of us climbed farther up to find a pool in which to bathe. Satisfied with the place, Blanca unselfconsciously stripped off all her clothing and sat in the pool like some life-size Zuñiga sculpture, throwing cold water over herself with abandon and washing her long black hair. At that hour it seemed to me as cold as any English bathroom (which I have abhorred since childhood), but as the sun rose higher I, too, found myself a deep, clear pool. The shock of the bracing water made me shiver, but it was wonderfully refreshing, and it did leave my skin and hair soft and satiny. As we strolled back to relieve Teofilo of his watch, Blanca casually told me that she had kept a sharp eye open while I was bathing, because water snakes hide in the pools, and when disturbed they hurl themselves out of the water and, with a lightning movement, wrap themselves around the intruder.

When we returned to the house, Francisca had a substantial breakfast waiting for us, and after that began a day so packed with activities that it would put any well-organized group tour to shame. First we went to the marketplace, where the people from distant villages high up in the Sierras, dressed in shabby but colorfully embroidered native garb, were selling their meager produce of corn, squash, chiles, or herbs. They collected their money in, or sold tortillas from, tall, narrow, round baskets called *tenates*. More often than not they would carry several of these, one set inside the other, the outer, largest one having a strong leather thong stitched to it to hang over the shoulder. Sitting around gossiping, or tending their animals in the fields, their hands would be in constant motion as they wove these baskets and broad-brimmed hats, holding under their armpits a roll of fiber made from stripping and drying the small local palm that grows prolifically in semiarid areas of Oaxaca. They greet each other by touching, not shaking, hands and, always smiling, chat incessantly to each other in their soft Mixtec tongue.

After our trip to market there was mass to attend, a visit to the father's grave, lunch with Teofilo's sisters, who had prepared a special Oaxacan stew called *amarillo*—chicken or pork with many vegetables prepared in a thin sauce flavored and colored with a dried yellow costeño. They had prepared tamales steamed in corn husks, and to finish the meal a delicious, grainy-textured paste of local guavas.

As soon as the meal was over and we could excuse ourselves, Teofilo, Francisca, and I went in search of provisions to take back to Mexico City while Blanca went to console her mother because we had not stayed there for lunch. First to the butcher's. At the back of his store we entered a small room completely screened against flies and hung densely with drying, thinly cut beef, *cecina*. The smell was overpoweringly strong, and I was glad when they had finally chosen several pounds of meat and folded it neatly into a basket as though it were the finest laundry. From there we went to the barrio, as everyone called it, about half a mile from the village. This was a small area of rich, black soil at the foot of a rocky escarpment. The smallholders there had planted it thickly with orchards, vegetable plots bordered with bushy rows of cilantro, and flowers. We bought bushels of guavas, a hundred sweet *"limas"* to make *agua fresca* (literally "fresh water," but in this case limeade, Blanca's and Teofilo's favorite mealtime refreshment), pumpkins, onions, and roses.

From there we went across the village to the tomato fields on the other side, where hampers of sweet, fresh tomatoes—plum-shaped ones for sauces and green ones for ripening later—were given to Teofilo and to Blanca, who had now joined us. Petra had added homemade cheeses, protectively wrapped in fig leaves, and some cakes of her famous drinking chocolate. Hundreds of tortillas completed the store of good country food to last them through the next few months, when they would return to stock up again. Surrounded by heady aromas, we drove slowly back to Mexico City the following morning, Teofilo still feeling the effect of his unaccustomed drinking bout.

BARBACOA

Meat cooked *en barbacoa* is Sunday food in Mexico, and varies tremendously from region to region. The word *barbacoa* refers to pit barbecuing (meat cooked on stakes over a wood fire is called *carne asada al pastor*, "roasted meat shepherd style"). There are specialists who dedicate themselves to this pit barbecuing, as it takes a great deal of preparation and long cooking. Perhaps the most popularly known barbacoa is that of central Mexico—the states of Hidalgo, Tlaxcala, and Mexico—where the unseasoned meat, usually mutton, is cooked in a pit lined with maguey (century plant) leaves. The head of the animal is included, as is the stomach—which is stuffed with the chopped kidneys, liver, intestines, and so forth, and seasoned with salt and chiles. A metal pan is placed under the meat to collect the juices—seasoned with onion, tomatoes, and chiles —which are served separately in small cups as *consomé de barbacoa*, a light and very tasty broth. This is almost the best part. Traditionally the very soft meat is eaten as tacos, wrapped in soft, steaming tortillas and doused with a fiery sauce of pasilla chiles and pulque called *salsa borracha* ("drunken" sauce).

In Coahuila, in the north, the whole sheep, including the head—but not the stomach and innards—is wrapped in several layers of sacking and tied securely with cord, which is then wound into a strong handle for lowering the "bundle" into the hot pit. I am told—I have not been fortunate enough to try it yet—that the meat is particularly succulent.

I think that one of the most delicious ways of cooking in the ground is that done in the Yucatán peninsula, in a *pib* (the Mayan word for pit barbecue). The young pig to be cooked is first seasoned with achiote ground with spices and diluted with Seville orange juice and finally wrapped in banana leaves, all of which gives the meat an exquisite flavor.

Another area where the barbacoa has always fascinated me is Oaxaca. And even there it varies in different parts of the state or region. I describe that of the northern part on page 310, and here is the home-cooked version from the area around the city of Oaxaca.

BARBACOA DE CARNERO OAXAQUEÑA
Oaxaca Barbecued Mutton
SEÑORA DOMATILA SANTIAGO DE MORALES
SERVES 6 TO 8

This is the "domestic" version of barbecued mutton from the central part of Oaxaca State. The chile seasoning, with its cinnamon and sesame seeds, has a wonderful flavor, and the fragrance that comes out of the oven—masa, chiles, and avocado leaves—is so tantalizing and satisfying in itself that you never want the cooking to end.

Señora Domatila cooked her own parched corn with lime, left it to soak overnight, and sent it to the mill the following morning with specific instructions that it be very roughly ground so the broken pieces of the kernels would give the dough a crunchy texture— quebrajada *or* martajada.

Obviously you don't need the more expensive cuts of lamb—mutton is preferable if you can get it. I have used lamb shanks and they were delicious. For this recipe you will want 3 to 4 pounds of meat (1.35 to 1.8 kg), depending, of course, on how much of it is bone.

THE BARBECUE SAUCE

3 ANCHO CHILES, SEEDS AND VEINS REMOVED

8 GUAJILLO CHILES OR IN OAXACA, CHILCOSTLES

2 TABLESPOONS SESAME SEEDS

¼-INCH (.75-CM) PIECE OF CINNAMON STICK, CRUSHED

2 TABLESPOONS MILD VINEGAR

1 ½ CUPS (375 ML) WATER, APPROXIMATELY

3 LARGE GARLIC CLOVES, TOASTED AND PEELED

6 SPRIGS FRESH THYME OR ¼ TEASPOON DRIED

1 TEASPOON DRIED MEXICAN OREGANO, OAXACAN IF POSSIBLE

1 ½ TEASPOONS SALT, OR TO TASTE

THE MEAT

2 TEASPOONS SALT

4 POUNDS (1.8 KG) ASSORTED CUTS OF MUTTON OR LAMB OR GOAT

2 LARGE SPRAYS OF AVOCADO LEAVES

THE DOUGH

¼ CUP (65 ML) PORK LARD, SOFTENED

2 TEASPOONS SALT, OR TO TASTE

2 POUNDS (900 G) TAMALE DOUGH (ABOUT 4 CUPS/1 L)

Toast the chiles well on a hot griddle or comal, taking care that they do not burn (as the guajillo chiles cool off, they should be crisp). Cover the chiles with water and bring them to a boil. Remove from the heat and let them soak for 5 minutes.

Meanwhile, put the sesame seeds into an ungreased frying pan over low heat. Keep turning them over until they turn a rich golden color, then set them aside to cool. When they are cool, put them, together with the cinnamon, into a spice grinder and grind as fine as possible. (This step may seem unnecessary, but if you put all the ingredients into the blender together the sesame seeds would remain whole for the most part.)

Drain the chiles and put the ancho chiles into a blender jar. Add the vinegar, 1 cup (250 ml) of the water, the garlic, herbs, salt, and ground sesame mixture and blend until almost smooth—the sauce should have a little texture, and it should be quite thick, rather like a paste. Add a little more water only if necessary to release the blades of the blender. Blend the guajillo chiles or chilcostles separately with the remaining water and pass through a strainer.

Salt the meat, then cover it liberally with the chile sauce, leaving about 2 tablespoons aside to add to the dough later. Set the meat aside to season.

Preheat the oven to 350°F (180°C). Have ready a roasting pan into which the meat and avocado leaves will just fit comfortably. Put a rack into the pan and add 1 cup (250 ml) of cold water. Pass both sprays of avocado leaves over a bare flame or a very hot electric burner—they should sizzle, crinkle, and send off a rich avocado smell.

Work the lard, salt, and reserved chile sauce into the tamal dough. Divide the dough into two equal parts. Pat each part out into a roughly circular shape about ¾ inch (2 cm) thick. Place the meat on one piece of dough and top with the second piece; press the edges of the dough together so that the meat is completely sealed.

Place the dough-covered meat on the avocado leaves and cover with the second spray. Cover the pan with a well-fitting lid or foil tightly secured to the edges of the pan so that practically no steam will escape.

Place the pan on the middle rack of the oven and bake for 1 hour. Turn the oven down to 325°F (165°C) and cook until the meat is tender—about 3 hours, depending on the quality and cut of the meat. During the cooking time make sure that there is still some liquid in the bottom of the pan—you may have to add ½ cup (125 ml) or so more of water to keep the dough moist (at the end of the cooking time the meat should be very soft; there should be some sauce around it and the dough should be spongy and moist).

Cut the meat and serve with plenty of the dough, along with freshly made tortillas, some Frijoles Refritos (page 155), and strips of jalapeño chiles en escabeche.

NOTE: The meat can be seasoned the day before—in fact this improves the flavor. The masa can also be prepared a day ahead. But this barbacoa is best eaten as soon as it comes out of the oven. I don't recommend freezing.

POULTRY

Guajolote en Mole Poblano ※ *Turkey in Mole Poblano*

Pato en Mole Verde de Pepita ※ *Duck in a Green Pumpkin Seed Mole*

Pollo en Salsa de Cacahuate ※ *Chicken in Peanut Sauce*

Manchamanteles ※ *Chicken and Pork Stewed with Fruit*

Tapado de Pollo ※ *Chicken and Fruit Casserole*

Pollo Almendrado ※ *Almond Chicken*

Pollo Estilo Guanajuato ※ *Chicken Guanajuato*

Pollo en Ajo-Comino ※ *Chicken in Garlic and Cumin*

Pollo Tepehuano ※ *Tepehuan Chicken*

Pollo Tekantó ※ *Tekantó Chicken*

Pollo en Naranja de China ※ *Chicken with Orange*

Pollo en Pipián Rojo ※ *Chicken in Red Sesame Seed Sauce*

Pollo Pibil ※ *Yucatecan Barbecued Chicken*

Pollo en Escabeche Oriental ※ *Chicken in an Onion and Chile Souse*

Pechugas de Pollo con Rajas

　　※ *Chicken Breasts with Poblano Chiles and Cream*

Pollo en Relleno de Pan ※ *Chicken Fried with Bread Crumbs*

Pollo a la Uva ※ *Chicken with Grapes*

Pollo en Barbacoa Comiteca ※ *Barbecued Chicken Comitán*

Pollo en Cuiclacoche ※ *Chicken in Cuiclacoche*

GUAJOLOTE EN MOLE POBLANO Turkey in Mole Poblano
SERVES ABOUT 10   PUEBLA

The French were somewhat surprised one Christmas Day, during a broadcast from Mexico, to hear the correspondent say: "Today while you eat your turkey and chocolate bûche de Noël *(chocolate log cake), just stop and think that what you are eating came originally from the New World. Chocolate and turkeys both came originally from the New World; chocolate and turkeys both came from pre-Columbian Mexico. We, too, are eating them in Mexico today; the only difference is that we are eating them together."*

No special festival is complete without Mole Poblano de Guajolote. It is prepared with loving care, and even today, more often than not, it is the one dish that brings out the metate: *chiles, spices, nuts, seeds, and tortillas are all ground on it. In the village fiestas each woman is given her allotted task: some clean and toast the chiles, others grind them; there are the turkeys to kill and prepare, the spices to measure, and the maize for the tamales to be soaked and cleaned meticulously.*

It would be impossible to say just how many versions there are; every cook from the smallest hamlet to the grandest city home has her own special touch — a few more mulatos here, less anchos, or a touch of chipotle cooked with the turkey; some insist on onion, others won't tolerate it. Many cooks in Puebla itself insist on toasting the chiles, often mulatos only, over an open fire and grinding them dry. And so the arguments go on forever.

In La Cocinera Poblana, *published in Puebla in 1877, it is interesting to note that there are at least seven recipes for mole poblano and not one of them lists cacao or chocolate in the ingredients.*

I can remember that just before Christmas, during my first years in Mexico, the traffic would be held up on the Paseo de Reforma while flocks of turkeys were being coaxed along by their owners. One by one they would be bought and for the rest of the week a constant gobbling was heard on the azoteas, *flat roofs, of the apartment blocks and houses around us. The turkeys were fattened up and killed for the Christmas Eve mole.*

The word mole *comes from the Nahuatl word* molli, *meaning "concoction." The majority of people respond, when mole is mentioned, with "Oh yes, I know — that chocolate sauce. I wouldn't like it." Well it* isn't *a chocolate sauce. One little piece of chocolate (and in Mexico we used to grind toasted cacao beans for the mole) goes into a large casserole full of rich dark-brown and russet chiles. And anyone I've ever served this to has been surprised and delighted, for in this, as in other Mexican sauces, the seasonings and spices are not used with* such a heavy hand that they vie with each other for recognition, but rather build up to a harmonious whole.

There are many stories attached to its beginnings, but they all agree that the mole was born in one of the convents in the city of Puebla de los Ángeles. The most repeated version, I suppose, is that Sor Andrea, sister superior of the Santa Rosa Convent, wished to honor the archbishop for having a convent especially constructed for her order; trying to blend the ingredients of the New World with those of the old, she created mole poblano. Yet another story goes that the Viceroy, Don Juan de Palafox y Mendoza, was visiting Puebla. This time it was Fray Pascual who was preparing the banquet at the convent where he was going to eat. Turkeys were cooking in cazuelas on the fire; as Fray Pascual, scolding his assistants for their untidiness, gathered up all the spices they had been using and put them together onto a tray, a sudden gust of wind swept across the kitchen and they spilled over into the cazuelas. But, as one present-day Mexican philosopher says, "Whether it was prepared for archbishop or viceroy, by the nuns or the angels, the very thought of it makes your mouth water" (Alfredo Ramos Espinosa, Semblanza Mexicana, page 216).

This is not the traditional way of cooking a turkey for a mole poblano—it is either boiled first or put raw to cook in the sauce—but the braising really enhances the flavor.

STEP 1—THE CHILES
APPROXIMATELY ½ CUP (125 ML) LARD
8 MULATO CHILES, SEEDS AND VEINS REMOVED
5 ANCHO CHILES, SEEDS AND VEINS REMOVED
6 PASILLA CHILES, SEEDS AND VEINS REMOVED
(RESERVE 1 TABLESPOON CHILE SEEDS FOR STEP 4)

STEP 2—THE GIBLET BROTH
THE TURKEY GIBLETS
1 SMALL CARROT, TRIMMED AND SLICED
1 MEDIUM WHITE ONION, ROUGHLY CHOPPED
6 PEPPERCORNS
SALT TO TASTE

STEP 3—THE TURKEY
APPROXIMATELY ⅓ CUP (85 ML) LARD
1 SMALL TURKEY, ABOUT 8 POUNDS (3.6 KG), CUT INTO SERVING PIECES
SALT TO TASTE

STEP 4—THE EXTRA SAUCE INGREDIENTS

2 CUPS (500 ML) TURKEY BROTH

½ CUP (125 ML) TOMATE VERDE, COOKED (SEE PAGE 492) AND DRAINED

3 GARLIC CLOVES, CHARRED AND PEELED (SEE PAGE 492)

4 WHOLE CLOVES

10 PEPPERCORNS

½-INCH (1.5-CM) PIECE OF CINNAMON STICK, TOASTED

⅛ TEASPOON CORIANDER SEEDS, TOASTED

⅛ TEASPOON ANISEEDS, TOASTED

1 TABLESPOON RESERVED CHILE SEEDS, TOASTED SEPARATELY

7 TABLESPOONS SESAME SEEDS, TOASTED SEPARATELY

APPROXIMATELY ¼ CUP (65 ML) LARD

2 TABLESPOONS RAISINS

20 UNSKINNED ALMONDS

2 OUNCES (60 G) RAW, HULLED PUMPKIN SEEDS (JUST OVER ⅓ CUP/85 ML)

1 SMALL DRIED TORTILLA

3 SMALL SLICES DRY FRENCH BREAD

1½ OUNCES (45 G) MEXICAN DRINKING CHOCOLATE

ABOUT 6 CUPS (1.5 L) TURKEY BROTH

SALT TO TASTE

Heat the lard in a skillet and briefly fry the chiles on both sides—the inside flesh should turn a tobacco color—taking care not to let them burn. Reserve the lard. Drain the chiles and transfer to a bowl of cold water and let them soak for about 1 hour. Drain but do not attempt to skin.

Preheat the oven to 325°F (165°C).

Put the giblets into a saucepan, cover well with water, add the carrot, onion, peppercorns, and salt, and bring to a simmer. Continue simmering for about 1½ hours, adding more water as necessary. Strain the broth and set aside.

Meantime, heat the lard in a Dutch oven, add the turkey pieces a few at a time, and fry until the skin turns a gold brown. Drain off the excess fat and reserve to fry the rest of the ingredients. Return all the pieces to the Dutch oven, sprinkle well with salt, cover, and braise in the oven until the meat is almost tender—about 40 minutes. Pour off the pan juices and add them to the giblet broth, then add water to make up to about 8 cups (2 l) liquid.

Put 1 cup (250 ml) water into the blender jar and blend the drained chiles, a few at a time, to a slightly textured puree, adding only enough additional water to release the blender blades. In a heavy flameproof casserole heat the reserved lard and fry the chile puree over medium heat (because it will splatter ferociously) for about 10 minutes, scraping the bottom of the pan almost constantly to avoid sticking. Set aside.

Put 1 cup (250 ml) of the broth into the blender jar, add the tomate verde and peeled garlic, and blend until smooth. Gradually add the rest of the ingredients in small quantities at a time as they are fried or toasted:

First, grind the spices together with the chile seeds in an electric coffee/spice grinder to a finely textured powder. Then grind all but 4 tablespoons of the sesame seeds again to a textured powder. Add to the blender jar.

Melt the ¼ cup lard in a frying pan and separately fry the raisins, almonds, pumpkin seeds, tortilla, and bread, draining each ingredient in a colander before adding to the blender jar. (It is easier if the almonds, bread, and tortilla are crushed a little before blending.) Add another cup (250 ml) of the broth, or enough to release the blades of the blender, until you have a thick, slightly textured paste.

Add the paste to the chiles in the casserole and continue cooking, again scraping the bottom of the pan well, for about 5 minutes. Break the chocolate into small pieces and add it to the mole with another cup (250 ml) of the broth and continue cooking for 5 minutes more. Dilute the mole with another 4 cups (1 l) of the broth, test for salt, and continue cooking over medium heat until well seasoned and pools of oil form on the surface—about 40 minutes. Add the turkey pieces and cook for another 20 minutes.

Serve each portion sprinkled with a little of the reserved sesame seeds.

NOTE: The mole sauce can be prepared days ahead using prepared broth and, in fact, improves in flavor. But naturally the cooked turkey or chicken should be added 20 minutes before serving.

The sauce freezes very well and will keep for several months.

PATO EN MOLE VERDE DE PEPITA

Duck in a Green Pumpkin Seed Mole

SERVES 6   MEXICO CITY AND PUEBLA

It is recorded that at the time of the Spanish conquest Montezuma and the other rulers were eating stews or chiles mixed with tomatoes and pumpkin seeds; long before that the Mayas to the south were cultivating pumpkins and using the seeds in their food. Pato en Mole Verde de Pepita has a lovely, smooth, pale green sauce, thickened with pumpkin seeds and subtly flavored with herbs — a true classic of the cuisine of central Mexico.

This is not a traditional way of cooking a duck in mole: it is either boiled first or put raw to cook in the sauce. But the method I give enhances the flavor enormously. Of course you could substitute a chicken but that would have to be poached as the flesh is too soft for braising and would then fall apart in the mole.

COOKING THE DUCK

THE DUCK GIBLETS

I SMALL CARROT, SCRAPED AND SLICED

I SMALL WHITE ONION, SLICED

I GARLIC CLOVE

6 PEPPERCORNS

SALT TO TASTE

5- TO 6-POUND (2.25- TO 2.75-KG) DUCK

PEPPER TO TASTE

THE SAUCE

3 ½ OUNCES (100 G) HULLED RAW PUMPKIN SEEDS (ABOUT ¾ CUP/188 ML;
    SEE PAGE 494)

6 BLACK PEPPERCORNS

⅛ TEASPOON CUMIN SEEDS

I CUP (250 ML) DUCK BROTH

I CUP (250 ML) TOMATE VERDE, COOKED AND DRAINED (SEE PAGE 492)

6 SERRANO CHILES, ROUGHLY CHOPPED

3 TABLESPOONS ROUGHLY CHOPPED WHITE ONION

2 SMALL GARLIC CLOVES, ROUGHLY CHOPPED

3 SPRIGS EPAZOTE

5 SPRIGS CILANTRO

1 SMALL BUNCH RADISH LEAVES

2 LARGE ROMAINE LETTUCE LEAVES, TORN INTO PIECES

3 TABLESPOONS RESERVED DUCK DRIPPINGS

2 CUPS (500 ML) RESERVED DUCK BROTH

SALT AS NECESSARY

Preheat the oven to 325°F (165°C).

Put the giblets with the vegetables and seasonings into a large pan, cover them with water, and bring to a boil. Lower the heat and simmer, covered, for about 1½ hours.

Heat a casserole well and brown the duck all over, pricking the skin (not the flesh) to render out the fat from the layer underneath it. Drain off the excess fat from time to time and reserve. Cover the casserole with a tightly fitting lid and braise the duck, about 40 minutes, depending on how tender the duck is.

Set the duck aside to cool a little, then cut into serving pieces. Skim the fat from the juices in the casserole and reserve and add the juices to the giblet broth. There should be about 5 cups (1.25 l); if not, add water to make up to that amount.

In an ungreased skillet, toast the pumpkin seeds about 5 minutes, stirring them from time to time until they swell—but do not let them brown. Set aside to cool, then grind them in a coffee/spice grinder together with the peppercorns and cumin.

Put the ground ingredients into a bowl and stir in the 1 cup (250 ml) broth until you have a smooth sauce. Set it aside.

Blend the tomate verde with the chiles, onion, and garlic until smooth. Add the greens and blend a little at a time until almost smooth, and set aside.

Heat 3 tablespoons of the reserved duck fat in a casserole and fry the ground ingredients over low heat, stirring and scraping the bottom of the pan to avoid sticking (it will quickly scorch), about 5 minutes.

Gradually stir in the blended ingredients and cook over low heat, stirring from time to time for about 10 minutes. Dilute with 2 cups (500 ml) of broth and continue cooking over very low heat for 10 more minutes. Adjust salt to taste.

Gradually add the rest of the broth. Let the sauce heat through, still over very low heat. When it is cooked, the mole should cover rather thickly the back of a wooden spoon. Add the duck pieces and just warm them through.

Serve immediately. I do not recommend freezing.

POLLO EN SALSA DE CACAHUATE Chicken in Peanut Sauce

SEÑORA LETICIA CASTRO

SERVES 6   CENTRAL MEXICO

I was having tea one afternoon with Señora Leticia Castro, who has a great reputation as a cook. During a discussion of the food of Oaxaca, she called in one of her maids who was from Oaxaca and asked her to dictate some of her favorite recipes to us. This she did, without a moment's hesitation and without needing to correct a quantity or an ingredient. Here it is just as she gave it to us—a most interesting and delicious way of preparing chicken.

The sauce is not very picante. There should just be a pleasant "afterglow" from the chiles.

4½ POUNDS (2 KG) CHICKEN PARTS

I TEASPOON SALT, OR TO TASTE

FRESHLY GROUND BLACK PEPPER

4 TO 5 TABLESPOONS FRESH LIME JUICE

I MEDIUM WHITE ONION, CUT INTO 4 PIECES

2 GARLIC CLOVES, UNPEELED

I-INCH (2.5-CM) PIECE OF CINNAMON STICK

6 PEPPERCORNS

6 WHOLE CLOVES

I¼ CUPS (315 ML) RAW (UNROASTED, UNSALTED) PEANUTS, MEASURED SHELLED AND WITH
    PAPERY HUSKS REMOVED

I POUND (450 G) TOMATOES, BROILED (SEE PAGE 490)

4 CHIPOTLE CHILES EN VINAGRE OR ADOBO, OR TO TASTE

3 TABLESPOONS VEGETABLE OIL OR RENDERED CHICKEN FAT

2 CUPS (500 ML) WATER

Sprinkle the chicken with salt, pepper, and the lime juice and set aside to season while you prepare the sauce.

Heat a small, ungreased frying pan or comal and toast the onion and garlic until soft. Peel the garlic. Toss the spices in the hot pan to toast them lightly, then toast the peanuts until they are golden (a toaster oven works even better).

Put the unskinned tomatoes, chiles, and the toasted ingredients, except the peanuts, into a blender jar and blend until quite smooth. Add the peanuts little by little and blend until almost smooth. Add a little water only if necessary to release the blades of the blender.

Heat the oil or chicken fat in a heavy casserole and fry the chicken pieces, a few at a time, until golden brown. Remove the chicken from the pan and set aside. There should be about ¼ cup (65 ml) oil in the pan. Remove, or make up to that amount. Reheat the oil and fry the blended ingredients over medium heat for 3 minutes, constantly stirring and scraping the bottom of the pan. Lower the heat and let the sauce cook for about 15 minutes longer, continuing to scrape the bottom of the pan from time to time.

Add the chicken pieces and the 2 cups (500 ml) of water. Adjust the seasoning and cook over low heat until the chicken is tender—35 to 40 minutes. The sauce will thicken—it should lightly cover the back of a wooden spoon—and pools of oil will form on the surface.

Serve the chicken with plenty of the sauce, accompanied by small boiled potatoes.

NOTE: This dish can be prepared several hours ahead. Surprisingly it freezes very well—and will keep for about 2 weeks.

MANCHAMANTELES Chicken and Pork Stewed with Fruit

SEÑORA MARÍA CORTÉS CHÁVEZ

SERVES 6 CENTRAL MEXICO AND OAXACA

Manchamanteles is traditionally made on Corpus Christi day. Of the many versions that exist of the recipe, with its fascinating name that translates as "tablecloth stainer," I think this is one of the most interesting and delicious. It was a prize-winning recipe that appeared in a column of the Mexican newspaper Excelsior *about twenty years ago.*

12 OUNCES (340 G) BONELESS STEWING PORK, CUT INTO 1-INCH (2.5-CM) CUBES

SALT TO TASTE

¼ CUP (65 ML) VEGETABLE OIL OR PORK LARD

1 LARGE CHICKEN (ABOUT 3½ POUNDS/1.5 KG), CUT INTO SERVING PIECES

25 ALMONDS, UNSKINNED

1½-INCH (4-CM) PIECE OF CINNAMON STICK

1½ TABLESPOONS SESAME SEEDS

5 ANCHO CHILES, WIPED CLEAN

12 OUNCES (340 G) TOMATOES, BROILED (SEE PAGE 490)

2 THICK SLICES FRESH PINEAPPLE, PEELED AND CUT INTO ½-INCH (1.5-CM) CUBES

1 PLANTAIN (ABOUT 12 OUNCES/340 G), PEELED AND CUT INTO THICK ROUNDS

1 SMALL JICAMA (ABOUT 12 OUNCES/340 G), PEELED AND CUT INTO ¼-INCH (.5-CM) SLICES

Put the pork cubes into a saucepan, add water to cover and 1 teaspoon of the salt, and bring to a simmer. Cover and cook for 25 minutes, then drain, reserving the broth. Strain the broth and skim off the fat, adding enough water to make 4 cups (1 l), and set aside.

In a heavy, flameproof casserole, heat the oil and fry the chicken pieces lightly, a few at a time. Remove and set aside. In the same oil, separately fry the almonds, cinnamon stick, and sesame seeds, draining each of excess oil. Crush the almonds and transfer the fried ingredients to the blender jar.

In the same oil, fry the chiles lightly on both sides, then drain and transfer to the blender jar. Add the broiled tomatoes and 1 cup (250 ml) of the broth to the blender jar and blend until smooth. (Be careful to add only enough broth to release the blades of the blender; the sauce must not be too watery.)

Pour off all but 3 tablespoons of the oil remaining in the casserole and fry the chile sauce for about 4 minutes, stirring and scraping the bottom constantly. Add 3 cups (750 ml) of the reserved broth and bring to a simmer. Add the chicken pieces, pork cubes, fruit, jicama, and salt to taste, then cover and cook over low heat for 1 to 1¼ hours, or until the meat and fruit are tender, stirring from time to time.

Serve hot, with freshly made tortillas.

NOTE: This dish may be prepared several hours ahead. However, I don't recommend freezing.

TAPADO DE POLLO   Chicken and Fruit Casserole
SERVES 6   VERACRUZ

This is one of those fruity stews, not too sweet but pleasantly acidy, that one finds in Oaxaca, Veracruz, San Luis Potosí, and throughout the central part of Mexico. It is served very simply, just with hot tortillas and pickled chiles on the side for those who like a bite to their food. To be truly authentic this dish should be cooked on top of the stove, but I think the flavor is improved by baking it in the oven.

4½ POUNDS (2 KG) LARGE CHICKEN PARTS
SALT
6 PEPPERCORNS
1 WHOLE CLOVE

$^{1}/_{2}$-INCH (1.5-CM) PIECE OF CINNAMON STICK

1 TABLESPOON GRANULATED SUGAR

$^{1}/_{4}$ CUP (65 ML) DRY SHERRY

3 GARLIC CLOVES, FINELY CHOPPED

$^{1}/_{4}$ CUP (65 ML) MILD VINEGAR

2 CUPS (500 ML) THINLY SLICED WHITE ONION

12 OUNCES (340 G) TOMATOES, SLICED (ABOUT 2 CUPS/500 ML)

1 SMALL APPLE, PEELED, CORED, AND CUT INTO THICK SLICES

1 SMALL PEAR, PEELED, CORED, AND CUT INTO THICK SLICES

2 MEXICAN BAY LEAVES

6 SPRIGS FRESH THYME OR $^{1}/_{4}$ TEASPOON DRIED

$^{1}/_{8}$ TEASPOON DRIED MEXICAN OREGANO

TO SERVE

$^{1}/_{4}$ CUP (65 ML) VEGETABLE OIL

1 LARGE, VERY RIPE PLANTAIN (ABOUT 12 OUNCES/340 G), PEELED AND CUT INTO
    LENGTHWISE SLICES

2 TABLESPOONS LARGE CAPERS, DRAINED

15 GREEN OLIVES, PITTED AND HALVED

Preheat the oven to 375°F (190°C). Sprinkle the chicken pieces with salt. Crush the peppercorns, clove, and cinnamon together and mix with the sugar, sherry, garlic, vinegar, and about 1½ teaspoons salt.

Spread one third of the onion on the bottom of a deep ovenproof casserole; cover with one third of the tomato slices and the fruits. Add the bay leaves and sprinkle with a little of the herbs, then put half of the chicken pieces on top of the fruits and vegetables and pour on half the vinegar–spice mixture. Repeat the layers, finishing up with a topping of onion, tomatoes, and fruit.

Cover the casserole and bake for about 1 hour, then uncover the casserole for 30 minutes longer, or until the chicken is tender and some of the juices have been reduced.

Meanwhile, heat the oil and fry the plantain pieces until a deep golden brown. Remove and drain. To serve, cover the top of the stew with the capers, olives, and fried plantain.

N O T E : This dish can be prepared several hours ahead. It does not freeze successfully.

POLLO ALMENDRADO　Almond Chicken

SEÑORA LETICIA CASTRO
SERVES 6　　　　　　　　　　　　　　　　　　　　COAHUILA

Chicken cooked in almond sauce is one of the milder, more elegant dishes of the Mexican cuisine, and there are many recipes for it. This one, a more unusual version, was given to me by Señora Leticia Castro, who comes from Coahuila in the north of Mexico. She generously let me take recipes from the family cookbook that have been handed down for several generations. The original recipe was for a "young and tender chicken" that was thickly covered, inside and out, with the almond "paste." However, the crust falls off when you serve the chicken, so I think this version is more practical.

I suggest you serve this with small, boiled new potatoes and a lightly dressed salad. Strips of jalapeño chiles en escabeche can be passed separately.

4 ½ POUNDS (2 KG) CHICKEN PARTS
2 ½ TEASPOONS SALT, OR TO TASTE
FRESHLY GROUND BLACK PEPPER
3 TABLESPOONS FRESH LIME JUICE
6 PEPPERCORNS, CRUSHED
2 WHOLE CLOVES, CRUSHED
2 MEXICAN BAY LEAVES
¼ CUP (65 ML) COLD WATER, APPROXIMATELY
1 POUND (450 G) TOMATOES, BROILED (SEE PAGE 490)
4 TO 6 TABLESPOONS PORK LARD
1 CUP (250 ML) PEELED ALMONDS, ROUGHLY CHOPPED
2 THICK ROUNDS OF STALE FRENCH BREAD OR HARD ROLL

Season the chicken with 2 teaspoons of the salt, pepper, and the lime juice and set aside for at least 1 hour.

Preheat the oven to 350°F (180°C).

Put the peppercorns, cloves, bay leaves, ¼ cup (65 ml) of water, and ½ teaspoon salt into a blender jar and blend thoroughly, then gradually add the tomatoes and blend again. Melt about half of the lard in a small frying pan and fry the almonds to a deep golden color, crush, and transfer to the blender jar. Adding a little more lard, fry the bread, break up roughly, and add to the blender, then blend all the ingredients to a slightly textured paste, adding a little more water only if necessary to release the blades.

Choose a shallow, ovenproof dish into which the pieces of chicken will just fit in one layer. Pour a little of the melted lard from the frying pan into the dish and spread the bottom of it with a little more than one third of the almond sauce. Place the chicken pieces over the sauce and then cover them with the remaining sauce. Bake, uncovered, basting from time to time with the rest of the lard until the chicken is tender and the sauce slightly crusty on top—about 45 minutes.

NOTE: While this dish may be prepared some hours ahead and left to season, it should be eaten as soon as it comes out of the oven. It does not freeze successfully.

POLLO ESTILO GUANAJUATO Chicken Guanajuato
SEÑORA MARÍA LUISA DE MARTÍNEZ
SERVES 6   GUANAJUATO

Oranges are grown on a very large scale in many parts of the Republic, and they are used in a great many regional dishes. Here is one from Guanajuato.

To prevent overcooking the chicken, the vegetables could be partially cooked beforehand.

4 1/2 POUNDS (2 KG) LARGE CHICKEN PIECES

SALT AND FRESHLY GROUND PEPPER

3 TABLESPOONS VEGETABLE OIL OR MELTED CHICKEN FAT

1 CUP (250 ML) THICKLY SLICED WHITE ONION

3 GARLIC CLOVES, FINELY CHOPPED

1 POUND (450 G) TOMATOES, BROILED (SEE PAGE 490)

6 SPRIGS FRESH THYME OR 1/4 HEAPED TEASPOON DRIED

6 SPRIGS FRESH MARJORAM OR 1/4 HEAPED TEASPOON DRIED

3/4-INCH (2-CM) PIECE OF CINNAMON STICK, BROKEN UP

1 1/4 CUPS (315 ML) FRESH ORANGE JUICE

ZEST OF 1/2 ORANGE

12 VERY SMALL NEW POTATOES, UNPEELED (ABOUT 12 OUNCES/340 G)

5 MEDIUM CARROTS (ABOUT 12 OUNCES/340 G), SCRAPED AND CUT INTO QUARTERS LENGTHWISE

Preheat the oven to 350°F (180°C). Season the chicken with salt and pepper.

Heat the oil in a flameproof casserole in which the chicken pieces will just fit snugly and fry them to a deep golden color. Remove from the casserole and sprinkle with more salt and pepper, then set aside.

Take out all but 2 tablespoons of the oil from the casserole. Fry the onion and gar-lic gently, without browning, until translucent.

Blend the unskinned tomatoes until smooth. Add to the pan, together with the thyme, marjoram, and cinnamon stick, and fry over high heat for about 3 minutes, stirring and scraping the bottom of the pan from time to time. Add the chicken pieces, orange juice, orange zest, potatoes, and carrots. Cover the casserole and bake for about 30 minutes, then turn the chicken pieces over and bake until tender—another 20 to 25 minutes, approximately.

Serve with plenty of the sauce and vegetables.

NOTE: While this dish should be served as soon as it is cooked, it could be pre-pared up until the last stage when you add the chicken. I do not recommend freezing.

POLLO EN AJO-COMINO Chicken in Garlic and Cumin

SEÑORA MARÍA SÁNCHEZ

SERVES 6   SAN LUIS POTOSÍ

This is one of those very simple stews served in the marketplaces of little towns in the eastern part of the state of San Luis Potosí, which forms part of the Huastec country. Within the state, there are three distinct geographic areas—the hot coastal lowlands, the more lush mountainous areas, and the bare, semiarid lands—and each has its own distinctive cuisine.

4 ANCHO CHILES, VEINS AND SEEDS REMOVED
I TEASPOON CUMIN SEEDS
12 PEPPERCORNS
I TABLESPOON SALT, OR TO TASTE
I WHOLE CLOVE
4 GARLIC CLOVES
3 ½ CUPS (875 ML) WATER, APPROXIMATELY
3 TABLESPOONS VEGETABLE OIL
4 ½ POUNDS (2 KG) LARGE CHICKEN PIECES

Cover the chiles with water and simmer for about 5 minutes, then leave to soak for 5 minutes. Drain. In a molcajete or mortar, grind the cumin, peppercorns, salt, and clove, then mash in the garlic gradually, adding ¼ cup (65 ml) of the water to dilute the mixture. Set aside.

Transfer the drained ancho chiles to a blender jar with ¾ cup (185 ml) of the water. Blend until smooth and set aside.

Heat the oil and fry the chicken pieces (a few at a time so as not to touch in the pan) to a pale gold. Add the spice mixture and fry over medium heat for about 3 minutes, stirring constantly. Add the blended chiles and fry for another 3 minutes, scraping the bottom of the pan constantly. Add the remaining water, then adjust the seasoning and cook slowly, uncovered, until the chicken is tender—about 40 minutes, turning the pieces over from time to time. (The sauce should not be thick; add more water if necessary.)

Serve hot, with freshly made tortillas.

NOTE: This dish can be prepared several hours ahead and cooked for about 20 minutes. It should be cooled and cooked in its final stage just before serving. It does not freeze successfully.

POLLO TEPEHUANO Tepehuan Chicken

SEÑOR GILBERTO NUÑEZ

SERVES 6   DURANGO

The recipe comes from a little town in Durango and was given to me by Gilberto Nuñez, who for some time was a chef in Mexico City and then returned to his native Durango to open his own restaurant. This dish is named after a small indigenous group called Tepehuanes found in the state of Durango.

For my taste, chicken and rice dishes are generally nice and comforting but rather dull. But there is something about this one, perhaps the cilantro and cumin, that gives it quite a fascinating flavor.

12 SCALLIONS (3 CEBOLLAS DE RABO IN MEXICO)

4½ POUNDS (2 KG) LARGE CHICKEN PIECES

8 CUPS (2 L) STRONG CHICKEN BROTH

1½ CUPS (375 ML) LONG-GRAIN UNCONVERTED WHITE RICE

SALT TO TASTE

2 TABLESPOONS VEGETABLE OIL

10 OUNCES (285 G) TOMATOES, FINELY CHOPPED (ABOUT 1⅔ CUPS/415 ML)

2 SERRANO CHILES OR ANY FRESH, HOT GREEN CHILES, FINELY CHOPPED (OPTIONAL)

10 SPRIGS CILANTRO, ROUGHLY CHOPPED

¼ TEASPOON CUMIN SEEDS, CRUSHED

Cut four of the scallions into quarters lengthwise, using the tender part of the green, and put, along with the chicken pieces and broth, into a large saucepan. Bring slowly to a simmer and continue to simmer covered for about 10 minutes.

Meanwhile, rinse the rice twice in cold water and leave to drain in a strainer. Shake it thoroughly and stir it gradually into the simmering broth, then add salt. Continue cooking until the chicken and rice are just tender—anywhere from 25 to 40 minutes (the time varies tremendously with the type of cookware used, the type of rice, and the quality of the chicken).

Meanwhile, chop the remaining scallions finely. Heat the oil and fry the scallions for about 2 minutes, without browning, then add the tomatoes, chiles, and cilantro and continue cooking for about 5 minutes (the ingredients should be reduced to a textured sauce). Carefully stir the tomato mixture and cumin into the pan with the chicken and rice and continue cooking for 5 minutes longer. The dish should have a soupy consistency.

Serve hot, with freshly made tortillas.

NOTE: While this dish is best eaten as soon as it is prepared it could, however, be held for a couple of hours, in which case I suggest warming it through in a 350°F (180°C) oven for about 20 minutes so that the rice does not stick and burn. It should not be frozen.

POLLO TEKANTÓ Tekantó Chicken
SEÑORA BERTA LÓPEZ DE MARRUFO
SERVES 6

YUCATÁN

Pollo Tekantó has become the celebration dish of the Marrufo family in Mérida. The recipe was handed down to Señora Berta by her husband's grandmother, who was half Spanish and half Mayan. She lived most of her life in the Hacienda of Tekantó and was renowned for her cooking.

While this is a delicate dish, it has a curiously lingering flavor from the almonds and even more from the onions and garlic, which are charred on the outside while the inside is only partially cooked—a characteristic of Yucatecan cooking. I have altered the recipe in only one respect. It calls for the seasoning paste recado para bifstek; I have simply substituted the separate ingredients—oregano, peppercorns, garlic, and salt.

This dish is particularly good cooked, as it was originally, with turkey. If you think of it in time, season the poultry and leave it to sit overnight.

12 OUNCES (340 G) WHITE ONIONS (ABOUT 2 MEDIUM)

3 X-CAT-IK OR GÜERO CHILES, OR FRESH, HOT ITALIAN PEPPERS

1 HEAD GARLIC, UNPEELED, PLUS 2 GARLIC CLOVES PEELED

¾ CUP (185 ML) WHOLE ALMONDS, UNSKINNED

SALT TO TASTE

½ TEASPOON DRIED MEXICAN OREGANO, YUCATECAN IF POSSIBLE

½ TEASPOON PEPPERCORNS, CRUSHED

2 TABLESPOONS MILD VINEGAR

3½ CUPS (875 ML) WATER, APPROXIMATELY

4½ POUNDS (2 KG) LARGE CHICKEN OR SMALL TURKEY PARTS

4 TO 5 TABLESPOONS VEGETABLE OIL OR MELTED CHICKEN FAT

1½ TABLESPOONS ALL-PURPOSE FLOUR

TO SERVE

½ CUP (125 ML) VEGETABLE OIL, APPROXIMATELY

12 THICK ROUNDS OF STALE FRENCH BREAD

1 LARGE PLANTAIN (ABOUT 12 OUNCES/340 G), PEELED AND CUT ON THE DIAGONAL INTO
    ½-INCH ROUNDS

LETTUCE LEAVES, PREFERABLY GREEN LEAF OR ROMAINE

6 RADISH "ROSES"

Put the whole onions, chiles, and unpeeled head of garlic straight onto the flame of a gas stove or charcoal (with an electric stove use a very hot griddle or comal) and let them char all over. The chiles should be lightly charred; the onion and garlic should have well-charred crusts and the inside flesh should be transparent but not too soft. Cut the outside crust off the onion and roughly chop the flesh. Set the head of garlic aside; do not peel. Leave the chiles whole; do not peel.

Meanwhile, cover the almonds with hot water, bring to a boil, and simmer for 5 minutes. Set aside to cool in the water. When the almonds are cool enough to handle, slip off the skins, crush lightly, and transfer to a blender jar (the object of boiling them is to soften them for the sauce). Add the salt, oregano, the two peeled (uncooked) garlic cloves, the cooked onion, peppercorns, ½ teaspoon of the vinegar, and about ½ cup (125 ml) of the water and blend until smooth. (You may need to add a little more water to release the blades of the blender, but do not add too much, as the consistency should be that of a loose paste.)

Spread one quarter of the almond mixture over the chicken pieces—it will be a *very* light coating—and set aside to season for a minimum of 2 hours or overnight.

In a heavy pan, heat 3 tablespoons of the oil to a medium temperature—if it is too hot the almond paste will burn. Add the chicken pieces, a few at a time, and fry very lightly until just changing color—you may need to use a little more oil.

Drain any remaining oil from the pan. Break up the head of cooked garlic and place the garlic cloves over the bottom of the pan, along with the chiles. Put the chicken pieces on top: Add the remaining 3 cups (750 ml) of water—it should almost cover the chicken —cover the pan, and simmer until the chicken is *just* tender—anywhere from 35 to 50 minutes. Change the position of the pieces from time to time so they cook evenly.

Meanwhile, prepare the toppings. Heat the oil and fry the bread until crisp and golden, then remove and drain. Fry the plantain rounds in the same oil until golden. Remove and drain.

When the chicken is almost tender, stir in the rest of the almond paste and vinegar and simmer, uncovered, for about 10 minutes.

Put the flour into a small bowl. Add a little of the hot sauce and stir until smooth. Add to the chicken, stirring it in well, and cook for a few minutes longer, or until the sauce thickens.

Line the edges of a serving platter with the lettuce leaves. Arrange the chicken pieces, coated with some of the sauce, on the lettuce and decorate with the radish roses and rounds of plantain. Arrange the fried bread around the edges of the platter and scatter the charred chiles and garlic over.

Serve the chicken hot, passing the rest of the sauce separately.

NOTE: This dish may be prepared a couple of hours ahead of time. I don't recommend freezing leftovers.

POLLO EN NARANJA DE CHINA Chicken with Orange

SEÑORA ISELA RODRÍGUEZ

SERVES 6   YUCATÁN

During a fairly recent cooking tour in Mérida, Yucatán, Isela Rodríguez came to visit me with a friend who wanted to meet me. I had cooked with Isela on numerous occasions and some of her recipes appeared in The Art of Mexican Cooking. *She had been thinking about new recipes for me from the family repertory and began to reel off several from memory until my head began to spin—I didn't have my tape recorder. Two of them particularly intrigued me so I grabbed my notebook and wrote them down. They had been handed down from her grandmother. This chicken recipe is one, the other is* Pescado en Ajo Quemado *(page 361).*

2 GARLIC CLOVES

SALT TO TASTE

2 TABLESPOONS BITTER ORANGE JUICE OR SUBSTITUTE (SEE PAGE 494)

1 TABLESPOON RECADO DE TODA CLASE (PAGE 484)

4 ½ POUNDS (2 KG) LARGE CHICKEN PIECES

3 TABLESPOONS VEGETABLE OIL OR MELTED CHICKEN FAT

1 LARGE RED BELL PEPPER, SEEDS AND VEINS REMOVED AND CUT INTO NARROW STRIPS

SALT TO TASTE

12 OUNCES (340 G) TOMATOES, SLICED

⅓ CUP (85 ML) RAISINS

2 HEAPED TABLESPOONS LARGE CAPERS, DRAINED OR RINSED OF SALT

20 PITTED GREEN OLIVES, HALVED

1 LARGE WHITE ONION, QUARTERED AND CHARRED

2 X-CAT-IK CHILES, OR YELLOW PEPPERS, CHARRED, SEEDS REMOVED, AND TORN INTO STRIPS UNSKINNED (SEE PAGE 464)

1 LARGE HEAD OF GARLIC, CHARRED

1 CUP (250 ML) ORANGE JUICE

½ CUP (125 ML) WATER

1 WHOLE ORANGE, THINLY SLICED (NOT PEELED)

Have ready an ovenproof dish at least 3 inches (8 cm) deep, into which the chicken pieces and vegetables will just fit in one layer.

In a small bowl, crush the garlic and salt with the bitter orange juice and mix in the *recado.* Spread the chicken very lightly with this paste and set aside to season for at least 2 hours or overnight.

Heat the oven to 350°F (180°C).

Heat the oil in a large skillet, add the bell pepper and a sprinkle of salt, and fry gently without browning for 1 minute. Add the tomato slices and cook over high heat to reduce for about 3 minutes. Add the raisins, capers, and olives and cook for a further 3 minutes. Spread half of this mixture over the bottom of the dish, place the chicken in one layer on top, and cover with the remaining tomato mixture.

Place the onion and chiles over the surface. Cut the head of garlic in half horizontally and place cut side down into the dish. Pour over the orange juice and water, cover, and bake for about ½ hour. Remove the cover and baste with the juices, re-cover, and bake for ½ hour more or until the chicken is tender. Serve with the slices of orange.

NOTE: I prefer to set this dish aside for about ½ hour before serving so that all the flavors meld. It is best eaten the same day. I do not recommend freezing.

POLLO EN PIPIÁN ROJO Chicken in Red Sesame Seed Sauce
SEÑORA DORA LARRALDE
SERVES 6   COAHUILA

THE CHICKEN
THE CHICKEN GIBLETS
½ WHITE ONION, SLICED
2 GARLIC CLOVES
1 SPRIG FLAT-LEAF PARSLEY
1 MEXICAN BAY LEAF
1 SPRIG FRESH THYME, OR A LARGE PINCH OF DRIED
SALT TO TASTE
A 3½- TO 4-POUND (1.5- TO 1.8-KG) CHICKEN, CUT INTO SERVING PIECES

THE SAUCES
6 ANCHO CHILES, SEEDS AND VEINS RESERVED (RESERVING 1 TABLESPOON OF THE SEEDS)
½-INCH (1.5-CM) PIECE OF CINNAMON STICK, CRUSHED
3 WHOLE CLOVES
5 PEPPERCORNS
¾ CUP (185 ML) SESAME SEEDS

3 TABLESPOONS LARD

1 GARLIC CLOVE, ROUGHLY CHOPPED

SALT TO TASTE

1 LARGE AVOCADO LEAF, FRESH OR DRIED

Put the giblets, onion, garlic, herbs, and salt into a pan, cover with water, and bring to a fast simmer. Continue simmering for about 30 minutes. Add the chicken pieces and cook over low heat until just tender—about 25 minutes. Strain, reserving the broth.

Toast the chiles lightly, cover with hot water, and leave to soak for 10 minutes.

Meantime, put the reserved chile seeds into an ungreased skillet and shake over medium heat until they turn a deep golden brown—take care not to burn. Set aside to cool a little. Transfer the toasted seeds together with the spices and grind to a powder.

Toast the sesame seeds to a deep gold color in the ungreased pan and set them aside to cool off a little. Add the toasted, cooled seeds and spices to the spice grinder and grind them very fine.

Melt the lard in a skillet and fry the ground seeds and spices over low heat for about 3 minutes, stirring constantly.

Transfer the chiles with a slotted spoon to the blender jar. Add ½ cup (125 ml) of the reserved broth and the garlic and blend to a smooth puree.

Add the blended chiles to the fried spice mixture and let it cook fast for about 5 minutes, stirring it constantly. Add 3 cups (750 ml) of the reserved broth and let the sauce continue cooking over low heat for about 20 minutes, or until it thickens and is well seasoned. Add the cooked chicken and salt, and let the chicken heat through.

Toast the avocado leaf briefly on a warm comal and then grind it finely. Add it to the sauce.

NOTE: The sauce can be made several days ahead if you have some good chicken broth handy. The chicken can then be poached ready and heated through in the sauce when you are ready to serve. The sauce freezes extremely well.

POLLO PIBIL Yucatecan Barbecued Chicken

SEÑORA BERTA LÓPEZ DE MARRUFO

SERVES 1   YUCATÁN

I have given the preparation instructions for just an individual portion, but if you want to extend the recipe for a large group set the seasoned chicken pieces in a large baking dish lined with banana leaves and after adding the tomato and onion, cover with a double layer of leaves. (Look at the reference to the pit barbecue, the pib, *in the recipe for Cochinita Pibil, page 277.)*

Start about six hours ahead or the day before.

¹/₄ LARGE CHICKEN

1 TABLESPOON ACHIOTE PASTE (SEE PAGE 485)

1 TABLESPOON WATER

SALT TO TASTE

A PIECE OF BANANA LEAF, ABOUT 12 BY 12 INCHES (30 BY 30 CM; SEE PAGE 462)

2 TABLESPOONS LARD OR VEGETABLE OIL

4 THIN SLICES WHITE ONION

4 THICK SLICES TOMATO

¹/₂ TEASPOON ACHIOTE PASTE

Prick the chicken all over with a fork. Dilute the seasoning paste with the water and set ¹/₂ teaspoon aside. Thoroughly rub the remainder, along with the salt, into the chicken.

Sear the leaf quickly over an open flame to make it more flexible, and wrap it around the chicken to make a small package. Set it aside to season, refrigerated, preferably overnight.

Preheat the oven to 375°F (190°C).

Melt the lard in a skillet and fry the onion until translucent. Add the tomato and the ¹/₂ teaspoon seasoning paste and fry it gently on both sides.

Unwrap the chicken. Put half the onion and tomato under the chicken and the other half on top. Wrap it up again in the leaf.

Place the "package" into the dish and cover it tightly. Cook for 20 minutes. Turn it over, baste with the juices, and cook for another 20 minutes, or until just tender. Do not overcook.

Turn the oven up to 450°F (230°C). Remove the cover, open up the leaf, and let the chicken brown on top.

Serve still wrapped in the banana leaf.

NOTE: This dish can be prepared and partially cooked well ahead and the cooking completed about ½ hour before you plan to serve. The seasoned chicken may be frozen up to about 1 month.

POLLO EN ESCABECHE ORIENTAL
Chicken in an Onion and Chile Souse
SERVES 6 TO 8

YUCATÁN

Pheasant in a light pickle, or souse, is one of the classic dishes of Spain that has been adopted, and adapted, in Valladolid, Yucatán. The recipe was presumably handed down through the years by the families that came originally from the Extremadura region of Spain and settled in the Yucatán.

It was Alberto Salum, of Alberto's Continental Restaurant in Mérida, who generously shared this recipe with me when I was first researching recipes in the Yucatán for The Cuisines of Mexico. *He took me into his kitchen where they were broiling this chicken over charcoal. Of course the flavor is enhanced if you can broil in this way.*

You will need either a large chicken or small turkey, better still, for this recipe. Some cooks prefer to use new onions while others insist they should be used only for fish.

4 MEDIUM WHITE ONIONS, THINLY SLICED (ABOUT 6 CUPS/1.5 L) AND PREPARED AS FOR
   CEBOLLAS ENCURTIDAS YUCATECAS (PAGE 248) BUT LEFT TO SOAK IN MILD VINEGAR
   FOR 1 HOUR ONLY

THE SEASONING PASTE
8 WHOLE ALLSPICE
10 WHOLE CLOVES
1 TABLESPOON PEPPERCORNS
1 TEASPOON DRIED MEXICAN OREGANO, YUCATECAN IF POSSIBLE, TOASTED
1 TEASPOON CUMIN SEEDS
10 GARLIC CLOVES
SALT TO TASTE
3 TABLESPOONS MILD WHITE VINEGAR OR SEVILLE ORANGE JUICE

COOKING THE CHICKEN

A LARGE CHICKEN OR SMALL TURKEY (ABOUT 5 POUNDS/2.25 KG), CUT INTO
  SERVING PIECES

3 CUPS (750 ML) WATER, APPROXIMATELY

4 GARLIC CLOVES, UNPEELED AND CHARRED (SEE PAGE 492)

1/8 TEASPOON DRIED MEXICAN OREGANO, YUCATECAN IF POSSIBLE, TOASTED

1 TEASPOON SALT

A LITTLE MELTED LARD FOR BRUSHING OVER THE CHICKEN

6 X-CAT-IK OR GÜERO WHOLE CHILES, CHARRED (SEE PAGE 464), BUT NOT SKINNED

Prepare the onions.

Grind the spices together to a powder. Crush the garlic and mix in the salt, vinegar, and powdered spices. The mixture should be like a rather thick paste.

Using one third only of the paste, coat each piece of the chicken very lightly. Set the pieces aside to season for at least 30 minutes.

Put enough water into a deep pan to barely cover the chicken. Add the garlic, oregano, and salt and bring to a simmer, then add the chicken pieces and continue cooking over low heat until the chicken is almost tender—take care not to overcook—about 25 minutes.

Drain the chicken and set it on a rack, reserving the broth and keeping it warm. As soon as the chicken is cool enough to handle, spread each piece lightly with the remaining paste.

Brush the chicken pieces with the lard and broil until the skin is just crisp and a pale golden color.

Put the prepared onion and lightly charred chiles (unskinned) into the broth and bring it to a simmer. Place the chicken pieces on a warmed serving dish and pour the broth with the onions and chiles over them.

NOTE: This dish can be prepared well ahead; it can even be eaten at room temperature, but it is not to be frozen.

PECHUGAS DE POLLO CON RAJAS

Chicken Breasts with Poblano Chiles and Cream

SERVES 6   MEXICO CITY

I am afraid I don't know the origin of this dish or from whom it came, but it has proved to be a favorite among aficionados of Mexican cuisine. It needs nothing to accompany it except plain white rice (see page 161).

6 SMALL CHICKEN BREASTS

SALT AND FRESHLY GROUND PEPPER

¼ CUP (65 ML) BUTTER

¼ CUP (65 ML) VEGETABLE OIL

2 CUPS (500 ML) THINLY SLICED WHITE ONION

2¼ POUNDS (1 KG) POBLANO CHILES, CHARRED, PEELED, SEEDS AND VEINS REMOVED, AND
     CUT INTO NARROW STRIPS (SEE PAGE 469)

SALT TO TASTE

½ CUP (125 ML) MILK

2 CUPS (500 ML) CRÈME FRAÎCHE OR THICK SOUR CREAM (SEE PAGE 489)

SALT TO TASTE

4 OUNCES (115 G) CHIHUAHUA (OR CHEDDAR) CHEESE, GRATED (ABOUT 1 CUP/250 ML)

Remove the bones and skin from the breasts and cut each of them into 4 parts. Season them well with salt and pepper.

Heat the butter and the oil together in a large skillet and fry the chicken for a few moments on both sides until lightly browned. Drain and set them aside.

In the same fat, fry the onion until translucent. Add all but ⅔ cup (165 ml) of the chile strips to the onion with salt. Cover the pan and cook over medium heat for about 5 minutes, shaking the pan from time to time to avoid sticking.

Blend the reserved chile strips with the milk until smooth. Add the sour cream and blend for a few seconds longer. Add the salt at the last moment since it tends to curdle the sauce.

Preheat the oven to 350°F (180°C).

Arrange half of the chicken pieces in an ovenproof dish. Cover them with half of the chile strips and half of the sauce. Repeat the layers.

Bake until the chicken is cooked—about 30 minutes. Sprinkle with the cheese and return to the oven until melted.

NOTE: You can prepare things well ahead of time—the breasts can be fried, the chiles cooked, and the sauce blended, but do not assemble it until a few moments before it is to go into the oven.

This dish is best eaten as soon as it is cooked; it is not to be frozen.

POLLO EN RELLENO DE PAN Chicken Fried with Bread Crumbs

SEÑORA MARÍA LUISA DE MARTÍNEZ
SERVES 6   MICHOACÁN

I first ate chicken cooked this way in the home of María Luisa and her husband, Dr. Pedro Daniel Martínez, two of the most knowledgeable people I know on Mexican regional food. María Luisa is one of the truly great creative cooks and has given me hours of her time, year after year, talking to me about food and explaining the nuances that make Mexican food something very special. She and her husband were born and brought up in Michoacán, a state which for me has some of the best regional food in the republic. They have never found this dish in restaurants or cookbooks: it is muy casero *(real home cooking).*

A 4-POUND (1.8-KG) CHICKEN, CUT INTO SEVERAL PIECES

$^1/_2$ SMALL WHITE ONION

2 GARLIC CLOVES, THINLY SLICED

5 PEPPERCORNS

SALT TO TASTE

3 MEDIUM CARROTS (ABOUT 8 OUNCES/225 G), SCRAPED AND CUT INTO $^1/_2$-INCH (1.5-CM) CUBES

3 MEDIUM ZUCCHINI (12 OUNCES/340 G), CUT INTO $^1/_2$-INCH (1.5-CM) CUBES

3 TABLESPOONS VEGETABLE OIL

$^1/_4$ CUP (65 ML) THINLY SLICED WHITE ONION

1 POUND (450 G) TOMATOES, BROILED (SEE PAGE 490)

3 TABLESPOONS RAISINS

2 TABLESPOONS SLIVERED ALMONDS

1 CHORIZO, CRUMBLED AND FRIED

3 JALAPEÑO CHILES EN ESCABECHE

2 TEASPOONS JUICE FROM THE CHILE CAN

$^1/_3$ CUP (85 ML) VEGETABLE OIL

1 $^1/_2$ CUPS (375 ML) DRIED BREAD CRUMBS

Put the chicken into a large pan with the onion, 1 garlic clove, the peppercorns, and salt, cover with cold water, and bring to a simmer. Continue simmering for about 15 minutes, add the carrots, and cook for 10 more minutes. Add the zucchini and continue cooking over low heat until the chicken is just tender and the vegetables still a little al dente, about 10 minutes. Strain, reserving the stock.

Heat the oil in a flameproof casserole and gently fry the onion and remaining garlic until translucent.

Blend the tomatoes to a fairly smooth sauce and add to the onion with ½ cup (125 ml) of the reserved stock. Let the sauce reduce over medium heat for about 5 minutes.

Add the chicken pieces and vegetables, the raisins, almonds, chorizo, chiles, and chile juice and cook slowly for 8 minutes more, stirring the mixture from time to time to avoid sticking. The sauce by then should be reduced.

Heat the oil in a skillet, add the bread crumbs, and fry them, stirring them all the time until they are an even gold color, about 8 minutes. Then sprinkle the bread crumbs over the chicken and vegetables and serve immediately.

NOTE: If you want to prepare everything ahead of time you can do so quite easily by cooking it up to the point of reducing the sauce. About 15 minutes before serving, reheat and reduce the sauce—this will heat the chicken through sufficiently. Even the bread crumbs can be fried crisp and kept warm.

I do not suggest freezing.

POLLO A LA UVA Chicken with Grapes
SEÑORA ANAMARÍA DE ANDREA
SERVES 8   AGUASCALIENTES

I first went to Aguascalientes in the early seventies and was struck by the elegance of the food at the Hotel Francia. I was introduced to the owner and his wife, Señora AnaMaría de Andrea, who very generously gave me this recipe and the one for stuffed guavas, which have remained favorites in my kitchen (see also My Mexico*) throughout the years.*

In those years grape growing and wine making were very important in Aguascalientes, now overshadowed by many "clean" industries, dairying, and the growing of guavas on a large scale.

Very early on in the colonial period, vines were brought over from Spain and grafted onto an indigenous wild grape. They began to flourish on a small scale, especially in the missions from Oaxaca to Baja California. As they began to extend, the Spaniards feared that the wines produced would start to compete with Spanish wines brought over to the New World, and legislation was started in 1543 to discourage their cultivation. The final death blow came in 1771, when very heavy penalties were imposed for anyone found growing either vines or olives.

For the banquets that she catered, Señora Andrea presented the chickens on oval platters decorated with vine leaves and alternating black and white sugared grapes. It may be easier for serving to cut the chickens into large serving pieces before pouring on the sauce.

2 LARGE CHICKENS, ABOUT 3 POUNDS (1.35 KG) EACH
2 TABLESPOONS BUTTER
2 TABLESPOONS VEGETABLE OIL
SALT AND FRESHLY GROUND PEPPER
1 CUP (250 ML) THINLY SLICED WHITE ONION
2 GARLIC CLOVES
2 CELERY RIBS, CHOPPED
2 POUNDS (900 G) TOMATOES, ROUGHLY CHOPPED (ABOUT 4¼ CUPS/1.65 L)
6 SPRIGS FRESH THYME OR ¼ TEASPOON DRIED
6 SPRIGS FRESH MARJORAM OR ¼ TEASPOON DRIED
⅔ CUP (165 ML) DRY WHITE WINE
1 POUND (450 G) SEEDLESS WHITE GRAPES

Preheat the oven to 350°F (180°C).

Truss the chickens. Heat the butter and oil together in a deep flameproof casserole and brown the chickens well all over. Season them with salt and pepper, remove, and set them aside.

In the same fat, fry the onion, garlic, and celery over low heat for about 5 minutes. Add the tomatoes and herbs to the pan. Place the chickens on their sides in the tomato mixture. Cover the pan and bake for about 20 minutes.

Turn the chickens over and continue baking them until they are tender—20 to 25 minutes. Turn off the oven. Transfer them to a warmed serving dish and return to a warm oven.

Blend the vegetables and juices in the pan to a smooth sauce. Return to the pan and cook it over medium heat until it has reduced and thickened—about 10 minutes. Add the wine and continue cooking the sauce for about 3 minutes, stirring it from time to time. Add the grapes and continue cooking the sauce over brisk heat for 3 minutes more.

NOTE: Pour the sauce over and around the chickens and serve immediately.

POLLO EN BARBACOA COMITECA Barbecued Chicken Comitán

SEÑORA IRMA ESPINOZA

SERVES 6

CHIAPAS

Some friends and I were visiting the archaeological ruins near Comitán, Chiapas, and stopped at a small hacienda on the way back to eat. The owner's wife, Señora Irma Espinoza, served us this delicious chicken dish. The next day the Zapatistas entered San Cristóbal and our excursions came to an end!

Banana leaves are not that difficult to get these days (see page 462), but if you don't have them available then use kitchen parchment (I am trying to get aluminum foil out of my kitchen).

It is best to season the chicken the day before.

6 LARGE PORTIONS OF CHICKEN

2 ANCHO CHILES, SEEDS AND VEINS REMOVED

6 OUNCES (180 G) TOMATOES, ROUGHLY CHOPPED (ABOUT 1 ¼ CUPS/315 ML)

4 OUNCES (115 G) TOMATE VERDE, HUSKS REMOVED AND ROUGHLY CHOPPED
  (ABOUT 1 CUP/250 ML)

1 CUP (250 ML) ROUGHLY CHOPPED WHITE ONION

2 GARLIC CLOVES, ROUGHLY CHOPPED

4 PEPPERCORNS, CRUSHED

2 WHOLE CLOVES, CRUSHED

SALT TO TASTE

3 SPRIGS FRESH THYME, OR ¼ TEASPOON DRIED

1 MEXICAN BAY LEAF, BROKEN UP

1 TEASPOON MEXICAN DRIED OREGANO

½ CUP (125 ML) ROUGHLY CHOPPED FLAT-LEAF PARSLEY

¼ CUP (65 ML) SLIVERED ALMONDS

¼ CUP (65 ML) RAISINS

12 PITTED GREEN OLIVES, HALVED

BANANA LEAVES OR PARCHMENT TO COVER THE DISH

Place the chicken pieces in one layer in an ovenproof dish at least 3 inches (8 cm) deep and set aside while you prepare the seasoning paste.

Cover the ancho chiles with hot water and leave to soak for 5 minutes.

Put the tomatoes into a blender jar and blend well. Gradually add the drained anchos, tomate verde, onion, garlic, crushed spices, and salt and blend until fairly smooth. Pour over the chicken, cover, and refrigerate overnight.

Preheat the oven to 325°F (165°C).

The following day, turn the chicken pieces over to thoroughly coat with the sauce. Scatter the herbs, almonds, raisins, and olives over the surface, cover with 2 layers of banana leaf, and bake for about 35 minutes. Turn the chicken pieces over and baste well with the sauce. Cover the dish and continue baking until the chicken is tender and the sauce thickened—about 35 minutes more.

NOTE: Once it's cooked, this dish can sit for a couple of hours, but reduce the initial cooking time to allow for reheating so as not to overcook the chicken. I don't recommend freezing.

POLLO EN CUICLACOCHE Chicken in Cuiclacoche

SEÑORA PAULA R. DE GONZÁLEZ
SERVES 6   PUEBLA

I was leafing through a cookbook published in Tehuacán, Puebla, in 1976 and found this recipe, which I have slightly modified. I hope that Señora Paula R. de González will forgive me because I do thank her most sincerely for the recipe.

I have chosen to include this recipe for chicken with cuiclacoche *first and foremost because it is delicious—although it looks a mess—and because of America's present love affair with this intriguing fungus.*

Incidentally, in the intial pages of the book there is one called "Propositos de una ama de casa"—Resolutions of a Housewife. Among them were: "I will make better meals, prepare more attractive dishes, discover the pleasure of setting a beautiful table. . . . I will invent ways of teaching my family to eat not only what they like, but what is good for them, and I will learn how to teach them good manners by setting the example." There were others which I found very touching.

I have modified the recipe by using melted chicken fat instead of oil and chicken broth instead of water. I would also suggest that the chicken be very slightly undercooked and the dish set aside to season for an hour before serving. It can then be reheated without overcooking the chicken. I serve this dish with plain white rice.

¼ CUP (65 ML) MELTED CHICKEN FAT OR VEGETABLE OIL

12 LARGE CHICKEN PIECES, ABOUT 3 POUNDS (1.35 KG)

2 CUPS (500 ML) THINLY SLICED WHITE ONION

2 GARLIC CLOVES, FINELY CHOPPED

1 ½ POUNDS (675 G) CUICLACOCHE, ROUGHLY CHOPPED (ABOUT 6 ¼ CUPS/1.563 L)

SALT TO TASTE

1 CUP (250 ML) LIGHT CHICKEN BROTH OR WATER

4 POBLANO CHILES, CHARRED, PEELED, SEEDS AND VEINS REMOVED, AND CUT INTO STRIPS
   (SEE PAGE 469)

⅓ CUP (85 ML) FIRMLY PACKED, ROUGHLY CHOPPED EPAZOTE LEAVES

1 CUP (250 ML) WATER OR LIGHT CHICKEN BROTH

Heat the fat in a deep flameproof casserole or skillet and fry the chicken pieces, a few at a time, until golden brown. Drain and set aside.

Remove all but ¼ cup (65 ml) fat from the pan. Add the onion and garlic and fry gently without browning until translucent—about 2 minutes. Add the *cuiclacoche*, sprinkle well with salt, and continue cooking, scraping the bottom of the pan to avoid sticking, for about 10 minutes.

Add the chicken pieces and broth, cover the pan, and continue cooking over low heat for about 30 minutes.

Add the chile strips and epazote and continue cooking covered over low heat until the chicken is almost tender—another 20 minutes. Set aside to season (see note above).

NOTE: I do not recommend freezing this dish.

Pescado en Tikin Xik ※ *Broiled Fish Seasoned with Achiote*

Sierra en Escabeche ※ *Yucatecan Soused Fish*

Pescado en Ajo Quemado ※ *Fish with Charred Garlic*

Ceviche ※ *Raw Fish Marinated in Lime Juice*

Pámpano en Salsa Verde ※ *Pompano in Green Sauce*

Pescado en Cilantro ※ *Fish Cooked in Cilantro*

Pescado Alcaparrado ※ *Fish in Caper Sauce*

Huachinango a la Veracruzana ※ *Veracruz Red Snapper*

Pescado Relleno ※ *Stuffed Fish*

Jaibas en Chilpachole ※ *Crabs in a Chile and Tomato Broth*

Jaibas Rellenas ※ *Stuffed Blue Crabs*

Arroz a la Tumbada ※ *Rice with Shrimps*

Camarones en Escabeche Rojo ※ *Shrimps Pickled in Red Chile Sauce*

Camarones en Pipián ※ *Shrimps in Pumpkin Seed Sauce*

Crepas de Camarón en Chile Pasilla

    ※ *Shrimp Crepes with Pasilla Sauce*

Saragalla de Pescado ※ *Shredded Fish Tamiahua*

Albóndigas de Camarones ※ *Shrimp Balls*

Pescado Enchilado ※ *Broiled Fish Seasoned with Chile Paste*

Relleno de Guavino ※ *Fish and Shrimp Sausage*

The show of fish . . . for it was of such variety and beauty, as I have never before witnessed, nor even conceived. I was aware that the finny race presented more resplendent hues and varieties of forms, when fresh from the water, than birds and insects, but now I became convinced of this truth. Hundreds of various species glowing in all the colors of the prism; surpassing the lustre of precious gems and all the brilliant tints of the humming birds, covered the stones of the market place of Vera Cruz.

—FROM W. H. BULLOCK, *Six Months Residence and Travel in Mexico,* NINETEENTH CENTURY

PESCADOS Y MARISCOS There is an awful lot of coast to Mexico, but some day I am going to do the grand tour. I suppose I would inevitably end up in my favorite places eating my favorite seafood, but I also want to fill in the gaps and see the rest. I would start off, of course, in Ensenada and look for the pismo clams—they are called just plain *almeja* (clam) there. Last time I could only find them cut up into a cocktail—and if there is one thing that is death to seafood it's a cocktail and that simply awful catsup-base sauce. I had wanted to see the shell and I had wanted to see it opened in front of me. After a compromise meal of a rather tough turtle steak ranchera, I came out of the restaurant only to find the clams I had been looking for on a little street-side stand. The pismo has a large whitish shell with a pink, juicy muscle inside— as sweet and delicious a clam as you will find anywhere.

As I work my way down the west coast, I would have several meals of *totoaba*, a large basslike fish that abounds in the northern part of the Gulf of California—wonderful eating. Then Guaymas for shrimps before heading to Mazatlán. The favorite midmorning snack from the street carts there is the fat, dark, ridged-shelled *pata de mula* (mule's foot). I would go to Mamucas for lunch before the crowd arrives to have a large bowl of *sopa marinera*, a wonderfully flavored and robust fish and shellfish soup, with lots and lots of *callos de hacha* to follow—they are pinna clams that could easily be taken for scallops.

I remember my last visit to Zihuatenejo with Paul just before we moved to New York. We were spending a few days fishing with friends. I remember we had just caught a large dorado—so beautiful in the water that it seemed a crime to pull it out and watch the lovely silvery-gold and blues fade. We pulled in to a sandy beach for a picnic and Goyo, the boatman, started a fire. In a crude frame of *huisache* branches, tied up well with strips of bark, he roasted half the dorado, cut off one large fillet, after seasoning it with lime juice and rough salt. When the time came for him to turn it over, before our astonished eyes he walked out knee-deep into the sea and held the fish under water for a couple of minutes. Then he returned to finish cooking it on the other side. There were hot tortillas; no more was necessary.

I remember eating oysters just brought in from the sea; the smallest, sweetest shrimps; and broiled sierra by the water's edge on the Gulf of Tehuantepec after a long, hot ride from Oaxaca one August. Even the sea was hot to swim in, but the beer was very cold and the metallic freshness of the oysters and the lime juice with our food refreshed us.

From there I would continue almost due east to Palenque. I was there once to visit the Mayan ruins, continuing on to Bonampak and up the Usumacinta River, which divides Mexico from Guatemala, to Yaxchilán. When our plane bumped down on what was no more than a few yards of loose stones, we were met by a reception committee.

It was the village schoolmaster's birthday, and our guide into the *selva*, a local rancher and hunter, had, with other friends, been helping him celebrate for quite some time that morning. So we were greeted warmly and driven off in the back of an old truck to share the ceremonial food. They were roasting a *peje-lagarto*—a prehistoric fish with thick tough scales, a species of gar—from the nearby river, over a wood fire. As the flesh was cooked, it was shredded, seasoned with some ground achiote, epazote leaves, and salt, and eaten in tacos.

By the next day I had persuaded the owner of a local restaurant to have a woman in the village, who was expert in preparing the native dishes, make us some *shote y momo*. *Shote* is the local name of a freshwater snail with an elongated shell about 1½ inches (4 cm) long. The snail is purged for a day or so in fresh water with *momo* leaves. *Momo* is the local name for *hoja santa*, the large heart-shaped leaf used a great deal in the cooking of Oaxaca, Veracruz, and Chiapas. It has a very strong flavor of anise and something more that defies description. The snails are then cooked and the broth seasoned with the ground leaves of chaya *(Cnidoscolus chayamansa)* and thickened with a little tortilla dough. It was served in deep bowls, and on the side, to extract the snails, were large tough thorns about 2 inches (5 cm) long.

And thence a brief stopover in Tabasco, where the large moro crabs are stuffed and then heated through in a pumpkin seed sauce, flavored and colored with achiote.

It would be worthwhile going back to the Bal Hai at Cozumel briefly to prevail upon Señora Moguel to prepare the regional lobster soup—*sac kol* in Mayan, which translated literally means "white broth." The lobster should be just out of the sea, freshly killed and cleaned of the spines and inedible parts. The rest is cut up with the shell and cooked, together with the head, in water seasoned in the typical Yucatecan way with toasted oregano, onion, and a roasted head of garlic. The broth is thickened with a little masa and colored with some ground achiote. While you're waiting for it, you have with your tequila the local appetizers—turtle egg sausage and the little, acidy berries of a bush that grows in the sandy soil in parts of southern Mexico—called nance *(Byrsonima crassifolia)*. The sausage is made by the local fishermen when they are out on their fishing and turtle-hunting expeditions. The turtle intestines are cleaned and stuffed with the eggs, and then the sausage is boiled so that the eggs are cooked. Señora Moguel also made a very good turtle stew—*ajiaco*—with spices, tomatoes, and white wine. But I prefer the more delicate river turtle as they prepare it in Tabasco, in a green sauce of various ground herbs and leaves of the chile plant.

I should never be forgiven by the Campechanos and Yucatecos if I didn't mention their favorite, *pan de cazón*. The *cazón* is a dogfish or small shark, the rather dry flesh of which is cooked and shredded and stuffed into an inflated tortilla with some bean paste—just like *panuchos*—and is then covered with a tomato sauce. The best cooks I talked to insisted that this was the correct version, and not the tortillas stacked in layers with the beans, fish, and sauce in between, as served in the restaurants.

Of all the fish in Mexico perhaps the greatest delicacy of them all is the *blanco de Pátzcuaro*—the famous white fish, a meal made upon which Calderón de la Barca said "would have rejoiced the heart of an epicure." You can, of course, eat it in the Mexico City restaurants, but it's much better to go to Lake Pátzcuaro itself in the lovely Michoacán countryside and eat it fried, fresh out of the water at El Gordo, the small restaurant at the embarcadero—the wharf for the little boats that ply to and fro across the lake. Or try the local *caldo michi*—a light vegetable broth, flavored with fresh coriander, and to which small white fish called *charales* are added at the very last moment so that the flesh is just tender but does not fall apart.

It is recorded that Montezuma and his nobles ate shrimps. Sahagún describes a casserole of shrimps with tomatoes and ground squash seeds. Their seafood was brought up from the gulf to Tenochtitlán, the Aztec capital—where Mexico City stands today—by relays of runners in about twelve hours, or so it is said.

I am frankly addicted to dried shrimps, which are used throughout the country. From as near the coast as Escuinapa in Sonora, and Nayarit, come the famous *sopes de vigilia*. As their name implies, they are prepared on days when meat is forbidden and, of course, are especially popular during Lent. Dried shrimps are ground up and mixed with tortilla dough; rather thick little tortillas are made and cooked on the comal and then well pinched up around the edges to form sopes to hold the scrambled eggs, nopales, and potato that are piled onto them. They are then sprinkled with a tomato sauce and topped with shredded lettuce and radish flowers.

Those who have eaten *cabrito* in the Correo Español in Mexico City will never forget the fiery little cups of dried shrimp soup that is served first; and there is the less harsh *caldo de camarón* (shrimp broth) served in the bars of Tuxtla Gutiérrez. And by far the most popular and esteemed dish served during Lent and at Christmas Eve dinner is *romeritos con tortas de camarón*, also called *revoltijo de romeritos*. (The *tortas de camarón* are fritters of dried shrimp in a mole sauce with stringy little greens called *romeritos*.)

Mexico has 6,000 kilometers of coastline touching on the Gulf of California or Mar de Cortes, the Pacific Ocean, the Gulf of Mexico, and the Caribbean, which provide endless varieties of seafood for home consumption and for export. But there are also fish and mollusks in the rivers and lakes of Mexico that provide ingredients for very special local dishes as well as a livelihood for many river and lakeside fishing communities.

In *Cuisines of Mexico* I described a wishful journey and a retracing of steps around the coastline and into the interior, so let me go back to that time, interpolating some more recent experiences in the recipes that follow.

PESCADO EN TIKIN XIK Broiled Fish Seasoned with Achiote

SERVES 6   YUCATÁN AND CAMPECHE

One could imagine that fishermen invented this method of broiling fish over mangrove wood. The words tikin xik *mean dried chile, although very little is in fact used in the seasoning.*

2 GROUPERS OR RED SNAPPERS, ABOUT 2½ POUNDS (1.125 KG) EACH
¼ CUP (65 ML) OLIVE OIL

THE SEASONING PASTE

1 TABLESPOON ACHIOTE SEEDS
¼ TEASPOON PEPPERCORNS
SALT TO TASTE
¼ TEASPOON DRIED MEXICAN OREGANO, YUCATECAN IF POSSIBLE, TOASTED
¼ TEASPOON CHILE SECO
3 GARLIC CLOVES
¼ CUP (65 ML) SEVILLE ORANGE JUICE OR MILD WHITE VINEGAR

TO SERVE

TOASTED MEXICAN OREGANO
HABANERO CHILES, CHOPPED
SLICED AVOCADO
CEBOLLAS ENCURTIDAS YUCATECAS (PAGE 248)
SLICED TOMATOES
SLICED SEVILLE ORANGES

Do not have the scales removed from the fish. Have the heads and tails removed and the fish opened out flat in one piece. Remove the backbone.

Grind and blend all the ingredients for the seasoning paste to a smooth consistency. Spread the paste, not too thickly, over the flesh (opened side of the fish) and set aside to season for at least 2 hours.

Brush the seasoned side of the fish with the oil and cook it, seasoned side down, over the charcoal or under the broiler for 5 to 8 minutes. Turn the fish over and cook it on the skin side for a slightly longer period or until flesh is *just* cooked through—about 15 minutes, depending on the thickness of the fish.

Serve the fish hot with fresh tortillas so that everyone can make his own tacos, with small dishes of the accompanying ingredients served separately.

SIERRA EN ESCABECHE Yucatecan Soused Fish
SERVES 6

This is a very fresh and fragrant dish and it far outshines any other regional variation of seafood en escabeche, or souse. I think it is best an hour or so after it is made and served at room temperature, although it will keep for a day or two in the refrigerator—however, the fish tends to toughen with long standing.

I have read recipes that call for added aromatics like the leaves of allspice, wild guava, or orange trees.

Although sierra—kingfish—is traditionally used, I sometimes like to prepare it in a more colorful way with salmon steaks.

PREPARING THE FISH

1 CUP (250 ML) WATER

¼ CUP (65 ML) FRESH LIME JUICE

1 TEASPOON SALT

6 1-INCH- (2.5-CM-) THICK STEAKS OF SIERRA OR SALMON (ABOUT 3 POUNDS/1.35 KG)

STEP 1

½ TEASPOON PEPPERCORNS

½ TEASPOON CORIANDER SEEDS

½ TEASPOON CUMIN SEEDS

2 WHOLE CLOVES

½-INCH (1.5-CM) PIECE OF CINNAMON STICK

2 WHOLE ALLSPICE

2 GARLIC CLOVES

½ CUP (125 ML) WINE VINEGAR

½ CUP (125 ML) WATER

½ TEASPOON DRIED MEXICAN OREGANO, YUCATECAN IF POSSIBLE, TOASTED

2 MEXICAN BAY LEAVES

10 SMALL GARLIC CLOVES, TOASTED (SEE PAGE 492), PEELED AND LEFT WHOLE

SALT TO TASTE

½ TEASPOON GRANULATED SUGAR

STEP 2

½ CUP (125 ML) OLIVE OIL

¾ CUP (185 ML) WINE VINEGAR

1 ¼ CUPS (315 ML) WATER

STEP 3

¹/₂ CUP (125 ML) VEGETABLE OIL

6 GÜERO CHILES, TOASTED (SEE PAGE 464)

4 CUPS (1 L) THINLY SLICED PURPLE ONIONS, BLANCHED AS FOR CEBOLLAS ENCURTIDAS
    YUCATECAS (PAGE 248)

Pour the water, lime juice, and salt over the fish and set it aside for 1 hour, turning it
once during that time.

Pulverize the spices in an electric grinder or mortar. Crush the 2 garlic cloves and
grind them to a paste with the spices. Put the spice-garlic paste into the saucepan with
the rest of the ingredients in Step 1 and bring the mixture to a boil. Add the oil, vinegar, and water and once again bring the mixture to a boil. Set aside and keep hot.

Dry the fish slices thoroughly. Heat the oil in a skillet and fry them about 5 minutes
on each side. They should be barely cooked. Place them in a serving dish and pour the
hot souse over them. Add the chiles and onions. Set the fish aside to season for at least
1 hour in the souse.

Serve at room temperature.

PESCADO EN AJO QUEMADO Fish with Charred Garlic

SEÑORA ISELA RODRÍGUEZ DE ALONSO

SERVES 6   YUCATÁN AND CAMPECHE

*This method and the flavors of the char-cooked ingredients are typical of the cooking of the
Yucatecan peninsula. Señora Isela also uses a fish head to give the sauce a more gelatinous
quality.*

I prefer to serve this dish with crusty French-type bread.

6 FISH STEAKS ABOUT ³/₄ INCH (2 CM) THICK, ABOUT 2¹/₂ POUNDS (1.125 KG)

A FISH HEAD, ABOUT 12 OUNCES (340 G)

3 TABLESPOONS FRESH LIME JUICE

SALT TO TASTE

2 GARLIC CLOVES, ROUGHLY CHOPPED

1 HEAPED TABLESPOON RECADO DE TODA CLASE (PAGE 484)

1¹/₂ TABLESPOONS BITTER ORANGE JUICE OR FRUITY VINEGAR

¹/₃ CUP (85 ML) PLUS 2 TABLESPOONS OLIVE OIL

1 ½ CUPS (375 ML) THICKLY SLICED WHITE ONIONS

1 LARGE GREEN BELL PEPPER, SEEDS AND VEINS REMOVED, THINLY SLICED

12 OUNCES (340 G) TOMATOES, THINLY SLICED

1 SMALL BUNCH FLAT-LEAF PARSLEY, ROUGHLY CHOPPED

2 SMALL HEADS GARLIC, WELL CHARRED AND CUT IN HALF HORIZONTALLY (SEE PAGE 492)

6 X-CAT-IK CHILES, CHARRED AND LEFT WHOLE, WITHOUT PEELING (SEE PAGE 464)

1 HEAPED TABLESPOON DRIED MEXICAN OREGANO, YUCATECAN IF POSSIBLE, TOASTED AND
  CRUMBLED

Season the fish, including the head, with the lime juice and salt and set aside for about 15 minutes.

In a small bowl crush the garlic together with the *recado* and dilute with the orange juice. Spread a thin coating over the fish (and head) and set aside to season for at least 1 hour.

Preheat the oven to 350°F (180°C).

Heat the ⅓ cup (85 ml) olive oil in a skillet, add the onions and bell pepper with a sprinkling of salt, and fry over low heat until wilted, about 2 minutes. Add the tomato slices and continue frying until some of the juice has evaporated—about 3 minutes.

Put one half of the tomato mixture in an ovenproof dish into which the fish and head will fit in one layer, sprinkle with half of the parsley, and cover with the rest of the tomato mixture. Place the garlic halves and chiles over the surface and sprinkle with the oregano and the remaining 2 tablespoons olive oil.

Cover the dish and bake for about 20 minutes. Remove from the oven and baste well with the juices, then cover and bake for 20 more minutes or until barely cooked. Set aside to season for about ½ hour before serving and then reheat gently to avoid overcooking the fish.

NOTE: The fish can be seasoned ahead and the tomato mixture cooked, but the dish should be assembled just before cooking.

CEVICHE Raw Fish Marinated in Lime Juice

BASED ON A RECIPE BY SEÑORA JOSEFINA VELÁSQUEZ DE LEÓN
SERVES 6   GUERRERO

Although I have capitulated and used the accepted spelling of ceviche, one of the leading gastronomes in Mexico in the sixties and seventies was a Spaniard by birth, Don Amando Farga. He insisted on using a b rather than a v, saying that the word came from the word cebar meaning—among other things—to saturate or penetrate. He also believed that this method of "cooking" without heat could be traced to the Orient when trade routes were opened up during the colonial period by the Spaniards between the Philippines and the Pacific ports of Latin America. Indeed many of these countries have their own recipes for preparing ceviche.

1 POUND (450 G) SKINNED FILLETS OF SIERRA (KINGFISH)
JUICE OF 6 OR 7 LARGE LIMES (1 ¼ TO 1 ½ CUPS/315 TO 375 ML), DILUTED WITH ABOUT
    ½ CUP (125 ML) WATER
12 OUNCES (340 G) TOMATOES, FINELY CHOPPED (2 SCANT CUPS/475 ML)
3 OR 4 CANNED SERRANO CHILES EN ESCABECHE
¼ CUP (65 ML) OLIVE OIL
½ TEASPOON DRIED MEXICAN OREGANO
½ TEASPOON SALT, OR TO TASTE
FRESHLY GROUND PEPPER

TO SERVE
1 SMALL AVOCADO, SLICED
1 SMALL PURPLE ONION, SLICED INTO RINGS
2 TABLESPOONS CHOPPED CILANTRO

Cut the fish into small cubes, about ½ inch (1.5 cm), and cover them with the lime juice. Set the fish aside in the bottom of the refrigerator until the fish loses its transparent look and becomes opaque, about 3 hours. Stir the pieces from time to time so that they get evenly "cooked" in the lime juice.

Add the tomatoes with the rest of the ingredients.

Set the ceviche aside in the bottom of the refrigerator for at least 1 hour to season. (You should serve it chilled, but not so cold that the oil congeals.)

Before serving, top each portion with slices of avocado and onion rings and sprinkle with a little chopped cilantro, if desired. Best eaten the same day.

PÁMPANO EN SALSA VERDE Pompano in Green Sauce

BALUARTES HOTEL, CAMPECHE
SERVES 6 AS A FIRST COURSE   CAMPECHE

I heard of this method of preparing pompano when I was traveling to collect recipes for The Cuisines of Mexico *in the late sixties. I could never find it on the menu of any of the popular restaurants, but I finally persuaded the cook at the Baluartes Hotel in Campeche, the only one on the* malecón *at that time, to prepare it for me. He rounded up the ingredients in the capacious but rather disorderly kitchen and cooked it in a shallow pan on top of the stove. It was delicious! I hate to say it, but it is perfect for anyone on a diet. The sauce should be blended and cooked at the last moment or it will lose its fresh color and flavor.*

2 POMPANO, EACH ABOUT 1 $\frac{1}{4}$ POUNDS (570 G)

$\frac{1}{4}$ TEASPOON PEPPERCORNS

$\frac{1}{4}$ TEASPOON CUMIN SEEDS

$\frac{1}{2}$ TEASPOON SALT

JUICE OF 1 LARGE LIME

THE SAUCE

$\frac{1}{3}$ CUP (85 ML) WATER

1 TABLESPOON MILD WHITE VINEGAR

2 GARLIC CLOVES, ROUGHLY CHOPPED

$\frac{1}{2}$ GREEN PEPPER, SEEDS AND VEINS REMOVED, ROUGHLY CHOPPED

1 SERRANO CHILE, ROUGHLY CHOPPED

3 SPRIGS FRESH CILANTRO, ROUGHLY CHOPPED

3 SPRIGS FLAT-LEAF PARSLEY, ROUGHLY CHOPPED

6 SCALLIONS

$\frac{1}{8}$ TEASPOON DRIED MEXICAN OREGANO, YUCATECAN IF POSSIBLE

1 POUND (450 G) GREEN (UNRIPE) TOMATOES

SALT TO TASTE

$\frac{1}{3}$ CUP (85 ML) OLIVE OIL

Have the fish cleaned, leaving the heads and tails on.

Grind the spices together dry, and mix with the lime juice.

Prick the fish all over with a coarse-tined fork and rub the seasoning in well. Set aside, in an ovenproof dish, to season for at least $\frac{1}{2}$ hour.

Preheat the oven to 300°F (150°C).

Put the water and vinegar into the blender jar and add the sauce ingredients except the oil a little at a time, blending after each addition until you have a slightly textured mixture.

Put a little of the oil under the fish, pour the sauce over the fish with the rest of the oil, and bake, loosely covered, for about 20 minutes. Turn the fish over carefully and bake for a further 15 minutes, basting with the sauce from time to time.

NOTE: This dish should be prepared and cooked right away or the sauce will discolor.

PESCADO EN CILANTRO Fish Cooked in Cilantro

SEÑORITA EVELYN BOURCHIER

SERVES 6 AS A FIRST COURSE   MEXICO CITY

This dish seems to call for an excessive amount of cilantro, but it cooks down to practically nothing and the flavor is not as strong as one would think—except, of course, for those who can't abide cilantro! The chile, onion, and cilantro flavors combined with the fiery juice from the can of chiles make for a unique sauce.

The friends in whose house I first tried this unusual fish dish also added large, unpeeled shrimps to the sauce. Although they did not know the origin of the recipe, they had found it in a charming little book printed privately in Mexico City: Herbs for Pot and Body *by Evelyn Bourchier and José Roldán Parrodí.*

A 3- TO 3½-POUND (1.35- TO 1.575-KG) RED SNAPPER

1 SCANT TEASPOON SALT

FRESHLY GROUND PEPPER

1½ CUPS (375 ML) THINLY SLICED WHITE ONIONS

⅓ CUP (85 ML) FRESH LIME JUICE

⅓ CUP (85 ML) OLIVE OIL

3 JALAPEÑO CHILES EN ESCABECHE

3 TABLESPOONS JUICE FROM THE CHILE CAN

2 CUPS (500 ML) ROUGHLY CHOPPED CILANTRO

Have the fish cleaned, leaving the head and tail on.

Prick the fish well on both sides with a coarse-tined fork, and rub it with the salt and pepper. Place the fish onto a baking dish with half the onions underneath and the rest on top. Pour the lime juice over it and set it aside for about 1 hour, turning it over once during that time.

Preheat the oven to 350°F (180°C).

Cover the dish and bake the fish for about 15 minutes on each side.

Add the rest of the ingredients and continue cooking the fish, covered, until it is just cooked, basting it from time to time with the juices in the dish—about 20 minutes.

NOTE: This dish is also delicious cold, if there is any left over.

PESCADO ALCAPARRADO Fish in Caper Sauce
SERVES 6

One of the many excellent cooks I met in Tabasco, alas whose name I cannot find, gave me this unusual recipe. The fish is covered with a pale green, creamy sauce.

An excellent fish for this dish is the robalo, a name you will often see on menus in Mexican restaurants. It is the robalo blanco *or snook, a pikelike fish of the* Centropomus *genus that has a rich, white flesh. With the red snapper, I suppose it is one of the most widely used fish in Mexico, particularly along the Gulf Coast, and apparently has been for a very long time. Robalo bones have been identified in kitchen hearths excavated at the Olmec site of San Lorenzo, dating back to 1200–1000 B.C. A very good substitute for robalo would be striped bass or wall-eyed pike.*

THE FISH BROTH

8 OUNCES (225 G) CARROTS, SCRAPED AND THINLY SLICED

8 OUNCES (225 G) TURNIPS, PEELED AND THINLY SLICED

2 MEXICAN BAY LEAVES

⅓ CUP (85 ML) THINLY SLICED WHITE ONION

12 PEPPERCORNS

2 TABLESPOONS FRESH LIME JUICE

4 CUPS (1 L) WATER, OR ENOUGH TO JUST COVER THE FISH

SALT TO TASTE

A 3-POUND (1.35-KG) STRIPED BASS OR SNOOK

THE SAUCE

3 OUNCES (85 G) BLANCHED ALMONDS, ROUGHLY CHOPPED (ABOUT ¾ CUP/170 ML)

1 ½ CUPS (375 ML) RESERVED FISH BROTH

½ CUP (125 ML) FRESH BREAD CRUMBS

4 LARGE LETTUCE LEAVES, TORN INTO PIECES

1 TABLESPOON LARGE CAPERS, RINSED

1 SPRIG FLAT-LEAF PARSLEY

4 GARLIC CLOVES

¼ CUP (65 ML) ROUGHLY SLICED WHITE ONION

½ CUP (125 ML) OLIVE OIL

SALT TO TASTE

THE TOPPING

THE HEART OF A ROMAINE LETTUCE

1 TABLESPOON LARGE CAPERS, RINSED

12 PITTED GREEN OLIVES

¾ CUP (185 ML) THINLY SLICED WHITE ONION

6 OUNCES (180 G) TOMATOES, THINLY SLICED (ABOUT 1 CUP/250 ML)

Put all the ingredients for the broth in a large saucepan and simmer for about 30 minutes. Strain and set aside but keep warm.

Clean the fish, leaving the head and tail on, and place in a shallow flameproof baking dish. Cover the fish with the warm broth and poach on top of the stove over low heat until just cooked—about 20 minutes. Pour off the broth and set aside.

Preheat the oven to 350°F (180°C).

In a coffee/spice grinder, grind the almonds as fine as possible—this should make about ½ cup (125 ml). Put 1 cup (250 ml) of the reserved broth into a blender jar, add the ground almonds, bread crumbs, lettuce leaves, capers, parsley, 2 garlic cloves, and the onion, and blend to a slightly textured sauce. Set aside.

Heat the oil gently, add the remaining 2 garlic cloves, and as soon as they start to brown, remove with a slotted spoon and discard. Stir in the blended sauce, add ½ cup reserved broth, and cook over low heat until well seasoned—about 8 minutes.

Pour the sauce over the fish and put into the oven until well heated through—about 15 minutes.

Put the lettuce leaves around the dish and top with the rest of the ingredients.

HUACHINANGO A LA VERACRUZANA Veracruz Red Snapper

ARQUITECTO JUAN O'GORMAN

SERVES 6 AS A FIRST COURSE   VERACRUZ

Huachinango a la Veracruzana is without doubt the best known and favorite Mexican fish dish, along perhaps with ceviche. There are many versions of this recipe, some including sweet red pepper and other ingredients, but this one remains first in my book. I first tried it at a dinner in the home of Juan O'Gorman, the famous painter, muralist, and architect, and his wife, Helen, a distinguished botanist and painter. It was a recipe he had brought back from Veracruz when working there on a school-architectural project. It has met with great success over the years, especially in Tokyo where I served it during a Mexican food promotion.

If the true Gulf red snapper is not available then you can substitute rock cod (on the West coast), red fish (Texas), or even — and it is delicious — wall-eyed pike (Minnesota).

A 3-POUND (1.35-KG) RED SNAPPER

I TEASPOON SALT, OR TO TASTE

2 TABLESPOONS FRESH LIME JUICE

$^1\!/_4$ CUP (65 ML) PLUS 3 TABLESPOONS OLIVE OIL

I CUP (250 ML) THINLY SLICED WHITE ONION

2 LARGE GARLIC CLOVES, SLICED

2 POUNDS (900 G) TOMATOES, FINELY CHOPPED (ABOUT 5 $^1\!/_3$ CUPS/1.335 L)

2 MEXICAN BAY LEAVES

$^1\!/_4$ TEASPOON DRIED MEXICAN OREGANO

12 PITTED GREEN OLIVES OR STUFFED WITH RED PEPPER, CUT INTO HALVES

2 TABLESPOONS LARGE CAPERS

2 JALAPEÑO CHILES EN ESCABECHE, OR CHILES LARGOS, CUT INTO STRIPS

$^1\!/_2$ TEASPOON SALT, OR TO TASTE

Preheat the oven to 325°F (165°C).

Have the fish cleaned, leaving the head and tail on. Prick the fish on both sides with a coarse-tined fork, rub in the salt and lime juice, and set it aside in an ovenproof dish to season for about 2 hours.

Heat $^1\!/_4$ cup (65 ml) oil in a skillet and fry the onion and garlic, without browning, until they are soft. Add the tomatoes, with the rest of the ingredients, to the pan and cook the sauce over brisk heat until it is well seasoned and some of the juice has evaporated—about 10 minutes. Pour the sauce over the fish.

Sprinkle the remaining 3 tablespoons oil over the sauce and bake the fish for about 20 minutes, loosely covered, on one side. Turn the fish over very carefully and continue baking it until it is just tender—about 20 minutes. Baste the fish frequently with the sauce during the cooking time.

PESCADO RELLENO Stuffed Fish

SEÑORA ROSINA GONZÁLEZ

SERVES 6

VERACRUZ

I was given this delicious recipe by the mother of a friend, Gonzalo González, who came from Veracruz and was an excellent cook. She was wonderfully patient with my endless questions as we sat for hours talking about her regional dishes.

While the original recipe calls for small red snappers, you could substitute flounder or other fish suitable for stuffing.

6 SMALL RED SNAPPERS (ABOUT 12 OUNCES/340 G EACH), ONE FOR EACH PERSON

6 GARLIC CLOVES

SALT AND PEPPER TO TASTE

1/3 CUP (85 ML) FRESH LIME JUICE

2 TABLESPOONS BUTTER

2 TABLESPOONS OLIVE OIL

1 1/4 CUPS (315 ML) FINELY CHOPPED WHITE ONION

1 POUND (900 G) TOMATOES, FINELY CHOPPED (ABOUT 2 2/3 CUPS/665 ML)

8 OUNCES (225 G) RAW SHRIMPS, PEELED AND DEVEINED

8 OUNCES (225 G) RAW SCALLOPS

2 TABLESPOONS FINELY CHOPPED FLAT-LEAF PARSLEY

SALT AND PEPPER TO TASTE

8 OUNCES (225 G) COOKED CRABMEAT

6 TABLESPOONS MELTED BUTTER

Have the fish cleaned, leaving the head and tail on. Have as much of the backbone removed as possible to form a good pocket for stuffing the fish without completely opening it up.

Crush the garlic and mix it to a paste with the salt, pepper, and lime juice. Prick the fish all over on both sides with a coarse-tined fork and rub the paste in well—inside and out. Set the fish aside to season for at least 1 hour.

Preheat the oven to 350°F (180°C) and prepare the stuffing.

Melt the butter with the oil in a skillet and cook the onion until translucent. Add the tomatoes and cook them over fairly high heat until some of the juice has evaporated.

Cut the shrimps into halves and the scallops into quarters. Add them, with the parsley and seasoning, to the tomato mixture and let cook over medium heat until the scallops and shrimps are just tender—about 10 minutes. Stir in the crabmeat.

Stuff each fish with about ½ cup (125 ml) of the filling and sew it up. Put half of the butter into a shallow ovenproof dish, place the fish side by side, and sprinkle them with the remaining butter. Cover the dish and bake until the fish are tender—about 20 minutes.

N O T E : Everything can be done well ahead of time up to the point of stuffing the fish. That should be done at the last moment so that the stuffing does not get watery.

JAIBAS EN CHILPACHOLE Crabs in a Chile and Tomato Broth
SEÑORA MARÍA CANO CARLÍN
SERVES 6
                                                              V E R A C R U Z

This is one of the most popular soups of Veracruz made with the little blue crabs from the Gulf of Mexico. I learned to cook it many years ago under the sharp eye of Señora María Cano Carlín, one of the several meticulous and enthusiastic cooks at Las Brisas del Mar Restaurant in Boca del Río a few kilometers south of the Port of Veracruz.

As you can imagine, there are variations, some cooks using anchos or chipotles. I have made some slight adjustments to Señora María's original recipe by adding an ancho chile for extra color and broiling the ingredients instead of cooking them in foil.

Many recipes call for crabmeat, instead of chomping on the crab shells. If you wish to make a more refined soup then use 6 crabs for the broth—and to extract the fat and eggs—and allow about 1 pound (450 g) of crabmeat.

Another cook I have heard of grinds some of the shell to add a little more substance to the broth. Try to buy female crabs, which can be distinguished by the orange tips on their claws and bell-shaped section on the breast (the male has a long, thin, penis-shaped marking).

12 LIVE FEMALE CRABS

1 ½ QUARTS (1.5 L) BOILING, SALTED WATER

1 ANCHO CHILE, SEEDS AND VEINS REMOVED

½ LARGE WHITE ONION, THICKLY SLICED AND BROILED

6 GARLIC CLOVES, BROILED AND PEELED (SEE PAGE 492)

1 POUND (450 G) TOMATOES, BROILED (SEE PAGE 490)

2 JALAPEÑO CHILES, BROILED

3 TABLESPOONS OLIVE OIL

3 LARGE SPRIGS EPAZOTE

If you dare, scrub the crabs well in cold water, and drop them into the pan with the boiling water. Let them cook for no more than 3 minutes. Remove all but 2 of the crabs and set aside to cool. Boil the remaining crabs for 10 minutes, then discard them.

When cool enough to handle, remove the bell-shaped piece of the shell, and pry off the back shell. Scrape out the orange eggs, if any, and pry out any fat lurking in the extreme points of the shell and reserve in a small bowl. Remove the spongy gills and grind them to a paste with the eggs and fat in a molcajete or blender. Reserve.

Cut each crab in half and crack the claws. Reserve. Return the shells and debris to the pan and let them simmer for about 10 minutes.

Strain the broth through a double thickness of cheesecloth and return to the pan, discarding all the debris. There should be about 5½ cups (1.375 l) broth. If not, add water to make up to that amount.

Put 1 cup (250 ml) of the reserved crab broth into the blender jar, add the ancho chile pieces, onion, garlic, tomatoes, and chiles, and blend to a slightly textured consistency.

Heat the oil in a skillet and fry the sauce over high heat, stirring from time to time to avoid sticking, until reduced and seasoned—about 5 minutes. Add to the broth in the pan and simmer for about 5 minutes. Add the paste of fat and eggs and simmer for a few minutes more. Then add the crabs, including the claws, and epazote and simmer again for yet another 5 minutes.

Serve in deep bowls with French bread or rolls.

NOTE: This soup can be prepared ahead, adding the crabs and epazote 5 minutes before serving.

It does not freeze.

JAIBAS RELLENAS Stuffed Blue Crabs
SERVES 6 AS A FIRST COURSE

These little stuffed crabs are a great favorite in the restaurants of the Gulf ports of Veracruz, Tuxpan, and Tampico.

When choosing the blue crabs, try to pick out the large females that have orangey colored tips to their claws; their eggs and fat add flavor to the stuffing.

You will see that I suggest you buy two extra crabs so that you can be sure to have enough meat for filling the six to be served.

8 LARGE BLUE CRABS
2 TABLESPOONS SALT
¼ CUP (65 ML) PLUS 3 TABLESPOONS OLIVE OIL
1 GARLIC CLOVE, FINELY CHOPPED
⅔ CUP (165 ML) FINELY CHOPPED WHITE ONION
12 OUNCES (340 G) TOMATOES, FINELY CHOPPED (ABOUT 2 SCANT CUPS/475 ML)
1 ½ TABLESPOONS FINELY CHOPPED FLAT-LEAF PARSLEY
2 SERRANO CHILES, FINELY CHOPPED
1 ½ TABLESPOONS LARGE CAPERS, RINSED
½ TEASPOON SALT, OR TO TASTE
6 TABLESPOONS FINELY GROUND, TOASTED BREAD CRUMBS

Drop the crabs into boiling, salted water and cover the saucepan. Bring them to a boil and cook them for about 3 minutes. Remove and drain.

When they are cool enough to handle, remove the heart-shaped breastplate and pry off the large black shell, keeping it intact. Scrape out any fat and eggs that have remained in the shell, as well as those in the crab itself. Set them aside.

Scrub 6 of the shells well and set them aside. Remove the meat from the crabs and set it aside. Preheat the oven to 350°F (180°C).

Heat the ¼ cup (65 ml) olive oil in a skillet and fry the garlic and onion until they just begin to turn golden. Add the tomatoes, parsley, chiles, capers, and salt, and cook the mixture over a medium heat until it is almost dry—5 to 8 minutes. Stir in the crab-meat and remove from the heat.

Fill the crab shells with the crabmeat mixture, sprinkle with the bread crumbs and remaining 3 tablespoons olive oil, and put the shells in the oven just long enough to heat them through.

Turn on the broiler and brown the surface of the stuffing.

NOTE: These stuffed crabs are nearly always prepared ahead and reheated. I don't recommend freezing because the filling becomes rather soggy.

ARROZ A LA TUMBADA Rice with Shrimps

SEÑORA LUCINA OCHOA DE ZAMUDIO

SERVES 4 AS A MAIN COURSE, 6 AS A FIRST COURSE   VERACRUZ

One of the very favorite dishes in the port of Veracruz is Arroz a la Tumbada—like many local names it has no adequate translation—but it is a very moist, but not too soupy, rice dish to which is added either just shrimp or assorted seafood, whatever is available and to suit individual tastes. Traditionally the flavor is enhanced by local wild herbs that are used from Tabasco, through the Tuxtepec area of Oaxaca, to Veracruz: a small chivelike onion (Allium scheonoprasum), *a large fleshy-leafed oregano extranjero* (Plectranthus aboinicus), *mint, and the long, serrated leaf* (Eryngium foetidum) *with the flavor of cilantro (available in New York and probably elsewhere where there is a population from the Caribbean, Dominican Republic in particular, where it is called cilantro while the more common cilantro is known as cilantrillo). I suggest you substitute ordinary chives, cilantro, mint, and Mexican oregano—the latter a poor substitute for the highly aromatic* Plectranthus *that I am sure will be available soon, since it is a native of Africa and I have seen it growing in Hawaii.*

Cooking time and the amount of liquid will vary depending on the type of rice.

1 CUP (250 ML) FRUITY (BUT NOT EXTRA VIRGIN) OLIVE OIL

1 ½ POUNDS (675 G) MEDIUM SHRIMPS, UNSHELLED (WEIGHED WITHOUT HEADS)

SALT TO TASTE

12 OUNCES (340 G) TOMATOES, FINELY CHOPPED (ABOUT 2 CUPS/500 ML)

¾ CUP (185 ML) FINELY CHOPPED WHITE ONION

1 SMALL RED BELL PEPPER, CLEANED OF VEINS AND SEEDS, THINLY SLICED

2 GARLIC CLOVES, FINELY CHOPPED

1 ½ CUPS (375 ML) LONG-GRAIN UNCONVERTED WHITE RICE, RINSED AND DRAINED

ABOUT 4 ½ CUPS (1.125 L) WATER

2 HEAPED TABLESPOONS FINELY CHOPPED CILANTRO (SEE NOTE ABOVE)

2 TABLESPOONS FINELY CHOPPED CHIVES

2 TABLESPOONS FINELY CHOPPED MINT

1 TEASPOON DRIED MEXICAN OREGANO

Heat the olive oil in a deep—about 5 inches (13 cm) deep—flameproof casserole. Add the shrimps and a good sprinkle of salt, and stir-fry over high heat for about 1 minute. Remove with a slotted spoon and set aside. In the same oil fry the tomatoes, onion, pepper, and garlic over medium heat until well amalgamated—about 5 minutes. Stir in the rice, add the water with salt to taste, and bring to a boil. Cover the pan and cook over medium heat for about 8 minutes. Add the shrimps and herbs and continue cooking, covered, still over medium heat, until the rice is tender—about 10 minutes. The consistency is between a soup and a rice dish—very moist and juicy (see note above.)

N O T E : This dish can be prepared ahead up until adding the shrimps and herbs, but I do not recommend freezing.

CAMARONES EN ESCABECHE ROJO
Shrimps Pickled in Red Chile Sauce
RESTAURANTE LAS DILIGENCIAS, TAMPICO
SERVES 6 TO 8 AS A FIRST COURSE

T A M A U L I P A S

Some people don't take to this pungent, hard-hitting dish at first, but it grows on you. I have served cold shrimps cooked in this way with cocktails and they were wildly popular.

The sauce was originally evolved, of course, to preserve shrimps or fish before the days of refrigeration in the hot, damp climate of the gulf ports. Veracruz has its own variations, but it is the specialty of Tampico. The busy port is a twin town of Ciudad Madero, a large petroleum-refining center. There is constant activity; a lot of money changes hands and the people live, laugh, and eat hard. In Tampico the shrimps are fried, added to the sauce as soon as it is made, and left to ripen in it. The first time I ate it there I wondered why the shrimps were rather tough and acidy. They had, of course, absorbed the vinegar. When I visited Tampico some years later I found that the recipe had been modified by restaurateurs. The sauce was not nearly as pungent and the shrimps were soft, as though they had just been immersed in the sauce. Oriental or pineapple vinegar (see page 495) would be ideal for this recipe.

Serve as a botana *with toothpicks or a main course with white rice. Begin the recipe at least five days ahead.*

THE SAUCE

½ CUP (125 ML) OLIVE OIL

5 ANCHO CHILES, WIPED CLEAN, SEEDS AND VEINS REMOVED

⅓ CUP (85 ML) ROUGHLY SLICED WHITE ONION

3 GARLIC CLOVES, ROUGHLY SLICED

¼ TEASPOON DRIED MEXICAN OREGANO

8 PEPPERCORNS

3 WHOLE CLOVES

1 ¼ CUPS (315 ML) MILD WHITE VINEGAR

2 MEXICAN BAY LEAVES

⅛ TEASPOON DRIED MEXICAN OREGANO

SALT TO TASTE

1 POUND (450 G) MEDIUM SHELLED AND COOKED SHRIMPS

Heat the oil in a skillet and fry the chiles lightly on both sides. Tear into pieces. Add the onion and garlic to the skillet and fry until translucent. Drain and transfer to the blender jar along with the chiles, ¼ teaspoon oregano, the peppercorns, and cloves.

Heat the vinegar and pour it over the ingredients in the blender jar. Set aside to soak for about 10 minutes, then blend to a smooth, thick consistency. No more liquid should be necessary, but if it is then add vinegar, not water (see note below).

Reheat the oil and add the sauce, together with the bay leaves, additional ⅛ teaspoon oregano, and salt. Once the mixture in the pan starts to bubble, lower the heat and continue to cook the sauce for about 15 minutes, stirring it from time to time to avoid sticking. Put a lid over the pan, as the thick sauce will splatter about fiercely.

Leave the sauce in the refrigerator to ripen for at least 3 days before using it.

Dilute the sauce with a little water, heat, and add the shrimps for just long enough to heat them through.

NOTE: If the sauce has no water in it, it will keep indefinitely in the refrigerator; it will also freeze well, but let it ripen first.

CAMARONES EN PIPIÁN Shrimps in Pumpkin Seed Sauce

SEÑOR ANGEL DELGADO, RESTAURANTE LAS DILIGENCIAS, TAMPICO

SERVES 6 TO 8   TAMAULIPAS

For the most part in Mexico, the unhulled, toasted seeds of certain varieties of pumpkins are ground as a base for the popular dish called pipián *(although this is sometimes made with a mixture of nuts or sesame seeds). But there are some notable exceptions where hulled pumpkin seeds are called for:* papadzules *of Yucatán and the* pipianes *of that specific area that encompasses the northern part of the state of Veracruz and the southern coast of Tamaulipas. In these areas a pumpkin is cultivated that bears the largest seed of them all, about 1 inch long (2.5 cm) and with a pretty green border around it to match the color of the very oily seed inside.*

This is an elegant and unusual dish—enough, because it is rich, for six portions as a main dish and eight as a first course. The recipe was prepared for me by Señor Angel Delgado, the owner of Las Diligencias in Tampico, which for many years has had the reputation of being one of the serious eating places outside of Mexico City—perhaps the best thing one can say of any restaurant. I have altered Señor Delgado's recipe slightly by reducing the amount of butter considerably—the sour cream is quite rich enough—and by using shrimp broth rather than milk to blend the sauce.

The shrimps of Tampico also deserve mention. I would go out of my way any day to have a plateful of camarones para pelar *in Tampico—served, as they should be, unskinned with head and tail still on. But you should specify whether you want those from the lagoons along the coastal area or from the sea.*

1 ½ POUNDS (675 G) MEDIUM-SIZE SHRIMPS, UNSHELLED

2 ½ CUPS (625 ML) COLD WATER, APPROXIMATELY

1 TEASPOON SALT, OR TO TASTE

1 CUP (250 ML) HULLED, RAW PUMPKIN SEEDS (ABOUT 4 OUNCES/115 G)

1 SMALL BUNCH CILANTRO

4 FRESH SERRANO CHILES OR ANY FRESH, HOT GREEN CHILES

½ SMALL WHITE ONION, ROUGHLY CHOPPED

1 TABLESPOON UNSALTED BUTTER

⅔ CUP (165 ML) THICK SOUR CREAM (SEE PAGE 489)

Shell and devein the shrimps and set aside. Put the shells, tails, and heads, if any, into a saucepan, add the water with salt, and cook over medium heat for about 20 minutes, to extract the flavor and make a light broth. Strain and discard the shells, reserving the cooking liquid. Allow the liquid to cool a little. Add the shrimps and cook over gentle heat for about 3 minutes, or until they are just turning opaque. Drain the shrimps, reserving the broth.

In a heavy, ungreased frying pan, toast the pumpkin seeds lightly, stirring them often, until they begin to swell up and start to pop about—do not let them brown. Set them aside to cool and then grind them finely in a coffee/spice grinder. (Alternatively they can just be added to the blender with the broth in the next step, but the sauce will not be as smooth.)

Place the shrimp broth, pumpkin seeds, cilantro, chiles, and onion in a blender and blend together until smooth.

Melt the butter in a heavy saucepan. Add the blended pumpkin seed sauce and cook over very low heat, stirring and scraping the bottom of the pan constantly, for about 5 minutes. Stir in the sour cream, adjust the seasoning, and just heat through—about 5 minutes. Then add the shrimps and heat through for another 5 minutes. The sauce should be of a medium consistency. Serve immediately.

Serve with fresh, hot tortillas or crusty French bread. Despite the temptation to do so, it is better not to serve it on top of rice or all that lovely sauce will be sopped up and lost.

N O T E : This *pipián* can be prepared ahead up to the point of adding the shrimps. I do not suggest freezing this dish.

CREPAS DE CAMARÓN EN CHILE PASILLA

Shrimp Crepes with Pasilla Sauce

SEÑORA MARÍA EMILIA DE FARÍAS

SERVES 6 AS A FIRST COURSE

TAMAULIPAS

When this recipe was given to me in the early days, I considered it a modern Mexican recipe; perhaps by now it could be considered a classic! This is a wonderful sauce and lends itself to many other ingredients, shredded chicken enchiladas for example or with veal, or other types of seafood.

6 PASILLA CHILES, WIPED CLEAN, SEEDS AND VEINS REMOVED

1 ½ POUNDS (675 G) TOMATOES, BROILED (SEE PAGE 490)

2 TABLESPOONS COARSELY CHOPPED WHITE ONION

⅓ CUP (85 ML) VEGETABLE OIL

½ TEASPOON GRANULATED SUGAR

SALT TO TASTE

1 ½ CUPS (375 ML) THICK SOUR CREAM (SEE PAGE 489), PLUS EXTRA FOR SERVING

1 ½ POUNDS (675 G) SMALL SHRIMPS COOKED AND PEELED

12 THIN CREPES, ABOUT 5 ½ INCHES (14 CM) IN DIAMETER, PREPARED ACCORDING TO
   ANY STANDARD CREPE RECIPE

1 ¼ CUPS (315 ML) GRATED CHIHUAHUA CHEESE OR MUENSTER

Preheat the oven to 350°F (180°C).

Heat a griddle or comal and toast the chiles lightly, turning them from time to time so that they do not burn. Crumble the chiles into a blender jar, add the tomatoes and onion, and blend to a smooth sauce.

Heat the oil in a large skillet. Add the sauce, sugar, and salt, and cook the mixture over medium heat, stirring it from time to time to avoid sticking. You will probably have to cover the pan with a lid, as the sauce splatters rather fiercely. After about 10 minutes the sauce will have thickened and seasoned. Set it aside to cool a little.

Stir the sour cream well into the sauce and let it continue to heat through for a minute or so.

Mix the shrimps into 1 cup (250 ml) of the sauce. Place a little of the mixture in each of the crepes and roll them up loosely. Place the crepes side by side on an oven-proof serving dish and pour the remaining sauce over them.

Sprinkle the grated cheese over the sauce and put some dollops of sour cream around the edge of the dish. Let the crepes heat through in the oven and the cheese melt. Serve immediately.

NOTE: The crepes and sauce can always be made the day before—the sauce freezes very well. They can be filled several hours ahead and the remaining sauce added just before they go into the oven.

TAMIAHUA Señora Santiago, the mother of a friend in Mexico City, had often talked to me about the small village on the Lagoon of Tamiahua, near Tampico, where she had lived for most of her married life and brought up her two children. She talked about her neighbors and friends and their peaceful, happy life: outings to the beach where they would catch and cook crabs and fish, boil potatoes to eat with them (an unusual custom for Mexico), and make enchiladas of *pipián*, a sauce of pumpkin seeds. She told me about her daughter's *comadre*, or godmother, who was renowned for her tamales and shrimp balls; the women bakers of the village; and Leoncio Arteaga, who owned and ran a small restaurant, famed for its local food, called El Veracruzano. I began to dream, and, as so often happens, a few days later there I was, in Tampico.

The morning after my arrival I found myself speeding south down the narrow highway in a bus that, in the fashion that seems typical for long-distance Mexican buses, had no regard for any life in its path. I arrived breathless at my destination, Naranjos, or Orange Trees—such a pleasant name for what turned out to be a dismal village, sprawling and untidy and fearfully hot. Waiting for me across the street was one of those squat village buses, the glass long disappeared from the windows and springs sticking up from the tattered seats. The rack on top of the bus was already piled with baskets, cardboard boxes, and live poultry precariously tied on with string. It said "Tamiahua" boldly on the front of the bus—but one never knows in Mexico. In any case, I climbed up and paid my fifty cents to a poorly dressed but very serious young man all of nine years old. There were a few other passengers, and very soon we were off, bumping along a deeply rutted dirt road. We stopped occasionally to let somebody on or off—a young rancher who had left his horse tethered under a wayside shelter, a woman whose chickens were squawking on top—or to deliver one of the boxes to a waiting figure at the side of the road. To the right and left there were small ranches, which were marked out by smooth, red-barked fence posts that had taken root and were already sprouting on their way to becoming trees. The land had been cleared for cattle raising; charred, twisted trunks were all that remained of what had been tall, old trees, and they made a rather sinister landscape.

Trucks passing us in the opposite direction seemed to be warning our driver of something that lay ahead. Soon we would see for ourselves what it was all about. Although it was now mid-October and the rainy season was over, it had rained heavily the night before and the river was full. We forded it easily, but as we began to climb the opposite bank, the wheels began to spin and the engine choked into silence. The driver asked the men aboard to get down and push, which they did with vigor, but to no avail. They examined the engine, and everyone offered his piece of advice. The driver tried to start the engine again by running back into the river, precariously trying to avoid the deepwater side of the dividing concrete. It started with a rude jolt and we were off again—but once more the engine died as the wheels spun in the mud.

Time and time again we backed into the river—the only other woman passenger and I exchanging fearful glances as the tires became more embedded, the men all the while insisting that we should not get down. An hour or more went by. We were joined by other drivers held up by our predicament. At least twenty voices were shouting advice now, and then twenty pairs of strong hands began pushing the bus from behind. The engine started up and the wheels bit into the earth. They held for one breathtaking moment, and then—amid resounding cheers and with mud churning up all around—we were finally off up the bank. About six miles farther on we finally entered Tamiahua, two and a half hours after leaving Naranjos. My rosy vision of it soon faded amid the signs of bygone prosperity and respectability. I set off immediately in search of the *comadre*, and while there were no street signs, it was a small town, and everyone knew everyone else; by chance I came across a neighbor who lived next door to her. As we walked along talking, I found out that my companion was one of the bakers I had wanted to meet. She invited me to visit her house and see for myself.

As I went into the house I could see a huge shelter at the back whose roof adjoined the house itself, and under it was a huge, round brick oven about six feet across. The area was piled high with logs, and to one side a shelf of rough wooden planks held trays of rising dough and loaves of cooling bread. She broke a roll open for me to try—and I found I was disappointed. I suppose one expects something else from these "ideally primitive" conditions, but the bread was soft and doughy, as so much bread is along the Gulf Coast of Mexico.

I went next door and found the *comadre*. She was drawn and gray with prolonged illness, and, since it obviously fatigued her to talk, I left as soon as I could—but not before she had given me some guiding hints about the local food, its essential flavors, and how it should be cooked.

By this time it was late for lunch, so I found my way back to the restaurante El Veracruzano, which turned out to be a large, simple wooden shack set out over the water. Off to one side was the open kitchen, and behind that were long tables piled high with thousands of oysters, which were sheltered from the sun by a primitive roof of coconut palm. I sat down at a table and chose a fish soup, a spicy tomato broth thick with generous pieces of fish, crab, and shrimp from the lagoon (which, as I could see, was now a scene of frenzied activity as little boats sped from one side to the other, stopping as their occupants inspected the nets slung across the narrow waterway). Next came fish roe with scallions, chiles, and cilantro, bound together by lots of beaten egg and fried into a large, flat cake, accompanied by the traditional *enchiladas de pipián*—made from the particularly large seeds of the pumpkins grown in the area—that are served with any fish dish in Tamiahua.

Finally Leoncio himself came to my table. He sat down and we talked for an hour or two about the local food, particularly the tamales of fish and shellfish that abound in the lagoon. Then with great pride he showed me his freezer, well stocked with fish; my heart sank at the thought of all that fresh seafood swimming right past his door.

It was now dark, and the restaurant was closing up for the night. I told myself I would try the oysters tomorrow, but I never did. After a miserable, fleabitten night I got up at five—and took the first bus out. Three of Leoncio's recipes follow: Saragalla de Pescado, Albóndigas de Camarones, and Pescado Enchilado. He would not divulge his recipe for *ostiones pimentados*, which was a closely guarded secret.

SARAGALLA DE PESCADO Shredded Fish Tamiahua

SEÑOR LEONCIO ARTEAGA, RESTAURANTE EL VERACRUZANO, TAMIAHUA
SERVES 6   VERACRUZ

Señor Leoncio uses a local fish, jurel, but I have used shark for this dish, which was very good —it shredded well and is dry and not at all fatty. Monkfish on the East Coast and yellowtail or mahimahi on the West are other suggestions; as a matter of fact, any leftover fish would be fine.

The Saragalla may be served hot or cold as a first course or as a filling for tacos. Señor Arteaga says it should be served topped with tomato and onion rings and strips of jalapeño chiles en escabeche, but I like it just as it is.

1 SMALL ANCHO CHILE

12 PEPPERCORNS, CRUSHED

1/4 TEASPOON CORIANDER SEEDS, CRUSHED

1/2-INCH (1.5-CM) PIECE OF CINNAMON STICK, CRUSHED

1/2 TEASPOON SALT, OR TO TASTE

2 GARLIC CLOVES

1/4 CUP (65 ML) WATER

3 TABLESPOONS LIGHT OLIVE OIL

ABOUT 6 OUNCES (180 G) TOMATOES, FINELY CHOPPED (ABOUT 1 CUP/250 ML)

1/4 CUP (65 ML) FINELY CHOPPED WHITE ONION

2 SERRANO CHILES, OR ANY FRESH, HOT GREEN CHILE, FINELY CHOPPED

6 GREEN OLIVES, PITTED AND FINELY CHOPPED

1 TEASPOON CAPERS, ROUGHLY CHOPPED

1 1/2 TABLESPOONS RAISINS

2 CUPS (500 ML) COOKED AND FIRM-FLESHED SHREDDED FISH (ABOUT 1 POUND/450 G)

Remove the seeds and veins from the ancho chile, cover with water, and simmer for 5 minutes. Soak for an additional 5 minutes, then drain and add to the blender jar. Add the crushed spices, salt, garlic, and water and blend, adding more water only if necessary, to a loose paste.

Heat the oil in a heavy skillet and add the tomatoes, onion, serrano chiles, olives, capers, and raisins. Fry over medium heat for about 5 minutes, stirring the mixture constantly. Add the spice mixture and cook, stirring from time to time, for about 5 minutes. Stir in the shredded fish and cook for 5 minutes longer.

Adjust the seasoning and serve either hot or cold, with freshly made tortillas.

ALBÓNDIGAS DE CAMARONES Shrimp Balls

SEÑOR LEONCIO ARTEAGA, RESTAURANTE EL VERACRUZANO, TAMIAHUA

SERVES 6   VERACRUZ

1 ½ POUNDS (675 G) SMALL SHRIMPS, SHELLED, CLEANED, AND ROUGHLY CHOPPED

THE TOMATO BROTH

3 TABLESPOONS VEGETABLE OIL

1 ½ POUNDS (675 G) TOMATOES, FINELY CHOPPED (ABOUT 4 CUPS/1 L)

⅓ CUP (85 ML) FINELY CHOPPED WHITE ONION

3 GARLIC CLOVES, FINELY CHOPPED

4 CUPS (1 L) WATER

2 TEASPOONS SALT, OR TO TASTE

5 PEPPERCORNS

⅛ TEASPOON CORIANDER SEEDS

1 CUP (250 ML) PEELED, DICED POTATOES (ABOUT 6 OUNCES/180 G)

1 ½ CUPS (375 ML) PEELED AND DICED CHAYOTE (ABOUT 8 OUNCES/225 G)

1 CUP (250 ML) NOPALES, COOKED (SEE PAGE 208)

SHRIMP BALL SEASONING

½ ANCHO CHILE, VEINS AND SEEDS REMOVED

¼ TEASPOON CORIANDER SEEDS

¼ TEASPOON PEPPERCORNS

½-INCH (1.5-CM) PIECE OF CINNAMON STICK

1 ½ TEASPOONS SALT, OR TO TASTE

1 ½ GARLIC CLOVES

3 TABLESPOONS WATER

1 TABLESPOON VEGETABLE OIL

Put the shrimps into the freezer for about 2 hours, until they are slightly frozen (this will make it easier to grind them in the blender or food processor).

Meanwhile, prepare the tomato broth. In a wide, heavy pan, heat the oil and fry the tomatoes, onion, and garlic, stirring them from time to time and scraping the bottom of the pan, until they are reduced to a thick sauce. Add the 4 cups (1 l) of water, salt, peppercorns, and coriander seeds and bring to a boil. Add the potatoes and cook for about 10 minutes, then add the chayote and cook until almost tender, about 15 minutes more. Add the nopales and just heat through. Adjust the seasoning.

Prepare the seasoning for the shrimp balls by first soaking the ancho chile in hot water for 15 minutes, then drain and put in a blender jar. Crush the coriander seeds, peppercorns, and cinnamon stick. Add the spices to the blender jar, along with the salt, garlic, and water, and blend to a paste. Heat the oil and fry the seasoning paste over high heat for about 2 minutes. Set aside.

Blend the slightly frozen shrimps to a fairly smooth consistency. Add the fried seasoning and work it in well with your hands. Lightly grease your hands, then form the mixture into balls about 1¼ inches (3.5 cm) in diameter—there should be 18 of them. Carefully place the shrimp balls into the simmering broth, then cover the pan and continue simmering for about 15 minutes, turning them once during the cooking time.

Serve the shrimp balls in deep soup bowls, with plenty of the broth and vegetables.

NOTE: This dish can be prepared several hours ahead but I do not advise freezing.

PESCADO ENCHILADO Broiled Fish Seasoned with Chile Paste

SEÑOR LEONCIO ARTEAGA, RESTAURANTE EL VERACRUZANO, TAMIAHUA

SERVES 6   VERACRUZ

One of Leoncio Arteaga's specialties is broiled sargo—a large local fish from the lagoon. On one occasion he had a four-pounder proudly displayed so you could see it immediately on entering the restaurant. A stake had been thrust up inside the fish, which had been liberally coated with a paste of ancho chile and broiled over a wood fire.

You can broil this fish successfully only if the bars of your broiler rack are very thin, because, no matter how much you grease them, the chile paste tends to stick rather badly as it dries out over the fire.

4 ANCHO CHILES, SEEDS AND VEINS REMOVED

4 PIQUÍN CHILES, LEFT WHOLE

3 GARLIC CLOVES

2 TEASPOONS SALT, OR TO TASTE

⅓ TO ½ CUP (85 TO 125 ML) MILD VINEGAR

1 4-POUND (1.8-KG) RED SNAPPER OR GROUPER, GUTTED BUT SCALES, HEAD, AND TAIL LEFT ON

3 TABLESPOONS VEGETABLE OIL

Cover the ancho chiles with boiling water and leave them to soak until soft—about 5 minutes. Drain the chiles, then transfer to a blender jar. Add the piquín chiles (whole), garlic, salt, and vinegar and blend until smooth. (The mixture should be like a thick paste. If any more liquid is needed to release the blades of the blender, use a minimum amount of water.)

Broil the fish briefly on both sides, unseasoned, and strip off the skin. Spread the outside of the fish with the chile paste, then baste with the oil and broil until cooked through—10 to 15 minutes on each side depending on the thickness of the fish.

Serve immediately, with hot, freshly made tortillas. Any leftover fish can be used for Saragalla (page 381).

RELLENO DE GUAVINO Fish and Shrimp Sausage

DON VICTORIANO

MAKES 4 FEET (1.25 M) SAUSAGE　　　　　　　　　　VERACRUZ

This recipe of Relleno de Guavino is Don Victoriano's. Nobody else I spoke to knows about it, and nobody remembers it.

You don't need an elegant and expensive fish for this recipe. Use whatever is the best buy—carp, sierra, or so forth. You could use the sausage immediately, but the flavor will be greatly enhanced if you leave it to ripen in the refrigerator for two to three days. The broth could be frozen and used for poaching fish or as a base for a fish soup.

I POUND (450 G) FISH, CUT IN ½-INCH (1.5-CM) SLICES, SKIN AND BONE REMOVED AND RESERVED

8 OUNCES (225 G) RAW SHRIMPS, CLEANED AND DEVEINED, SHELLS RESERVED

THE BROTH

2 SPRIGS FLAT-LEAF PARSLEY

I CELERY RIB, ROUGHLY CHOPPED

2 SMALL CARROTS, SCRAPED AND SLICED

4 CUPS (I L) WATER

2 BAY LEAVES, MEXICAN IF POSSIBLE

3 SPRIGS FRESH THYME, OR ⅛ TEASPOON DRIED

I TABLESPOON FRESH LIME OR LEMON JUICE

6 PEPPERCORNS

2 TEASPOONS SALT, OR TO TASTE

THE SAUSAGE

6 OUNCES (180 G) TOMATOES, FINELY CHOPPED (1 SCANT CUP/250 ML)

¼ CUP (65 ML) FINELY CHOPPED WHITE ONION

1 MEDIUM CARROT, SCRAPED AND DICED SMALL

1 ½ TABLESPOONS FINELY CHOPPED FRESH PARSLEY

1 MEDIUM RED BLISS OR OTHER WAXY POTATO, PEELED AND DICED SMALL

⅔ CUP (165 ML) PEAS

1 TABLESPOON FRESH LIME JUICE

1 TEASPOON SALT, OR TO TASTE

6 TABLESPOONS OLIVE OIL, APPROXIMATELY

1 JALAPEÑO CHILE OR ANY FRESH, HOT GREEN CHILE, FINELY CHOPPED

FRESHLY GROUND BLACK PEPPER

4 ½ FEET (1.35 M) SAUSAGE CASINGS (NOT PLASTIC), APPROXIMATELY

TO SERVE

¼ CUP (65 ML) DRAINED, CHOPPED LARGE CAPERS

¼ CUP (65 ML) PITTED, CHOPPED GREEN OLIVES

Put the fish and shrimps into the freezer and leave for about 2 hours or until half frozen. Prepare the broth. Put the debris from the fish and shrimps into a wide saucepan, together with the rest of the broth ingredients. Bring to a boil and simmer for about 40 minutes. Strain the broth and return to the saucepan.

Put the fish and shrimps, a small quantity at a time to prevent the blades from clogging, into a blender jar or food processor and grind until fine. Mix the fish paste with the rest of the sausage ingredients, using only 2 tablespoons of the oil. Fry one spoonful of the mixture now for taste, then adjust the seasoning if necessary and stuff into the casing, using any standard stuffing method; make two lengths about 1 inch (2.5 cm) thick, then prick all over with a very sharp pointed fork.

Reheat the broth, and when it starts to simmer, add the sausages in flat coils. The broth should completely cover the sausages; if it does not, then add more hot water. Bring to a simmer and cook for about 15 to 20 minutes, then remove and drain. Let ripen in the refrigerator for a few days—this *will* improve the flavor—then proceed.

Cut the sausage into slices about ½ inch (1.5 cm) thick. Heat the remaining 4 tablespoons oil until it smokes, then lower the heat and fry the sausage slices until golden brown. Serve hot, sprinkled with the capers and olives.

DON VICTORIANO I don't know how it had escaped me during my many years of living in Mexico, but it wasn't until 1973 that friends told me about a very special restaurant, outstanding for its regional dishes. They are cooked with great care, my friends said, many using sweet and delicate crayfish, crabs, and shrimps from the river that flow past the restaurant's door. Of course I had to go.

I had crossed the Papaloapan River, miles farther down from my destination, in a boat that was small and crowded but that flaunted a little awning to protect us from the sun. I joined the other passengers waiting for the bus who, as they waited, ate tortillas crammed with carnitas, those small, delicious chunks of crisply cooked pork, or cracked the large white crab claws they had bought from the small food stands grouped around the ferry dock. The bus was standing by, empty, and it was beginning to seem that we would be there forever when suddenly, out of nowhere, the driver appeared at the wheel. There were two staccato hoots on the horn and we scrambled aboard, sensing the urgency of his message—and as the last ones clung to the hand rail and got a footing on the bottom step we went roaring off in a cloud of dust.

On our left was the broad river, full to the brim, its muddy waters carrying logs, uprooted shrubs, and other debris swiftly down to the sea. The roadsides were alive with brilliant wild flowers; on the right, colorful birds skimmed over a narrow stream choked with pale mauve water hyacinth. On the marshes around the lagoons beyond, humped zebus grazed peacefully with their attendant herons standing watchfully by.

Half an hour later we were in Tlacotalpan, a small, compact town on the riverbank. At first all you could see was a mass of low, tiled roofs weathered to a rich red-brown, accented by a white dome and spire, a few palm trees towering like sentinels above them all. As I stepped down from the bus, I found myself in a Mexico I didn't recognize. Many of the streets were unpaved. They were soft and grassy and so quiet, with flowering hibiscus and oleander bushes here and there. Many of the houses had recently been painted, in colors ranging from deep-hued pinks, greens, and blues to delicate pastels; their classical pillars and arches, picked out in white, gleamed in the midday sun. At every turn there seemed to be another little plaza—deserted, colorful, and almost unreal, as though one had stepped into a neglected set for an eighteenth-century movie. Along the riverbank the fishermen's boats strained at their moorings in the swift current; the deserted docks nearby were a reminder of the days when the town was a flourishing port, and nineteenth-century ocean-going vessels brought in Spanish, Italian, and Portuguese passengers and cargo.

I established myself in the only hotel in town, and it was not long before I was deep in a conversation with the hotel owner about the local food. She was a mine of information, and very soon I began to realize that here was something very special indeed. For it was she who told me about Don Victoriano, who had taught the cooks in the famous little restaurant I had been told about.

Without a moment's delay I set out to find his house—which I did quite easily, for everyone knew him. In fact, he lived in two houses, adjoining and at right angles to each other, one painted a deep, violent red, the other a brilliant blue. I walked up to an open door and three people beckoned me in. I found them all seated in the locally made rocking chairs that seemed to be in every house, highly varnished, dark wooden frames with cane backs and seats, arms and headrests draped with spotlessly white antimacassars.

I was told to wait a moment, and very soon Don Victoriano came shuffling quickly into the room in his worn leather *huaraches*. He was of medium build, slim; his tightly curling black hair was receding and tinged with gray at the temples; his eyes were a lively blue-gray and his dark skin was mottled with pink. He was dressed like the fishermen of the town, in baggy blue pants and a white sweatshirt. He welcomed me in the open, friendly manner typical of the coast, as though I were an old friend and he had been expecting me.

No formal introduction seemed necessary. I loved good food; I loved to cook and wanted to learn about the regional specialties. "Come to lunch tomorrow at one o'clock. I am just cooking a *galápago en moste*, and by tomorrow it will be well seasoned and ready to eat."

The dish he had described—terrapin in a black sauce—sounded too good to miss, and the hollow, toneless church bell was just striking one o'clock when I returned the following day. Don Victoriano welcomed me by rushing out from the kitchen, noisily punctuating his greeting by sucking at the pineapple pulp that was lodged between his lower lip and teeth. We were very soon joined by an old lady and her companion, both carrying big black umbrellas against the afternoon sun.

Don Victoriano proudly ushered us into his new dining room, which was also the kitchen. The burners were set into a countertop that ran the width of the room and was completely tiled. The whole room, in fact, was covered with highly glazed blue and white tiles—floor, walls, buffet, stove, even the table.

The meal began. The fresh rolls that he himself had brought from the bakery only minutes before were carried into the room, along with a pile of carefully wrapped tortillas and a jug of iced, crushed papaya drink. The maid brought in large plates of shrimp soup—the small, sweet shrimps from the river, which reminded me of those I used to eat at home in England—then white rice and fried plantain. These were followed by the pièce de résistance, *galápago en moste quemado*.

The terrapin was delicious. Gelatinous and much more tender than sea turtle, it had been cooked in a thin, blackish sauce that had a musky flavor and was colored by the burnt, ground leaves of the moste bush that he had by his back door. "This dates from Zapotec times," said Don Victoriano.

I was beginning to feel very full—and then another steaming, fragrant dish was brought in. Don Victoriano apologized profusely for not serving something more elegant; apparently relatives had arrived unexpectedly, and because he had served them breakfast at ten-thirty that morning he couldn't get out to the market. He said the new dish was a duck in *lo que queda* sauce. I soon realized it was literally *lo que queda*; "that which was left over" had gone into the sauce, which resembled a light *pipián*, or pumpkin seed sauce.

A huge mountain of sliced pineapple was now placed on the table, along with cookies made of unrefined sugar and grated fresh coconut, but the real dessert was on the buffet: enormous portions of a light egg custard thickened with finely ground almonds and topped with swirls of beaten egg white.

After the meal was over at last, I tried to concentrate on Don Victoriano's conversation and his never-ending string of recipes, while our lunch companions dozed, their heads bent over peacefully while their chairs rocked. He cooked and catered for hundreds—a baptism upriver, a wedding in the mountains, a breakfast for the President and his entourage. He never drank or smoked, had never had a day's illness, and was in his seventies.

"I want to give a large fiesta to celebrate that day and a good first year in my new house. I shall cook it all; come back then and cook with me and learn. The *galápagos* will be at their best and heavy with eggs, the wild ducks will be flying, and with any luck there will be fresh *tismiche* [newly hatched fish] from the river. We shall have to catch and skin the *galápago*; the best ones come from the river up near the mountains. Yes, come back then."

That December the house was due to be finished, so I wrote asking when the fiesta was to take place. I had a formally typed letter in reply, obviously composed and written by one of the town's official letter writers. It seemed the house was still not finished, and the inaugural fiesta postponed.

The following years were busy ones; I traveled but never to Tlacotalpan. Finally, three years later, I found myself once again on the road heading toward the little town to visit Don Victoriano. This time I was in a more predictable first-class bus, which roared along over the wide bridge that had now replaced the ferry.

When I got there, it didn't seem the same Tlacotalpan. Many streets were now paved and there was noise and activity, with young men screaming around on raucous motorcycles. I hurried along through the quieter back streets to Don Victoriano's. He no longer lived there. The man who had never had a day's illness in his life had died quite suddenly—and to that day nobody knew why.

It wasn't until twenty years later that a local resident told me Don Victoriano had died of pneumonia. Apparently, or so the story goes, some local macho rowdies put him on a block of ice where he was made to sit all night. He died soon after.

SWEET YEAST BREADS

LA PANADERÍA ❋ THE BAKERY

Let me say at the outset that I love all manner of baked goods, from heavy British fruit-cakes to light cream puffs, so little wonder that I can always remember from my childhood in England the fascination of bakeries. That wonderfully yeasty smell would waft out of the bakehouse door as trays of freshly baked teacakes, scones, and currant buns were brought out, all ready to be rushed home, toasted on a brass toasting fork over glowing coals, and slathered with butter to make teatime such a consoling affair. Depending on where you were, there would be pikelets, crumpets, lardy and eccles cakes, or coiled Chelsea buns generously filled with currants.

When I first came to Mexico in 1957 I found it very difficult to walk past a bakery. I almost automatically stopped, entered, took up my metal tray and pair of tongs, and began the round, mentally savoring all the different types of sweet breads and finally emerging with tray piled high—far too many, but I had to try them all, just once more.

In Mexico you eat freshly made breads every day. From early morning to late afternoon constant streams of sweet rolls, shiny pastries, crusty, white rolls, croissants, and cupcakes are loaded onto the already full trays in the windows and around the walls of the bakery. All shapes and sizes, intricately worked doughs with sugar toppings or sprinklings of sesame seeds and candied peel, they bear the entrancing names of *besos* (kisses), *novias* (brides), *monjas* (nuns), *tortugas* (turtles), *bigotes* (mustaches), *yoyos*, *suspiros* (sighs), and so on without end, as far as I can discover.

For years I favored a bakery in Mexico City, very near where, year after year, I stayed with friends, and one day it occurred to me to go in and ask to be shown how to make the breads. Like many other bakeries in Mexico City, this one was owned and operated by a Spanish family. They provided the premises, sales staff, supervisor, and bakehouse equipment and contracted with a master baker *(el maestro)* and his team to make bread on a piecework basis. My bakery had a particularly formidable supervisor, who always snapped and never smiled. However, heartened by a wave of publicity on television and in the papers about my work, I approached him. He said he would have to ask the *maestro* and led me through a door at the side of the shop into the huge bakehouse.

The bakehouse, as big as a warehouse, was stacked to the ceiling with large sacks of flour. There were two huge, diesel-fired ovens, worktables, large mixers, and various machines to cut and roll the dough, as well as movable racks containing trays full of rising or freshly baked breads. One group of about eight men were working around a rectangular table making hundreds of the elongated Mexican yeast rolls called *bolillos*, while at the back of the room, at workbenches set at right angles to one another, were my future teachers and friends. They were all dressed in aprons and caps in different shades of white. Maestro Miguel was a quiet-spoken man, and I could hardly hear him above the roar of the ovens. But he agreed to let me come in and learn, and thus began an apprenticeship I shall never forget.

The *maestro* and his son Jorge started every morning at three o'clock to prepare some of the more complicated doughs ahead of time, readying them for the arrival of the rest of the team at six. The first sweet rolls had to be baked by the time the store opened at seven, or sometimes even earlier. A lot of the slow-rising doughs had been prepared the day before and had to be taken out of the cooler rooms in which they were stored (the temperature in the main room was well over 80 degrees). So, when I arrived that first morning at eight, everything was in full swing. An old sack was torn up for my apron and a bit of old cloth to cover my hair. I was told to measure out the ingredients for the starter for conchas, those round, spongy, sugar-topped buns. And so my apprenticeship began in earnest.

I soon settled into the daily routine, and I rapidly came to admire my hardworking colleagues. The team, with no more than a quiet word to each other, went about their work each morning with a dedication and coordination that many a department in government would be wise to emulate. The *maestro* whispered a few instructions and answered an occasional question, but that was all; during the months I worked there I never heard a quarrel or cross word. As the morning wore on, the workers began to gossip and tease each other, with an occasional guffaw or a piercing whistle of approval when one of the shop girls came in. Occasionally the radio would be turned on, and those making the *bolillos* would fall into a hypnotic rhythm of pounding, kneading, and rolling the dough without stopping to catch a breath for hours on end. I came to be fascinated by the terminology I heard as these busy mornings flew by so rapidly. I found it curious how the terms for mixing dough were related to heat and cold. When a dough was mixed to the right point and had to be worked into shape immediately, someone said, "Don't let it get cold" *(no se deje enfriar)*. To beat the dough to its correct consistency, it was "Let it get warm" *(se calienta la masa)*. And the admonition "Don't let it burn" *(no se queme)* meant that the dough should not be allowed to go past its correct point in beating.

The mornings were so busy that I was always relieved to see ten o'clock drawing near, for it was then that Rubén, the special pastry cook, who was in charge of the food for the *almuerzo*, started his preparations. It fascinated me to see what he would do next with only a baking tray to cook on. Often he would cut tortillas into strips and fry them lightly in the doughnut fryer (to do which, of course, he always asked permission). He would broil tomatoes and chiles under the jets of the oven and pound them into a sauce in an ingeniously improvised molcajete (after putting the broiled ingredients into an empty tin can, he would place a plastic bag over the top so it dipped down inside, covering the contents, and then he would pound them with an empty Coke bottle!). The sauce went over the fried tortillas, was topped with lots of crumbled cheese, and then back it all went into the oven once more. There were always fresh *teleras*—flat, crisp rolls—that were torn open and stuffed with the *chilaquiles* Rubén had made. I was always expected to help myself first, and they would wait to see my expression. How they laughed when I found my torta too picante.

I never failed to look with awe on Miguel's incredible expertise. There were two huge drawers under the worktable for flour. I could never get right which drawer I was to use or what the difference was in the flours, but the *maestro* just had to run his fingers through the flour once to tell whether the amounts of salt, yeast, or water should be increased or diminished for that particular lot. He would inspect each new shipment of flour to judge the quality of the grain and milling and would occasionally make up one batch of dough with it, to test it. I often saw him with Jorge, breaking open the new-baked bread and discussing at some length just what adjustments were necessary for that shipment.

I soon found that the baking processes were not without their impediments. Something was missing on the scales, for which we always had to compensate when we weighed something. I sometimes forgot, but just as I was about to make a mistake a quick hand would come out of nowhere and make the adjustment for me. There was a large hole in the bottom of the mixer, so I was warned to put flour and sugar in first and then the eggs and liquids. There were no bowls or spoons; we used hands and table—and I found it disconcerting at first to roll out dough in the deep, curved well that was the working surface of our table deformed by constant use.

Nothing was thrown away in the bakehouse, either. I was taught how to fold and cut brown paper bags to make icing decorating bags that were simple, strong, and efficient. Every little chile can was kept from the *almuerzo*, too. They were just the right height to use as supports for stacking trays of rising dough when there was not enough room in the special racks. New uses were found for other old containers as well.

Hundreds of eggs were cracked, ready for the day's work, into a recycled lard drum. They were measured out for the rich doughs with an old tin can—seventeen eggs to the can—about ⅜ of a liter, I believe it was. And I shall never get over our *biscuits de queso*. In that bakery they were cut out with hollowed tin cans, and the characteristic little circle in the top stamped with an empty, upended Coke bottle!

I learned never to waste one teaspoon of flour or sugar. On completing a batch of dough I was handed a small dustpan and brush to sweep the surface clean; the gathered crumbs went into a special bin, to be used again. And once, when I held up impossibly greasy hands with a helpless look on my face, a large lump of soft dough landed in front of me, thrown by someone from the other table who had seen my plight. Most efficient and ecological, too—no greasy towels to wash up, and that surplus grease went to enrich some other dough that would be used later in the day.

The days sped on, and it seemed to me that my apprenticeship came to an end almost before it had begun. My hands, though, were proof of the work I had put them through. The strenuous kneading and pulling and stretching of dough in which they had engaged themselves had softened them, had emblazoned them with the badge of the baker (had Jorge not told me you could always tell a baker by his hands?), a badge I bore proudly in the less hectic—in fact I would almost say boring—days that followed.

GENERAL NOTES

Apart from liking to eat Mexican *pan dulce*, I found that I was fascinated by the very different techniques of making them, techniques I had never seen elsewhere. I know they sound terribly complicated. Try them once and the instructions will become clearer; after several tries you will become quite expert. I hope these recipes won't be ignored by all but the real aficionados and the homesick Mexicans.

You really have to be in the mood, with an undisturbed weekend ahead, to embark on a new type of baking such as this for the first time. (Once in the mood I myself find it hard to break out of it. I like my own bread and cakes, I like dough rising around the kitchen and a yeasty smell permeating the house. I even happen to like the crusty coating of flour on every handle and knob in the kitchen!) You will find that once you get in the habit you can arrange your baking time to stretch over work, play, or shopping periods; you will become critical of the oversweet, overrefined baked goods of this type generally around and your palate will begin to demand the real thing.

1 While I have no time for dough hooks in regular bread making, I do recommend a heavy-duty mixer with a dough hook attachment for all these yeast recipes (with the exception perhaps of the Biscuits de Queso on page 405). They require long, hard beating, which I certainly wouldn't do by hand.

2 You will need a warm, draft-proof area to proof the doughs, ideally at a temperature of 75°F (24°C), so I suggest you keep a room thermometer handy.

3 You may wonder why I make a starter and then only use half of it in the recipe. First, the half quantity is hard to mix and beat in the standard bowl the heavy mixers provide, and second, it will encourage you to try the recipe a second time.

4 Why aren't they rich in butter? In Mexico *pan dulce* are bought and eaten in great quantities daily. They would be too rich, too heavy, and too expensive eaten on such a scale with morning and evening café con leche or chocolate.

5 All breads baked with a high proportion of yeast such as these tend to dry out quickly. Eat as many of them as you can freshly baked and then follow the ways I have suggested of freezing, reheating, or toasting whenever feasible.

6 Weather affects this sort of baking. A damp, heavy, warm day will not produce the same nice, light dough as a clear, dry day, so be warned.

7 To make the lumpy sugar used in decorating some of the *pan dulce*, spread a good, thick layer of granulated sugar on a large baking sheet. Dampen it thoroughly with water and let it dry out completely before crumbling it roughly, ready to use.

8 Never use your fingers when working and kneading dough, only the flat of your hands and the heels of your palms. When the dough is strong, use your whole forearm to break it down.

9 For predictable results, use cake yeast and not dried.

SPECIAL EQUIPMENT FOR MEXICAN BAKING

A kitchen scale indicating both pounds and kilos is to my mind essential. A postal or diet scale for weighing small quantities, if your ordinary scale does not measure these accurately, is a possible substitute.

In addition to a normal-size wooden rolling pin, you should have a skinny wooden rolling pin, 12 to 15 inches (30 to 38 cm) long and just under 1 inch (2.5 cm) in diameter. You probably won't find this anywhere, so do what the Mexican bakeries do:

buy a broom handle or dowel cut to the appropriate length and have the ends smoothed off.

A plastic dough scraper. Nothing else can really take its place.

A cutter for decorating Conchas (page 398), not essential but nice.

A room thermometer to enable you to judge and adjust temperatures when your dough is rising.

2 large rubber spatulas.

2 thick pieces of old toweling and some large plastic bags for raising the doughs.

A heavy-duty electric mixer with dough hook attachment. I don't think it would be honest of me not to give the result of my experience in so many kitchens with so many different pieces of equipment, in England, the United States, Mexico, and France. I much prefer the KitchenAid. So many mixers are designed for design's sake—and this is particularly true of English and German machines. Those with bulbous bottoms— although the beater may be designed for them—very rarely beat as thoroughly and as quickly as the more tapered mixing bowl the KitchenAid offers.

CUERNOS Croissants
MAKES 20 TO 24 CROISSANTS, ABOUT 4¹⁄₂ INCHES (11.5 CM) ACROSS WHEN BAKED

The large, fat, well-browned croissants made in Mexico are one of the most popular pan dulce. *Eaten with* café con leche *or* chocolate *at breakfast or suppertime, when they are always brought fresh and hot from the bakery, they are made of a rich brioche-type dough and given plenty of slow rising time to develop flavor and character. They need a lot of beating, so I do advise you to use a heavy-duty mixer with dough hook attachment.*

In Mexico, for economy's sake they are made with margarine and vegetable shortening. I have compromised and put in some butter to improve the flavor.

Start at least 12 hours ahead.

THE STARTER (FOR 2 BATCHES)
8 OUNCES (225 G) UNBLEACHED ALL-PURPOSE FLOUR (1 SCANT CUP/225 ML), PLUS EXTRA FOR DUSTING

1 OUNCE (30 G) CAKE YEAST (2 TABLESPOONS/32 ML) FIRMLY PACKED

2 TABLESPOONS LUKEWARM WATER, APPROXIMATELY

3 LARGE EGGS, LIGHTLY BEATEN

THE FAT MIXTURE

7 OUNCES (200 G) UNSALTED BUTTER, AT ROOM TEMPERATURE (HEAPED ¾ CUP/ABOUT
    200 ML)

4 OUNCES (115 G) UNSALTED MARGARINE, AT ROOM TEMPERATURE (½ CUP/125 ML)

2 OUNCES (60 G) SOLID VEGETABLE SHORTENING, AT ROOM TEMPERATURE (¼ CUP/65 ML)

THE FINAL DOUGH MIXTURE

I POUND (450 G) UNBLEACHED ALL-PURPOSE FLOUR, (2 SCANT CUPS/475 ML), PLUS
    EXTRA FOR DUSTING

I CUP (250 ML) EGGS, ABOUT 4 LARGE ONES

3½ OUNCES (100 G) GRANULATED SUGAR (ABOUT ⅓ CUP/85 ML) PLUS 2 TABLESPOONS

2 OUNCES (60 G) UNSALTED MARGARINE, AT ROOM TEMPERATURE (¼ CUP/65 ML)

¼ CUP (65 ML) LUKEWARM WATER

THE GLAZE

2 LARGE EGGS, WELL BEATEN

Sift the flour into the mixing bowl of a heavy-duty mixer. Crumble the cake yeast into a small bowl, add the warm water, and press out the lumps with the back of a wooden spoon until it has the consistency of a thin, smooth cream. Add the eggs and yeast cream to the flour and beat with a dough hook at high speed until the dough forms a cohesive mass and starts to come away cleanly from the side of the bowl. The dough should then be soft, sticky, smooth, and shiny. This should take about 5 minutes.

Throw a little more flour around the edge of the bowl and beat for 2 seconds longer. Flour your working surface well and scrape the dough out onto it. Flour your hands and quickly work the dough into an oval-shaped "cushion." Butter a small baking sheet and sprinkle it with flour. Place the dough on it and make three deep diagonal slashes across the top. Cover with a piece of buttered waxed paper and then with a length of toweling and set it aside in a warm, draft-free place to rise until it has more than doubled in size—1 hour at 75°F (24°C).

During this time, prepare the fat mixture. Mix the fats with your fingertips until they are well incorporated and smooth. Refrigerate briefly; when it is ready to use, the fat mixture should be soft and pliable, neither hard nor oily.

Divide the risen starter into two equal portions. Store one half in the refrigerator for the next batch of Cuernos (it will last 3 days refrigerated and about a month frozen). The other half should be broken up roughly and put into a mixing bowl. Add the rest of the ingredients (but not, of course, the mixed fats) and beat at high speed with the dough hook until the dough forms a cohesive mass and starts to come away from the sides of the mixing bowl—about 10 minutes.

Stop the mixer occasionally during this time and scrape off the dough that collects at the top of the hook. The dough should now be soft, sticky, smooth, and shiny. Throw a little more flour around the edge of the bowl and beat for 2 seconds more.

Flour your working surface well and scrape the dough out onto it. Flour your hands and quickly form the dough into an oval-shaped "cushion." Let it rest for 1 minute.

Flour your hands again and flatten the dough out into a rough rectangular shape with the long side toward you. Then, with a thick rolling pin, roll the dough out to a rectangle about 19 by 10 inches (49 by 25.5 cm) and ¼ inch (.75 cm) thick, lifting the dough constantly as you roll it out to make sure that it is not sticking. Throw more flour underneath when necessary.

Starting from the right side, smear the mixed fats, as evenly as possible, over two thirds of the dough (there will be quite a thick layer of fat), leaving a 1-inch (2.5-cm) border free of fat around the edge of the dough. Sprinkle the fat liberally with flour. Starting from the left-hand side, fold the ungreased third of the dough over onto the greased middle third. Then fold the right-hand third over on top of them both to form a neat rectangular "package." Make sure that all the edges meet as evenly as possible, as if you were ironing table linen. Press the edges together firmly with the rolling pin so that the fat will not be able to ooze out. Give the dough one turn to the right clockwise, so that the long side will again be toward you.

Again, flour your working surface well. Roll the dough out a second time into a rectangular shape. Sprinkle flour over the surface of the dough, fold as before, and give one turn clockwise. Flour your working surface again and once more roll out the dough—although this time the rectangle will be a bit smaller, about 17 by 8 inches (43 by 20 cm) or thereabouts. By this time the yeast will be in action and the dough becoming thicker and more resilient. Sprinkle with flour and fold for the third time.

Set the dough aside to rest for about 10 minutes. Do not refrigerate unless the day is very hot and sticky. For this type of baking, the ideal temperature in the working area of the kitchen is 75°F (24°C); this will not be too hot for working and resting the dough.

Flour the surface again and roll the dough out twice more, folding and turning it in the same way. Cover the folded dough with a piece of buttered waxed paper and a thick piece of toweling and store in the bottom of the refrigerator, to allow the dough to rise very slowly, for at least 6 hours (a maximum of 12).

At the end of the rising time, remove the dough from the refrigerator. Flour your working surface well and turn the dough onto it. If the dough is very cold and stiff and hard to roll, then let it sit at room temperature for about 15 minutes. Roll the dough out until it is about ¼ inch (.75 cm) thick. Using a plastic pastry scraper or knife, cut the dough into strips 5½ inches (about 13.5 cm) wide. Then cut each strip into triangles with a 3-inch (7.5-cm) base.

Pick up one of the triangular pieces of dough and stretch the wide base gently outward to form elongated "ears." Gently pull the pointed end to stretch the dough a little. Place the triangle of dough down on the surface, with the point toward you, and then, using your palms, quickly and lightly roll it up, from the "ears" down toward the tip, making an even, compact roll. Curve the ends around to complete the crescent shape; make sure that the pointed tip is visible on top of the Cuerno.

Place the Cuernos about 2 inches (5 cm) apart on lightly greased baking sheets and set aside in a warm place, free from drafts but uncovered, until they have doubled in size—about 2½ hours in a temperature of 75°F (24°C).

Just before the end of the rising period, place the oven racks in the top half of the oven. Preheat the oven to 425°F (225°C).

Brush the Cuernos liberally with the beaten egg and bake until they are a deep brown (not golden brown)—about 12 minutes. Halfway through the baking time, reverse the position of the trays so the Cuernos will bake and brown evenly, top and bottom.

CONCHAS Sugar-Topped Sweet Buns
MAKES 16 TO 18 BUNS, ABOUT 5 INCHES (12.5 CM) ACROSS WHEN BAKED

Conchas (literally, shells) are probably the most generally known and popular of the sweet Mexican yeast rolls. They are round, spongy buns with a thin, sugar topping etched with a curved, shell-like design, from which their name is derived. Others are topped with a criss-cross design and should strictly speaking be called chicharrones *(the same name, interestingly enough, that is given to the fried pork skins), although they are usually all lumped together and called* conchas. *They are delicious when fresh and well made and the dough has been given the long, slow rising that develops the flavor. Like all bread with a higher percentage of yeast, they dry out very quickly, and instead of reheating them I prefer to cut them into thickish horizontal slices and toast them. They are also very good sliced thick, put onto well-buttered cookie sheets, and toasted crisp like Swedish rusks, to be eaten with tea or coffee or even with ice cream.*

You really do need to use a mixer with a dough hook attachment for this type of dough, which requires such a lot of beating—unless, of course, you have a very strong arm and are a glutton for punishment!

Start one day ahead.

THE STARTER (FOR 2 BATCHES)

½ POUND (225 G) UNBLEACHED ALL-PURPOSE FLOUR (2 CUPS/500 ML), PLUS EXTRA FOR
  WORKING

¾ OUNCE (22.5 G) CAKE YEAST, 3 TABLESPOONS CRUMBLED

3 TABLESPOONS LUKEWARM WATER, APPROXIMATELY

2 LARGE EGGS, LIGHTLY BEATEN

THE FINAL DOUGH MIXTURE

1 POUND (450 G) UNBLEACHED ALL-PURPOSE FLOUR (4 CUPS/1 L), PLUS EXTRA FOR
  WORKING

6 OUNCES (170 G) GRANULATED SUGAR (¾ CUP/170 ML)

½ TEASPOON SALT

1 OUNCE (30 G) UNSALTED BUTTER, SOFTENED (2 TABLESPOONS)

1 CUP (250 ML) EGGS (ABOUT 4 LARGE ONES), LIGHTLY BEATEN

¼ CUP (65 ML) LUKEWARM WATER, APPROXIMATELY

THE SUGAR TOPPING

4 OUNCES (115 G) UNBLEACHED ALL-PURPOSE FLOUR (1 CUP/250 ML)

4 OUNCES (115 G) CONFECTIONERS' SUGAR (1 CUP/250 ML MINUS 2 TABLESPOONS)

2 OUNCES (60 G) UNSALTED MARGARINE, AT ROOM TEMPERATURE (¼ CUP/65 ML)

2 OUNCES (60 G) SOLID VEGETABLE SHORTENING, AT ROOM TEMPERATURE (¼ CUP/65 ML)

2 TABLESPOONS UNSWEETENED COCOA POWDER

1 TABLESPOON GROUND CINNAMON

Sift the flour into a mixing bowl. Crumble the yeast roughly into a small bowl. Add the warm water and press out the lumps with the back of a wooden spoon until it has the consistency of a thin, smooth cream. Add the eggs and yeast cream to the flour and beat with the dough hook for about 2 minutes—the dough should be fairly stiff and sticky. Throw a little extra flour around the bowl and beat for 2 seconds longer so the dough comes away cleanly from the side of the bowl.

Flour the working surface well. Scrape the dough onto the surface and let it rest for 1 minute, then flour your hands well and quickly shape the dough into an oval "cushion." Place on a well-greased and floured baking sheet and make three deep diagonal slashes across the top. Cover with a piece of buttered waxed paper and a thick towel and set to rise in a warm place—it should double its size in $1\frac{1}{2}$ hours at a temperature of 75°F (24°C), which is ideal.

At the end of the rising period, cut the dough into two equal parts; weigh to make sure they are equal. Put part into the refrigerator for a later batch of Conchas (it will last about 3 days refrigerated or 2 months frozen). Tear the other half of the starter into rough pieces and put the pieces into a large mixing bowl.

Add the ingredients for the final dough, except for 2 ounces (60 g) of the sugar, to the starter in the bowl, and beat with a dough hook at high speed for 5 minutes. Add the rest of the sugar and beat for 5 minutes longer, or until the dough is soft, sticky, and shiny and forms a cohesive mass. Throw a little more flour around the edge of the bowl and beat for 2 seconds more so that the dough cleans itself away from the side of the bowl.

Flour your working surface and hands well. Scrape the dough out onto the surface and quickly form it into a round, even cushion shape. Let it rest for 1 minute while you butter and flour another large mixing bowl, leaving your mixer bowl free for other purposes.

Put the dough into the bowl, cover with a piece of buttered waxed paper and a thick cloth or towel, and set aside in a warm, draft-free place—about 75°F (24°C)—for 2 hours. At the end of the rising period, place the covered bowl with the dough into the bottom of the refrigerator and leave it to rise more slowly for 16 hours.

Just before the end of the long rising period, prepare the sugar topping for the buns. Sift the flour and confectioners' sugar together. Cut the fat into the flour mixture and work it in with your fingertips until thoroughly and evenly incorporated and you have a soft, pliable mixture. Divide the mixture into two equal parts. Add the cocoa to one part and cinnamon to the other and mix each one until the flavoring is evenly distributed. Set aside.

After the dough has completed its long rising period, turn it out onto a well-floured surface and let it rest for 1 minute. Flour your hands and quickly work the dough into a round cushion shape. With a plastic dough scraper or a sharp knife, cut the dough into 4 equal portions. Divide each portion again into four, making 16 portions. I like to make sure that each portion is equal, so I weigh each one and cut off any dough over 2 ounces (60 g); this way I usually end up with 18 pieces.

Butter some cookie sheets well.

Dust your hands very lightly with flour, and taking a ball of the dough in each hand, cup your palms and fingers around each of them and press them down firmly onto your working surface. Move your hands in a circular motion to form, very quickly, completely even, round balls of dough. (This is a baker's trick, and it takes a little practice before you can do it perfectly. If the countertop has too much flour you can't get any traction; if it is too sticky, then the dough will stick and have an uneven surface.)

Place the balls of dough onto the prepared sheets about 3 inches (7.5 cm) apart. When they are all set out, grease your hands well and press each ball down firmly to flatten it slightly. Then take a small piece of the sugar topping and roll it into a ball about 1 inch (2.5 cm) in diameter. Dust your hands with flour and with the fingers of your left hand—or right, whichever the case may be—press the ball of topping out onto the palm of your other hand until you have a flattened disk about 3 inches (7.5 cm) in diameter. Press this disk very firmly onto one of the balls of dough so that it adheres well. Repeat until all the balls of dough have a sugar topping, some of cinnamon, some of chocolate. Cut a crisscross or curved pattern in the sugar toppings with a knife, or use an authentic cutter.

Set the Conchas aside to rise, uncovered, in a warm, draft-free place until they are almost double in size—about 3½ hours at a temperature of 75°F (24°C).

Set two oven racks in the top half of the oven. Preheat the oven to 375°F (190°C).

Bake the Conchas until the dough is light and springy and a golden color appears around the sugar topping—about 12 minutes.

CAMPECHANAS Sugar-Glazed Flaky Pastries
MAKES ABOUT 32 PASTRIES

Next time you go into a bakery in Mexico, look for those shiny-topped, oval pastries that break into a thousand flaky pieces as you bite into them. Those are Campechanas. I had always wanted to make them, and it was such a proud day for me when trays full of my very own Campechanas were drawn out of the bakery oven. Everyone in the place craned their necks, curious to see how they had come out, and congratulated me as the pastries were whisked away into the front shop, actually to be sold.

Once you get the knack of rolling and stretching the dough, they are not difficult to make. I always think of this as an exercise in dexterity. If you look at it like that, perhaps it won't be so frustrating the first two or three times you make them! The baking procedure, however, has to be just right or you will end up with whitish layers of uncooked dough in the middle; or the sugar on top will not melt and caramelize as it should. The commercial campechanas *are always made with a mixture of vegetable fat and margarine—in Mexico I have never tasted them made with butter—but I have used a bit of butter here to improve the flavor.*

You really have to use an electric mixer; 15 minutes beating by machine is at least *half an hour by hand.*

THE BASIC DOUGH
1 POUND (450 G) UNBLEACHED ALL-PURPOSE OR STRUDEL FLOUR (ABOUT 2 CUPS/
    450 ML)
1/4 HEAPED TEASPOON SALT
1 OUNCE (30 G) GRANULATED SUGAR (2 TABLESPOONS)
1 1/3 CUPS (335 ML) COLD WATER
1 OUNCE (30 G) VEGETABLE SHORTENING (2 TABLESPOONS)

FAT FOR HANDS AND WORKING SURFACE
8 OUNCES (225 G) SOLID VEGETABLE SHORTENING (1 CUP/250 ML), APPROXIMATELY, FOR
    HEAVY GREASING OF HANDS AND WORKING SURFACE

THE FAT/FLOUR MIXTURE
5 OUNCES (140 G) UNBLEACHED ALL-PURPOSE OR STRUDEL FLOUR (1 1/4 CUPS/315 ML)
4 OUNCES (115 G) UNSALTED BUTTER, AT ROOM TEMPERATURE (1/2 CUP/125 ML)
4 OUNCES (115 G) UNSALTED MARGARINE, AT ROOM TEMPERATURE (1/2 CUP/125 ML)
2 OUNCES (60 G) SOLID VEGETABLE SHORTENING, AT ROOM TEMPERATURE (1/4 CUP/65 ML)

THE TOPPING

I CUP (250 ML) GRANULATED SUGAR, APPROXIMATELY

Put all the ingredients for the basic dough into the mixing bowl of a heavy-duty mixer and beat about 15 minutes with the dough hook until you have a stiffish, very smooth, very elastic dough that cleans itself in thick skeins from the side of the bowl. (Test by stretching a piece of the dough. If it breaks easily, then it needs some more beating.)

Grease your working surface well with some of the extra fat. Turn the dough out onto it. Grease your hands well and divide the dough into two equal parts. Roll each part into a large ball. Grease your hands again and press each ball out to a flat, even circle about 8 inches (20.5 cm) in diameter and ¾ inch (2 cm) thick. Smear the dough liberally with fat and set it aside to rest for about 10 minutes. Meanwhile, prepare the fat/flour mixture.

Work the flour and softened fat together with your fingertips until the mixture is completely smooth. Divide into two equal portions. The mixture should be soft enough to spread easily, but on no account let it become oily. Refrigerate briefly, if necessary. Set aside.

Smear your hands and the working surface with plenty of the extra fat. Pick up one of the disks of dough and turn it upside down (that is the rough side; you can see the joins of the dough that resulted from rolling it into a ball). Flatten the dough out as evenly as possible to a rectangular shape about ¾ inch (2 cm) thick, with the width toward you and the length extending away from you. Grease a thin rolling pin generously, ideally 15 inches (38 cm) in length (see note page 394), and roll the dough out thinner, still keeping the rectangular shape, until it is about ⅛ inch (.5 cm) thick.

Take one portion of the fat/flour mixture and smear it, with your hands, as evenly as possible over the top of the extended dough. Smear the rolling pin again with more fat, and carefully pulling out the near end of the dough, press it onto the rolling pin. Give a turn to the rolling pin, covering it with a thin layer of the dough and leaving about 3 inches (7.5 cm) of the pin uncovered at each end so you can grasp it firmly.

Taking the rolling pin in one hand, smooth the dough out evenly over the pin with the other. Then, very carefully, start the rolling and stretching movement, lifting the dough up quite high off the counter as it stretches out. Your hands will quite naturally be working like pedals as you roll the dough, working them backward and forward. Stretch the paper-thin dough out as much as you can without tearing it. (Note, however, that even the most expert bakers do have tears in their dough at times, so if it does happen, don't despair. It will also happen if the dough has not been beaten enough in the first place.) The last few inches of the dough must be rolled and stretched very carefully, since they will form the outer layer of the Campechanas.

Grease your hands with more fat, and smear it liberally over the outside of the rolled dough. Grasping the end of the rolling pin with one hand, with the other push the roll off the pin—it will be in the form of a sausage about 3 inches (8 cm) in diameter. Grease your hands once more and gradually stretch the roll, easing it at different parts until it has extended to form a longer, thinner roll about 28 inches (71 cm) long and 1½ inches (4 cm) in diameter. Set the roll onto a well-greased surface while you repeat the procedure for the second roll. Leave the dough to rest for about 20 minutes.

To form the Campechanas, grasp the roll between your left thumb and forefinger, about 2½ inches (6.5 cm) from the end. Flatten that small section of dough with your other hand until it is about ½ inch (1.5 cm) thick. Then, squeezing the dough hard between your thumb and forefinger, give a quick twist, severing it from the rest of the roll. (Maestro Miguel would not hear of using a knife or other convenient cutter. He says it spoils the form of the Campechanas and they would have ragged edges.)

Have ready some ungreased baking sheets. Place the piece of broken-off dough on one of them. Greasing your hands very well, flatten the dough out into a thin oval shape about 5½ by 2½ inches (14 by 6.5 cm). Smear another good layer of fat over the flattened surface. Repeat the procedure until all the dough has been used up—each roll should yield about 16 pastries. (Mathematically it doesn't look correct, but the dough stretches out even more as you work with it).

Preheat the oven to 375°F (190°C), setting the oven racks in the top half of the oven. Sprinkle the sugar for the topping liberally over the finished trays of flattened dough. Turn the trays upside down and give them several sharp taps in different places so that the excess sugar falls off. (Note: If you have not greased the top of the dough sufficiently, the sugar will not adhere properly and make a nicely glazed topping.)

Unless you have a very big oven, bake one tray at a time, on the middle shelf of the oven, until the pastry has puffed up and browned lightly—15 to 20 minutes. Turn the oven up to 450°F (230°C), move the tray to the top shelf, and bake for another 5 minutes, by which time the sugar should have melted and caramelized. Be careful— the baking is tricky, and every oven is different. You will have to experiment a bit with the first tray for the desired result. Gas ovens tend to be temperamental and run out of control at 450°F (230°C) and the sugar burns.

BISCUITS DE QUESO Cream Cheese Yeast Biscuits
MAKES ABOUT 40 BISCUITS, 3 1/2 INCHES (9 CM) ACROSS WHEN BAKED

These rich, yeasty biscuits, or scones, are a favorite pan dulce *in Mexico. Of course they are better eaten the day they are made, and preferably straight from the oven, but they freeze perfectly well and can be reheated or cut in half and toasted. Those that are not frozen and have become a little dry should be quickly dipped into milk and reheated in a 400°F (205°C) oven for about 15 minutes, or, without being dipped into milk, cut horizontally into thick slices and toasted. They are very good either by themselves or with preserves for breakfast or tea.*

For reasons of economy, Biscuits de Queso are made in the Mexican bakeries with all margarine. For reasons of flavor, as they are really rich enough with the cream cheese and large number of eggs, I substitute a small amount of butter for part of the margarine. Ordinary packaged cream cheese could be used, but I prefer, if possible, to buy the best but most reasonable loose cream cheese available in the delicatessen section of specialty shops or supermarkets.

Start at least five hours ahead.

THE STARTER (FOR 1 BATCH)
6 OUNCES (180 G) UNBLEACHED ALL-PURPOSE FLOUR (1 1/2 CUPS/375 ML), PLUS EXTRA
   FOR DUSTING
2 OUNCES (60 G) GRANULATED SUGAR (1/4 CUP/65 ML)
1/4 TEASPOON SALT
1 OUNCE (30 G) CAKE YEAST
1 TABLESPOON LUKEWARM WATER
1/3 CUP (85 ML) LIGHTLY BEATEN EGGS
2 OUNCES (60 G) UNSALTED MARGARINE, SOFTENED (1/4 CUP/65 ML)

THE FINAL DOUGH MIXTURE
8 OUNCES (225 G) GRANULATED SUGAR (1 CUP/250 ML LESS 2 TABLESPOONS)
8 OUNCES (225 G) CREAM CHEESE
2 TEASPOONS SALT
1 1/3 CUPS (335 ML) LIGHTLY BEATEN EGGS
1 CUP (250 ML) WHOLE MILK
2 1/2 POUNDS (1.125 KG) UNBLEACHED ALL-PURPOSE FLOUR (10 CUPS/2.5 L)
3 ROUNDED TABLESPOONS DOUBLE-ACTING BAKING POWDER
8 OUNCES (225 G) UNSALTED MARGARINE, AT ROOM TEMPERATURE (1 CUP/250 ML)

5 OUNCES (140 G) UNSALTED BUTTER, AT ROOM TEMPERATURE ($\frac{1}{4}$ CUP/65 ML PLUS
   2 TABLESPOONS)

THE GLAZE

2 LARGE EGGS, WELL BEATEN

Put the flour, sugar, and salt together into a mixing bowl; mix well. Crumble the cake yeast into a small bowl, add the warm water, and smooth out the lumps with the back of a wooden spoon until it is the consistency of a thin cream. Add the yeast cream, eggs, and softened margarine to the flour and mix just until the eggs are well incorporated and you have a soft, sticky dough—about 3 minutes.

Scrape the dough out onto a floured surface. Let it rest for 1 minute, then, with well-floured hands, shape it into an elongated cushion shape. Grease and lightly flour a small baking sheet and place the cushion of dough on it. Make three deep, diagonal slashes across the top of the dough, then cover with a piece of buttered waxed paper and a thick towel and set in a warm place—75°F (24°C) is ideal—to rise and almost double in volume. This will take about 2 hours.

Tear the starter up roughly and put into a mixing bowl. Add the sugar, cream cheese, salt, and eggs and mix until all are well combined, which should take about 3 minutes. Add the milk and mix for 1 minute longer, then set aside.

Sift the flour and baking powder together. Cut the fat into the flour, and when it is in small pieces rub lightly with your fingertips until the mixture resembles fine bread crumbs. Gradually add the flour mixture to the rest of the ingredients, mixing only until just combined. The result should be a soft, sticky dough.

Throw a good dusting of flour—no dainty little sprinkle from a perforated metal can—over your working surface. Scrape the dough out onto this and let it rest for 1 minute, then flour your hands well and quickly work the dough into a round cushion shape. Leave for 1 minute more. Flour your hands again and press the dough out to a thick rectangular shape. Then, with a thick rolling pin, flatten the dough to a rectangular shape—long side toward you—about 21 by 13 inches (53.5 by 33 cm) and about $\frac{1}{2}$ inch (1.5 cm) thick.

Dust the surface of the dough lightly with flour. Starting from the left-hand side, fold one third of the dough over onto the middle third, making sure that the edges meet neatly, then fold the right-hand over on top to form a neat package. Lift the package up and dust the working surface well with flour. Give the dough one turn to the right, clockwise. Roll out again, roughly to the same size. Dust the surface of the dough with a little more flour, fold as before, and again give a turn to the right. Repeat this process once more, to give three turns in all. Leave the dough to rest for 1 minute.

Dust the surface of your counter again liberally with flour and roll the dough out until it is about ¾ inch (2 cm) thick. Using a plain, round cookie cutter about 2½ inches (6.5 cm) in diameter, cut the dough out into rounds and place about 1½ inches (4 cm) apart on greased baking sheets. Gather up the remaining dough, press together well, and roll out again until it is ¾ inch (2 cm) thick; cut into biscuits. When all the biscuits are cut out, flatten them slightly with the palm of your hand and then stamp each one in the center with a circular cutter about ½ inch (1.5 cm) in diameter. Set the biscuits aside to rise, uncovered, until they almost double in size—about 2 hours in a temperature of 80°F (30°C), free from drafts.

Arrange two oven racks in the top half of the oven. Preheat the oven to 375°F (190°C). Brush the surface of the biscuits liberally with the beaten egg and bake, two trays at a time, for about 10 minutes. Reverse the position of the trays—the one on top to the second shelf, and so forth—and bake for another 5 to 10 minutes, or until they are spongy, cooked throughout, and golden brown on top.

Remove the trays from the oven and let the biscuits cool off away from drafts and cold air.

DESSERTS AND COOKIES

Flan de Naranja ✳ *Orange Flan*

Flan a la Antigua ✳ *Old-Fashioned Flan*

Cocada Imperial ✳ *Imperial Coconut Flan*

Queso de Nápoles ✳ *Neapolitan Cheese*

Capirotada I ✳ *Bread Pudding I*

Capirotada II ✳ *Bread Pudding II*

Buñuelos del Norte ✳ *Buñuelos from the North of Mexico*

Buñuelos de Viento ✳ *Fritters in Anise-Flavored Syrup*

Buñuelos Chihuahuenses ✳ *Buñuelos from Chihuahua*

Sopaipillas

Cajeta de Celaya ✳ *Goat's-Milk Dessert*

Cajeta de Leche Envinada ✳ *Cow's-Milk Dessert with Wine and Almonds*

Cajeta de Piña y Plátano ✳ *Pineapple and Banana Dessert*

Guayabas Rellenas de Cocada ✳ *Guavas Stuffed with Coconut*

Dulce de Camote ✳ *Sweet Potato Dessert*

Chongos Zamoranos ✳ *Curds in Syrup*

Mangos Flameados ✳ *Flambéed Mangoes*

Crema de Piñon o Nuez Encarcelada ✳ *Pine Nut or Pecan Cream*

Calabaza en Tacha ✳ *Pumpkin Cooked in Raw Sugar*

Torta de Cielo ✳ *Almond Sponge Cake*

Polvorones ✳ *Mexican Shortbread Cookies*

Roscas ✳ *Ring Cookies*

On a visit to a convent: "We came at length to a large hall, decorated with paintings and furnished with antique high-backed arm chairs, where a very elegant supper, lighted up and ornamented, greeted our astonished eyes; cakes, chocolates, ices, creams, custards, tarts, jellies, blancmanges, orange and lemonade and other profane dainties ornamented with gilt paper cut into little flags."

—FRANCES CALDERÓN DE LA BARCA, *Life in Mexico*

POSTRES Y GALLETAS

Almost every day when I was in Mexico City in the early seventies, I would walk through Chapultepec Park to the metro station just in front of the statue of the Niños Héroes—is there anywhere else in the world where you would find, instead of the usual signs forbidding you to spit or loiter, one saying *Prohibido pasar con globos* (It is forbidden to carry balloons into the subway)? If you have seen Chapultepec Park on a Sunday or holiday, with its clouds and clouds of brilliantly colored and bizarrely shaped balloons, you understand why. From early morning to late afternoon, just outside the station, there used to be a young woman selling *postres* from an ingeniously devised little cart. It had an enclosed glass top for the more delicate ones, and a folding extension with gently sloping ramps on which the little brightly colored jellies

shivered. Some were brilliant and clear, red and green, others opaque and creamy looking, pinks, greens, and browns; there were some with creamy bottoms and crystalline
tops displaying a whole unhulled strawberry or some chopped pecans, little cups of rice
pudding, or custards with caramel bottoms—the flavors, among others, pistachio,
walnut, blackberry, or wine. But you wouldn't need such a complicated cart. On Saturday evenings in the streets of Puebla near the market little boys scurried along with trays
of wobbling *natillas* and *jaleas* on their heads or in various artfully designed little cages
with lots of shelves and glass sides that sat comfortably on the back of a bicycle.

I am not going to try to draw the impossible line between the candies and desserts
of Mexico, because what we would call candies are so often served as *postre*, the end of
a meal. Undoubtedly the nuns from Spain during the colonial period were the greatest
innovators, and many of their sweetmeat creations still exist today in the same form and
made with the same recipes.

You don't have to go to Puebla to see the varied "convent" *dulces*. When you are
next in Mexico City, take a walk from the Palace of Fine Arts down Calle Cinco de Mayo
toward the Zócalo. On the right-hand side you will come across a shop called Dulces
de Celaya, owned by the same family who founded it in 1874. Its showcases, windows,
fittings, and lamps—nearly everything about it—are the same as they were then except
for a background of constant, sharp traffic noises from the busy street outside.

One window is usually filled with crystallized fruit—whole sweet potatoes, thick
slices of pineapple, rich dark-red watermelon, hunks of the whitish *chilacayote* with its
black seeds, and whole shells of orange peel. On the opposite side are the *gaznates*—
cornets of a thin, fried dough filled with a pineapple and coconut paste; thin triangles
of almond *turrón* between layers of rice paper, and thick disks of chocolate ground on
the metate with almonds and sugar and perfumed with vanilla and cinnamon. Inside
the shop those that specially caught my eye were the small, brilliant green limes stuffed
with coconut; almond paste miniatures of earthenware milk pitchers about one inch
high, a mamey with a piece of its light-brown skin curled back to display the rich,
salmon-pink fruit inside; or the papaya, also in miniature, with a slice cut out of it to
see the flesh and small seeds inside. There are large rectangular *jamoncillos* of Puebla
decorated with pine nuts and raisins; the acid-sweet tamarind candies from Jalisco and
small fudge-like rolls covered with pecan halves from Saltillo. The variety was, and is
still, overwhelming, and I always wanted to try everything—just once more.

For the present-day traveler who accepts what is on the menu of the average modest restaurant—although the more expensive restaurants now offer an array of much more sophisticated desserts—there is very little to choose from beyond the usual ice creams and canned fruit (there are some excellent Mexican commercial brands on the market), canned *chongos,* and the inevitable flan of very varied quality. But if you are traveling around the country, look for some of the regional specialties.

In San Luis Potosí there is a dark preserve of prickly pears—*queso de tuna*—served with slices of the very good local cream cheese or the dried pressed peaches—*duraznos prensados.* Go into one of the many shops selling the pastes of thinly rolled *láminas* of guava, quince, or crabapple under the arches of the buildings around the central plaza of Morelia; in the supermarket of La Paz in Baja California I bought some delicious paste of mango many summers ago. After a good meal of *cabrito* and frijoles rancheros in Monterrey, the industrial capital of the north, make sure that you get with your coffee the round candies of crystallized goat's-milk *cajeta—bolitas de leche quemada*—a specialty of the little town of General Zuazua. Irpuato and Zamora are great centers of strawberries, and besides some of the most delicious jams, they sell little packages of pressed crystallized strawberries.

On my first visit to Acolman, a lovely convent and a very early one of the colonial period, situated on the road out to the pyramids of Teotihuacán, I was rather astounded to see carved on the stone arch over the main door an unmistakably round and solid flan, along with grapes and other fruits and vegetables. Dairy cattle were introduced by the Spaniards as early as 1530, and the nuns lost no time reproducing their favorite sweetmeats and desserts, combining what they had brought with them from Spain with local products.

Just as I suppose most people make a beeline when they are traveling for a famous church or museum, I head first for the market. It's the key to my eating for the next few days. It seems to me that the most interesting part of Mérida's market is spread outside its walls for about a block on either side. Under the covered arches of the buildings nearby are the candy vendors. Most of their candies seem to be based on coconut, and my favorite of all, though death to one's fillings, is the *coco melcochado*: finely grated coconut in a well-burned caramel brittle.

I came across the *marañón*—the fleshy fruit of the cashew nut—the first time I was in a market in Campeche. The nut grows on the outside of its red and yellow fruit, which ripens in May. There is quite an industry in Campeche bottling them in alcohol and syrup. But try those preserved in syrup—*en almíbar*—they need the sweetness; those preserved in alcohol are curiously bitter. I remember seeing in the bus station, of all places, a small, sealed plastic bag containing what looked like a large, fleshy prune—it was a dried *marañón*. The flavor is subtle, and although I ate it every day for the best part of a week, I simply can't relate it to anything else.

The "pickled" peaches and quinces, as they are called (and they are pickled in every sense of the word in a sugarcane spirit called *aguardiente*), are still the specialty of the Chiapas highlands. The air is damp up in San Cristobál, and as in England, from time to time you need to stoke up to drive out the penetrating cold. It was in the Dulcería Santo Domingo where I first saw the fruit in huge glass jars. What a find the Dulcería was! They had the freshest, richest *pan dulce* that I had ever found in Mexico at that time, and if you happen to be there about five o'clock in the afternoon, the lightest, flakiest empanadas arrive hot from the oven with a slightly sweet meat filling.

Yes, there is a tremendous variety of wonderful sweetmeats to eat in Mexico, but you have to be prepared to look for the really good ones.

FLAN DE NARANJA Orange Flan
SEÑORA MARÍA LUISA CAMARENA DE RODRÍGUEZ
SERVES 6   PUEBLA

Señora María Luisa Camarena de Rodríguez invited me to stay with her family in Tehuacán for a few days at the end of October to try the local specialty, mole de cadera, *which is prepared each year at the time of the mass killing of goats. (I was fascinated by it—a strong, soupy stew made from the spine and hip bones of the goats and seasoned with chiles and avocado leaves—but I confess that I couldn't eat anything after the first mouthful.) However, during the few days I was there, she took me to meet the well-known cooks of the town and lent me the family cookbook, to choose and copy any recipes that I liked. Many were almost completely Spanish in origin, and this one, for an orange flan, particularly caught my eye.*

I think it's quite sensational. However, if the oranges are very sweet you will need to add a little more lime juice. I have also made it with a proportion of tangerine juice, which was unusual and delicious. I have reduced the sugar to ¹⁄₄ cup (65 ml; aside from the sugar for the caramel) and added the grated zest, which I think improves the flavor. Don't be surprised that this flan has no milk or at how much the mixture reduces during the cooking time. And if you do not let the froth from the beaten eggs subside sufficiently before you put it into the oven, it will puff up and stick to the lid of the flan mold.

¾ CUP (185 ML) GRANULATED SUGAR
FINELY GRATED ZEST OF 2 ORANGES AND ½ LIME
1 CUP (250 ML) ORANGE JUICE PLUS JUICE OF ½ LIME
6 LARGE EGGS, SEPARATED

First make the caramel. Melt ½ cup (125 ml) of the sugar in a heavy pan over low heat. When it has completely melted, turn the heat up and stir the syrup with a wooden spoon until it darkens (the color will depend on how dark you like your caramel). Pour the caramel into a flan mold, or a 1-quart (1-l) charlotte mold, and turn it around quickly, tipping the mold from side to side until there is an even coating of caramel over the bottom and halfway up the sides. Set aside.

Preheat the oven to 350°F (180°C). If you are not using a flan mold, set a water bath on the lowest shelf of the oven (improvising with a roasting pan into which the mold will fit and putting in hot water to a depth of 1½ inches [4 cm]), or so that it will come almost halfway up the side of the mold *after* it has been filled with the flan mixture.

Add the grated zest to the juice and stir the remaining ¼ cup (65 ml) sugar in gradually so that it dissolves.

Beat the egg yolks until they are thick, then, in a separate bowl, beat the whites until stiff. Gradually add the yolks to the whites, beating all the time. When they are thoroughly incorporated, gradually beat in the orange juice. Let the froth subside before pouring the mixture into the prepared mold. Grease the lid of the mold, cover, and set in the water bath. Bake until the flan is set—about 2 hours. (Test by inserting a cake tester. If the blade comes out clean, then it is cooked.) Set aside to cool, *not* in the refrigerator, before attempting to unmold.

FLAN A LA ANTIGUA Old-Fashioned Flan
BASED ON A RECIPE BY SEÑORA JOSEFINA VELÁZQUEZ DE LEÓN
SERVES 6

This is a truly superb flan with a satiny texture.

1 QUART (1 L) MILK
½ CUP (125 ML) GRANULATED SUGAR
A VANILLA BEAN, ABOUT 2 INCHES (5 CM)
A PINCH OF SALT
4 LARGE EGGS
6 LARGE EGG YOLKS

Have ready a flan mold coated with caramel (see page 413).

Preheat the oven to 350°F (180°C).

Heat the milk in a heavy saucepan, add the sugar, vanilla bean, and salt, and let it simmer for about 15 minutes. The milk should be reduced by about ½ cup (125 ml). Set it aside to cool.

Beat the eggs and egg yolks together well. Add them to the cooled milk and stir well. Pour the mixture through a strainer into the coated mold. (Rinse the vanilla bean, let it dry, and store it for use again.)

Cover the mold and set it in a water bath on the lowest shelf in the oven. Cook the flan for 2 hours and test to see if it is firmly set. When it is done, set it aside to cool.

COCADA IMPERIAL Imperial Coconut Flan
SEÑORA NORMA DE SHEHADI, MEXICO CITY
SERVES 6

Despite its name, this cocada *is a type of flan and a textured and delicious one at that. It will, of course, have a much better flavor if made with a fresh coconut since the water can be used as well. I warn you that it will separate into layers when cooked!*

Like all flans it is better made several hours or the day before for the custard to set more firmly and make it easy to cut.

¾ CUP (185 ML) GRANULATED SUGAR
2 CUPS (500 ML) MILK

1 SMALL COCONUT

1 CUP (250 ML) RESERVED COCONUT WATER

4 LARGE EGGS, SEPARATED

A PINCH OF SALT

Have ready a flan mold coated with caramel (see page 413).

Preheat the oven to 350°F (180°C).

Melt the sugar in the milk over low heat in a heavy saucepan, then raise the heat and boil it briskly. Take care that it doesn't boil over. As soon as it begins to thicken, stir the mixture so that it does not stick to the bottom of the pan. After about 30 minutes, it should be the consistency of a thin condensed milk and should have been reduced to about 1 cup (250 ml).

Pierce a hole through two of the "eyes" of the coconut and drain the water from it. Set the water aside. Put the whole coconut into the oven for about 8 minutes. Crack it open; the flesh should come away quite easily from the shell.

Pare the brown skin from the flesh with a potato peeler and grate the flesh finely; 2¼ cups (565 ml), loosely packed, will be needed for the flan.

Add the grated coconut to the coconut water and boil it over brisk heat for about 5 minutes, stirring it all the time. Add the "condensed" milk and continue cooking for another 5 minutes. Set the mixture aside to cool.

Beat the egg yolks together until they are creamy and stir them well into the coconut mixture. Beat the egg whites until they are frothy, add the salt, and continue beating until they are firm but not too dry. Fold them into the mixture.

Pour the mixture into the prepared mold. Cover the mold with a well-greased lid and put it into a water bath. Cook the flan on the lowest shelf in the oven for about 1½ hours, then test to see if it is done. When it is done, set it aside to cool.

QUESO DE NÁPOLES Neapolitan Cheese
SERVES 6

There are many variations of Queso de Nápoles, or queso Napolitano, *and how it came to be named remains a mystery. If you ask for it in Yucatán, you will be given a very solid flan made with canned condensed milk, with or without ground almonds. And it may also be cooked without the caramel. I have chosen this version because I think it is by far the best: a white, delicate flan, with a spongy, nutty layer at the bottom. It is also a marvelous way of using up those egg whites which always have a way of accumulating.*

2 CUPS (500 ML) MILK

¼ CUP (65 ML) GRANULATED SUGAR

¼ CUP (65 ML) FINELY GROUND ALMONDS (ABOUT 1 ½ OUNCES/45 G)

4 EGG WHITES

A PINCH OF SALT

Have ready a flan mold coated with caramel (see page 413).

Preheat the oven to 350°F (180°C).

Bring the milk to a boil in a heavy saucepan and let it simmer for 5 minutes.

Add the sugar and the almonds to the milk and let the mixture simmer for another 5 minutes. Set it aside until it is cool.

Beat the egg whites until frothy, add the salt, and continue beating until they are stiff. Fold the beaten whites into the milk mixture. Pour the mixture into the prepared mold.

Cover the mold with a well-greased lid and set it in the lowest part of the oven in a water bath. Cook for 1½ hours, then test to see if the *queso* is firmly set. When it is done, set it aside to cool.

CAPIROTADA I Bread Pudding I
SERVES 6

One of the favorite Lenten desserts of Mexico is Capirotada, using slices of the small yeast rolls called bolillos *(slices of French bread would do equally well). Slice the bread and leave it overnight on a wire tray to dry out, or you can dry it out in a slow oven.*

In some recipes for Capirotada, you are told to fry the bread, which absorbs an enormous amount of fat, so I have changed the cooking method here.

Don't look askance at the fig leaf listed below; if it is available it gives a distinctive and delicious flavor to the pudding. And if you are using piloncillo, the raw sugar of Mexico, I suggest that you leave it to soak in the water several hours ahead of time, as it tends to be rather hard.

Traditionally, Capirotada is eaten as a dessert or with a glass of milk at supper.

¼ CUP (65 ML) MELTED PORK LARD

¼ CUP (65 ML) VEGETABLE OIL

4 BOLILLOS, OR 16 HALF-INCH (1.5-CM) SLICES FRENCH BREAD, DRIED OUT

8 OUNCES (225 G) PILONCILLO OR DARK BROWN SUGAR

1 CUP (250 ML) WATER

4-INCH (10-CM) PIECE OF CINNAMON STICK OR 1 LARGE FIG LEAF

4 OUNCES (115 G) QUESO AÑEJO OR ROMANO, FINELY GRATED

¼ CUP (65 ML) RAISINS

¼ CUP (65 ML) SLIVERED ALMONDS OR PINE NUTS

3 TABLESPOONS UNSALTED BUTTER, SOFTENED AND CUT INTO SMALL PIECES

Preheat the oven to 350°F (180°C) and place the oven rack on the middle level.

Butter generously a shallow dish just large enough to accommodate half of the bread slices in one layer—a dish 8½ by 8½ inches (21.5 by 21.5 cm) should be perfect.

Choose a cookie sheet onto which all the bread slices will just fit comfortably. Mix the melted lard and oil and coat the cookie sheet well. Arrange the pieces of bread on the cookie sheet and paint the top of them liberally with the rest of the oil–lard mixture. Bake for about 10 minutes, then turn the pieces over and bake for another 10 minutes, or until the bread is crisp and a deep golden color.

Over low heat, melt the piloncillo or sugar in the water, along with the cinnamon or fig leaf (if using the piloncillo, see the note above). Bring the resulting syrup to a boil and cook for 8 minutes *only* (the syrup should have some body but not be too thick).

Put one half of the bread slices into the prepared dish and very slowly pour about one third of the syrup onto the bread (*not* the dish), then sprinkle with one half of the cheese, raisins, and nuts. Dot with half the butter. Cover with the remaining bread slices and syrup and sprinkle on the rest of the cheese, raisins, and nuts, and dot with the remaining butter. (Note: it is particularly important to pour the syrup little by little onto the bread, waiting for each batch to be absorbed before adding more. If you don't do this, the syrup will run to the bottom of the dish and the top layer will remain dry.) Cover the dish with foil and bake for about 20 minutes, by which time the bread should be soft but not mushy and the top slightly browned.

Serve either hot or cold.

CAPIROTADA II   Bread Pudding II

SEÑORA MARÍA ELENA LARA
SERVES 6   MEXICO CITY

This is a totally different version from the preceding recipe. While that one calls for stale bolillos or French bread, this version calls for the slightly sweet yeast bread called pechuga *(a suitable substitute for which would be any semisweet yeast bread made with eggs, such as challah). This bread, too, is sliced and left to dry out overnight—or is dried out in a slow oven.*

Señora Lara uses chopped acitrón (candied biznaga cactus) between the layers, but I find this too sweet—a problem I have with most Mexican desserts—and prefer using dried pineapple plus ¹/₃ cup (85 ml) white raisins and currants as a substitute, harking back, I am sure, to my youth in England and the bread-and-butter pudding that was an inevitable favorite at home.

An ideal dish for this recipe would be a round glass dish about 8¹/₂ inches (21.5 cm) in diameter and 2¹/₂ to 3 inches (6.5 to 7 cm) deep.

2 ¹/₂ CUPS (625 ML) MILK
¹/₃ CUP (85 ML) GRANULATED SUGAR
2-INCH (5-CM) PIECE OF CINNAMON STICK
¹/₃ CUP (85 ML) GOLDEN RAISINS AND CURRANTS, MIXED
¹/₃ CUP (85 ML) BLANCHED, SLICED ALMONDS OR PINE NUTS
5 ¹/₂ TABLESPOONS VEGETABLE OIL
3 DRIED TORTILLAS, 6 INCHES (15 CM) IN DIAMETER
4 TABLESPOONS UNSALTED BUTTER
15 SLICES SWEET YEAST BREAD, EACH APPROXIMATELY 6 INCHES (15 CM) LONG,
    2 INCHES (5 CM) HIGH, AND ¹/₂ INCH (1.5 CM) THICK
¹/₂ CUP (125 ML) CUBED ACITRÓN (SEE PAGE 497) OR DRIED PINEAPPLE

THE TOPPING
4 LARGE EGGS, SEPARATED
PINCH OF SALT
2 TABLESPOONS GRANULATED SUGAR, APPROXIMATELY

Put the milk, sugar, cinnamon stick, raisins, and almonds into a saucepan and bring to a simmer. Continue simmering until the sugar has melted, then set aside to cool.

Heat 1¹/₂ tablespoons of the oil and fry the tortillas on both sides; they should be leathery. Drain on paper toweling, then cut them into pieces so that they completely cover the bottom of a round baking dish.

Melt 2 tablespoons of the butter in 2 more tablespoons of the oil. Quickly dip both sides of the bread slices into the mixture so they are lightly covered but do not absorb too much. Add the rest of the oil and butter and repeat the process for the remaining slices. Put the pieces back into the frying pan, a few at a time, and fry over low heat until golden on both sides. (The original recipe used up a great deal more fat because the slices were just fried. This is a more laborious method but uses less fat.)

Put one third of the fried bread into the prepared pan in one layer, completely covering the bottom. Pour over about one quarter of the sweetened milk, raisins, and almond mixture, then sprinkle on one third of the acitrón. Cover with another layer of the bread. Pour about one third of the remaining milk and fruit evenly onto the bread, then sprinkle on another third of the acitrón. Repeat the layers with the remaining ingredients and set aside for the bread to absorb the milk—about 15 minutes.

Place an oven rack on the lowest shelf of the oven; preheat the oven to 350°F (180°C).

Beat the egg whites together until fluffy. Add the salt and beat until stiff (you should be able to turn the bowl upside down without the eggs sliding out). Add the yolks, one by one, beating well after each one is added, until they are well incorporated.

Spread the top of the pudding evenly with the beaten eggs, then sprinkle with the sugar and set in the oven to bake for about 30 minutes. When cooked, all the liquid should be absorbed and the top lightly browned.

Serve either hot or cold.

BUÑUELOS DEL NORTE Buñuelos from the North of Mexico

SEÑORA ALMA KAUFMAN

ABOUT 22 10-INCH (25.5 CM) BUÑUELOS   CHIHUAHUA

Somewhere, every day in Mexico, churches celebrate the day of their patron saint. Small stands appear out of nowhere overnight, and by morning have set themselves up in business on the sidewalk outside the church, ready to feed the early worshippers. They may be gaily hung with elaborately decorated fiesta breads of all sizes, they may be cooking up the usual enchiladas and tacos—but no matter what, there will always be a buñuelo stand.

In the villages of Michoacán the buñuelo seems to have become daily food. As evening falls, there is a hum of activity under the arches of the central plazas as everyone gathers to gossip over a bowl of pozole (pork and corn soup) or eat buñuelos. It is the tradition there to break them up into a hot syrup flavored with cinnamon stick, and you are even given a choice of having them acaramelizados (still crisp) or garritos (cooked in the syrup until soft). And no Christmas Eve supper in Mexico is complete without hot chocolate and buñuelos. This is the time of year when the family recipes are brought out and everyone helps to stretch out the paper-thin rounds of dough, which are then fried crisp and sprinkled with sugar and cinnamon or perhaps a vanilla-flavored syrup. Naturally, every recipe varies slightly, and families vie with each other, proclaiming theirs to be superior and authentic. Alma Kaufman, who was born in Chihuahua, showed me how to make the buñuelos traditional to her family.

As she sat, cross-legged, pulling out each piece of dough to a paper-thin circle with rapidly moving fingers, she reminisced about her childhood. Every Christmas she went to visit her grandmother in the Sierra de Chihuahua, and would watch her sitting in the sun, stretching out the dough either over her knee or over an inverted pottery jug. She believes that there is something very special about the air and sun at that time of year that contributes toward making the festive buñuelos superior to those made during the rest of the year. Her grandmother always made hundreds of them for family and friends, but they were kept under lock and key from the children, whose appetites knew no limits, and for the few days before Christmas frantic efforts were made to try and discover where the key had been hidden.

Señora Kaufman mentioned that her grandmother's original recipe used an infusion of the papery husks of tomate verde to both mix the dough and provide the acid raising agent now supplied by baking powder. And because the family prefers to eat their buñuelos just as they are, instead of sprinkling them with sugar and cinnamon or a cinnamon-flavored syrup, the dough has a larger proportion of sugar than most recipes call for. (They can also be made with butter, or pork lard, or a mixture of shortenings, according to one's taste.)

The furniture in the room was piled with pale golden disks, and Señora Kaufman's son was just finishing off the last batch from twelve pounds of flour. He was punching and pulling it until it reached its punto. To test this, he formed the dough into a thick circle and put it over his clenched fist. The dough rolled softly over his hand, covering it like a closely fitting cap. Another way he tested the dough was to form it into a thick roll and slash it to a depth of about 1½ inches (4 cm) with a sharp knife. If the dough sprang back immediately like elastic, it was ready.

THE BUÑUELOS

1 CUP (250 ML) COLD WATER, APPROXIMATELY

½ CUP (125 ML) GRANULATED SUGAR (IF NOT USING THE SYRUP; ONLY 1 ROUNDED
    TABLESPOON SUGAR IF USING THE SYRUP)

½ TEASPOON SALT

1 POUND (900 G) UNBLEACHED ALL-PURPOSE FLOUR (ABOUT 4 CUPS/1 L)

2 TEASPOONS BAKING POWDER

4 TABLESPOONS PORK LARD OR BUTTER, CUT INTO SMALL PIECES

1 LARGE EGG, LIGHTLY BEATEN

VEGETABLE OIL FOR FRYING

THE SUGAR SYRUP (OPTIONAL)

1 CUP (250 ML) LIGHT BROWN SUGAR

½ CUP (125 ML) COLD WATER

2½-INCH (6.5-CM) PIECE OF CINNAMON STICK, BROKEN IN HALF

Put the water into a small saucepan. Add the sugar and salt and warm through over low heat until the sugar has melted. Let the mixture cool off to lukewarm while you start the dough.

Sift the flour and baking powder together, then rub with the fat through your fingertips until the mixture resembles fine crumbs. Add the beaten egg and then, gradually, the sugared water. Work the dough very hard, kneading, pulling, and throwing it down onto the table until it is smooth and elastic. Test by making a cushion of the dough and slashing it with a knife to a depth of about 1 inch (2.5 cm); the dough should spring back immediately. This will take 10 to 15 minutes, depending, of course, on how much strength you put into it.

Press the dough out to a thick oval, then roll up into an elongated sausage shape. Tuck both ends in to form a cushion and place inside a plastic bag. Set the dough aside, in a warm place, for a minimum of 3 hours.

After the dough has rested, divide up and roll into balls approximately 1 inch (2.5 cm) in diameter. Place the balls on a tray; cover first with plastic wrap and then with a damp towel, and set aside in a warm place for at least 30 minutes.

Cover your table with a cloth. Sitting in a comfortable chair, cross your legs and put a dry, clean kitchen towel over your knee. Press one of the balls of dough firmly between your palms until you have a circle about 2½ inches (6.5 cm) in diameter. Take the dough between the thumbs and forefingers of both hands and gently stretch it out into a larger circle about 4 inches (10 cm) in diameter; do this in such a way that the center will be almost transparent while the edges are still thick.

Place the center of the dough on your knee and, using the thumbs and forefingers of both hands, gently ease out, rather than pull, and at the same time stretch, the thick edge in quick little movements, working clockwise, until you have a circle about 10 inches (25 cm) in diameter. Place the buñuelo carefully onto the tablecloth to dry (you can hang them around the edge of the table, too) while you proceed with the remaining balls of dough.

It will take about 45 minutes for the buñuelos to dry out on one side; they will then feel dry and papery to the touch. Turn them over and let them dry out completely on the second side. The drying process should take about 1 hour 15 minutes, depending, of course, on how humid the air is.

Pour oil to a depth of ½ inch (1.5 cm) into a large, heavy frying pan and heat until it is hot but not smoking. Spread a large tray with a double layer of paper toweling.

Put one of the buñuelos carefully into the hot oil—it will most probably balloon up—and holding a sharp-tined fork in each hand, prick the dough in various places and lift up the edge at one side to let the air out. In perhaps 2 seconds light golden spots will appear through the dough or at the edge, the sign that the buñuelo should be turned over and cooked for a few seconds more on the other side. The buñuelo should be pale gold in color, with some creamy-colored patches. If it is too dark in color (commercially made ones usually are), lower the heat and let the oil cool off a little before cooking the next one.

As each buñuelo is cooked, drain well of any excess fat by holding it over the pan and then lay on the paper toweling to drain further. Serve immediately or keep hot if you are going to dribble them with syrup first.

If you are using the sugar syrup, put the ingredients for the syrup into a small saucepan. Set over low heat and stir until the sugar has melted. Raise the heat and cook fast until the syrup reduces and forms a soft thread—120°F (49°C) on a candy thermometer. Dribble the syrup over the hot buñuelos and serve.

Buñuelos should be kept only a few days in a cool place—they will have a rancid flavor if kept longer.

BUÑUELOS DE VIENTO   Fritters in Anise-Flavored Syrup
MAKES 12 SMALL BUÑUELOS   VERACRUZ

Most countries have their version of buñuelos, or fritters, either sweet or savory, and they are certainly great favorites throughout Spain and Latin America.

In many parts of Mexico buñuelos are made of a stiffer dough, which is rolled out thin anywhere up to 12 inches (30 cm) in diameter and then fried crisp and stacked ready for use. In Uruapan I have wandered around in the evenings under the portales of the central plaza looking for the crispest and freshest to eat with a cup of hot chocolate. There they are broken into small pieces and heated quickly in a thick syrup of piloncillo, the raw sugar of Mexico. These of Veracruz are very much like the churros of Spain — in texture if not in shape — but flavored with aniseeds and served with a syrup.

Thirty eggs went into the batch that were being made in the Brisas del Mar Restaurant, in a small village a few miles south of Veracruz. Señorita Duarte, whose recipe this is, showed me how to make them, and I must say everyone was very good-humored about the bizarre shapes that some of their customers had to eat that day.

THE SYRUP
1 ½ CUPS (375 ML) DARK BROWN SUGAR
SCANT ¼ TEASPOON ANISEEDS
3 CUPS (750 ML) WATER

THE DOUGH
1 CUP (250 ML) WATER
¼ TEASPOON SALT
¼ TEASPOON ANISEEDS
3 TABLESPOONS LARD
4 OUNCES (115 G) SIFTED FLOUR (ABOUT 1 CUP/250 ML)
2 LARGE EGGS
¼ TEASPOON BAKING POWDER

THE BUÑUELOS
VEGETABLE OIL FOR FRYING—AT LEAST 1 ½ INCHES (4 CM) DEEP IN THE PAN

Add the brown sugar and aniseeds to the water in a saucepan. Cook over medium heat until the sugar has melted, and then bring it quickly to a boil. Let the syrup boil for about 20 minutes; by then it should have reduced to about 1½ cups (375 ml). Set it aside to cool.

Put the water, salt, aniseeds, and lard into a saucepan and bring to a fast simmer. When the lard has completely melted and the mixture is still simmering, stir the flour into it quickly. Beat the mixture, while continuing to cook it, until it shrinks away from the sides of the pan. Set it aside to cool.

When the dough is cool enough to handle, knead it until it is quite smooth.

Beat the eggs lightly and stir them into the dough, a little at a time, reserving some of the egg until you have tested the dough. You should be able to roll it into a soft ball that will just hold its shape. Add the rest of the egg if necessary.

Mix the baking powder into the dough.

In a deep skillet heat the oil to about 375°F (190°C). Wet your hands well, take a piece of the dough, and roll it into a ball about 1½ inches (4 cm) in diameter.

Place the ball on your fingers—*not on your palm*—and flatten it to make a cake about ¾ inch (2 cm) thick. Make a large hole in the center of the dough and drop it into the hot oil. Cook it on both sides until it is golden brown and well puffed up.

Remove the buñuelos from the fat with a slotted spoon and drain them on the paper.

Pour ¼ cup (65 ml) syrup over each serving of two buñuelos and serve immediately.

NOTE: These can be cooked several hours ahead and doused with syrup just before serving, but they do not keep successfully from one day to another.

BUÑUELOS CHIHUAHUENSES Buñuelos from Chihuahua

SEÑORA ROSA MARGARITA J. DE MEJÍA

MAKES 12 8-INCH (20.5-CM) BUÑUELOS   CHIHUAHUA

These buñuelos are from Chihuahua, as are Señora Kaufman's on page 419, but how different the two are! These are sprinkled with granulated sugar and cinnamon while they are still hot and can be eaten hot or cold. At Christmas time in Chihuahua they are served with café con leche, as chocolate is rarely drunk in the north.

The leavening agent, as in many parts of Mexico, is tequesquite *(a natural salt used as a raising agent), for which I have substituted cream of tartar.*

12 OUNCES (340 G) UNBLEACHED ALL-PURPOSE FLOUR (ABOUT 3 CUPS/750 ML)

2 TEASPOONS BAKING POWDER

$^{1}/_{4}$ TEASPOON CREAM OF TARTAR

$^{1}/_{4}$ TEASPOON SALT

3 TABLESPOONS GRATED CHIHUAHUA CHEESE OR MILD CHEDDAR

1 $^{1}/_{2}$ TABLESPOONS SOLID VEGETABLE SHORTENING, CUT INTO SMALL PIECES

1 $^{1}/_{2}$ LARGE EGGS, LIGHTLY BEATEN

$^{1}/_{3}$ CUP (85 ML) WARM WATER, APPROXIMATELY

VEGETABLE OIL FOR FRYING

THE TOPPING

$^{1}/_{2}$ CUP (125 ML) GRANULATED SUGAR, APPROXIMATELY, MIXED WITH 2 TABLESPOONS
GROUND CINNAMON

Sift the flour, baking powder, cream of tartar, and salt together. Stir in the cheese. Add the shortening and rub in lightly with the tips of the fingers until it is well incorporated.

Gradually stir in the eggs and water, then knead the dough lightly until it is soft and pliable—about 2 minutes. Cover the dough with waxed paper and set aside for about 2 hours. Do not refrigerate—unless, of course, the weather is very hot and sticky.

Divide the dough into 12 equal balls about 1½ inches (4 cm) in diameter. Lightly sprinkle a pastry board or cloth with flour. Using a thin rolling pin (see page 394), roll four of the balls of dough out very thin; they should each make a circle about 8 inches (20 cm) in diameter.

Pour the oil into a heavy 10-inch (25-cm) frying pan to a depth of 1 inch (1.5 cm) and heat until smoking. Carefully place a thin round of dough in the hot fat and fry until it is a deep golden color on the underside (you may need to use two spatulas toward the end of the frying period to keep the buñuelo down in the fat); this should take about 2 minutes. Turn it over carefully and fry the second side. (The whole process should take from 3½ to 4 minutes.) Remove and drain on paper toweling. While still hot, sprinkle with the sugar and cinnamon.

Repeat with the remaining three circles, then roll out four more balls of dough and continue until the remainder of the buñuelos have been fried.

Serve the buñuelos immediately or let cool and store in an airtight container for a few days only as they will develop a rancid flavor.

SOPAIPILLAS
MAKES ABOUT 120 SOPAIPILLAS

CHIHUAHUA

For years I have been denying to aficionados of the sopaipillas of New Mexico that they have a Mexican counterpart. I have now discovered that they can be found, though rarely, in the state of Chihuahua. Made of the same dough as flour tortillas, they are rolled out thin, cut into small pieces, and fried puffy and crisp. They are then sprinkled with confectioners' sugar or cinnamon and eaten cold in the early evening, with coffee. I have yet to see them on any restaurant menus in the north.

When rolling out the dough, try not to pick up too much extra flour. It will sink to the bottom of the frying pan and burn, and eventually you will have to strain the oil and start again — which is a nuisance, and very messy besides.

¹/₂ TEASPOON SALT
I CUP (250 ML) WARM WATER
2 OUNCES (60 G) PORK LARD (¹/₄ CUP/65 ML), CUT INTO SMALL PIECES
I POUND (450 G) UNBLEACHED ALL-PURPOSE FLOUR (ABOUT 4 CUPS/I L)
VEGETABLE OIL FOR FRYING
CONFECTIONERS' SUGAR AND GROUND CINNAMON FOR DUSTING

Dissolve the salt in the water and set aside to cool to lukewarm. Rub the fat into the flour with your fingertips until it resembles very fine bread crumbs.

Add the salted water to the flour and mix the dough with your hands until it comes cleanly away from the sides of the bowl. Turn the dough out onto a lightly floured surface and knead and pull it out for about 5 minutes. Knead the dough into a round cushion shape, put into a plastic bag, and set aside for a minimum of 2 hours, but preferably overnight. Do not refrigerate.

Cover a tray with a smooth, clean cloth. Remove the dough from the bag and knead for a minute or so on a lightly floured surface, then divide into small balls approximately 1¹/₄ inches (3.5 cm) in diameter; there should be about 30 of them. Set them onto the tray and cover with a slightly damp cloth or plastic wrap so the outside of the balls does not dry out and form a crust.

Have ready a small frying pan containing vegetable oil to the depth of ¹/₂ inch (1.5 cm). Have ready another tray, covered with two layers of paper toweling. You will then need an ordinary kitchen fork, a metal spatula, and a thin rolling pin (see page 394).

Start heating the oil over low heat while you roll out the first ball.

Dust your working surface *very* lightly. Roll one of the balls out until it is about 5½ inches (14 cm) in diameter—don't worry if the circle is a bit uneven, as sopaipillas can be cut into any shape at all. The dough should be thin but not transparent. Cut the dough into four or even six triangular pieces—or what you will—and immediately, *while the dough is still damp*, put the sopaipillas into the hot oil. Keep pressing the sopaipillas down lightly with the back of a fork. If your oil is the correct heat the dough should begin to bubble and puff up in about 2 seconds. As soon as the sopaipillas are a light golden color on one side, turn them over and continue cooking on the second side for a few seconds more. Remove with a slotted spoon and drain on paper toweling. While they are still warm, sprinkle with confectioners' sugar and ground cinnamon. Repeat the process with the rest of the balls.

A NOTE ON HEAT OF THE OIL: The oil should be heated to just below the smoking point. If the sopaipillas cook too fast on the first side, then they will not puff up as readily. Keep adjusting the heat and test if necessary with a small piece of the dough.

CAJETA DE CELAYA Goat's-Milk Dessert
BASED ON A RECIPE BY SEÑORA JOSEFINA VELÁZQUEZ DE LEÓN
MAKES ABOUT 1 QUART (1 L) CENTRAL AND NORTHERN MEXICO

Cajeta *was the name originally given in Mexico to the small wooden boxes especially made to store sweetmeats, although it has come to mean the sweetmeat itself: a paste made of fruits, nuts, or thickened milk. Evolved presumably to preserve these products before the days of refrigeration, the present-day Cajeta de Leche—known in other parts of Latin America as dulce de leche—is now sold in glass jars; indeed, it would be a frustrating job to keep it in a box, as it would ooze out.*

The Cajeta de Celaya, which takes its name from the bustling town in the Bajío where the making of it has become quite a large industry, can be bought in different flavors: wine, caramel, strawberry (strawberries grow in abundance in that part of the country). As with many other products all over the world, the demand has become so great that poor-quality cajetas *are selling in great quantities, even though they have lost the characteristics of the original through the addition of too much cane syrup. Still the best is the musky goat's-milk* cajeta *from San Luis Potosí that I first came across in Mexico.*

I have seen it made commercially in huge vats in San Luis, and I thought that the dark color was due to the long cooking time—but when I made it at home I found out that it wasn't so. None of my friends could tell me how to get that rich, dark brown of the San Luis cajeta, *and no cookbook mentioned it, but in the same little book that told me about the pineapple and banana* cajeta *I came across the rather obvious method that I have included in this recipe.*

Traditionally in Mexico it is eaten by itself, and that is how I think it is best. However, it has come to be used over small dessert crepes or over vanilla ice cream, which I personally find too sweet a combination.

1 QUART (1 L) GOAT'S MILK
1 QUART (1 L) COW'S MILK
3/4 TEASPOON CORNSTARCH
SCANT 1/4 TEASPOON BAKING SODA
1 1/2 CUPS (375 ML) GRANULATED SUGAR

THE CARAMEL
1/2 CUP (125 ML) GRANULATED SUGAR

Put the goat's milk and 3 1/2 cups (875 ml) of the cow's milk into a large, heavy saucepan and bring to a boil.

Mix the cornstarch, baking soda, and remaining 1/2 cup (125 ml) of the cow's milk together and stir the mixture into the boiling milk.

Stir the 1 1/2 cups (375 ml) sugar gradually into the saucepan and keep stirring until it has dissolved. Continue cooking the mixture. Meanwhile prepare the coloring.

Caramelize the 1/2 cup (125 ml) sugar (see page 413). Remove the milk mixture from the heat and very gradually add the hot caramel. Take care as it will foam up alarmingly.

Continue boiling the mixture until it is just beginning to thicken—40 to 50 minutes, depending on the depth of the *cajeta* in the pan. Then continue to cook, stirring it all the time, until it forms a thread and coats the back of a wooden spoon.

Pour the *cajeta* into a dish to cool before serving. From start to finish it will take about 1 1/2 hours to cook.

NOTE: Cajeta de Celaya will keep indefinitely in screw-top jars in a cool place.

CAJETA DE LECHE ENVINADA
Cow's-Milk Dessert with Wine and Almonds
SERVES 6

CENTRAL MEXICO

6 CUPS (1.5 L) MILK

1 POUND (450 G) GRANULATED SUGAR (ABOUT 2 CUPS/500 L)

A PINCH OF BAKING SODA

3 YOLKS OF LARGE EGGS

1/3 CUP (85 ML) ALMONDS, BLANCHED AND SLIVERED

1/2 CUP (125 ML) MEDIUM-DRY SHERRY OR MADEIRA

Put the milk, sugar, and baking soda into a heavy saucepan and set it over medium heat until the sugar has melted. Then raise the heat and boil it as fast as possible for 30 minutes. Put ³⁄₄ cup (185 ml) of the milk–sugar mixture aside to cool. Beat the egg yolks until creamy and add them to the cooled milk.

Continue boiling the rest of the milk mixture until it becomes thick, like condensed milk. As it thickens, stir the mixture continually or it will stick to the pan. This should take about 30 minutes.

Remove from the heat and add the egg mixture to the thickened milk, stirring all the time. Continue cooking the mixture over medium heat until it starts to come away from the bottom and sides of the pan.

Stir the almonds and sherry into the mixture. Pour the mixture into a serving dish and let it get thoroughly cool before serving.

NOTE: This *cajeta* will keep indefinitely in screw-top jars in a cool place.

CAJETA DE PIÑA Y PLÁTANO Pineapple and Banana Dessert
SERVES 6

JALISCO AND COLIMA

This is a thick, dark paste of fruit with an unusual and refreshing flavor.

Whenever I make it I think of Luz, our first Mexican maid. Although she came only to clean for a few brief periods each week, somehow she managed to give me my first Mexican cooking lessons. At that time I didn't think to ask her where she had come across this recipe, and I had never been able to find it in any cookbook, or find anyone else who knew of it, at least in Mexico City. But one day I was reading through a book I had just acquired, Recetas Prácticas para la Señora de Casa published in Guadalajara in 1895, and there it was.

And I shall remember her also for sentimental reasons, for she was our maid when Paul decided he would take the plunge and get married again. It was the day of our civil wedding, and when we returned home Luz was standing at the entrance of the apartment house, almost blocking the door with the biggest flower arrangement I have ever seen. She was beaming, and in her excitement had apparently told everyone she could find about the wedding, for she was surrounded by the caretaker and his family, various maids, and curious onlookers. Indeed she had informed everyone, for that evening as I went into the bathroom—and I must explain that our bathroom window was extremely large and low and opened into a well immediately opposite the bathroom window of our French neighbor—with true Gallic courtesy Monsieur the neighbor rose, threw open his arms, and exclaimed: "Felicidades, señora, I hear that you and the señor are getting married." And with that he shut the window.

1 ½ CUPS (375 ML) DARK BROWN SUGAR
3 CUPS (750 ML) WATER
2-INCH (5-CM) PIECE OF CINNAMON STICK
1 PINEAPPLE, ABOUT 4 POUNDS (1.8 KG)
2 POUNDS (900 G) BANANAS (NOT TOO RIPE)
2-INCH (5-CM) PIECE OF CINNAMON STICK, BROKEN IN HALF
JUICE AND ZEST OF ½ LIME

Preheat the oven to 350°F (180°C).

Bring the brown sugar, water, and cinnamon to a boil in a heavy pan and let them continue to boil fast for about 20 minutes. The liquid will have reduced to about 2½ cups (625 ml). Remove the cinnamon stick.

Clean and dice the fruit and blend it with the syrup to a medium texture.

Pour the mixture into a shallow ovenproof dish, ideally not much more than 3 inches (8 cm) deep, and stir in the broken cinnamon stick and lime juice and zest. Set the dish in the oven and let the mixture cook for about 4 hours. From time to time, scrape the mixture from the sides of the dish and stir it well. This is particularly important toward the end of the cooking period.

When the mixture is thick, sticky, and a rich, dark brown, transfer it to a small serving dish and glaze it quickly under the broiler. Set it aside to cool.

Serve the *cajeta* with queso fresco or Thick Sour Cream (see page 489).

NOTE: This should keep for 10 to 15 days in the refrigerator—but I doubt whether that will be necessary. I'm afraid I always dip a finger into it each time I open the refrigerator door. I don't suggest freezing.

GUAYABAS RELLENAS DE COCADA Guavas Stuffed with Coconut
MAKES 12 PIECES

This recipe was inspired by one given to me by Señora AnaMaría de Andrea, of Aguascalientes, whom I have mentioned elsewhere, and it has been one of my "entertaining" desserts for many years.

I usually make double the amount of cocada *and freeze it ready for the next batch. It will last in perfect condition for one year.*

8 OUNCES (225 G) GRANULATED SUGAR (ABOUT 1 CUP/250 ML)
½ CUP (125 ML) WATER, PREFERABLY THE WATER FROM THE COCONUT
8 OUNCES FINELY SHREDDED COCONUT, APPROXIMATELY ½ FRESH COCONUT
2 YOLKS OF LARGE EGGS, LIGHTLY BEATEN
FINELY GRATED ZEST OF 1 ORANGE
⅓ CUP (85 ML) FRESH ORANGE JUICE
½ TEASPOON FRESH LIME JUICE
12 CANNED OR COOKED FRESH GUAVA "SHELLS" (SEE PAGE 432)

Melt the sugar in the water in a heavy saucepan over medium heat, then bring the syrup to a boil. Let it boil fast until it forms a thin thread—225°F (110°C) on a candy thermometer.

Add the coconut to the syrup and cook it until it is transparent but not too soft—about 5 minutes. Set aside to cool.

Add the rest of the ingredients except the guava shells, return to the heat, and continue cooking the mixture over medium heat for about 15 minutes, until the mixture is almost dry, scraping the bottom of the pan continuously. Set the *cocada* aside to cool.

Fill each guava shell with a large tablespoon of the *cocada*, covering the top of the guava shell completely.

Place the filled shells under the broiler and let the *cocada* brown a little. *Take care: it will burn very quickly.* Set them aside to cool before serving.

GUAVAS AND GUAVA "SHELLS" The guava (*Psidium guajava*) is a fruit native to tropical America. While there are wild guava trees in many parts of Mexico, the guava is also cultivated extensively. There are also many varieties but I consider the small, squat criollo, or native, to be the most fragrant and delicious. It has a very thin skin, which is lightish green at first, then ripening to a pale yellow. The firm flesh, about ⅛ inch thick, encases many small hard seeds set in an opaque, mucilaginous substance.

These guavas and some "improved," larger varieties are now being imported into some areas of the United States where I have seen them on sale in supermarkets catering to Latin American and Caribbean communities. Guava shells are also available canned—often the pink-fleshed variety. Be careful not to confuse these guavas with the feijoas (also known as pineapple guavas, which have a dark green skin and elongated shape.

Here is my method for preparing guava shells for stuffing:

1 pound (450g) yellow Mexican guavas, ripe but still firm
2 cups (500 ml) water
½ cup (125 ml) soft light brown sugar

Rinse the fruit well and dry but do not peel. Remove the small circular base of the shriveled flower and cut into halves horizontally. Now you have a choice: either remove the fleshy insides containing the seeds, or poach and remove them later, which is easier.

Put the water and sugar into a wide, shallow pan into which the guava shells will just fit in one layer and bring up to a boil. Lower the heat and simmer the syrup for about 5 minutes.

Place the guava halves, cut side down, into the syrup and cook gently, uncovered, for about 5 minutes on each side. Drain, cut side down, and when cool remove the fleshy center if you have not already done so.

DULCE DE CAMOTE Sweet Potato Dessert
SERVES 6

This recipe was given to me soon after I first arrived in Mexico by Elizabeth Borton de Treviño, whose book My Heart Lies South, *about her early married life in Monterrey, Nuevo León, gives a fascinating picture of a northern Mexico provincial town in the late forties.*

This Dulce de Camote was originally called "yam dessert" and then we all learned that the orange-fleshed tubers were in fact sweet potatoes and not yams. Whom do we thank? After 3 days of ripening, to develop flavor, this dessert can be very successfully frozen for up to one year.

This recipe is more attractive made with the orange-fleshed sweet potatoes but if not available use the white. It can be enhanced by the quality and mixture of dried fruit used. In Mexico very sweet candied fruits are used, but I prefer to use white and black raisins, candied orange and lemon peel, candied pineapple, dried apricots, and even some angelica, which adds a delicious crunch.

2 POUNDS (900 G) SWEET POTATOES, PREFERABLY ORANGE

½ CUP (125 ML) GRANULATED SUGAR

¼ CUP (65 ML) WATER

1 TEASPOON VANILLA EXTRACT

1 TEASPOON GROUND CINNAMON

½ CUP (125 ML) COARSELY CHOPPED WALNUTS OR PECANS

½ CUP (125 ML) MIXED CANDIED AND DRIED FRUITS, CHOPPED (SEE NOTE ABOVE)

1 OUNCE (30 ML) DARK RUM

1 OUNCE (30 ML) TEQUILA, PREFERABLY AÑEJO

UNSWEETENED WHIPPED CREAM OR THICK SOUR CREAM (SEE PAGE 489)

Three days before serving, preheat the oven to 375°F (190°C).

Bake the sweet potatoes on a cookie sheet until they are quite soft—about 2 hours. Set them aside to cool. Remove the skin and process the flesh in the food processor. There should be about 2 cups (500 ml).

Put the sugar and water into a large saucepan and set over low heat until the sugar has dissolved. Turn the heat up and boil the syrup until it threads—225°F (110°C) on a candy thermometer.

Add the pulp to the syrup and mix well. Transfer to a glass bowl. Mix in the rest of the ingredients except for the whipped cream, cover, and leave it to ripen for at least 3 days at the bottom of the refrigerator. (The longer the better.)

Turn the mixture into a serving dish and serve with unsweetened whipped cream or sour cream.

NOTE: The longer this dessert is left to season the better—I have even frozen it for one year and it was still excellent.

CHONGOS ZAMORANOS Curds in Syrup

BASED ON A RECIPE BY SEÑORA JOSEFINA VELÁZQUEZ DE LEÓN

SERVES 4   MICHOACÁN

Chongos Zamoranos are small rolls of custardlike curds in a thin syrup formed by the sugar and the whey.

According to Spanish dictionaries, one of the meanings of the word chongo *in Mexico is "topknot." The Mexican* Diccionario de Cocina, *published in 1878, describes it as a "sweet soup made of bread or dried cake with cheese—made in innumerable ways." Going down the list I find that the "whey chongos" or "whey conserves" are just like those of today.*

Those most generally known and popular in Mexico are the canned chongos zamoranos. *The curd of these is very rubbery and squeaks just a little as your teeth bite into it; and they are overly sweet. I have followed Mexican recipes, vague as they are, and careful instructions from Mexican friends to the letter; I have tried every brand of milk that I can lay my hands on; I have varied the shapes and sizes of the dishes, used different amounts of rennet and tried longer cooking times. In all, I would say, without exaggeration, I have tried a hundred variations to try and get them more like the authentic Mexican version. And then I stop and wonder why, when the* chongos *here are more delicious.*

1 QUART (1 L) MILK

2 YOLKS OF LARGE EGGS

RENNET (TABLETS OR LIQUID) SUFFICIENT TO CLABBER THE MILK
    (SEE MANUFACTURER'S INSTRUCTIONS)

1/2 TABLESPOON COLD WATER

1/2 CUP (125 ML) DARK BROWN SUGAR

2-INCH (5-CM) PIECE OF CINNAMON STICK

Heat the milk gently to 110°F (44°C)—a little hotter than lukewarm.

Beat the egg yolks lightly and mix them well into the milk. Crumble the tablets and let them dissolve in the water.

Pour the milk mixture into a flameproof dish at least 3 inches (8 cm) deep and 8 (20 cm) to 10 (25 cm) inches in diameter. Stir in the rennet solution. Set the dish in a warm place until the milk has set—about 30 minutes. Then, with a pointed knife, carefully cut across the junket, dividing it into 8 equal wedges.

Put the dish over low heat, and as soon as the curds and whey start to separate, sprinkle the brown sugar between the segments of the curd. Break up the cinnamon stick a little and put the pieces into the whey.

Leave the dish over the lowest possible heat for 2 hours. Watch it carefully to see that it does not come to a boil. If necessary, put an asbestos mat under the dish. The curds will get firmer as the cooking time lengthens and the sugar and whey will form a thin syrup. At the end of the cooking time, remove the dish from the heat and set it aside to cool.

When cool, starting from the pointed end of each piece, roll the curd up carefully. Put the rolled pieces onto a serving dish and pour the syrup, with the cinnamon pieces, over the *chongos*. Serve at room temperature.

NOTE: *Chongos* will last for several days in the refrigerator, but they get sweeter as they absorb the syrup and darker in color.

MANGOS FLAMEADOS Flambéed Mangoes
HOWARD BROWN
SERVES 2 TO 3

An acquaintance of my husband Paul, Howard Brown, the first General Manager of the Ramada Inn at Monterrey, invented this recipe and was generous enough to give it to me for the first edition of The Cuisines of Mexico.

I know that mangoes are delicious raw, but there are so many varieties now available for many months of the year that one is always looking for new ways of preparing them. The best mangoes for this recipe, in my opinion, are the slender, yellow Manilas that come into the Mexican markets in May and are available for about three months. Unfortunately I have never seen them in the United States. However, the fleshy Haydens that are available and varieties like them can be used very successfully.

This recipe can be prepared ahead up to the point of adding and reducing the juices, but don't add the mangoes until you are ready to finish the dish and serve. It is delicious served over a not-too-sweet sorbet or ice cream that is firmly packed and still partially frozen.

2 MANILA MANGOES OR I LARGE HAYDEN, ABOUT I POUND (450 G)

I ½ TABLESPOONS UNSALTED BUTTER

I ½ TABLESPOONS GRANULATED SUGAR

ZEST OF ½ ORANGE, THINLY PARED AND JULIENNED

ZEST OF ½ LIME, THINLY PARED AND JULIENNED

I OUNCE (30 ML) TRIPLE SEC OR COINTREAU

JUICE OF ½ ORANGE

JUICE OF ½ LIME

I OUNCE (30 ML) WHITE TEQUILA

Peel the mangoes, slice the flesh off the pits, and cut into thick strips. Set aside.

Melt the butter in a chafing dish, stir in the sugar, and continue stirring until it has dissolved. Add the zests together with the Triple Sec, heat the mixture, and flame it. When the flames have died down, add the juices and cook until reduced—about 2 minutes.

Add the mango strips and heat until the syrup begins to bubble. Add the tequila, heat through, and flame again. Serve immediately.

CREMA DE PIÑON O NUEZ ENCARCELADA

Pine Nut or Pecan Cream

SERVES 6   CENTRAL AND NORTHERN MEXICO

This is clearly one of those desserts of Spanish origin that were often changed, embellished, or adapted to local ingredients by the nuns in Mexico during the colonial period. Although I find them too cloying, I have included this one example to appease my Mexican friends who have accused me of leaving out some of their favorite desserts.

I have changed the recipe slightly. Because I have reduced the amount of sugar, which helps thicken the mixture, I have included two egg yolks—which is not atypical—and I have suggested rum or brandy rather than the innocuous white wine, and pecans as a possible

substitute for the pine nuts. If you can find them, the pink Mexican pine nuts do give a delicate flavor and pale pink color to the dessert.

1 TABLESPOON UNSALTED BUTTER FOR THE DISH

3 CUPS (750 ML) MILK

4-INCH (10-CM) PIECE OF CINNAMON STICK, ROUGHLY BROKEN UP

¾ CUP (185 ML) GRANULATED SUGAR

2 TABLESPOONS RICE FLOUR OR CORNSTARCH

8 OUNCES (225 G) PINE NUTS OR PECANS (APPROXIMATELY 2¼ CUPS/565 ML), ROUGHLY
    CHOPPED, PLUS A FEW WHOLE NUTS FOR DECORATION

2 LARGE EGG YOLKS, WELL BEATEN

⅓ CUP (85 ML) BRANDY OR RUM OR ⅔ CUP (165 ML) WHITE WINE, OR TO TASTE

10 LADYFINGERS, ROUGHLY BROKEN UP

Lightly butter a shallow dish, ideally about 9 inches (23 cm) in diameter and 1½ inches (4 cm) deep.

Bring the milk to a boil, then add the cinnamon and stir in most of the sugar, reserving a little to grind with the nuts. Lower the heat and stir until the sugar is melted. Stir ¼ cup (65 ml) of the warmed milk into the rice flour and work to a smooth paste. Stir this into the milk–sugar mixture and continue cooking, stirring all the time, until it thickens slightly.

Grind the nuts with the reserved sugar until very fine and stir into the boiling milk mixture. Cook until the mixture has reduced and thickened—20 to 30 minutes. Add about 1 cup (250 ml) of the hot mixture to the egg yolks and beat together well. Return to the pan and continue to cook, stirring and scraping the bottom of the pan constantly, until the mixture thickens to the extent that you can see the bottom of the pan as you stir. (It should coat the back of a wooden spoon thickly.) Stir in about two thirds of the brandy or wine.

Pour half of the mixture into the prepared dish. Cover with the ladyfingers, sprinkle with the rest of the brandy or wine, and cover with the remaining cream. Decorate the top with the whole nuts and set aside to cool to room temperature—do not refrigerate—before serving.

NOTE: This dessert keeps for several days in the refrigerator, but always bring it up to room temperature before serving.

CALABAZA EN TACHA Pumpkin Cooked in Raw Sugar

SEÑORA CONSUELO DE MENDOZA

MAKES ABOUT 30 PIECES

MICHOACÁN

There are many regional recipes for pumpkins cooked with raw sugar, either piloncillo *in the form of cones, or* panela, *in thick rounds—the darker the color the richer the flavor. This recipe comes from the eastern part of Michoacán, where it is eaten preferably for breakfast with a glass of cold milk. During Holy Week a favorite breakfast food is pumpkin or other fruits cooked in the same way stuffed into* teleras, *flattish bread rolls.*

I MEDIUM PUMPKIN, ABOUT 5 POUNDS (2.5 KG)

8 CUPS (2 L) WATER

I ½ POUNDS (675 G) PILONCILLO OR PANELA, BROKEN INTO SMALL PIECES, JUST UNDER
    4 CUPS (960 ML) OR DARK BROWN SUGAR

3 2-INCH (5-CM) CINNAMON STICKS

10 GUAVAS (OPTIONAL), HALVED, SEEDS LEFT IN

Pierce the shell-like outer rind of the pumpkin in several places to enable the syrup to penetrate the flesh and cut into pieces about 3 inches (8 cm) square, leaving the fibrous flesh and seeds inside.

In a wide, heavy saucepan put enough water to completely cover the pumpkin. Add the brown sugar and cinnamon sticks and bring to a boil. Add the pieces of pumpkin and guavas and cook over fairly high heat, moving the pieces around from time to time to avoid sticking. Cover the pan and cook for about 15 minutes, then remove the lid and continue cooking until the syrup has reduced and the flesh of the pumpkin is a rich brown.

TORTA DE CIELO Almond Sponge Cake

SERVES 12

YUCATÁN

I had eaten this cake—literally "cake of heaven"—many times in the Casa Chalam Balam in Mérida and loved it. In Yucatán it is served at weddings and first communion receptions. I was told that the recipe was kept a secret by the old ladies who made it for the hotel. After many experiments I think this recipe comes as close as possible to the version I like so much. The soaking of the almonds keeps the cake rich and moist; it is sometimes also flavored with anise.

8 OUNCES (225 G) WHOLE ALMONDS, UNSKINNED (ABOUT 1 ²/₃ CUPS/415 ML)

5 LARGE EGGS, SEPARATED

A GOOD PINCH OF SALT

8 OUNCES (225 G) GRANULATED SUGAR (1 HEAPED CUP/265 ML)

¹/₄ TEASPOON BAKING POWDER

1 TABLESPOON ALL-PURPOSE FLOUR

1 TABLESPOON BRANDY

A DROP OF ALMOND EXTRACT

Line the bottom of a 9-inch (23-cm) springform pan with parchment paper. Butter the paper and sides of the pan well, and dust with flour.

Pour hot water over the almonds so that they are well covered and leave them to soak for about 4 hours. (Remove the skins—they should slip right off.)

Preheat the oven to 325°F (165°C) and place a rack on the middle level.

Chop the nuts roughly and grind them a little at a time in a coffee/spice grinder. They should be neither too coarse nor too fine. Set aside.

Beat the egg whites until they are fluffy. Add the salt and continue beating until they are firm. Add the yolks one by one and continue beating until they are all incorporated.

Mix the dry ingredients with the almonds and, beating at a low speed, gradually add them to the eggs. Add the brandy and almond extract and pour the batter into the prepared pan. Bake for 1¾ hours. Remove the cake from the pan or cool on a rack.

POLVORONES Mexican Shortbread Cookies

SEÑORA MARÍA LUISA DE MARTÍNEZ, MEXICO CITY

MAKES ABOUT 2 DOZEN COOKIES

Polvorones are small, round cookies, so short that they crumble to the touch. Traditionally they are made with all lard, but that is dying out—I myself find the flavor too strong and the texture too greasy. A combination of butter, shortening, and lard seems to give the best results.

Polvorones may be flavored with cinnamon or orange, and made of ground pecans, walnuts, or pine nuts instead of almonds. While they are still warm from the oven, tradition has it that they are then liberally sprinkled with confectioners' sugar and, when cool, each one is wrapped in white tissue paper. The paper is bunched at each side and twisted, and the ends are cut into shreds, making the cookies look like bonbons.

$\frac{1}{3}$ TO $\frac{1}{2}$ CUP (85 TO 125 ML) UNSKINNED ALMONDS (ABOUT 2 OUNCES/60 G),
    PLUS 10 EXTRA ALMONDS
8 OUNCES (225 G) UNBLEACHED ALL-PURPOSE FLOUR (2 CUPS/500 ML)
$\frac{1}{8}$ TEASPOON SALT
I TEASPOON BAKING POWDER
2 $\frac{1}{2}$ TABLESPOONS GRANULATED SUGAR
2 OUNCES (60 G) UNSALTED BUTTER ($\frac{1}{4}$ CUP/65 ML)
2 OUNCES (60 G) VEGETABLE SHORTENING ($\frac{1}{4}$ CUP/65 ML)
$\frac{1}{3}$ CUP (85 ML) CONFECTIONERS' SUGAR, APPROXIMATELY

Preheat the oven to 350°F (180°C).

Spread the unskinned almonds and flour on separate cookie sheets and toast each on the top shelf of the oven or in a toaster oven until the nuts are crisp and the flour a deep creamy color—about 15 minutes. Set both ingredients aside to cool off completely. Turn off the oven.

Sift the cooled flour together with the salt and baking powder and put onto a marble slab or pastry board. Make a wide well in the center of the flour. Put the cooled nuts into the blender with the granulated sugar and blend until fine, then put the mixture, along with the butter and shortening, into the center of the well in the flour and mix until the dough is crumbly, like pie crust. Put the dough onto a large square of plastic wrap and gather it into a ball, pressing the "crumbs" lightly together. Set the dough aside for a minimum of 2 hours in the refrigerator.

Preheat the oven again to 350°F (180°C). Butter a cookie sheet well.

Unwrap the ball of dough, and leaving the dough on top of the wrap, put another square of the wrap over the surface of the dough. Press the dough out between the wrap with quick, short movements of your rolling pin until it is about $\frac{1}{4}$ inch (.75 cm) thick; it will be very crumbly around the edges. Using a cookie cutter 2 inches (5 cm) in diameter, cut out as many cookies as you can. Gather up the remaining dough and roll out and cut more cookies.

(Note: the cookies should be transferred to the cookie sheet on a spatula with very great care or they will break up.) Repeat until all the dough has been used up.

Bake the cookies on the top shelf of the oven until they are a pale golden color— 10 to 15 minutes. Sprinkle them well with the confectioners' sugar and set aside to cool before attempting to remove them from the sheet.

Carefully remove the Polvorones to an airtight container or wrap in tissue paper, as follows: cut 24 squares of tissue paper 8 by 8 inches (20 by 20 cm). Place each cookie in the middle of a square and fold two sides over to cover it. Gently bunch the ends of the paper and twist them firmly. With scissors, cut the paper at each end into a fringe about 1½ inches (4 cm) deep.

ROSCAS Ring Cookies
MAKES 20 TO 22 COOKIES

I learned about Roscas during my apprenticeship in the bakery. Practically any type of yeast dough or pastry, salted or sweet, was rolled out to a thin strand, doubled, then twisted and joined up at the ends, sprinkled with sugar or sesame seeds, and baked until crisp. So, when some very sad Roscas turned up at breakfast one morning, when I was on holiday, I thought I would find out exactly what the baker was doing wrong.

I got up at five the following morning and went into the kitchen as the baker was just beginning. Instead of measuring the flour—he said he was using about a kilo—he deftly sprinkled handfuls of it into a perfectly even ring with sloping sides. On the ridge he sprinkled the baking powder—evenly, neatly, not one grain out of place. He mixed butter, sugar, and canned milk in the center, but as he reached for the coloring and flavoring cans I stopped him. A little more butter this time, a little less liquid next, and fresh aniseeds. The following day was better, the third day was perfect. All the kitchen help tried and approved, and he was very proud of the result.

8 OUNCES (225 G) UNBLEACHED ALL-PURPOSE FLOUR (2 CUPS/500 ML)
½ TEASPOON BAKING POWDER
¼ TEASPOON GROUND CINNAMON OR ½ TEASPOON ANISEEDS
¼ TEASPOON SALT
2 OUNCES (60 G) UNSALTED BUTTER, AT ROOM TEMPERATURE (¼ CUP/65 ML)
2 OUNCES (60 G) VEGETABLE SHORTENING, AT ROOM TEMPERATURE (¼ CUP/65 ML)
2 OUNCES (60 G) GRANULATED SUGAR (¼ CUP/65 ML), PLUS 2 TABLESPOONS FOR DUSTING
¼ CUP (65 ML) WATER
2 TABLESPOONS HEAVY CREAM

Sift the flour, baking powder, cinnamon, if you are using it, and salt onto a marble slab or pastry board. Make a well in the center, and into this put the butter, shortening,

¼ cup (65 ml) of the sugar, the water, and cream. Work the ingredients in the center together with your fingers until they are completely incorporated and smooth.

Gradually work in the dry ingredients, and the aniseeds, if used, and knead the mixture well. Work the dough *hard* for about 5 minutes, pressing it out with the palms of your hands, using them like pedals, against the working surface until it is smooth and pliable. (If you do not work it well enough, you will not be able to form the Roscas as indicated.)

Preheat the oven to 350°F (180°C) and set an oven rack on the top shelf. Lightly grease two baking sheets.

Roll the dough into balls of about 1¼ inches (3.5 cm) in diameter. Take one of the balls and work it under your palms (on an unfloured surface, if possible) into a rounded, even strip of dough about ¼ inch (.75 cm) in diameter. Double the strip, then press the ends together. Holding the ends firmly down onto the surface with one hand and starting from the other end, quickly and lightly twist the two strands together. If you have trouble rolling and twisting them, then make a simple ring with one strand of dough, rolling each ball out to a strip about ½ inch (1.5 cm) thick. Join the ends to make a circle, or "bracelet," about 2 inches (5 cm) in diameter, then place carefully onto the prepared baking sheet.

Proceed with the remaining balls of dough, and, when you have one baking sheet filled, bake until a deep golden color—15 to 20 minutes. As soon as you remove the cookies from the oven, sprinkle them liberally with the extra sugar. Let them cool off thoroughly before attempting to remove them from the baking sheet, then store in an airtight can or cookie jar.

DRINKS

TEQUILA

MEZCAL

Margarita

Tequila Sunrise

Sangrita

Agua Fresca de Flor de Jamaica ⁕ *Jamaica Flower Water*

Rompope ⁕ *Mexican Eggnog*

Tepache ⁕ *Fermented Pineapple Drink*

Horchata de Melón ⁕ *Melon-Seed Drink*

CHOCOLATE

Chocolate ⁕ *Hot Chocolate*

COFFEE

Café de Olla ⁕ *Coffee with Cinnamon and Brown Sugar*

ATOLES

Champurrado ⁕ *Chocolate-Flavored Atole*

Atole Masa ⁕ *Preparation of Corn for Atole*

Atole de Zarzamora ⁕ *Blackberry Atole*

Atole de Piña ⁕ *Pineapple Atole*

B E B I D A S Mexico is justly famous for such diverse drinks and beverages as tequila, pulque, aguas frescas, chocolate, atole, and its beer and coffee, all of which, discussed in detail later, are readily accessible to the visitor. Many of the regional drinks are much more difficult to come by. Usually made at home, they are often produced from the fermented juice of local, often wild fruits. There is the pineapple *tepache* of Jalisco; the *sangre de Baco* (blood of Bacchus) made of wild grapes from Guerrero; and teshuin, maize fermented with raw sugar from the mountainous regions of Chihuahua and Nayarít. On the coast of Colima and Guerrero, the sap from the coconut palm is made into *tuba,* and there are innumerable other concoctions based on sugarcane and/or flavored with wild cherries; there are the mezcales of Oaxaca; the much-esteemed *baconora* of Sonora; the anise-flavored liqueur made of flowers and called *Xtabentún,* from the Yucatán—and, of course, the world-famous Kahlúa. The central plateau of Mexico, besides, is rich in mineral springs. There are small spas dotted here and there, and the thermal, therapeutic waters attract people from all over the Republic. Some of the larger ones bottle and distribute quite widely the naturally gaseous and still mineral waters.

TEQUILA

Tequila is made from the distilled liquid of the baked and crushed, pineapple-like bases of the *Agave tequilana*. It is named after the small town where it originated, not too far from Guadalajara, in Jalisco, which is *the* tequila-producing state. The Spaniards introduced the process of distillation to Mexico, and it is generally believed that tequila was first made around the middle of the eighteenth century, although it was not until a hundred years later that it became an industry set up by two of the best-known families in the business today, Cuervo and Sauza.

There are now well over a hundred types of "boutique" tequilas, some costing more than $100 a bottle. The ordinary whites are best for mixed drinks; the pale-gold tequilas, which have usually been aged for one year, and the much heavier añejos, which have been left to mature for six to eight years, are better for sipping. There is one very special tequila, Centenario, which is brought out every six years to coincide with the inauguration of each new presidential term. The label is designed with miniature portraits of the preceding presidents. There are now many excellent books devoted to the subject of tequila.

If you are drinking tequila by itself you may wish to have an aged one, añejo, which has a very pale, gold color and more body and flavor, although I always prefer the white. The Mexican way of drinking it is with a piece of lime and some salt. Hold a quarter of a lime in your left hand and place a little salt in the well at the base of the thumb and index finger of the same hand. Hold the tequila glass in the other hand. Lick the salt, swallow some tequila, then suck the lime.

MEZCAL

Mezcal, an alcoholic drink akin to tequila, is gaining in popularity both in Mexico itself and abroad. It is distilled from the juice extracted from the cooked pineapple-like base of several species of agave. The main production comes from the Valley of Oaxaca, where it is still made in *palenques*—partially roofed areas where the cooking and shredding of the base and the distilling of the extracted liquid takes place in rustic surroundings. Mezcal produced under these artisanal conditions has a discernible, and agreeable, smoky flavor, while the more common mezcals now being made using industrial machines are more highly refined and do not have that characteristic flavor.

MARGARITA

CARLOS JACOTT
SERVES 1

No book on Mexican food should omit that happiest of drinks for which Mexico is justly famous, the Margarita. I have never found a better recipe than that given to me by Carlos Jacott and served in his very popular New York restaurant, El Parador, during the sixties and seventies.

Of course, the secret is fresh lime juice!

His Tequila Sunrise is another favorite, which I include next. Thanks to Carlos for so many years of great Margaritas (it deserves a capital M).

A SLICE OF LIME

A LITTLE SALT, EITHER ORDINARY TABLE SALT OR FINELY GROUND ROCK SALT

1 ½ OUNCES (45 ML) WHITE TEQUILA

½ OUNCE (15 ML) TRIPLE SEC

1 OUNCE (30 ML) FRESH LIME JUICE

A FEW ICE CUBES, CRUSHED

Chill a large cocktail glass well. Rub the rim with a slice of lime. Put the salt onto a plate. Press the rim of the glass into it, giving it a turn to make sure that the rim is ringed with salt.

Put the tequila, Triple Sec, lime juice, and ice cubes into a cocktail shaker. Cover and shake together well. Pour the mixture through a strainer into the prepared glass, or over shaved ice if preferred.

TEQUILA SUNRISE

CARLOS JACOTT

SERVES 1

2 OUNCES (60 ML) WHITE TEQUILA
1 ½ OUNCES (45 ML) FRESH LIME JUICE
1 TABLESPOON GRENADINE SYRUP
1 TEASPOON EGG WHITE
SOME ICE CUBES, CRUSHED

Chill a large cocktail glass well.

Put the tequila, lime juice, grenadine syrup, and egg white into a blender with the ice cubes. Blend the mixture until frothy and pour into the prepared glass.

SANGRITA

MAKES ABOUT 1 ½ CUPS (375 ML), ABOUT 8 SERVINGS

Friends in Jalisco always said that Sangrita was originally made with the juice of sour pomegranates, but since this fruit is difficult to come by they suggested using Seville orange juice and grenadine syrup. Of course every family, especially those from in and around the town of Tequila, has its own recipe, swearing that theirs was the original.

1 ¼ CUPS (315 ML) SEVILLE ORANGE JUICE OR SUBSTITUTE (SEE PAGE 494)
3 ½ TABLESPOONS GRENADINE SYRUP
SALT TO TASTE
A GOOD PINCH OF POWDERED RED CHILE, PIQUÍN, OR CAYENNE

Mix all the ingredients well and chill. Serve in small glasses, about 2 ounces (60 ml) per person, accompanied by a shot of tequila.

Another bullfight last evening! It is like pulque, one makes a wry face at first and then begins to like it.

—FRANCES CALDERÓN DE LA BARCA, *Life in Mexico*

PULQUE The landscape of the high central plateau is dominated by the impressive century plants, or magueys (*Agave americana y spp.*), which have provided so much sustenance to wandering tribes throughout history. Today they are chiefly cultivated for pulque, which is made of the fermented, milky sap, *aguamiel*, that is drawn off from a hollow scraped out in the base of the plant just before it sends up its long flowering stalk.

The sap can be reduced to a syrup, or crystallized to a sugar. Once fermented, the slightly alcoholic pulque can be used as a leavening agent for breads, to cook meats, for chile sauces, or to make a type of *tepache* or vinegar.

Pulque is often cured with fruits, like other drinks in Mexico, and even canned and exported.

If you happen to be traveling in the Mexican countryside after the rains in the fall and see a peasant drawing off the *aguamiel* with a long, thin gourd, stop and ask to try it.

It is sweetish and acidy at the same time and curiously refreshing.

Great quantities of earthenware are also exposed in the markets, and the stranger will be pleased to observe the beautiful way in which Indian women produce a variety of liquors of every colour and flavour. A vase, much larger than any made in Europe, of red earthenware resembling the Etruscan, is filled with water, and nearly buried in wet sand. A variety of flowers, principally poppies are stuck in, among which stand the glasses containing the showy colored beverages, which, with chocolate, pulque, and ices are served out for a trifle.

—W. H. BULLOCK, *Six Months Residence and Travel in Mexico*, NINETEENTH CENTURY

AGUA FRESCA DE FLOR DE JAMAICA Jamaica Flower Water
MAKES 4 CUPS (1 L)

Despite the tremendous popularity of commercial bottled drinks all over the country, from the capital to the smallest mountain hamlet, the red watermelon, pale green lime, or orangey-brown tamarind waters, sweetened and kept cool with huge chunks of ice, are sold from huge glass or earthenware containers in the marketplaces, by the street vendors, or in a few of the more traditional restaurants. This is one of them: acidy and refreshing, it is colored by the deep red calyx of the Hibiscus sabdariffa.

⅔ CUP (165 ML) JAMAICA FLOWERS
4 CUPS (1 L) COLD WATER
⅓ CUP (85 ML) GRANULATED SUGAR, OR TO TASTE
GRANULATED SUGAR, IF NECESSARY

Put the flowers and 3 cups (750 ml) of water together into a saucepan and bring them to a boil. Continue boiling the flowers for about 5 minutes over brisk heat.

Add the rest of the water and the sugar and set it aside for at least 4 hours or overnight.

Strain the liquid into the jug. Add more sugar if necessary. Serve well chilled.

ROMPOPE Mexican Eggnog
MAKES 1 QUART (1 L)

4 CUPS (1 L) MILK
1 CUP (250 ML) GRANULATED SUGAR
4-INCH (10-CM) PIECE OF CINNAMON STICK OR 1 VANILLA BEAN
¼ TEASPOON BAKING SODA
12 LARGE EGG YOLKS
¾ CUP (185 ML) PURE CANE ALCOHOL OR RUM OR ½ CUP (125 ML) BRANDY, OR TO TASTE

Put the milk, sugar, cinnamon, and baking soda into a saucepan. Bring to a boil, then lower the heat and simmer for about 20 minutes, or until the sugar has melted completely and the mixture is reduced to about 3 cups (750 ml). Set aside to cool a little.

Meanwhile, beat the egg yolks until they form thick ribbons on the beater—about 10 minutes, depending on the efficiency of your beater.

Remove the cinnamon from the milk mixture. Gradually add the milk mixture to the egg yolks, still beating. Return to the pan and cook over low heat, stirring and scraping the bottom and sides of the pan constantly, until the mixture thickens enough to coat the back of a wooden spoon. (Take care, as it can quickly turn to scrambled eggs. At the first sign of this tragedy, pour into the blender and blend until it is smooth.) Set aside to cool completely.

Meanwhile, sterilize a 1-quart (1 l) bottle in boiling water.

Gradually stir the alcohol into the "custard," pour into the bottle, and use immediately or store in the refrigerator up to one month for future use.

TEPACHE Fermented Pineapple Drink
MAKES ABOUT 2 QUARTS (2 L)

One of the most refreshing drinks on a hot day is the slightly fermented infusion of pineapple called tepache. *Possibly it originates, or so it is said, in the state of Jalisco, but there are of course many regional variations. It should be made, if possible, in a large earthenware jug or pot and served ice cold or over ice cubes.*

1 VERY RIPE PINEAPPLE, ABOUT 2 POUNDS (900 G)
2 WHOLE CLOVES
2 WHOLE ALLSPICE
4-INCH (10-CM) PIECE OF CINNAMON STICK
9½ CUPS (2.4 L) WATER
1 POUND (450 G) PILONCILLO, CRUSHED, OR DARK BROWN SUGAR
1 CUP (250 ML) LIGHT BEER

Remove the stem and base of the pineapple and scrub the outside well. Cut into 1½-inch (4-cm) cubes, skin and flesh together. Crush the spices roughly and add them, together with the pineapple and 8 cups (2 l) of the water, to a large earthenware jug. Cover and set in the sun or a warm place until the mixture begins to ferment and become bubbly on top—about 3 days, depending on the temperature.

Put the remaining 1 ½ cups (375 ml) of water and the brown sugar into a saucepan and bring to a simmer. Simmer, stirring from time to time, until the sugar has melted. Let it cool slightly, then add, along with the beer, to the pineapple infusion and stir well. Cover the jug and leave in a warm place for 1 or 2 days longer, until it has fermented. Strain and serve very cold or over ice.

HORCHATA DE MELÓN Melon-Seed Drink
SERVES 1   CENTRAL AND SOUTHERN MEXICO

Horchata, *a milky-looking drink originally made of almonds or a small white tuber called chufa, was brought from Spain to Mexico, where it became popular in the Yucatán. There it is generally made by soaking and grinding raw rice, often with the addition of a few almonds, then straining and serving over ice. It is considered delicious, healthy, and refreshing, but what drink wouldn't be refreshing in that heat? I had always thought it was just plain dull — but there are always surprises in Mexico.*

After lunch one day at a friend's house, I went back to the kitchen and saw that the maids were saving the seeds from the cantaloupes that we had been eating for lunch. They were going to make horchata *from the seeds. Some cooks rinse, drain, and dry the seeds, but I think this is the most delicious version of all.*

Scrape the center fleshy part from 1 cantaloupe, seeds and juice included, into a measuring cup, and for every cup add:

1 CUP (250 ML) COLD WATER
1 ½ TABLESPOONS GRANULATED SUGAR, OR TO TASTE
1 ½ TEASPOONS FRESH LIME JUICE, OR TO TASTE

Put all the ingredients together in a blender jar and blend until very smooth. Set aside in the refrigerator for a minimum of ½ hour, then strain through a fine strainer and serve over ice cubes.

CHOCOLATE

Here are also two cloisters of nuns [in the Dominican convent in Oaxaca], which are talked of far and near, not for their religious practices, but for their skill in making two drinks, which are used in those parts, the one called chocolate and the other atole, which like unto our almond milk, but much thicker, and is made of the juices of the young maize or Indian wheat, which they so confection with spices, musk and sugar that it is not only admirable in the sweetness of the smell, but much more nourishing and comforting to the stomach. This is not a commodity that can be transported from thence, but is to be drunk there where it is made. But the other, chocolate, is made up in boxes, and sent not only to Mexico [City] and the parts thereabouts, but much of it is yearly transported into Spain.

—THOMAS GAGE, *Travels in the New World*, SIXTEENTH CENTURY

When I am in Oaxaca, I love to go to the grind-it-yourself place. The women buy their kilos of cacao beans, and a certain quantity of sugar and almonds to go with them, depending on what they can afford—if they are very poor, then they buy fewer cacao beans and almonds and more sugar. Each woman picks up a zinc tub, which she places under one of the several grinding machines around the store. The cacao and almonds are poured into the hopper, and very soon a satiny, tacky chocolate sauce oozes out of the spout—which has been sprinkled with sugar so that none will stick and be wasted— and falls onto the pile of sugar in the tub below. The women bring with them two large wooden spoons to mix it all well, and some even have brushes so that not one speck of the valuable chocolate is left sticking to the metal. Then the chocolate is carried to another machine for a second grinding—this time with the sugar—and it is at this point that you persuade someone to let you stick your finger in and try. It is then carried home and set to dry in small molds in the sun.

The subject of chocolate is inexhaustible, and certainly fascinated all the early writers about Mexico. Sahagún tells us that it was drunk only by the rich and noble, and even then in moderation, for it was thought to have deranging qualities like the mushroom. There was orange, black, and white chocolate; it was made with honey or mixed with purple flowers and served at the end of a feast with great ceremony. The distinguished men drank from painted cups, or black cups on a base covered with jaguar or deer skin. Perforated cups were used as strainers and the spoons were tortoiseshell. All this equipment was carried in special net bags.

Thomas Gage devotes a lot of space to chocolate in *Travels in the New World*. He tells how the women of Chiapas flouted the bishop and were excommunicated because they would not give up their comforting cups of chocolate to sustain them during Mass. Only the British seemed to scorn chocolate; when they captured a Spanish ship on the high seas laden with cacao they threw it overboard in disgust, calling it sheep's dung.

CHOCOLATE Hot Chocolate
MAKES ABOUT 1²/₃ CUPS (415 ML)

The name itself is derived from the Nahuatl word xocotl *(fruit) and* atl *(water).*

The drinking chocolate of Mexico is quite different from the chocolate available here. It is lighter bodied, and it has a definite texture. Luckily, several varieties of Mexican chocolate are available here, because there is really no substitute for it.

Some people prefer to make hot chocolate with milk.

1 ½ CUPS (375 ML) WATER
1 ½-OUNCE (45-G) TABLET OF MEXICAN CHOCOLATE

Heat the water in an earthenware pot. As it comes to a boil, break the chocolate into it and stir until the chocolate has melted. Let it boil gently for about 5 minutes so that all the flavor comes out, then beat it with a molinillo or blend in a blender until it is frothy.

NOTE: If you are making it with milk, first dissolve the chocolate in ½ cup (125 ml) water, bring to a boil, and then add the milk and bring again up to a boil.

COFFEE

So many mornings in the early days in Mexico I was awakened by the gentle swish of brooms. Some of the maids in the street would be sweeping sidewalks, terraces, or patios, slowly, rhythmically, while they gossiped, and others scuttled into the cool morning air to bring back crisp *bolillos* and hot *pan dulce* from the *panaderías*. The time to go is either early morning or late afternoon, just as the baker is sending out his huge trays of freshly baked goods. You pick up a small, round metal tray and a pair of tongs and wander around trying to decide what you really want from dozens of varieties: *triangulos, yoyos, kekis, suspiros, besos, yemas,* among so many others. I always choose the sugar-glazed flaky *campechanos*, or the rich, yeasty *puros* (cigars), which are so good with a large glass of café con leche.

And then my mouth waters as I remember my breakfasts in the Hermosillo market. Cele's scrupulously clean concession was always doing a roaring trade from huge pans of freshly brewed coffee and milk covered with a thickly matted skin of deep yellow cream: at intervals the baker next door would send fresh batches of *pan dulce*. Or sitting outside under the arches in Veracruz, where the waiter fills your glass halfway with strong, rich coffee and then taps it sharply so that its ringing tone summons with a sense of urgency his helper, who is scurrying to keep up, with a jug of steaming milk. Driving back to Mexico City, once more in the mountains, you'd stop at Córdoba—one of the important coffee centers of Mexico—to sit in a streetside café and drink a strong, fragrant brew with the smell of roasting coffee heavy in the air. Now, alas, standards of quality have been considerably diluted.

We hear very little about it, but Mexico is among the leading producers of excellent coffees. It is served in every way—Italian, Austrian, American—but a few traditional restaurants still have Café de Olla on the menu. It is served in small pottery mugs.

CAFÉ DE OLLA Coffee with Cinnamon and Brown Sugar
SERVES 1

2 CUPS (500 ML) WATER
¼ CUP DARK-ROASTED, COARSELY GROUND COFFEE
1-INCH (2.5-CM) PIECE OF CINNAMON STICK
PILONCILLO OR RAW DARK BROWN SUGAR TO TASTE

In an earthenware pot, bring the water to a boil. Add the dark-roasted coffee, the cinnamon stick, and the dark brown sugar to taste. Bring to a boil twice, then strain and serve.

ATOLES

There is no translation of the word *atole*—gruel perhaps, but that sounds so very boring and the word has long since disappeared from most people's vocabulary.

The word *atole* comes from the Nahuatl, *atolli* (although some etymologists think it should have come from *atl*, water, and *tlaoli*, corn) and is pre-Columbian in origin. The *Diccionario de Cocina* published in the nineteenth century describes atoles as "very healthy and nutritious for the poor . . . but it is also good for invalids and well-to-do families." I can vouch for it that atole is the most comforting of drinks when made of the correct masa (see page 456) and not overly sweet—which is a tendency in Mexico.

There is an endless number of ingredients and flavors for atoles, varying from one region to another, or perhaps from one village to another. Many are flavored with seasonal fruits: blackberries, wild cherries, strawberries, tamarind, or, from one village in Veracruz, Seville orange juice. In Michoacán there is one with fresh corn kernels and wild anise or the husks of the cacao bean. There is a most extraordinary atole in the Sierra Norte de Puebla flavored with orange flowers, sweetened with raw sugar, and fortified with little balls of masa mixed with lard and stuffed with cheese. There are the *chileatoles*, picante and sweet at the same time, and the atole of soured masa topped with toasted sesame and chile seeds from Oaxaca, while in Puebla an atole of soured masa of blue corn, enriched with beans and seasoned with a chile sauce, is served.

Atole is the traditional accompaniment to tamales, for supper or breakfast, or to drink, thin and cold, as a refreshment in the daytime. The subject is almost inexhaustible.

I am giving three here: a chocolate-flavored atole; the blackberry atole of Michoacán, made when the fruits are gathered in the higher altitudes just before the rains; and another of pineapple that I always order in Chilpancingo, Guerrero, to drink with the enticing and crisp little regional *chalupas* (see *The Art of Mexican Cooking*).

CHAMPURRADO Chocolate-Flavored Atole
MAKES ABOUT 4½ CUPS (1.125 L)

In the seventies it was rare to find little merenderos *(cafés for breakfast and supper) like the Café Meléndez in Torreón. It was run by a middle-class family who made delicious tamales and simple regional dishes in the tradition of the grandmother who started the business in the early 1920s. I thought their version of Champurrado (normally made with masa) was particularly delicious, especially with the addition of the orange zest and, of course, the won-derfully rich milk of that area.*

2 CUPS (500 ML) WATER

THIN ZEST OF 1 WHOLE ORANGE

4-INCH (10-CM) PIECE OF CINNAMON STICK, BROKEN UP

2 TABLESPOONS GRANULATED SUGAR, OR TO TASTE, DEPENDING ON THE CHOCOLATE

4 CUPS (1 L) WHOLE MILK

3 OUNCES (90 G) MEXICAN DRINKING CHOCOLATE

2 TABLESPOONS CORNSTARCH

Put the water, orange zest, cinnamon, and sugar into a pan and boil quickly for about 20 minutes, or until you have an infusion and the liquid has reduced by at least 1 cup (250 ml). Add the milk, and just before it comes to a boil, the chocolate. Simmer the mixture until the particles of chocolate have completely dissolved (Mexican drinking chocolate will take longer than the others)—about 10 minutes.

Put the cornstarch into a small bowl. Stir in about 2 tablespoons of the milk mixture and smooth out the lumps with the back of a wooden spoon. Add ½ cup (125 ml) more of the milk mixture to dilute the cornstarch thoroughly. Stir this into the saucepan and cook until the mixture thickens slightly, stirring almost constantly for about 10 minutes. Strain and serve hot.

ATOLE MASA Preparation of Corn for Atole
MAKES ABOUT 2¼ POUNDS (1.15KG), ABOUT 4 CUPS (1 L) MASA

Traditional cooks will only use corn cooked without lime for atoles. Of course many don't have the time and will use tortilla masa, but the taste will not be as pure. This preparation may be a little too esoteric but I give the recipe for all the devoted aficionados.

It is hardly worthwhile making a smaller quantity while you are at it, and besides, the mill does not like to grind smaller amounts. The excess freezes perfectly for several months.

1 POUND (450 G) WHITE DRIED CORN

6 CUPS (1.5 L) WATER

Rinse the corn and remove any unwanted bits and pieces, put into a deep saucepan, and cover with the water. Set the pan over high heat and bring to a boil. Lower the heat to medium, cover the pan, and cook for 15 minutes—it should cook at a fast simmer.

Remove from the heat and set aside to soak overnight. The following day, drain the corn and have it ground to a fine, very soft dough, masa.

NOTE: Since this masa is not cooked with lime it will sour quickly unless refrigerated. Any masa you are not going to use will keep for one day, but after that it should be frozen.

ATOLE DE ZARZAMORA Blackberry Atole
MAKES ABOUT 8 CUPS (2 L)

This is the most popular atole when the wild blackberries are brought down from the mountains to the market in Zitácuaro, Michoacán, in May, just before the rains start.

Some people prefer to eat or drink this atole when it has cooled and the flavor heightened. Thickness is very much a matter of taste; but this is how my neighbors like it.

It is not worth making a smaller amount; besides, this atole will keep several days in the refrigerator and even freezes well for several months. I always put it into the blender after defrosting and before reheating.

1 POUND (450 G) BLACKBERRIES
2 CUPS (500 ML) WATER
1 CUP (250 ML) ATOLE MASA (SEE PRECEDING RECIPE)
ABOUT 6½ CUPS (1.6 L) WATER
PILONCILLO OR RAW DARK BROWN SUGAR TO TASTE

Put the blackberries into a saucepan with the 2 cups of water and bring to a boil. Lower the heat and simmer for 5 minutes. Strain the blackberries into a bowl, pressing out as much of the flesh as possible. Discard the seeds. Set the blackberry puree aside. There should be about 3 cups of puree.

Dilute the masa with 1½ cups (375 ml) of the water. Put the rest of the water into a Mexican clay *olla* or heavy saucepan and bring to a boil. Add the diluted masa through a strainer, pressing out any lumps with a wooden spoon. Cook over medium heat, stirring from time to time to avoid sticking, until the mixture is just beginning to thicken—5 minutes.

Stir in the strained blackberry puree with sugar to taste and continue cooking over medium heat, stirring and scraping the bottom of the pan to avoid sticking, until the mixture thickens—it should make a thin coating over the back of a wooden spoon—about 15 minutes.

Serve either warm or at room temperature.

ATOLE DE PIÑA Pineapple Atole
MAKES ABOUT 8 CUPS (2 L)

ABOUT 6 ½ CUPS (1.6 L) WATER
1 ¼ POUNDS (565 G) CLEANED AND FINELY DICED PINEAPPLE (ABOUT 3 ⅓ CUPS/835 ML)
1 CUP (250 ML) ATOLE MASA (SEE PAGE 456)
PILONCILLO OR RAW DARK BROWN SUGAR TO TASTE

Put 5 cups (1.5 l) of the water into a Mexican clay *olla* or heavy saucepan, add 1 cup (250 ml) of the diced pineapple, and bring to a boil.

Meanwhile, dilute the masa with the remaining water and add through a strainer to the boiling water, pressing out any lumps with a wooden spoon. Cook over medium heat, stirring and scraping the bottom of the pan to avoid sticking, until just beginning to thicken—5 minutes.

Blend the remaining pineapple as smooth as possible and add to the pan through a strainer, pressing out the pulp to extract as much of the flesh and juice as possible. Stir in the sugar and continue cooking over medium heat, stirring and scraping the bottom of the pan to avoid sticking, until the mixture thickens—it should make a thin coating over the back of a wooden spoon—about 15 minutes.

Serve warm or at room temperature.

GENERAL INFORMATION

COOKING EQUIPMENT

MEASURES AND EQUIVALENTS

PREPARATION OF WRAPPINGS FOR TAMALES

Fresh Corn Husks ❋ *Dried Corn Husks* ❋ *Banana Leaves*
❋ *Lime (cal) for Tortilla Masa*

FRESH CHILES

Chile de Agua ❋ *Chilaca* ❋ *Güero Chile* ❋ *Cera Chile* ❋ *X-cat-ik Chile*
❋ *Largo Chile* ❋ *Habanero Chile* ❋ *Jalapeño Chile* ❋ *Manzano Chile*
❋ *Poblano Chile* ❋ *Serrano Chile* ❋ *Chile Verde del Norte*

DRIED CHILES

Ancho Chile ❋ *Mulato Chile* ❋ *Pasilla Chile* ❋ *Guajillo Chile* ❋ *Puya Chile*
❋ *Chile de Árbol* ❋ *Cascabel Chile* ❋ *Chile Seco del Norte* ❋ *Chilacate*
❋ *Chipotle Chile* ❋ *Mora Chile* ❋ *Morita Chile* ❋ *Pasilla Chile de Oaxaca*
❋ *Chilhuacle Negro, Rojo, Amarillo* ❋ *Piquín Chile* ❋ *Chile Seco Yucateco*

MEXICAN CHEESES

Queso Añejo ❋ *Queso Asadero* ❋ *Queso Chihuahua* ❋ *Queso Fresco*
❋ *Quesillo de Oaxaca* ❋ *Queso Panela*

SPICES

Recado de Toda Clase ❋ *Simple Recado Rojo*

COOKING HERBS

Fresh Herbs ❋ *Dried Herbs*

OTHER INGREDIENTS

Sugar ❋ *Salt* ❋ *Cooking Fats and Oils—Homemade Lard* ❋ *Sour Cream—
Thick Sour Cream; Prepared Sour Cream* ❋ *Vegetables* ❋ *Citrus Fruits—Seville
Orange Substitute* ❋ *Pumpkin Seeds* ❋ *Plantains* ❋ *Vinegars—Pineapple
Vinegar* ❋ *Avocados* ❋ *Chicharrón* ❋ *Cuiclacoche* ❋ *Flor de Calabaza* ❋
Acitrón ❋ *Nopales* ❋ *Dried Shrimp* ❋ *Basic Recipes—Caldo de Pollo; Chicken,
Cooked and Shredded; Pork, Cooked and Shredded; Beef, Cooked and Shredded*

COOKING EQUIPMENT

In Mexico one cannot visualize a kitchen without a comal, cazuelas, a tamale steamer, and a molcajete and tejolote. The metate is no longer commonly used.

A *comal* is a disk of thin metal or unglazed clay that goes over a heat or fire for cooking tortillas or char-roasting ingredients mainly for table sauces. Use a heavy cast-iron griddle if you have no comal.

Cazuelas are wide-topped glazed clay pots for cooking on gas heat or over wood or charcoal. They are not suitable for an electric burner. Heavy casseroles, such as Le Creuset, or heavy skillets of different sizes can be substituted.

A *tamale steamer* can be as simple as a Mexican metal steamer with four parts: a straight-sided, deep metal container with a perforated rack that sits just above the water level, an upright divider to support the tamales in three sections, and a tight lid. This type of steamer can often be found in a Mexican or Latin American grocery along with molcajetes and tortilla presses. Failing that, any steamer can be used as long as the part holding the tamales is set deep down near the concentration of steam—tamales must cook as fast as possible so that the beaten masa firms up and the filling doesn't leak into it, a messy affair! A couscous steamer is not suitable for that reason.

I have had to improvise a tamale steamer on many occasions: I think the most successful was a perforated spaghetti or vegetable holder, which normally sits down into the water, set onto four upturned custard cups so as to hold it just above the level of the water—which should be about 3 inches (8 cm) deep. To hold in as much steam and heat as possible, cover the top of the pot with tightly stretched plastic wrap. (But remember to prick and deflate the plastic before inspecting the tamales.)

A *molcajete* and *tejolote*, the traditional Mexican mortar and pestle, are indispensable pieces of equipment for any cook who wishes to reproduce truly authentic Mexican table sauces, guacamole, and the like. They are very practical for crushing spices and grinding ingredients to obtain maximum flavor and texture. The molcajete is in essence a thick bowl of either black or gray volcanic rock with a pestle made of the same material. Before using, the surface of the molcajete has to be ground. To do this, grind a small handful of rice with the pestle until it is reduced to a grayish powder. Rinse the molcajete well and repeat the grinding several times until the rice powder is slightly whiter. It is then ready to use.

Of course it would be better to carry one back from Mexico to make sure you are getting a good quality—it should be very heavy and not very porous. Failing that, many Mexican stores and supermarkets where there is a big Hispanic population in the United States now carry them, but beware, they are of varying quality. A good molcajete should not have a deeply pitted surface and it will hold water. If a test grinding turns up lots of gritty dust, pass it by.

The *metate*, a rectangular grinding stone, and its muller, the *mano*, is also made of volcanic rock. It is now only used, even in Mexico, by the most traditional of cooks for grinding ingredients for moles and sauces. It is not indispensable, but it does look nice!

If you want to make your own tortillas from scratch, or some of the *antojitos*, then a tortilla press is a must, unless of course you are a whiz at patting them out by hand—a dying art even in Mexico. The metal presses are available in Mexican markets and in large supermarkets catering to a Hispanic community. But be sure to buy a very heavy one and not the light and brittle aluminum ones that seem to have flooded the markets; they are not effective and break easily. I find the most useful size to be 6 inches (15 cm) in diameter.

A *blender*, preferably with two jars, is endlessly useful. A food processor is useful for only a few recipes, where stated. It will never blend a chile or other sauce as efficiently as a blender.

MEASURES AND EQUIVALENTS

I have attempted to give both weights and cup measures where feasible.

For *liquid measures*, I use a standard 8-ounce (250 ml) glass cup, and for *solids*, an 8-ounce (250 ml) metal cup. Preferably measuring cups should be the standard ones with straight sides and not those plastic ones in fancy shapes.

When I refer to 8 ounces (225 g), I mean weight, not the 8-ounce liquid measure. For example, 1 cup (250 ml) of corn tortilla masa weighs about 9 to 9½ ounces (250 to 262 g) and may even weigh a little more if it is very damp. A cup of dry tamal masa weighs about 6 ounces (180 g).

I always try to persuade cooks to buy a good heavy-duty scale, not the light ones that hang from a wall and bounce or those that have a container that slips off its base with the slightest movement. Not only will you weigh more accurately but you also are spared the messy business of forcing fat into cups and then having to scrape it out and deal with a greasy sink.

PREPARATION OF WRAPPINGS FOR TAMALES

FRESH CORN HUSKS Uchepos (page 106) and Tamales Dulces de Elote (page 107) are wrapped in fresh corn husks. After they are carefully cut from the ears of corn, rinsed, and shaken dry, they are ready to be used. If some of the outer husks are very thick and inflexible, they could be used to line the steamer.

DRIED CORN HUSKS I always hope that one day dried husks will be sold in the United States as they are in Mexico, with their curved base intact, and not severely cut off.

Put the husks to soak some hours ahead in cold or hot water and when they are flexible, shake or wipe them dry before filling the tamales. If you wish to give yourself extra work and tie the tamales (which is pretty but not absolutely necessary), tear some of the larger husks into threads and use them as ties.

BANANA LEAVES If you can buy fresh, pale green banana leaves—already cut from the thick central rib of the whole leaf—so much the better; they are sold in packages in some Mexican and Latin American supermarkets in the Southwest. Cut the leaves into the sizes indicated in the recipe and wipe clean. Hold the pieces one by one over the flame of a gas stove, or over the hotplate of an electric stove, until they wilt and become flexible. This process will take a few seconds on each side of the leaves; be careful not to overdo them so that they discolor and become brittle when cool.

Nearly all Asian markets carry packages of frozen banana leaves that tend to be thick and rather inflexible requiring a longer wilting process. They also need to be cleaned thoroughly with a damp cloth.

LIME (CAL) FOR TORTILLA MASA

Lime, or calcium oxide, known as *cal* in Mexico, is used when cooking dried corn for tortilla or tamale dough—masa. It is generally available in Mexican or Latin American markets or *tortillerias*—where tortillas are made—unless of course they are using one of the dried preparations for their tortillas.

Lime is available either slaked in powder form and ready to use, or unslaked still in hard lumps. If you buy the unslaked, put it into a nonreactive container, sprinkle with water, and watch it crumble. It will send off a steam as it releases its heat.

When handling lime, always take care to keep it clear of your eyes.

FRESH CHILES

CHILE DE AGUA ❀ WATER CHILE

This is very much a local Oaxacan chile and is rarely exported outside the region. However, it features in an important relish in the Oaxacan cuisine and as such deserves a mention, albeit an esoteric one, for visitors to Oaxaca and aficionados. The chile de agua is a large, light green chile that ripens to a fiery, orangey-red. Although sizes can vary tremendously, an average one would measure 5 to 6 inches (13 to 15.5 cm) long and about 1¼ inches (3.25 cm) wide. It has a very good fresh flavor but is extremely hot.

Chiles de agua are generally prepared for a sauce or relish by first charring, peeling, and cutting them into strips, without seeds and veins.

Although the flavor will not be the same, a good fresh relish can be made from any large hot chile pepper.

This chile is rarely used in its dried state. Since it is not available in the United States, any light green, large hot pepper can be substituted.

CHILACA Chilacas are long, thin, dark to blackish green chiles that ripen to a deep brown and are grown mainly in the Bajío—the central area north of Mexico City. Most of them are destined to be dried and transformed into pasilla chile. In their fresh green state they are used in relatively small quantities in and around Mexico City, while they are an important ingredient in the cooking of Michoacán. There they are referred to as *cuernillo* chile (big horn) or *chile para deshebrar*—the latter because they are torn into strips after being charred and peeled.

The skin of this chile is shiny, and the surface is formed by shallow, undulating vertical ridges. They have an excellent flavor and can be very picante. They are now imported from Mexico on a limited scale in the United States (e.g., Fiesta Supermarkets in Texas). Although sizes can vary, an average one measures about 7 inches (18 cm) long (not counting the stem) and ¾ to 1 inch (2 to 2.5 cm) wide.

Charred and peeled, cleaned of veins and seeds, and shredded, they are used as a vegetable or in vegetable dishes, with fried onion and potato for instance, with cheese as a filling for tamales, or in a tomato sauce to accompany Uchepos (page 106) and stewed pork.

TO CHOOSE *Always choose those chiles that are smooth and shiny, not those that have a tired-looking, wrinkled skin. Apart from losing flavor, they will be hard to peel.*

TO STORE *If you are not using them right away, wrap them in two layers of paper toweling, then in a plastic bag, and store them in the refrigerator. They do not freeze when whole. After they have been prepared (see below) and torn into strips, they can be frozen, but not for more than a month or so, or they will lose their texture and flavor when defrosted.*

TO PREPARE *With few exceptions these chiles are charred and peeled for use in sauces, vegetables, and so on, as mentioned above. Leave the stems intact so you can turn them more easily; place them directly onto a gas burner or outdoor charcoal or wood grill and allow them to brown and blister, turning them from time to time until they are evenly charred. Take care not to let the flesh burn through since it is not very thick. If you are using an electric stove, lightly grease the chiles and broil them under a hot broiler, turning them from time to time until evenly charred.*

Place them in a plastic bag and set aside to "sweat" for about 15 minutes. Do not let them cool off before putting them into the bag as this will make peeling more difficult. The skin should now slip off easily; be sure to work over a strainer because the skin is tough and can stop up the sink drainage system. Rinse the chile briefly; do not soak it in water, or the flavor will be impaired.

With a sharp paring knife, cut off the top with the stem attached and discard. Slit the chile down the side and scrape out veins and seeds and discard. Tear the chile into thin—about ¼-inch (.75-cm)—strips, which are now ready to use or freeze (see note above).

GÜERO CHILE In Mexico any pale yellow or pale green chile is referred to as *güero*, or blond. There are several that fall into this category (listed below). They are used fresh or canned and not dried.

CERA CHILE Also referred to as caribe chile or Fresno, this is a small, triangular yellow chile with a smooth, waxy surface. An average one is about 2½ inches (6.5 cm) long and just over 1 inch (2.5 cm) at its widest part. It is used mostly in the northern states and Jalisco for pickling with vegetables and fruits, or whole, slashed at the bottom to be added to stews, sauces, or lentils to give flavor. It can be mild or fairly hot. In Jalisco I have seen it labeled variously as hungaro, California Gold #5, or even Anaheim, none of which names I take very seriously.

This chile is widely available in the United States, called wax or Fresno.

X-CAT-IK CHILE *X-cat-ik* means blond in the Mayan language. This is very much a locally grown and distributed Yucatecan chile. It is pale yellow in color, long and thin, pointed at the end, rather than thin-fleshed. An average one is $4\frac{1}{2}$ to 5 inches (12 to 13 cm) in length and $\frac{1}{4}$ inch (.75 cm) wide; it varies from mild to fairly hot. It is generally used charred, unpeeled, and whole in sauces or in fish and chicken sauces (escabeches) in the Yucatecan cuisine. It is not available in the United States; an Italian or banana pepper can be substituted.

LARGO CHILE OR CARRICILLO To my mind this is the most flavorful of the güero chiles. Unfortunately its distribution is very limited and seasonal, owing, I suppose, to the fact that most of the production goes to the canning industry. This is a long, curling, thin chile with a smooth, thin skin but an undulating surface. Although grown in the central part of Mexico, it is used in the dishes of Veracruz, generally added whole for flavoring rather than for piquancy. Most of the chiles produced are canned in a light pickle and labeled *chiles largos,* the only form in which they reach the United States.

HABANERO CHILE The habanero chile plant in full production is a spectacular sight with its broad, dark green, glossy leaves and the fully ripe chiles hanging down in clusters like brilliant orange lanterns. When mature, the chile is mid-green and ripens to yellow and then orange. It looks as though it has been burnished and is almost translucent. An average-size habanero chile, which is grown commercially exclusively in the Yucatán with very limited distribution elsewhere, is about $1\frac{1}{4}$ inches (3.5 cm) long and about $1\frac{1}{4}$ inches (3.5 cm) wide. It is considered the hottest of the chiles in Mexico, although I would rate the manzano and the chile de árbol in the same category. Not only are its looks exceptional but it also has a distinctive flavor, which is lingering and perfumed—so much so that it is often put into sauces to give flavor and not piquancy.

It is impossible to find an adequate substitute for the habanero chile. The nearest thing to it, grown under different climatic conditions, which alters its physical appearance a little and makes for a softer flavor, is the Haitian piment—called Scotch bonnet in Jamaica and chile Congo in Trinidad—which comes into the Caribbean stores of New York.

The habanero chile is not used in a dried state in Mexico.

TO USE *The chile should have a smooth, unwrinkled skin. It should be resilient, not soft, to the touch and firm around the base of the stem.*

TO STORE *If you are not going to use the chiles immediately, cover them well with two layers of paper toweling and put them into a plastic bag in the refrigerator. They will keep quite well for a week or more.*

Another way of storing them for use in sauces is to char them lightly and allow them to cool off and then pack in thick wrapping for the freezer, where they will keep for about three months.

TO PREPARE *This chile is used raw in fresh sauces like the one for Cochinita Pibil (page 277), and in Cebollas Encurtidas para Panuchos (page 249). Simply rinse the chile and chop it with seeds and veins included.*

To make a simple, very hot Yucatecan sauce, the chile should be charred whole, and then ground into a mortar with lime juice and sea salt. If it is for Frijoles Colados Yucatecos (page 158) or a Yucatecan tomato sauce, it can be added whole, raw, or whole and slightly charred to release the flavor.

That lovely expression, "the chile takes a walk through the sauce," comes from Yucatán. A raw habanero chile is shredded at the pointed end and then dunked into the sauce several times just to leave behind a slight piquancy and flavor.

JALAPEÑO CHILE Jalapeño chiles are perhaps the best-known chiles outside of Mexico since much of the crop is pickled and canned. There are a great many varieties of this chile, but their shape is unmistakable: an elongated, blunt triangle varying from mid- to dark green, some with dark patches on them, others with a vertical brown intermittent striping. The jalapeño chile is called by different names according to the type and the season in which it is harvested or just local usage: *gordo* chile in Veracruz, *chilchote* in the Sierra de Puebla, or *tornachile* in old cookbooks, *cuaresmeño* in central Mexico. An average jalapeño chile is about 2½ inches (6.5 cm) long and just under 1 inch (2.5 cm) wide; it can range from mild to hot to very hot. It is used either in its mature but green stage or when fully ripened and bright red in color.

Jalapeño chiles, widely available in the United States, are used mostly in strips (rajas), either in fresh sauces or pickled. Generally speaking they will be chopped and blended for sauces only if serranos are not available in your area.

TO CHOOSE *The skin of these chiles when fresh is smooth and shiny and the flesh firm to the touch. When dull and wrinkled, they have lost their fresh flavor and crisp texture. Always make sure there is no deterioration around the base of the stem.*

TO STORE *If you are not going to use them right away, store them as for the other fresh chiles, wrapping them first in paper toweling and then in plastic bags; even then it is best to keep them only about a week, for after that time the flavor and texture are impaired.*

TO PREPARE *First rinse the chiles well in case traces of insecticide remain. Wipe them dry, cut them into strips, and fry them with onion for a tomato sauce. Seeds may be removed for appearance' sake.*

Fry them whole with onion and garlic for pickled chiles before adding herbs and vinegar.

In Veracruz they are stuffed with tuna, sardines, or cheese — and they are very potent. For these recipes (not given in this book), the chiles are charred over a flame as for poblanos, peeled, slit open, seeded, and stuffed. Occasionally they will be stuffed with meat, fish, or cheese and covered with a batter as for chiles rellenos.

MANZANO CHILE The manzano chile, called *perón* in Michoacán and *canario* in Oaxaca, is a fleshy, bulbous chile with an average length of 2 inches (5 cm) and width of about 1¾ inches (4.5 cm). It is one of the hottest chiles I know.

It is an uncommon chile for various reasons: the plant, which can grow into a high bush, can withstand cold and is cultivated in Michoacán, in the high country around Lake Pátzcuaro, where it is picante; and in the Chiapas highlands, where it is milder. It has a purple, rather than the normal white, flower and quite large woody seeds that are jet black in color. There are two distinct plants: on one, the green mature fruit ripens to a bright yellow; on the other, it turns from green to a brilliant red. The real aficionados say they prefer the yellow because it has more flavor than the red, which they say is hotter, if that is possible.

The surface of the chile is smooth and shiny, and once picked it seems to keep its fresh appearance longer than other types of chiles. In Mexico the unpeeled chile is used in pickles and relishes. Charred but not peeled, it is ground in a tomato sauce; charred and peeled, it is stuffed for chiles rellenos. But in none of these cases are the seeds used.

The manzano chile is never used in a dried form and is now being imported from Mexico on a limited scale (e.g., Fiesta Supermarkets in Texas). I have seen plants in window boxes of the Latin American Mission District of San Francisco, where it is called *rocoto*.

TO CHOOSE *Make sure that the surface is smooth and shiny and firm to the touch; when it's wrinkled and dull and soft, the best has gone out of the chile. Also be sure that there is no deterioration around the base of the stalk.*

TO STORE *If you are not going to use the chiles right away, wrap them in paper toweling and put them into a plastic bag in the refrigerator — even then they tend to lose their crisp texture for use when raw.*

TO PREPARE *Rinse and dry the chiles. For use in fresh relishes, remove the stalk, cut open the chile, and remove seeds, then cut the chile into strips. It is usual to leave the chiles to macerate in lime juice with salt to cut the heat a little.*

To use a manzano chile in a tomato sauce, place it whole on a hot comal and turn it from time to time until the skin is slightly charred and blistered. Cut it open, remove the seeds and veins, and blend the chile with the tomatoes—only part of one chile will be necessary to make the sauce picante.

Manzano chiles are also prepared like poblanos for chiles rellenos. They are charred and peeled in the usual way and slit open, and the seeds and veins are removed. They are then covered with hot water and simmered for about 1 minute. The water is changed, a little salt is added, and they are left to soak for 5 minutes more. They are drained, stuffed with a picadillo of shredded meat or with cheese, covered in an egg batter, and fried. They are served in a tomato broth, again just like chiles rellenos.

POBLANO CHILE The poblano chile is also known by the names *chile para rellenar, chile gordo* (Jalisco), *jarál* (state of Mexico), and, most incorrectly in the United States, pasilla, or fresh pasilla.

This is a large, fleshy, triangle-shaped chile with a shiny, smooth, mid- to black-green color that ripens to a deep red and ranges from mild to hot with a distinctive taste. An average-size chile is 4½ inches (12 cm) long and 2½ inches (6.5 cm) wide at the shoulder—the widest part—and is distinguished by a deep ridge around the base of the stalk. With rare exceptions it is charred and peeled, and the veins and seeds are removed before it's cooked. Used as a vegetable, it is stuffed, as chiles rellenos, or cut into strips and fried with onion and potato, added to a tomato sauce with eggs or stewed pork, used as a topping for soups, blended with cream for a rich sauce, or blended to add to rice. Dried when ripe, it becomes the ancho chile; charred and peeled when still green and then dried, it becomes pasado chile.

TO CHOOSE *Always choose chiles that are smooth and shiny and not those that have a dull, wrinkled skin. Apart from loss of flavor in this condition, they will be harder to peel.*

TO STORE *If you are not going to use them right away, wrap them in two layers of paper toweling and then in a plastic bag; in this way they keep their moisture for a few days in the refrigerator.*

They do not freeze in their raw state, but once they have been charred and peeled they can be frozen for a month, no more, or they lose their flavor and texture when defrosted.

TO PREPARE *As mentioned above, with few exceptions, the poblano chile is charred or fried and peeled before using.*

Leave the stem, if any, on the chile intact — it makes it easier to turn the chile — and place it directly over an open flame of a gas stove or a wood or charcoal grill. If using electricity, then smear the chile with a light coating of oil and place it right up under the broiler. Turn the chiles from time to time to allow the skin to blister and char lightly all over. Do not allow the flesh to be burnt right through.

Place them immediately into a plastic bag and leave them to "sweat" for about 10 minutes. This helps to loosen the skin. The skin can now be slipped off easily, and this should be done over a strainer because the little pieces are tough and can block up the sink drain. Rinse the chile briefly, but do not soak it in water, or the flavor will certainly be impaired.

FOR CHILES RELLENOS

Leaving the top of the chile and the stem's base intact, carefully make a slit down one side. Opening it up halfway, carefully cut out the placenta (the white bulky part with the seeds) and discard. Scrape out the remaining seeds and detach the veins running down the chile carefully so as not to tear the flesh. It is now ready to stuff. But it is best to mark any very picante chile, for they vary, for family or guests who like them that way. They should be used right away but can be stored overnight — no longer, or they will lose much of their juiciness and flavor. They can also be frozen, but no longer than one month because on defrosting they lose both texture and flavor.

FOR RAJAS (CHILE STRIPS)

With a sharp paring knife, cut off the top of the chile with stem attached. Slit the chile down the side and scrape out veins and seeds and discard. Cut the chile into vertical strips about ¼ to ½ inch (.75 to 1.5 cm) wide.

CHILE SQUARES FOR TOPPING

Follow the instructions for chile strips, but cut the flesh into ½-inch (1.5-cm) squares. Heat a little butter or oil in a frying pan and sauté the chile squares, turning them over from time to time, for about 3 minutes. This helps to take away the raw taste and gives them a sweeter flavor.

SERRANO CHILE The name *serrano* or *verde* for this chile (not to be confused with the chile verde of the Yucatán) seems to be in general use throughout Mexico with the minor, local exception of the Sierra de Puebla, where it is often referred to as *tampiqueño*.

It is a small, mid- to dark-green chile, depending on the variety of seed used, that ripens to a bright red. The new varieties tend toward a lighter color and larger size—about 2 inches (5 cm) long and ½ inch (1.5 cm) wide—while the "unimproved" (but often more flavorful) serrano chile tends to be a darker green, more pointed at the tip, and smaller in size, an average one being 1 to 1½ inches (2.5 to 4 cm) long and ¼ inch (.75 cm) wide.

They all have shiny, smooth skin and can range from hot to very hot. While they are generally preferred for fresh or cooked sauces in their mature but green stage, they are still used when very ripe and red.

TO CHOOSE   *The skin of the chiles should be smooth and shiny, not dull and wrinkled. When they reach this latter stage, they have lost their crisp texture and fresh flavor and taste of earth.*

Make sure that there is no deterioration in the form of black patches on the skin (there are some natural dark spots, again depending on the type of seed used), especially around the base of the stem, and that they are firm and not soft to the touch.

TO STORE   *If you are not going to use them right away, wrap them in two layers of paper toweling and store them in a plastic bag in the refrigerator; in this way they will not dry out. Even then they will last only about one week without losing flavor and texture.*

If you wish to store them well ahead for use in cooked sauces, simmer them for 5 minutes in water, cook them, then freeze or broil and freeze (see details below).

TO PREPARE   *Always rinse chiles well because you never know what traces of insecticides remain.*

For fresh sauces, chop or blend the chiles without removing seeds and veins. For a cooked sauce, with tomate verde, simmer the whole chiles with the tomate verde and then blend.

For a sauce of broiled red tomatoes or tomate verde, broil or char the chiles on a comal, turning them until slightly charred and blistered.

Toreados are serrano chiles that have been rolled on a hot comal until they begin to color and soften; they are usually left whole and demolished in two bites by the true aficionado.

CHILE VERDE DEL NORTE ❋ ANAHEIM PEPPER

The large, long, skinny green chile used in northwestern Mexico, principally in Sonora but also in Chihuahua, is also referred to as the Magdalena chile, named for the town in Sonora near where it is grown in quantity. It is in fact the same as the Anaheim, or California, chile pepper. It is light green in color and can range from mild to hot. In Mexico it is usually charred and peeled; left whole with seeds and veins removed, it is often stuffed for a chile relleno, or it is cut into strips and used in tomato sauces and for chile con queso in Chihuahua.

In Chihuahua it is also charred and peeled and then dried to become the black and wrinkled pasado chile.

While it is usually in its green, mature state, it is also ripened to a fiery red for drying to become the Chile Seco del Norte or Chile de la Tierra (see page 477).

DRIED CHILES

This section on dried chiles does not set out to be complete—it would take a whole book to do that—but it does describe some of the more commonly used chiles, their characteristics, their uses, and how they are prepared. There is also a brief mention of some of the lesser-known chiles that are very important to some of the regional cuisines and of special interest to travelers to these regions, apart from aficionados—among them food writers and chefs—who are on a constant quest for more information about these uniquely Mexican ingredients.

Drying chiles is, of course, a way of preserving them; so is smoking them, and in northern Mexico there is another method for preserving chiles (see *pasado chile*, page 468) that is unknown, and probably unacceptable, elsewhere.

Methods of dealing with dried chiles vary slightly from region to region and are set out in each recipe. For example, in some areas cooks toast chiles lightly before soaking and blending them for a cooked sauce, while others simmer them in water and then blend them. Proponents of the former method say that their sauce has a better flavor and is more digestible.

There are two important rules when dealing with the preparation of the fleshy chiles like anchos, mulatos, and pasillas for thick sauces and moles: they should not be soaked longer than the time specified, or their flavor will be left in the soaking water. Second, never attempt to skin the chiles once they have been soaked, because the skin provides flavor and color and acts as a thickening agent for the sauce.

> **CHOOSING AND STORING** *Always try to buy chiles that are loose so you can see what you are getting; all too often, dried-out, third-rate chiles tend to be disguised by the fancy packaging.*
>
> *Do not go by the name on the package—many chiles are mislabeled. Study the pictures and descriptions and decide for yourself. While sizes do vary legitimately, the best-quality chiles should approximate the average sizes given for each type.*
>
> *The best chiles will be of the most recent crop and still flexible. If they are damp, you know you are paying for the moisture, but no matter; let them dry out in an airy place in the sun. But do not dry them until they're brittle; they should be just flexible. Although chiles that are dried to a crisp can be used, they will have to be soaked for a longer period and then cleaned of veins and seeds. If you attempt to clean them before soaking them, they will break into 100 pieces.*
>
> *Try to avoid buying chiles with transparent patches of skin; a fruit fly has been at work and eaten the flesh from the skin. It has probably also laid eggs inside and in time, with the right damp, hot conditions, little grubs will hatch out.*
>
> *Stored properly, dried chiles will last for years. It is best to store them in a cool, dry place and, if you have the space, in the refrigerator or freezer. This will prevent insects from getting at them. In any case, inspect the chiles every month or so to make sure they are not deteriorating. Open one up and see if it has any traces of mildew, which will spread quickly under very damp conditions. If it does, it should be thrown out or, preferably, burned.*

ANCHO CHILE The ancho chile—sometimes confusingly called *pasilla roja* in parts of Michoacán—is the most commonly used chile throughout Mexico. It is in fact the poblano chile ripened to a deep red and then dried. It is widely available in the United States.

A good-quality ancho is flexible, not dried out to a crisp, with a deep reddish-brown wrinkled skin that still has some shine to it. A good, average-size chile is $4\frac{1}{2}$ inches (12 cm) long and about 3 inches (8 cm) wide. As it dries out it becomes increasingly dark in color and more difficult to distinguish from the dried mulato chile for one who is not thoroughly familiar with chiles. To make sure, open one up and look at it through the light; it should be a reddish brown rather than the brownish-black color of the mulato. Once the chiles are soaked it is easier to tell the difference as these tones are more pronounced. The flavor of the ancho is decidedly sharper and fruitier than that of the mulato, which is softer and more chocolatey in flavor.

PREPARATION   *There are several different methods for preparing these chiles for recipes in this book, and each one will be indicated specifically in the recipe.*

Generally speaking the ancho chile is not used for fresh table sauces, or salsas de molca-jete as they are called in Mexico, with one exception. That is more of a relish than a sauce, salsa de tijeras — the raw chile is cut into strips and marinated in oil and vinegar, etc.

FOR CHILES RELLENOS

Leaving stem and top intact, slit the chile open very carefully and remove veins and seeds. Cover with hot water and leave to soak for about 15 minutes or until the chile is fleshy and has been reconstituted. It is then ready to be stuffed with cheese, a meat filling, chorizo and potato, etc.; fried in batter; and served in tomato sauce in the usual way.

FOR COOKED SAUCES, MOLES, ETC.

Remove the stem, if any, slit the chile down the side, and remove seeds and veins. Flatten the chile out as much as possible, then use one of these methods:

METHOD 1 *Cover with hot water and leave to soak until fleshy, about 15 minutes. Note: Soaking time will depend on how old and dry the chile is; 15 minutes is for a reasonably flexible chile. Drain and transfer to a blender jar, discarding the water.*

METHOD 2 *Put the cleaned chiles into a pan of hot water, bring to a simmer, and continue simmering for about 5 minutes more, until fleshy and completely reconstituted.*

METHOD 3 *Heat a comal over medium heat — it must not be too hot, or the chiles will burn and make the sauce bitter — and press the chile, inside down, on the comal as flat as possible. Leave for about 3 seconds, turn over, and repeat on the second side or until the inside flesh turns an opaque, tobacco brown — about 3 seconds (if the chile is fairly moist, it will blister, but that is not the sign). Remove, cover with hot water, and leave to soak for about 15 minutes.*

METHOD 4 *For some moles the dried chile should be fried. Heat enough lard or oil to cover the bottom of the frying pan. When hot — but not smoking, or the chile will burn — place the chile, inside out, as flat as possible in the hot oil. Fry for about 5 seconds, pressing down well into the oil. Turn it over and fry it on the second side for about the same time or until the* *inner flesh is an opaque tobacco brown. Remove and cover with water. Add more oil to the pan as you continue with the chiles.*

METHOD 5 *For grinding ancho chile to a powder—which is often used in the North as a condiment to add to menudo, etc.—place a comal over low heat and press the chile down as flat as possible without burning. Turn the chile over and toast on the second side for about 1 minute or until the chile is completely dehydrated; when cool, it should be crisp. Tear the toasted chile into pieces into a blender jar or coffee/spice grinder and grind to a fine powder. To store it most effectively, put it into an airtight container and store in the freezer section of the refrigerator.*

MULATO CHILE The mulato chile plant is essentially the same as that of the poblano but with slightly different genes that affect the color and taste. It is rarely used in its fresh state, since a grower can get a higher price for his crop of mulatos dried than fresh, and they usually fetch a higher price than many other types of dried chiles. Although size can vary considerably, an average one is 5 inches (13 cm) long and 3 inches (8 cm) wide. It is black-ish brown in color, and the skin—again in a first-class one—may be smoother than that of the ancho. The flavor is sweetish, rather chocolatey, and can range from quite mild to rather hot. Unfortunately, many chile purveyors, especially those along the border, are mixing anchos and mulatos and will swear to you that they are the same. They are not. A test to distinguish them is given under Ancho Chile (see page 472). It's important to do so because, for instance, a mole poblano that calls for a certain proportion of mulatos can be altered substantially in appearance and flavor if anchos are used instead. Mulatos are widely available in the United States.

PREPARATION   *See methods listed for ancho chile.*

PASILLA CHILE The pasilla chile is the dried chilaca, sometimes referred to as *negro* chile (black chile) and in Oaxaca as the *pasilla de Mexico* to distinguish it from the *chile pasilla de Oaxaca* (see page 479). It has a shiny, black, wrinkled surface with vertical ridges and a rich but sharp flavor—in contrast to the other black mulato chile—and can range from fairly hot to hot. An average one is 6 inches (15.5 cm) long and 1 inch (2.5 cm) wide. It is widely available in specialty stores and some supermarkets in the United States.

The pasilla chile is used to garnish soups, for rustic table sauces, and for moles or other cooked sauces.

PREPARATION   *For many dishes it is prepared in the same way as the ancho chile, and methods 1 through 4 on pages 473–474 would apply. However, there are three distinctive ways in which it is used:*

1. As a topping and condiment for soup. *If the chile has a stem, leave it intact. Wipe thoroughly with a damp cloth. Heat oil in a small frying pan to a depth of ¼ inch (.75 cm) over medium heat. When hot—but not smoking, or the chile will burn—put the whole chile into it and fry slowly, turning from time to time, until it is shiny and crisp. If it is not punctured or broken, it will inflate impressively, which not only makes it look nice but also makes it crisp evenly. Either serve the fried pasilla chiles whole on top of each soup bowl or crumble them roughly with seeds and veins and pass them separately to sprinkle on the soup as a condiment.*

2. As a rustic table sauce. *If the chile has a stem, leave it intact to help turn the chile more easily. Wipe the chile thoroughly with a damp cloth. Heat a comal over medium heat—it should not be too hot, or the chile will burn. Place the whole chile onto it and toast, turning from time to time, for 5 to 7 minutes or until it is evenly crisp all around. Crumble the chile, with seeds and veins, into a molcajete or blender jar and blend briefly to a textured sauce with the other ingredients called for.*

3. The veins as a condiment. *When a recipe calls for the veins and seeds to be cleaned from the pasilla chile, save the veins, toast them on an ungreased comal until a rich golden color, and crumble on top.*

GUAJILLO CHILE The guajillo chile (along with the ancho) is the most commonly used dried chile in Mexican cooking, probably because it is more widely available and cheaper than many others. The guajillo chile has a smooth, tough skin that is a deep maroon color. It is long and thin, tapering to a point; an average one is 5 inches (13 cm) long and 1¼ to 1½ inches (3.5 to 4 cm) at the widest point. It can vary from fairly hot to hot and has a pleasant, sharp flavor. In the north central region of the country it is called *cascabel* (rattle) because it rattles and resembles a rattlesnake's tail. It belongs to a family of chiles that when fresh are sometimes called *mirasol* (looking at the sun)—erroneously, for the majority of these chiles hang down on the plant and do not point up to the sun.

While the guajillo is occasionally used for a table sauce, it is more often used after being soaked and blended for spreading on meat for a *carne enchilada*, for enchilada sauces, and for thick stews. However, the sauce nearly always has to be strained since the skin is so tough and not all of it is ground sufficiently in the blender. It is widely available in the United States.

PREPARATION   *Remove the stems, slit the chile open, and scrape out the veins and seeds. Follow methods 1, 2, and 3 on page 473 for ancho chile.*

METHOD 4 *When used as a substitute for the black Oaxacan chile, it is toasted on the comal or straight on the fire until it is black and crisp. It is then rinsed twice in cold water to get rid of some of the bitterness and then soaked in hot water.*

PUYA CHILE The puya, or *guajillo puya* as it is often called, is a thinner and hotter version of the guajillo with an average length of 4 inches (10.5 cm) and width of ¾ inch (2 cm). It is cleaned and prepared in exactly the same way as the guajillo. It is widely available in the United States.

CHILE DE ÁRBOL The chile de árbol is not from a tree as its name implies but from a rangy, tall plant. It ripens from green to a bright red and retains its brilliant color when dried. It is a long, smooth-skinned, slender chile with an average length of 3 inches (8 cm) and width of ⅜ inch (1.25 cm) and it is very, very hot.

While the dried chile de árbol is used mostly for table sauces, occasionally a few will be blended in with other, more fleshy chiles for a meat stew, etc. It is widely available in the United States.

PREPARATION   *Nobody in Mexico would dream of taking the veins and seeds out of this chile; they know it is hot, and they like it that way.*

METHOD 1 *Place the whole chile with stem, if any, intact onto a fairly hot comal—but not too hot, or the chile will burn—and keep turning it around until it is toasted to a light brown color and becomes crisp. Crumble it into a blender jar without soaking it and follow the instructions in the recipe.*

METHOD 2 *Heat a little oil in a small frying pan, add the chiles, and fry until lightly browned and crisp, about 3 minutes. Remove, do not soak, and blend following the recipe instructions.*

CASCABEL CHILE The chile cascabel is in the form of a little round rattle, as its name suggests. It has a smooth, tough, reddish-brown skin, and an average-size chile measures 1¼ inches (3.5 cm) in diameter and 1 inch (2.5 cm) long. This chile can best be appreciated in an uncooked table sauce, although quite often it is blended with tomatoes or tomate verde for a cooked main-dish sauce. Available in the United States.

PREPARATION

METHOD 1 *If it is in the form of a nice even sphere, and the flesh is not pushed in in places, then it can be toasted whole on a medium-hot comal, and the stem, if any, can be used to turn it around. It should be toasted slowly until crisp — about 5 minutes — but care should be taken not to let it burn, or the sauce will be bitter. Then remove the stem, cut open, remove the seeds and veins, toast the seeds (if required in the recipe), and crumble into a blender jar.*

METHOD 2 *If it is not even, remove the stem, cut open, and scrape out the veins and seeds. Toast by flattening it down onto a medium-hot comal until the inside of the flesh is an opaque tobacco brown. By then it should be toasted crisp. Crumble into a blender jar, unsoaked.*

METHOD 3 *In the Northwest the cascabel chile is often just soaked or simmered in water until the tough skin begins to soften and is then blended with tomatoes or green tomatoes for a cooked sauce. However, the wonderful nutty flavor of the chile is lost when it is toasted.*

CHILE SECO DEL NORTE OR CHILE DE LA TIERRA ❀ DRIED ANAHEIM, CALIFORNIA CHILE PODS This chile is also called *largo colorado* and is used exclusively in northern Mexico, particularly in Sonora. It is the dried Anaheim chile (or *Magdalena* on the other side of the border) and is sold in the United States labeled "California chile pods."

Its thin, shiny skin can best be described as a deep, burnished coppery red color. The skin is tucked around the base of the stem, forming irregular "pleats" from base to tip. It can vary from mild to fairly hot.

The chile seco is soaked and blended and used in sauces for *chilaquiles*, enchiladas, carne con chile, and other northern dishes. When it is ground to a powder and used for sauces, it is often thickened with lightly browned flour.

PREPARATION   *Remove stems, slit open vertically, and remove veins and seeds. Cover with boiling water and simmer until soft — about 10 minutes. Then drain and follow the instructions in the recipe.*

CHILACATE The chilacate is grown in the Jalisco/Colima area and used, dried, in the cooking of that region. It is a smooth, shiny, tough-skinned chile, sweetish in flavor, that can range from mild to fairly hot. Its color could best be described as "raisin" (according to the color chart in *Webster's International Dictionary*), and an average size is 5 inches (13 cm) long and 2 inches (5 cm) at the widest part. In Colima it is used interchangeably with anchos and guajillos, mixed in a ratio of 2 to 1 respectively. You will often see chilacate packaged in the United States and marked (incorrectly) "guajillo." There is also a New Mexican dried chile that resembles it and can be used as a substitute. When soaked and blended, the chilacate is used for enchilada and other cooked sauces.

PREPARATION   *Remove the stem, if any, slit open from base to tip, and remove seeds and veins. Cover with hot water and leave for about 15 minutes to soak. Drain and blend or simmer in hot water for 5 minutes and leave to soak for 5 minutes longer. The tough skin, unlike that of the guajillo, softens fast and blends well.*

CHIPOTLE CHILE The chipotle chile (as it is known colloquially) or *chilpocle* is the jalapeño chile ripened and smoke-dried, as its Nahuatl name (*chil*, chile; *pectli*, smoke) suggests. It is a tough, leathery, wrinkled chile that gives the appearance of a piece of old tobacco, although it is actually a darkish brown color highlighted with golden brown ridges. An average one—depending on the quality of the crop—is 2½ inches (6.5 cm) long and 1 inch (2.5 cm) wide at its widest part.

Canned chipotles are a very popular condiment, either in a light pickle or in an adobo—mild red chile—sauce. And in these forms they can be used in most dishes where chipotles are called for. The plain dried—and smoked—ones can be used for pickling to flavor soups and pasta dishes, or soaked and ground with other ingredients in a sauce for meatballs, shrimps, or meat. They are extremely hot. They are available dried or canned in adobo sauce in the United States; don't try to remove the seeds.

PREPARATION   *The chipotle chile is always used with seeds and veins intact.*
For pickling, it is briefly stewed in water or vinegar to soften before the other ingredients are added. For sauces it (not the canned type) is often very lightly toasted and then put to soak before being blended with other ingredients. The soaking time depends on how dry it is—from 15 to 30 minutes.

MORA CHILE In parts of Veracruz and Puebla the mora chile is called chipotle, or chipotle mora. It tends to be smaller than the full-blown chipotle, about 2 inches (5 cm) long and ¾ inch (2 cm) wide, and is a deep mulberry color as its name implies. It is extremely hot.

The mora chile is prepared and used in the same way as chipotles and is favored by the canning factories for its more convenient size. It is sometimes available in the United States, canned; don't try to remove the seeds.

MORITA CHILE The morita chile is a small, dried, smoked chile, triangular in shape with a smooth, shiny, mulberry-colored skin. An average one is 1 inch (2.5 cm) long and ¾ inch (2 cm) wide. It is very picante and should be used with discretion. It is sometimes available in the United States. I am told the moritas are the last picking of the serrano chile crop.

PREPARATION *The chile is either toasted lightly and blended with other ingredients or soaked in boiling water until soft, but veins and seeds are not taken out.*

PASILLA CHILE DE OAXACA The chile pasilla de Oaxaca is very much a local chile used only in the cooking of Oaxaca and part of Puebla. To me it is one of the most interesting and delicious chiles, and all Mexican aficionados should be aware of it (and if they go to Oaxaca, they can buy and experiment with it).

It is the most wrinkled of all the chiles. It is smoked and very hot. An average one is about 3½ inches (9 cm) long and 1¼ inches (3.25 cm) wide with shiny skin that varies from mulberry to wine red. While the chile is stuffed and fried in a batter like any chile relleno, it is also used in table and cooked sauces. The closest substitute would be the mora, although it would be too small for stuffing well.

PREPARATION *If the chile is to be stuffed, it is probably too dry to cut open and clean, so put it on a warm comal to heat through and become flexible, then slit it open carefully, retaining the stem, if any, and scrape out the veins and seeds. Cover with hot water and simmer for about 5 minutes. Leave to soak for about 10 minutes longer. Then stuff and fry in the usual way. For sauces: toast the whole chile lightly on a comal or directly over a low flame or in hot ashes, turning over so both sides are toasted evenly (shake but do not wash off the ash). Then tear it into pieces with seeds and veins and blend with the other ingredients for a table sauce or cooked sauce.*

CHILHUACLE NEGRO, ROJO, AMARILLO The chilhuacles are uniquely Oaxacan chiles that are gradually disappearing and quite expensive now to buy for the local people, who are substituting guajillos (and charring them to get the correct color for the mole negro of Oaxaca, for instance).

These are squat, full-bodied chiles, some slightly pointed at the end but most blunt, almost square; 2 inches (5 cm) long and 2 inches (5 cm) wide is an average size. The black, yellow, or red skin is matte and very tough; when soaked, the flesh has a sharp licorice flavor. These chiles are used mostly for moles.

> PREPARATION   *Remove seeds and veins, toast well on a comal without burning, rinse in cold water, then put to soak in hot water for about 20 minutes. They can also be cleaned, rinsed, and fried, then blended without soaking, depending on the recipe.*

PIQUÍN CHILE Chile piquín, pequín, *chiltepe* (Puebla), *chiltepin* (Sonora), chile *max* (Yucatán), *amashito* (Tabasco): they are all very small, very hot chiles. Triangular, round, or cylindrical in shape, they are generally either pickled in vinegar or ground dry as a condiment. Usually no more than ½ inch (1.5 cm) long and ¼ inch (.75 cm) wide—the round ones are about ¼ inch (.75 cm) in diameter—they have shiny skins that range from orangey to deep red in color.

CHILE SECO YUCATECO I have included the seco chile of Yucatán because it is an interesting one and significant in the Yucatecan cuisine. It is in fact the dried chile verde of Yucatán—a small, thin, light green chile that has a unique flavor. It ripens and dries to a golden orangey color and has a shiny, transparent, tough skin with an average length of 2 inches (5 cm) and width of ¾ inch (2 cm). It is very hot.

In the Yucatán it is ground to a powder and used as a condiment, but perhaps most interesting of all, it is charred black and ground with other spices to a paste used for the black *chilmole* and *rellenos negros* seasoning. While the chile is not available in the United States—use hot paprika as a substitute—the black seasoning pastes are.

MEXICAN CHEESES

The cheeses used in Mexican traditional cooking are relatively unsophisticated and in many cases purely regional.

QUESO AÑEJO Queso añejo (properly called *añejo de Cotija* for the farming town of Cotija on the border of Michoacán and Jalisco where it was first made), or aged cheese, is a very dry, whitish, salty cheese with some acidity that comes in a barrel shape and is usually grated very finely to resemble fine bread crumbs. It is used on top of *antojitos*, enchiladas, soups, and pasta and does not melt.

There is one excellent brand made in the United States, near Los Angeles, with a fairly wide distribution, called simply Queso Cortija, but if it's not available in your area, use romano or sardo.

QUESO ASADERO Queso asadero is a flattish, soft, braided cheese like mozzarella. It is made in northern Mexico with a percentage of sour milk, has a good fat content, is pleasantly acidy, and melts well. In Sonora it is known as *queso cocido*, cooked cheese, because the curds are cooked to form the skeins that are then wound into balls. This cheese is used for *queso fundido* (melted cheese), for *chile con queso*, and to stuff chiles.

I have not found a good asadero in the United States, but a Jack, Teleme, or domestic block muenster can be substituted.

QUESO CHIHUAHUA This cheese was originally made in the Mennonite communities in Chihuahua, and large wheels of it were stamped with the name of the community. The real thing is rare now as the Mennonites are migrating to other countries, but there are many passable substitutes. This cheese resembles a fairly soft cheddar, and is pleasantly acidy, with a good proportion of fat, which means that it melts nicely.

Queso Chihuahua is used for stuffing chiles, grated on top of sopas secas and pastas, and for melting in *queso fundido* or *chile con queso*. The so-called Chihuahuas made in the United States bear little resemblance to the original, so it is best to substitute a good medium-sharp cheddar (not the soapy packaged ones), a domestic block muenster, or a Monterey Jack.

QUESO FRESCO Queso fresco is a crumbly soft cheese with a pleasant acidity that melts and *hace hebra* (makes strings) when heated. It is made of cow's milk, as are the other cheeses mentioned here (goat's-milk cheeses are not very popular) and is sometimes called *queso ranchero* (not to be confused with the brand name Queso Ranchero); in one isolated village near a friend's ranch it is called *de metate* because traditionally the curds are pressed and ground on a metate.

Queso fresco is used in many different ways: to eat uncooked as a botana (snack with drinks); crumbled, to sprinkle on top of *antojitos*, in enchiladas, and in soups; cut into strips for chiles rellenos, etc.

While several United States companies are now making this type of cheese, they fall far short of the real thing except for the Mozzarrella Cheese Company, in Dallas (see Sources), which makes a very good product. The Cacique brand Queso Ranchero is acceptable and widely available. The various types of queso blanco will not do; they are too white and rubbery and innocuous, so you may have to use what is available in your area.

QUESILLO DE OAXACA This is a braided, cooked cheese made and sold in the markets of Oaxaca in all sizes, from a 1-inch (2.5 cm) ball used as a botana (snack with drinks), to 6 inches (15.5 cm) in diameter. Of course it is made on a large commercial scale in big blocks to be sold in Mexico City and around the country.

The quesillo de Oaxaca has a tougher consistency than the asadero and a higher melting point. It is used for chiles rellenos, quesadillas, etc., as well as eaten raw, as mentioned above.

It is difficult to find a good substitute for this cheese. The usual commercial American mozzarellas do not have enough acidity or character but can be used in a pinch. A young Mexican chef in New York, however, has located an excellent string cheese called Lataia that acts and tastes exactly right. If it is not available in your area, use, as for asadero, a Jack, Teleme, or domestic block muenster (never the small, packaged kind).

QUESO PANELA The traditional queso panela is a flattish, round fresh cheese marked with the weave of the basket in which the curds are set to drain. I first came across it years ago at its best, made in every household in the hot coastal area of Jalisco. The temperature there is hot enough to ferment the cheese so that it has a spongy, porous texture.

It is the simplest of all the cheeses to make. Clabber the milk as for chongos, omitting the egg yolks (see page 434), cut the curd into large pieces, and transfer the pieces with a slotted spoon to a draining basket, sprinkling sea salt liberally between layers of curds. Hang up to drain overnight. When the curds are drained but still moist, set them aside on a rack for the acidity to develop, 12 to 24 hours in a warm place.

SPICES

Traditional Mexican cooks use whole spices and in very small quantities with minor exceptions.

ALLSPICE PIMENTA DIOICA The tree from which this berrylike seed comes is a native of tropical America and grows wild in the southern part of Veracruz and Tabasco. The seed when ripened and dried is a mid- to dark brown. It is round with an average size of about ¼ inch (.75 cm) in diameter. The leaves are also highly aromatic and used to flavor some dishes in Tabasco and the Yucatán.

The seeds are known by various names: *pimienta gorda*, *pimienta de Jamaica*, *malagueta*, and in Tabasco, *pimienta de la tierra*.

ANISEEDS PIMPINELLA ANISUM Aniseeds, or *anís* as it is known in Mexico, is used mostly, although not exclusively, for flavoring syrups for desserts, or is added to the dough of some *pan dulce*, semi-sweet yeast breads. Very small quantities are used in some recipes for mole poblano. They are also added to corn masa for some of the *antojitos* of Hidalgo.

CINNAMON CINNAMOMUM VERUM The true cinnamon is the brittle, flaking bark of a tree native to Sri Lanka and southwest India. It is lightish brown in color and should not be confused with what often passes as the real thing, cassia bark, which is harder and darker in color. Whole pieces are used to flavor syrups or coffee, or smaller quantities are ground with other spices for moles or other cooked chile sauces. Cinnamon in its powdered form is used for desserts, cakes, and semi-sweet yeast breads.

CLOVE SYZYGIUM AROMATICUM Cloves, *clavos* or *clavos de especia*, are mostly used whole or ground with other spices for moles or other cooked chile sauces, broths, or pickles. Cloves are the aromatic dried flower buds of a tree native to the Molucca Islands but grown extensively in the Caribbean "spice island" of Grenada. Like other spices, they are used in very small quantities.

CORIANDER SEEDS CORIANDRUM SATIVUM Coriander seeds, *semillas de cilantro*, are used in small quantities either whole in pickles or ground for some of the more complex cooked sauces like moles. They were used frequently in recipes recorded around the turn of the century.

CUMIN **CUMINUM CYMINUM** Whole cumin seeds, *comino*, never the powdered, are used in traditional Mexican food. They are often ground with garlic or other spices, and are used sparingly so that their flavor does not dominate, except in some of the northern food, especially that of Nuevo León.

PEPPERCORNS **PIPER NIGRUM** Mild black peppercorns are used extensively, but generally in small quantities (except for the seasoning pastes of the Yucatán Peninsula). They have various local names: *pimienta*, *pimienta negra* or *chica*, or *pimienta de Castilla*. They are often ground with other spices, or used crushed or whole in broths or to season meats.

ACHIOTE—ANATTO **BIXA ORELLANA** Achiote, the coloring and flavoring agent used extensively in the Yucatán Peninsula, comes from the outer coating of the very hard seed of a tropical American tree. The whole seeds are ground in combination with other spices for seasoning foods. While commercially prepared pastes, *recado rojo*, are widely available in Mexican and Latin American markets and many supermarkets carrying products for ethnic foods, you can easily make your own.

RECADO DE TODA CLASE
MAKES ¼ CUP (65 ML)   SEÑORA ISELA RODRÍGUEZ

2 tablespoons mild black peppercorns
7 whole cloves
8 whole allspice
¼-inch (.75 cm) cinnamon stick
¼ teaspoon cumin seeds
2 tablespoons toasted and crushed dried Yucatecan oregano

Put all the dry ingredients into an electric coffee/ spice grinder and grind as finely as possible. Pass through a fine strainer and grind the residue once more until you have a fine powder.

Transfer the powder to a small bowl and add just enough water to mix to a stiff paste. Store the recado *in this form in the refrigerator or freezer.*

TO USE THIS RECADO
FOR 1 TABLESPOON OF THIS PASTE:

2 garlic cloves, crushed
2 tablespoons bitter orange juice or substitute (see page 494)
Salt to taste

Mix the ingredients to a loose paste; you may need to add a little water.

SIMPLE RECADO ROJO ❈ ACHIOTE PASTE
MAKES ¹/₂ CUP (125 ML)

A simple achiote paste for general use and for any pibil *recipe (although not included here).*

4 rounded tablespoons achiote seed
1 teaspoon crushed dried Mexican oregano, Yucatecan if possible
1 teaspoon cumin seeds
¹/₂ teaspoon mild black peppercorns
12 whole allspice
3 tablespoons water, approximately

Mix the spices and grind one third of the quantity at a time — or as much as your electric grinder can accommodate efficiently — as finely as possible. Sift through a fine strainer and grind the residue once again. Stir the water in gradually and mix well to a stiff paste.

If you are not going to use the paste immediately, form it into a round thick cake and divide into four pieces. Wrap well and store in the freezer compartment of the refrigerator. Storing it in this way makes it easier to take out a small piece at a time.

To dilute for use, crush this amount with about 20 small garlic cloves and sea salt to taste, and dilute to a thin cream with bitter orange juice or its substitute, a mild vinegar.

COOKING HERBS

The three *hierbas de olor* used most commonly in Mexican food are thyme, marjoram, and bay leaf. In Mexico they are sold together tied in little bunches, either fresh or dried—although generally used when dried. You can sometimes find them in Mexican markets in the United States. Fiesta Supermarkets in Texas were selling the fresh herbs on a recent visit. However, while thyme and marjoram are no problem, the bay leaf is quite different from the usual, strong-flavored *Laurus nobilis* most commonly found and used; its scientific name is *Litsea glaucescens*.

FRESH HERBS

CILANTRO CORIANDRUM SATIVUM Although native to the Old World, cilantro has been adopted wholeheartedly into the cuisine of Mexico, and both the fresh leaves and the seeds are used—in different ways in different dishes. The tender leaf and small stems are used in raw and cooked sauces, in some green moles, and with seafood, rice, and soups.

In Latin American and Caribbean stores, cilantro is known not as cilantro but as cilantrillo, and the word *cilantro* is given to another herb with a tough, dark green, serrated leaf but with the same flavor. Its botanical name is *Eryngium foetidum,* and in Mexico it is used chiefly in the cooking of Tabasco, southern Veracruz, parts of Oaxaca, and also in the Yucatán.

Cilantro leaves are delicate and should be stored with care. Buy cilantro, if possible, with the roots still attached—it will last longer. Wrap the roots and main stems in a damp paper towel and the leaves in a dry one, then store them in a plastic bag in the refrigerator. Remove any yellowing leaves daily.

EPAZOTE, MEXICAN TEA OR WORMSEED TELOXYS (FORMERLY CHENO-PODIUM) AMBROSIOIDES Epazote is, in my opinion, the most Mexican of the culinary herbs. Although it can be found growing wild in many parts of North America and in Europe, only in Mexico does it seem to be used to the fullest extent.

The fresh leaves, or a whole stem with leaves (not the dried, which is innocuous and has lost essential air), are used extensively in the cooking of central and southern Mexico. It is a sine qua non for the cooking of black beans, for tortilla and other brothy soups, in quesadillas, chopped with fresh corn, and elsewhere.

Epazote has a pointed, serrated, mid-green leaf with a pungent, addictive flavor, and its flower/seeds are in the form of minuscule green balls clustered around the stem tips. A source for seeds is given at the back of the book, but now many nurseries both on the West Coast and in the East sell the plants along with those of other culinary herbs.

HOJA SANTA PIPER AURITUM This large heart-shaped leaf of a tropical shrub, with a pronounced anise flavor, is used to season foods in the southern part of Mexico. It also grows wild along Texas riverbanks, I am told; it is often referred to as the rootbeer plant and the flavor likened to sarsaparilla.

In some recipes the flavor may be replaced by avocado leaves, but for others there is no substitute.

AVOCADO LEAVES PERSEA DRYMIFOLIA In some parts of Mexico these slightly anisey leaves are used whole or broken up as a seasoning, and you may sometimes see the powdered leaves for sale as well. Because there's been some concern about toxicity among some California aficionados, I think it's time to set the record straight.

The toxicity reports relate back to a study done in 1984 at the University of California at Davis, which showed that dairy goats suffered some toxic effects from ingesting very large amounts of avocado leaves (the toxic agent remains unknown). The crucial point, according to Dr. Arthur L. Craigmill, toxicology specialist at Davis and one of the authors of the study, is that the toxic effects were traced to the Guatemalan avocado *(Persea americana)*. When the goats were fed Mexican avocado leaves *(Persea drymifolia)*, a different species, there were no problems.

The Hass avocado, the best-tasting one grown in America, is a hybrid of indeterminate origin, though its DNA tests positive for a Guatemalan ancestor, hence the suspicions. No one has ever tested the Hass leaves for toxicity, but it seems unlikely that the small amounts used in cooking would cause any problems in any case.

The aromatic (most of them) Mexican leaves are available by mail order (see Sources).

DRIED HERBS

OREGANO There are many regional wild plants called orégano in Mexico about which there is, if I may quote a botanist friend at the time of writing, some "taxonomic confusion." They are used dried. The most commonly used Mexican oregano *(Lippia graveolens)* can be found, usually packaged, in stores where Mexican ingredients are sold.

The types of local oreganos mentioned in this book include one from the Yucatán, a larger-leafed variety that grows into a bush and when dried is toasted to a darkish brown, found in stores where Yucatecan ingredients are sold. The Oaxacan is a light, minty-flavored oregano (probably species *satureja*) which is used in much larger quantities than the others. There's also the small long-leafed variety used in Nuevo León.

OTHER INGREDIENTS

SUGAR ❋ AZÚCAR

Ordinary granulated can sugar is used generally in Mexican baking recipes, desserts, and sweetmeats except where piloncillo, or raw sugar in the form of cones, is called for. The latter is available in Mexican and Latin American markets, but ordinary dark brown cane sugar can be used as a substitute.

SALT ❋ SAL

I recommend sea salt for all the recipes, rather than ordinary table or kosher salt.

Pure sea salt is very cheap in Mexico, either in its soft form or in harder crystals, and is now being imported to the United States.

COOKING FATS AND OILS

Without doubt, vegetable oils are the most commonly used fat in Mexican cooking. They are generally made from either safflower, corn, sunflower, or more recently, rape, or a combination of two or more.

Vegetable fats are used for many types of pan dulce, some pastries, and flour tortillas.

Butter is used for better-quality pastries and breads, while in parts of southern Mexico, the Isthmus and Tabasco in particular, a soft, slightly acidy (and delicious) *mantequilla de rancho,* or ranch butter, is used for certain types of fresh corn confections.

Rendered beef fat is used in parts of northeast Mexico for the *bocoles* of Veracruz and Tamaulipas.

Olive oil, generally Spanish, is used for recipes of Spanish origin, particularly in Veracruz, the Yucatán, Campeche, and even parts of Michoacán, among many other areas.

Pork lard is still preferred by traditional cooks, especially for frying moles, for tamales, and for *antojitos.* Some cooks prefer a whitish lard, while in southern Mexico—Oaxaca, Tabasco, and Veracruz in particular—the caramel color from the chicharrón vats is preferred, often together with the crisp chicharrón "crumbs" that sink to the bottom. If you cannot find a really good lard—not the whitish stuff made solid with stabilizers—then have a shot at making your own with the fat trimmed from the pork and often sold packaged in supermarkets or ethnic butcher shops.

HOMEMADE LARD
MAKES ABOUT 1½ POUNDS (680 G), ABOUT 4 CUPS (1 L)

2 pounds (900 g) unsalted fatback or pork fat

Heat the oven to 325°F (165°C). Have ready two large, heavy skillets.

Cut the fat into small cubes and, taking about one fourth at a time, pulse briefly in the food processor just to break the pieces down to render the fat more efficiently. Divide the fat between the pans, taking care not to overfill so that the rendered fat spills over, and place on the top and middle sections of the oven.

Check the pans after about 20 minutes and pour off any liquid fat into stoneware or glass containers. Stir and press down on the remaining pieces from time to time, straining off as much of the lard as you can.

Discard the crisp fatty residue, or add it to masa for gorditas, or put it out for the birds, whatever . . .

When the lard is cool, cover and refrigerate. It will keep for several months.

SOUR CREAM

In the large urban areas it is difficult, if not impossible, to find pure, naturally soured cream, just like the crème fraîche of France. The commercial brands certainly have fillers and preservatives, and much that is sold in the local marketplaces in central Mexico has been extended with some sort of vegetable fat. While these sour creams are adequate as toppings for *antojitos* and the like, they are not suitable to be cooked in a sauce. You can buy some delicious sour cream in markets like Juchitán in southern Oaxaca, for instance, and some that has been churned for *mantequilla de rancho*, a soft slightly cheesey "ranch butter" that is delicious spread on tortillas.

Some very good brands of crème fraîche are now available in the United States, and they are worth the extra cost. I could never recommend the product sold under the name Mexican Crema in a glass jar; it is certainly not worth the price.

Of course, you can always make your own, as Julia Child taught us many years ago.

THICK SOUR CREAM
MAKES ABOUT 1 CUP (250 ML)

1 cup (250 ml) heavy (not ultrapasteurized) cream
Approximately 3 tablespoons buttermilk or yogurt (not low-fat)

Mix cream and buttermilk in a glass container and set in a warm place (oven with a pilot light, in a yogurt maker, etc.) overnight. It should have soured slightly and thickened in about 8 hours if you have natural products, but it may take longer. To have it really thick, make this home-made version several days ahead.

PREPARED SOUR CREAM

A thinner, slightly soured, cream is used lavishly over many antojitos. *For this I suggest a short cut—which is also cheaper—by diluting sour cream with milk to the desired consistency.*

VEGETABLES

TOMATOES LYCOPERSICUM ESCULENTUM Y SPP. Tomatoes are a native and indispensable ingredient in many regional dishes. When I first came to Mexico in 1957 we used only large, round tomatoes—*de bola*; I don't recall when the elongated plum tomatoes, *jitomate guaje* or *guajillo*, were introduced. Now they are ubiquitous—in fact, in many regional markets they are the only tomatoes available. You can occasionally find a tomato that looks like a small beefsteak tomato, the only difference being its thin, orangey-red skin and very juicy and fairly acidy nature. (I have found them in Malinalco, in the state of Mexico, and Chilapa, Guerrero, among other more remote places.) Some large tomatoes are in fact now being imported into the United States. But my favorites are the very tiny (about 1 cm in diameter) *cuatomates*, as they are known in the Sierra de Puebla Norte. They are like very small cherry tomatoes with an intense flavor and enormous amount of tiny seeds. These little tomatoes are known by several names, especially in different parts of Veracruz: *menudo* (small), Zitlali (presumably the name of a village where they are grown and not to be confused with the village of that name in Guerrero), *ojo de venado* (deer's eye), *tomato de monte* (mountain tomato), among others.

Owing to their tough skins a sauce made in the traditional way in a molcajete is very roughly textured. In the area around Tuxpan, Veracruz, cooks like to mix ripe and green, unripe little tomatoes for a sauce that is not as sweet. In the past I have come across recipes calling for green, unripe tomatoes in Oaxaca and Campeche.

Regional cooks I have known are most specific about how tomatoes are to be prepared for sauces, and I give some of their methods below:

RAW For raw sauces, those akin to *salsa mexicana* with their slight regional variations, for adding to seafood cocktails, to scrambled eggs or salads, the unskinned tomatoes should be chopped finely and not seeded.

SIMMERED For some cooked sauces, tomatoes are covered with water and simmered until soft—about 10 minutes for medium-size tomatoes. Generally, and with few exceptions, they are then skinned before blending—the skin of plum tomatoes tends to be particularly tough—or the tomatoes are blended, unskinned, and the sauce strained.

COOKED AND LIGHTLY CHARRED ON A COMAL This is a very roundabout way of expressing the (Mexican) Spanish word *asado*. (The word is often applied to roast or grilled meat.)

In traditional peasant cooking many of the ingredients are prepared in this way—for example, rustic table sauces or for including in more complex moles. Whole unskinned tomatoes are cooked on an ungreased comal or griddle over medium heat until soft right through, while the skin is lightly charred. This method intensifies the flavor and brings out the sweetness of the tomato. Some cooks I know then remove the skin while others—and I go along with them—do not, and opt for a sauce that is superior in flavor and texture but is not so colorful.

Many of the traditional foods of the Mayan villages in the Yucatán Peninsula are cooked in a *pib*, or pit, and ingredients to be included in the meal—chiles, tomatoes, onion, and garlic—are roasted *asados* on the hot stones lining the bottom of the pit. Locally they are referred to as *enterrados*, or "buried."

Of course, if neither method seems practical, then place the tomatoes in one layer in a shallow pan and place under a broiler about 3 inches (8 cm) from the heat and broil, turning them once, until mushy and slightly charred. (This is an excellent method if you are going to freeze an abundant crop of tomatoes, when they are at their best in season.)

STEWED Preparing tomatoes by this method is rare, but a few cooks use it in Oaxaca. Cut the unskinned tomatoes into eight pieces and, for say 1 pound (450 g) of tomatoes, add 1 tablespoon vegetable oil and about ¼ cup (65 ml) water. Cover the pan and cook over gentle heat, shaking the pan from time to time to avoid sticking, until mushy—about 10 minutes. This is a particularly good method when tomatoes are not at their best or are rather dry.

GRATED The first time I saw this method was in Sonora many years ago, and I use it in the recipes on pages 133 and 179. It is best to have large round tomatoes. Cut a slice off the top of the tomato and, using the coarse side of a grater, grate the flesh with all the seeds and juice. With pressure the tomato is almost flattened and you end up with most of the skin in the palm of your hand.

MEXICAN GREEN TOMATOES PHYSALIS SPP. The indigenous *tomate verde* is an indispensable ingredient in Mexican food. The fruit itself, with its shiny green skin often blotched with deep purple, is encased in a papery grayish-green husk that is often slightly sticky to the touch. Its name often varies with the region: *fresadilla* in northern Mexico, *tomate de capote* in Colima, *miltomate* in Oaxaca, *tomate milpero*, and when very small in Michoacán, *tomatillo*, among other names. There are several varieties of this green tomato. The smallest (about 1 cm in diameter) grows wild in the cornfields; it is very compact and therefore has an intense flavor. There is also a large fleshy variety that I have seen in markets in the state of Mexico; the bright green skin is patched with yellow, and the fruit is referred to as *tomate manzano* or apple tomato. In the United States, *tomate verde* are sold as *tomatillos*.

With one exception, when you prepare these green tomatoes, remove the papery husks and rinse them well, but do not try to skin them. For some sauces they are chopped and blended raw, but more often they are simmered in water until soft.

Here are the methods for preparing them.

COOKED WHOLE ON A COMAL For a rustic table sauce, remove the husks from the whole tomatoes, place them on an ungreased comal or griddle, and cook over medium heat, turning from time to time, until they are fairly soft and slightly charred. They are then ground or blended, skin included.

I once saw a Oaxacan cook place the unhusked tomatoes into still hot, but not glowing, ashes and let them soften and char slightly.

SIMMERED Simmering the *tomate verde* whole in water is by far the most general way of preparing them. Cover in cold water, then simmer over medium heat until soft but not breaking apart—10 to 15 minutes depending on size.

I have seen Oaxacan cooks cut them into quarters and stew them slowly with very little water until very soft and mushy.

GARLIC Influences from the United States are changing garlic. Years ago heads of garlic were smaller; the cloves were smaller and mostly purple. The heads and cloves seem to get larger by the year, with the notable exception of those sold in the markets of the southern states, particularly Oaxaca and Guerrero. They are tastier, too. (A type of elephant garlic tied firmly into rings with red ribbon has always been considered a lucky charm.)

With the exception of dishes of Spanish origin—*en mojo de ajo* and *en ajillo*—garlic is not used heavily in Mexican food. In the recipes of central Oaxaca, for instance, a whole head of garlic may be called for, but it is an extremely small head and the taste is not discernible in the finished sauce.

Peeled and finely chopped garlic gently fried with finely chopped onion until translucent forms the base for traditional Mexican food. *Ajo asado*, or toasted cloves, or a head of garlic is often called for. The unpeeled cloves (pricked so they don't explode) are put onto a comal over medium heat; then turned from time to time until slightly charred on the outside and soft inside. They are then peeled and blended according to the recipe's instructions. If a whole head is called for, first remove the loose papery outside husk, then place the whole head onto a hot comal (not too hot) and again turn it from time to time until evenly cooked. The head is sometimes added whole to a broth or, in some Yucatecan dishes, broken apart and the unpeeled cloves added to a broth or escabeche (light pickle). As mentioned above, the dishes of Spanish origin are those that have peeled and fried garlic in abundance.

CITRUS FRUITS

LIME ❀ LIMÓN

The name is a little confusing to anyone outside Mexico where the yellow lemon is unknown. The most commonly found limes are small, green, and thin-skinned, akin to the Key lime. There are, of course, other similar varieties and in some areas the larger Persian lime is grown commercially (and alas in Veracruz, waxed).

I wonder if there is another country that uses the lime so profusely: in limeade, or *limonada*; to accompany beer, especially Tecate; in some fresh sauces; in seafood cocktails; with broths of all types, to season meats; with jícama; and with some fresh fruits like papayas (as well as applied to an insect bite). A shot of tequila without a lime quarter to suck on after each sip is inconceivable. And a delectable sweetmeat is a hollowed-out candied lime stuffed with a *cocada*, a paste of shredded coconut.

LIMA AGRIA The sour lima is a squat, light green citrus fruit with a pronounced nipple at its extremity. The peel has an extraordinarily complex flavor that I can only liken to the bitter orange in intensity and bitterness, while the flesh is highly acidic.

The bitter lime is mostly associated with the Yucatecan *sopa de lima*, but I have seen it served to accompany the moles of Chilapa or Guerrero; a fresh sauce is made of the flesh in parts of Jalisco. I am sure there are other examples of its use.

LIMA DULCE Until you try it, the lima dulce, or limetta, could be mistaken for the lima agria except for the fact that it generally has a smoother surface. Despite its fragrant peel, the flesh is sweet and innocuous. I was once given the juice to drink to accompany a meal in the state of Mexico; I have seen the rind used in cooking only in a dish of *rellena*, pig's blood cooked with hot fresh manzano chiles and flavored with rue. Most popularly, limas dulces are an indispensable item for loading the Christmas piñatas along with other fruits, sugarcane, and candies. They also make a fragrant, pale green infusion when simmered for about 10 minutes in water.

BITTER OR SEVILLE-TYPE ORANGE A variety of bitter or Seville orange, introduced from Spain during the colonial period, is used in many parts of the Republic, but more commonly in Tabasco and the Yucatán Peninsula. The juice is used with other condiments to season meats or fish, or as a base for onion and chile sauces, or in the pickled onions used as a topping for *panuchos*, or in escabeches in Yucatán.

The bitter orange is most commonly a bright orange color except in the Yucatán Peninsula, where it is greenish even when ripe, and the juice, although acidic, is slightly sweeter. It is an ugly-looking fruit, squat with a thick, rough skin. It can be seen growing wild or as an ornamental tree (lining even the residential streets and Capitol Park in Sacramento) in northern Mexico, southern Texas, and Arizona.

In colder northern areas the main crop is ripe in February, but farther south the trees produce year-round.

Bitter oranges are almost always available in Caribbean markets (or *boticas*, mostly Dominican herbalist stores where they are used as a remedy, probably for gall bladder problems) and the Fiesta Supermarkets in Texas. When you do find a supply that varies, squeeze out the juice and freeze it with very little of the finely grated rind. In southeast Mexico, the outer layer of peel is removed before juicing to avoid the bitterness of the oils it contains.

As a substitute for the recipes in this book, you can use either a mild fruity vinegar or a combination of juice and rinds, as follows:

SEVILLE ORANGE SUBSTITUTE
MAKES ABOUT ½ CUP (125 ML)

1 teaspoon finely grated grapefruit or green Meyer lemon rind
2 tablespoons fresh orange juice
2 tablespoons fresh grapefruit or ripe Meyer lemon juice
4 tablespoons fresh lime juice

Mix all together and use as indicated.

PUMPKIN SEEDS (PEPITAS)

Ground raw pumpkin seeds, either unhulled or hulled, are used in many Mexican dishes. The type of seed used will vary with what is grown in a particular area. Generally speaking the very flat seeds are toasted and used as a snack; the tiny, fattish ones, called colloquially *chinchilla*, are used unhulled in dishes of the Yucatán, like Sikil P'ak (page 4).

The raw hulled seeds are readily available in health food stores, some supermarkets, and specialty stores. Whole, unhulled seeds are now more readily available but avoid if possible the enormously expensive, very small packages of these seeds in the Latin American section of supermarkets and specialty stores.

Pumpkin seeds are always toasted in an ungreased pan over low heat and cooled before grinding. Care should be taken not to let them get too dark or the sauce will be bitter.

PLANTAINS

Many delicious varieties of bananas are grown in the tropical areas of Mexico, among them the plantain or "vegetable" banana. These *platanos machos* are used mainly, but not exclusively, in the traditional food of tropical areas in the southern states. Plantains are easily distinguishable by their triangular, long curving shape and thick skin.

The most common ways of preparing plantains, when they are very ripe, is peeled, cut into slices lengthwise, and fried. In this form they are often served with a *sopa seca* of white rice. In Veracruz and Tabasco, they are cooked and mashed to a dough and used for empanadas with a meat or cheese filling or blended for a soup.

My favorite way of eating plantains is when they are still slightly green—fried and smashed flat and then fried a second time until they are semi-crisp *tostones*, as in Tabasco.

Plantains can become addictive. The most delicious plantains of all are the smaller, thinner, and more pointed *dominicos*, as they are called in Tabasco, and the *plátano de Castilla*, in Oaxaca.

VINEGARS

The vinegars used in Mexican cooking are usually very mild, fruity ones. Many cooks in the provinces still make their own vinegar from pineapple and raw sugar (see recipe below); in Tabasco, overripe bananas are used, while one small market stand that I deal with in Zitácuaro uses a mixture of fruits—whatever is in season—and always has on sale a delightful, light amber vinegar. Once you have a good "mother" going, you can go on making your own vinegar ad infinitum, with any fruit you like.

PINEAPPLE VINEGAR

When you are using a pineapple for other purposes, save the peelings, along with a little of the flesh.

Half the peelings of a fresh pineapple
4 heaped tablespoons crushed piloncillo (raw sugar) or dark brown sugar
1½ quarts (1.5 l) water

Mix ingredients well and set, uncovered, in a sunny, warm spot to ferment. The mixture should begin to ferment in about 3 days; keep it fermenting until all the sugar has been converted and the liquid becomes acidy. It may be cloudy to begin with, but as it sits it will clear and gradually turn to a dark amber color. This may take 3 weeks or more. By this time a mother—a gelatinous white disk—should be just beginning to form. Leave until it is quite solid—up to another 3 weeks—then strain the liquid and cork, ready for use. Put the mother with more sugar and water—and a little more pineapple if you have it, but it is not really necessary—and leave to form more vinegar.

Yes, you need patience, but it is worth it. While you can never quite duplicate that which you make, a good substitute would be half good-quality white wine vinegar and half mild Oriental rice vinegar.

AVOCADOS

Even in California it is best to anticipate and buy avocados several days ahead—the state of ripeness is usually uneven—and let them ripen, wrapped in paper and stored in a warm place. More Mexican avocados are being imported during the winter, thanks to NAFTA. The large avocados coming from Florida have a more watery flesh and do not make a good guacamole, but they are better sliced and served as a topping for *antojitos* or dishes where indicated.

CHICHARRÓN (CRISP-FRIED PORK RIND)

Chicharrón is the skin of the pig that is first dried in the sun, then stewed in hot lard. It is then fried in even hotter lard until it is golden brown and has a crisp, porous texture. Many Mexican markets in the United States make their own chicharrón and display it in large sheets, but it can also be purchased in supermarkets commercially packed as "fried pork skins" or pork rinds. Avoid any brands that are tough and chewy, which means, of course, that they have not been prepared properly.

CUICLACOCHE, OR HUITLACOCHE (CORN FUNGUS)

Cuiclacoche is the silvery-gray fungus that occurs accidentally—although it can be induced—on some varieties of corn generally during the rainy season. The flesh is moist and inky black. *Cuiclacoche* has been used since pre-Columbian times and is popularly used, cooked with other ingredients, for soups, casseroles, as a filling for quesadillas, and even for sauces. The fungus is shaved off the corn cob and roughly chopped, first removing any corn silk that has adhered to it.

Cuiclacoche can be purchased fresh from specialty sources in the United States (or if you have a farmer acquaintance who is bothered by a plague of it, you could pick it yourself). There are some very acceptable canned products exported from Mexico and sold in supermarkets in some areas.

FLOR DE CALABAZA (SQUASH FLOWERS)

The name is slightly misleading, since it means pumpkin flowers, while in fact the flowers of smaller types of squash are used in Mexican cooking. The flowers are cooked with other ingredients for soups, casseroles, or as a filling for quesadillas.

In Mexico the flowers are sold in the public markets and supermarkets and are at their best during the rainy season. In the United States they are usually available at farmers' markets or ordered through specialty suppliers unless, of course, you have a garden and grow squash. If that is the case, pick only the male flowers, easily recognizable by their penis-shaped stamen, but leave 1 in every 25 for pollination.

To prepare the flowers for cooking, cut off the green stems and strip off the stringy sepals, leaving the fleshy base and stamen intact (sadly many Mexican cooks remove these parts which, in actual fact, add a delicious flavor and texture). Chop the flowers roughly and follow the recipe's cooking instructions.

ACITRÓN

Acitrón—not to be confused with citron, which is a large citrus fruit—is the name given to the candied biznaga cactus, the large round *Echinocactus grandis*. Small cubes of acitrón are used mainly in sweet tamales, meat stuffings (*picadillos*), and some desserts. It is usually

sold in square bars and marked either acitrón or biznaga, and can often be found in Mexican bakeries or groceries in the United States.

Acitrón does not have a pronounced flavor. I have often substituted candied or dried
pineapple. Both will keep for several months if stored sealed in a cool, dry place.

NOPALES

Nopales or cactus paddles are the fleshy joints or "leaves" of several varieties of edible *Opuntia*
cactus. With rare exceptions they are cooked first before being added to certain dishes.

Nopales are now readily available in large supermarket chains and in specialty stores
like Mexican groceries. They are best when used fresh and firm.

To prepare nopales, first scrape off the tiny thorns—taking care not to get them into
your fingers—then cut them into either narrow strips or small squares. For cooking them,
see the recipe on page 208 for Nopales al Vapor.

DRIED SHRIMP

The concentrated flavor of dried shrimp enhances soups, rice, tamales, beans, and table
sauces; once you acquire a taste for it (it is too strong for many visitors), it becomes quite
addictive. In Oaxacan markets, dried shrimp are sorted and priced according to size, from
the large 2½-inch (6.5-cm) ones to the smallest of about ¾ inch (2 cm), not forgetting
the minuscule ones, ¼ inch (.75 cm), found along the Pacific coast.

Good-quality dried shrimp are now to be found in Mexican food markets and in the
Mexican food section of some supermarket chains in the United States, but take care in
choosing them. Do not buy the small packages of bright-orange–colored shrimp bodies,
peeled and headed—they have no flavor. Nor should you buy the packages marked "dried
shrimp powder," a great proportion of which is pure salt. Try to find whole unpeeled
shrimp.

Most dishes call for shrimp with heads and legs removed. The heads are very flavorful
and—without the black eyes—should be stored for making shrimp fritters. They are very
salty at best. Rinse in cold water, drain them, and cover with fresh cold water. Leave them
to soak for about 10 minutes—no longer, or they will lose a lot of flavor. Store in a dry place
for up to several months.

BASIC RECIPES

CALDO DE POLLO ❈ CHICKEN BROTH
MAKES ABOUT 14 CUPS (3.5 L) OF STRONG BROTH

A large boiling fowl or 5 pounds (2.5 kg) chicken carcasses
The giblets and feet or 1 pound (450 g) extra giblets
1 small white onion
2 garlic cloves
Sea salt to taste

Cut the fowl into pieces. Place in a stockpot with giblets and cover with cold water. Add onion and garlic, and bring to a boil. Lower the heat and simmer for about 3½ hours. Add salt. Cool and leave, unstrained, overnight.

Heat the broth, then strain, discarding the debris. Skim the fat carefully from the top and store the broth ready for use. Cool and skim before using or storing.

NOTE: To store, pour the broth into ice-cube trays and freeze. When solid, transfer to refrigerator bags. Mark with amount and date and store in the freezer compartment.

CHICKEN, COOKED AND SHREDDED
MAKES ABOUT 2½ CUPS (625 ML) FIRMLY PACKED SHREDDED CHICKEN

6 cups (1.5 l) chicken broth
1 large chicken, about 3 pounds (1.35 kg), cut into serving pieces
Sea salt to taste

Bring the chicken broth to a simmer in a large saucepan, add the chicken pieces, and cook over low heat until just tender—about 25 minutes. Remove from heat and let the chicken cool in the broth.

Drain the chicken, reserving the broth for soups or sauces.

Remove meat from the bones and shred coarsely with some of the skin for extra flavor. Season with salt as necessary.

PORK, COOKED AND SHREDDED
MAKES ABOUT 2¹/₃ CUPS (585 ML)

2 pounds (900 g) boneless pork
Pork bones, if any
¼ medium white onion, roughly sliced
1 large garlic clove
Sea salt to taste
5 peppercorns

Cut the meat into large cubes, put it into a large saucepan with the other ingredients, and cover with cold water. Bring to a boil, then lower the heat and simmer until just *tender*—about 45 minutes. Remove from the heat and let the meat cool in the broth. When the meat is cool enough to handle, drain, reserving the broth. Shred the meat and add more salt as necessary. Be careful not to overcook the meat, remembering that the cooking process goes on as the meat cools off in the broth.

The meat can either be shredded by hand, with the tines of two forks back to back, or lightly pounded in a mortar just until the fibers separate.

BEEF, COOKED AND SHREDDED
MAKES ABOUT 2 CUPS (500 ML) FIRMLY PACKED SHREDDED BEEF

1 pound (450 g) skirt or flank steak, cut into 1-inch (2.5-cm) cubes
1 small onion, roughly chopped
1 garlic clove
Sea salt to taste

Put the beef and other ingredients into a large saucepan, cover well with water, and bring to a simmer. Continue simmering over low heat until the beef is tender—about 40 minutes. Leave the meat to cool in the broth, then drain, reserving the broth for another purpose.

When the meat is cool enough to handle, shred coarsely, removing any sinew or gristle.

SOURCES

With the deluge of foods coming in from Mexico and the steady stream of workers coming back and forth across the border, we may soon see the day when a sources section in a Mexican cookbook is unnecessary, at least for city dwellers. Meanwhile, here are a few suggestions for mail-order foods, plants, and equipment. Other sources are mentioned with discussion of specific ingredients.

TEXAS

The most extensive products from Mexico can be found in the Fiesta Supermarkets, in Houston and Austin in particular. The HEB markets, and their upscale Market Place in Austin and San Antonio, carry a large variety of ingredients for authentic Mexican cooking, including many types of fresh and other fresh and dried products.

THE MOZZARELLA CHEESE CO.
2944 Elm Street
Dallas, TX 75226
214-741-4072

Carries a very good queso fresco. You can send for a list of cheeses and prices.

MASSACHUSETTS

THE HARBAR CORPORATION
30 Germania Street
Jamaica Plain, MA 02130
617-524-6107

Has some of the best pure corn tortillas and corn masa in the United States. Mail order also.

SID WAINER & SON
2301 Purchase Street
New Bedford, MA 02746
508-999-6408

Stocks fresh and dried chiles, etc.

MAIL ORDER

KITCHEN MARKET
218 Eighth Avenue
New York, NY 10011
212-243-4433

Stocks dried chiles, several Mexican herbs, as well as a variety of Mexican products and equipment.

THE CMC COMPANY
P.O. Box 322
Avalon, NJ 08202
800-262-2780

Stocks dried chiles (including chipotle morita and pasilla de Oaxaca), Mexican avocado leaves, chorizo, masa (Masteca brand from Texas), pozole, piloncillo, and equipment such as tortilla presses, comales, and molcajetes. No fresh foods.

SHEPHERD'S GARDEN SEEDS
30 Irene Street
Torrington, CT 06780-6658
800-482-3638

Sells seeds for many chiles, tomate verde (tomatillos), and several Mexican herbs, including epazote.

KING ARTHUR FLOUR
P.O. Box 876
Norwich, VT 05055-0876
800-267-6836

Stocks Nielsen-Massey's real Mexican vanilla.